ROADFOOD
and
GOODFOOD

ROADFOOD

and

GOODFOOD

Jane and Michael Stern's Coast-to-Coast Restaurant Guides Combined, Updated, and Expanded

ALFRED A. KNOPF   New York   1986

THIS IS A BORZOI BOOK
PUBLISHED BY ALFRED A. KNOPF, INC.

Library of Congress Cataloging-in-Publication Data

Stern, Jane.
Roadfood and Goodfood.

Updated ed. of 2 works previously published separately: Roadfood (1980)
and Goodfood (1983).
Includes index.
I. Restaurants, lunch rooms, etc.—United States—
Directories. I. Stern, Michael. II. Stern,
Jane. Roadfood. III. Stern, Jane. Goodfood.
IV. Title.
TX907.S7325   1986   647′.9573   85-45784
ISBN 0-394-74396-2 (pbk.)

Manufactured in the United States of America

FIRST EDITION

to Bob Cornfield

Contents

There is a map locating restaurants at the beginning of each section.

Original Introduction to Goodfood

Goodfood is meant to be a source book for people passionate about American regional food; people who not only want to eat well but who also want to eat authentic local food from coast to coast.

We traveled more than a hundred thousand miles looking for restaurants that serve the best indigenous specialties. It didn't matter whether it was a linen-napkin joint with tuxedoed waiters or an Oklahoma grocery store with a back-room pitmaster in bandana and cowboy boots, downtown or out in the boondocks—we asked ourselves the same questions: Is this restaurant the best of its genre? Does it express the culinary soul of its region?

Having written *Roadfood*, a gustatory survival guide for highway travelers, we set out thinking we knew what we would find: Key lime pie in Florida, baked beans in Boston, Hoosier fried chicken in Indiana. But as we traveled we discovered a wealth of lesser-known specialties, too: from geoduck steaks in the northwest to fried dill pickles in the Mississippi delta. We came to realize that, despite the vogue for American cookery, many of the country's best dishes remain unexplored and unappreciated.

What people of each region eat is as singular and well defined as a fingerprint. If you don't believe it, just try to pass off spaghetti-based Cincinnati chili to a New Mexican. Lifetimes might go by before a Massachusetts chef would allow tomatoes in his quahog chowder, but just over the border, in Rhode Island, tomato-clam chowder is, *by law*, part of the state's official shore dinner.

The *character* implicit in regional cooking made the research for this book the best kind of adventure. It brought us face to face with people whom we might ordinarily fly over or zoom past in a car . . . like the wilderness fisherwoman who displayed her box of home-smoked lake trout to us with more pride than a salesperson at Tiffany's laying out a diamond necklace, or the fat man who sauntered up to us in a bar in Mobile, Alabama, the one we pegged as the worst sort of redneck, who instead of killing us as we expected, took us out to dinner in an oyster restaurant we would never have found by ourselves, then wouldn't let us leave until we Yankees got a taste of southern hospitality, which meant filling up our car's back seat with his homegrown watermelons, his wife's hot pepper jelly, and enough home brew quince wine to keep our car fueled up to California and back.

We have friends—serious eaters—who say they don't give a hang for atmosphere and ambience; that food is the only criterion. We put food atop the list, too, but relish the fringe benefits of good food in a good place. For us, it's bogus atmosphere that is a bore; you can't buy character from a restaurant design firm. On the other hand, a cliffside lobster shack with a view—and the scent—of the ocean crashing below adds immeasurably to the pleasure of a downeast meal. We believe it is worth traipsing up to the

Bronx to savor a New York egg cream in its rightful environment—in a candy store under the tracks of the El, where the soda jerk knows how to squirt the seltzer off the spoon with a flourish.

Because of our strong feelings for savoring food in its natural setting, we haven't included regional restaurants that are outside their region. There may be a great oyster bar in Kansas or gumbo parlor in Manhattan, but you won't find it here.

American cooking is an expression of place and soul, with all the unvarnished charm of an Ozark folk song. Even at its most sophisticated, it is a people's food—more folk art than high art. That is why "new American cuisine," which combines native produce in tricky ways, is not part of this book. We believe that American cooking is something more than a novel amalgam of regional groceries. As little appreciated as it has been, there is a culinary tradition in this country. It is that tradition (actually, many traditions) that *Goodfood* celebrates.

We have included maps to help locate towns that may not be familiar, or ones so small they aren't in an ordinary atlas. You will notice certain states and areas clustered with restaurants, others devoid of even one. That's the way it is. As many times as we have driven through Montana, we've yet to find a meal worth the trip; on the other hand, it's impossible to turn around in Acadian Louisiana without being offered a plate of fabulous food.

We hope you enjoy the restaurants in *Goodfood* as much as we did . . . although please be aware that the best kitchen can stumble over its own feet on occasion.

Prices—especially for seafood—can fluctuate wildly. *The prices we do list are for one meal, without drinks.*

We have tried to be as accurate as possible about hours of operation, but they too can vary. If you are making a special trip, call ahead. More than once we have detoured out of our way to eat at a favorite place, only to find a "gone fishing" sign hanging on the door.

Goodfood was immeasurably enriched by tips from readers, old friends, and new friends we met along the way. We invite your suggestions for future editions; send them to us care of Alfred A. Knopf, 201 East 50th Street, New York, N.Y. 10022. There is always going to be a cafe in some vest pocket town or city neighborhood that makes a magical fried chicken or gumbo or blackberry pie, and we intend to try it.

Introduction to Roadfood and Goodfood

When we set out to write *Roadfood*, our goal was to find honest and inexpensive meals near the highway. By the second edition, the book had begun to zero in on unique regional foods. Often these local specialties were far from the highway and more expensive than the *Roadfood* limit of $5 per meal would allow. So we wrote *Goodfood*, a guide without limitations of cost or geography.

Shortly after *Goodfood* was published, our files again began to bulge with readers' tips, and we have spent the last three years discovering new restaurants, revisiting old favorites, updating *Roadfood* and *Goodfood* to produce what we intend to be the ultimate guide for adventurous eaters.

Eight years ago, some people questioned who would want a guide to restaurants that serve American food. Now American food is hot: upscale, downscale, all over the map.

Restaurants flaunt regional cuisine. Buffalo chicken wings, once known only to tavern-goers in upstate New York, are served from Miami to Seattle. You can eat Creole pan-blackened redfish in New Hampshire and Arizona *chimichangas* in Des Moines. No longer does anyone think of American food as merely hot dogs and hamburgers; this country has left its culinary inferiority complex in the dust.

We couldn't be happier.

Except for this: regional restaurants outside their own regions remind us of dioramas in a natural history museum: interesting, educational . . . but you cannot smell the mountain air. The joy of eating regional food is not just what's on the plate. It is sitting shoulder to shoulder with Amish farmers in Indiana, beach bunnies in Corona del Mar, and cowboys in Amarillo. It is seeing the sun set over Puget Sound and listening to the strident honk of the waitresses at Durgin-Park in Boston. There is no seasoning as pungent as authenticity.

This book is a guide to all the restaurants we know that offer an authentic taste of America.

Acknowledgments

The pleasures of writing a book like this cannot be denied, but there was more to it than eating pie for breakfast. To help us turn good food into a good book, we counted on three special people: Bob Gottlieb, who, miraculously, made publishing a creative joy for us; Robert Cornfield, our agent and friend, whose expert advice is always accompanied by generous helpings of home-cooked pasta; and especially our editor, Martha Kaplan, whose guidance and good sense were a beacon for us, whether we were lost on a mountain in Utah or in the convolutions of a run-on sentence.

Harry and Florence Stern of Chicago, Judy Peiser of the Center for Southern Folklore in Memphis, Ella King Torrey of Oxford, Mississippi, and Mark Criden and Nicole Urdang of Buffalo provided us with homes away from home, and grand tours of their cities. Special thanks to Alan Mc-Dermott, Donna Martin, and Lee Salem, who hosted us royally in Kansas City, and to John McMeel, who gave us a place to stay and a pep talk that stayed with us coast-to-coast.

It is difficult to find foster parents for two 125-pound dogs. But Beulah and Edwina were never happier than when Jim and Judy Monteith or Kim and Doug Green took care of them.

The Robohm family, friends and neighbors, never failed to provide the tall cool drink at the end of the trail.

For invaluable help in guiding us to some of the best places in this book, we thank Paul Arthofer, Merton and Helen Baldwin, Jerry and Alice Barone, Mrs. William F. Becker, Betty Brandt, Mr. and Mrs. Gregg Burmeister, Ort Carlton, Sylvia Carter, Connie Crump, Pat Davison, Freeman F. Dodge, Tom Edmondson, Alison and Margaret Engel, Tom Englehardt, Clayton H. Farnham, Cora Faye, Bill Ferris, Susan and Gary Fine, Rob and Jeanne Goldfarb, Alicia Lane Greis, Debbie Hartz, John Hendricks, Ed Hitzel, Garietta Jackson, Brooke Jennings, Jackie Kaufman, David Kershaw, Donna Lee, Jeff Lyons, Eric Jones and Susan Miller, Mr. and Mrs. Richard Koch, Polk Laffoon IV, John Landsberg and Fran Lantz, Laverne M. Lasobeck, Hillary Leavitt, Matt Lewis, Joe Manning, John Mariani, Sally McMillan, Megan McCaslin, Steve L. Morton, Frank Muhly, Jr., Russ Parsons, Tom Pasavant, Robert A. Pease, Paul Pintarich, Marcia and Richard Poole, Paul Rayton, Bart Ripp, Edith Rosenthal, Carol Sama, Gary Sanders, Albert A. Schaufelberger, Susan Seager, Leslie Seeche, Janice Shindeler and Harry Crofton, Kevin Sellers, Art Siemering, Pat and Heather Sparkuhl, John A. Staedler, Bud Stiker, Richard David Story, Mrs. Henry Thomas, Jean Tolbert, Mildred Tuchten, Sandra L. Vander Zicht, Ben and Suzanne Van Vechten, Daniel Wendland, Charles Wilson, L. Wayne Wirtanen, Byron and Kathy Wise, Howard Wong, Carolyn Wyman, Bill Yankee, Mark Yates, and the anonymous Carolinian we met over Indian pudding in Boston, who told us about Maurice's Piggy Park.

New England

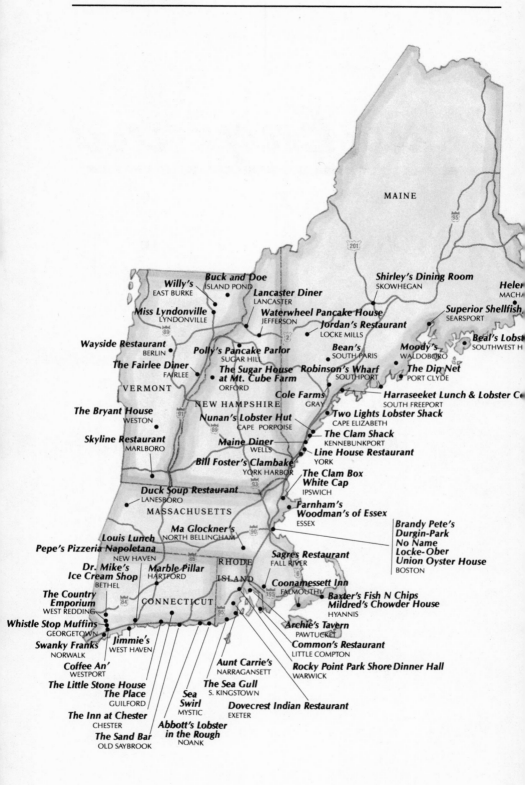

MAINE

Willy's
EAST BURKE

Buck and Doe
ISLAND POND

Shirley's Dining Room
SKOWHEGAN

Hele
MACHA

Lancaster Diner
LANCASTER

Miss Lyndonville
LYNDONVILLE

Waterwheel Pancake House
JEFFERSON

Superior Shellfish
SEARSPORT

Jordan's Restaurant
LOCKE MILLS

Wayside Restaurant
BERLIN

Polly's Pancake Parlor
SUGAR HILL

Bean's
SOUTH PARIS

Moody's
WALDOBORO

Beal's Lobst
SOUTHWEST H

The Fairlee Diner
FAIRLEE

The Sugar House
at Mt. Cube Farm
ORFORD

Robinson's Wharf
SOUTHPORT

The Dip Net
PORT CLYDE

VERMONT

Cole Farms
GRAY

Harraseeket Lunch & Lobster Co
SOUTH FREEPORT

The Bryant House
WESTON

NEW HAMPSHIRE

Nunan's Lobster Hut
CAPE PORPOISE

Two Lights Lobster Shack
CAPE ELIZABETH

Skyline Restaurant
MARLBORO

Maine Diner
WELLS

The Clam Shack
KENNEBUNKPORT

Line House Restaurant
YORK

Bill Foster's Clambake
YORK HARBOR

The Clam Box
White Cap
IPSWICH

Duck Soup Restaurant
LANESBORO

MASSACHUSETTS

Farnham's
Woodman's of Essex
ESSEX

Ma Glockner's
NORTH BELLINGHAM

Brandy Pete's
Durgin-Park
No Name
Locke-Ober
Union Oyster House
BOSTON

Louis Lunch

Pepe's Pizzeria Napoletana
NEW HAVEN

RHODE
ISLAND

Sagres Restaurant
FALL RIVER

Dr. Mike's
Ice Cream Shop
BETHEL

Marble Pillar
HARTFORD

Coonamessett Inn
FALMOUTH

The Country
Emporium
WEST REDDING

CONNECTICUT

Baxter's Fish N Chips
Mildred's Chowder House
HYANNIS

Whistle Stop Muffins
GEORGETOWN

Archie's Tavern
PAWTUCKET

Swanky Franks
NORWALK

Jimmie's
WEST HAVEN

Common's Restaurant
LITTLE COMPTON

Coffee An'
WESTPORT

Aunt Carrie's
NARRAGANSETT

Rocky Point Park Shore Dinner Hall
WARWICK

The Little Stone House
The Place
GUILFORD

The Sea Gull
S. KINGSTOWN

Sea
Swirl
MYSTIC

Dovecrest Indian Restaurant
EXETER

The Inn at Chester
CHESTER

Abbott's Lobster
in the Rough
NOANK

The Sand Bar
OLD SAYBROOK

New England Specialties

Where we list several places, we have starred the one we think best.

American Chop Suey—A casserole of macaroni and ground beef

★ Bean's (South Paris, ME)   24
  Cole Farms (Gray, ME)   26
  Wayside Restaurant (Berlin, VT)   68

Baked Beans and Brown Bread

  Bean's (South Paris, ME)   24
  Cole Farms (Gray, ME)   26
★ Durgin-Park (Boston, MA)   43
  Aunt Carrie's (Narragansett, RI)   57
  The Bryant House (Weston, VT)   63
  The Fairlee Diner (Fairlee, VT)   65
  Wayside Restaurant (Berlin, VT)   68

Boiled Dinners and Red Flannel Hash—For dinner, corned beef is slow simmered with beets, potatoes, and cabbage; the next day it is chopped into a vivid red hash and fried on the grill

  Moody's (Waldoboro, ME)   33
  The Fairlee Diner (Fairlee, VT)   65
★ Wayside Restaurant (Berlin, VT)   68

Chowders and Fish Stews

  Abbott's Lobster in the Rough (Noank, CT)   10
  Bean's (South Paris, ME)   24
  Cole Farms (Gray, ME)   26
  The Dip Net (Port Clyde, ME)   28
  Line House Restaurant (York, ME)   31
  Maine Diner (Wells, ME)   32
  Moody's (Waldoboro, ME)   33
  Two Lights Lobster Shack (Cape Elizabeth, ME)   38
  Baxter's Fish N Chips (Hyannis, MA)   39
★ Coonamessett Inn (Falmouth, MA)   41
  Durgin-Park (Boston, MA)   43
  Mildred's Chowder House (Hyannis, MA)   47
  White Cap (Ipswich, MA)   51
  Aunt Carrie's (Narragansett, RI)   57
  Common's Restaurant (Little Compton, RI)   58
  Rocky Point Park Shore Dinner Hall (Warwick, RI)   60

Aunt Carrie's (Narragansett, RI)   57
Willy's (East Burke, VT)   69

Hot Lobster Roll

Abbott's Lobster in the Rough (Noank, CT)   10
★ Jimmie's (West Haven, CT)15
Maine Diner (Wells, ME)   32

Indian Pudding—A warm molasses and cornmeal pudding

Bean's (South Paris, ME)   24
Coonamessett Inn (Falmouth, MA)   41
★ Durgin-Park (Boston, MA)   43
Locke-Ober (Boston, MA)   45
Mildred's Chowder House (Hyannis, MA)   47
Aunt Carrie's (Narragansett, RI)   57
Dovecrest Indian Restaurant (Exeter, RI)   59
Rocky Point Park Shore Dinner Hall (Warwick, RI)   60
The Bryant House (Weston, VT)   63
The Fairlee Diner (Fairlee, VT)   65
Skyline Restaurant (Marlboro, VT)   67

Lobster Dinners

Abbott's Lobster in the Rough (Noank, CT)   10
The Little Stone House (Guilford, CT)   16
The Place (Guilford, CT)   21
Beal's Lobster Pier (Southwest Harbor, ME)   24
Bill Foster's Clambake (York Harbor, ME)   25
Harraseeket Lunch & Lobster Company (S. Freeport, ME)   28
★ Nunan's Lobster Hut (Cape Porpoise, ME)   34
Robinson's Wharf (Southport, ME)   35
Superior Shellfish, Inc. (Searsport, ME)   37

Lobster Pie

The Little Stone House (Guilford, CT)   16
★ Maine Diner (Wells, ME)   32

Maine Blueberries—Cake, pie, grunt, and cobbler

Beal's Lobster Pier (Southwest Harbor, ME)   24
The Dip Net (Port Clyde, ME)   28
★ Helen's (Machias, ME)   29
Shirley's Dining Room (Skowhegan, ME)   36

Muffins, Sweet Rolls, and Doughnuts

New England Portuguese

Pancakes

Pickled Tripe

Rhode Island Chicken Dinner

Rhode Island Jonnycakes—Small pancakes made from white cornmeal

Rhode Island Shore Dinners—Steamers, clam cakes, chowder, lobsters, clam broth, and corn on the cob

    Aunt Carrie's (Narragansett, RI)   57
★ Rocky Point Park Shore Dinner Hall (Warwick, RI)   60
    The Sea Gull (S. Kingstown, RI)   62

Snail Salad

★ Archie's Tavern (Pawtucket, RI)   56
    The Sea Gull (S. Kingstown, RI)   62

Strawberry Shortcake on a Biscuit

    Bean's (South Paris, ME)   24
    Line House Restaurant (York, ME)   31
    Two Lights Lobster Shack (Cape Elizabeth, ME)   38
★ Durgin-Park (Boston, MA)   43
    The Bryant House (Weston, VT)   63
    Skyline Restaurant (Marlboro, VT)   67

Vermont Cheese and Crackers

    The Bryant House (Weston, VT)   63

Wooster Square Pizza—A regional style of pizza baked in ancient coal-fired ovens

    Pepe's Pizzeria Napoletana (New Haven, CT)   19

Yankee Chicken Pie

    Marble Pillar (Hartford, CT)   18
    Bean's (South Paris, ME)   24
    Lancaster Diner (Lancaster, NH)   53
★ The Bryant House (Weston, VT)   63
    Buck and Doe (Island Pond, VT)   64

Types of New England Restaurants

CONNECTICUT

Abbott's Lobster in the Rough

117 Pearl St., Noank, Conn.
(203) 536-7719

Summer daily noon–9 p.m.

Lobster dinners about $10–$20; other meals $10 or less

At Abbott's, "in the rough" means sea air, a warm summer sun, and the occasional screech of a gull overhead. The dining area is a lawn and pier scattered with multicolored picnic tables. The tables look out on a harbor filled with sailboats and lobstermen's trawlers: ambience no inland seafood restaurant can duplicate; the best appetizer in the world.

Behind the order window, you can see the massive iron steaming tanks—very industrial, and a superior way to cook a lobster. Crack into the hard bright red claws and knuckles: here is the tenderest pink meat, its natural sweetness brought to blossom by the steam; even the tail is extra-ordinarily delicate, with a full, satisfying succulence. At Abbott's you will never get waterlogged or rubbery lobsters because they do not linger in a pot of water; only seconds transpire between the time they're cooked and served.

Abbott's clam chowder is a simple preparation—little more than clam broth, diced potatoes, chunks of clam, and a whisper of pepper. It is bracing food, the essence of the ocean.

Raw littlenecks are served freshly opened, on the half-shell: tiny pink folds of flesh, glistening in brine. They are sold on a platter along with topnecks—larger clams, similar to cherrystones, in fact rather gross.

Mussels from Rhode Island are usually on the menu, by the plate—about twenty-five of them. The shells are blue-black, sharp as a killer whale; the bodies full and clean, steamed to a peak of plump clamitude. For a couple of dollars and a lot of work, you can plow through a bowl of steamers—approximately fifty small clams. Remove the loose black membrane, grab the little clam by its neck, dip it in melted butter and/or broth, and pop it down the hatch. Steamers are a delicious shoreline treat, but they must be eaten fast; by the time you get to the last dozen, their juicy fresh bodies will have begun to dry.

Abbott's hot lobster roll, a Connecticut specialty, is an opulent sandwich of buttered lobster meat mounded high onto a large sesame bun: lobster indulgence without fuss. You can also get a lobster salad roll—mayo-diluted, served cold in a split wiener bun.

Be prepared: on a sunny day, Abbott's gets mighty crowded. There is a long wait in line to get to the order window, then another twenty minutes while the lobster steams. This, however, is one of the few restaurants where you could hardly mind loitering. Abbott's seafood market next door is great for browsing; the lobster pound is open for inspection; and Noank is a delight. It is a small fishing village, its hilly streets a patchwork of shoreline homes and small shops. Just up the road from Abbott's is a general store that's been around for seventy-five years, its sign advertising SMOKES, COFFEE, CONVERSATION.

Coffee An'

343 N. Main St., Westport, Conn.
(203) 227-3808

Mon.–Fri. 7 a.m.–5:30 p.m., Sat. 7 a.m.–4 p.m.

Under $5

Connecticut and Rhode Island are New England's doughnut belt, south of Yankee muffin country and north of where the bagels are. Sugar-fried dough is hawked at every county fair. Seafood shops sell doughboys and doughballs to accompany fish. It might even be argued that the ubiquitous clam fritter is a sort of mutant doughnut.

No doubt about it: doughnuts are the dough of choice in southern New England, and it's no secret that 99 percent of all the doughnuts eaten here are atrocious. However, not all are lardy junk food, and not all shops that sell them are ugly franchised eateries catering to guys with big necks and no taste buds. Coffee An' in Westport makes the best doughnuts in Connecticut —probably the best in America.

According to Derek Couturas, who starts making them every morning at four, there are no secret recipes; there is only close attention to detail. "For instance," he said, "any recipe will tell you to glaze the doughnuts when they are hot, so the glaze looks good, all nice and shiny. But if you do it when they're *too* hot, the glaze runs off. You get the shine but not the taste. I know exactly when the glaze must be put on."

After twenty-one years at it, he is a master. Every morning at seven, you can see him in the back room, surrounded by cooling doughnuts hung on long wood dowels, busily glazing or sprinkling powdered sugar onto trays of hot round beauties. They sell fast, dozens at a time over the glass take-out case, so fast that they always come warm to the people who occupy the fifteen or twenty places at the low counter, or the few high chairs at the window.

Our favorites are the chocolate doughnuts, knobby circles that are as dense as pound cake—so rich with devil's food they are raven black, their crust iced with a clear glaze. And cinnamon twirls—stupefying items, a full three inches high and six around, billowy yeast cakes threaded with dark circling veins of cinnamon and sheathed in sweet sugar gilt. We estimate one twirl to be the caloric equivalent of five ordinary doughnuts.

The Country Emporium

West Redding, Conn.   At the Redding train station
(203) 938-2484

Tues.–Fri. 11 a.m.–3 p.m., Sat. & Sun. 10 a.m.–3 p.m. Closed for two weeks after Labor Day   Reservations advised on weekends

About $5

The Country Emporium is an old-fashioned Connecticut country store, a hodgepodge of odd tools, penny candies, and silly gag postcards. It is also a great place for breakfast. The house specialty: pancakes.

An order consists of three substantial six-inchers—your choice from a list of eight varieties. We recommend buckwheat, dark and pleasantly coarse; kernel-dotted corn pancakes; and the strange cheddar-cheese pancakes, which are made with enough cheese so that when they fry on the griddle, whole areas near the edge turn crisp and the cakes develop a piebald skin of yellow-gold and brown.

A small fragrant disc of sausage can be had on the side. It's made by a local butcher with herbs brought to him by Emporium owner Anita Galer.

For fancier palates, there are crepes: sour cream and lingonberry; chocolate chip with ice cream; and when strawberries are available at a reasonable price, strawberry and sour cream. The Emporium also serves lovely— if rather diminutive—hamburgers on baked-here dill buns, hot chili, soups, a few sandwiches, and cream and fruit pies.

The tone of the small two-room restaurant is, like the store, eclectic: a big wood cookstove, hundreds of old implements hung on the ceiling and walls, bolts of calico fabric for sale, and, just like the Seventh Avenue Deli, a gallery of signed publicity photos of famous people who have eaten pancakes here. ("The place to be in Conn.," says Jack Klugman. Beverly Sills smiles happily in agreement.)

Dr. Mike's Ice Cream Shop

158 Greenwood Ave., Bethel, Conn.   In Bethel Commons
(203) 792-4388

March–Christmas Summer daily noon–11 p.m. Shorter hours in cooler weather

$5 or less

We grant that ice cream is a specialty not unique to New England, but anyone who has tasted Cote's ice cream in Maine or a Bailey's hot fudge sundae in Boston can tell you that the northeast is where the best ice cream is.

Being somewhat fanatical about this subject, we have made it our business during the last dozen years to sample *every* kind of ice cream all across the country for which any believable claim of greatness can be made. In the Pantheon are the Dove Bars of Chicago, Graeter's turtle sundaes in Cincinnati, Angelo Brocato's Italian gelati in New Orleans' French Quarter, and Vivoli in Berkeley. But above them all towers Dr. Mike's of Bethel, Connecticut—the best ice cream in America.

We were worried when original owner Peter Seltzer sold the business to Robert Allison in 1983. But Robert hasn't franchised or expanded or in any way diminished Dr. Mike's magic. In fact, he has done the impossible—made ice cream better than ever.

The rich chocolate is thick and creamy, flecked with occasional fine cocoa powder still dry in the dark custard. Its deep flavor is poised perfectly between bitter and sweet. There are more sophisticated ice creams, sweeter, more dense with chocolate; the artistry of Dr. Mike's rich chocolate is its tantalizing balance of qualities.

Less intensely flavored, but richer, is chocolate malt ice cream—pale, toffee-colored, the density of the cream accentuated by pure malt.

A third regular flavor we recommend is something called chocolate lace and creme. The "creme" is simply cream, sweetened and iced, no flavorings, the way all Dr. Mike's varieties begin. The "chocolate lace" is a confection manufactured in Danbury, broken up into small crunchy chunks of bitter-chocolate-covered candy, sprinkled throughout the cream like supreme chocolate chips.

If you take your coffee with two lumps of sugar, you may find Dr. Mike's coffee ice cream too adult. It is nothing but coffee with cream and only a dash of sweetness. We like it topped with one of Dr. Mike's extras, such as a sprinkle of malt powder or M & M's. The coffee ice cream also makes a swell base for a hot fudge sundae. The fudge is champion, grainy and intense; it is topped with freshly whipped heavy cream.

Other varieties in the repertoire: coconut, prune, cinnamon, and an unsurpassed vanilla—pure, genuinely vanilla (not *plain*) flavored.

Malts are made without syrup. They are simply your choice of ice cream flavor, thinned by whole milk, enriched by malt powder, mixed a few moments in one of the two single-wanded milk-shake machines.

Dr. Mike's is difficult to locate, behind Bethel's main street, down a small alleyway. It is a tiny place, with barely room for five stand-up customers at one time. Outside is a porch with three small tables.

The Inn at Chester

318 W. Main St., Chester, Conn.   Rte. 148
(203) 526-4961

Breakfast, lunch, & dinner daily, Sun. brunch   Reservations advised

$15–$30

A lovely backroad setting, just where you'd hope to find a cozy New England inn. The inside is appropriately rustic, yet smells deliciously of new-hewn wood. The main room is tall, with a stone fireplace and a view into an arboreal greenhouse. A low-ceilinged, quieter dining room is adjacent. And there is a smaller room with a single large table that can be reserved for two to a dozen people. It is a proper dining room, like you'd expect in a decorous colonial home, so private it seems secret. What a setting for romance or celebration!

"American country" describes the food: honest cooking with a boutique flair, good ingredients, skillfully cooked, put together with a sense of design. You will eat things that are familiar, but seldom boring.

First, warm bread—grainy corn sticks, white and onion-topped dark rolls. What other restaurant dares serve cranberry shrub? Here's a taste of old New England—lemon sherbet atop a tall glass of apples and minced berries: tart, musty, cool.

There is no better meal for a cold winter night than the Inn's pork, each slice edged with crackling skin. Its accompanying apples are firm, exactly tart enough to balance the sweet meat. Pork and apples are coddled in a nostalgic ginger raisin sauce that tastes like Christmas. On the side comes a cup of creamy corn pudding.

It is rare to be served game hen as robust as the one prepared here. Beneath a crunchy skin, the meat is naturally flavorful, accented by a cornbread stuffing of sausage, spinach, and a dash of garlic.

You like chocolate? Taste the marble cheesecake, with its cocoa swirls through svelte cream curd—a tantalizing composition. Hazelnut cake, fresh and nutty, is edged with mild chocolate frosting.

The pecan diamond is small, deadly, and delectable—profoundly sweet brittle, soft enough to chew, served with good whipped cream; it is pecan pie reduced to its essence. Bread pudding is another killer, a brick of it, packed with nuts and raisins, strongly cinnamoned, running with boozy bourbon sauce.

Jimmie's

Savin Rock, West Haven, Conn.
(203) 934-3212

Sun.–Thurs. 11 a.m.–11 p.m., Fri. & Sat. to 1 a.m.

$5–$10

Pure-palated clam connoisseurs scoff, but Jimmie's turns out some great fried seafood. The sad part is that the shoreline rude food is served indoors, at tables, by waitresses, with knives and forks and napkins. Formerly the height of raunch at Savin Rock Amusement Park, Jimmie's has gone uptown with the neighborhood. It is an architect's notion of a restaurant with shingle siding inside and out, and a pleasant (but protected) view of the water. No longer is the thrill of dining here intensified by the fear that a gull will swoop down and steal a french fry.

Even with its veneer of civilized dining, Jimmie's beach cuisine cannot help but be mucho fun. The lobster roll is a crumbling-to-pieces mess, a frankfurter bun so sopped with butter that it threatens to fall apart, grilled crisp and packed with nothing but sweet chunks of buttered lobster. Get a side of onion rings—individual circles of sweet crunchy onion in a pale crust.

Clams, shrimp, and scallops are available as platters, higher-than-wide heaps composed half and half of good french fries and golden seafood. Occasionally there are oysters, big-bellied clods of deep-fried goo. The scallops are sweet and tender; shrimp are fresh, sheathed in the gentlest breading; and clams are exemplary: gnarled and nutty-flavored, with full round bodies and circular thin strips, looking like some briny fry basket monster's diamond ring.

"Clams are one of nature's health foods," says Jimmie's menu. We can think of many good reasons for chowing down at this seaside clamatorium, but that isn't one of them.

The Little Stone House

Whitfield St., Guilford, Conn.
(203) 453-2566

Tues.–Thurs. noon–8:30 p.m., Fri. to 9 p.m., Sat. to 9:30 p.m.,
Sun. to 8 p.m.   Closed in Jan.

$10–$20

A cute place, all stone and dark wood, set low against a marsh across from the docks. Inside, bright flowers adorn the larger tables; the clientele is well-heeled. And yet, for all that, it is very plain, very Yankee.

The waitresses, for instance: some are young and eager, but many are old-timers who, however efficient, are brusque. No-nonsense women in nylon uniforms.

The menu has not changed in the last fifteen years. Good sole, bluefish, scrod, scallops—but the most interesting item in the house is the colonial favorite, lobster pie. Quite formidable in appearance, it is a boat-shaped casserole of lobster meat (whole sections of the beast) in a svelte white sauce, the casserole covered with a many-layered crust. The crust fairly oozes butter from between its thin sheets—a complement to the lobster beneath. The waitress sets this unwieldly dish by your plate, and then she's gone. You are on your own.

Only slightly less rich is what the menu lists as "fresh picked lobster"—nothing more than a bowl of lobster meat in butter. Like the lobster in the pie, it is unimpeachably fresh.

Some of the best things come free with dinner: zingy bright red chow-chow and garlic/chive cottage cheese; moist gingerbread and cranberry nut bread.

Many regulars begin their dinner with lobster bisque, a pale soup that we have always thought too thick with cream, skimpy with the flavor of lobster, not unlike Stouffer's lobster "Newberg." Clam chowder, on the other hand, is excellent. It is a toasty soup with plenty of clams and just the right balance of potatoes.

A chiffon fruit pie is made each day: strawberry, lime, lemon, or the like, served atop a graham cracker crust and topped with a blanket of unpleasant pseudo-whipped cream.

"The Story of The Little Stone House" on the back of the menu informs that "for over thirty years, The Little Stone House has been synonymous with embarrassingly fresh seaford [*sic*]."

Louis Lunch

261 Crown St., New Haven, Conn.
(203) 562-5507

Mon.–Fri. 9 a.m.–4:30 p.m.

$5 or less

Walking into Louis Lunch to eat a hamburger is the culinary equivalent of engaging Socrates himself in a lively dialogue, or pulling pen from shirt shield in Independence Hall to sign your name to the Declaration of Independence. To eat at Louis Lunch is to become part of history; for it was here, in 1903, that Louis Lassen invented the hamburger.

Louis was a thrifty man who didn't like throwing out the trimmings from the steaks he served at his lunch wagon. So he ground up the leftovers, seared them on a fire, and put the result between two pieces of toast. *Voilà!*

Errant food historians contend that the hamburger was invented in Germany as a "Hamburg steak" and imported to America. What cheek! In fact, what we call a hamburger is known in Hamburg as an "American steak." Never mind who first ground up beef anyway (it was probably the Tartars, centuries ago); it was Louis Lassen's genius to put the ground-up patty on bread. *That* is the essence of hamburgerhood.

A small brick building with school desk seats and an ancient initial-carved counter, Louis Lunch is a bit of otherwise-vanished New Haven—New Haven with charm, where the collegians meet the townies. At a recent breakfast we watched counterman Ken Lassen (Louis III) kibbitz with customers as he nimbly doled out eggs. "Are you scrambled?" . . . "Who's onions?" . . . "Want me to cut those up for you, Professor?"

The "Professor" was an elderly, wizened gent who comes in regularly (with his own coffee cup), but on this day, had his arm in a sling. Louis . . . or, rather, Ken filled his cup and cut his eggs. "So, Professor, what do you think of Dallas and New York?"

The old man swirled his coffee, took a feeble sip, set down the cup, pointed a finger skyward, and said with total assurance, "This year, I am certain . . . the Giants are the team of destiny."

Marble Pillar

22 Central Row, Hartford, Conn.
(203) 247-4549

Mon.–Sat. 7 a.m.–8 p.m.

$5–$10

The Marble Pillar is a hundred-and-twenty-year old institution; so institutional that its walls are painted canned-pea green, like at the Motor Vehicle Bureau. It is in its glory at high noon, dishing out hot lunch on sectioned plates amidst a cacophony of full-volume table conversations, with the strong-armed serving staff bellowing orders to the kitchen from the middle of the dining room.

Coat hooks on the wall, large tables shared by strangers, yeomanly cooking, buck-and-a-half cold sandwiches at lunch: here is a forthright downtown lunch room; a restaurant that is, above all, *real*.

With one horrible exception: mashed potatoes that are far too powdery for our sensitive palates. But if you can get past that, you're on easy street.

Chicken pot pie, recently saved from extinction by nouvelle American chefs, never went out of fashion in Hartford, Connecticut. An obscure southern cousin of the better-known Vermont chicken pie, Connecticut's own version is at its steamy best right here, brought warm to the table in a foil tin, heaped onto your plate by the waitress. In the cornucopic spill, you find plump peas (*bright* green ones), fresh carrots, hunks of potato, and big squares of white meat chicken, plus a rugged array of crisply broken tan crust. Superb!

You know that the liver, for $3.50 including onion, gravy, spuds, peas, black bread and butter, is not from an expensive young calf. This is dark, hearty, grown-up beef liver; and it is delicious—strong and loud, for liver lovers only.

Of the menu's three wursts, knockwurst is the jumbo pink tube, mildly garlicked, like a frank; mettwurst is pork and beef, like kielbasa; and bratwurst, the best of them, is two lengths of lush veal sausage—long pale links with crackling skin. All varieties come with pork-enriched sauerkraut and a mound of paprika'd potatoes.

The Marble Pillar's German accent is thicker at dinner, when the dining room takes on the look of an Edward Hopper painting, the pace becomes a maudlin dirge, and you can order from a variety of schnitzels, pork chops, and dumplings.

Get a side order of spaetzel if it doesn't come with your dinner. These oddly shaped little dumpling ribbons are distinctive—buttered and fried, cozy food.

Schweinhaxe (pig hocks) are an autumn specialty, highly recommended by the waitress, who gleefully describes the "few hairs still sticking from the circle of fat that surrounds the tenderest pork you will ever eat." Ulp.

Strudel is the house dessert, bought elsewhere, frozen. Other highlights include Jell-O, which the waitress, when asked what flavor it is, says straight out, "red"; fat canned plums in nectar; and a surprise pièce de résistance— fruit rum sundae. This bagatelle is nothing but vanilla ice cream, a splash of liquor, and the yellow and orange things from a can of fruit cocktail. Similar to the Princess Cup served at New Orleans' estimable Galatoire's, it's a dish that transcends its ignoble ingredients.

There was once a time when every city in America had its Marble Pillar: Old Reliable, where citizens from all walks of life could count on honest blue-plate specials and fast service without frills. In an era of culinary classism, such gastronomic democracy is something to treasure.

Pepe's Pizzeria Napoletana

157 Wooster St., New Haven, Conn.
(203) 865-5762

Mon., Wed., & Thurs. 4 p.m.–11 p.m., Fri. & Sat. 11:30 a.m.–1 a.m., Sun. 2:30 p.m.–11 p.m.   Closed in Aug.

$5–$10

It may seem odd to list pizza as a regional specialty, but anyone who has been to Wooster Street in New Haven can tell you that the pizzas made here are not merely different, but extraordinarily delicious—America's best.

Pepe's opened in 1925, and was New Haven's first "pizzeria Napoletana." On the back wall, there is a portrait of Frank Pepe The Founder gazing out over the Bay of Naples. The artist's perspective renders Signor Pepe a full forty feet tall—*hommage*, we assume, to the man who invented the coaloven pizza.

The cooking process is virtually unchanged from Pepe's techniques of sixty-one years ago. It starts in the traditional Neapolitan manner, with dough that has been allowed to lie in a wood trough to "rest" before being pounded—by hand—into a flat circle. The flattening of the dough takes place on the business end of a six-foot-long wooden spatula, where the pizza is assembled by a man clad in a sauce-splattered apron, his shoes white with fallen flour. He distributes a sauce lumpy with tomato bits around the circle; then, for most pizzas, cheese is spread about (if you don't order mozzarella as an ingredient, you get a tomato-only pie), followed by large chunks of fennel-specked sausage, sliced pepperoni, whatever you choose. With a fancy flourish of one hand, he dusts on seasoning, then hoists up the spatula and slides the pie into the oven. The kitchen is open, allowing patrons to watch the pizzaiolo's virtuosic preparation of the pie—a unique ritual that is one of the small wonders of Naples', New Haven's, and America's gastronomy.

The ingredients used at Pepe's are the best you can get; but it is the oven that makes the pies unique. It is coal-fired, and as the pizza cooks on the oven's brick floor, the crust absorbs a faintly ashy taste. Adhering to the crust's underside are tiny burnt crumbs, creating a charred, almost friable texture. The circle of crust at the pie's circumference swells into a variegated ring of chewy puffs and brittle pockets, and sometimes blackens at its outermost edges.

Drawn from the oven, the pizza is slid onto a battered metal pan, then cut by your waiter or waitress at a table just outside the kitchen. It takes a while for a pie to cook, but Pepe's veteran staff hurries it to the table with a special kind of walk they have all developed for ferrying pizzas down the two aisles—best described as a speeded-up trudge.

The house specialty is the white clam pie. Available only when the kitchen decides to shuck fresh clams, it is an oval of rugged crust topped with whole clams, olive oil, oregano, and a harvest of garlic bits (fresh garlic would be too sharp). It is an elementary, perfect communion. Although other pizzerias in Connecticut serve similar oceanic ovals made with anchovies or minced clams, none compares to Pepe's version—a dish that elevates the humble pizza to a level of culinary grandeur alongside the best original Italian-American creations of the legendary Mosca's outside New Orleans.

Once you have tasted this white clam pie, all other pizzas diminish by comparison. Many are the times we have trundled into Pepe's, only to be told that there were no clams today. Our offers to run out to a seafood store and fetch and open our own fell on deaf ears. With perfection out of reach, we settled for one of Pepe's other—merely magnificent—pizzas.

If Pepe's is packed, or if it's Tuesday, there are two alternative coal-oven pizzerias on Wooster Street, both offering a taste of Neapolitan New Haven. Next door to Pepe's (underneath the laundry hanging out to dry) is The Spot, Pepe's original home, now with ferns and a skylight and artistic prints on the wall; and at 237 Wooster Street is Sally's Apizza, its wall hung with pictures of Sal ("Sally") Consiglio's brother Tony standing with celebrities like Dean Martin, Frank Sinatra, and the Kennedys.

The Place

891 Boston Post Rd., Guilford, Conn.
No phone

Mid-May–Sept., Mon.–Fri. 5 p.m.–11 p.m., Sat. & Sun. 1 p.m.–
11 p.m.—weather permitting

$5–$10

Guilford, Connecticut, is a shoreline town known for wealthy summer residents whose go-to-hell casual attire is the last word in prepdom. The Place
is a taste of Connecticut with just a dash of unstuffy alligator ambience.

Although right across the road from a shopping center of drugstores and
supermarkets, this is a pastoral setting. You sit on tree stumps; you eat off
overturned wooden spools that once held phone cables; the sun or the stars
serve as a roof. There is an FM radio hung in a tree. The breeze in this
restaurant-without-walls is scented with smoke from an open fire.

The menu is second cousin to a clambake, but a la carte. The specialties
are littleneck clams roasted over wood in the shell, split open, daubed with
hot sauce, and broiled a few moments more. There are steamers, small lobsters, and sweet corn cooked in the husk, then brushed with butter.

You are welcome to run across to the mall for a bottle of wine. Simply
hold your breath, dodge the traffic on Route 1, and, with jug in hand, jump
back like Pan into this enchanted glade in the midst of civilization.

The Sand Bar

Old Saybrook, Conn.   At the Point
(203) 388-3243

Summer daily 11 a.m.–9 p.m. or 10 p.m.

$5 or less

"Our clams have bellies," says the menu at The Sand Bar. Pictured next to
the list of pints and platters, steamers, stuffies, and salads is a clamoid
creature in a sailor suit sitting happily in the "c" of the word "clam."

The connoisseur of fried clams insists on going belly-up. Clam strips—
tiny rubber-band-like squiggles that remain when the bellies have been removed from sea clams—are considered by mollusk mavens to be strictly for
pantywaists. At The Sand Bar, bellies are full and tender, the clams crunchy,
light brown, with an alluring oceanic aroma. They come on clam plates with
french fries and cole slaw, on a clam roll, or in pints or half-pints—festively

striped trapezoidal boxes. You can also get steamers and clams on the half-shell, as well as soft-shell crabs, shrimp, and scallops.

The Sand Bar is a jolly place to eat, on the water, with a big open terrace that affords a view of sailboats skimming the horizon. The gulls that linger on the railings near the picnic tables are remarkably well-mannered, always allowing you to finish your meal before buzz-bombing for the crumbs left behind.

Sea Swirl

Rte. 1, east of downtown Mystic, Conn.
(203) 536-3452

Summer daily 10 a.m.–11 p.m.

$5 or less

There is something wrong about a fried clam on a china plate served in a restaurant with a maitre d' or a wine list. Its full glory can best be savored at a picnic table, or at least in the front seat of your Impala, hopefully near enough the ocean for the salty air to stimulate the appetite.

Sea Swirl offers little in the way of salt air, but there are picnic tables, plus a view of teenagers cruising up and down Route 1 in muscle cars with heavy engines. It appears to be a defunct Carvel stand. It is not pretty.

But Sea Swirl clams are superb, the best you can get this far south. They are sweet and oily, with tender bellies and a sharply seasoned crust: rich, raunchy roadfood. Sexy. We admit that even we peeled out of the parking lot with a squeal of rubber on pavement, the remnant teenage souls in both of us tickled by this unexpected encounter with greatness.

Swanky Franks

182 Connecticut Ave., Norwalk, Conn.   At exit ramp 14
(203) 838-8969

Mon.–Sat. 10 a.m.–9 p.m., Sun. 11 a.m.–7 p.m.

Under $5

About once each month, the craving strikes. And when we are hit with this particular urge, nothing else will satisfy. It is the Swanky Franks siren call, and if we have heard it, you could offer us dinner at Lutèce or Troisgros or Julia Child's kitchen, and we would pass them all up in favor of a place at Swanky Franks counter and a couple of crinkly garlic-loaded weiners piled high with mustard and relish and onions and kraut in a steamy white bun, with a side of dark greasy french fries and a can of Coke.

There are other things on the Swanky Franks menu, like clam rolls and sandwiches, but only weirdos don't get weiners. The one up-and-up deviation is a split and *grilled* weiner for a nickle more. (Grilled is the choice if you are watching your weight, as the regular Swanky Franks are deep-fried in oil.)

Swanky Franks aficionados had a scare a couple years ago when the original owner, a bellicose counterman who kept the conversation crackling, sold the place to new owners. But not to worry. The franks are still as deliciously awful, the fries as greasy, the service as lightning fast. And the steady clientele remains—a motley assortment of Broderick Crawford look-alikes who just pulled off the highway, plus local white-collar types who don't mind advertising where they ate their lunch. They're a stinking meal, these dogs, and their odoriferous aftermath sticks with you all day long—a steady, uncouth pal.

Whistle Stop Muffins

Branchville Station, Georgetown, Conn.
(203) 544-8139

Mon.–Fri. 5:30 a.m.–11:30 a.m.; tentative weekend hours 8 a.m.–noon Sat. & Sun.

Under $5

We live in Fairfield County, where muffins are somewhat exotic food, Yankee fare not encountered until you cross the state line into Rhode Island. Then one day, motorvating up Route 7, scarcely a mile from home, we saw a small, scrawny-lettered sign pointing the way to Branchville Station.

The muffins sold here every morning, hot out of the oven, are bulky behemoths, with great curved domes twice as wide as their bottoms. Still in the pan, they appear to be a single wide sheet cake, their batter having run completely together. When you order, Lolly Turner takes her knife and separates one from all the others, creating a round-bottomed, square-topped pastry. She pulls it from the pan, and if it is a fruit-filled muffin, she dusts it with powdered sugar.

Granular, steamy corn muffins; bran muffins with raisins and a giddy kick of spice; cake-heavy blueberry muffins laden with purple fruit: the repertoire is not special. But the muffins are.

The place is nice, too. The train still stops, but the station, as a station, is defunct. The ticket window has become the muffin window; the waiting room now serves as a two-table dining room (carry your own muffins and coffee). We like to arrive a little after nine o'clock, when the commuters have gone. We sit over coffee and buttered muffins, surrounded by the aged wood-slat station walls, inhaling the aroma of new batches emerging from the oven, and gazing out over the tracks. By golly, southern Connecticut really is part of New England!

MAINE

Beal's Lobster Pier

*Clark's Point Rd., Southwest Harbor, Maine Next to Mount Desert
Island Oceanarium*
(207) 244-3202

Summer daily 9 a.m.–8 p.m.

Usually $10 or less, but lobster prices vary

Beal's Lobster Pier is truly a lobster pier, piled high with traps, surrounded by the lobstermen's boats. At one end is a shed where customers select a live lobster by weight, and choose raw or steamed clams. At the other end of the pier is another, even smaller shed called the Captain's Galley, which sells clam chowder and very good, moist blueberry cake. Along the pier are picnic tables.

As we waited for our clams and lobsters to boil, a fisherman told us that the farther north you go along the Maine coast, the colder the water—and the firmer and better-tasting the lobster.

The lobster sure did taste good, as did the clams and quahog chowder and cake. Of course, the sound of the boats rocking in their berths, the smell of the sea, and the sight of the sunset over the mountains of Acadia National Park didn't hurt at all.

Bean's

6 Main St., South Paris, Maine
(207) 743-6493

Mon.–Sat. 6 a.m.–8 p.m.

About $5

When we were told we hadn't eaten good food in Maine if we hadn't been to Bean's, we had our doubts. Of course we knew the name; ordered from their famous catalogue many times. But food there? What could it be? Stew served in a hunting boot . . . chicken à la canvas tote bag? It wasn't long before we found that Maine is the home of two famous Beans—L. L. and Bean's of South Paris.

Bean's opened for business in 1945. It was once decorated with scenes of Oxford County life by Paris Hill painter Ellie Viles, but over the years it has spruced up to the point of resembling a nondescript lunchroom. Happily, the food hasn't modernized one bit. It's downeast cooking all the way.

As you might expect, Bean's cooks beans, quite good ones in fact—slow simmered the old-fashioned way with pork and molasses, served with a moist hunk of brown bread on the side. Saturday is the traditional day for partaking, and that is when they're always on the menu.

You can come here any day and get exemplary chowder—a mild milky broth with hunks of tender fish, dusted with paprika.

A Kate Hepburn look-alike at a neighboring table leveled a blue-eyed gaze at us as we surreptitiously scribbled notes about her vegetableless chicken pie, noting the flaky crust and rivulets of saffron-colored sauce.

Served with most main dishes at Bean's are baked potatoes—big flavorful native spuds that have never known the shame of wearing an aluminum foil dinner jacket.

Bean's desserts are plain and good: gingerbread crowned with fresh whipped cream; or strawberry shortcake served on a biscuit rather than a piece of sponge cake. Bean's Indian pudding, topped with ice cream, is a light puree, toothsome with the pleasant grit of cornmeal.

What else makes Bean's a favorite spot? Hot popovers, homemade pies, and that silly New England favorite, American chop suey—ground beef stretched with macaroni noodles and tomato sauce, a parsimonious Yankee tradition since long before the invention of Hamburger Helper.

Bill Foster's Clambake

Rte. 1A, York Harbor, Maine
(207) 363-3255

Summer Wed.–Sat. 7 p.m., Sun. 5 p.m., Sat. only in Sept.
Reservations required

About $15

If Bill Foster's place were any other kind of restaurant, we wouldn't give it a second glance. It's rowdy, crowded, and confused—especially so after dinner, when the sing-along begins: just the way a downeast clambake ought to be.

Never mind the crush of tourists, this is a lovely place: a screened pavilion set among tall trees and a colorful spray of flowers. Inside, the eating hall is set with long communal tables—rough-hewn furniture, the kind that encourages you to be messy.

And messy you will be as you crack into a full shore dinner of lobsters, clams, corn on the cob, chowder, baked potato, onions, hot dogs, rolls and butter, and watermelon. There is a raw bar for insatiable molluskophiles, an ice cream booth, and an open bar serving beer, wine, and liquor. Bill Foster's Clambake is a carnival, a whole evening's entertainment.

The lobsters, clams, corn, potatoes, and onions are slow cooked by bake-master Bill Foster over an open fire. The food is layered with rockweed into a wire-bottom wood box, each course set in to steam according to how long it takes to cook. The seaweed is the secret of a clambake, imparting a musky ocean-smoke flavor to the food, a flavor that mixes just about perfectly with the briny vapor of the steaming clams.

Mr. Foster has been hosting his shivarees at the York Harbor bake-ground for thirty-six years. His staff is available for private clambakes, wherever you choose.

The Clam Shack

Kennebunkport, Maine   At the bridge
(207) 967-2560

Summer daily 11 a.m.–11 p.m.

$5 or less

The Clam Shack is a minuscule take-out stand. As you wait for your clams to fry, you have a good opportunity to observe the regular customers—summer Kennebunkportians, many of whom favor expensive sportswear in colors that exactly replicate the Day-Glow palette of the spray-paint graffiti artists who decorate New York subways.

Clam Shack clams are excellent—dark brown and chewy, served as a lunchbox platter with french fries and cuts of dill pickle. As a side order, you can get sweet onion rings or clam cakes that are a dough-fancier's delight.

Many Clam Shack customers take their order around back and eat standing up, overlooking the water.

Also on sale at the Shack are clam hods, baskets fishermen use to keep clams cool and wet. The sign suggests you take one home for use as a planter.

Cole Farms

Rte. 100, north of Gray, Maine
(207) 657-4714

Daily 5 a.m.–11:30 p.m.

$5 or less

Cole Farms, less than a half hour west of coastal Yarmouth, is a different Maine, a Maine of pickup trucks and horse farms and stores that sell western boots. No sea gulls, no sailors, not a lobster on the menu, not a tourist in the house.

Although the culinary clichés are missing, a connoisseur of American regional cuisine could be led blindfolded to Cole Farms and easily pinpoint the restaurant's location. You know it's New England, because baked beans are on the menu as a main course and a list of the day's muffins is always posted near the door. Plus, Cole Farms serves that old downeast favorite, American chop suey.

You could further narrow down the geography by observing the predominance of blueberries (in muffins and pies) and noting that Cole Farms' list of ice cream specialties (Maine is *fanatical* about homemade ice cream) lists both "milk shake" and "frappe." The frappe is what the rest of America calls a milk shake. The milk shake is simply milk and flavoring: a taxonomy unique to Maine.

The astute gastronomic detective would only have to take one look at a Cole Farms clam cake to tell you that the restaurant is within fifty miles of Portland. Clam cakes in this area are less frittery and more like pancakes— flat crunchy circles with sweet clam-dotted insides.

Finally, our gourmet gumshoe would discover that while corn and fish chowders are made here daily, the kitchen seldom bothers with clam chowder. Ergo, we are away from the shore. The restaurant is either in the town of Gray, or afloat on Sebago Lake.

The point is this: if you've had your fill of lobsters and clams and pretty seaside picnics, veer west a bit and taste something tourists seldom experience—inland Maine, with a tart Yankee flavor all its own. Cole Farms' muffins are so lacking in sugar you want to call them dour. The genuine lemonade served here is really no more than stretched-out lemon juice, thick with pulp. The grape-nut pudding is not for Cool Whip palates. And plate lunches, although not particularly regional, are stern fare, too: hot roast beef with chunky mashed potatoes, meat loaf, baked ham.

Square, square meals—so honest that the menu lists a cup of Cole Farms chowder for 95¢, and Campbell's soup for 85¢.

Cole Farms manages to be at once huge and cozy. There are four or five attached dining rooms, with most booths nestled in small separated screened-in areas. Service, by pretty country girls, is very fast and surprisingly solicitous. Our waitress, recognizing we weren't regular customers, brought us a dish of her favorite grape-nut ice cream to taste.

The Dip Net

Port Clyde, Maine   On the Dock
No phone

Summer Mon.–Sat. 8 a.m.–4 p.m.

$5 or less

Poor Betty Koelle. She's too good a cook. She got forced out of her first restaurant in Camden because she couldn't stand all the business. Too much work. So she moved to The Dip Net, a waterfront shed with no more than a dozen stools around the counter. "We never told anybody; we never advertised; but people found out we're here. I've baked twelve hundred pies so far this summer. I just can't take it!"

Baking is the main reason for her fame—about ten or twelve varieties of pie every day: raspberry glaze, walnut angel graham cracker, coconut macaroon, German chocolate, custards of all kinds, and just about every fruit that grows in Maine. There are muffins and cakes and puddings, too, and bright crustless fruit cobblers set on the counter.

Don't be so dessert-crazed that you miss out on the other mini-masterworks turned out of this open kitchen: seafood casserole, a bubbling ramekin of shrimp and crabmeat; first-rate chowders and seafood stews. If so versatile a cook can be said to have a specialty, Betty's broccoli is it. A cool, garden green salad of crisp raw broccoli bits and mayonnaise, it is the filling for sandwiches and the center of sensational omelettes.

Betty Koelle's artistry doesn't stop with cooking. Although it seems like nothing more than a shack over the water, The Dip Net is in fact a beautifully decorated place: eclectic, to be sure—what with the net hanging from the ceiling and the mismatched chairs—but with great style. Look, for instance, at the varnished floor. Betty hand-painted tiny buoys across a field of yellow on the wood.

We only hope that those loyal customers who have stalked Betty Koelle up and down the Maine coast don't chase her out again.

Harraseeket Lunch & Lobster Company

South Freeport, Maine   At the Freeport Town Landing
(207) 865-3535

Summer daily 11 a.m.–9 p.m.

$5 or less

Freeport is a town of many wonders: the L. L. Bean showroom, open twenty-four hours a day; the Desert of Maine, vintage tourist attraction and source of all manner of kitsch souvenirs; and Harraseeket Lunch & Lobster, a breezy clam shack overlooking the South Freeport Harbor.

HL&L serves some of the best fried clams north of Ipswich, real giants —globes of chewy crust hugging whole clams thick with sea flavor. Clam cakes offer less clam, more breading—but this breading is good, the frying oil absolutely fresh. HL&L's onion rings are large individual circles with a satisfying crunch.

SEAFOOD BASKETS A SPECIALTY, says the sign, and in Maine, baskets are always assortments of fried things: excellent here, but do explore the non-fried menu. Try a lobster or crab roll on a buttered toasted bun. Or better yet, get the ubiquitous shoreline combo, lobster and clams. The clams are your basic copious steamers; the lobster is boiled, and it was one of the cheapest ones we found anywhere in Maine—less than $5 for a 1½-pounder.

HL&L is an eat-in-the-rough establishment: place an order, wait for your number to be called, then find a picnic table overlooking the harbor. Your dining companions will be an equal mix of L. L. Bean customers, visiting fishermen, and people lucky enough to spend their summers in this sunny part of the world.

Helen's

32 Main St., Machias, Maine
(207) 255-6506

Daily 5 a.m.–9 p.m.

$10 or less

Wild blueberries are as dear a Maine food as lobsters, and even more difficult to harvest. Whereas the king of crustaceans obliges fishermen by walking right into the parlor part of a lobster trap, the wild Maine blueberry has defied all attempts at mechanical harvesting. Lowbush blues must be raked by hand from their ground-hugging shrubs; they are tiny fruits, much smaller than the more easily gathered highbush berries grown in the southeastern states; their season is short—two months at the most, in late summer.

For all these reasons, wild blueberries are seldom found outside the state of Maine. But in Maine, especially in the far northeast, August is a banquet of blue. In Machias, for three days late in the month, the blueberry harvest is celebrated with blueberry pancake breakfasts, cooking contests, and festivities to honor this most American of berries.

And at Helen's restaurant, in August and early September, you can eat what is surely the best blueberry pie in the universe: "down-Maine" blueberry pie, a rudimentary concoction—wild blueberries heaped onto a crust and topped with whipped cream. Simple enough, but Helen's genius is that the blueberry filling contains both cooked and uncooked fruit, a dramatic combination of soft and firm textures. The resonant taste of these berries is absolutely nothing like the big bland blue balls sold as blueberries everywhere outside northeastern New England.

Helen's makes a similar pie with strawberries (from Mexico or California), and some dandy double-crusted pies as well; but if you come here in August, down-Maine blueberry pie is a ticket to rapture.

A fixture on Main Street since the 1940s, Helen's is more than a pie shop. It is the one good place in town to eat (probably the one good place between Bar Harbor and New Brunswick). Seafood is the house specialty: great fried clams, plump and crisp; local scallops; small native fried shrimp; fresh broiled halibut, and haddock (usually fried, but also available broiled—a meaty, delicately flavored fish).

Helen's bakery is downstairs, source of The Pie, as well as muffins, turnovers, rolls, bread, and brownies.

Helen is retired, and the dining room on the left has been remodeled in a rather dull colonial style; but the back dining area, overlooking the river, is as charming as can be. Given our druthers, though, we like to sit at the counter. From here, the view is Helen's pie case.

Jordan's Restaurant

Rte. 26, Locke Mills, Maine
(207) 875-3515

Thurs.–Tues. 8 a.m.–9 p.m.

$5 or less

Jordan's is an oasis of good eating in a barren land. Western Maine is dotted with grocery store/gas stations that sell big fat sandwiches to big fat men, and we were almost hungry enough to settle for lunchmeat ourselves when we spotted it. We were on safari, stalking the perfect fried clam, and while the clams were . . . interesting, if not nearly the best, we realized mid-meal that otherwise Jordan's was A-1 country cooking.

The waitress set down a basket that contained only two cupcake-shaped dinner rolls. We could smell the steamy yeast even before the basket neared our table. "Tell me when you want more," she said. "We like to serve them warm." We assured her that we like to eat them warm, too; and now, insured against the possibility of starch deprivation, we tore into our ration. When seconds arrived, she told us we really ought to come back for breakfast one day, because Jordan's specializes in thick-sliced toast made from their own bread.

Now about those clams. The bad news is they are canned. But the good news is what Jordan's does to compensate. The clams are batter-dipped and fried in clear oil, resulting in something that is a cross between a fritter and a fried clam—a bulbous shape like a teeny-weeny down jacket. These will never win approval from clam purists, but for the rest of us, they're fun.

Better than the clams was the chicken pie, with plenty of shreds of tender chicken and vegetables, topped with a batter crust. The fish chowder was a milky soup, agreeably bland and buttery. Even a liver and onions platter tasted especially good, served with a side of potato salad dotted with red onions.

We then tried a fruit plate, which had slices of apple, orange, cantaloupe, and grapefruit around a hill of cottage cheese. After that came a dense wedge of sugary pecan pie and a slice of apple, which was true to the western Maine style, in that its filling resembled a strudel mash. Jordan's mince pie is made from scratch—suet, brown sugar, raisins, etc. It's highly spiced, delicious. Mellow coffee was the meal's denouement.

Jordan's is a comfortable truckstop-like cafe with a semicircular counter in one room and upholstered chairs at tables in the other. Someone has taken the time to make enormous salt and pepper shakers out of old 7-Up bottles. Most of the clientele seems known to the waitresses. We noted a trucker's cap on a wall hook and assumed its owner had been transferred to another route or felt casual enough about Jordan's to leave it hanging there until he returned.

Line House Restaurant

Rte. 1, York, Maine   On the Kittery border
(207) 439-3401

March–Nov. Wed.–Mon. 7 a.m.–8 p.m.

About $5

Line House oyster stew is an example of just how good plain Yankee cooking can be. In the northeast, seafood *stew* (oyster, fish, clam, or otherwise) differs from the more commonly known *chowder* in that it lacks potatoes or any other vegetable. It is a primal milk or cream broth, seasoned with butter, salt, and pepper, powdered with paprika, ballasted with large hunks of seafood. At the Line House, each batch of butter-yellow oyster stew is individually built when ordered, beginning with large oysters, sauteed just enough to yield their oceanic juices. It's the best oyster stew we've tasted in our travels up the coast.

The Line House has been in business for nearly fifty years, beginning as a clam shack, and is now a modern roadhouse with a smattering of rustic touches such as old implements and walking sticks hung on the wall and blue gingham curtains in the windows. It's a decidedly local haunt, with a shelf of personalized coffee cups in the back room for the regulars. "When I see them pull up, I get their order ready," the waitress explained. "It's always the same every morning—coffee and a muffin."

The muffins are blueberry, so fluffy they break into pieces from the weight of the butter. The crumbles are ribboned with purple fruit.

We also recommend the fried clams and clam cakes, and the strawberry shortcake on a baking-powder biscuit. When you order coffee, real cream comes alongside in a small pitcher.

Maine Diner

Rte. 1, Wells, Maine
(207) 646-4441

Daily 7 a.m.–7 p.m., until 8 p.m. in summer

$10 or less

The Maine Diner has been a Route 1 fixture for years, but it was formerly open only on an inverse seasonal basis. As soon as tourists started coming up the coast in the spring, the coot who owned it shut down until the winter, when the out-of-staters disappeared. Strictly local.

In fact, it was such a favorite of Bruce and Myles Henry of nearby Drake's Island, that when they saw it for sale, they bought it, spruced it up, painted the outside white with snappy blue trim, and went about perfecting their grandmother's lobster-pie recipe.

Of all the good downeast things you can eat at the Maine Diner, grandmother's luxury casserole is the one that mustn't be missed. Your individual ceramic dish contains whole big portions of lobster—tail, claw, knuckle meat—drenched in butter, topped with a mixture of breadcrumbs and tomalley. It is a strange, punk-colored dish, green and brown and pink, shockingly rich.

The menu describes the hot lobster roll as *FANTASTIC!* The menu is correct. It is a Connecticut-style roll, nothing but sweet, resilient lobster meat spilling out of a grilled weiner bun. You cannot eat it with your hands, because the bun is soaked with butter and falls apart under the weight of the meat. But you *do* eat it with your hands, and fingers glisten as they pick tender claws and strings of pink, and occasional hunks of butter-sopped bread.

Fried clams are extraordinary, too—vigorously oceanic, just a wee bit oily; so fragile the crust seems to melt away as you sink into them.

Maine Diner pies are literally homemade, brought and sold to the Henry brothers by the waitresses, whose specialties include red raspberry, blueberry, pistachio, and banana cream.

There is always grape-nut custard on the menu—a layered pudding, its eggy balm atop a bed of moistened cereal. This kindly nutmeg-dusted bowl of bliss is a true New England antique, reminiscent of a time before gourmets made dessert sinful and decadent.

Occasionally, the Henry brothers bake up a batch of pale Indian pudding, dotted with raisins. On this subject, our waitress couldn't help but volunteer a passionate opinion: "to me Indian pudding tastes like . . . yech!"

Other than that prejudice, the help at the Maine Diner is friendly and proud of the food. We could see them beam with joy as we happily plowed our way through one of the best inexpensive roadside meals along Maine's southern coast.

Moody's

Rte. 1, Waldoboro, Maine
(207) 832-7468

Always open, except Fri. midnight–Sat. 5 a.m. & Sat. midnight–Sun. 7 a.m.

$5 or less

When we first stopped at Moody's, a decade ago, they were selling black-and-white souvenir postcards that showed 1949 Fords pulled up around the old wooden diner. Now there are new cards, in color. They show 1963-vintage Cadillacs parked in the same place.

Moody's may be a little slow, but it's sure. It is an old, steady friend—the place to go when you want coffee, a little conversation with a waitress, and the best diner meal in the northeast.

With the exception of high-ticket items like lobster and salmon, the menu is a primer of Maine specialties: chowders, tripe, haddock in egg sauce; grapenut pudding; freshly baked muffins, molasses doughnuts, hermits, and cupcakes. Moody's is the only place in New England that always has a traditional boiled dinner on the menu—a colorful platter of corned beef, turnips, boiled potatoes, cabbage, and carrots.

Moody's blueberry muffins are superlative, New England's best. At the slightest pressure, they pull into moist halves, twin textured landscapes of ivory-colored dough, streaked purple with tart Maine blues. You hardly want butter with a muffin this rich; just an occasional sip of coffee.

The menu lists "milk shakes" and "velvets." Our waitress explained that a milk shake is "just a cabinet without the ice cream." She must have been from Rhode Island, where Maine velvets, known also as frappes, are called cabinets—what the rest of us know as milk shakes. In Maine, if you order a chocolate milk shake, you will get chocolate milk. (Soda fountain names are a gastrolinguistic maelstrom outdone only by the diversity of names and varieties of hot roast beef sandwiches across the country—French dip, beef Manhattan, wet beef, beef on weck, etc.)

As years go by, Moody's weathered beauty grows more striking. The ancient wood booths are worn soft, warm with age; the green-upholstered chrome counter stools are genuine antiques. Doors are still hung on heavy spring hinges. The exterior is natty, painted white and pine-tree green. A neon sign outside glows EAT twenty-four hours a day.

Nunan's Lobster Hut

Rte. 9, Cape Porpoise, Maine   Two hundred feet from the Texaco station *(207) 967-4362*

Daily June 5 p.m.–8:30 p.m., July–Labor Day to 9 p.m.

Dinner about $10–$15, lobster prices vary

Lobsters are plentiful in restaurants along the southern coast of Maine. Plain or fancy: firm, ocean-fresh beauties filling out their bright red shells, or wizened undead zombies living in a fish bowl—you will find all manner of *Homarus americanus,* served every way including a "Lazy Lobster" platter, which calls for the waitress to extract meat from the shell piece by piece for her dainty patron in a bib.

But Maine natives know that the ultimate in crustaceous grandeur is an unadorned crimson lobster flavored with nothing but the salt water in which it has been cooked. If you really like lobster, you don't want breadcrumbs stuffed where the tail ought to be, or "turf" to balance your "surf," or diablo sauce to smother it. A little butter on the side, thank you, and that's it.

This perfect lobster will be found in a clapboard shack perched above a salt marsh in Cape Porpoise, Maine: Nunan's Lobster Hut, a place designed for lobster eating. It is a long, segmented building, with sinks and rolls of paper towels hung along the wall for cleansing butter from hands and face during the meal. You sit in a hardwood booth or at a small Formica table with ribbed edges to keep shells and juice from running off.

A few wooden buoys hang from the ceiling. But these are not carelessly chosen pieces of "seafood decor" from Restaurant Central; they are Nunan family buoys, red on white—the colors flown by Nunan lobster boats. There are nets hung up, too—retired from use. And there is a picture of the family's favorite from their fleet, the *Sadie Nunan.* The Nunans have been selling the lobsters they catch since 1951, when Captain George set up a kettle and a cookstove near the marsh. Little has changed since then. Certainly nothing's gotten fancy.

When you dine at Nunan's, you get your lobster served on a pizza pan, along with a two-bit bag of potato chips and a paper cup of butter. The only thing the kitchen does between lobster pot and table is crack the claws.

At the risk of repeating ourselves, this is the best boiled Maine lobster you can get. Actually, it isn't boiled; it's steamed—in a mere two inches of salt water in a blue enamel pot, a process that guarantees the lobster won't be waterlogged, as happens when it spends too long cooking underwater or when a lobster is precooked and then reimmersed when an order is brought into the kitchen.

It takes twenty minutes to cook the lobsters in the steam pot, just enough time for each of the various parts to attain the pink of perfection. The tail is resilient but not at all rubbery the way overcooked or landbound ones can get. The knuckle meat and claws are tender and sweet; the legs succulent; the moist jelly called tomalley is the lobster-lover's manna.

Before you consider yourself finished with this most Maine of meals, be sure to have one of Bertha Nunan's chocolate brownies or a piece of her sweet-crusted blueberry pie for dessert. She makes both every morning in her kitchen at home, while her son Richard is out tending to his lobster traps in the waters off Cape Porpoise.

Robinson's Wharf

Rte. 27, Southport, Maine   Southwest of Boothbay Harbor
(207) 633-3830

Mid-June–early Sept. daily 11 a.m.–9 p.m.

$10 or less

Robinson's Wharf is so loosely run, it's easy not to realize just how nifty it is. It seems simply a part of the scenic shoreline heading out of Boothbay Harbor. It looks pretty nice, so you drop in and ask the boys in their rubber fishermen's boots to boil you a 1½-pound lobster and a bucket of steamers, and what the heck, some chowder or lobster stew for starters, and a couple of ears of corn on the cob.

The lobster, clams, and corn all get tossed into the same boiling seawater while you meander out on the dock and find a picnic table overlooking the gully known as Townsend Gut. Or you might want a place in the indoor dining room—a large ship's mess with varnished wood tables, wrought-iron chairs, and a sink at one end for washing up after the lobster and steamers have been tackled.

The food is served on paper plates; the only real utensil is a nutcracker. When finished, most diners stroll back inside to get brownies or carrot cake or Round Top ice cream for dessert, then return to the dock and the water view: a great *digestif.*

You drive away from this meal with a scent of seafood clinging to your hands, and the clean oceany taste of freshly boiled lobster slowly fading out on well-served taste buds, and you go back home. One day in the fall or winter, you remember the meal on Robinson's Wharf, and you know that all the money in the world can't duplicate that lobster feast—at least not until next summer, when once again it will be easy to enjoy.

Shirley's Dining Room

37 Greenwood Ave., Skowhegan, Maine   Turn off Rte. 201 north at the
Belmont Motel
(207) 474-2470

Mon.–Sat. 5 a.m.–7 p.m., Sun. 5 a.m.–3 p.m.

$1–$8

We have always liked stories about wolfish appetites: lumberjacks' ten-thousand-calorie breakfasts, Diamond Jim Brady's customary two-pound chocolate bonbon snack, Calvin Trillin's garlic shock after a week in New Orleans. With the same fascination for prodigious eating, we treasure Shirley's Dining Room, a restaurant that closely approximates a mess hall in a lumber camp.

It isn't large, actually just an annex of a private home. Tables-for-eight line the wall, and there is one especially large table near the kitchen where local workmen come to chat 'n' chew. The only decor is a single sign reading, THIS IS A HIGH CLASS PLACE. ACT RESPECTABLE. There aren't two chairs in the whole restaurant that match.

The food at Shirley's is big food. How big? How hot is Tigua Indian chili? How strong is white lightnin? How long does it take to drive across Montana? Very big food. The menu (a mimeographed sheet in a tattered manilla folder with *Shirley's Dining Room* inscribed across the front in ball-point pen) offers everything in three sizes: Regular, Small, or Baby. Note there is no "Large." "Baby" no doubt refers to a baby whale, because each of the "Regular" turkey dinners we got was nearly enough for both of us.

It is an honest menu. You get what you pay for. Sandwiches are offered on "store bread" or "homemade," with a dollar premium for the latter. A buck seems a lot, until you see the homemade bread—enormous slabs (white, wholewheat, or raisin) that appear to have been axed from the loaf. These are actually two-fisted sandwiches.

Shirley's bread is the basis of some grandiose breakfasts. For about a dollar, you can get a cup of coffee and simply one slice of buttered raisin toast. The chewy toast is heavily buttered, dense with raisins—a hearty meal all by itself. French toast is even more substantial.

There are pancakes, too—or should we make that singular? One blueberry pancake completely covers a large dinner plate, and is filled with approximately a half-pound of blueberries: a beautiful study in blue and gold, with amber maple syrup.

Shirley's may be a workingman's eating hall, but that doesn't mean the food is plebeian. Throughout the spring, summer, and early fall, fresh fruit is on the menu—blueberries, strawberries, raspberries, peaches. They come alone in a cereal bowl, or drenched with cream: fancy stuff, plainly priced. Shirley's strawberry shortcake comes covered with cream that has been only loosely whipped, and mixes easily with the berries and moistened biscuit.

An exuberant, endearing restaurant, much better than it has to be—a boon in mid-Maine. "You should come back for Sunday dinner," our waitress told us when last we visited. "Is it good?" we asked. "Mmm-hmm," she said. "Ham, turkey, roast beef. Really big. I mean huge." Shirley's *huge* is something we would like to see.

Superior Shellfish, Inc.

Just off Trundy Rd., Searsport, Maine
(207) 548-2448

Summer daily 11:30 a.m.–8 p.m.   Shorter hours in spring and fall

$10 or less

The clams served at Superior Shellfish are "clean." Once dug up, their shells are washed; they then spend two full days in vats of running seawater, where the mollusks' natural siphoning action removes all internal grit. They are put into a net and tossed into boiling water along with kicking 1½-pound lobsters. About fifteen minutes later, the pulley-operated tank cover is lifted and out come the aromatic steamers and lobsters, ready to eat. Both have a zing imparted by boiling salt water.

There is a very homemade-tasting milky clam chowder to have as an appetizer while the seafood boils, and some lobster rolls already made up. Across from the boil tanks is a full bar.

The food is the thing here. Although you can see Penobscot Bay beyond the railroad tracks, Superior Shellfish is not a pretty place. It is a large wooden hangar, painted green, two-thirds of which is devoted to the clam-cleaning operation and wholesale seafood business. The other third is the serve-yourself restaurant, plus a retail market.

Decor is plain Maine. On each gray-blue picnic table is a small Styrofoam cup filled with daisies and dandelions; in the corner of the building there is a woodstove, for when the weather's cool. A few local crafts are offered for sale.

What it lacks in natural beauty, Superior Shellfish makes up for with good, inexpensive clams and lobsters—and the charm of utter simplicity.

Two Lights Lobster Shack

Two Lights Rd., Cape Elizabeth, Maine
(207) 799-1677

Mid-Apr.–mid-Oct. daily 11 a.m.–8 p.m.

$10 or less

North of Portland, there are many fishing villages with quaint lobster shacks at the ends of picturesque piers, where you can eat at picnic tables overlooking peaceful harbors. They're swell.

South of Portland, there is Two Lights Lobster Shack. It is breathtaking. It's on the water, too, and picnic tables are set out under the sun for lobster-eating, but there is no pretty harbor to view. What you see as you dine is the north Atlantic surf crashing up against the great gray rocks of the seacoast. Two Lights is Maine in the raw: an awesome, fiercely romantic place to eat.

The lobsters are swimming in a tank as you enter the Shack; pick one and wait for your number to be called. The lobster is boiled in seawater and yanked out after about twenty minutes—just enough time to attain a peak of flavor. The meat is snapping firm, yet with that characteristic tenderness found in only the freshest (not frozen, not iced, not overcooked) Maine lobsters.

The lobster monomaniac needs nothing else to be happy. For the rest of us, Two Lights offers a plenteous seaside menu. We especially like the clam chowder, a milk-white broth in which the tang of whole clams is balanced by chunks of firm potato, still edged with bits of skin. Lobster stew is a fine bland dish—pale orange, with only a faint oceanic backtaste. There are steamer clams, boats and plates (larger boats) of fried seafood, and lobster rolls with just a dash of mayonnaise spooned atop the meat. And there are Portland-style clam cakes—flat golden pancakes of oniony clam-speckled batter that are fried on a griddle. Clam *latkes*.

Drive to Two Lights Lobster Shack in July, and you will probably pass several u-pick-em strawberry fields. Strawberry shortcake will likely be on the menu. Made with strawberries that burst with sunny nectar when bitten, the cake is two biscuits, berries, and a mound of freshly whipped cream. Nice. You can also get a piece of cheesecake ladled with blueberries, or a traditional New England grape-nut pudding.

We knew that Casco Bay had been settled by a lot of Irish people (film director John Ford was born in Cape Elizabeth), and there was one peculiar dessert we sampled here that must have migrated with them from the British Isles: oatmeal pie. This is a real rib-sticker, its filling like a thick macaroon; a very serious thing, close to health food more in name than taste.

There is a small dining area inside, decorated with old implements and set with varnished distressed-wood tables. But if the weather's right, dine outdoors. Sit at a picnic table, or at one of the lovers' benches positioned to look out over the sea. The ocean breeze can be strong (we lost half a state's notes to it) and you will have to hold down any empty plates, but the sting of salt air, combined with the flavor of a lobster you have just cracked open, is simply one of the most sensuous eating experiences in America.

MASSACHUSETTS

Baxter's Fish N Chips

177 Pleasant St., Hyannis, Mass.
(617) 775-4490

Apr.–early Oct., Tues.–Sun.   Also open Mon. holidays
11:30 a.m.–8:30 p.m.

$5 or less

This is what Cape Cod summer is all about: clams and beer and chowder, the heat of the sun, the smell of the sea, and gulls flapping overhead, waiting for a chance to steal your lunch. At Baxter's self-service condiment bar, a sign warns SEAGULLS ARE ROBBERS. PLEASE DON'T LEAVE YOUR PLATE UNATTENDED. Above the sign is a mug shot of a masked gull swooping through the air with a purloined fried clam in its beak.

Wait in line, place your order, then carry your own food to a picnic table on the pier, overlooking the Hyannis Harbor. Or you can eat inside, at nautical map-topped varnished tables, or on *Gov. Brann*, a retired and permanently docked barge. Buy beer at a bar with a grouchy sign that carps, NO CHECKS, NO CHARGES, NO CUFFING.

The menu is the familiar eat-in-the-rough repertoire: fish, clams, scallops, shrimp, and fritters—all expertly fried to order. On the side, you will hear locals order bottles of "tonic," which is Massachusettsese for soda.

The chowder, although packed with potatoes and clams, is middling, without clammy zest. But the fried clams are excellent—rich, grainy-crusted, with a salty snap. And the fritters, big red-gold spheres, are agreeably oily, their soft bready insides packed with bits of clam. Bubble-packs of honey come alongside.

Mooring is available for those who arrive by boat.

Brandy Pete's

267 Franklin St., Boston, Mass.
(617) 439-4165

Mon.–Fri. lunch & dinner

$10 or less

Brandy Pete's is Boston's temple of meat and potatoes. The menu, typed and printed every day, always includes an amusing bit of persiflage, such as "God made the garden of Eden a perfect paradise, without pain, without misery, without parking meters." The list of foods is so square it's cubic.

At Brandy Pete's, turkey dinner isn't just for Thanksgiving; it's a regular lunchtime item, "yesterday's roast stuffed turkey," according to the menu, served with cranberry sauce and mashed potatoes, blanketed, natch, with gravy. And when was the last time you saw turkey croquettes on a menu? Here they are, bigger than life, in a silky white sauce. And welsh rarebit or cheese-topped asparagus on toast points? Come and get 'em.

Boston oddities as well: codfish cakes and baked beans; and a grand meal called "gravy meat and spaghetti"—a slab of pot roast, cooked to a fare-thee-well, stacked upon a pallet of well-done spaghetti, covered with smoky meat sauce.

The only way to end such a meal is anachronistically, with pudding. Rice, bread, tapioca, or grape-nut: two or three are made each day. Grape-nut is heavy, its thick egg custard layered with a soft ribbon of sweetened cereal. There are better versions elsewhere. But Pete's tapioca is angelic, a meek, quivering hill of the most fragile fluff, faintly sweet with a pinch of salt to keep it on the level.

Gruff and yet ingratiating, with a staff of waitresses who give no quarter, Brandy Pete's is Beantown in the raw. Above the dining room hangs a large portrait of the late Pete himself, declaring his irascible and thoroughly Bostonian credo: THE CUSTOMER IS ALWAYS WRONG.

The Clam Box

Rte. 1A at Mile Lane, Ipswich, Mass.
(617) 356-9707

Summer Mon.–Thurs. 11 a.m.–9 p.m., weekends to 10 p.m.
Shorter hours in spring & fall   Closed in winter

$5 or less

If regions had official regional animals the way states do, New England's
would undoubtedly be the clam. There are plenty of epicurean things to do
with clams, but it's clams in their ignoblest form—fried—that get Yankees'
juices going. They are celebrated and argued over by devotees from Green-
wich, Connecticut, to Eastport, Maine, and most especially along the clam-
rich coast of Massachusetts's north shore.

Any clam-lover can tell you that while the recipe for frying clams is easy,
it takes a skill bordering on magic to make the difference between an ordinary clam as served at any one of a hundred shacks along the seacoast and
the crème de la clam, as served at The Clam Box.

You can order clams by themselves, or as most people do it, on a platter.
Clam Box platters are sectioned cardboard plates, but the sectioning is ignored in the kitchen; the plate comes piled high with clams, onion rings or
french fries, cole slaw, tartar sauce, and lemon wedges. It's a miracle the
jumbo portions don't overflow the plate; and if you can manage to carry it
and a Coke to a table, plan on a half hour of first-rate eating.

The clams, the onion rings, the french fries all stay crisp throughout the
meal. If you finish up and hit bottom, the cardboard plate is quite amazing:
not a grease stain in sight, not a drop of oil. These are the cleanest clams on
the coast.

The Clam Box is easy to find. It is shaped just like a clam box—the
trapezoidal container used for take-out orders.

Coonamessett Inn

Jones Rd., Falmouth, Mass.
(617) 548-2300

Breakfast, lunch, & dinner daily   Reservations advised

$5–$25

We were embarrassed during our first stay at the Coonamessett Inn when
Michael came down to breakfast woefully underdressed in an open shirt
instead of the repp tie and club blazer worn by every other man in the house.
It's that kind of place.

And because it is a lah-de-dah inn catering to travelers, the kitchen indulges in fanfaronade beyond our care: escargots bourguignons and tournedos of beef, sauce Périgordine, and French pastries.

Yet the menu is anchored by tradition, and even though Carl Johnson, the third chef at the "Cooney" in twenty-eight years, is experimenting with gourmet versions of old-fashioned Yankee fare, he wouldn't dare get rid of the enshrined favorites.

Such as Indian pudding, the best outside of Boston. Made of cornmeal, molasses, and a jolt of ginger, it is served in a stemmed glass dish with a dab of vanilla ice cream. Staunch, serious porridge, its nearly microscopic grainy texture is pure pleasure on the tongue. Long hours in a slow oven steam away moisture, leaving luscious crusty body. It is always on the menu, and even in the heat of summer, we are told, they sell eight gallons a week.

Chowder is silver-gray, the color of quahogs more than cream or potatoes, a ton of briny clam flavor in every spoonful. Likewise, lobster bisque is essence of lobster meat, coral pink and cream thick, laced with sherry, topped with glistening specks of roe. You find, intact, the meat from one whole claw in every bowl.

Time-honored house specialties are Yankee pot roast in vegetable sauce, broiled scrod, broiled lobster stuffed with claw meat, and out-of-shell lobster, sauteed in butter. In the Vineyard Room, where Chef Johnson experiments with variations of familiar themes, one can order salad of smoked Cape scallops with strawberry horseradish dressing, or an item known as lobster Coonamessett, sauteed in butter and cognac, glazed with Béarnaise sauce.

Forget the pastries; we'll take pudding for dessert, either the superlative Indian, or grape-nut (a gelatinous New England favorite), or bread pudding, made from the pecan rolls served in the mealtime bread basket, topped with bourbon sauce.

Rooms and individual cottages, on fancy landscaped grounds, are $50–$100.

Duck Soup Restaurant

Rte. 7, Lanesboro, Mass.
(413) 443-1106

Wed.–Mon. 7 a.m.–8 p.m.

$3–$10

Along a route of soigné inns with mediocre and predictable "fare," here is a comfy cafe serving good inexpensive food.

Yes, duck soup is the centerpiece of the menu, but it's no gimmick, no *hommage* to the Marx Brothers, just a tasty brew of duck meat, rice, carrots, and celery, seasoned with tarragon, mild and only slightly ducky. Try it with a loaf of warm bread—or, better yet, the cinnamon bread made here daily, tear-apart soft like a good babka, woven with streaks of cinnamon.

Duck Soup's lunch menu features omelettes made with ham, asparagus, or good cheeses, as well as a full list of sandwiches. At dinner, things go upscale, and the house specialty, roast duckling, takes center stage. "I can make it half a dozen ways," owner Douglas McClelland boasted. "Sweet and sour, orange brandy, mandarin flavored . . ." This is not nouvelle cuisine half-baked duck; it is expertly prepared—fatless, with savory crisp skin.

For dessert, there are fruit pies and crisps, and grand bread pudding in which massive torn slices of bread retain their individuality but take on the texture of eggy custard. There is also weighty cheesecake made by the nuns of New Skete, an Eastern Orthodox nunnery in Cambridge, New York. The cake is a rarity for which many people travel miles to the source. It's nearly impossible to find in any other restaurant.

The Duck Soup is a homey place. When we found it, Mr. McClelland's son was putting together a model ship in one booth while Mr. McClelland roasted ducks in the kitchen for that evening's dinner. "My dream someday is to run a country inn," he told us. "Here we serve the kind of food that's usually sat down to with a bottle of wine. Without the wine, we have to succeed on the food alone. So it's got to be good." It is.

Durgin-Park

30 N. Market St., Boston, Mass.
(617) 227-2038

Daily lunch & dinner

$5–$15

Durgin-Park is an original—one of our favorite restaurants, despite the fact that *Boston* magazine once described it as a cross between a meal with the Pilgrims and mess at boot camp.

It is an eating hall with rows of long communal tables. Exposed pipes and overhead fans hang from the ceiling, but don't look up—bare bulbs will blind you. Once seated, it is necessary to adjust your speaking voice to measure up to the din of other diners, and the clatter of pots and pans from the open kitchen. This is a joyous restaurant, perking with exuberant people who like to eat in a big way.

The waitresses are another story. From behind, one will toss napkins onto your table and wait grumpily while you peruse the menu. If you aren't ready to order right away, she's gone. She will return soon, even grumpier. But don't let Mrs. Battleaxe throw you—she's just Beantown gruff; and, you see, most of her customers know what they want without looking at the menu.

In keeping with values of plainness and thrift, everything at Durgin-Park is prepared without fancy flourishes, and served in the largest portions imaginable. We have yet to try a single item that disappoints.

A Durgin-Park meal automatically begins with a square of cornbread. It is real Pilgrim food; taste this block of baked grain, and you can never again believe the trendmongers when they tell you that American gastronomy is some kind of new idea. It's just that, as Seymour Britchky wrote, "when our traditions get old, we throw them out." Except at Durgin-Park.

The house specialty is a Brobdingnagian cut of prime rib, which every carnivore really ought to try on his first visit, if only to clear the way for other specialties like broiled swordfish or that shoreline favorite, lobster stew.

Beyond the dishes on the menu listed as house specialties (steaks and various lobster casseroles), there are at least a dozen more that are Boston cuisine at its unpretentious best: roast turkey, Yankee pot roast, oyster stew, cherrystone stew, Boston "schrod," fried cod . . . chowders, too, and heart-warming side dishes like stone-crock baked beans, fresh apple sauce, and a glorious mountain range of the most delicious mashed potatoes into which the kitchen staff unceremoniously slides several pats of butter, still in their paper wrappings.

Durgin-Park's Indian pudding dessert is awesome, one of America's great—and most distinctively American—desserts. It is no secret how they make it. The recipe is available at the cashier's desk, in a little brochure that informs you that Durgin-Park bakes enough pudding in one year to float the Queen Mary and the Queen Elizabeth. The ingredients are cornmeal, molasses, sugar, butter, milk, eggs, and a sprinkling of spices, baked in a stone crock in a slow oven for five to seven hours. During this time, the sugar caramelizes, and the cornmeal swells to an intense granularity. The pudding turns dark and heavy. There is nothing sophisticated about it. It makes you think of the mettle of the Founding Fathers. A classic.

Also on the dessert menu is strawberry shortcake on a biscuit; hot apple pie so ungainly it tumbles into an avalanche of cinnamon-dusted apple chunks and crust long before it reaches your table; and another New England legend: apple pan dowdy, a homely cobbler made from spiced apples in a biscuit-dough crust.

Half the fun of dining at Durgin-Park is people-watching. It is a tradition in this city to eat here, whether you are a pushcart vendor on a splurge or a blue-blooded Brahmin. On our last visit, two vegetarians sat next to us and ordered platters of potatoes, corn, peas, beans, and tomatoes. Farther down the table, a Harvard man in a football jersey polished off his prime rib in record time, then waited impatiently as his svelte date tried to make some headway into hers.

"Established before you were born" is inscribed on the Durgin-Park menu; and although the Faneuil Hall Marketplace all around it has modernized, sprouting a crop of chromy boutiques and the latest in urban renewal food stands, this dowdy restaurant smack in the middle of it all remains majestically unchic.

Farnham's

88 Eastern Ave. (Rte. 133), Essex, Mass.
(617) 768-6643

Summer Tues.–Sun. 5 a.m.–10 p.m.   Weekends only and shorter hours in other seasons

$5 or less

To devotees of the fried clam, Cape Ann, Massachusetts, is Mecca. Here towns have names like Ipswich and Little Neck; and clam platters, cooked to order, far outnumber chicken buckets or McBurgers as the fast food of choice. Of all the region's clamatoria, Farnham's is probably the most beloved.

"We are a clam-eating institution," a waitress proudly informed us. "Been here X number of years." We didn't pry the algebraic solution to "X" from her, but we did enjoy two platters of what must be described as the champagne of fried clams: tingly fresh, veiled in an amber crust.

Farnham's clams come as a "box" (clams only—Small, Medium, or Large), a "boat" (half clams, half french fries), or a "plate" (clams, fries, and onion rings). Get the plate for Farnham's magnificent onion rings, believed by many to be the best on the north shore, if not the earth.

Most of Farnham's business is take-out, but there is a counter and a few varnished pine booths, lovingly reshellacked over the restaurant's "X" years in business. It is an adorable place to eat. Outside, there are flower boxes bursting with pansies, and inside, there are sarsaparilla and Moxie on the menu.

Locke-Ober

3 Winter Place, Boston, Mass.
(617) 542-1340

Mon.–Sat. 11 a.m.–10 p.m.   Reservations advised

$25–$50

Locke-Ober is a relic. Its famous specialties are outré gourmet food, richly sauced, like seafood Newburg and chicken Richmond (under glass), and the palate-boggling lobster Savannah—an eighteen-inch trough of a lobster shell packed with hunks of lobster meat in a cognac-spiked mushroom sauce.

Locke-Ober isn't all Continental frippery. Originally a merger of Louis Ober's luxurious French restaurant and Frank Locke's neighborhood saloon, the kitchen also offers simply cooked New England seafood and grilled meats. Our calves liver was tender, piquant, served with a heap of sweet-smelling sauteed onions. Oysters Gino, baked with seasoned crumbs and bacon, were beautiful.

The list of side dishes makes for a nostalgic read, its scope suggesting *fin-de-siècle* luxury. "Grilled sweets" as our white-haired waiter called the sweet potatoes, are simple orange spud circles, not candied, but grilled until the edges begin to char. Marvelous. Hash browns are served as a large crisp pancake—the best accompaniment to a steak or chop.

The dessert worth knowing about is called Sultana roll, an ice cream and claret wine confection that has been on the menu since The Beginning. And of course, this being Boston, Locke-Ober makes top-notch Indian pudding, more genteel than Durgin-Park's primeval brew, suited to a classy restaurant. But it is dumpy, nonetheless: buttery, not too sweet, as thick and smooth as freshly mixed concrete, with a heady brown-sugar aroma.

"A trip to Boston without visiting Locke-Ober," Ogden Nash wrote, "would be like going to Agra and ignoring the Taj Mahal." Except this dark clubby place is more intimidating. It is truly a *serious* eating establishment: mahogany woodwork, heavily flocked wallpaper, sober waiters in tuxedos. The upstairs dining room could be a funeral parlor. Even out-of-towners and tourists who come to gawk at this famous culinary landmark (with its painted nude who gets draped in black when Harvard loses to Yale) know to wear dark suits.

Ma Glockner's

Maple St. between Rtes. 126 & 140, North Bellingham, Mass.
(617) 966-1085

Tues.–Sat. 4 p.m.–10 p.m., Sun. noon–8 p.m.

About $5

Travel north out of Providence, and you're in Rhode Island Red country, where the favorite eating-out ritual calls for large groups of people to go to a large restaurant and order large plates of chicken.

The most famous place to feast on native poultry is just a hop over the Massachusetts border in North Bellingham: Ma Glockner's, which began life on Thanksgiving Day in 1937 as a twenty-four-seat dining area in Ma Glockner's living room. The business passed from Ma to her sons, then to the Blias family, and through the years the original home was expanded a half dozen times. Today, Ma Glockner's seats five hundred, but still serves only one thing—chicken dinners, according to the original recipe.

We stopped at a store called Chicken Power in Woonsocket and asked directions of a man who was literally up to his elbows in buckets of breasts and thighs he was sorting.

His directions were complex, and we were soon lost—our natural state any time we look for anything in Rhode Island. We passed dozens of chicken stands and an equal number of doughnut shops. What makes Rhode Island-ers love fried dough and poultry so much? Before we found the answer to this gastronomic riddle, we spotted a sign with a neon hen roosting on top.

Despite its expanded size, there is something undeniably homey about Ma Glockner's. Inside are several small rooms, done up in varnished pine wood, looking straight out of a 1948 decorating how-to book.

All your menu choices have been made. You get half a chicken, pressed nearly as flat as a Chinese duck, fried in butter but not breaded. This is a tender bird made for sleeves-up eating, requiring stacks of napkins to daub the iridescent chicken juices from your chin. Along with it come french fries, cranberry sauce, salad, and large hot cinnamon buns (called Swedish rolls), the requisite accompaniment for chicken dinner in these parts. "People kill for our rolls," the waiter casually noted as we devoured our allotment and called for more. They are big chewy spirals, heavily spiked with spice and glazed with sugar. With the chicken—or without it—they are stupendous.

Mildred's Chowder House

290 Iyanough Rd., Hyannis, Mass.   Rte. 28
(617) 775-1045

Daily lunch & dinner

$5–$10

So you want to know why New Englanders make such a fuss over clam chowder? Dip into Mildred's and taste the tartness of the sea infused with salt pork, the starchy granularity of soft potato nuggets, and a thousand briny bits of clam. It's got bite, but the strong clammy teeth are cosseted in tender warmed-milk whiteness. You are spooning up New England's most wonderful culinary paradox: invigorating comfort food.

Mildred's reputation was built on chowder, which she started serving in a small roadside cafe almost forty years ago. Since then, the restaurant has grown, Ted Kennedy has praised the chowder (there's his letter on the wall, along with one from the JFK White House), and droves of summer tourists have joined the year-round Hyannis natives who have made Mildred's a habit.

The new Mildred's is a vast, efficient chowder house served by waiters and waitresses in brown pants or skirt and yellow polo shirts, each equipped with a beeper so the kitchen can call them from the far reaches of the dining room. If you choose, you can eat fast and beat it; or you can linger over Irish coffee.

Even plainer than chowder is the downeast preparation known as stew, nothing but cream and butter and seafood. Mildred's lobster stew is especially good, aromatic pools of melted butter coating each morsel of meat you spoon up from the warm cream below. Here is proof that bland can be grand.

Local fish are expertly broiled. Scrod, served with paprika-seasoned breadcrumbs, falls into firm flakes at the prodding of a fork. Fried scallops are sweet and tender.

Whatever the weather, many regulars order hot Indian pudding for dessert. It is red-brown and pasty, mildly gingered, not too sweet, served with a small scoop of ice cream. Grape-nut custard is an unwieldy heap of eggy pudding in a small bowl, topped with real, unsweetened whipped cream.

No Name

15½ Fish Pier, Boston, Mass.
(617) 338-7539

Mon.–Sat. lunch & dinner

$10 or less

It truly has no name, no sign outside, nothing to tell you that this hole in the wall serves some of the best, freshest seafood in town. But if you come at a normal eating time, you will find it easily . . . by the line of hungries waiting to get in. Cognoscenti know to dine at 11 a.m. or 4 in the afternoon.

Outside, on the pier, is atmosphere you can smell: fishermen and seagulls fighting it out over the daily catch, wholesalers loading up trucks. It is the real thing, guaranteed authentic; a wharf piled with fish whose natural habitat is not a restaurant freezer. Amazing as it seems, they actually come from the ocean!

No Name began years ago as a small Greek-run lunch counter for the men who work on the pier. Now there is a dining room adjacent to the counter. At all hours, it is bedlam, waiters calling orders, patrons chowing down with gusto, happy to have finally gotten a table. The back seats are the best, where the view out the window is tubs of fish being unloaded and airplanes swooping low overhead on the flyway into Logan Airport.

The burly man who pointed you to the table brings a pitcher of water. Help yourself to a paper cup from the high stack, and think fast about what you want to eat. There isn't time to dally here. The menu is small, not very interesting—common fare like scrod, sole, bluefish, clams, and scallops.

But taste this scrod, served in a golden pool of butter, its crust faintly charred, its flesh falling into big moist hunks, clean and pure and sweet— and you suddenly know that you have never really tasted fresh fish before. Milky paprika-orange chowder is overloaded with heavy hunks of fish. Order a fried clam roll and you get a long length of bread, cleaved in two, stuffed with clams, served with a herbed tartar sauce so special that we ask our waiter what its secret is. "The Greek touch," he laughs back over the din.

Sagres Restaurant

181 Columbia St., Fall River, Mass.
(617) 675-7018

Daily 11 a.m.–10 p.m., weekends to 1 a.m.

$10 or less

Fall River is home to a large population of Portuguese fishermen who migrated here over a century ago, adding a dash of spice and a spritz of olive oil to the region's cuisine—a fact your food-seeking radar will pick up as you approach town and note the *linguiça* sausage on otherwise ordinary diner menus, or luncheon specials of *chouriço* and fried potatoes.

For a quick study of how to fall in love with New England-style Portuguese food, we suggest a visit to Sagres Restaurant. It's a dimly lit place, decked out in shades of Iberian red and black. Although it has a postage-stamp-sized dance floor and a bandstand, it is a decidedly simple place to eat, so not-for-tourists that the only obstacle to a fine meal might be making yourself understood in English.

We came for lunch and tried *Caldurada de Mariscos & Peixe*, a hearty farrago chock full of clams, shrimp, and fish, crunchy with *al dente* vegetables, seasoned with a medley of spice in a light tomato sauce. It was served like a paella for two, and was so generously filled with seafood that we barely had room for the vivid "Spanish style" stuffed clams we had ordered as a backup dish. A basket containing Portuguese sweet bread fresh from the oven was perfect for mopping up the last of the *Caldurada*.

Our meal concluded with strong *Cafe Bustelo* and *Beirao* liqueur—a toasty anisette. We then strode onto the streets of Fall River, listening to the lyrical accents, warmed by Sagres's charm, aglow with good spirits brought on by our luck at discovering this unspoiled sample of exotic fare unique to the coast of southern New England.

Union Oyster House

41 Union St., Boston, Mass.
(617) 227-2750

Sun.–Thurs. 11 a.m.–9:30 p.m., Fri. & Sat. to 10 p.m.

$5–$20

The Union Oyster House is America's oldest restaurant.
   It was Daniel Webster's favorite place to eat.
   It introduced toothpicks to America.

But in our book of worthies, the Union Oyster House is inscribed for its clam chowder. Diced potatoes, salt pork, minced clams, a little seasoning, plus plenty of butter and half-and-half: the soul of New England.

New England chowder is like New York cheesecake. It can be tricked up in all kinds of ways, many of which are good, sometimes thrilling, and fun for a change. But none of the deviations offers the profound comfort to be found in this confluence of simple tastes. Oyster House chowder is made from a recipe that simply cannot be improved.

Boston is the home of the bean and the cod, both of which you will find in equally elemental form at the Oyster House. The beans might surprise a non-Yankee accustomed to the gooey kind that come from the supermarket in tomatoey syrup. These beans, enriched by salt pork and molasses, are baked for hours, during which a kind of magic occurs. Instead of dissolving into a pasty brown sugar mush, the dowdy legume is reborn, complex and intriguing. (If you've had good red beans and rice in New Orleans, you know what we're talking about.)

The cod served by the Oyster House is called scrod, a firm filet cut from a small Atlantic cod. Broiled with a few seasoned breadcrumbs, it is one of the northeast's royal treats. On Friday, you can get a whole baked scrod in cheesy rarebit sauce.

A lesser-known regional specialty is salmon, a festive dish customarily served on the Fourth of July between Boston and Portland as a midsummer celebration of the fish's run in coastal rivers. Midsummer is also when the traditional salmon side dishes—new potatoes and green peas—are ready for a kind of premature harvest. The Oyster House is one of the few restaurants in New England that still serves this esoteric dish in exactly the manner it has always been served—the fish poached, sided by peas and small boiled potatoes flecked with dill.

The menu is large, with plenty of other kinds of fish, and steaks, and lunchtime sandwiches, even seafood quiche, and, for children, "Ye Olde Peanut Butter and Jelly Sandwich." Of course there is a raw bar, by the front window, where Cotuits, cherrystones, and littlenecks are shucked to order. The top-of-the-line at the Union Oyster House is a shore dinner, another classic: clam chowder, a bucket of steamers, boiled lobster, salad, an ear of corn, and a chunk of gingerbread topped with whipped cream.

Gingerbread is fine, and Boston cream pie shouldn't be overlooked; but if you are here to savor gastronomic history, Indian pudding is the dessert of choice. It is made the old-fashioned way, namely baked for an eternity until the simple ingredients of molasses and cornmeal meld into something quite extraordinary.

The Oyster House takes no reservations, and can get crowded at times. But the wait is never as bad as it is at any of the Legal Sea Food restaurants, which Bostonians like so much. We actually enjoy hanging about this red brick tavern, where you can soak up two centuries of history along with dozens on the half-shell.

White Cap

185 High St. (Rte. 133), Ipswich, Mass.
(617) 356-5276

Summer Thurs.–Sun. 11 a.m.–8 p.m.

$5 or less

PLACE YOUR ORDER AND STAND BACK, commands the sign above the White Cap counter. This is a businesslike place, stripped down for good eating, devoid of menu foolishness.

White Cap provides an opportunity to taste some of Massachusetts's best seafood—in particular, fish chowder: exceptional chowder, luxuriant with butter and chunks of firm fish filling up the bowl . . . or rather, the Styrofoam cup. That's right, the table settings are polystyrene and the spoon is hard plastic; but shoreline cookery has always thrived on simplicity.

In fact, the dine-in-the-rough style is exactly right for picniclike fare: steamers in all combinations with broth, butter, or hot sauce; fried clams with crunchy onion rings—this is food that tastes best when you can roll up your sleeves and dig in without a fuss. That's the charm of no-frills White Cap.

Woodman's of Essex

121 Main St. (Rte. 133), Essex, Mass.
(617) 768-6451

Summer daily 11 a.m.–10 p.m.   Shorter hours in other seasons

$5 or less, more for lobsters or the clambake

On July 3, 1916, Lawrence Woodman was frying up a batch of homemade potato chips to go with the clams on the half-shell he served at his small seafood stand in Essex. The chips were themselves a relatively nouvelle bit of cuisine, having only recently been invented by George Crum, chef at Saratoga Springs' Moon Lake House. But Saratoga chips were nothing compared to the leap of culinary genius Woodman was about to make.

A fisherman stopped by for his usual order of clams and chips, and when he heard Woodman complain that business was slow, he whimsically suggested throwing the clams in to fry with the potatoes. "Ridiculous," said Lawrence Woodman. "Clams have shells."

"Just a joke," said the fisherman, but a creative fever had begun to burn in Woodman's brain. The next day, when the fisherman came in for his usual order, he got something new—shucked clams, dipped in batter, then fried. It was the Fourth of July, 1916. Lawrence Woodman had invented not only the fried clam, but with his chips on the side, the fried clam *platter* as well.

There must be a lot of history buffs in Essex, because Woodman's today is almost always mobbed. HAPPINESS IS FINDING A TABLE AT WOODMAN'S reads a sign, and it's no joke. At night during the summer season, there is a Woodman's "scene," the main activities of which appear to be drinking beer and going back for more fried seafood. Woodman's is scenically located on the edge of a salt marsh, and is what's known in Massachusetts as an eat-in-the-rough restaurant, the custom being that you place your order and stand back to wait, as your belly growls and dozens of other customers parade past you from the pick-up window with trays mounded high with clams, shrimp, fish, scallops, fries, onion rings, and an occasional lobster.

While you wait, it's fun to watch the chefs at work. They belong to the short-order school of culinary wizardry, seemingly able to juggle five fry baskets and a couple of skillets at one time, while expertly heaping fried food onto platters that soon appears taller than the plate is wide.

Woodman's clams are superior, crusty and copious, as fresh as any here in the heart of the fried-clam belt, with the added fillip that they are the clams from which all modern versions, even Howard Johnson's, sprang. This is a genuine taste of history, with tartar sauce on the side.

During July and August, on Wednesdays, Saturdays, and Sundays, Woodman's stages a clambake over an open wood fire: steamers, broth and butter, a lobster, corn on the cob, hot dogs, and watermelon.

NEW HAMPSHIRE

Lancaster Diner

Rte. 2, Lancaster, N.H.
(603) 788-4087

Daily 6 a.m.–7 p.m.

$5 or less

We arrived late, almost lunchtime, and got the last two coffee rolls: dense, cake-sized spirals etched with cinnamon. Four construction workers with necks the size of our waists clomped in a few minutes after us, ordered coffee rolls, and were told the last two had just been sold. We bravely tore into the magnificent cinnamon sweet rolls we had claimed for our own, trying to ignore the men who glowered at us from their booth, eating buttered toast.

Actually, the steel-booted guys didn't have it all that bad. Toast at the Lancaster Diner is made from baked-here bread; and besides, they get coffee buns every day. Those of us who are passing through must seize our pleasures when we can.

Even if you don't arrive in time for breakfast, the Lancaster Diner has a lot to offer: chicken pot pies, roast turkey dinners, extraordinarily creamy grape-nut custard pudding, apple pie, mince pie, fig squares, and raisin-filled cookies. All made here.

The Lancaster is one of the most dazzling diners in the northeast. (To be accurate, it isn't a diner; it's a storefront designed to look like a diner.) The façade of primary red and yellow is a study in symmetry: on either side of the door, oval windows are bordered with the slimmest tubes of blue and red neon. Inside, the red and yellow color scheme spills onto the booths' upholstery, here lined with polished wood. The vaulted ceiling and wood walls are trimmed in the house livery, and behind the wood fixtures at the counter is a brilliant wall of chromium.

The Lancaster Diner is most comely after dark, when all the coffee rolls are sure to be gone, but the neon is turned on and the stainless steel sparkles. The red and yellow booths look like candy.

Polly's Pancake Parlor

Rte. 117, Sugar Hill, N.H.
(603) 823-5575

Early May weekends only   Memorial Day–mid-Oct. daily 7 a.m.–7 p.m.

$10 or less

Polly's is northern New England distilled to its sweetest essence: stone-ground wholewheat, buckwheat, and cornmeal pancakes, served with country sausage or cob-smoked bacon, and a tray of maple toppings in burnished pewter pots—fancy-grade syrup, granulated maple sugar, and thick maple spread. The dining room is a glass-walled porch that overlooks the rolling wooded hills of Hildex Maple Sugar Farm. After a meal, you can stroll across the small country road to say hello to the goat or horses in the barn, or you can meander through surrounding fields, reminiscing about the pancakes you just ate.

It was 1938 when Polly and "Sugar Bill" Dexter converted their carriage shed into a tea room as a means of getting people to sample the maple products they made. Hildex Farm is still in the sugaring business; the tea room has been expanded by Sugar Bill's daughter Nancy, but maple remains the focus of her menu.

You can get waffles and French toast, muffins made with maple-sweetened pancake batter, freshly baked English muffins, sandwiches on made-here bread—you can even get a bowl of oatmeal; but nearly everybody comes to Polly's for the pancakes. One order consists of half a dozen three-inch cakes—buckwheat, corn, wholewheat, or plain, filled with your choice of blueberries, walnuts, or coconut. We advise experimental types to spring for the all-you-can-eat sampler, served in batches of three until you tell the waitress you've had enough. That way, it is possible to taste—if not every-thing—at least the astonishing range of Polly's pancakes.

If you can swing dessert, try ice cream with Polly's hurricane sauce—a topping made by slicing apples into slivers, then boiling them down with the maple syrup. Or there is a wondrous Maple Bavarian Cream—nothing more than gelatin, whipped cream, and maple syrup, alchemically blended to create the closest thing on earth to manna.

Polly's serves the best pancakes in America, but that is not the only reason we love it. There is a *style* here, a care for aesthetic values you might expect to find in only the finest (read "expensive") restaurant. Although it is the most casual of places, nothing is accidental. Look at the wooden service plates, each hand-painted with a single maple leaf; or the miniature scoops, also hand-painted, for sprinkling granulated maple sugar on an order of fresh strawberries, blueberries, or nectarines. A pewter pitcher holds cream, thick as Devonshire cream, bought exclusively by Polly's from a local dairy farmer. The antique tools on the wall are relics that have been in the Dexter and Aldrich families since approximately 1798, when they started farming this land.

Then, of course, there is the view—a devastating sight in the fall, when the Hildex Farms sugarbush goes out in a blaze of color.

The Sugar House at Mt. Cube Farm

Rte. 25A, between Orford and Wentworth, N.H.
(603) 353-4814

Breakfast only   Seasonal, usually weekends

$5 or less

At the foot of Moosilauke Mountain there is a sugar house surrounded by scenic mountain trails, vegetable gardens, and small clusters of apple trees. There is a syrup evaporator in the back room, and card tables set up for people who come to eat breakfast. The menu is nothing but pancakes or doughnuts, served with made-here maple syrup. It's a postcard perfect place; why, there's even a colorful old gent in a red flannel shirt and hunting cap who tidies up the premises.

As we paid our breakfast bill to the colorful man, we remarked how nice it was to pay no tax in New Hampshire. "No, sir," he said proudly. "No sales tax. No income tax. That's why I was Governor for six years."

The man who tidies up and owns this pancake parlor is Meldrim Thomson, Governor of New Hampshire from 1973 to 1979. When he lived in the Governor's Mansion, he began a tradition of inviting legislators in for pancake breakfasts, made from his wife Gale's batter, and served with syrup he had boiled at his farm in Orford. "I came here every weekend," he told us, petting Sheba, the old black Labrador who tags along with him outside. "And after a while I said to myself, 'Why on earth do I go to Concord every Monday, when I have all this?' " Now that he's retired from politics, he has opened this little restaurant to continue the tradition of pancake breakfasts, as many mornings as he and his family can manage.

Ordinarily, the Governor keeps to his farming and syrup making, and leaves customer relations to his daughter-in-law, Glynetta, who happens to be Orford's representative to the state legislature. In another life, Glynetta might have been a truck-stop waitress. "Sorry," she said to us as she brought our pancakes. "I didn't mean to be so long, but we had a crisis with the pancake batter . . . these are the crisis ones."

She was kidding. The pancakes are grand—made from a batter that is equal thirds corn, white, and wholewheat flour, all ground here.

The Governor's doughnuts are very plain, raised, unfrosted. That makes them just right for dunking in the cups of maple syrup provided.

Waterwheel Pancake House

Rte. 2, Jefferson, N.H.
(603) 586-4479

Mid-June–mid-Oct. daily 7 a.m.–2 p.m.

$2–$8

Gastronomically, New Hampshire is a two-faced state. There is Portsmouth, with its tricked-up trendy cuisine, where the best-known purveyor of preciosity has the nerve to place joyless advertisements in tourist booklets that announce "dining by confirmed reservation only." (What, we would like to know, is an *un*confirmed restaurant reservation?)

In contrast to the seacoast's slavish following of culinary fashion, there is the north country, where values have shaped a genuine . . . cuisine? No, let's say *cookery*. Here you find inns (like Sugar Hill's venerable Homestead) that still make New England boiled dinners; and you find maple-sugar houses like the Waterwheel with small dining areas for sampling all the ways in which farmers have traditionally used the product of the spring sugaring season.

Of course there is maple syrup—clear amber, its elusive flavor nearly fugitive; a revelation for anyone who has only sampled gummy blends of corn syrup and maple flavoring a la Mrs. Butterworth. The Clukay family, who run the Waterwheel, have been winning first prizes for their syrup in county and state fairs for years.

Waterwheel pancakes—cornmeal, buckwheat, or plain, with or without blueberries—are made from coarse stone-ground flour. Doughnuts are made every morning—heavy, farm doughnuts, just ready to be moistened with a little of that syrup.

Oatmeal is served with maple crumbles on top; toast is available with maple cream instead of jelly; side orders of baked beans are enriched with maple. You can even get a maple milk shake.

Whatever ways you sample maple at the Waterwheel, you will want to save room for a slice of pie. The maple cream is good—pleasant and refreshing; but the mince pie, made in autumn, is profound. It is an authentic mince pie, made not just with raisins and goo, but with finely chopped beef brisket, and plenty of it. It is mostly meat, as aromatic as a pomander ball, intensely clove and orange flavored; a dark, heavy piece of pie with more character than all the flaming bombes in Portsmouth.

The Waterwheel is offhanded in the extreme, with ceiling lamps fashioned from inverted maple buckets hanging over its vinyl booths. The dining room shares space with a gift shop where hand-knit sweaters and maple souvenirs are sold. It isn't a beautiful restaurant, nor is its setting by the side of well-traveled Route 2 idyllic; but it is honest and simple—and hereabouts, those are the highest compliments you can pay.

RHODE ISLAND

Archie's Tavern

47 Mendon Ave., Pawtucket, R.I.
(401) 727-1700

Tues.–Thurs. & Sun. 11 a.m.–10 p.m., Fri. & Sat. 11 a.m.–11 p.m.

$5–$15

Hidden in a clot of heavy industry, Archie's looks exactly like the low-slung factories that surround it. There is no door or sign in front.

"We face the neighborhood, not the street," explains the host. Actually, the back entrance faces a vast parking lot. The interior is an above-ground cavern, dinner-hall size, multiple mismatched rooms (the result of many expansions over the years) with large tables of large people consuming large portions of food. The host, a thin man in a pastel pink jacket that seems three sizes too big, halts at each table to share a laugh, then glides on, like an itinerant Unknown Comic, but without the bag on his head.

It is not only the giant-size surreal setting that makes Archie's an essential Rhode Island eatery. It is the cinnamon rolls that everyone is eating with their meal, just like in the chicken dinner halls. These warm beauties have no peers anywhere in the state.

Or you can sample the local oddity, snail salad, a mountain of sweet thinly sliced snails, not too chewy, in a zesty marinade. They're a good appetizer, but you hardly need to pique the tastebuds after laying waste to the complimentary tray of jumbo marinated mushrooms, crackers, and spackle-thick California dip.

Exuberant portions: three-to-an-order pork chops, plate-size slabs of swordfish, nearly a whole chicken (plus mussels, shrimp, et al.) in the paella. "We serve over two tons of prime rib every week," says the menu; most of them in the form of the "Neanderthal Cave Man Cut": large indeed, but you have seen bigger.

Many people come to Archie's for the ritual family-style chicken dinner, where for about $5 a head, the table is piled high with roasted (and well-herbed) chicken, antipasto, macaroni and red sauce, vegetables, and Jell-O. This is the meal that cinnamon rolls perfectly complement.

Ocean State cuisine is mostly oceanic: shore dinner halls and clam shacks, swordfish and scallops. Archie's Tavern is the place to taste the other, inland Rhode Island with a style of cooking all its own and character to spare.

Aunt Carrie's

Ocean Rd., between Point Judith and Narragansett, R.I.
(401) 783-7930

Summer Wed.–Mon. noon–9 p.m.   Sept. weekends only

$10 or less, more for lobster

A meal at Aunt Carrie's suggests what eating must have been like in the Ocean State years ago, when the shore was rimmed with summery restaurants serving that bigger-than-life Rhode Island feast known as a shore dinner.

Aunt Carrie's still serves shore dinners, and although they're not as copious as the heroic non-stop calorific feeds of the nineteenth century, it's hard to imagine coming away hungry. You get chowder, a bucket of steamers, and a side of broth; you get clam cakes, broiled flounder, lobster, corn on the cob, french fries, brown bread, and Indian pudding or watermelon for dessert.

There is no need to go all the way, though; most people stop by for nothing more than pints or platters of fried seafood. Be sure to try the Rhode Island favorite, clam cakes—amusingly quirky puffs of dough dotted with morsels of clam. Aunt Carrie's fried clams are slim, nutty, and mild. Onion rings or french fries provide a suitable crunch to accompany the freshest broiled fish filets.

As a chowder house, Aunt Carrie's shines. All three varieties are available: tomato-based; buttery white milk chowder; and a superb clear chowder—not much more than broth and clams.

In the kitchen you will see an antique pie safe; during most of the summer it holds rhubarb pie, made from rhubarb picked in Aunt Carrie's garden.

There really was an Aunt Carrie who ran the place many years back; a sense of graceful seniority hovers about this grande dame of a restaurant. Although it's easy to get your food to go, and nice picnic benches are set outside, we recommend lingering over a shore dinner in the screened dining room, where you can enjoy the appetizing sea air and an unobstructed view of the beach and ocean.

Common's Restaurant

On the green, Little Compton, R.I.
(408) 635-4388

Mon.–Sat. 6 a.m.–6 p.m., Fri. 6 a.m.–7 p.m., Sun 6 a.m.–noon

$5 or less

The wonderful thing about Rhode Island's endlessly winding backroads is that none of them are marked. No street signs anywhere. If you ask directions, nobody can give them, because everyone who lives here just kind of *knows* the way, by little landmarks like the house with blue shutters or the gas station with the golden labrador out front.

The point is not to panic when you cannot find Little Compton. Enjoy the drive through the oceanside landscape, and pretty soon you will come upon a pastoral village green.

At the north end of the green is a gray clapboard building with flower boxes in its windows and a few cars—all local license plates—pulled up. Inside, newspapers are strewn about on a waist-high partition between two small dining rooms. Customers read while they eat, chitchat table to table among themselves and with the waitresses.

This town lunchroom, far off the tourist-trod path, is a citadel of Rhode Island cuisine. Jonnycakes, for instance, are made every day until 11:30 a.m. (but we found it easy to twist the cook's arm at 2 in the afternoon). They are lace-thin, golden brown, crisp webs of fine white cornmeal, served fanned out on oval dishes. Melting butter comes on top, and corn syrup on the side.

The flavorful behemoth clams known as quahogs are chopped up and mixed with chunks of potato into crisp-crusted quahog pie. On occasion, there is salmon pie, too.

A stuffed quahog, known hereabouts as a "stuffie," is both halves of the humongus clam shell pocketing a mountain of dazzling peppers-bread-and-clam stuffing. A couple of stuffies and a cup of chowder make a memorable Ocean State lunch.

The chowder is Southern New England style, meaning it is made without tomatoes, more like the plain briny broths you will find further south, around Mystic, Connecticut. This clam-dotted brew is enriched with butter and served with three monumental fritters. Dark red, crusty, heavy with oil, they are awful . . . and irresistible, great for gnawing.

The menu features a roster of familiar lunch-counter sandwiches, plus "Egg McCrowther" (the Crowthers run this place), and grinders (the southern New England term for a hero or hoagie sandwich) made with spicy Portuguese *chouriço* sausage.

Small-town cafe pies for dessert: homely, hand-formed, generously heaped with fruit fillings. We liked the prune-apricot pie—whole dried apricots and chunks of prune under a glazed flaky crust.

Dovecrest Indian Restaurant

Summit Rd., Exeter, R.I.
(401) 539-7795

Daily 11:30 a.m.–9 p.m.   Closed in Feb.

$10 or less

Rhode Islanders are so fond of making much ado about their jonnycakes—the small cornmeal pancakes that traditionally accompany breakfast, lunch, or dinner—that even an incorrect spelling of the word (jo*h*nnycake) is liable to result in some South County food chauvinist expelling great gusts of hot air concerning the sanctity of regional cuisine.

At the Dovecrest Indian Restaurant, the menu offers "Johnny Cake" (two words, with an *h*!); nonetheless, here is the best jonnycake you can eat. Dovecrest jonnycakes are exquisite: small griddle-cooked patties, each only slightly larger than a silver dollar, their frail crusts pocketing fluffy, finely grated cornmeal. Jonnycakes are served with butter and syrup on the side, but we recommend, for your first taste at least, savoring these without any condiment at all.

For the jonnycakes alone we have traveled half a day to eat at Dovecrest, but there is more: Indian pudding, its stark molasses and cornmeal character enlivened by Dovecrest cooks with ginger and grated orange peel, served steaming hot with vanilla ice cream melting fast on top. There is a full, absolutely ordinary menu of steaks, chops, and seafood, but explore *off* the menu, and you will likely find at least one authentically Indian game dish— buffalo roast, venison steak, rabbit stew with dumplings.

The Dovecrest is a bastion of rare Rhode Island and Indian specialties. It is a genuinely quaint place in a tiny village called Arcadia, which you find by getting lost along a seemingly endless series of roads, past Narragansett Long Houses (Indian churches), and through a dense tangle of forest. The restaurant is wood paneled, with a glass porch annex that looks out onto a peaceful countryside. There are a few Indian rugs about for decoration, a trading post and a museum just outside, and a lazy dog lounging by the back door.

Rocky Point Park Shore Dinner Hall

Rocky Point Park, Warwick, R.I.
(401) 737-8000

Summer daily noon–8 p.m.   May & Sept. weekends only

Shore dinner $8–$18, clam cakes & chowder $5 or less

It is one of the paradoxes of American gastronomy that the smallest state serves the biggest meals. Nowhere else, not even in Texas, are the culinary customs so bountiful, the restaurants so enormous, the scale of feasting so grand. Ocean State exuberance reaches its zenith in a traditional shore dinner, served in a shore dinner hall. A hundred years ago there were dozens of eating halls along the Narragansett Bay, selling clam cakes and chowder, baked fish, lobster, and corn on the cob.

A sign outside the Rocky Point Park Shore Dinner Hall says WORLD'S LARGEST SHORE DINNER HALL. It seats 4,000 people at one time, in one room, at tables-for-36. On a busy day, 20,000 people will dine here, consuming 750 gallons of clam chowder and a ton of clam cakes *every hour*. The noise level recalls a large high school cafeteria, but the food is a quantum leap above.

RPPSDH is a souvenir of America's culinary past, utterly old-fashioned in every way. The menu is identical to the one offered on opening day in 1847, the same menu described by Judge Louis Cappelli of the Rhode Island Superior Court in a 1949 ruling to be "the sum total of the various foods that comprise an official Rhode Island shore dinner": olives, cucumbers, Bermuda onions, clam chowder, white bread, brown bread, steamed clams and drawn butter, clam cakes, baked sausage, baked fish in Creole sauce, french fries, corn on the cob, boiled lobster, watermelon, and Indian pudding. "It might be permissible to send chicken in for lobster," Judge Cappelli ruled, "but beyond that simple act, man is creeping towards the outer edges of society."

Did we mention that you get all of the above, and you get unlimited amounts of all of the above (except lobster) for as long as you care to continue eating?

The amazing thing about this orgy of excess served in the army-sized chowderdrome is that the food is good. The clam cakes, made by shooting golfball-sized squirts of batter into hot oil from overhead guns, emerge from the oil as toasty gold squiggles in festive shapes, some round billows, others little crunches, the hot batter studded with bits of clam. A nostalgic shoreline treat.

Clam cakes are made to go with chowder, but not just any chowder. Understand that New Englanders are very picky—downright jingoistic— when it comes to clam recipes; as soon as you cross the line into Massachusetts, they will tell you that tomatoes in chowder are an abomination. But in Rhode Island, clam chowder is tomato-orange.

"Oh, like Manhattan chowder," we said to one of RPPSDH's chefs, who stood over a vat. "Phoo!" said he. "You know what Manhattan chowder is? It's yesterday's vegetable soup with clams thrown in." So, Rhode Island chowder, a huge silver tureen of which is set by your table, is made *with* tomatoes, *with* potatoes, but definitely *without* any other vegetables.

Indian pudding is the one optional item on the shore dinner menu, for the simple reason that on a summer day most people prefer dessert of watermelon over hot porridge. But this Indian pudding is excellent—loose molasses-sweetened cornmeal, freckled with bits of "skin" from the top of the crock where it cooks for approximately five hours. If any one dish could be called New England soul food, it is this frumpy cereal. RPPSDH garnishes it with a little spoonful of hard sauce made with lemon, ginger, and vanilla.

Service is brisk. Bright young men and women in white aprons ladle out the chowder, fetch drinks from the bar, and carry steamers to the table in the all-but-vanished seaside resort manner—bunched up in their aprons. It is quite amazing to watch them set the twenty-foot-long tables after each service—deftly rolling up the old paper, then re-covering the table by plunking down a mother roll and spinning out another twenty-foot-length of paper —all in seconds.

At the entrance, you may be startled by the meanness of a sign warning PEOPLE HAVING CHOWDER AND CLAM CAKES CANNOT BE SEATED WITH PEOPLE HAVING SHORE DINNERS. This is because meals are paid for in advance by purchasing one of several tickets—for a full shore dinner, for a shore dinner with chicken instead of lobster (cheaper), or for clam cakes and chowder (cheaper still). Since each version is a family-style all-you-can-eat proposition, the clam cake and chowder people must be segregated from those who get everything.

A monumental restaurant, but in its own way, quaint. The Caribbean pink and aqua walls create for us a sense of déjà vu, but it is only in dreams that we have ever seen anything like the shore dinner hall at Rocky Point

Park. It is a surviving dinosaur from another time: nineteenth-century New England intact. Outside, in the amusement park that surrounds it, the summer air is filled with the screams of people riding roller coasters and splashing in the flume.

The Sea Gull

Succotash Rd., S. Kingstown, R.I.   E. Matunuck Beach exit off Rte. 1
(401) 789-2000

Summer Sun.–Thurs. 11 a.m.–8 p.m., Fri. & Sat. until 9 p.m.
Shorter hours in spring

$5 or less

In Rhode Island, clam cakes and chowder are as inseparable as catfish and hushpuppies in Arkansas or country ham and biscuits in Virginia. You wouldn't think of having one without the other. And the two of them together are a paragon seaside meal, a short-form shore dinner, sold in every eating hall and casual cafe along the coast.

Native Rhode Islander and *Roadfood* connoisseur Carolyn Wyman told us without any equivocation that the best place for clam cakes and chowder is The Sea Gull, a certain fact based on a South County–wide search she and several journalist colleagues had made for the ultimate clam cake-and-chowder house.

What is great about the clam cake here is how sweet it tastes, almost like the dough is enriched with butter. Pure white fluffy inside, dotted with moist clam morsels, encased in a knobby brittle crust. You want to eat a dozen.

Three kinds of chowder are available: red, white, and clear, clear being the steel-gray broth commonly found in southern New England (Rhode Island and Connecticut) and in our opinion, the best companion for the doughy cakes. It is strong-flavored, as rank as bilge water, yet sweet with the irresistible smack of clams and potato chunks.

If you are in the market for a major meal, The Sea Gull will set you up with a full-scale shore dinner, including clam cakes and chowder plus steamers and a lobster. And true to Rhode Island custom, the menu lists snail salad —a cool, oily mélange of snails, celery, and onions.

Although beach clothes are not allowed in the dining room, this is a casual place, for chowing down with gusto after a day at the beach.

VERMONT

The Bryant House

Rte. 100, Weston, Vt.
(802) 824-6287

Mid-May–Dec. Wed.–Sat. lunch & dinner, Mon.–Tues. lunch only

Lunch $5 or less, dinner $5–$10

Located next to the Vermont Country Store, The Bryant House is a bastion of indigenous Yankee cooking. It's great fun to eat here, then amble next door to stock up on such hard-to-find products as Bag Balm (a cream for sore udders) or red flannel long johns with a back door.

As far as we know, this is the only restaurant where you can lunch on that most basic Vermont meal—a piece of cheddar, a bowl of cold milk, and a stack of common crackers. According to Vrest Orton, The Bryant House's owner, "*Crackers and milk* means not just *any* cracker but Vermont crackers, and if you think you can dislodge this long-relished supper or snack pièce de résistance by suggesting that some *other* kind of crackers, sweet, salty, or in any other form, are better, you will soon discover that nothing is so firmly established as this inseparable and natural combination."

Vermont crackers are small hard discs, which with a smart blow can be separated (like English muffins) into two halves. Vermonters either put their cheese on the halves or crumble the crackers into the milk. If you want to prove that you're a real Yankee, try to split your crackers neatly in two using only one hand.

There was a time when every family in the state bought their crackers at a general store. Today, even old-timers make a trip to the one place that still manufactures them and sells them by the barrel—the Country Store, or to the one restaurant that serves them—The Bryant House.

Vermont is also known for its chicken pie, made here in the traditional way with a biscuit crowning the yellow gravy. New England baked beans are always on the menu, served with a wedge of brown bread on the side.

Bryant House pancakes are made from whole grains ground in Vrest Orton's mill. They come with ham that has been smoked over corn cobs or bagged farm sausage, and they're topped, natch, with Vermont maple syrup.

Indian pudding at The Bryant House is unique. Neither sweet nor spicy, it is a coarse porridge dominated by the taste and texture of stone-ground cornmeal. A basic foodstuff, we imagine it would be as easy to gum down for breakfast as dessert. Also noteworthy on the dessert menu is strawberry shortcake, served on biscuits with real whipped cream; and apple pie with Vermont cheddar.

The Bryant House is an artfully restored home with several small dining rooms that have bookshelves built into the walls and pictures of Republican Presidents to look at. "I believe in sentiment and a sense of history," Orton says on the cover of his menu. The foods listed inside are testimony to that belief.

Buck and Doe

135 Main St., Island Pond, Vt.
(802) 723-4712

Daily lunch & dinner   Closed Mon. in winter

Lunch $10 or less, dinner about $15

You know you are getting close to Buck and Doe when your nose, cleared by the knife-sharp mountain air, sniffs pecan rolls tumbling from cast-iron pans, pea soup soaking up the juices of a ham-bone, apples sizzling in brown sugar, squash glazed with maple syrup . . .

We arrived an hour before Buck and Doe opened, so we made a promenade around the vest pocket village, stopping in the variety store, the food mart, and the hardware store to sample hometown opinions. "Buck and Doe is the best." "You won't believe it." "Wait till you see the pies." The raves were unanimous.

When the hot roll basket came, we began to understand. Baseball-size sticky buns, dotted dead center with pecans, were glazed amber; and when the brittle caramelized crust broke apart, they vented steam.

Our next course was soup: fish chowder rich with butter and cream; pale green pea soup topped with garlicky croutons.

Then came a platter of broiled Gaspé Bay salmon, and another with Buck and Doe's hot fish balls—flaked white fish rolled in cornmeal and deep-fried, served with horseradish cocktail sauce; they were sided by buttercup squash and a "Franconia potato"—baked skinless so that a new spicy crust develops as it cooks. Traveling past us to other tables were lobster rolls overflowing with big chunks of pink-speckled lobster meat, chicken pies, and stuffed peppers with Creole sauce. We were tempted to get more entrees, but we wanted to leave plenty of room for dessert.

Buck and Doe's banana cream pie is a legend among pie aficionados. Ronald Langford, the chef and owner, calls it "mile-high banana pie," and high it is—inches of banana-packed custard. Langford's apple goody is a hot brown-sugar apple cobbler served with a scoop of ice cream on top. For less ambitious eaters, there are primitive desserts, too—strawberries and freshly whipped cream, or Vermont cheddar and crackers.

We watched Ronald Langford pull the sweet buns out of the oven, fretting that the single pecan that adorns the top of each wasn't sitting quite right. "Nothing leaves this kitchen unless it's perfect," he said, and his assistant chef began lining up the pecans.

We asked him if he served venison. "Can't serve deer," he lamented. "Health regulations forbid it." Then why name the restaurant Buck and Doe? "There were plenty of white-tailed deer when we moved up here fifteen years ago," Langford said. "My wife Helen and I would sign our Christmas cards 'The Buck and the Doe,' and when we opened the restaurant, that seemed like the perfect name."

Even though it's not expensive, Buck and Doe is the sort of place one wants to go on a big date. There is a fancy wine list (including directions for pronouncing Châteauneuf-du-Pape and Dom Perignon), and at dinner the lights are lowered and the prices raised. We think the motto on the paper placemats sums it up just right: "A really nice place to eat."

The Fairlee Diner

Rte. 5, Fairlee, Vt.
(802) 333-9798

Mon.–Sat. 6 a.m.–9 p.m., Sun. 8 a.m.–4 p.m.   Closed Sun. in winter

$5 or less

We went back to the kitchen of this tiny diner to compliment the chef on his butterscotch pie. "It's an old recipe," Butch Roberts told us. "A lot of people remark about it, because they've never tasted real butterscotch before—just candy and ready-made puddings. It's so seldom you get a chance to taste the real thing."

The Real Thing is exactly what you'll get at The Fairlee: freshly made doughnuts every morning, glazed or jelly filled; lunches of ham with raisin sauce or roast turkey and dressing; good hearty chowders or milky oyster stew topped with a thin film of butter; warm dinner rolls—this is honest food, nothing phony, nothing fancy. What could be more true to the character of Vermont cuisine?

For dessert, select from a repertoire of puddings that includes apple tapioca, raisin rice, and raisin bread; or get a wedge of prune apricot or vanilla-scented custard pie; or, in the summer, choose fresh peach shortcake capped with whipped cream. The lemon meringue pie at The Fairlee is breathtaking—precariously tall, vibrantly lemon-flavored, crowned with frothy meringue. And the rare treat of real butterscotch pie is not to be missed. Its ambrosial filling is thick as peanut butter, spread with a layer of whipped cream for textural balance.

Not everything at The Fairlee is traditional. On our last visit, we sampled a unique Indian pudding—very moist and spicy, the classic recipe unconventionally perked up with small apple slivers.

In an understated way typical of this part of the country, The Fairlee is pretty. Its white wood siding is accented by sharp forest-green trim; flower boxes decorate the doorway; and inside, six gleaming pine booths are lined up opposite the counter. In the winter, locals linger comfortably over freshly brewed—and freshly ground—coffee. In the summer, at mealtimes, the pace is faster, the booths less cozy. Any time, though, a meal at The Fairlee Diner is sure to be a square one.

(The Roberts family, who have run The Fairlee for years, also operate a branch, Roberts' Country Cooking, just down Route 5 in East Thetford. The new place, while lacking big sister Fairlee's visual charms, serves the same good food.)

Miss Lyndonville

Rte. 5, Lyndonville, Vt.
(802) 626-9890

Mon.–Thurs. 5 a.m.–2 p.m., Fri. 5 a.m.–9 p.m., Sat. 6 a.m.–3 p.m., Sun. 8 a.m.–1 p.m.

About $5

From the tables in the older part of this rejuvenated monitor-roof diner, our view toward the counter was rustic indeed: a row of stools capped by a row of workmen having coffee. Between the bottoms of the men's plaid jackets and the tops of their jeans was a row of lower backs, at the precise point the backs bisect into pink buttocks. How's that for local color?

The men come to Miss Lyndonville for breakfast of deep-fried French toast, which tastes extremely fried. Pancakes are highway-style flapjacks, able to soak up gallons of syrup. But they are served with real maple syrup that is light amber and delicious. Many of Miss L's loyal regulars get them topped with blueberries or strawberries and whipped cream.

Forget about the so-called muffins, which are squares of undistinguished coffee cake with blueberry goo in the center.

On the other hand, the homemade toast is excellent; the coffee is strong. And at lunch, there is a hearty "North Country special," a burger on grilled homemade bread, with Vermont cheddar, tomato, onion, special sauce, with slaw and good greasy hash browns.

We like Miss Lyndonville for its nonchalant ambience, the oil-cloth-covered tables, the local radio station playing loud, the table-to-table chitchat, and good coffee. It's a William Least Heat Moon kind of place. And if you are looking for a square meal, diner style, it's yours too.

Skyline Restaurant

Rte. 9, Hogback Mountain, Marlboro, Vt.
(802) 464-5535

Summer daily 8 a.m.–8:30 p.m.   Fall 8 a.m.–8 p.m.   Winter Wed.–Sun. 8 a.m.–8 p.m., Mon. & Tues. 8 a.m.–3 p.m.

$10 or less

"A Vermont restaurant," says the Skyline brochure, "operated by a native Vermonter for over 37 years." Does that explain why it looks frozen in time, about 1950?—weathered pine paneling, plaid rug, a fireplace and easy chair near the door, and the "famous 100 mile view," just over the top of the antique store and "wildlife museum" across the road. What a sweet taste of old-fashioned roadside tourism. You imagine Duncan Hines stopping in on one of his "Adventures in Good Eating."

Every table affords not only a breathtaking panorama (with a placemat key to what's what), but also a close-up view of bright-colored birds attracted to the dozen birdhouses at the side of the building.

All the charm would be a waste if the chow didn't measure up, but it too is a taste of Vermont foodways as they were. Pancakes and waffles, made from stone-ground meal, are served in stacks with Vermont maple syrup, sugar-cured ham, and homemade sausage liberally spiced with peppers.

We stopped in for lunch and had a club sandwich. No big deal, you say? This was *real* turkey on the overstuffed triple decker, cut from the bird that just the night before had been made into roast turkey dinners, with all the fixings, made from scratch.

Vermont cheddar comes on sandwiches, soups are made fresh each day, and with our salads we ate wonderful date-nut bread, sticky, warm and cakelike.

For dessert, many Skyline patrons get a waffle, topped with syrup, whipped cream, and a cherry. In strawberry season, strawberry shortcake is served the traditional way, on unsweetened baking powder biscuits.

Maple pecan pie—its eggy maple-sweetened custard topped with sticky pecans and a smear of whipped cream—was the major discovery of our lunch. Apple pie was a corker, too: spicy, homey, made with firm, tart fruit. And you will always find Indian pudding on the menu: not too sweet, a pale, grainy pillow of ginger-accented gruel, served with a dainty dose of vanilla ice cream.

Our only disappointment at the Skyline was its selection of postcards. All of them are modern. We expected cards more in keeping with the spirit of the setting and the cuisine: linen-finish, feverishly tinted, showing cheerful tourists at table eating farmers' breakfasts and pointing with great interest through the picture window toward the White Mountains and the Berkshires.

Wayside Restaurant

Rte. 302, Berlin, Vt.   On the Montpelier border
(802) 223-6611

Mon.–Sat. 6:30 a.m.–9:30 p.m.

About $5

If you want to sort out the old Vermonters from the newly arrived, ask which food is their favorite. The arrivistes might tell you maple syrup or chicken pies, but only the hard-core coot will give the right answer: boiled dinner.

Boiled dinner begins with corned beef. It's cooked in the same water with beets, cabbage, potatoes, and carrots (each for its own proper length of time), and then all the vegetables are arranged in a circle on a platter around the thickly sliced corned beef. It's a formidable sight; there is no other dish that provides so strong a feel for the sturdy character of this region's gastronomy. The Wayside doesn't make a big deal out of boiled dinner. On those occasions when they make it, it is listed plainly as corned beef. This is not the type of restaurant that tries to impress patrons with its authenticity. No need for that. The patrons, almost all regular customers, know a real Vermont menu when they see it.

It is customary to make too much boiled dinner, so that the next day all the leftover ingredients can be chopped up together and fried on the grill. The beets tint the coarse hash shocking red, and that is how it got its name —red flannel hash, another of the Wayside's occasional specialties.

The last time we were here, they had served roast beef the day before— and this day's lunch special was old-fashioned beef hash (not red), baked in the oven. It was served with small powdery biscuits.

Another specialty of the house—and a north mountain dish even harder to find in a restaurant—is salt pork and milk gravy, usually made on Thursday. The pork is sliced thin and cooked in a pan until the strips crackle and turn crisp; then a milky white gravy is ladled on, and the hearty dish is accompanied by carrots or beets.

They don't make salt pork, hash, or boiled dinner every day at the Wayside, but the changing menu is replete with regional favorites: deep-fried native perch, broiled haddock, fried pickled tripe, milk oyster stew, fish chowder, blueberry muffins at breakfast, and for dessert, a couple of real winners made with local syrup—maple sundaes and maple cream pie.

The maple cream pie is a deep layer of maple filling as grainy and dense as toffy, topped by an equally tall layer of light whipped cream. The polar contrast of textures between intense maple and breezy cream makes for one hell of a piece of pie.

The Wayside is a wide wood-paneled restaurant, plain and rather square (in the cultural, not geometrical sense). You can come here and get hamburgers or other uniform foodstuffs, but you won't find a better informal place to sample a changing bill of authentic Yankee fare.

Oh, yes—one other north country specialty served at the Wayside; a dish you're not likely to find in any traditional New England cookbook, but one that's served in dozens of restaurants from Vermont to western Maine: American chop suey. It's ground beef and macaroni in tomato sauce, listed on the menu as the Vermont Special!

Willy's

Rte. 114, East Burke, Vt.
(802) 626-8475

Dinner Wed.–Sun.   Reservations advised

$10–$15

Willy's is one mighty room, on a scale unheard-of in modern restaurants, except perhaps the perch dinnerdromes of Hammond, Indiana.

An enormous red building snugged close to the road in the middle of nowhere, with a door a full ten feet tall, it is a former Methodist church built in 1838 from Bunyanesque cuts of lumber: 10×10 sills, fifty feet long, 8×8's, 10×12 kingposts, beams and posts held together by hand-forged bolts.

The spectacle of space means trouble for the waitresses, local girls working hard for their money trying to cover the vast reaches of the dining room, trudging yet again to the seats in the balcony.

The meal begins in the fashion of an inn with a tray of spreadable cheddar cheese, crackers, scallions, and carrots. Then you make your way to the salad bar, and it is a looker, a farmy spread of corn relish, pickled vegetables, watermelon pickles, marinated mushrooms, leafy things, all sorts of peppers, sourdough and wholewheat bread.

The menu is Yankee/German with gourmet aspirations. Scallops and fisherman's stew are listed alongside veal à la Holstein and pork chops Grand Marnier.

Kässler Ripchen, roast smoked loin of pork, was marinated in garlic and maple syrup—a surprisingly harmonious combination, and served with a heap of homemade sauerkraut that is really sour.

With sauerbraten came spaetzel that looked exactly like fried clams, little twisty knots, but of course the pastry pinches were blander, with a mellow butter-egg flavor, sauteed lightly, then fried. Three round slices of sauerbraten in their spicy sauce were accompanied by coarsely cut cabbage, sweet and wine vinegar sour. On the side we dug into a large casserole of creamy whipped potatoes, the real thing.

Our American-flavored meal wasn't as distinctive, merely good. Pale fried clams could not compete with the snappy oceanic beauties one eats nearer the shore; sauteed oysters, breaded with zesty whole wheat flour and sauteed in butter and wine, were succulent to the point of being oily. The German egg pancake, on the other hand, was a masterful puff of baked and rolled batter stuffed with sweet stewed apples.

On a table near the salads, desserts are on display: chocolate cake, short-cakes ready to be topped with strawberries, eclairs waiting to be cut and stuffed with custard.

The original Willy's was a downtown New York restaurant. Salad plates, with black gothic letters spelling out *Willy's,* are a déjà vu of a vanished kind of urban man's restaurant. George Willy III, on the back of the menu, says, "the New York City rat race was not at all what I had planned for my life. So in 1979, I packed it up and moved Willy's to East Burke."

(Given one week's advance notice, Willy's will prepare suckling pig for fifteen or more people, served family style on the balcony.)

Mid-Atlantic

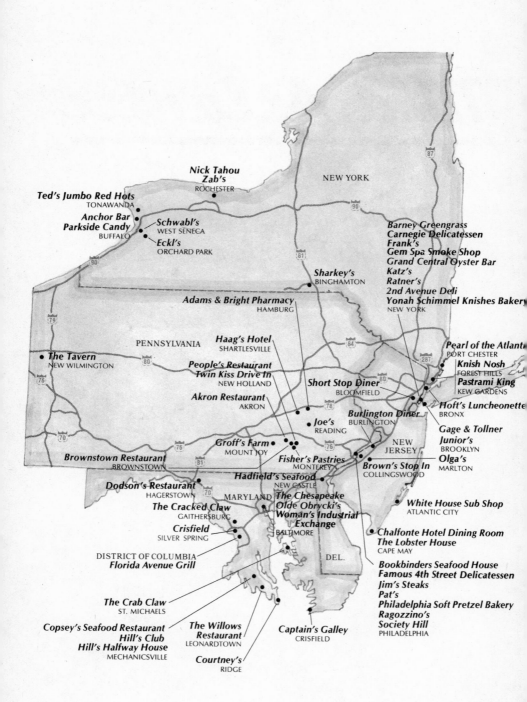

Nick Tahou
Zab's
ROCHESTER

NEW YORK

Ted's Jumbo Red Hots
TONAWANDA

Anchor Bar
Parkside Candy
BUFFALO

Schwabl's
WEST SENECA

Eckl's
ORCHARD PARK

Barney Greengrass
Carnegie Delicatessen
Frank's
Gem Spa Smoke Shop
Grand Central Oyster Bar
Katz's
Ratner's
2nd Avenue Deli
Yonah Schimmel Knishes Bakery
NEW YORK

Sharkey's
BINGHAMTON

Adams & Bright Pharmacy
HAMBURG

PENNSYLVANIA

The Tavern
NEW WILMINGTON

Haag's Hotel
SHARTLESVILLE

People's Restaurant
Twin Kiss Drive In
NEW HOLLAND

Akron Restaurant
AKRON

Short Stop Diner
BLOOMFIELD

Pearl of the Atlantic
PORT CHESTER

Knish Nosh
FOREST HILLS

Pastrami King
KEW GARDENS

Hoft's Luncheonette
BRONX

Joe's
READING

Burlington Diner
BURLINGTON

Gage & Tollner
Junior's
BROOKLYN

Groff's Farm
MOUNT JOY

NEW
JERSEY

Olga's
MARLTON

Brownstown Restaurant
BROWNSTOWN

Fisher's Pastries
MONTEREY

Brown's Stop In
COLLINGSWOOD

Hadfield's Seafood
NEW CASTLE

Dodson's Restaurant
HAGERSTOWN

MARYLAND

The Chesapeake
Olde Obrycki's
Woman's Industrial
Exchange
BALTIMORE

White House Sub Shop
ATLANTIC CITY

The Cracked Claw
GAITHERSBURG

Crisfield
SILVER SPRING

DEL.

Chalfonte Hotel Dining Room
The Lobster House
CAPE MAY

DISTRICT OF COLUMBIA
Florida Avenue Grill

Bookbinders Seafood House
Famous 4th Street Delicatessen
Jim's Steaks
Pat's
Philadelphia Soft Pretzel Bakery
Ragozzino's
Society Hill
PHILADELPHIA

The Crab Claw
ST. MICHAELS

Copsey's Seafood Restaurant
Hill's Club
Hill's Halfway House
MECHANICSVILLE

The Willows
Restaurant
LEONARDTOWN

Captain's Galley
CRISFIELD

Courtney's
RIDGE

Mid-Atlantic Specialties

Where we list several places, we have starred the one we think best.

Bagels and Onion Rolls

    Carnegie Delicatessen (New York, NY)   104
    Junior's (Brooklyn, NY)   112
★ Ratner's (New York, NY)   120
    Yonah Schimmel Knishes Bakery (New York, NY)   125
    Famous 4th Street Delicatessen (Philadelphia, PA)   131

Blintzes—Crepes rolled around sweetened pot cheese

    Carnegie Delicatessen (New York, NY)   104
    Junior's (Brooklyn, NY)   112
    Pastrami King (Kew Gardens, NY)   117
★ Ratner's (New York, NY)   120
    Famous 4th Street Delicatessen (Philadelphia, PA)   131

Chicken Corn Soup

    Twin Kiss Drive In (New Holland, PA)   143

Chicken Stoltzfus—Chicken in cream gravy topped with diamond-shaped pastry squares

    Groff's Farm (Mount Joy, PA)   133

Chopped Chicken Liver

    Carnegie Delicatessen (New York, NY)   104
★ 2nd Avenue Deli (New York, NY)   122
    Katz's (New York, NY)   114
    Pastrami King (Kew Gardens, NY)   117
    Famous 4th Street Delicatessen (Philadelphia, PA)   131

Crab Cakes

    Hadfield's Seafood (New Castle, DE)   81
★ Captain's Galley (Crisfield, MD)   84
    The Chesapeake (Baltimore, MD)   85
    Copsey's (Mechanicsville, MD)   86
    Courtney's (Ridge, MD)   87
    The Crab Claw (St. Michaels, MD)   88

The Cracked Claw (Gaithersburg, MD)   89
Dodson's Restaurant (Hagerstown, MD)   89
Hill's Club (Mechanicsville, MD)   91
Hill's Halfway House (Mechanicsville, MD)   91
Old Obrycki's (Baltimore, MD)   92
The Willows Restaurant (Leonardtown, MD)   93
The Woman's Industrial Exchange (Baltimore, MD)   94
The Lobster House (Cape May, NJ)   98

Crab Feasts

Copsey's (Mechanicsville, MD)   86
The Crab Claw (St. Michaels, MD)   88
The Cracked Claw (Gaithersburg, MD)   89
★ Olde Obrycki's (Baltimore, MD)   92

Crab Imperial—Backfin crabmeat baked in a white wine sauce

Captain's Galley (Crisfield, MD)   84
The Crab Claw (St. Michaels, MD)   88
The Cracked Claw (Gaithersburg, MD)   89
Olde Obrycki's (Baltimore, MD)   92
★ Bookbinders Seafood House (Philadelphia, PA)   129

Crab Soup

The Chesapeake (Baltimore, MD)   85
Copsey's (Mechanicsville, MD)   86
★ Courtney's (Ridge, MD)   87
The Willows Restaurant (Leonardtown, MD)   93

Egg Creams—A soda fountain drink of seltzer, milk, and chocolate syrup

Carnegie Delicatessen (New York, NY)   104
Gem Spa Smoke Shop (New York, NY)   109
★ Hoft's Luncheonette (The Bronx, NY)   111
Parkside Candy (Buffalo, NY)   116
Pastrami King (Kew Gardens, NY)   117
Famous 4th Street Delicatessen (Philadelphia, PA)   131

Funeral Pie—Amish raisin pie

People's Restaurant (New Holland, PA)   139

Hoagies and Subs—A cold-cut-packed loaf of Italian bread, especially popular in the Delaware River Valley

★ White House Sub Shop (Atlantic City, NJ)   100
  Ragozzino's (Philadelphia, PA)   141

Hot Pastrami/Corned Beef Sandwiches

★ Carnegie Delicatessen (New York, NY)   104
  Junior's (Brooklyn, NY)   112
  Katz's (New York, NY)   114
  Pastrami King (Kew Gardens, NY)   117
  2nd Avenue Deli (New York, NY)   122
  Famous 4th Street Delicatessen (Philadelphia, PA)   131

Knishes—A hot potato dumpling

  Knish Nosh (Forest Hills, NY)   115
  2nd Avenue Deli (New York, NY)   122
★ Yonah Schimmel Knishes Bakery (New York, NY)   125
  Famous 4th Street Delicatessen (Philadelphia, PA)   131

Kosher Hot Dogs

  Carnegie Delicatessen (New York, NY)   104
★ Katz's (New York, NY)   114
  Pastrami King (Kew Gardens, NY)   117
  Famous 4th Street Delicatessen (Philadelphia, PA)   131

Lancaster County Sausage

★ People's Restaurant (New Holland, PA)   139

Manhattan Clam Chowder—A tomato-based clam chowder made with potatoes, celery, peppers, carrots, etc.

  The Chesapeake (Baltimore, MD)   85
  The Lobster House (Cape May, NJ)   98
★ Grand Central Oyster Bar (New York, NY)   110
  Bookbinders Seafood House (Philadelphia, PA)   129

Milk Shakes

  Brown's Stop In (Collingswood, NJ)   95
  Olga's (Marlton, NJ)   99

Hoft's Luncheonette (The Bronx, NY)   111
Junior's (Brooklyn, NY)   112
★ Famous 4th Street Delicatessen (Philadelphia, PA)   131
Twin Kiss Drive In (New Holland, PA)   143

New York Cheesecake

The Lobster House (Cape May, NJ)   98
Gage and Tollner (Brooklyn, NY)   107
Grand Central Oyster Bar (New York, NY)   110
★ Junior's (Brooklyn, NY)   112
Ratner's (New York, NY)   120

New York Strip Steak—An aged boneless sirloin cut from the top section ("shell") of the short loin

★ Frank's (New York, NY)   106
Gage and Tollner (Brooklyn, NY)   107
Bookbinders Seafood House (Philadelphia, PA)   129

Oysters on the Half-Shell

The Chesapeake (Baltimore, MD)   85
Copsey's (Mechanicsville, MD)   86
Hill's Club (Mechanicsville, MD)   91
Hill's Halfway House (Mechanicsville, MD)   91
The Lobster House (Cape May, NJ)   98
Gage and Tollner (Brooklyn, NY)   107
★ Grand Central Oyster Bar (New York, NY)   110
Bookbinders Seafood House (Philadelphia, PA)   129

Oyster Pie

Akron Restaurant (Akron, PA)   128
★ Brownstown Restaurant (Brownstown, PA)   130

Pan Roasts and Shellfish Stews

The Lobster House (Cape May, NJ)   98
★ Gage and Tollner (Brooklyn, NY)   107
Grand Central Oyster Bar (New York, NY)   110
Bookbinders Seafood House (Philadelphia, PA)   129

Pennsylvania Dutch Chicken Pie—A crustless chicken stew served on broad noodles

Akron Restaurant (Akron, PA)   128

★ Brownstown Restaurant (Brownstown, PA)   130
   People's Restaurant (New Holland, PA)   139

Pennsylvania Dutch Preserves and Jellies

★ Fisher's Pastries (Monterey, PA)   132
   Groff's Farm (Mount Joy, PA)   133
   Haag's Hotel (Shartlesville, PA)   134

Pennsylvania Mushrooms

Joe's (Reading, PA)   136

Pepper Hash—A zesty Delaware Valley cabbage slaw

The Lobster House (Cape May, NJ)   98
★ Bookbinders Seafood House (Philadelphia, PA)   129

Pepper Pot—Stout tripe soup, unique to Pennsylvania

Bookbinders Seafood House (Philadelphia, PA)   129

Philadelphia Cheese Steaks—An Italian loaf filled with thinly sliced steak, cheese, and sauteed onions

White House Sub Shop (Atlantic City, NJ)   100
Brown's Stop In (Collingswood, NJ)   95
Jim's Steaks (Philadelphia, PA)   135
★ Pat's (Philadelphia, PA)   138
Society Hill (Philadelphia, PA)   142
Twin Kiss Drive In (New Holland, PA)   143

Philadelphia Soft Pretzels

Philadelphia Soft Pretzel Bakery (Philadelphia, PA)   140

Raisin-Pumpernickel Rolls ("Black Russians")

Gage and Tollner (Brooklyn, NY)   107

Rivel Soup—Either milk or chicken broth soup, afloat with pinches of eggy dough

Brownstown Restaurant (Brownstown, PA)   130

Root Beer (homemade)

Fisher's Pastries (Monterey, PA)   132

St. Mary's County Stuffed Ham—Country ham stuffed with kale or turnip greens and bits of red pepper

Copsey's (Mechanicsville, MD)   86
Courtney's (Ridge, MD)   87
Hill's Club (Mechanicsville, MD)   91
★ Hill's Halfway House (Mechanicsville, MD)   91
The Willows Restaurant (Leonardtown, MD)   93

Scrapple—A loaf made of pork and cornmeal, served by the slice

Akron Restaurant (Akron, PA)   128
★ Brownstown Restaurant (Brownstown, PA)   130

Shad Roe—Broiled shad eggs, usually wrapped in bacon and served on toast; a springtime dish

★ The Chesapeake (Baltimore, MD)   85
The Crab Claw (St. Michaels, MD)   88
The Lobster House (Cape May, NJ)   98
Grand Central Oyster Bar (New York, NY)   110
Bookbinders Seafood House (Philadelphia, PA)   129

Shoofly pie—A crumbly brown sugar crunch over a molasses-rich filling; either "wet" or "dry"

Akron Restaurant (Akron, PA)   128
Fisher's Pastries (Monterey, PA)   132
Haag's Hotel (Shartlesville, PA)   134
★ People's Restaurant (New Holland, PA)   139

Snapper Soup—A thick gumbo made with snapping turtle meat and sherry

The Lobster House (Cape May, NJ)   98
★ Bookbinders Seafood House (Philadelphia, PA)   129

Soft Clam Belly Broil—Lightly breaded broiled soft clam bellies

Gage and Tollner (Brooklyn, NY)   107

Sponge Candy—Chocolate-covered spun molasses

Parkside Candy (Buffalo, NY)   116

Sticky Buns—Sugar-and-cinnamon–topped yeast rolls

* ★ Akron Restaurant (Akron, PA)   128
  Fisher's Pastries (Monterey, PA)   132

White Hot Weiners

Nick Tahou (Rochester, NY)   115
Ted's Jumbo Red Hots (Tonawanda, NY)   124
★ Zab's (Rochester, NY)   126

Types of Mid-Atlantic Restaurants

Bakeries

Knish Nosh (Forest Hills, NY)   115
Yonah Schimmel Knishes Bakery (New York, NY)   125
Philadelphia Soft Pretzel Bakery (Philadelphia, PA)   140

Candy Stores

Gem Spa Smoke Shop (New York, NY)   109
Hoft's Luncheonette (The Bronx, NY)   111
Parkside Candy (Buffalo, NY)   116

Crab Houses

Captain's Galley (Crisfield, MD)   84
Copsey's (Mechanicsville, MD)   86
Courtney's (Ridge, MD)   87
The Crab Claw (St. Michaels, MD)   88
The Cracked Claw (Gaithersburg, MD)   89
Olde Obrycki's (Baltimore, MD)   92

Delicatessens

Carnegie Delicatessen (New York, NY)   104
Junior's (Brooklyn, NY)   112
Katz's (New York, NY)   114
Pastrami King (Kew Gardens, NY)   117

2nd Avenue Deli (New York, NY)   122
Famous 4th Street Delicatessen (Philadelphia, PA)   131

Diners

Burlington Diner (Burlington, NJ)   96
Olga's (Marlton, NJ)   99
Short Stop Diner (Bloomfield, NJ)   99

Drive-Ins

Brown's Stop In (Collingswood, NJ)   95
Twin Kiss Drive In (New Holland, PA)   143

Farm Restaurant

Groff's Farm (Mount Joy, PA)   133

Hot Dog Stands

Nick Tahou (Rochester, NY)   115
Ted's Jumbo Red Hots (Tonawanda, NY)   124
Zab's (Rochester, NY)   126

Hotels & Inns

Chalfonte Hotel Dining Room (Cape May, NJ)   97
Haag's Hotel (Shartlesville, PA)   134
Society Hill (Philadelphia, PA)   142
The Tavern (New Wilmington, PA)   142

Kosher Dairy Restaurants

Ratner's (New York, NY)   120
Yonah Schimmel Knishes Bakery (New York, NY)   125

Landmarks

Gage and Tollner (Brooklyn, NY)   107
Grand Central Oyster Bar (New York, NY)   110
Haag's Hotel (Shartlesville, PA)   134

Roadside Stand

Fisher's Pastries (Monterey, PA)   132

Soda Fountains

Brown's Stop In (Collingswood Heights, NJ)   95
Hoft's Luncheonette (The Bronx, NY)   111
Parkside Candy (Buffalo, NY)   116
Adams & Bright Pharmacy (Hamburg, PA)   127

Taverns

Hill's Club (Mechanicsville, MD)   91
Hill's Halfway House (Mechanicsville, MD)   91
The Willows Restaurant (Leonardstown, MD)   93
Society Hill (Philadelphia, PA)   142

DELAWARE

Hadfield's Seafood

192 S. Dupont Hwy., New Castle, Del.
(302) 322-0900

Tues.–Thurs. 10 a.m.–9 p.m., Fri. & Sat. 9 a.m.–10 p.m.,
Sun. 10 a.m.–9 p.m.   Closed Mon.

Under $10

Hadfield's is the *New York Times* of Chesapeake Bay seafood: all the fish that's fit to eat—whole, fileted, on the half-shell, fried, or stuffed . . . by the pound or bushel, by the gallon or by dozens. Finned and shellfish, clams, oysters, he-crabs and she-crabs, and whole fish of every imaginable size and shape are laid out on ice in a row of glass cases as long as a football field.

Most of what's sold at this enormous emporium is raw, for cooking at home, but for travelers there are picnic tables inside; and on a recent visit, we noted several happy diners in the parking lot, enjoying their crabs and clams to the sound of car radios.

There are dinners of crab cakes, fish cakes, flounder, soft crabs, or stuffed lobsters, along with fries and slaw; or, as we prefer, you can build your own meal, crab by shrimp by filet. Despite the grocery-store look of Hadfield's, some of the prepared dishes have a homey flavor—especially the Manhattan clam chowder, a zesty tomato-red soup packed with vegetables and big hunks of clam.

The fried foods, breaded in advance, vary in quality. When fresh, in the early summer, soft-shell crabs are juicy and wrapped in a delicate paper-thin crust. If your preference is raw oysters or clams or broiled filets, you won't find fresher.

Once you've chosen from the vast menu, give your order to the girl behind the counter, then sit in a molded plastic chair and wait for her to call your name. There is a supplemental menu of "seafood extras" that includes cocktail sauce by the cup, two ounces of melted butter, crab mallets, cocktail forks, even whole tomatoes, and something called "clam baggies," apparently for catching your own.

DISTRICT OF COLUMBIA

Crisfield

8012 Georgia Ave., Silver Spring, Md.
(301) 589-1306

Tues.–Thurs. noon–10 p.m., Fri. & Sat. to 10:30 p.m., Sun. to 9 p.m.
Closed 2 weeks in August   Expect to wait at peak mealtimes

$10–$25

Crisfield doesn't look like the kind of place where you'd spend a lot of money; they don't even take credit cards. But don't be fooled by appearances. With a few dozens from the raw bar, it's easy to drop a sawbuck for dinner (actually, in the Washington area, that's a bargain).

Although Crisfield is the plainest-looking seafood house in the Capital vicinity (its decor was once described as "early shower tile"), the provender is fresh from local waters, perfectly prepared—the best fish in town. That explains why it's so busy, and why there is a buoyant feeling in the dining room. This is not a restaurant for social climbing or showing off; it's a happy place because people come to Crisfield for one reason only—to eat well.

The menu is extensive, and unless you know what you want before you sit down, you are going to have to deal with an impatient waitress. Don't let these veteran kvetches throw you; while we've never actually met a Crisfield waitress we would call *friendly*, they get the job done.

There is every kind of fried or broiled local fish available, plus a repertoire of seafood Norfolk-style, sauteed in butter. We like crab Norfolk the best. Imperial crab, baked in the shell, and baked shrimp stuffed with lump crabmeat are two favorites that have been on the menu here for decades. Crisfield crab cakes are moderately spiced, tasting more of sweet crabmeat than crumbs. In cool months, you can count on brilliant Chincoteague oysters from Tidewater country.

Crisfield is a good place to try rockfish (Washingtonians' name for Chesapeake Bay striped bass); the piece we had was sweet and clean, not at all polluted-tasting, the way so much eastern bass can be.

Side dishes are nothing much: french fries, slaw, rolls; for dessert, a few pies or some fair cheesecake. If you're in the mood for something special in the way of sweets, just up the street, at 8101 Georgia Avenue, is Gifford's ice cream place.

Florida Avenue Grill

1100 Florida Ave., Washington, D.C.
(202) 265-1586

Mon.–Sat. 6 a.m.–9 p.m.

$5 or less

The city of Washington is too cosmopolitan to have much in the way of indigenous food. Good Italian, expensive French, Vietnamese, Afghani: a person can eat well all around the world here, with the conspicuous exception of American food, either of the south or the eastern seaboard.

But for genuinely regional fare, there *is* one place to go—and it is a beaut—the Florida Avenue Grill. Here is what must be admitted as *the* regional cuisine of Washington, D.C., a cuisine that existed for about two hundred years in the south before it got its name in the 1960s: soul food.

You can eat breakfast at the Grill any time of day, but we suggest arriving early so your buttermilk biscuits are oven-fresh. Get them with a slab of mid-Atlantic scrapple; or, for the more adventurous, work your way through gristly ham hocks. Somehow, even the fried eggs have extraordinary character. And the corn muffins, thick and crusty with steamy insides, are without peer.

If you come for lunch you will be presented with a choice of vegetables, each of which is a homely but delicious example of the soul kitchen's way with produce: collard greens soaking in their pot likker, bacony black-eyed peas (a not-too-distant cousin of the southern classic "hoppin John"), sweet potatoes, stewed okra, butter beans, pinto beans—a seasonal variety that changes depending on availability at the produce market. The Florida Avenue Grill's vegetables are substantial; a person could make a hearty meal out of them with a couple of corn muffins on the side.

A lot of soul cooking is the creation of resourceful chefs who were relegated the lesser parts of the hog—the hock, fatback (used to flavor greens), chitlins, and the like. We have yet to find pig's tails in the mustard greens, or ears or hog maw on the menu, but the Grill does have a way with pig: pork chops, ribs, and chitlins are regular lunchtime fare.

The spare ribs are baked, coated with an emphatic hot sauce, a sauce that is similar—if not identical—to that which permeates the excellent meat loaf. We could not abide the malodorous chitlins; this dish is an acquired taste—acquired only, we suspect, when one is young and southern. The Grill's chicken and cornbread dressing, on the other hand, is an aromatic delight that will conjure up farm suppers in Dixie for even the soul-food novice.

The Florida Avenue Grill is a humble place. In fact, it's rather shabby. But you wouldn't expect to find authentic soul food in the dining room of the Watergate.

MARYLAND

Captain's Galley

Main St., Crisfield, Md.   On the town dock
(301) 968-1636

Daily 7 a.m.–10 p.m.   Shorter hours in winter

About $10

Except for a panoramic picture window over Chesapeake Bay, there is nothing exciting about the look of the Captain's Galley: wood paneling, a small salad bar, a few decoys displayed on the wall. But do not be discouraged by the lack of grandeur; this, after all, is Crisfield, Maryland, the crab capital of America, immortalized in the Pulitzer Prize–winning book *Beautiful Swimmers*. It is the home of "watermen" (the local name for crabbers) like Captain James Dodson, who owns the Captain's Galley and supplies virtually all the seafood to its kitchen.

Crabs pulled from the waters around Crisfield are sweeter than those from anywhere else, a quality accentuated by Captain's Galley crab cakes, made from backfin meat. They are clouds of creamy crab bound together by a fissured crust so delicate it threatens to fall apart at the slightest touch.

An equally grand use for crabmeat is the locally popular dish called crab imperial. For this, backfin meat is mixed into a sherry-tinged white sauce and baked briefly. Crabmeat au gratin, crab balls (miniature crab cakes), soft-shell crabs sauteed in butter, tomatoey crab soup: the Captain's Galley is a crab-lover's paradise, with everything but a Baltimore-style crab feast on the menu.

When you have eaten your fill of crab, take a walk along the dock. Inhale the tang of salt air and watch the weatherworn workboats bringing in their haul.

The Chesapeake

1701 N. Charles, Baltimore, Md.
(301) 837-7711

Mon.–Fri. noon–10 p.m., Sat. 5 p.m.–midnight, Sun. 5 p.m.–10 p.m.
Reservations advised

$15–$25

The last time we stayed in Baltimore, we did exactly the thing that all savvy eaters know not to do. We asked the hotel desk clerk where to eat. "We've got great places," she boasted. "There's one real fancy one that plays chamberpot music while you dine, and another that's in a rough neighborhood; but use your indiscretion getting there, and you'll be fine."

We ignored the advice, left the hotel lobby and told our cabbie "The Chesapeake," letting out long mutual sighs of salvation. This is the grand old dowager of Baltimore restaurants, the "nice place in town" for years, recently renovated and reopened by its original owners. It is understated, with deep cozy banquettes and impeccable appointments: a tie-and-jacket place; your fellow diners will speak in soft voices and know which fork to use.

The menu is broad, offering duck and lamb and steaks ("cut it with a fork or tear up your check and walk out"). Salads are impressive, especially the huge "Hollywood salad," a stripped-down Caesar without the anchovies, and the official Caesar with the works, tossed in a wooden bowl. But let's focus in on the kitchen's forte—seafood.

For starters, you can go the clean and easy route with saltwater oysters on the half shell, or shrimp steamed hot pink in a cloud of uniquely Baltimorean spices. Or you can get messy with a kettle of superb steamed Chesapeake Bay clams. We like The Chesapeake's oysters Rockefeller, too; the oysters remain clear and tender, although the green stuff on top lacks the strong kick of Pernod you get in definitive New Orleans versions.

Chesapeake clam chowder is what's called Manhattan (or Rhode Island) chowder elsewhere; that is, it's tomato-based, not as clammy as milk chowder. The crab soup is a standard of Maryland's eastern shore: peppery orange, served hot enough to trail a sassy bouquet of steamy *eau de* crab above the bowl.

Of The Chesapeake's many ways with Maryland crabmeat, we recommend the old standby, crab imperial, which is nothing more than crabmeat suspended in a sheer white sauce. The Chesapeake's crab cakes are adequate, but pale in contrast to their spicier cousins on the eastern shore.

Crab lumps Chesapeake is a Norfolk-inspired combination of sauteed crabmeat and Smithfield ham. The range of this single dish—between the soft, buttery crab lumps and resilient, salty ham—is breathtaking; the flavors never meld: an artful meal, the best in the house.

Seasonal variations: stone crab claws are often available in the early spring, served cold with mustard sauce. In May there is shad roe. Soft-shell crabs are sold all summer—The Chesapeake does well with them, pan-fried in butter, or pan-fried and stuffed with lump crabmeat.

As at many fancy fish places, desserts are outrageous: flamed cherries or peach jubilee (more show than tell); a coconut sno-ball; killer cheesecake; and the chocolate marquis—chocolate, sour cream, butter, and walnuts, described on the menu as "a chocoholic's dream."

Copsey's Seafood Restaurant

Rte. 5, Mechanicsville, Md.
(301) 884-4235

Summer daily 10 a.m.–10 p.m.   Rest of year 10 a.m.–9 p.m.

$10 or less

We headed south out of Baltimore with two regional foods in our sights: crab cakes and stuffed ham, both specialties of St. Mary's County. The wide peninsula from Waldorf to Point Lookout is an unspoiled land, rimmed by the coves and bays of the Patuxent and Potomac rivers, dotted with crab houses and taverns specializing in seafood. We tried them all, and found the best crab cakes at our first stop, Copsey's—where, as a bonus, we also sampled the unique stuffed ham of St. Mary's County, and a brilliant orange crab soup.

Copsey's crab cakes are tidy ovals made from the meat of blue crabs, with only a trace of crumbs to bind them. They are seasoned with plenty of pepper, which perfectly brings forth the crab's natural sweetness; and they go best with a cold beer. You can get the crab cakes alone or, as we had them, on a fried platter that includes buttery local perch, mighty three-inch oysters, mannows (sea clams), and a soft-shell crab. We generally shun fried seafood platters, but in this part of Maryland that would be a big mistake. They love their seafood fried; and they know how to do it without overwhelming the crustaceans' natural flavors.

Most of the stuffed ham we sampled up and down Routes 5 and 235 was spiced like fire. But Mary Copsey likes hers cool; and so she balances the pink ham with kale/cabbage/onion greens that are less pungent. "You can always add hot sauce," she told us. "But I wouldn't. I like to taste that ham."

Copsey's is a squat cinderblock building with one table in a small grocery store area and two dining rooms—one with brown paper "tablecloths" for hot crab feasting, the other wood-paneled, a bit dressier, for less messy meals. The single table in the store is the roost of Mary Copsey, where she sits and smokes and chats with friends. Here she has a good view of the trophies declaring her son the 1980 oyster-shucking champion, and her daughter the first woman shucker champ ever.

Courtney's

Rte. 252, Ridge, Md.   At the water, 5 miles north of Point Lookout
(301) 872-4403

Summer Mon.–Thurs. 8 a.m.–10 p.m., Fri.–Sun. 6 a.m.–11 p.m.
Winter hours vary

$10 or less

"Yes! We have crab soup," said Courtney's menu; so we tried a bowl, and yes! It is good: bright orange and thick with filaments of sweet crabmeat. Topnotch crab cakes, too—loosely packed, coarsely shredded meat enveloped in a craggy, dark red crust. Both dishes have the distinct peppery taste unique to Maryland seafood.

Courtney's oyster stew was a smoky milk broth, also prodigiously sprinkled with pepper, and glutted with whole tender oysters. It was topped with pools of melted butter that never quite blended with the soup, but rather, broke into small savory droplets that were easy to spoon up with the oysters.

Although it's nothing more than a long shed of a building on raised concrete steps, there are few places as picturesque as Courtney's for sampling the Chesapeake Bay's harvest. To get here, you veer off Route 5 and drive along a flat, winding road through marshes, past boat sheds and fishermen's cabins. When you see the water, you've arrived. Through big windows you look out at Courtney's Crab House across the road; and beyond that, the Maryland shoreline stretches out as far as you can see.

The Crab Claw

Navy Point, at the end of Mill St., St. Michaels, Md.
(301) 745-2900

Tues.–Sun. 11 a.m.–10 p.m.   Closed mid-Nov.–mid-March

About $10

Maryland's eastern shore is the place to let your hair down, roll your sleeves up, and feast on hot crabs and cold beer. The Crab Claw, perched on a pier overlooking the Miles River, is the ideal setting. In its dining room a sign proclaims BLUE CRABS REIGN SUPREME.

If you choose to partake of what our placemat called "one of the great traditions in Maryland eating"—the crab feast—you will be presented with a pile of crabs, steamed in their shells, mildly spiced. With wooden mallet and pick you then go to work (dissection instructions and diagrams are on the placemat). Hard crabs are priced according to size, and you buy as many as you think you want.

Instructions or not, crab feasting requires some skill, and we well remember our first attempts, which left us frustrated. While all around, veteran crab eaters were happily ingesting big savory hunks of sweet meat, we sat over a pile of broken shells trying to extract a few edible morsels. If you have a low frustration level, lack good motor skills, and are a novice, you may want to forgo the crab feast. The menu says, "Crabs—All Ways," so try one of the other specialties, which get you more crab for less work.

We like something called a crab fluff. It is a ball of crabmeat dipped in batter spiced with crab seasoning, then fried. The plain crab cake is a good balance of meat and bread crumbs, flecked with parsley. All meals are served with corn muffins and miniature French bread rolls brushed with melted butter.

The Crab Claw's soft crabs are grilled, unbreaded, giving them a toasty parchment-red skin, with bodies of moist, well-seasoned meat.

Fried hard-shell crab is a horrifying dish, a whole blue crab with a giant lump of crab cake on top, batter-dipped and fried. It arrives at the table with a wooden mallet by its side and a kitchen knife plunged into its crab-cake sac, looking something like a B-movie monster: "The Crab That Devoured Baltimore . . . They tried to kill it with knives and hammers, but it KEPT ON COMING!" In fact, once you get over the initial shock of presentation, you are faced with an even more complex crab-eating problem: how to eat the crust and the meat while avoiding the hard shell.

In the spring, when fish spawn in the Atlantic, The Crab Claw sells dinners of shad or herring roe.

If you know a cozy spot along the shore for a picnic, you can buy steamed seasoned crabs by the dozen, to go, along with cold beer. And for those who arrive by boat, there is a Crab Claw dingy that shuttles customers from their own craft to the restaurant. The Crab Claw takes no reservations. Expect to wait, especially on weekends.

The Cracked Claw

19815 Frederick Rd., Gaithersburg, Md.
(301) 428-9199

Tues.–Fri. 11:30 a.m.–10 p.m., Sat. & Sun. 5 p.m.–10 p.m.

$10–$15

You have to admire the honesty of a restaurant that rates its own provender every day on a blackboard in the dining room. Some days, the board announces the supply is downright POOR; more often, it's GOOD; and you can be sure, with a system like this, that when the board says EXCELLENT, you are in for some mighty fine eating.

The food in question, as the name of this establishment suggests, is hard-shelled crabs, spiced and steamed and served with the same no-baloney forthrightness as the blackboard. Disposable brown paper serves as table-cloths; a heavy wooden mallet is the only tool provided. Crabs are served by the bushelful until you tell the management you have had enough.

When they are at least *good*, the peppery crabs are meaty fellas; none-theless, expect to expend plenty of energy extracting the good parts. Lazy crab fanciers can also order crab cakes or crab imperial . . . which come with utensils.

Dodson's Restaurant

32 Summit Ave., Hagerstown, Md.
(301) 733-7920

· Mon.–Fri. 7 a.m.–3 p.m.·

About $5

If you're planning to pass through Hagerstown, the crucial thing is to get there on a weekday between 7 a.m. and 3 p.m. In other words in time for breakfast and lunch. Those are the meals available at Dodson's Restaurant, and that's where you want to eat in Hagerstown . . . right next to the county courthouse, and just across the street from the Mount Hope Prison Ministry

Outreach. But its proximity to the courthouse isn't the main reason for the town's lawyers, judges, clerks, et al. drifting in all morning for coffee and pie, or swarming in for breakfast and lunch. The real reason, of course, is the food—the honest and generous cooking of basic American restaurant fare, at criminally low prices.

We tooled into Hagerstown at about ten in the morning, desperate for anything plausible to eat, and there was Dodson's—totally empty except for a nice young woman who turned out to be the waitress. When she brought our order of hotcakes—crisp on the edges, rich and buttery inside—and we began to rave, she started telling us about the place with ingenuous pride. It's owned by Mitch and Bette Dodson—Mitch does the cooking, Bette makes the pies—and they're both perfectionists. Mitch is obsessed with his raw materials—he makes his own salad dressings, and for hamburgers and spaghetti sauces he doesn't trust store-bought ground meat: he buys beef and grinds his own. What are the crab cakes like, we asked—and followed the hotcakes with a plate of them. They were perfect—piping hot, filled with large hunks of crab (no bread stuffing) and accompanied by a Mitch-made tartar sauce. Breakfast includes all the usuals—eggs any style; omelettes, French toast, bacon, ham, sausage—even good coffee. By this point we wouldn't have been surprised to hear that Mitch grew his own beans.

As for lunch, it's ribeye steaks, fried country ham, pork chops, liver and onions, fried chicken, soft-shell crabs, fried oysters (in season), and so on, with all the usual side dishes and a few not so usual—pickled beets, stewed tomatoes, cottage cheese, and apple butter. Plus salads and salad plates— even a Pineapple & Cottage Cheese Salad, though we're not sure how even Mitch could pull that one off. Plus endless sandwiches, from Kraut Dogs to Sweitzer Cheese to Steamship Roast Beef to Submarines. And don't forget Bette's pies! Needless to say, Mitch makes all his own soups—and according to our waitress, "They're so good, even the hot soups sell out in the summertime!"

Dodson's is as pleasant, airy, and unpretentious as its food is good. There's a low counter, and two small dining rooms, all with colonial-type wallpaper; the colonial motif extends to the ornaments, but not obnoxiously so. By the time we had washed down our last crab cake, the place was beginning to fill up for midmorning snacks. Other waitresses come in at lunchtime, and when things really get crowded, Bette abandons her pies and helps out serving, and if there's any justice in this world, that must happen just about every day! As we said goodbye, we asked our waitress her name. "Mitcha," she said. "Like Mitch?" we asked. "That's right," she said. "He's my father." Lucky girl . . .

Hill's Club

Rte. 235, Mechanicsville, Md.
(301) 884-3262

Daily lunch & dinner

$10 or less

As you travel through the undulating low hills of St. Mary's County, past colonial plantation houses and lush tobacco fields, it's like driving into the past. Here people still take their food in pubs and taverns, the way it must have been in eighteenth-century Maryland.

At first we were disconcerted by the coexistence of booze and food. It's rare to find good eats and serious drinking under the same roof, but in St. Mary's County there is something convivial about the taverns, and something appetizing about the notion of spicy seafood or stuffed ham accompanied by plenty of beer.

One of the best pubs we know in these parts is Hill's Club, where you can sample the full repertoire of southern Maryland cuisine, from rockfish (known as striped bass farther north), oysters, and crab cakes to good stuffed ham.

The Hill's ham on our platter was thick and sweet, stuffed with great pockets of oily greens—not the snapping fresh kale we found in Copsey's ham; rather, marinated and soft—in contrast to the fibrous ham. Oysters on the half-shell were large, clean, and freshly shucked, oceanic flotsam still clinging to their gnarled shells. The crab cakes were good, too—all crab and little else—just enough crust to bind them together.

Hill's Club is a dark, cozy place with a lot of character. There's an old-fashioned pinball machine and a case full of bowling trophies to admire in the barroom. And to the side of the sweeping circular bar is a dining area decorated with seascape paintings and a stuffed fish, complete with a small salad bar. "Dining Elegance & Your Favorite Cocktails," is the Hill's motto.

Hill's Halfway House

Junction of Rtes. 5 & 235, Mechanicsville, Md.
(301) 884-3287, DC hotline: (202) 870-2133

Daily 6 a.m.–10 p.m.

$10 or less

Ham-stuffing is a culinary custom unique to St. Mary's County, originated by slaves who took the hog jowls they were relegated and dressed them up with turnip greens. The results were so good that the soul food went "up market," from jowls to hams, and today there is hardly a restaurant or grocery store around where you can't buy stuffed ham in the autumn, winter, and spring. "Hams are best when the weather turns cool," we were informed by a veteran ham-stuffer who does a ham each weekend for family and friends to enjoy on Sunday.

The ham-stuffer assured us that the Halfway House was where we would find the county's best. She was right, too. Hill's Halfway House stuffed ham is piquant but not so hot it numbs your tastebuds. The crunchy greens are fresh with only the gentlest sting, leaving plenty of room for the good sweet ham to hog the show. You can get sandwiches or platters any time between September 15th and May 30th.

Be sure to try the crab cakes, too—finely minced crab molded into succulent patties and fried just long enough to form a crisp skin. Oysters on the half-shell are opened when ordered, and the soft-shell crabs we sampled were sheathed in the frailest spiced crust.

The Halfway House is a casual joint, with Formica tables and molded plastic chairs unceremoniously lined up as in a crab house. There is a jukebox, and a discount liquor store in the adjoining bar.

Hill's Halfway House is just down the road from Hill's Club, and we were curious to find out more about these prolific Hills; but when we asked in both places, nobody would own up to any familial ties between the two like-named restaurants.

Olde Obrycki's

1729 E. Pratt St., Baltimore, Md.
(301) 732-6399

Apr.–Oct. Tues.–Sat. lunch & dinner

$8–$15

Steamed crabs are a Baltimore obsession in the summer, and while there are many restaurants in town that feature crab feasts with all the accoutrements—picks and mallets and pitchers of beer, all set out on newspaper nappery—there is one place every connoisseur of America's regional foodways must experience: Olde Obrycki's. It is Baltimore's preeminent crab house, serving what Craig Claiborne described as "the finest crabmeat feast I have ever been witness to or participated in."

The star of the crab feast is the hard-shell blue crab; its preparation a ritual. The crabs are layered in a pot of vinegar water, covered with a mixture of salt, pepper, ginger, mustard, and who-knows-what-else, and steamed just long enough for the shells to turn an appetizing dark red. At Obrycki's one pays by the crab ($1 or more each), and has a choice of small, medium, or large. Go with the medium or large ones, and your efforts will be rewarded with plenty of crabmeat, more brilliantly spiced at Obrycki's than at any other crab house we know. The order is set right out on the table, on brown wrapping paper, along with the tools necessary for extracting the meat.

Crab-eating requires a significant expenditure of energy—the claws and legs have to be twisted off, the "apron" underneath must be pried away, and the shell must be cracked in two.

Easier to eat than hard-shell crabs—and in our book even more delicious —are Obrycki's soft crabs sauteed in butter. They are a summertime dish; lovely creatures—light gold, delicate, slightly crusty.

Every crab dish at Obrycki's is a small masterwork: peppery deviled crab, deep-fried or broiled, mounded into a shell; fresh crab cakes (also available fried or broiled); or crab imperial in cream sauce. The prices are low enough so you can try some of just about everything—and discover why Marylanders are so crab crazed.

If you are planning to dine at Obrycki's in April or October, call ahead to make sure they are open. When crabs stop coming fresh from the Chesapeake Bay, Obrycki's doors close until spring. Almost any time, there will be a wait for seats.

The Willows Restaurant

Rte. 5, Leonardtown, Md.
(301) 475-2711

Tues.–Sun. lunch & dinner

$10 or less

The Willows is a white brick roadhouse with lacy curtains in the windows, motherly waitresses, and divine crab cakes.

When we refer to these mounds of crabmeat bound together in gold crust as divine, or if we say their steamy aroma of fresh crabmeat, dotted with *al dente* greens and peppery spice is heavenly, we are not being flip. At a table near us sat the local minister and his flock. Before the parishioners dug in, they waited, and Father blessed the crab cakes.

We followed the congregation's lead and ordered crab soup; it was powerful stuff, thick with crab, spicy enough to clear your sinuses for the day. Even the stuffed ham had an extraordinary nip—it was the zestiest we tasted in our St. Mary's County quest.

The Willows is among the more demure crab houses on Route 5. It proudly displays a fraternal order flag right alongside a blue ribbon won for pie baking at the county fair. We've got to say, however, that the lemon meringue pie we sampled was slim and gluey; the chocolate pie little better than My-T-Fine in a crust. Stick to the seafood, and you won't go wrong.

The Woman's Industrial Exchange Restaurant

333 N. Charles, Baltimore, Md.
(301) 685-4388

Mon.–Fri. breakfast 7 a.m.–11 a.m., lunch 11 a.m.–2:30 p.m.

$5 or less

As we sat in The Woman's Industrial Exchange, eating crab cakes and chicken jelly with deviled eggs, a man entered the dining room. His clothes were tattered. He needed a shave. He looked beat. And yet he did not seem like a bum, just a man down on his luck. "I have two dollars," he told the hostess. "What can I have for two dollars?"

A nylon-uniformed waitress sat him down at a table and told him to relax. She hurriedly conferred with two of her colleagues. They whispered: "Croquettes? Soup? A sandwich?" A decision had been reached. "Pancakes," they concluded. "They're filling."

The man ate pancakes and bacon and drank coffee; and when he left, the lady at the cash register told him to keep his two dollars.

Lest you get the wrong idea, let us tell you that the Woman's Industrial Exchange is hardly a soup kitchen. It was conceived over a century ago in a spirit of self-help, as a place where women could sell handiwork to support themselves. And it remains a lunch haven for single ladies. To get to the dining room, you walk through a showroom: needlepoint pillows, hand-knit sweaters, clothes for Barbie and Cabbage Patch kids. "Whenever you purchase any of the merchandise," the menu advises, "you receive good value and are aiding a very deserving woman."

The long, narrow eating area, with its black-and-white linoleum and cream-colored walls, is a quiet museum exhibit that shows ladies' lunch as it used to be. Pictures of flowers and birds hang above the red leather banquette; jellies are for sale in a cluster of mismatched jars by the cash box. The menu features creamy croquettes, chicken or egg salads, and powdery, shortening-rich biscuits.

Crab cakes, with their red-gold crust, are loaded with hunks of sweet meat, accompanied by pickly cole slaw and cool, carrot-crunchy macaroni salad. Chicken jelly, just in case you haven't read your 1924 *Fannie Farmer* recently, is aspic made from chicken stock. Invalid food, but it packs substantial chicken flavor. Served as an amber block, chicken jelly arrives at the table jiggling beneath hard-cooked egg slices and between two deviled egg halves.

Tall meringue pies are featured at dessert, still warm if you eat early in the lunch hour. And of course there are layer cakes and floating islands. Very nice sweets, although none are jaw-droppers; you wouldn't expect confectionery pyrotechnics in a seemly place like this.

There is a lady stationed at the entrance of the Woman's Industrial

Exchange. She appears frail, and old enough to be our grandmother. Her job: to hold the door open for customers. She wields it with aplomb, wishing everyone who eats here a happy afternoon.

NEW JERSEY

Brown's Stop In

Rte. 130, one block south of Nicholson Rd., Collingswood, N.J. (609) 456-4535

Daily 11 a.m.–11 p.m. until 10 p.m. in winter

$5 or less

Big mugs sit in a chiller, frosted with ice, waiting to be filled with root beer; an old-fashioned milk-shake machine stands next to an equally venerable malt dispenser; you can smell steaks and onions sizzling on the grill: on the rim of Philadelphia, where cheese steaks, ice cream, and root beer are the people's choice, Brown's has it all.

"This place has to be great," one of us remarked, pointing to a large wooden testimonial on the wall. On closer inspection, it proved to be our *Roadfood* write-up from 1978—blown up, glued on a piece of pine, antiqued, distressed, and varnished. Wow, we had never seen ourselves on wood before. Beside it, clippings from *New Jersey* magazine and various Philadelphia newspapers cited Brown's as the best cheese steak outside of the city—at least according to "experts" Jane and Michael Stern. With swelled heads, we tottered back to our stools.

Brown's cheese steaks tasted even more delicious than we remembered. We got ours the way they do it in Philadelphia, with onions. It came on a hot roll with lots of cheese and an ample mound of oily, shredded beef. We thought the bread slightly *too* crisp, without the softness necessary to assimilate the distinctive flavor of sauteed steak and onions. But for the best cheese steak in New Jersey, that's a quibble we can live with.

Our only complaint about Brown's milk shakes was we didn't get enough! Here in the milk shake belt, you're allowed to get fussy if you are served only a glass, without the silver container with a refill in it. But this shake tastes of nature's finest cream; and so, feeling fat and sassy, we sprang for seconds.

Philadelphians are a restless bunch, especially when it comes to sandwiches. Never satisfied with one or two ingredients if more can be fortuitously stuffed into a roll, they are forever improving on the native hoagie. All around us, as we ploddingly sampled traditional cheese steaks, Brown's adventurous patrons were eating Texas Tommies—hot dogs grilled with bacon and cheese, and Brownie Specials—cheese steaks layered with slices of ham. People of the mid-Atlantic states, we salute your spirit of invention!

Burlington Diner

Hwy. 130 & High St., Burlington, N.J.
(609) 387-0658

Always open, except Mon. 8 p.m.–Tues. 4 a.m.

$10 or less

The Burlington Diner is a classic beanery full of sass: all Jersey and a mile wide—or nearly so, being two diners put together end-to-end. What do you eat in a classic Jersey diner? Breakfast, sure, Mac, but what else? Why, chicken croquettes, of course! Croquettes are diner food, see, and we're talking the real McCoy here, not those flat gummy discs in grocers' freezers. We're talking tall golden pyramids of spiced and flaked poultry topped with a ladies' luncheon la-de-dah cream sauce.

The Burlington, this diner of diners, this hash house supreme, this jernt we nominate as the official state restaurant, makes chicken croquettes like nobody's business.

Before our butts hit the booths, waitress Stella had menus in our hands. We ordered and she moved on to a Ricardo Montalban look-alike straight from the Atlantic City casinos. "I'll wait on you any time," she cooed at him, then turned to us, the eavesdroppers, and shrugged. "What can I do? I'm in love with beauty."

We came at lunchtime, and the Burlington was jammed with New Jersey natives gobbling up platters of blue-plate special food under autographed pictures of pro wrestlers, Joe Frazier, gorgeous-gammed beauty queens, and other local luminaries. Waitresses were running through the aisles like Knute Rockne, one arm out, clearing the path, shouting "Coming through! coming through!" to amblers.

Like the Alps, our chicken croquettes caused us to draw sharp breaths before expounding on their majesty. Twin peaks of poultry the color of the mesas in the Navajo nation, they stood mired in the white cream gravy flowing down their sides; beside them sat a volcano-shaped mound of mashed potatoes, gravy bubbling out from a deep crater formed by a heavy ice cream scoop. Completing the plate's geological formation were fibrous, clay-orange sweet potatoes. We plowed through the landscape in record time, our metabolisms goosed by the diner's contagious celerity.

In the wink of an eye, Stella tallied up our check tableside. "I was a mathematician before I was a waitress," she said. "I've got a mind like a Univac." And she was off again to wait on Mr. Suave.

Chalfonte Hotel Dining Room

301 Howard St., Cape May, N.J.
(609) 884-8409

Mid-June–Sept. breakfast & dinner   Reservations advised, jackets required for men

$15 or less

The meal you are served in the Chalfonte Hotel Dining Room, in the charming Victorian community of Cape May, is probably exactly the same menu visitors to the Jersey shore enjoyed at the beginning of this century, right down to the freshly made mayonnaise that chef Helen Dickerson stirs up, not from any written recipe, but from forty years of experience.

The Chalfonte Hotel is 109 years old, and Helen, an elderly black lady, has overseen the kitchen more than one-third of that time. Many of the unwritten recipes predate her arrival; they were invented by her mother, who worked here first. "I quit my stirrin when it tastes good," is how she explains her formidable culinary skills.

It *does* taste good: traditional Southern country cooking (Cape May is below 39° latitude), served family style, not from any long menu, but from what the kitchen has prepared that day.

During the week, breakfast consists of bacon and eggs, hot biscuits, and a downy spoonbread casserole, made of cornmeal, eggs, and evaporated milk. Fresh broiled bluefish or flounder—once-popular shoreline breakfast items—are served, too, and on Sunday morning all this is supplemented by kidney stew.

Dinner varies by day: Monday, leg of lamb or broiled fish: Tuesday, roast beef; Wednesday and Sunday, fried chicken; Thursday, country ham or roast turkey; Friday, deviled crab; and Saturday, roast beef. Helen's fried chicken is beautiful, chewy-crusted bird, served with three-piece dinner rolls and a cheddar-cheese-laced eggplant casserole, plus four or five platters of fresh vegetables. For dessert, there was vanilla bread pudding, aromatically nutmegy.

You will not get these exact items when you dine at the Chalfonte; side dishes change, depending on what's available, and what Helen Dickerson decides to prepare. Of course, Helen doesn't do all the cooking herself. She has a chief assistant, her daughter Dot, who is in turn helped by *her* children, the fourth-generation Dickerson cooks.

Rooms at the Chalfonte Hotel run between $75 and $100, including breakfast and dinner.

The Lobster House

Fisherman's Wharf, Cape May, N.J.
(609) 884-8296

Mon.–Sat. noon–3 p.m. & 5 p.m.–10 p.m., Sun. 2 p.m.–9 p.m.
Reservations advised

$10–$20

Food writers of our ilk much prefer quaint undiscovered eateries with surprisingly good food to huge well-known restaurants where for a large amount of money, you darn-tooting *expect* the food to be good; but in the case of The Lobster House, we happily make an exception. This isn't merely a big restaurant; it is a small conglomerate, including a fish market, a coffee shop, a schooner with a cocktail lounge inside, a ritzy dining room, and, not least, a working fishing fleet that catches much of what's served inside.

Our favorite way to enjoy The Lobster House is to head around back of the restaurant, where there are umbrella'd tables set out on a sunny pier. For a fancier (and costlier) dinner, you'll want the restaurant, where on a nice summer weekend a long wait must be expected.

The food is just what one wants on the Jersey shore: flounder, fileted thick and broiled perfectly so the fish retains firm body and a rich nutty flavor; broiled bluefish, dark and rich; Jersey scallops; swordfish steaks; and an array of clam specialties, including a voluptuous clam stew made with cream, served with tangy fresh pepper hash on the side (a New Jersey specialty). The barbecued clams are also excellent, brought to the table on a bed of hot rock salt. Of course there are clams on the half shell, and steamers with butter and broth. In deference apparently to people who have been dragged against their will to the shore, the menu also lists "Landlubber's Specialties" like steak or chicken.

We especially liked the Lobster House's snapper soup, a mid-Atlantic dish that is a gelatinous gumbo thick with shreds of turtle meat and bits of hard-boiled egg, flavored heavily with sherry. Another good item is deviled crab, which is sold at the take-out counter but not available in the restaurant. It is a plump oval that is virtually all crabmeat, mildly spiced, with the thinnest of crusts.

For dessert: creamy cheesecake, rice pudding, or strawberry shortcake (made only when fresh strawberries can be had).

Olga's

Junction of Rtes. 70 & 73, Marlton, N.J.
(609) 596-1700

Always open

Under $10

Olga's is an enormous baroque diner whose milk shakes and architectonic pastries are famous. The baked goods are on display in a glass case near the door, and it is hard not to notice that the hairdo on the hostess who leads you to your table resembles the fanciest piece of cake in the showcase.

As we waited for our pies and shakes, we marveled at this diner deluxe, with its menu as long as the Dead Sea Scrolls and its pastry case topped with bowling trophies shaped like the Chrysler building. The separate dessert menu has a cover drawn in psychedelic swirls like an old Donovan album, depicting a girl mooning wistfully over a big gloppy piece of cake.

The Boston cream pie, despite its having been proclaimed the best in the world by none other than *Boston* magazine, was not great, its traditional center strip of vanilla cream replaced with a layer of flavorless marshmallowy goo.

But the chocolate shakes made us as weak in the knees as the mod lass on the dessert menu. The first jolt of creamy, deep chocolaty goodness reminded us that any place within a fifty-mile radius of Philadelphia is Milk Shake Country, where fountain treats are king. Each glass came sided by a silver blender pitcher that yielded two and a half servings. It was rich with little unblended lumps of ice cream. And it gave just the right resistance coming up the straw.

Short Stop Diner

315 Franklin St., Bloomfield, N.J.   Exit 148 off the Garden State Pkwy.
(201) 429-1591

Always open

Under $5

Unequivocally, New Jersey is diner land; a state whose distinct accent never sounds better than when bouncing off a hot griddle, or reverberating in pink Formica and Naugahyde booths. Diner slang sounds *right* when you hear it called out by a native son of Ho-Ho-Kus or Hackensack.

Now if there is one thing diners do best, it's breakfast. And the Short Stop Diner dishes it out twenty-four hours a day.

The specialty of the house is "eggs in the skillet," a happy local custom of cooking up a mess of Jersey eggs in a silver skillet, adding bacon or steak or sausage, then setting the skillet right before the customer, on a wood trivet. The logic to this method is that the skillet keeps the food warm, eliminating the ghastly sight of two chilly eggs staring balefully up from a cold china plate. There is also something aesthetically pleasing about the eggs and meat nestled together in a pan of sizzling butter.

The Short Stop is not a fancy diner, unless you consider a big electric clock on which "Time to Eat" has been printed in magic marker to be the last word in chic. Nor is it a place to linger. 15 MINUTE PATRON PARKING, says the sign in the lot. But for a well-brewed "cup of mud" (coffee) and a couple of "cackles, wrecked" (scrambled eggs), you can't beat it. The repartee from griddleman to waitress, and from waitresses to customers is pure Jersey . . . and so are the thirty dozen eggs per day and mounds of creamy butter that are the makings for the Short Stop's good breakfast meals.

White House Sub Shop

2301 Arctic Ave., Atlantic City, N.J.   At Mississippi Ave.
(609) 345-1564   For pick-up call 345-8599

Mon.–Sat. 10 a.m.–midnight, Sun. 11 a.m.–midnight

$5 or less

We realized just how important hoagies were to the people of the mid-Atlantic states when we came across a travel article in a Philadelphia magazine that advised its readers who planned to head east over the Delaware that they should be aware that "sub is New Jerseyese for hoagie."

Known across America as a hero, po boy, grinder, wedge, blimp, zep, Cuban mix, rocket, bomber, Garibaldi, or Italian, the stuffed loaf of bread is the pièce de résistance of street food in south Jersey.

In Atlantic City it is called a submarine, and there is one place in the ocean resort that not only makes the best, but boasts that it invented them. Having seen similar claims of sub authorship in Philadelphia, New Orleans, and New London, Connecticut, we wouldn't touch the murky subject of the submarine's gastronomic genealogy with a ten-foot baguette. Suffice it to say that the White House Sub Shop has been in business since 1946, about the time *hero* sandwiches took on the *submarine* moniker in homage to the activities of the silent service during WWII.

More than 9 million subs have been made here, a fact written for all to see on the sign outside that reads WHITE HOUSE: HOME OF SUBMARINES, on a neon loaf.

However dubious its lineage, the sub created by the White House is without peers. A whole sub (you can also get half) is a full two feet long, stuffed into a slim tube of bread turned out by a local bakery. This bread is magnificent, always absolutely fresh, sturdy, with a good tough crust (essential for holding copious ingredients), but still somehow light, almost fluffy inside. You can order any individual ingredient, such as salami, ham, or turkey, or you can go all the way and get the White House Special—Genoa salami, prosciutto, capicola, provolone, lettuce, tomatoes, and sweet peppers. The special is a pulchritudinous knockout, the meat layered into a bouquet of pink ruffles with red pepper highlights. It weighs maybe three or four pounds, but it is tightly packed, neat, easy to hold in one hand.

The White House cuts its own choice round steak for cheese steak subs, makes its own meatballs for meatball subs. The cheese steak is delicious, as neat as the cold-cut sandwich, and as overstuffed. We would stack it up any day against Philly's best.

As at all the great sub or hoagie shops in the Delaware Valley, the walls of the White House are lined with pictures of celebrities who frequent the place, presumably as a demonstration that they have never lost touch with the little people and the little people's humongous sandwiches. Dozens of testimonials indicate that not only has Jerry Lewis eaten here "numerous times," but so have the astronauts, Sinatra, and Joe Frazier. The White House photo gallery is especially interesting because not all the pix are publicity 8 × 10's. Many are candid shots, catching the likes of Ray Charles, Paul Anka, or Joan Rivers mid-mouthful with sub in hand.

NEW YORK

Anchor Bar

1047 Main St., Buffalo, N.Y.
(716) 886-8920

Daily 11 a.m.–3 p.m. & 4 p.m.–2 a.m.

$5 or less

People ate chicken wings before Theressa Belissimo cooked up a batch to serve with drinks in her corner tavern; but it was Theressa's recipe that put wings into orbit. She halved them, forming one "drumette" and another bow-shaped morsel with two thin bones; she deep-fried them; and then—her stroke of genius—she brewed butter, vinegar, and hot sauce to pour atop the fried wings. She served her invention on a plate with celery stalks and a bowl of blue-cheese dressing. Chicken wings have since become citywide *inamorati*, the definitive Buffalo dish, displacing even the venerable beef on weck sandwich (roast beef on a caraway roll) as western New York's proudest contribution to American gastronomy.

Nearly every pizza parlor and bar in town serves them, in exactly the same configuration on the plate, beneath an overturned wooden bowl (for bones). But they are not, not on your life, all the same. The Buffalonians we know need little prompting to engage in refined debates over the relative crispness or meatiness of one place's wings over another, or historical colloquies concerning wings' genealogy (claims are made by a man named John Young that *he* invented wings; but his are not served with blue-cheese dressing and celery).

The Anchor Bar, which has been officially recognized by the city of Buffalo as the original wingery, remains a humble corner tavern; except for wing-related newspaper clippings on the wall and a testimonial from Durkee congratulating the Anchor for its copious use of "Red Hot! Sauce," it could be Archie Bunker's tavern.

Anchor wings are small and crisp, with yellow-orange sauce brushed onto the crust. Because of the relatively small amount of meat on both drumette and bow, each bite of wing is an endearing variety of textures—shreds of tender meat, crunchy skin, slippery sauce. Fun food: great bar vittles or appetizers. If ordered mild, they are more butter-flavored, but nonetheless spicy. The hot ones are lip-scorchers, so redolent of Tabasco they could be used as smelling salts. That's where the blue cheese and celery come in handy: a cool respite from the zest of the wings.

The Anchor Bar also sells clams, sandwiches, potato skins, something called chicken lips, which the menu describes as breaded and barbecued turkey breast, and "scalone," which our waitress said was scallops and abalone crumbs. We stuck to wings.

Barney Greengrass

541 Amsterdam Avenue, New York, N.Y.   At 86th Street
(212) 724-4707

Tues.–Sun. 8:30 a.m.–4 p.m.   Closed Passover week & first three weeks in August

$5–$15

In Manhattan, on the Upper West Side, bagels and lox is as much a breakfast habit as grits and red-eye gravy in Tuscaloosa. Saturday night or Sunday morning, you go to the deli for lox and maybe sturgeon or sable or whitefish, cream cheese, a bit of garniture such as olives, onions, or tomatoes; you buy your bagels; then you eat it all at home, where you can read the Sunday *New York Times.*

To the rule that bagels and lox is home-food, here is one fine exception: Barney Greengrass, a West Side tradition since before there was a Zabar's. A humble delicatessen with a dining room attached, it is the best place in town to eat what the rest of America considers the classic New York breakfast.

On weekends after ten a.m., one must wait for a table. The line extends outside, and each time a customer enters or exits, an aromatic puff of frying onions wafts out the door. Inside, you can see the waiters serving baskets of bagels, plates of smoked fish, and the house special—from which that tantalizing aroma emanates—a scramble of eggs, onions, and Nova Scotia salmon.

It is an inspired combination, this special, a perfect paradox of plain and fancy, lean and oily foods. The salmon is firm silk, ritzy pink nuggets of smoked luxury infolded within a mess of eggs whose flavor is brilliantly heightened by soft shreds of sweet fried onion. It is not immense, just one small plateful; but it is immeasurably satisfying.

Barney Greengrass's unique breakfast special (served any time) is famous, not to be missed, but Moe Greengrass (Barney's son) calls himself "The Sturgeon King." So you order a platter of sturgeon. It is expensive, about $15, and it tastes expensive. The fish is cut into thick slices: lean food, drier than the glistening pink Nova Scotia salmon. A platter of either (or both) is a feast for one, or a cozy shared brunch for two—fish, slaw or potato salad, lettuce, tomato, onion, olive, pickle, cream cheese, plus two bagels or bialys.

For less than half the price of a platter, you can get a nice little sturgeon or Nova sandwich on your choice of rolls. There is snowy Great Lakes whitefish too, rich garlicked sable, plus a repertoire of deli cold cuts on crispcrusted rye bread. One of these days we will be brave and order what the menu lists as broiled Nova Scotia heads and wings.

Barney Greengrass borscht is classic. Served in a glass, it is beet-sweet, enriched with enough sour cream to turn the cold red soup milk-shake pink.

The house coffee is a mellow brew, perfect for lingering over. And on weekdays, Barney's is a place where West Siders do linger. Lots of jogging suits in evidence; well-scrutinized newspapers at many tables; conversations about a film at the Thalia, or about a film in production (the low budget kind, e.g. "I found a great location, but there's no place to put my tripod.")

When things are slow, you will see Moe Greengrass lounging at a table between the take-out area and the dining room. A genial man of kingly proportions, Moe inherited the sturgeon crown after his father moved his fish store here from Harlem in 1929. This is a real family business, with son Gary manning the register, wife Shirley behind the counter (or as we saw her on a recent visit, showing a particularly handsome smoked fish platter around the dining room), and Moe supervising everything, pointing entering customers to tables, or occasionally squeezing through the narrow aisles to take orders. "That's a winner," he says when you pick the breakfast special. And: "You did very well," when you clean your plate.

Carnegie Delicatessen

854 Seventh Ave., New York, N.Y.   At 55th St.
(212) 757-2245

Daily 6:30 a.m.–4 a.m.

$10 or less

"They all eat here," proprietor Leo Steiner assures us, pointing to the long table in back that has for years been a favorite gathering place for standup comics after hours. "Henny . . . Milton . . . Joey (he likes lox, eggs and onions). Warren Beatty and Nicholson eat here, too. They get matzoh ball soup and stuffed cabbage. And Falk, for him we have to burn the cabbage," Steiner shrugs the shrug of an expert shrugger. "Burnt is the only way he'll eat it."

The Carnegie (since 1935) is the prototype of the celebrity delicatessen, where Jewish (and non-Jewish) New Yorkers who have made it big—and some who haven't made it big—come to feel at home. They are mothered, fussed over, adored, and needled by a staff that consists entirely of semiprofessional performers: kvetchers, yentas, smart alecks, all in their gold deliman jackets and orthopedic waiters' shoes. The waiters and countermen, with Leo Steiner at the fore, are the show at the Carnegie. Watch them lean and slouch against the counter griping that a customer barely meets the minimum charge; they schlep, they twirl their towel, they call you "Doctor" or "Professor," "Dear," "Darling," or "Beautiful Lady."

It is a show built upon a sandwich. A corned beef sandwich. Corned beef that is cooked and seasoned in Mr. Steiner's kitchen in the basement. Brick red, lean, with a faint spicy tang, the meat is piled a full four inches high between slices of seeded rye. "I will not tell you the name of my baker," Mr. Steiner grins. "I won't even tell you what borough he's in." The secret is worth a million. The aromatic bread, with its glossy tan crust and chewy, sour insides, speckled with a thousand caraway seeds, is the best rye in America.

You want a sandwich with more pizzazz? Get the pastrami, which is spicier, luxuriant with veins of fat, rimmed with peppery zest. Can't decide? Get a corned beef and pastrami combo, six inches high, impossible to eat like a sandwich. So you dismantle it, and stuff the excess meat between the extra bread that comes with hot meals.

They're good, too, the full dinners: brisket in gravy with potato pancakes, boiled beef flanken, and plain roast chicken ("Woody's favorite," a waiter confides). Chicken soup is golden comfort, served with excruciatingly delicate matzoh balls or little meat-filled kreplach (dumplings, like ravioli, but redolent of schmaltz).

Unlike its imitators (which are legion), the Carnegie does not list sandwiches named for currently famous celebrities. There is a Henny Heaven on the menu (Nova Scotia salmon and cream cheese on a bagel). "You don't have to be a genius to figure out who Henny is," Leo Steiner tells us. "But let me tell you something. Henny doesn't even like novi! Henny likes tongue. But I've got to keep it ambivulous, or else Hackett would kill me."

Eckl's

4936 Ellicott Rd., Orchard Park, N.Y.   Southeast of Buffalo
(716) 662-2262

Daily 5 p.m.–11:30 p.m.

$5–$10

You can get the two Buffalo specialties here—chicken wings and beef on weck—but it's the ambience of Eckl's that's definitively upstate.

It's dark, lit with sconces; the paneled walls are decorated with heraldic gold keys and leaping deer pictures lacking only a cross-hairs in the foreground. Couples dine at Eckl's, big men in Sansabelts and acrylic-sweatered women topped with heavy hairdos, stalwarts who begin dinner with shrimp cocktail (for the lady) and a massive crock of French onion soup (for the gent). Dale Eckl, ubiquitous in the dining room, wears a short blue coat made of nylon, like a hairdresser. Eckl's is a supper club for citizens of the solid variety, who drink highballs and eat meat.

The food is square and somber, the meat high quality. "We refuse to succumb to the so-called advances of portion control, blast freezing, and chemical tenderizers," says the menu. "At Eckl's we simply endeavor to bring you the finest flavor possible in steaks, prime rib, and roast beef."

The specialty of the house—and of western New York—is beef on weck, a sandwich of hand-sliced roast beef piled onto a kummelweck (caraway seed) roll that is encrusted with a layer of pretzel salt. The beef is thin and virtually fatless, bland without gravy—a quality overcompensated for by the unbearably salty roll. We found it necessary to scrape salt off the top; that done, a good balance of taste was attained.

The leanness of the tender pink meat is admirable, too, although in concert with the spongy roll, the overall effect is dry. We should have asked for the roll to be dipped for a moment in gravy. Understand these are minor quibbles with what would in any other city be a top-rated sandwich. But Buffalonians take their beef on weck as seriously as Memphians do ribs; thus, severe standards must be applied.

Eckl's also sells an upmarket version of Buffalo chicken wings—meaty morsels, garnished not merely with the usual local accoutrements—celery and a bowl of blue-cheese dressing—but with radishes, a sprig of parsley, lettuce, and tomato.

Frank's

431 West 14th St., New York, N.Y.
(212) 243-1349

Mon.–Sat., breakfast & lunch, Wed.–Sat. dinner   Reservations advised

$25–$40, $5 or less for breakfast

Frank's is a forthright steak and chop house with the kind of square-jawed honesty that uptown steak houses mimic, at twice the price. But the sawdust on these floors is no affectation.

During the early morning, West 14th Street is crowded with trucks hauling "swinging beef" to and from the Gansevoort meat market. Frank's is where the big-neck crowd congregates for coffee and cafeteria-style chow. The doors open at approximately 2 a.m., for workingmen to come for breakfast. Hard hats and bloody aprons hang on the wall.

By nightfall, the meat market is closed. All the businesses board up—except for Frank's, where fresh sawdust is strewn about, and white linen is set on the tables. The cafeteria line closes, and George Molinari (Frank's son-in-law) puts on a suit and tie. Soon the tables are packed with a crowd of culinary cognoscenti who gloat in the knowledge that they are relishing a diamond in the rough. How rough? Frank's is so far from Manhattan's beaten paths that you can actually find a parking space on the street outside the restaurant!

Meat is the star: choose a double rack of lamb, mammoth prime rib, or a skirt steak that completely covers the plate on which it is served. Frank's strip steak is the primest of prime beef, agreeably resilient, with a profound mineral tang. Broiled to a glistening sheen on its tender charred crust, plump and livid pink, packed with juices, it is the definitive New York steak.

In the heart of the market, Frank's has an inside track on the freshest and best variety meats in town. Thick-cut calves liver, sauteed or broiled and served with bacon and a heap of onions, is just about as gentle-textured as it can be without falling apart when you look at it. For serious innards-eaters, sweetbreads, kidneys, and similar icky things are regularly chalked on the blackboard menu. But you don't have to love tripe to be won over by Frank's tripe Florentine, sold as an entree or appetizer, simmered to painful tenderness in a cumin-spiked wine and tomato sauce.

No one on earth enjoys all this good food more than Mr. Molinari, the proprietor, who greets each guest at the door. George is a husky fellow with a gruff voice, a meat-market kind of guy who somewhere along the line learned excellent manners.

When the subject is meat, when George is asked to describe the steak or the pound-plus veal chop, you might almost feel you have demanded too much to ask him to put his feelings into words. How can one expect a man to describe what he knows to be perfection? But he perseveres, and with endearingly awkward politeness, his voice cracks with rapture as he describes the canneloni, the pasta alla panna (with cream), or the pasta puttanesca (a raunchy mix of olives and anchovies). "Puttanesca means in the manner of a prostitute," he says, a rosy blush coloring his face.

Gage and Tollner

372 Fulton St., Brooklyn, N.Y.
(718) 875-5181

Mon.–Fri. 11:30 a.m.–9 p.m., Sat. 4 p.m.–11 p.m., Sun. noon–9 p.m.
Closed Sun. in July & Aug.

$10–$25

Midway through a meal at Gage and Tollner, as the uniformed, white-aproned waiters set down corn fritters, Duxbury stew, and hash browns afloat in white cream gravy, it occurred to us that New York City is not the culinary island we had always thought it to be. We looked at the soft white napkins cushioning each silver dish of food, we tasted the suave things that Gage and Tollner does with clams and oysters, and we realized that we were dining in the city that is the crown jewel of a distinctive culinary region of America, the mid-Atlantic states.

The Gage and Tollner style, basically unchanged since the restaurant opened in the 1880s, is—or was—unique to the eastern seaboard south of New England and north of Norfolk. You might still find such polished luxury at an eating club in Philadelphia or a private home in Baltimore, but it is, for the most part, a thing of the past, a style reminiscent of dining cars in the golden days of train travel. And we don't say that just because most of the waiters are black, carry themselves with the demeanor of a Pullman porter, and wear "service emblems" indicating twenty-five, thirty, and in one case forty years of employ.

It's the menu, too: mostly seafood offered in a startling variety of preparations, as if the kitchen wants to be conspicuous about the wealth of its larder and the skills of its staff. Delmonico's and Rector's had menus like this. Gage and Tollner sports sixteen different ways to prepare soft-bellied clams, ten ways with bay scallops, as many with oysters, shrimp, and crab, and four different Welsh rarebits, or as the menu correctly lists them, rabbits. (You can double your capacity for experimentation by getting half-portions.)

A basket of warm breads is set on the table, covered with a white napkin (if you had G & T's laundry business for white napkins, you'd be rich). New York breads: oyster nuggets, flat soda cracker discs, light rye with caraway seeds and raisins, and raisin pumpernickel rolls ("black Russians," invented by a New York City bakery).

The finest way to start a meal is the soft clam-belly broil appetizer, a dish of a dozen clam bellies in frail cornmeal breading—buttery nuggets with a broiled-crisp tip here and there. They are evocative of fried Ipswich clams, but only dimly so, for these stimulating morsels are transcendent; born-again fried clams.

Among the soft-belly entrees, we recommend the Duxbury stew (clams in a heavy cream sauce), the succulent fritters, and, most especially, the Dewey pan roast—one of the grandest and simplest seafood dishes on the east coast. It is a silver plate (if you also had G & T's silver polish business, you'd be rich) of soft bellies broiled in their own juices with *al dente* green and red peppers and chunks of cooked tomato. Miraculously, the clams seem to have been softened and relaxed, rather than toughened, by their roasting. What a savory dish!

Beware of the Welsh rabbit. A full order is a full meal. A half-order is nearly a full meal. But it is good food, like you'd expect to get in the dining room of a swell hotel. In addition to classic Welsh rabbit, there are variations of the molten cheese theme: Long Island rabbit, golden buck, and Yorkshire buck. The last has a fried egg and bacon atop its toast. The other two are made with eggs—or is it just the golden buck that's made with eggs? If interested, ask your waiter. He knows, and with only a little coaxing, will explain.

The shrimp curry is strong, hot, and granular; steamed lobsters are impeccable (if peccably priced); bisques are nearly as stout as the rabbits; bay scallops, plainly broiled, are as fresh and delicate as the ones at Christ Cella, which is to say they are unsurpassed.

The steaks (sirloins, mostly, known as "New York cut" elsewhere) are carried, one by one, when ordered, to the kitchen by waiters who get them (as well as raw half chickens and fish filets) from the food locker behind the bar at the center of the restaurant.

Fried chicken is a good dish, served with corn fritters and maple syrup —a taste of the more southerly mid-Atlantic.

Gage and Tollner's mutton chop is relatively mellow, still a shocker if you expect lamb. The chop is thick, cooked to just the degree of pinkness you specify, available the English way with sausage and kidneys.

Gage and Tollner's cheesecake is excellent—unadulterated New York-style cake, pure white with just a hint of burnished gold across the top of the slice. It is on the light side of the cheesecake spectrum (you can actually eat an entire piece), not too sweet, either. A skinny crumb crust at the bottom lends a slight almond flavor. The cake comes on a doily on a cold plate, straight from the fridge. Let it sit a few moments; nearer room temperature, the flavor blooms. With a pot of this restaurant's rich Colombian coffee, the cake is a primary eating experience.

Gage and Tollner is, in appearance, exactly the place it was in the 1880s (by law now—it has been declared a historical landmark, inside and out). Purple flocked paper alternates with arched mirrors along the wall. The gas lamps hanging from the stamped tin ceiling are real, lit every night. Tables are ancient wood; each place is set with a white napkin. It's an old-fashioned middle-class American restaurant, a bit like Galatoire's in New Orleans, but ritzier, in that characteristically eastern way.

Although outside Manhattan, Gage and Tollner is easy to reach. It's just a few blocks from the spidery Brooklyn Bridge—the historic link between the boroughs, built four years after Charles M. Gage opened his restaurant.

Gem Spa Smoke Shop

131 Second Ave., New York, N.Y.
No phone

Always open

Under $5

We like the menu at the Gem Spa; it makes life simple. Do you want a regular egg cream, made with chocolate? Or do you want coffee or vanilla? Will a single pretzel rod be enough? Those are the decisions that must be made; but even within those limited choices, we are quite frankly suspicious of the deviates who get vanilla or coffee.

Chocolate egg cream—syrup, milk, and seltzer—mixed in a twelve-ounce glass, served forth with a foamy head, salty foot-long pretzel on the side: this is one of the unimprovable culinary combos on earth, like champagne and caviar or milk and graham crackers.

There is plenty of mysticism about how to make a proper egg cream. The secret of the Gem Spa, it is said, is the milk—so cold it is crystalline. It is mixed in seconds . . . and it must be drunk fast. When an egg cream begins to warm, the bubbles dissipate, and the magic—a drink rich as eggs and cream, brewed from merely milk and soda water—is gone.

The smoke shop, we ought to mention, is in a less-than-wonderful neighborhood, and a large percentage of its shelf space is devoted to nudie magazines or worse. There is no place to sit; scarcely room to stand at the cramped counter. Although the egg creams are impeccably authentic, seekers of Lower East Side lost memories may need to wear earplugs and blinders to appreciate the nostalgic thrill.

Grand Central Oyster Bar

Lower level of Grand Central Station, 42nd St. & Vanderbilt Ave.,
New York, N.Y.
(212) 490-6650

Mon.–Fri. 11:30 a.m.–9:30 p.m.   Reservations required for a table,
but not the oyster bar or counter

$8–$25

Is there another restaurant in the United States where it is possible to attempt to distinguish the differences among Cotuit, Wellfleet, Apalachicola, Chincoteague, Box, and Kent Island oysters? Five days a week, every week of the year, the Grand Central Oyster Bar offers at least this many. In the "R" months, there may be another half dozen—Malpeques from Canada, Olympias from the northwest, even famous French Belons, small numbers of which are now grown in Maine.

You pay per oyster, so it is possible to get one or two of each and create from the profusion a joyous meal entirely on half-shells. The Maine Belons seem to have the sharpest deep sea bite, similar to the assertive, nearly metallic oysters from New Orleans (which are occasionally sold here, too). The biggest of the bunch are box oysters from Long Island; the smallest are Olys from Washington. Variations can be slight (dependent as much on season as species). The real point is that these are perfect icy oysters, expertly opened before your eyes (if you dine at the bar itself) in such a way that they sit in their shells in a shining pool of dipsey liquor: food of the gods.

Beyond raw mollusks, the menu of the Grand Central Oyster Bar is a roster of over a hundred dishes made with seafood from the waters of America and the world: sand dabs, she-crab soup, Lake Winnipeg goldeye, mako shark, catfish, pompano, Dover sole, etc. There are cold salads; broiled, poached, and fried filets; mussels and scallops and clams. Whatever is available (i.e. fresh) on any particular day has a price written next to it on the all-inclusive menu.

But let us zero in on the local specialties:

If you sit at the raw bar, you can see stews and pan roasts made in gleaming silver pots—in approximately sixty seconds. Oyster stew is a northeastern preparation—oysters, half-and-half, butter, and a few dashes of seasoning—warmed, but not boiled. The pan roasts are unique: heartier than stew, made with heavy cream and chili sauce, served on toast.

You can get rich white New England clam chowder, but this is Grand Central Station, New York. Could there be any better place in America to sample *Manhattan* clam chowder? Tomato-based, flavored with salt pork, redolent of thyme, and chocked full of diced carrots, celery, green peppers, potatoes, and of course minced clams, it is massive soup—cold-weather food.

If the swordfish steak is firmer and richer than any you have had, it is because the Oyster Bar sells only steaks cut from harpooned fish, which are taken from the sea immediately rather than lingering in an underwater net, where the meat can soften. A summer dish, from the waters north of Montauk.

Between January and May, shad make their way north to the Jersey coast, where they spawn—which means that in the spring the Oyster Bar offers a rare mid-Atlantic delicacy, shad roe. It is broiled, served on toast, topped with bacon: a gelatinous dish, perhaps not one for squeamish fish-o-phobes.

Oyster Bar biscuits are little more than flour, milk, and shortening. A bit salty with the flavor of baking powder, they are aromatic, creamy white inside, dusted with flour: a grand companion for broiled fish. Arrive early enough at lunch, and they are hot.

Fancy desserts: many-layered, Cointreau-scented chocolate truffle cake; blueberry pie; strawberry shortcake (on sponge cake); apple pie in a whole wheat crust. And there is, natch, New York cheesecake—slightly cakey, pure white with a hint of vanilla and citrus flavors, set on a sugary pastry crust.

Lunch can be hectic at the Oyster Bar. It is a cavernous place, quite a beautiful slice of old Manhattan, with high vaulted tile ceilings and large railroad clocks hung on aged wood walls. The size amplifies the noise when it's jammed, which it always is between noon and two. (If you want a quieter meal, head for the small dining room to the side.) The push of throngs angling for a counter seat plus the razzle-dazzle of the countermen at the red marble bar shucking and brewing adds up to a lot of commotion. At the tables, nicely decked out with checked blue cloths, service can be rushed.

At dinner, the pace is much slower, the room is quiet as an underground tabernacle, and the waiters have more time to explain what, please, is wolf fish? All things considered, though, the flavor of the Oyster Bar is fullest at noon. *That's* New York.

Hoft's Luncheonette

3200 White Plains Rd., Bronx, N.Y.   At Burke Ave.
(212) 654-5291

Mon.–Fri. 7 a.m.–6 p.m., Sat. 7 a.m.–5:30 p.m.

Under $5

To New Yorkers who grew up in the Bronx or on the Lower East Side, an egg cream is mother's milk.

The ingredients are simple: syrup, milk, and soda water. The setting is all. An egg cream must be made at the soda fountain in a small drug or candy store, preferably one on the corner, under the tracks of the El. It must be made in the correct shapely soda fountain glass; and it must be made fast, with the bold finesse of a Bronx bomber. "A sophisticated drink," Avery Corman called it in *The Old Neighborhood*, "for the candy store connoisseur."

The properly made New York egg cream hardly needs any stirring, because after squirting in the syrup (usually Fox's U-Bet Chocolate, but you can get vanilla or strawberry) and splashing in the milk, the soda jerk uses fountain-dispensed seltzer to agitate the liquid as it hits the glass. A few swirls of a spoon is all that's needed to complete the mixing. The resulting drink has a foamy head, creamy flavor (rich as eggs—how it got its name), and a champagnelike tingle.

You will find this perfect egg cream, in its perfect setting, at the corner of White Plains Road and Burke Avenue in the Bronx, under the El, at Hoft's Luncheonette.

Hoft's is so intensely nostalgic that it will induce déjà vu even if you grew up in Nebraska and never heard of egg creams. Surely, you used to go to the five-and-dime for banana splits with lengthwise-sliced bananas. Or Cokes made from syrup plus plain soda. You remember thinner-than-Hershey's chocolate sauce? Sundaes with names like The Burke Special or The Broadway Flip, served in small silver cups? Real chocolate malts, so cold they're nearly frozen, so enriched with malt powder they make your throat tighten when you swallow? Those are some of the confections you can still get at Hoft's.

The ice cream used in shakes, sundaes, and frappes (sundaes without whipped cream or sprinkles) is homemade, good and creamy, but not overly rich. Nothing here is extravagant or overlarge; this place predates the age of ice cream excess.

The fixtures are dark mahogany, the floor is a pattern of tiny black and white checked tiles, the ceiling is stamped tin. Opposite the soda fountain are Hoft's candies—chocolate panatellas, chocolate shoes, chocolate brides and grooms, even chocolate-covered graham crackers.

You can get for 25¢ plain.

Junior's

386 Flatbush Ave., Brooklyn, N.Y.
(718) 852-5257

Sun.–Thurs. 6 a.m.–1:30 a.m., Fri. & Sat. 6 a.m.–3 a.m.

$5–$10

For better and for worse, with brashness and charm, from crunchy pickle appetizers to incomparable cheesecake for dessert, Junior's *is* Brooklyn. Fifty years old, burnt down a couple of years ago and now risen gaudier than ever from its ashes, this restaurant is the laughingstock, and the pride, of New York City's most colorful borough.

Most American cities with large Jewish populations have their Junior's —late-night, brightly lit delis featuring overstuffed combination cold-cut sandwiches, but nowhere outside of Brooklyn will you find kibbitzing raised to the art it is at Junior's; and nowhere in the world can you eat cheesecake like this.

Legendary New York cheesecake: the richest dessert in history; pure edible ivory, like some new element on the atomic chart—perhaps a fusion of lead and satin. In fact, it is little more than cream and cream cheese and eggs, with scarcely a hint of vanilla flavoring. The pale crust at the bottom is insignificant; and although it is possible to buy Junior's cheesecake with pineapple or cherry or some other kinds of goo on top, no real New Yorker ever does. Cheesecake is cake made of cheese, not jelly.

Junior's is distinct among New York cheesecakes for its texture—thicker than most, barely gummy, so dense that it requires some effort of mouth to wrench it from the tines of the fork where it wants to stick. Coffee, preferably black, is required to help float it down.

Dozens of cakes are lined up at the bakery counter to your right as you walk in. Each is identical, a minimalist sculpture; not, like other Junior's desserts, obscenely large. The top of the cake is burnished brown, light in the center, getting darker toward the edge, perfectly symmetrical, as if the color were blown on by an airbrush artist.

Beyond cheesecake, the menu is immense: combo sandwiches, pastrami and corned beef, blintzes, good borscht and matzoh ball soup, potato *latkes*, pickled herring, derma, bagels, broilings, a few dozen cakes and pies, and "skyscraper sodas" topped with syrupy burgundy-colored cherries.

As for ambience, there are times when Junior's, with its orange Naugahyde booths, relentless noise, and waiters cum stand-up comedians, is the last place on earth you want to be. But there are other times—like if we've been off in Kansas or California, or for that matter, Connecticut, too long, and miss the kind of racy street smarts you find only in Brooklyn or the cheesecake you find only in New York; if, in other words, we crave a jolt of city soul in the raw: times like that, Junior's is "cherce."

Katz's

205 E. Houston St., at Ludlow, New York, N.Y.
(212) 254-2246

Sun.–Thurs. 7 a.m.–11:30 p.m., Fri. & Sat. 7 a.m.–1:30 a.m.

$5 or less

We stepped up to the counter and ordered a couple of sandwiches from a man who looks like he was born when Katz's opened, in the late 1800s. Just to get him going, we asked for pastrami on white with mayonnaise. He looked at us as though we had said wallpaper paste on a Brillo pad; he shrugged wearily; and in a heavy New York accent, he called out to the sandwich-maker next to him, "Sold American!" He grumpily dipped into a cup of mayo; but before he could smear it on a slice of white, we let him know we were just pulling his leg. "Pastrami on rye with hot mustard, please"—and he went to work.

As he began cutting the pastrami (with knife and fork—no automatic slicers here), he forked a thick piece and held it out over the glass case. "Here, I'll give y'a sample." When one of us devoured it, he held out another slice, "So you shouldn't starve."

There are other delicatessens in New York that make sandwiches that are probably as good as Katz's, but there is no other place in America where you can go one-on-one with countermen like this. Even the new ones, the ones who aren't old Jewish men, have learned the Katz's shoulder shrug, the world-weary philosophy—and the finesse with knife and fork.

The hot pastrami *is* hot, tender and streaked with fat (unless you coax your man to slice it lean), its edge peppered with zesty cracked coriander. Brick-red corned beef is leaner, but every bit as luscious. Katz's hot dogs are the best in the city, Nathan's be damned: heavily garlicked dogs tightly cased in crackling crisp skin. On the side, have a plate of thick french fries, each one a small block of soft fluffy potato with six crunchy yellow-gold sides. Eggs are fried into pancake-shaped omelettes with either tongue or salami.

Two drinks go well with this food: either hot tea served in a glass, Russian-style (use paper napkins as a pot holder); or Dr. Brown's Cel-Ray (yes, celery-flavored) tonic.

Quite a sight, this Katz's; it looks unchanged since about the mid-1940s. Unfortunately, the neighborhood around it has changed a lot. It's a grungy area, and it's tough to park; better you should arrive by cab or, as we saw three people do on our last visit, by limousine, so your driver can wait outside.

Katz's is a large lunchroom. Lighting is bright overhead neon; tables are lined up evenly in rows. Toward the back, in the mail-order department, salamis of all sizes dangle, and a row of enormous scales hang from the ceiling. By the cash register, a sign advises SEND A SALAMI TO YOUR BOY IN THE ARMY.

Knish Nosh

67th Rd. & Queens Blvd., Forest Hills, N.Y.
(718) 897-5554

Daily 9 a.m.–7:30 p.m.

Under $5

Three kinds of knishes—liver, kasha, or potato. Round balls, about a pound apiece, the filling wrapped in a papery tan crust all around except for a vent hole on top, where you can see and smell what's inside.

Liver filling is more mealy than meaty, laced with onion and lubricated with ample schmaltz. Although it does not seem possible, kasha is even heavier than liver, with a toasty cereal aroma. Potato filling is the raciest of the three, highly seasoned, shimmering with onions, and still a little lumpy. These are real knishes, authoritative lumps of Eastern European soul food, served by an all-black staff in a storefront knishery in Queens.

"Hot or cold?" asks the counter man when you place your order. *Hot* is for eating here, at one of three wobbly tables in the window, to the hum of the soft drink cooler at the side of the room. Take them home, and as they warm in the oven, they make your whole house smell like a Sunday visit to grandmother's.

Nick Tahou

2260 Lyell, Rochester, N.Y.
(716) 647-2296

Always open

$5 or less

Some travelers seek great food; others have garbage plates thrust upon them. In Rochester, we were in the latter group.

On the prowl for white hot weiners, the pale, veal-based dogs they like so much upstate, we sauntered into Nick Tahou, a raffish round-the-clock weiner hut that has specialized in hots, both red and white, since 1918. The menu looked good: Texas hots, pork hots, burgers topped with Nick's special sauce. Instead of charcoal grilled like in Buffalo, these were split and fried on a griddle. We ordered an assortment at the stand-up counter where everybody places their order and waits; and as we waited, we heard customer after customer call out for a "garbage plate."

The waitresses didn't flinch at the call; they went to work, piling a cardboard plate with cool baked beans on one side, home-fried potatoes on the other, onions on top of both, then a double order of split red hots, mustard, and finally meat sauce.

"What is that?" we had to know. The menu did not list anything of the sort.

"A garbage plate, honey," said the waitress. "Want one?"

"You bet." And customers, pegging us as novices, began to volunteer testimonials about the joys of the garbage plate. "Everybody eats them," they proclaimed with glee. "Get macaroni on the side," a garbage eater called out from a nearby table.

We went full bore, got the macaroni, and carried our garbage plate et al. to a table. Holy cow, what a load of grub! And on the side, in case there isn't enough nourishment on the platter, you get bread. It is an eccentric combination, the only possible comparable being Cincinnati 5-Way chili, with which Nick's strangely spiced, fine-grained meat sauce shares a few Greek-scented ingredients (nutmeg? cinnamon? clove?). But this all-American melting pot extravaganza is—as its aggressively déclassé name suggests—in a culinary class by itself. Call it *cuisine maudite*, soul food of the working man of upstate New York.

By the way, the pork hots at Nick Tahou are delicious, very porcine, sweet, and peppery. The Texas hots, loaded with garlic, aren't nearly as subtle. But then, subtlety is not a quality greatly valued in a restaurant where the garbage plate is king.

Parkside Candy

3208 Main St., Buffalo, N.Y.
(716) 833-7540

Mon.–Fri. 8 a.m.–10 p.m., Sat. & Sun. 10 a.m.–11 p.m.

$5 or less

Parkside Candy is like a grand old movie palace. Enter, and the space transports you to another world of grandiose, classic-minded form. Although it looks like a normally shaped corner store from outside, the interior is a clean oval, with soft, recessed lighting in a rim around the domed ceiling. Around the circumference of the room are cut-out areas, vending windows in which candies are displayed and sold. One window is for ice cream; another for barks and brittles. At the back of the room, a single cut-out, little more than a notch in the wall, houses one table, for lovers with a soda and two straws.

The candy counters are spaced by ornate carved columns and mirrors. In the center of the room stand massive floor lamps, spreading light upward. Quiet music creates a reverential mood for candy buying or sundae eating. You have entered a museum of candy, unchanged since it opened in 1927. "No smoking," says the menu, "due to the fact that chocolate quickly absorbs odors."

Behind the store is the candy factory, specializing in salt-water taffy, chocolates, and a Buffalonian bonbon called sponge candy. Made only in cool-weather months, sponge candy (also known as honeycombs) comes in large square chocolate-covered hunks, light or dark. Inside is spun molasses, which at first seems dry. As you bite into the honeycomb, it moistens and shrivels, turning chewy and blending with the chocolate into the sweetest sugar-coated melody.

A special place to buy candy; and a nostalgic dining room, its checkerboard tile set with wooden tables. The menu is pure ice cream shop, where sandwiches have names like "The Englewood" or "The University." "The Main Street" is a traditional Buffalo beef sandwich, thin sliced, au jus, served on a caraway-crusted hard roll. And there is a vast assortment of soda fountain specialties, from candy mountain frappes and dusty roads to a peanut-butter fudge parfait and an old-fashioned egg cream. Top of the line is "The Old Granada Special": eight ice cream flavors, four toppings, two kinds of nuts, whipped cream, and a single cherry. "Share it with a friend!" suggests the menu.

Pastrami King

124–24 Queens Blvd., Kew Gardens, N.Y.
(718) 263-1717

Daily 8 a.m.–11 p.m.

$10 or less

Most delicatessens buy their pastrami from a meat supplier; and because suppliers' stuff is all pretty much alike, the differences among pastrami sandwiches are subtle matters of bread and mustard quality, and how the meat was handled after it was bought.

Pastrami King is a shocking exception to the rule. "We cure our own pastrami, corned beef, and tongue," says the menu. When your teeth sink into a piled-high sandwich and the smoldering flavor of the meat reverberates in your mouth, suddenly pastrami becomes an entirely new and wonderful taste sensation.

Although leaner than most, it looks like the usual—beet red, fine-grained, rimmed by a thin halo of fat and blackened spice. Machine sliced into tender flaps, the meat is firm; but if you want to pick a *schmeck* from inside the overstuffed sandwich, it pulls apart easily with a gentle tug.

What is most amazing about this pastrami is that it isn't salty at all. Instead of salt, you taste a long garlic and pepper cure, and as that initial punch of flavor fades, you are left with a marvelous haze of the cedar-chip smoke in which the curing brisket was enveloped.

The King's corned beef packs a wallop too, its pickly tang undiluted by quick-cure sodium injections. And the plain brisket is unsurpassed: dark brown, succulent, ineffably tender.

These magnificent meats of Queens Boulevard are dished out with deli panache by a serving staff whose crabbyness is as pungent as any on the Lower East Side. "What the hell are you doing?" cries the waitress when we try to order chicken in the pot at noon. "That's dinner! Why don't you get the lunch—chicken fricassee. It's $4.95." She sets crusty potato pancakes and a side order of noodle pudding on the table next to ours and momentarily stumbles. We apologize for being in her way. "I knew it would happen," she grumps. "You got big feet."

Pearl of the Atlantic

Fox Island Rd., Port Chester, N.Y.
(914) 939-4227

Mon.–Fri. lunch & dinner, Sat. & Sun. noon–11 p.m.
Reservations advised

$10–$20

Salvador Carlos, like many of the Portuguese who have settled on the Atlantic coast, is a fisherman—a lobsterman to be exact. Several summers ago he and his wife Maria opened a small clam bar catering mostly to his fellow Portuguese fishermen. Word spread quickly into Port Chester and Connecticut about the delicious mussels in red sauce and clams *algarve* served in this little out-of-the-way place, and pretty soon Pearl of the Atlantic became a real restaurant, featuring clams and mussels and lobsters from Salvador Carlos's traps.

It's still in the same unlikely place, past the town incinerator on a road you are *sure* is leading nowhere. The restaurant is a pretty place, its small dining room offering a panoramic view of the Byram River.

Success becomes Pearl of the Atlantic. Dressy Westchester and Fairfield County gourmets sit table-by-table with old salts in fishermen's sweaters and families of local Portuguese. Service, by men who can explain to you the difference between lobster Carlos and lobster Cointreau, is brisk and masculine. The food is better than ever.

Our favorite way to start a meal here is steamed clams "Carlos style": six jewel-like littlenecks in a bowl, swimming in a nectar of olive oil, clam broth, bits of parsley, a dash of lemon perhaps, and maybe garlic, too. We aren't quite sure, and Mr. Carlos won't tell. All we know is what is written at the bottom of the menu, an unhelpful but accurate understatement: "Carlos style cooking consists of blending various spices."

The various spices are put to good use in another appetizer called clams Atlantic, larger cherrystones baked in broth with red peppers and flavored with butter rather than olive oil. Clams *algarve* is an even milder dish, littlenecks in a butter and lemon-parsley sauce.

Food historians credit the Portuguese for introducing fish stews to plain-palated New England; and the best entrees on Pearl of the Atlantic's menu are those that combine a variety of shellfish with tomatoes, olive oil, garlic, and herbs. They are brought to the table in rough aluminum kettles, along with wooden bowls for disposing of shells, and bibs to keep your shirt from getting squirted.

The most beautiful of the casserole dishes are the *paellas:* marineira—lobster, clams, mussels, squid, scallops, shrimp, peppers, peas, rice, and onions; and valenciana—all of the above, plus sausage, hard-boiled egg, chunks of pork, and shredded chicken. You get nearly a whole lobster in each —cut into large hunks, stunning red against a field of saffron-yellow rice, punctuated by black mussel shells and green peas.

Mariscada is a similar gallimaufry, but without the Spanish rice, served in a red sauce laced heavily with port wine: rich and powerful food, highly flavored but not fiery hot.

Of the Pearl's seven different ways of doing lobster, we recommend Madeira the highest. It is a whole lobster, steamed, stuffed with crabmeat, sauteed in heavy red wine and onions. For a wholly different, much lighter taste, try lobster chablis—a casserole dish with a sauce made of white wine and mushrooms.

For dessert there is flan, the Iberian custard. It is bland and eggy, covered with a sharp burnt-sugar sauce. To top things off just right, there is inky espresso, and Portuguese coffee with a kick.

Ratner's

138 Delancy St., New York, N.Y.   By the Williamsburg Bridge
(212) 677-5588

Sun.–Fri. 6 a.m.–11:30 p.m., Sat. 6 a.m.–1:30 a.m.
Closed Jewish holidays

$5–$10

Ratner's is New York's premier kosher dairy restaurant. There is no meat at all on the menu, but you can have a banquet of fish, eggs, cheese, milk, and sour cream in more ways than you ever thought possible—even baked vegetable cutlets, vegetarian chopped liver, kasha chop suey, meatless kreplach and pirogen.

Vegetable oddities are not this kitchen's strong suit. The best dishes at Ratner's are classics: the legendary onion rolls on every table; borscht (beet soup) turned flamingo pink from its dollop of sour cream (served in a bowl or, as most get it, in a glass); pickled herring; Nova Scotia salmon or belly lox; sable and carp; matzoh brei (a distant Jewish relative of an omelette); simple luxuries like a bowl of sour cream and bananas or a block of cheesecake.

Ratner's potato pancakes are good: very crisp, dark brown, almost hard-edged, their insides at once coarsely textured and creamy, with a sharp onion taste. They are served with tart apple sauce.

There are all kinds of blintzes (crepes rolled around sweetened cheese) —pineapple, cherry, apple, and kasha; but forgo the snazzy ones. Stick with the excellent basic cheese blintz, fully packed with vanilla'd farmer cheese, served with a scoop of sour cream.

"Ratner's own sour milk" is milk mixed with sour cream and allowed to stand in a warm place long enough to become firm. It is served in a glass with a spoon, and it has an agreeable bitter undertaste, not unlike buttermilk. It goes fabulously well with fresh fruit, although it isn't listed on the menu that way; so you'll have to convince your poor, put-upon waiter to see what he can do.

"I'll try and get it for you more or less," is what our man told us when we placed a big order. And he did get it all, including sour milk with blueberries—an elegant and simple combination.

It apparently looked so good that the people at the next table wanted a taste. "Mmm, like yogurt," said the little chubette who dipped her spoon in our glass. Now you must understand that such behavior is not just *likely* in Ratner's; it is positively encouraged by the arrangement of the furniture. Down the center of the restaurant runs a partition, and on either side of it is a row of tables. The problem is that the partition is only six inches higher than the tables. Therefore, unless you get a place along the wall, your dining (and conversation) partners necessarily include the strangers seated next to you.

The decor in Ratner's is what you might call poodle moderne. Along the Formica paneling dangle aqua-colored lamps, set in pink and black frames. The host greets you under a sign with arrows pointing in two directions, one for PARTIES OF 5 OR MORE, the other for PARTIES OF 4 OR LESS.

A boisterous, refreshingly unchic place: a New York tradition since 1918, still a source for grand Jewish food.

Schwabl's

789 Center Rd., West Seneca, N.Y.   At Union
(716) 674-9821

Mon.–Thurs. 11 a.m.–midnight, Fri. & Sat. 11 a.m.–12:45 a.m.

$5 or less

A fresh caraway-seasoned hard roll, crusted with coarse grains of salt, is dipped momentarily in unthickened beef gravy, then layered with a sheaf of tender—but not tenderized—roast beef. This is western New York's famous beef on weck, an ideal balance of crisp crust and gravy-softened bread, of salt's sting and roast beef's moist luxury—prepared at Schwabl's better than anywhere else.

You can see the man at the end of the bar slicing a great haunch of beef, carefully selecting the lean slices for sandwiches: rare, medium rare—there really is a difference, and even though the nylon-uniformed waitresses never write down a thing, they remember who gets which. The traditional condiment for Buffalo beef on weck is horseradish, jars of which you will find along the bar and at every table.

Schwabl's also specializes in a hot ham sandwich, hand-sliced, on white bread in a pool of clove-perfumed tomato gravy. A pungent warm potato salad is available on the side.

Although there is a touch of striving in the decor—gold-embroidered wallpaper and curtains, tables covered with brown textured Naugahyde (reminiscent of a deluxe suite in an unremodeled Holiday Inn), Schwabl's is a pleasant informal beef house, bright and bustling at lunch. "We cater to nice homey family trade," says the menu.

2nd Avenue Deli

156 Second Ave., New York, N.Y.   At 10th St.
(212) 677-0606

Daily 6:30 a.m.–11:30 p.m.   Closed Passover

$5–$10

Oy vay. Our poor waiter, the hangdog man in his rumpled mustard-colored jacket and orthopedic shoes, he schleps the corned beef and pastrami sandwiches to the table, and now we tell him we've got no pickles. "So *nu?* So here," he says, whisking a silver bowl of sea-green kosher dills from an empty table to our own. And off he trudges to the sandwich counter to lean. He's tired. This man has been tired since he was born.

We have been to deli restaurants in other cities with friendly help, cheerful pink-cheeked youngsters who are actually *nice!* And let us tell you that like corned beef on white bread, *it don't go.* Crabby old men are as important an ingredient in a deli as schmaltz is in chopped liver.

You will find ample amounts of both at Second Avenue and Tenth Street, in the most authentic Jewish deli in New York, and therefore, America. There are perfectly adequate delicatessens uptown (The Stage, Carnegie, Madison Avenue Deli), selling fine matzoh ball soup and corned beef sandwiches and the like, but they're . . . well, they're *uptown.* Kishka and kasha and kugel (respectively: stuffed cow's intestine, buckwheat groats, noodle pudding) are not uptown food.

Such chopped liver you'll get on Second Avenue! It's an earthy, pale brown paste, dotted with little grainy bits of liver (beef and chicken) and finely chopped sweet onions. Plenty of schmaltz (that's chicken fat) gives it a delectably silky, yet heavy texture. It is the schmaltz that makes the liver taste like a grandmother's kitchen with a chicken-in-the-pot bubbling on the stove. (Chicken-in-the-pot is, in fact, a Lower East Side specialty, perfectly prepared here.)

The hot pastrami is relatively mild, its black pepper crust only a small jab of spice edging the coral-colored meat. Sandwiches are overstuffed (of course), the 1/8-inch thick ribbons of pastrami spilling out the edges. You can get "extra lean" at a premium, but don't; the glistening streak of fat that bisects a beef brisket belongs in a pastrami sandwich.

Soups: mushroom barley, matzoh ball, plain consommé with kasha—humble food, the most comforting in the world.

2nd Avenue gefilte fish is the genuine article: carp and whitefish ground up with matzoh meal, egg, and onions, formed into irregular ovals and served with stinging horseradish. The fish is highly flavored, and each piece has a dense yet somehow fragile consistency—nothing like the fish-flavored breadcrumb balls sold in stores as gefilte fish.

A big menu, pure deli: cold cuts of every kind, kasha varnishkes (bowtie noodles on kasha), knishes (bad news; go to Yonah Schimmel's instead), beef- or chicken-in-the-pot, Nova Scotia lox. No bagels.

There are a few celebrity pictures about, like in the delis uptown, but a majority of the clientele is neighborhood. Out on the street, old men sit in their chairs, tongues clucking, as young men saunter by with noisy street radios. The avenue is a mix of bodegas and kosher dairy restaurants, old and new newcomers to New York. Inside, a testimonial letter from President Reagan is posted next to the cash register: "Just because we're Californians doesn't mean that we don't appreciate the unique delights of fine New York kosher cooking. There's nothing like it anywhere else!" You want we should argue with the President?

Sharkey's

56 Glenwood Ave., Binghamton, N.Y.
(607) 729-9201

Daily 11 a.m.–1 a.m.

$5 or less

The best, or at least the most interesting, food in western New York is served in bars: wings and beef on weck in Buffalo, spiedies in Binghamton.

Spiedies—charcoaled chunks of marinated lamb (occasionally pork or venison)—are a totally localized specialty, as popular in Binghamton as burgers in L.A. For a sample of their contribution to regional gastronomy, Binghamtonians gleefully directed us to the city's leading spiedi stop, a neighborhood tavern called Sharkey's in the Polish and Ukrainian part of town.

Sharkey's is a family place, sharing a front with an ancient barber shop. At a table, ladies in housecoats were having a discussion about the insoles their chiropodists prescribed. Men sipped beer and watched the afternoon soaps at the bar. At the booths and tables in back, people ate early dinners of clams, kielbasa, or chicken wings. Sharkey's has been in business nearly forty years, and is run now by Bob and Larry Sharak, sons of the man who started it.

"We want spiedies," we told Bob Sharak, a rotund man who works the bar. "Two sticks," he called out, and one of the housecoated ladies left her chiropodic conversation to cook the food over an open fire in the next room.

"Spiedies are as old as the hills," Bob told us, but he had no idea where the name came from, or why they are unique to Binghamton. "We were the first to sell raw spiedi meat to cook at home," he said, popping a stick of gum in his mouth and chewing with vigorous pride. "The secret's in the marination."

Our spiedies arrived on skewers, on a paper plate, with a stack of thinly sliced French bread. We were instructed to take hold of the cool handle of the skewer in one hand and use the bread as a mitt in the other, pulling off a few hunks of still-sizzling lamb to create a rolled sandwich.

The sandwiches taste like a picnic, flavored by the coal fire, with a tasty charred surface all around each cube of meat. The lamb is rich and resilient, its tang softened by the marinade. Spiedies go just about perfectly with the locally brewed beer Sharkey's serves up in tall mugs from the tap.

Ted's Jumbo Red Hots

2312 Sheridan Dr., Tonawanda, N.Y.
(716) 836-8986

Sun.–Thurs. 10:30 a.m.–11 p.m., Fri. & Sat. 10:30 a.m.–midnight

$5 or less

"You have made one terrible, terrible mistake," wrote David Shribman when *Goodfood* was published in 1983. The heinous error was omitting Ted's from our roster of great Buffalo-area restaurants. Our choice for charcoal-grilled red hots had been Pat's, which we thought pretty fair. "Ted's," Mr. Shribman assured us, "is far superior. Besides, the onion rings rank with the world's best."

On our last trip to Buffalo, we found Pat's defunct. So we hurried to Ted's, funct and thriving, with a few branches in town and one in Tempe, Arizona.

Shribman had been right. Ted's are the *ne plus ultra* of upstate weenies. They are grilled over coals; as they cook, the chef pokes them, cuts their skin, squishes them down against the grill. The brutalization encourages the dogs to suck up a maximum amount of smoke taste from the fire, so what you get is a blackened tube steak, firm and lean and crusty-edged.

As it cooks, you deal with a "dresser" behind the counter. The dresser is in charge of condiments—all the usual, plus Ted's special hot sauce. First let us say that these hot dogs are terrific naked; they don't even need mustard. Now let us say that Ted's sauce is not to be missed, with a spicy tingle that perfectly complements them. It is tongue-sizzling hot, laced with bits of relish.

French fries are boring, but onion rings are a kick: hard-crusted, with some sweet onion squiggles still uncoated, other rugged circles intertwined. A cardboard basket of these salty circles perfectly rounds out a foot-long dog. All you need on the side is a tall glass of loganberry juice (A.K.A. bug juice), and you are in Tonawanda red hot heaven.

Yonah Schimmel Knishes Bakery

137 E. Houston St., New York, N.Y.
(212) 477-2858

Daily 8 a.m.–6 p.m.   Closed Jewish holidays

$5 or less

"Where are you from?" asked Lillian Berger, the fourth generation of Yonah Schimmel bakers, when she saw us puzzling over which knishes to try.

"Connecticut," said we.

"Canada?"

"*Connecticut.*"

"You never saw food like this, did you?" piped in a coffee drinker from a nearby table; then added, for Lillian Berger's sake, "In Canada, they don't know from a knish."

"We know all about them!" we insisted. "I was born and raised in New York," Jane cried in vain.

But we had been spotted. As much as knishes were the soul food we were raised on, we had strayed far from our roots. We had come to think of knishes as those square machine-made potato cakes that resemble fast-food fish filets and are sold all over the city. We had forgotten what a real knish looks and tastes like.

"Give the Canadians some muhn cake, too," the kibbitzer added.

"Sure, fine," we said. "Muhn cake so we can tell our friends in Canada what Jewish food is like. And a potato and a kasha knish, a cheese bagel, and a bit of that potatonik."

A knish—in case you are Canadian and have never seen one—is a Ukrainian- (or possibly Polish-) ancestored hot dumpling. An authentic one, as made at Yonah Schimmel's (since 1910) is a round, hand-formed sculpture a little bigger than a baseball. Its crust is dark tan, nice and flaky. The customary filling is potatoes, like mashed potatoes, but twice as heavy. There are also spinach, cabbage, and sweet potato knishes, as well as knishes filled with kasha (buckwheat groats compressed into a dense lump); but there are no knishes filled with meat—Yonah Schimmel's is kosher.

Knishes are, in a literal sense, monumental. It is impossible to overstate their gravity or the sense of fixity they induce when eaten. You don't eat a knish, then play tennis or jog. You eat a knish and sit.

Yonah Schimmel's cheese bagel was an oddity, nothing like the common shiny doughnut-shaped roll. It was more like a danish stuffed with sweet/sour pot cheese; the dough was soft, very moist—like a bagel that's been boiled but not baked. Lillian Berger insisted on calling the potatonik a pudding, but to us it looked and tasted like a cake, with a wonderful rugged brown crust on top. The coffee drinker had steered us right with his suggestion of muhn (poppy seed) cake. This was a square of sweet cake speckled with thousands of poppy seeds throughout, served with a schmear of butter.

We came to Yonah Schimmel's on a Sunday, and as we ate, business at the front counter boomed. Most is take-out, but the few thin tables are lovely places to sit—like elongated squares on a chess board, rimmed in red. This is an ancient room with uneven plaster walls, a stamped tin ceiling, and a dumbwaiter that hoists food up from the bakery in the cellar.

It was impossible to eat everything we had ordered. As we got up from the table, hoping to exit unnoticed, Lillian Berger called out in the best guilt-inducing voice either of us have heard since we were ten years old: "You didn't finish?"

Zab's

3340 Monroe Ave., Rochester, N.Y.
(716) 248-8624

Daily 11 a.m.–10 p.m.

$5 or less

Zab's is a small local chain ("Not in 5 locations," boasts a misspelled ad in the Yellow Pages) specializing in red hots and white hots, cooked over charcoal. White hots, made with veal, ham, and beef, are mildly seasoned and absorb a strong smoke flavor from the coals. Red hots are porky and more vigorously spiced. Even more aggressive is the taste of a Polish dog, loaded with pepper, tightly packed, with a solid snap to its firm-textured meat. All these top-notch tubes are dished out with fast-food efficiency in a clean modern environment completely lacking the outlaw thrill of most upstate hot dog dumps. That's OK, because the taste of the food is what counts most; and these are among the best.

We were fascinated by the "Polish King" plate, a Zab's variation of what weiner-king competition Nick Tahou calls a garbage plate—that is, *the works*, piled up helter skelter. Toasted rye bread forms the foundation of a King. It is topped with a split red weiner, then melted Swiss cheese. Then comes hot sauce, sauerkraut, and Russian dressing. Macaroni and beans are available, at extra cost, on the side. As the plate was assembled, the hot sauce was ladled on with the exact same wrist motion Nick Tahou assemblers use: precise, but with a sharp flourish as the ladle reaches the end of the dog.

The Polish King presented a serious problem: how to get it from plate to mouth. It was far too messy to lift by hand. And yet the split dog was so firm and chewy that it resisted the plastic flatware provided. We ate with our hands, lowering our heads like pigs at a trough to minimize spillage.

Zab's sauce is startlingly hot, a fierce pickle-pepper blend that we feel overwhelms the mild white hots but perfectly complements the odoriferous reds. We bought a bottle to take home, where we get endless raves for its pizzazz as a seafood cocktail sauce.

PENNSYLVANIA

Adams and Bright Pharmacy

State St., Hamburg, Pa.
(215) 562-2738

Mon.–Sat. 8:30 a.m.–9 p.m.

Under $5

It was in Philadelphia that George Washington decided he liked the cool sweet custard he tasted at a Frenchman's party, and so imported America's first cream icing machine for himself. A hundred years later, ice cream starred at the 1876 Centennial Expo in Philadelphia; and until not too long ago, a small Philly confectionery named Sauter's made ice cream that was the stuff of legend.

A lot of that's past now, but not far from Philadelphia, in Hamburg, Pennsylvania, at Adams and Bright Pharmacy, we found a milk shake that can take you back to swell butterfat days when yogurt was for health-food nuts, and ice cream was the great American dessert.

It's nothing more than a counter in a pharmacy, with a vintage malt dispenser, a stack of Lilly paper cups for punching onto silver bottoms, and tall silver milk shake makers that hook up to a triple-wanded mixing machine.

Our malts were just about perfect—creamy, afloat with little islands of unblended ice cream. There's nothing extraordinary about the ingredients, but there was something grand about sitting in the pharmacy and watching the ice cream, milk, and syrup being thrown together. Each silver shaker delivered three full glasses, but in a moment of total immaturity, we made awful noises through our straws, sucking out the dregs of these great shakes.

Akron Restaurant

Rte. 272, Akron, Pa.
(717) 859-1181

Mon.–Sat. 6 a.m.–8 p.m., Sun. 11 a.m.–7 p.m.

About $5

At the farmers' market in Ephrata we wandered among the stalls sampling sticky buns and the mashed-potato-based doughnuts called *fasnachts*, and asking the traditionally garbed Mennonites where they thought we could find good examples of local food. "Try this," suggested a farmer, handing us a taste of cup cheese from a thick enamel dish. Cup cheese is strong, ripened from sour milk into a silky, keen-flavored custard. Once the farmer saw we liked it, he decided to clue us in to his favorite local restaurant—the Akron.

One look at the menu, and we understood why it was the farmer's choice. The Akron kitchen turns out dishes unique to Pennsylvania Dutch cuisine; the daily specials include baked oyster pie, beef heart, creamed beef on toast, and chicken pie—a regional crustless stew that is a warming mélange of chicken and broad homemade noodles.

Scrapple, a specialty of the Akron, is a food that many people raised outside the mid-Atlantic region can't abide. But those who like this loaf of pork shavings, cornmeal, and spice (heavy on the sage), love it. We'll warn you now, the Akron's scrapple is scary to look at. The slab is cut six inches long, three inches wide, and a half an inch tall. It's heavy, crisp around the edges, with a moist center. Most people have it with breakfast, but there is a scrapple lunch here too.

We also recommend the Akron's sticky buns, as good as the ones we had nibbled at the farmers' market. Glazed amber and rolled in nutmeats, they are chewy and filling, and come to the table warm.

Only the shoofly pie was disappointing—disappointing because it looked so profoundly delicious: a spill of cake crumbles atop a glistening molasses filling. At first taste, it was perfect . . . and yet, its flavor was a mirage, disappearing instantly as the pie hit the taste buds.

The Akron's not a pretty place. It looks more like a suburban steak house than the Amish farmer's choice. But weigh its mansard roof and Muzak against the buns, the scrapple, and the baked chicken pie on the scales of good food justice, and the verdict clearly points to the Akron as a fine regional place to eat.

Bookbinders Seafood House

215 S. 15th St., Philadelphia, Pa.
(215) 545-1137

Mon.–Fri. 11:30 a.m.–11 p.m., Sat. to midnight, Sun. to 10 p.m.
Reservations advised

$10–$30

Bookbinders is probably as close as we'll ever get to old Philadelphia dining (save the unlikely possibility of our being invited to join one of the exclusive eating clubs). Yes, tourists eat here (the smart ones, anyway; the chumps are at the *other* "Old Original Bookbinder's" on Walnut); and yes, there are lobster bibs that say "I'm a Booky."

But where else in town can you find such delicious snapper soup, or Philadelphia pepper pot, or that strange, unique, and utterly vanished local favorite, oysters and chicken salad? Bookbinders is Philadelphia before nouvelle cuisine swept into town, before purveyors of preciousness turned the city's head with their dubious "new Philadelphia cuisine," which really isn't any different from what's served in trendy bistros in a dozen self-renovating American cities.

There is a long menu of lobsters and broiled fish; stews of clams and oysters; and even some very expensive—and we are told terrific—prime steaks. But we suggest you zero in on the unique city dishes Bookbinders does so well.

A hundred years ago, pepper pot was Philadelphia's most popular street food, sold by vendors in milk cans, hot and ready to eat. Legend says it was invented by a Pennsylvania Dutch cook to feed George Washington's troops during their long winter at Valley Forge. Bookbinders' version is hearty: soothing creamy green soup dotted with red pimiento, afloat with cubes of tripe and tender little dumplings, seasoned with red and black pepper and sage.

A second uniquely Philadelphian soup is snapper: freshwater snapping turtle meat laced into a reddish-brown base as thick as stew. It is faintly piquant, the meat gamey, the soup dotted with bits of hard-boiled egg and spiked with the strong tang of sherry. There are other restaurants in town that still make snapper soup, but no other version tastes as . . . historically *right* as this.

A third soup—more uniquely Bookbinders' than Philadelphia's—is a Friday offering called bouillabaisee [sic]. It bears little resemblance to the Mediterranean variety; rather, it is thick and creamy—pale orange like a bisque, filled with hunks of scallop, shrimp, and crab: very square, very American.

Three fried oysters with chicken salad is the kind of entree one sees on a menu and wonders, "Who'd ever order that?" We'll tell you who—the elderly Chestnut Hill lady and gent sitting at the table next to us, the ones who read the menu with matching magnifying glasses. This odd combo is in fact an old Philly favorite. The oysters are gargantuan, each three by two inches at least. Beneath the red-brown crust is a thin line of breading enveloping the plumpest, firmest, freshest oysters ever fried—clean and sweet, without grit or goo. On the other half of the plate is a scoop of fresh chunked chicken salad. On the side comes pepper hash, chopped very fine, sweet and sour and peppery, a brilliant refresher between the oysters and the chicken.

We also recommend the mountain of pure white crabmeat called simply baked crab (or crab imperial, the same with peppers and mushrooms added); and the creamy spiced deviled crab. On the side, we loved Bookbinders' baked macaroni, a cheesy pudding reminiscent of good hotel food, the likes of which you can't ever—or would never—make at home. Likewise the rice pudding for dessert: a big dopey serving of the stuff, with fat raisins and a cinnamon skin on top. These unfashionable dishes, as much as the rare Philadelphia specialties, are why we love Bookbinders.

But there is more: a comfortable wood-paneled dining room, with the unhidden hiss of lobsters steaming up front; waitresses in pink and white, too busy doing their job to waste time introducing themselves by name; food served on sturdy no-frills plates that have seen a thousand meals. You know you are in an *honest* restaurant, where tradition and expertise are the kitchen's strong points, not clever packaging of the latest urban food fad.

Brownstown Restaurant

Main St., Brownstown, Pa.   Rte. 772
(717) 656-9077

Wed.–Sat. & Mon. 6 a.m.–8 p.m., Tues. 6 a.m.–2 p.m., Sun. 11 a.m.–7 p.m.

$10 or less

The Brownstown is our favorite restaurant for Pennsylvania Dutch cuisine. Plus they make the best scrapple you're likely to find anywhere in scrapple-happy Pennsylvania.

Candy, the waitress, first replied to our question, "What's good here?" by running to get us a slab of coffee cake: yellow buttery cake with veins of brown sugar and a thick crumble crust.

"Have you tried our rivel soup?" she asked. "It's wonderful. We make it with a beef base and add pinches of dough." Rivel soup is nearly impossible to find outside of Lancaster County. Brownstown's isn't creamy like some others we've tried, but so much the better: it's hearty, without undue weight.

"And what about scrapple?" Candy asked. "Don't you just love it?" We confessed we had yet to find scrapple that we could honestly say we loved. "You haven't tried ours," and she was off for a third time to bring back a plate of Brownstown's best. She was right. This is great scrapple—redolent more of corn than hog; a soft lovely loaf with a sizzling crisp skin and tender body, not at all oily or rank.

Candy reeled off some other specialties: Monday, chicken and waffles; Tuesday, baked ham with potato filling; Wednesday, pork with sauerkraut. On Friday the menu swings even more regional, with oyster pie or corn pie, made with hard-boiled eggs, milk, and butter in a pastry crust. Meals are served with a long parade of vegetables, including classic "red beet eggs" (hard-boiled eggs marinated in beet juice), lettuce with hot bacon dressing, and most of the "seven sweets and seven sours" that customarily grace the Amish table.

The minute you enter, you know the Brownstown is a special place, nothing like the tourist traps that hawk local culture along Route 30. Instead of out-of-towners with cameras, the tables are populated with locals sipping coffee and chatting about the Grange or the garage. It's an old-fashioned place, with pale green walls, overhead fans, and a big case near the door filled with a hodgepodge of patent medicines, souvenirs, and automotive aids. There's a three-foot-tall pickle jar, an ancient portrait of Abe Lincoln, and some framed headlines from local papers. In back, for families, they've got another dining room, a bit fancier, with wallpaper and wood paneling. Washrooms (with plumbing) are outside.

Famous 4th Street Delicatessen

4th and Bainbridge Sts., Philadelphia, Pa.
(215) 922-3274

Mon.–Sat. 7 a.m.–6 p.m. Sun. 7 a.m.–3 p.m.

$5 or less

Philadelphia is famous for its ice cream. There were once dozens of small stores that specialized in ice cream fancies, and at that yearly congregation of the city's elite known as the Assembly, Philadelphia society still indulges in ice cream shaped into little flowers, fruits, and what-have-you. But look around the streets of Philly today, and it becomes apparent that the ice cream tradition has pretty much hit the skids. There are some decent franchised operations, but short of crashing the Assembly, you won't find anyplace like the old Sauter's, where fanciful handmade ice cream was everyday fare.

We found the Famous 4th Street Delicatessen while on the ice cream trail, and although they don't do anything fancier with ice cream here than make it into shakes and malts, the shakes and malts they do make are distinguished—worthy of the city's exalted reputation. The ice cream used is Breyer's, like anyone can buy, but added to that are the best flavorings, real malt, and milk that has been enriched to the consistency of light cream. The shakes are ridiculously thick; they simply don't come up a straw—you have to use a spoon or gulp them from the paper metal-bottomed cups or silver milk shake motherships they come in.

We came to the Famous for milk shakes, but found much more. Owner David Auspitz spotted us as we downed the shakes and tried to surreptitiously take notes, and he wouldn't let us leave until we tasted a little of everything, especially the chocolate chip cookies. Chocolate chip cookies are such a cliché already, it seems hard to imagine getting excited about them, but these are the best: rich and toasty, big round beauties filled with large chips and nutmeats, an ideal balance between crispness and chew.

So our meal shouldn't be unbalanced, we went on to corned beef sandwiches—great lean corned beef on sour rye. On the side: kugel (noodle pudding) and a potato knish.

As we ate, Dave philosophized about the restaurant business. "We don't use any portion control or ready-mades. We get our fish seven days a week. Nothing is frozen but the ice cream." He brought out a copy of *Restaurant Business* magazine and slapped it angrily. "They send me a questionnaire: 'What mixes do you use?' I wrote them back and said 'Take your [expletive] mixes and get back to me when you want to talk to a real restaurant.' Restaurants are so bad now, most people have forgotten what a real cup of coffee tastes like!" And he described how he found a man in town who roasts the coffee beans for him, and how Famous coffee is ground fresh and brewed ten cups at a time.

"We are a living museum," Dave said. "You can bring your kid and see what a real delicatessen is like." Except for the fact that the people who work here don't seem especially cranky, Dave is absolutely right.

Fisher's Pastries

Hess Rd. & W. Newport Rd., Monterey, Pa.   Rte. 772
No phone

Mon.–Fri. 9 a.m.–5 p.m.   Hours vary in bad weather

Under $5

For anyone suffering overexposure to Ronald McDonald, Jack in the Box, or any other franchised clown or puppet, we prescribe a trip to Fisher's Pastries, a stand run by the Fisher family on their farm.

It's a too-good-to-be-believed place, with characters who look like they were sent by Central Casting, set in a rural vista where the buggy traffic outnumbers cars. The day we found it, the large open booth was manned by an Amish girl of about 17, who looked not unlike Natassia Kinski in a bonnet and sober black shoes. With level-eyed charm she explained what the family had set out this day. "We have Montgomery pie, chocolate shoofly pie, and regular wet-bottom shoofly. We have chowchow, peppers and relishes, apple dumplings, snickerdoodles, sugar cookies . . ."

She was interrupted by her father's horse-drawn buggy pulling up the pathway. "Are the sticky buns ready yet?" he asked her as he dismounted. A red-cheeked boy scooted down in a wagon to greet him.

As it was impossible to buy the stand, the farm, and the Fisher family for mementos of our visit, we settled for the two kinds of shoofly pie, Montgomery pie, a whoopie pie, and a half gallon of root beer. We resisted the impulse to cram our already crowded car trunk with mason jars of heartbreakingly beautiful peppers and preserves.

The shoofly pies were delicious, with a thick ribbon of molasses running along the bottom, a layer of sponge cake above that, and a sugary topping that called out for a dollop of ice cream we couldn't provide. The Montgomery pie is a lemon sponge creation. And whoopie pies are the prototype of Ring Dings—chocolate moon-shaped circles filled with cream.

The Fishers' homemade root beer will jar a palate accustomed to the sweet carbonated stuff. It is what its name implies, a brew made from roots —serious; as earnest as the men and women who make it, a drink with earthy character and not a bit of fizz.

Groff's Farm

Fourth farm on the left on Pinkerton Rd., Mount Joy, Pa.   Off Rte. 141 (717) 653-2048

Tues.–Sat. lunch & dinner   Reservations required

About $15

A while back we read that Chang was the most common name in the world, outnumbering Smith and Jones by the thousands. As we drove along the rural roads of Pennsylvania Dutch country, we wondered if the nameographers had counted the number of Stoltzfuses. You see this name everywhere —on mailboxes, street signs, and store windows. We weren't a bit surprised, then, when the menu at Groff's Farm listed the house specialty as Chicken Stoltzfus.

Chicken Stoltzfus, as invented by this rural restaurant in the unspoiled hills of Lancaster County, is made with large pieces of chicken smothered in cream sauce and served with small squares of pastry crust. It is saffron colored—a warm, sunny-hued stew. According to Betty Groff, it was named after her Amish friends Elam and Hannah Stoltzfus—a spur-of-the-moment choice while she was being interviewed by the Philadelphia *Bulletin*.

Originally the Groffs' meals were informal affairs, served to groups of visitors lucky enough to know someone who knew someone who knew Abe or Betty Groff. But word spread quickly, and while the restaurant is still a rustic farmhouse, it is necessary to make reservations in advance to dine here, and most men wear jackets and ties.

Eating is one of the few rituals not strictly regulated by the Amish and Mennonite religions, and so moderation is unknown at their dinner table. Traditionally, every course is set out when the meal begins; pies and cakes are eaten right alongside the meat and potatoes and "seven sweet and seven sour" relishes. This practice is modified somewhat at Groff's Farm, where the first course of the meal is chocolate cake and cracker pudding—so that you can enjoy them while you still have room, according to Mrs. Groff. As kids who always ate our Twinkies before the lunchbox sandwiches, we can appreciate the logic.

The Farm's menu is brief. Everyone gets Chicken Stoltzfus, along with a choice of ham, prime rib, or some seasonal seafood. The table is loaded with traditional relishes like pickled celery and cinnamon- and clove-spiced cantaloupe. Everything is served family-style in large bowls.

On Wednesday nights, son Charlie Groff, a graduate of the Culinary Institute of America, has free reign in the kitchen to try out gourmet specialties.

Haag's Hotel

Just south of Rte. 22, Shartlesville, Pa.
(215) 488-6692

Daily 11 a.m.–7 p.m.

$5–$10

We visited Haag's Hotel in the dead of winter; so dead, in fact, that we were the only patrons in the dining room. Locals sat in the adjoining saloon drinking Corby ale, munching on pretzels, and talking about that ever-popular rural topic, the weather.

The bar and dining rooms are on the ground floor of a small stone building whose antiquity is a pleasant contrast to the nearby Interstate. The walls are painted landlord green and hung with papier-mâché pretzels that are sallow with age. The floor is worn green and white checkerboard linoleum. Wooden chairs and white oilcloth-covered tables complete the distinctly Pennsylvanian tableau.

We were presented with two menus. One listed sensible repasts of fried ham, roast beef, or chicken sided by a choice of three vegetables. The alternative to this small selection is the family-style dinner, which includes chicken, ham, and beef, plus twenty side dishes—all you can eat. (Hard to believe, but twenty is an *abbreviation* of the traditional Lancaster County hotel meal, which often featured fifty different foods!)

If twenty side dishes isn't impressive, then it's been a while since you've eaten Pennsylvania Dutch food. A people of robust appetite, they like their food heavy, sweet, and starchy. Among the twenty extras are potato filling, pot pie (noodles simmered in chicken broth), tapioca pudding, dried apricots, apple butter, peaches, shoofly pie, and sugar cookies.

Feeling unusually restrained (and rather foolish to have the staff carry twenty platters to our table-for-two), we ordered from the first menu. The chicken and ham dinners were cozied up to large mounds of filling. Filling looks like mashed potatoes, and that's how it begins, but to make it heavier and more "filling," the hale cooks of this region add bread-crumbs, approximately tripling the density of the potatoes. Filling approaches critical mass; it's the kind of food every dieter dreams of in moments of extreme hunger.

Also on our plates were hills of dried corn, dehydrated kernels that are boiled in water and reconstituted. It's an old Amish custom that allows people who don't use electricity to store produce without having to freeze it.

A tub of apple butter was set on the table along with the meal, and this too seemed to have an unusually high specific gravity. It's darker than most apple butters, prune colored, and highly spiced. We thought it was a perfect way to perk up the dour filling and salty ham.

Our shoofly pie was good, but a little dusty due to an overabundance of sugar and spice that lay atop the cake part. A scoop of ice cream—like the apple butter—helped even out the score. An even better choice—and a regional dish harder to find than the locally ubiquitous shoofly pie—was sugar pie, a moist concoction of brown sugar, cream, and vanilla, topped with nutmeg and bits of butter that melt into a glistening sheet of gold as the pie bakes.

Haag's has been around for five generations. It's a genuine antique, not pretty, but long on character. With twenty courses of exemplary Pennsylvania Dutch food available for under $10 a person, it's the best introduction we know to a unique cuisine.

Jim's Steaks

400 South St., Philadelphia, Pa.
(215) 928-1911

Mon.–Thurs. 10 a.m.–1 a.m., Fri. & Sat. 10 a.m.–3 a.m., Sun. noon–10 p.m.

Under $5

It is said that the only thing that will help you if you're drunk in Philadelphia is a cheese steak, guaranteed to kill or cure. It is true that most versions of this rough street sandwich are strong medicine, and most places that serve them are, to put it plainly, dumps.

Jim's Steaks (the second oldest cheese steak place in Philly, after Pat's) is, if not an exception to the rule, a minor deviation. For one thing, Jim's is pretty, art-deco sharp, all shiny chrome with tiny black and white octagon tiles on the floor. For another thing, it is clean. There's a tidy dining room upstairs where you can eat after getting your steak in the cafeteria line on the first floor, and the counter opposite the line is regularly swabbed of sandwich crumbs and dribbles.

Finally, Jim's steaks are less greasy than most. The meat is a bit drier, almost—but not quite—healthy-seeming; and if you don't want the traditional Cheez Whiz dribbled on top, you can get actual pre-sliced squares of American cheese or—get this—provolone.

The sandwich is still a delectable mess. If you get slices instead of drippy Whiz, the slices, cold when put into the roll, melt as soon as hot beef and onions are put on top of them, blending with both the bread and the meat so what you have is a layering the reverse of the traditional cheese-on-top-of-meat configuration. Jim's uses a single torpedo-shaped roll for each sandwich, a tough, chewy loaf that admirably stands up to the melting cheese, the meat, the onions, and even the optional peppers or pizza sauce.

Joe's

7th and Laurel, Reading, Pa.
(215) 373-6794

Tues.–Fri. 5 p.m.–9 p.m., Sat. 4:30 p.m.–9:30 p.m.   Reservations advised

$15–$25

Joe's is a classy restaurant in a dowdy town, but it is not for its incongruous couth that traveling gourmets have inscribed it in the little black book of out-of-the-way treasures. The southeastern corner of Pennsylvania is mushroom-rich, and Joe's is the only restaurant that takes full advantage of the natural bounty.

When it opened as a workingman's bar in 1916, Joe's specialized in cream of mushroom soup made from wild mushrooms that Mr. and Mrs. Joe Czarnecki gathered in the pine forests outside of town. Today, a third generation of Czarneckis still forage in the fields and woods around Reading, and use their catch as the basis for one of the most unusual indigenous menus anywhere in America.

Joe's is a fancy place—old-Pennsylvania fancy, with a cabbage-rose carpet and walls covered with burgundy tiles and gold-flocked paper. One chandelier hangs in the center of the small dining room; each table is garnished with a little shaded lamp and a vase of fresh flowers; and each place setting's napkin is wound into an impressively tall tower on the serving plate. Large photographic close-ups of mushrooms are displayed in lieu of art.

Expensive wines are set out in the vestibule.

It is the house policy to automatically add 18 percent to the check as a service charge; you *will* spend a lot of money at Joe's.

Despite the flourishes, it is a homey place with a strong family feeling. Heidi and Jack Czarnecki are ubiquity itself in the dining room; they have a proprietary concern for their mushrooms, and they genuinely want customers to share their enthusiasm.

We began our meal with the rarest of rustic delicacies—morels, a mushroom that cannot be cultivated, but must be painstakingly hunted in the forest's underbrush. Joe's version, stuffed morels Marie, is a pretty plate of eight honeycomb-ridged conical caps. They are stuffed with puree of veal, arranged in a circle on little squares of toast, and covered with clear brown sauce.

Joe's soup is still the best dish in the house—a fragrant woodsy puree of wild mushrooms, presented with a mushroom shape traced in cream on the soup's surface.

Marinated wild mushrooms—cepes and chanterelles—are another good appetizer, gamey in taste, smoothly textured.

Our favorite entree at Joe's is the simplest—wild mushrooms Cracow-style—nothing more than large fragile *Boletus edulis* mushrooms in a rich cream sauce, heaped onto a bowtie of puff pastry. Most of the dishes are more elaborate (the fellows at the serving carts have to have something to do), such as snails *suillus pictus*, an intensely seasoned combo of breathtaking Reading mushrooms and earthy snails. You can also get swanky stuff like venison in game sauce or veal sweetbreads with wild agaric mushrooms.

Desserts are very, very rich: almond cream cheese cake, white chocolate mousse, or a tortlet of crumbly meringue and amaretto butter creme, flecked with bits of almond, topped with heavy chocolate sauce. Good espresso is served with a plate of complimentary little pinches of chocolate mint truffles (the confectionery kind).

If Joe's inspires you to set out on the mushroom trail, we recommend heading south to Kennett Square, Pennsylvania, where there is a Mushroom Museum, tracing mycological history back to the Egyptians, who believed mushrooms conferred immortality on all who ate them.

Pat's

1237 E. Passyunk, at Wharton & 9th, Philadelphia, Pa.
(215) 468-1546 or 339-9872

Always open

$5 or less

What Nathan's is to hot dogs or Woodman's of Essex is to fried clams, so Pat's is to the Philadelphia cheese steak sandwich. It was invented here in 1930 by Pat and Harry Olivieri, and it has since become a citywide obsession that cuts across all class and ethnic lines. There are probably a hundred restaurants in the Philadelphia area that specialize in Pat's invention, a good many of them calling themselves "The Original." But there is only one Pat's —on the concrete triangle formed by Ninth, Wharton, and Passyunk.

Pat's is a take-out stand in a neighborhood that could be Naples. To the north is the Italian market, where fresh fruits and cheeses and fish are sold from open-air bins. Soft pretzel and Italian ice vendors stake out every street corner. Old men sit out on sidewalks watching life go by. This is the quintessential *street* neighborhood. How appropriate that it is the home of the cheese steak, the aristocrat of street foods.

Well, maybe *aristocrat* isn't exactly right. The cheese steak reigns in Philly, but not because of anything royal in its makeup. It is, in fact, composed of lowly ingredients: thin, chipped beef sizzled on a grill alongside onions. The meat and onions are hoisted onto half a loaf of Italian bread (sliced length-wise); a trowel of molten Cheez Whiz is dripped onto the steak; and then, if you wish, you can add peppers or hot sauce from one of the big glass cookie jars. Cheese steaks are greasy, gooey, and incomparably delicious, best enjoyed about 3 a.m. as the grand finale to a big night on the town.

Cheez Whiz? Minute steak? Greasy onions? Absolutely yes—accept no substitutes. Alter any of the simple, essential elements, and the cheese steak magic evaporates. The roll, obtainable only in Philadelphia's Italian bakeries, has just the right consistency to absorb the meat's oil, yet stay chewy and retain its rough crust; the onions and cheese and meat meld together perfectly.

Pat's is patronized mostly by Sylvester Stallone look-alikes and South Philly girls in skinny halter tops. There are 8 × 10s of steak-loving Philly celebrities taped onto the roof of the canopy that hangs over the sidewalk (so you can eat cheese steaks in the rain), and the counterman doesn't have to be pressed hard to start telling you all about how Frank Sinatra's chauffeur comes by for a load of steaks every time the Chairman of the Board comes to town. It is de rigueur for Philadelphia politicians to be photographed scarfing down a cheese steak here.

The ambience of Pat's—yellow neon tubes of light overhead, sidewalks paved with dripped cheese and sauce, and trucks rumbling past—is an ambience that no restaurateur, however ambitious, could ever duplicate or improve on.

People's Restaurant

140 W. Main St., New Holland, Pa.   Rte. 23
(717) 354-2276

Mon.–Fri. 7 a.m.–8 p.m., Sun. 11 a.m.–7 p.m.

$10 or less

The Pennsylvania Dutch are pie-happy; and People's is one of the best places we know to experience this fact for yourself. Here is where we first sampled "funeral pie," a traditional raisin pie which, despite its name, couldn't be more cheerfully, molar-zingingly delicious. (It dates back to the days of cool cellars where ladies stored their baked goods in anticipation of family occasions such as weddings—or wakes.)

People's shoofly pie is the best you can get. It's wet-bottom shoofly, as opposed to dry-bottom (which is more like a crumbly coffee cake, customarily served in the morning, and suitable for dunking). People's wet-bottom shoofly has a moist filling made with dark barrel molasses, topped with only a sprinkle of brown-sugar crumbs. It's served warm, with a scoop of vanilla ice cream.

Food historian Evan Jones says that today's Pennsylvania Dutch cooks have a repertoire of over fifty different pies. The last time we visited People's, the menu included shoofly and raisin, pumpkin, pumpkin pecan, graham cracker custard, cherry crumb, apple crisp, pure white coconut, and grasshopper pie.

But to come to People's for the pie alone is to miss out on regional specialties like Lancaster sausage, served with horseradish made in the nearby community of Ephrata; or chicken pie, a crustless stew of chicken and cream gravy over broad noodles; or roast turkey with sausage filling; or pork and sauerkraut; or an array of vegetables that includes wonderful creamy whipped potatoes. After writing down our orders, a sweet hairnetted waitress told us, "Those are nice selections, dears." And she was back in a flash with two salads of wilted lettuce and hot bacon dressing and a basket of tea-roomy rolls.

For so weighty a cuisine, the food at People's is prepared with a blessedly light touch, and will leave you satisfied instead of stuffed. It really seems to be a people's place, judging by the tables of organdy-hatted Mennonites sitting to our left, and the sheriff and his deputy to our right.

Philadelphia Soft Pretzel Bakery

4315 N. 3rd St., Philadelphia, Pa.
(215) 324-4315

Mon.–Sat. 6 a.m.–about 1 p.m.

Under $5

Southeastern Pennsylvania is America's pretzel belt, from Lancaster County, where they like them so much they even make pretzel soup, to Philadelphia, where vendors sell soft pretzels on every street corner.

Although they look like nothing more than overgrown hard pretzels, soft pretzels are a totally different eating experience. They are not designed to be munched by the handful with beer in an easy chair; one is a snack unto itself, made to be eaten outdoors, preferably while walking somewhere or at least sitting in a park. Most people get them with a squirt of mustard on top. As one might expect in a city as bread-crazed as Philadelphia, the soft pretzels sold on street corners are seldom more than hours out of the oven.

The oven that the best of them come out of is at the Philadelphia Soft Pretzel Bakery, way up north on Third Street. Here, every morning between six and ten you will see the vendors stocking up on soft pretzels by the gross —and the city's pretzel mavens buying them by the bag, at the bargain rate of seven for a dollar. If you arrive early enough, it's quite something to see the pretzel twisters at work in back—eight of them, each turning out a thousand per hour.

In the back room are pictures of Philadelphia cops and celebrities, even a famous local horse, who all like the Soft Pretzel Bakery's pretzels best. For the pretzel connoisseur who insists on going to the source, this is the only place. There is no way to get them fresher.

They are distinguished by their neat, nearly rectangular shape—easy to hold. They have a consistency like the best water-boiled bagel, pleasingly plump and chewy. They are bland, toasty, and sprinkled with grains of coarse salt, which gives them a mouth-watering sharp edge.

Bring your own mustard squirter.

Ragozzino's

737 S. 10th, at Fitzwater, Philadelphia, Pa.
(215) 923-2927

Mon.–Fri. 8:30 a.m.–9 p.m., Sat. 9 a.m.–7 p.m.

$5 or less

The sign outside says RAGOZZINO'S: ALL KINDS OF SANDWICHES, and that is technically correct, but the one kind of sandwich you want to get here is a hoagie, Philadelphia's own version of a hero or po boy. There are two things that make Philly's hoagies superior to other regional versions of the bread loaf stuffed with meat: great bread and good cold cuts from the Italian market on the South Side. And at Ragozzino's there is a third component, an artistic *je ne sais quoi* in the sandwich's construction. For years, *Philadelphia* magazine has proclaimed Ragozzino's the city's best hoagie, a judgment with which we happily concur.

The bread is a long half-loaf, sliced lengthwise. The sandwich-maker prepares the inside of the loaf with a few squirts of olive oil. Into it he builds a towering arrangement of floppy layers of Genoa salami, capicola, and provolone, then covers the coiled sheafs of meat and cheese with a chef's salad worth of lettuce, tomatoes, and sweet peppers. These in turn are sprinkled with Italian dressing and lots of oregano.

The ham and peppers are racy red, the roll supple; it is an exciting sandwich, like a fine Italian car, sexy and beautiful, but likely to fall apart as you enjoy it.

Ragozzino's is a wonderful place, a small cafe that provides an unequaled taste of Italian Philadelphia. There are little world-weary laminated signs everywhere: IF YOU CAN'T STAND THE HEAT, STAY OUT OF THE KITCHEN, and TRUST IS GOOD; NO TRUST IS BETTER, and a rather enigmatic one, NO MORE HERMAN. We thought perhaps Herman was a good customer who had died, but when we asked, we were told, "Herman is a friend who loses at the track every night, and every morning he comes in and says, 'No more.'"

We stopped in for our hoagie mid-afternoon in the summer. An animated conversation about the Phillies was in progress, held between the counterman, an elderly chap standing by the door, and five or six other old men, each sitting at his own table over a cup of coffee. There were women in here too, but they were all seated at the counter, having their own conversation, in quieter tones, in Italian.

Society Hill

3rd & Chestnut, Philadelphia, Pa.
(215) 925-1919

Daily noon–2 a.m.

$5 or less

Cheese steak aficionados are going to lynch us for this one: Society Hill is about as far from a traditional cheese steak stand as you can go. For one thing, they don't specialize. They serve omelettes and salads and sandwiches. For another, the steak they make here, while generically related to what you get at Pat's in South Philly, is practically—forgive us—gourmet food.

Society Hill begins with a circular roll, more delicate than the traditional cheese steak torpedo. The roll is hollowed out, and into it are inserted strips of good meat, meat that has not sizzled on the grill amidst a pile of onions forever, meat that is buttery textured, tender like pot roast. Lots of meat—so much meat, in fact, that midway through the sandwich, all this meat begins to weigh too heavily on the bread; and the bread, being a bit of a lightweight to begin with, gets mushy, like a French dip roll. By the end of the sandwich, the bread has softened and lost its character. It isn't street tough like the customary hero roll; it doesn't have the oomph to stay strong all the way through.

Nonetheless, we recommend it—for beginners, or perhaps for cheese steak fanciers who develop stomach trouble and have to have theirs mild. This steak isn't in the least bit oily, nor is it salty like most. The toppings— cheese, onions, tomato sauce, peppers, or mushrooms—are all top quality.

And although Society Hill lacks the color and the cachet of Pat's, it's a cozy place—a former flop house that has been turned into a chichi bread-and-breakfast hotel, now frequented by artists, musicians and other avant-garde types. Rooms upstairs run between $50 and $75.

The Tavern

108 N. Market St., New Wilmington, Pa.
(412) 946-2020

Mon., Wed.–Sat. lunch & dinner, Sun. noon–7:30 p.m.
Closed Tues.   Reservations essential

$10 or less

Pennsylvania country cooking is a rarity outside of Lancaster County; near Interstate 80, it does not exist, except at The Tavern. Here in a white clapboard inn, you sit at white linened tables with blue gingham skirts; and you are presented a menu of regional delights like potato soup, ham stacks, ham loaf with brown sugar syrup, pork chops with crisp dressing, creamed chicken on biscuits, and a variety of pies baked by local Amish women.

Cora Durrast opened for business in this 1830 building more than fifty years ago. "All the furnishings you see now, I bought then," she told us. "You know where? . . . at Macy's, in New York. I paid a dollar fifty for each chair."

As we talked with Mrs. Durrast in the central hallway, patrons strolled out of the dining rooms on either side, and it seemed as if she knew all of them, and they all knew her. Some bought booklets that tell about The Tavern's history and had her sign them. Others asked when she next planned to serve her ham loaf, a traditional Pennsylvania dish fast disappearing from most restaurants' repertoires.

Except for honey rolls, the heavy sugar and butter sticky buns that precede each meal, The Tavern's menu varies from day to day. Vegetables, served family style in bowls, might be as simple as corn on the cob or what Mrs. Durrast laughingly calls "lead dumplings," absolutely plain flour-and-water dough pinches served in ham or chicken broth; or you might get fresh cabbage with sour cream and red peppers; or zucchini, onions, and cheddar cheese, baked in a casserole with breadcrumbs.

Entrees are mostly stick-to-the-ribs farmer food: chicken pies, smoked pork, chicken pancakes (crepes with oomph). There is usually a fancy French silk pie for dessert, and plainer offerings like butterscotch pie or filled chocolate cake, and occasionally, shoofly pie.

A lovely inn serving local food: an oasis north of Pittsburgh.

Twin Kiss Drive In

Rte. 23, west of New Holland, Pa.
(717) 354-5518

Mon.–Fri. 10:30 a.m.–10:30 p.m., Sat. 10:30 a.m.–8 p.m.

$5 or less

Why go to a cheese steak parlor in Lancaster County, miles from Philadelphia's great cheese steaks? Because, as cheese steaks go, these are beauties —and you get the bonus of watching them made.

First onions are laid on the Hotpoint Rocket 12 Griddle; then a steak patty is set on top of the onions. As the steak cooks, a grillwoman with twin spatulas mashes it hard, hacks it, cuts it, finally mincing the meat with the frying onions. Now the mélange is topped with a slice of cheese, and as the cheese melts, a bun is set on the grill to warm. The steaming meat and onion mixture is scooped off with a spatula, put into the bun, and topped with a small ladle of sweet red tomato sauce.

What you get is a good messy cheese steak, oily and sharply flavored with onions, nicely gilded by the sauce. It's an homage to the griddle chef's art, far from fast food, requiring vigilance and a lot of elbow (and other) grease.

Twin Kiss is a small white diner that supplements its main specialty of cheese steaks with some good local foods—like hearty, well-spiced chicken corn soup, and root beer by the gallon (bring your own jug and save 40¢). The day we tried it, Twin Kiss was fragrant with grilling steak and onions, its stools occupied by a dozen plaid-shirted workmen, most of whom sipped thick milk shakes as they watched the laborious construction of their sandwiches.

(There are two other Twin Kisses—one in Mount Joy, the other in Manheim—but neither provides as clear a view of the chef at work.)

Mid-South

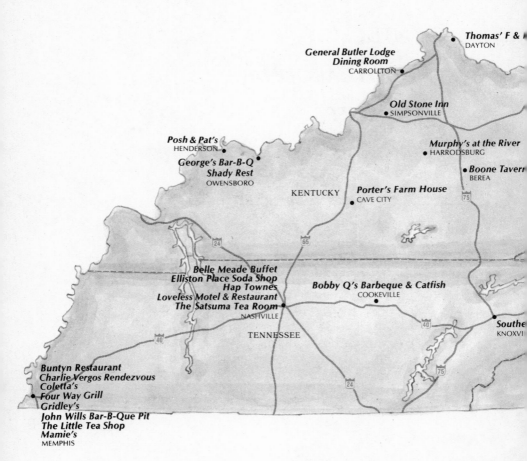

Thomas' F & F
DAYTON

General Butler Lodge
Dining Room
CARROLLTON

Old Stone Inn
SIMPSONVILLE

Posh & Pat's
HENDERSON

Murphy's at the River
HARRODSBURG

George's Bar-B-Q
Shady Rest
OWENSBORO

Boone Tavern
BEREA

KENTUCKY

Porter's Farm House
CAVE CITY

Belle Meade Buffet
Elliston Place Soda Shop
Hap Townes
Loveless Motel & Restaurant
The Satsuma Tea Room
NASHVILLE

Bobby Q's Barbeque & Catfish
COOKEVILLE

TENNESSEE

Souther
KNOXVI

Buntyn Restaurant
Charlie Vergos Rendezvous
Coletta's
Four Way Grill
Gridley's
John Wills Bar-B-Que Pit
The Little Tea Shop
Mamie's
MEMPHIS

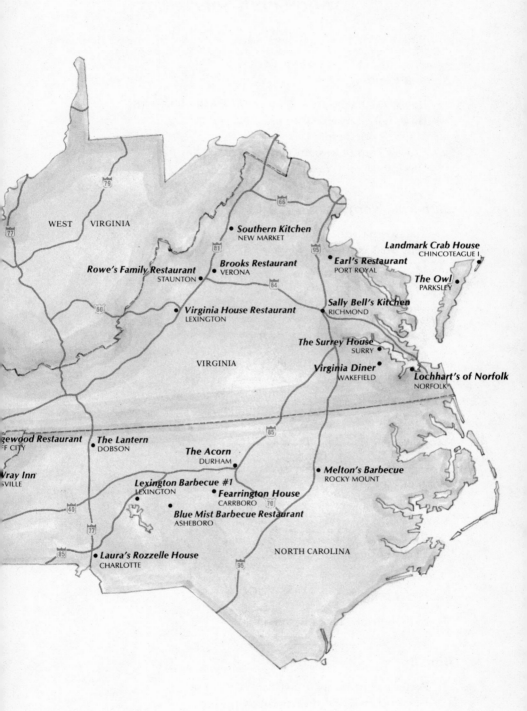

● Southern Kitchen
NEW MARKET

Landmark Crab House
CHINCOTEAGUE I.

● Earl's Restaurant
PORT ROYAL

Brooks Restaurant
● VERONA

The Owl
PARKSLEY

WEST   VIRGINIA

Rowe's Family Restaurant
STAUNTON

Sally Bell's Kitchen
RICHMOND

● Virginia House Restaurant
LEXINGTON

The Surrey House
SURRY

VIRGINIA

Virginia Diner
WAKEFIELD

Lochhart's of Norfolk
NORFOLK

gewood Restaurant
F CITY

● The Lantern
DOBSON

The Acorn
DURHAM

● Melton's Barbecue
ROCKY MOUNT

Vray Inn
SVILLE

Lexington Barbecue #1
LEXINGTON

● Fearrington House
CARRBORO

Blue Mist Barbecue Restaurant
ASHEBORO

● Laura's Rozzelle House
CHARLOTTE

NORTH CAROLINA

Mid-South Specialties

Where we list several places, we have starred the one we think best.

Banana Pudding

★ Bobby Q's Barbeque & Catfish (Cookeville, TN)   172
Buntyn Restaurant (Memphis, TN)   173
Mamie's (Memphis, TN)   183
Rowe's Family Restaurant (Staunton, VA)   191
Virginia Diner (Wakefield, VA)   195

Barbecue, North Carolina Style

The Acorn (Durham, NC)   163
Blue Mist Barbecue (Asheboro, NC)   164
Lexington Barbecue #1 (Lexington, NC)   168
★ Melton's Barbecue (Rocky Mount, NC)   168

Barbecued Mutton

George's Bar-B-Q (Owensboro, KY)   156
Posh and Pat's (Henderson, KY)   160
★ Shady Rest (Owensboro, KY)   161

Barbecued Pizza

Coletta's (Memphis, TN)   175

Barbecued Pork

Bobby Q's Barbeque & Catfish (Cookeville, TN)   172
John Wills Bar-B-Que Pit (Memphis, TN)   179
★ Ridgewood Restaurant (Bluff City, TN)   184
Earl's Restaurant (Port Royal, VA)   187

Beaten Biscuits

Sally Bell's Kitchen (Richmond, VA)   192

Biscuits

Porter's Farm House (Cave City, KY)   158
Fearrington House (Carrboro, NC)   165

Burgoo—Traditionally, a game stew; now made with mutton

Chess Pie—Very sweet, made with cream, egg yolks, and sugar

Chicken and Dumplings

Chitlins—Formally, chitterlings: pig intestines

Cobblers

Cornbread Cakes

Country Ham

Porter's Farm House (Cave City, KY)   158
Fearrington House (Carrboro, NC)   165
Laura's Rozzelle House (Charlotte, NC)   167
Nu-Wray Inn (Burnsville, NC)   169
★ Loveless Motel & Restaurant (Nashville, TN)   181
Southern Grill (Knoxville, TN)   186
Brooks Restaurant (Verona, VA)   187
Southern Kitchen (New Market, VA)   193
The Surrey House (Surry, VA)   194
Virginia Diner (Wakefield, VA)   195
Virginia House Restaurant (Lexington, VA)   196

Fried Pie

★ Shady Rest (Owensboro, KY)   161
Mamie's (Memphis, TN)   183

Greens and Pot Likker

The Acorn (Durham, NC)   163
Buntyn Restaurant (Memphis, TN)   173
★ The Little Tea Shop (Memphis, TN)   180
The Satsuma Tea Room (Nashville, TN)   185

Ham Hocks, Feet, Ears, etc.

Four Way Grill (Memphis, TN)   176

Hot Brown—A sandwich made with chicken and bacon or ham, topped with bubbling cheese sauce

General Butler Lodge Dining Room (Carrollton, KY)   155

Hushpuppies—Deep-fried puffs of cornmeal

The Acorn (Durham, NC)   163
Blue Mist Barbecue (Asheboro, NC)   164
★ Lexington Barbecue #1 (Lexington, NC)   168
Bobby Q's Barbeque & Catfish (Cookeville, TN)   172

Memphis Ribs

Charlie Vergos Rendezvous (Memphis, TN)   174
John Wills Bar-B-Que Pit (Memphis, TN)   179
★ Gridley's (Memphis, TN)   177

Norfolk-Style Seafood (sauteed in butter)

★ Landmark Crab House (Chincoteague, VA)   188
  Lockhart's of Norfolk (Norfolk, VA)   189

Peanut Pie

  Virginia Diner (Wakefield, VA)   195

Peanut Soup

  Southern Kitchen (New Market, VA)   193
★ The Surrey House (Surry, VA)   194

Pecan Pie

  Belle Meade Buffet (Nashville, TN)   171
  Gridley's (Memphis, TN)   177
  Brooks Restaurant (Verona, VA)   187
  Virginia House Restaurant (Lexington, VA)   196

Preserves

  Laura's Rozzelle House (Charlotte, NC)   167
  Nu-Wray Inn (Burnsville, NC)   169
★ Loveless Motel & Restaurant (Nashville, TN)   181

Red-Eye Gravy—Ham drippings and coffee, served with grits and/or biscuits

  The Lantern (Dobson, NC)   166
  Nu-Wray Inn (Burnsville, NC)   169
★ Loveless Motel & Restaurant (Nashville, TN)   181
  Southern Grill (Knoxville, TN)   186

Southern Fried Chicken

  Boone Tavern (Berea, KY)   154
  Old Stone Inn (Simpsonville, KY)   158
  The Acorn (Durham, NC)   163
  Laura's Rozzelle House (Charlotte, NC)   167
  Nu-Wray Inn (Burnsville, NC)   169
  Belle Meade Buffet (Nashville, TN)   171
★ Buntyn Restaurant (Memphis, TN)   173

Loveless Motel & Restaurant (Nashville, TN)   181
Southern Grill (Knoxville, TN)   186
Rowe's Family Restaurant (Staunton, VA)   191
Southern Kitchen (New Market, VA)   193
Virginia Diner (Wakefield, VA)   195

Spoonbread—Made from white cornmeal, with a consistency between a soufflé and pudding

★ Boone Tavern (Berea, KY)   154
The Owl (Parksley, VA)   190

Sweet Tater Pie

The Owl (Parksley, VA)   190

Types of Mid-South Restaurants

Barbecue Pits

George's Bar-B-Q (Owensboro, KY)   156
Posh and Pat's (Henderson, KY)   160
Shady Rest (Owensboro, KY)   161
The Acorn (Durham, NC)   163
Blue Mist Barbecue (Asheboro, NC)   164
Lexington Barbecue #1 (Lexington, NC)   168
Melton's Barbecue (Rocky Mount, NC)   168
John Wills Bar-B-Que Pit (Memphis, TN)   179
Ridgewood Restaurant (Bluff City, TN)   184
Earl's Restaurant (Port Royal, VA)   187

Box Lunch Take-Out

Sally Bell's Kitchen (Richmond, VA)   192

Cafeterias

Belle Meade Buffet (Nashville, TN)   171
Hap Townes (Nashville, TN)   178

Ham Houses

Ballance Country Hams (Oakland, KY)   159
Country Ham Apartments (Bowling Green, KY)   159
Porter's Farm House (Cave City, KY)   158
Loveless Motel & Restaurant (Nashville, TN)   181

Old Southern Inns

Boone Tavern (Berea, KY)   154
Old Stone Inn (Simpsonville, KY)   158
Laura's Rozzelle House (Charlotte, NC)   167
Nu-Wray Inn (Burnsville, NC)   169

Plate Lunchrooms

Buntyn Restaurant (Memphis, TN)   173
The Little Tea Shop (Memphis, TN)   180
The Satsuma Tea Room (Nashville, TN)   185
Southern Grill (Knoxville, TN)   186

Small Town Cafes

The Lantern (Dobson, NC)   166
Bobby Q's Barbeque & Catfish (Cookeville, TN)   172
Rowe's Family Restaurant (Staunton, VA)   191
Southern Kitchen (New Market, VA)   193
Virginia House Restaurant (Lexington, VA)   196

KENTUCKY

Boone Tavern

Ky. 25, Berea, Ky.   Exit 76 off I-75
(606) 986-9358

Mon.–Sat. breakfast, lunch, & dinner, Sun. lunch & dinner
Reservations required

Dinner $10–$15

Students who attend Berea College do so on a work-study program. One of the jobs they can choose is work at the Boone Tavern. The college champions mountain culture; and here in the college-run restaurant, southern food is the order of the day—standards like fried chicken, honey ham, and spoonbread.

Despite the bright lights and family atmosphere, rules are strict: no smoking or drinking in the dining room; a row of house jackets hang by the entrance for gentlemen who fail to wear "suitable attire."

If it sounds a little uptight, don't worry. The rules are balanced out by the staff's eagerness to please, and by the fact that you will be too busy eating to feel any strain. The moment our behinds hit the chairs (made by college students, as is all the furniture in the dining room), a perky waiter was by our elbows, relish tray in hand. We chose marinated carrots, watermelon pickle, etc., which Mr. Eager doled onto our tiny bread plate, on top of a pat of butter. No sooner had he made his exit than a waitress appeared, with a casserole of hot spoonbread. Boone Tavern spoonbread is legendary, so of course we said yes. The spoonbread girl dropped a ladleful on top of the pickles and butter.

What could we do? We ate it. Delicious, especially the spoonbread, a cornmeal-based soufflé reminiscent of Yorkshire pudding. With clean plates, we welcomed back the spoonbread girl for seconds, this time *sans* relish. She returned often with more. There is *lots* of service at the Boone Tavern.

Instead of the mountain girl we expected, our waitress was a lyrically accented black exchange student. We admired her colorful dress. She said it was a gift from Mom back in Zimbabwe. She told us she was homesick.

After the spoonbread, dinner began in earnest with three-tone punch, a dramatic name for a less than dramatic local grapefruit drink, flavored with mint. Excellent native Kentucky turkey was served with herby dressing and topped with giblet gravy, the plate's landscape brightened by fresh cranberry relish. The honey ham was dark red and somewhat dry, twin slices of meat over which the diner pours a little cup of sweet lemon sauce, afloat with cloves. Chive-buttered new potatoes and orange-sauced beets were the vegetables of the day. The spoonbread girl was superseded by someone with a basket of chive rolls.

The Boone Tavern is famous for something called chicken flakes Elsinore, a cream-based chicken dish served in a "bird's nest" of potatoes.

The students make their own ice cream, which is quite good. We had French vanilla custard in a super-abundant chocolate peanut butter sundae. It was far better than "red velvet cake," which is the color of a red shag rug, and nearly as dry.

The way we see it, things balance out at the Boone Tavern. Four-star spoonbread makes up for icky cake; the staff's enthusiasm for its lack of savoir faire. If you don't like eager helpful kids and homely but warming southern food, don't come here; but then again, if you're such a grouch you probably don't go out much to begin with.

General Butler Lodge Dining Room

General Butler State Resort Park, Carrollton, Ky.   *Off Ky. 227*
(502) 732-4384

Daily breakfast, lunch, & dinner

$3–$12

If you think food served in state parks is nothing more than Twinkies and slush puppies, you haven't been to Carroll County, Kentucky, lately. This state-run recreation ground boasts a darn good restaurant.

The waitresses look like runaways from the old days at Schrafft's, their demure black uniforms banded by white aprons. They pour coffee while handing you the menu, an amenity usually reserved for the "professional driver" section of truck stops. But Kentuckians love their coffee, and even in the nicest places, it flows like winter-weight Valvoline.

The menu lists "Bluegrass hot brown," a complex layering of country ham, sliced bread, turkey breast, sliced tomatoes, crisp bacon, rich cheese sauce, and a sprinkling of parmesan. Hot browns are unique to the Louisville area. This is an excellent version, served bubbling hot in a casserole.

Another Kentucky habit is eating pancakes for lunch—in this case, not just any old pancakes, but super-rich pecan pancakes, sided by sausages. At lunch or dinner, you can get country ham, not all that old or gamey, but the real thing for sure. Have baked apple or oven-browned potatoes on the side, along with a mess of long-simmered mustard greens.

There is at least one genius in the General Butler Lodge kitchen; it was here we found the best chess pie in the south. It is served just barely warm, a light custardy wedge with a crust like a microfine layer of macaroon. It is eggy and sweet and achingly moist, the kind of dessert one wants to eat in the tiniest increments, prolonging the pleasure.

The dining room is all decked out with white wrought-iron furniture, ferns, and green rugs; a pretty ladies-lunch–type place, clean and modern. Upstairs is a surprisingly good gift shop, where for a reasonable price we found an antique calico cat—a genuine piece of Kentucky folk craft.

George's Bar-B-Q

E. 4th & Montgomery Ave., Owensboro, Ky.
Pay phone (502) 926-9276

Mon.–Sat. 10 a.m.–midnight

$5 or less

Burgoo, a western Kentucky specialty, was invented during the Civil War, some say by a Lexington chef named Gus Jaubert for the Confederate troops, others contend by a Union soldier with a speech impediment who threw blackbirds into a pot and tried to call it bird stew.

Whatever its origins, burgoo means one thing to the people around Owensboro. It is a conglomeration of pork, beef, mutton, and chicken, stewed together in a tomato sauce with okra, cabbage, peppers, potatoes, and at least that many more vegetables, set on fire with Tabasco sauce and cayenne pepper. As served in area restaurants, burgoo lacks its traditional game meat —opossum or squirrel—but it is nonetheless a gutsy all-American dish, best sampled at a workingman's cafe such as George's.

At lunchtime, George's is a crush of blue collars and white collars all vying for booths or counter stools, all ordering either mutton or burgoo. The jukebox blares Tammy Wynette oldies. Beer is sold by the can and bottle, on tap and in six-packs.

The burgoo is served in a large plain bowl, the kind of heavy tableware favored by truck stops. It is a chocked-to-the-brim tomato-red mulligan stew of meat shreds and vegetables, the keen nip of smoked mutton prevailing: spicy enough to make a long-neck Coke or beer seem like a perfect idea.

If you're one of the brawny guys at George's, you find that the burgoo just stimulates the appetite for more food. So you get a barbecued mutton plate. We like George's way with mutton. It is heavily smoked, hacked to pot roast consistency, and mixed with a generous amount of seething red sauce.

Not a place for elegant dining; but then barbecue and burgoo would look rather silly on a silver plate.

Murphy's at the River

U.S. 68 east, Harrodsburg, Ky.   At the Brooklyn Bridge
(606) 734-9739

Wed.–Sun. lunch & dinner, Fri.–Sun. only in Jan. & Feb.

$5–$12

Murphy's wasn't always so picturesquely located on the banks of the Kentucky River. About five years ago it was *in* the river, when a catastrophic flood swept up to the roofline. The waters receded; when we stopped by, the river was nothing more than a muddy stream. Murphy's is back in business, a quaint wood cabin tucked beside the road: a darling place to eat.

You don't need a menu to figure out what to order—not if you recognize that the festive decorations on Murphy's indoor tree are catfish skeletons, dyed pastel colors appropriate to the season (pink for Mother's Day; red, white, and blue for the Fourth of July, etc.). Hanging fish skeletons may not be everyone's idea of pleasant restaurant decor, but they're not really repulsive; and somehow they fit the riverside ambience.

Murphy's catfish is served whole; unless you are a do-it-yourselfer, the waitress will be glad to remove and spirit away the bones. The fish is fresh, available either broiled or fried. Fried is better; catfish is perhaps the only lake creature that benefits from a crust and a dunk in hot oil. With the fish comes a pass to a salad bar with homemade dressings; the waitress brings cornbread, muffins, and hot biscuits; you also get hushpuppies, potatoes, and seasonal vegetables.

If catfish is not your dish, try the Kentucky ham—it's a good salty chaw, firm and delicious, served with Murphy's-made hot mustard. There are a few steaks to be ordered, deviled crab, and broiled trout. Murphy's will pan-fry the trout if requested.

Lemon chess pie is the dessert we like best; it is pure and tender, a warm translucent patch of sugar and egg, tinged with lemon. Peach cobbler is good, too, topped with real whipped cream.

Old Stone Inn

U.S. 60, Simpsonville, Ky.
(502) 722-8882

Apr.–Nov. Wed.–Sat. 5:30 p.m.–8 p.m., Sun. 12:30 p.m.–7:30 p.m.
Reservations required

$10–$15

We were sorry to hear when we last dined at the Old Stone Inn that Tom Marshall, waiter for sixty years, has semi-retired. Now the staff is "newcomers," retainers with a mere twenty or thirty years of service. The Inn was built in 1791; it *is* old Kentucky: pressed linens on the table, fine old sideboards, horsy prints on the walls, creaky wood floors, and ancient listing portals at the entrance to each of the fourteen rooms.

The menu is a short one, posted on a board in the vestibule. Start with one of two soups, potato or chicken mushroom, served in bowls made by the Hadley Pottery people of Kentucky. Move on to skillet-fried chicken or country ham, both expertly prepared, available separately or as a half-and-half proposition; or choose "chicken Eugenie," a chicken and ham dish in a gentle cream sauce: country cooking gone gourmet. For nonregional dining, the board also lists sirloin strip steak or fried shrimp.

Side dishes are time-honored Stone Inn classics: eggplant casserole, a house specialty that has appeared in cookbooks too numerous to count; fabulous corn pudding; hot dinner rolls; salad with a luxurious Thousand Island dressing. For dessert, cobblers are made each day, using the season's fresh fruit, usually apples or peaches.

Good food, plus a large measure of southern hospitality: it is impossible not to like this place.

Porter's Farm House

Hwy. 90 & 31W, Cave City, Ky.
(502) 773-2202

Daily 7 a.m.–9 p.m. in summer, until 8 p.m. rest of year

$10 or less

Porter's Kentucky ham is beautiful: dark pink, edged with lustrous fat that has turned speckled gold from frying. Each slice is substantial; if you were to cut a salt-cured ham this thick, the rugged flavor would be overwhelming. But the hams served at Porter's are cured with sugar at a ham house in

Mansville. That means they are more delicate, with a graceful nutlike taste. As fibrous as all country ham is (only water-packed ham gets tender), Porter's Kentucky ham is uniquely juicy. Perhaps that's why it goes so well with the little fluffy biscuits Porter's makes.

Ham and biscuits, along with slaw, sliced tomatoes, stewed apples, boiled potatoes, green beans, and red-eye gravy are all part of the family-style meal that is Porter's specialty. Everything is dished out in bowls and serving platters and you help yourself until you've had enough. Then it's time for a wedge of one of Porter's cream pies, their feathery meringues towering a full three inches high. We tried butterscotch, which was soft and creamy, not a bit toffee-like. The chocolate pie was wonderful, too—dark rich chocolate on the flakiest of crusts.

Porter's moved and expanded since the days it was a small cafe in Sulphur Well, but it is still the same delicious paradox of rare and regal food (authentic country ham) served with utmost small-town informality.

If you cannot get to Porter's in southwestern Kentucky, but want a genuine Kentucky ham of your own, we suggest contacting one of the following ham houses, both of which are small family businesses that specialize in mail-order. It's fun to get hams in the mail—they come in grungy burlap sacks shaped like mandolins—and both of these places include a full set of instructions for cleaning and cooking. (If you are passing through Kentucky, both welcome visitors.) Hams generally reach their peak in autumn. They run 10 to 20 pounds, and cost $2–$3 per pound.

Ballance Country Hams
Rte. 1, Box 15, Oakland, Ky. 42159
(502) 563-3956

Put in your order early. These hams go fast. You will be notified by mail that "The hams are *ready!*" Ballance uses a salt and sugar cure; then the hams are smoked over green hickory wood. The Ballance family has been curing hams since the 1850s.

Country Ham Apartments
521 State St., Bowling Green, Ky. 42101
(502) 842-0153

When we visited the Country Ham Apartments, they were called the Country Ham Motel, and they were hopping mad about a so-called ham house down the road that "shoots up" hams with brine to quick-cure them. None of that goes on here. The hams and bacons that hang proudly in the window for all passersby to see are slow-cured in the traditional Kentucky way. Early in the year, there still may be a few two-year-old hams available. They are prized by connoisseurs, and are priced accordingly. "We ship anywhere" is the Ham Apartments motto. (Yes, this really is an apartment complex, with about half a dozen "units" in back, although none were available for occupancy when we drove through. Perhaps the rooms were occupied by curing hams.)

Posh and Pat's

2201 Hwy. 41N, Henderson, Ky.
(502) 827-4714

Tues.–Thurs. & Sat. 10 a.m.–6 p.m., Fri. 10 a.m.–7 p.m.

$5 or less

We hadn't been to Posh and Pat's for five years, but it was just as we left it—Pat behind the counter, gabbing with her customers. "It looks the same," we said to her. "Yup," said she, "jes trying to keep the smoke out. Barbecue is a smoky business." Pat and her husband Posh have done a good job of keeping the smoke out of their tidy lunch counter, and an even better one of keeping it in the meat; the lamb we had was excellent—its muttony jangle finely muted by the smouldering wood.

The meat chunks come already sauced on sandwiches. The meat is heavy, the sauce is thin; the sandwich dissolves within twenty seconds—because the bread is strictly ersatz. Understand that nowhere in America is good barbecue served with good bread, for the simple reason that in order to fully appreciate the pitmaster's art, one requires a starchy chaperone for the barbecue, a companion utterly without character of its own, a neutral background, as it were. Posh and Pat's will provide you with same, white or rye.

If you forgo the sandwich and get a platter, it will come with the bright yellow egg salad favored in the mutton belt; also pickles, onions—and spongy bread.

We asked Pat if she had added burgoo to her menu yet; burgoo is sold by every other mutton joint between here and Owensboro. "Nope," she said. "I guess I'm lazy." Nobody who makes mutton this good could possibly be lazy. We see her more as a specialist.

Shady Rest

Hwy. 60 east, Owensboro, Ky.
(502) 926-8234

Mon.–Thurs. 7 a.m.–9 p.m., Fri. & Sat. 7 a.m.–10 p.m.

$4–$8

The cover on the menu at the Shady Rest depicts a country child cozying up to a cute little lamb. Above the pastoral scene is inscribed, "Little Mary had some lamb . . . Won't you have some too?" When you realize that the Shady Rest is famous for its barbecued mutton, the image of the little girl sneaking up on the lamb takes on whole new shades of meaning.

Owensboro is the heart of Kentucky mutton country, the only place in America where ewes are the smokehouse meat of choice. Those accustomed to southern pork or Texas beef will be startled; this lamb is potent, the vigor of the meat just barely rounded off by its fourteen-hour sizzle in the smoke pit.

The waitress will ask if you want the meat "off the pit" or "regular." Off the pit means that the meat is not already doused in barbecue sauce, allowing the customer to customize it using three different varieties that are brought to the table. Off the pit meat is fairly dry and Shady Rest's blend of sauce is a good one; so we recommend getting it regular. No need to worry that the strong flavor of mutton will be compromised.

The mutton platter includes a very yellow, very eggy potato salad, pickles, onion slices, a pile of barbecue beans that is a rich little stew all by itself, and beige sliced bread that purports to be rye, but is in fact more like Wonder bread with a suntan. The bad brown bread, good for mopping up sauce, is one of Kentucky lamb's traditional accoutrements.

Shady Rest burgoo is less muttony than most, less pepper-hot, too. Although it isn't cooked outdoors in a washtub or gunpowder kettle (the traditional method), and although it lacks squirrel meat, it is an agreeably invigorating stew, russet red, country hearty.

The menu describes fried apple pie as "our own kitchen special." It is a stupendously good variation of the fried pie theme. A very thin envelope of butter crust is filled with cooked cinnamon-spiced apple slices, then griddle-fried to a golden turn. It is soft and fragrant, served warm. The waitress will ask if you want ice cream on it. A cool scoop of vanilla tastes just right.

The Shady Rest used to serve its meals on old-fashioned wooden plates, which the health inspector nixed. Even without the tableware, it is a charming place to eat: nice wood paneling, cozy booths, helpful waitresses, and Ohio River Valley food par excellence.

Thomas' F & N Steak House

Rte. 8, Dayton, Ky.
(513) 261-6766

Lunch & dinner daily

$10–$20

As the name suggests, beef is Thomas' claim to fame, but what we like best is the french-fried eggplant. Puffy golden strips, barely salted, with a gossamer crunch; they are served with breathtaking horseradish cocktail sauce.

After the eggplant, you choose from among T-bones, sirloins, filets mignon, or porterhouses—the latter sold in one or two-pound sizes. Butchered and aged in Thomas' back room, the steaks cut easily into nice-to-chew forkfuls. They are high-quality meat, with a blunt beefy savor, rounded by the aging process. Slabs of prime rib—sliced thin, regular, or heavy—are weighed down with natural juices.

The steaks' supporting cast at Thomas' consists of a baked potato, iceberg lettuce with creamy garlic or acidic champagne dressing (served in lovely pewter bowls inscribed with an F & N insignia, "since 1929"), and a warm round of bread that arrives on a cutting board with a knife plunged into its crust. Plus there are some cooked-to-death—and quite deliciously seasoned—cut green beans, as soft as warm butter. And there is dessert of frothy "French" cheesecake or calorific carrot cake.

Thomas' interior decor is an eyeful: walls covered with a patchwork pattern of pictures, posters, prints, some of them antique, some going back only to the early 1960s, a collection with no discernible theme or logic whatsoever. There are Victorian lamps, six fireplaces, an ancient wood cookstove, and—in the entryway—a million little statuette collectibles.

It is impossible to gather any sense of the shape of the place, since it is a roadhouse made of several strung-together dining rooms, all dark, some secretive, others built for parties. We sat in the most capacious round leatherette booth, with a seat cushion as soft and bouncy as a waterbed.

NORTH CAROLINA

The Acorn

3311 Guess Rd., Durham, N.C.
(919) 477-9879

Sun.–Thurs. 11 a.m.–8 p.m., Fri. & Sat. 11 a.m.–9 p.m.

$5 or less

A hunkering cinderblock commons, tables lined up in rows and covered with green-checked oilcloths, The Acorn is the long-standing barbecue of choice among citizens of Durham. It is prettier than most North Carolina pits, with frilly curtains on the windows, and the requisite assorted hot sauces contained in a berry-pickin' basket that's been decorated with hand-painted acorns; but the food, local epicures assure us, is as good as it was years ago, when this family-size mess hall was nothing but a drive-in called The Little Acorn.

The meat is finely minced pork, lean and greaseless, smoke flavor clinging to every shred. As is Carolina custom, little is added in the kitchen, just a dash of pepper hot sauce; if you want more, reach into the basket and sprinkle away. With the meat come smooth-skinned hushpuppies and slaw or vegetables.

They are serious about their vegetables, fifteen each day: still-crunchy turnip greens, killer strong; syrupy, falling-apart candied yams with a strong clove kick; crunchy fried okra; real whipped potatoes. For about $3, you can get a plate of four vegetables and hushpuppies. The only one we would not order again is the baked potato, a hoary monster that made us think that the kitchen had been saving it for us since *Roadfood* was first published in 1978.

To do things properly in this part of the world, accompany your barbecue with a bowl of Brunswick stew, the hot orange gallimaufry of chicken, pork, corn, tomatoes, beans, and hot peppers.

But to *really* do it right, come to The Acorn with a large group, order family style, and help yourself to platters of barbecue and Brunswick stew, hushpuppies, mashed potatoes, beans, plus superior fried chicken and pitchers full of iced tea. This kind of Carolina cooking was meant to be eaten *en masse*, with gusto.

Dessert is a choice of icebox lemon pie, pecan or chocolate pie, or banana pudding, the latter sold in two sizes. The large portion is Homeric; but you'll be sorry if you order only small. It's that good.

Blue Mist Barbecue Restaurant

Hwy. 64, four miles east of Asheboro, N.C.
(919) 625-3980

Daily 6:30 a.m.–10 p.m., Sun. 7 a.m.–10 p.m.

$5 or less

"If there were such a thing as a state food," *Town and Country*'s Jim Villas wrote a few years back, "North Carolina's would without question be barbecue." From Asheville to the Atlantic Ocean, the Carolina hills and flatlands are dotted with barbecue pits. Some are shacks, some huge eating halls, but they all follow the same ritual of slow-cooking hogs over hickory coals, and in most cases, mopping them as they smoke with some manner of secret sauce.

In the western mountains, they like their barbecue smoky and topped with a deep red tomato sauce; in the tobacco belt farther east, the "Que" is pale, redolent of vinegar. Asheboro is smack in the center of this spectrum, but there's nothing middling about Blue Mist barbecue. It's great North Carolina eats—flaky minced pork infused with the perfume of hickory smoke, spread lightly with a sweet and sour tomato sauce. The meat is infinitely mottled: on the tray you will find chunks and shreds; crackling tidbits and soft fibers; dry, lean pieces interlaced with juicy fat ones. The sauce has a pepper bite, but not enough to overwhelm the tender woody taste of the pork.

If you order a "tray" of barbecue, it comes with knobby hushpuppies and forgettable cole slaw. If you get a sandwich, the slaw is automatically piled on top of the meat—an appalling local custom that makes about as much sense as dumping ketchup on a great steak. This barbecue is too good to be buried under chopped cabbage!

The Blue Mist is a modern restaurant with pretty ocean-blue booths and a counter—a comfortable choice for those who find the more ramshackle pits intimidating. When we stopped in, there was no outside sign saying "Blue Mist" anywhere. As we got out of our car we asked a group of four elderly ladies on their way out if this was indeed the Blue Mist. "Well, of course it is, boy," their leader replied, shaking her cane in the direction of the smoking pit. "Can't you smell?"

Fearrington House

U.S. 15-501, Carrboro, N.C.   Eight mi. south of Chapel Hill
(919) 967-7770

Lunch Tues.–Fri., dinner Tues.–Sat., Sun. brunch
Reservations advised

$10–$20

Nineteen-twenties-vintage Fearrington Farm is the center for a planned village of 200 families. In what used to be the granary, there is a market selling fine food and country-themed housewares; in the milk barn, there is pottery for sale; in the smith's shop, a post office. And the elegant white farmhouse is a restaurant, surrounded by flowering crabapple trees and herb gardens, its dining rooms perfumed with fresh roses. One can eat outside, shaded by pecan or oak trees; indoor dining rooms look out on gardens, arbors, terraces, and, in the spring, a Wizard of Oz field of daffodils.

The menu was formulated by esteemed southern cook Edna Lewis, and although she has moved on, her mark on the Fearrington kitchen is indelible. Nowhere else will you find buttermilk biscuits like these—devoid of baking powder's bite and of sugar's sweetness, hardly more than a pure light puff of flour with a wispy sour tang.

A salad plate of black-eyed peas and summer savory is brilliantly seasoned with fresh chervil. Summer tomatoes are real, from the garden; the potato salad is made with breathy dilled mayonnaise. Biscuits are stuffed with razor-thin slices of resilient country ham, sided by honeycup mustard. Even the green salad is extraordinarily *southern*, its tender leaves of bibb lettuce garnished with toasted pecans. Shrimp salad is an appropriately ladylike mélange, on a bed of tangy watercress, balanced by a single ham biscuit.

The menu is small, changing with the seasons. Spring dinner might include sauteed baby trout, baked North Carolina crab, a meal of sauteed and baked vegetables, or an appetizer of oysters broiled with buttered bread crumbs. At Sunday brunch, buttermilk pancakes are served with fried apples and country sausage, honey-maple syrup on the side.

We got a warning from the waitress when we ordered "Edna's chocolate soufflé" for dessert. "It takes a good ten minutes," she said. No problem; we were having a fine time sipping our unsweetened iced (Twining's) tea and gazing out at the neatly lined-up hay bales that so resemble shredded wheat. "And it's bittersweet," she added. "I tell you because some people are disappointed that it's not sweet enough."

Only in this sorghum-sopped land of presweetened tea and Goo Goo Clusters could anyone be disappointed with such a chocolate soufflé, which happens to be the best dessert in the history of the United States of America.

An ethereal swell of chocolate rises high above the rim of the dish, moist yet fully poised, its crusted top begging to be torn so that clouds of cocoa steam can waft across the table. Into the heated center, pour silky bittersweet fudge from a pitcher, then, for a dash of sugar flavor to counterbalance all that dusty chocolate, dollop in some of the sweetened whipped cream that comes in a ramekin alongside.

No dessert can compare to such a consummate triumph, not even Fearrington's lemon frost pie, which is merely spectacular: creamy egg-white icebox filling atop a golden braided crust, its intense lemon color splashed by a sauce of vibrant blueberries, the whole beautiful tableau garnished with a geranium and white petunia leaves.

In a state known for sleeves-up country vittles and ramshackle barbecue halls, Fearrington House's Ciceronian menu and its bucolic setting are a culinary *Brigadoon* . . . but accessible seven days a week.

The Lantern

Rte. 601, Dobson, N.C.   Exit 93 off I-77
(919) 386-8461

Mon. 6 a.m.–2 p.m., Tues.–Sat. 6 a.m.–9:30 p.m., Sun. 11:30 a.m.–9:30 p.m.

$5 or less

In 1980 we got a letter from *Roadfood* reader Laverne Lasobeck of Rockledge, Florida. "Needing both gasoline and food," she wrote, "we traveled down off I-77 into Dobson, N.C., and found The Lantern. Voila!—the ultimate in southern biscuits!! As you often hear in joking references, it is a wonder they didn't float away, off the plate! We had discovered the 'pièce de résistance' of exceptional small-town eating places. Please make a note of it for your future excursions."

Thanks, Laverne. We followed your lead to one of North Carolina's choice cafes. We agree about those biscuits, too—airy beauts they are, but not so light they don't stand up nobly to milk gravy and lusty country ham on the side.

We asked owner Clinton Dockery why they are so good. He leaned back in his chair, took a slow puff of his cigarette, looked level-eyed at us foolish Yankees, and said simply, "Some people can make biscuits better than others." Amen.

But biscuits aren't the end of the Lantern story. Come for lunch and sample inexpensive cafe food like chicken and gravy or ham with raisin sauce, sided by your choice from more than a dozen regionally favored vegetables, including black-eyed peas, buttery puffs of hominy, candied yams, squash or broccoli casserole.

In keeping with the Carolina sweet tooth, there is a long list of desserts: fruit pies, custards, and cakes. We recommend you try one of the cobblers, but not necessarily peach or cherry. In our book, the best choice was a sensational sweet potato cobbler—a local favorite, according to Mr. Dockery, who told us, "Yes, sir, they eat that one real well. It's good." From a man as imperturbable as he, that was a rave review.

Laura's Rozzelle House

Hwy. 16, north of Charlotte, N.C.   At the river
(704) 392-7561

Tues.–Fri. lunch & dinner, Sun. dinner noon–3 p.m.
Reservations required for dinner

$10 or less

We hit Charlotte after days on the trail of Carolina barbecue. We were pigged out, up to our snouts in pork. So we called our friend Sally McMillan in Charlotte and challenged her to suggest some other food with a Carolina flavor.

Sally's description of Laura's Rozzelle House soon had us hoggishly squealing in happy anticipation of dinner. "Good country food," is what she called it, and that it was: fried chicken, crisp-skinned and moist, cooked slowly in cast-iron skillets, sided by rice and gravy, green beans, cole slaw, potato salad, candied yams, boiled okra, squash casserole, and hot "cat head biscuits" (named for their whopping girth), complemented by native crabapple jelly. Oh, yes, there was another entree—country ham; and despite our porcine saturation, we couldn't resist. It's sugar-cured, resilient enough to yield a fine sweet flavor as it's chewed.

Desserts are traditional southern cobblers—peach, strawberry, or blueberry, depending on the seasonal yield of the mountains.

All the food is served family-style, in bowls and on platters that are replenished by the waitress as often as you empty them.

Laura's is a small plantation house near the Catawba River, built in 1849 by Dick and Laura Rozzelle, once used by travelers as a meal stop and overnight resting place en route from Charlotte to the north or west. It's still an atmospheric old building, with walls and ceiling made of wide pine boards: a refreshing contrast to the airplane-hangar architecture that characterizes so many restaurants on the outskirts of Charlotte.

Lexington Barbecue #1

Hwy. 29-70 south, Lexington, N.C.
(704) 249-9814

Mon.–Sat. 10 a.m.–10 p.m.

$5 or less

We asked two policewomen outside City Hall where the best barbecue in town could be had, and both drawled "Lexington Number One" in unison. We tried it, and the results confirmed our belief that when it comes to locating good food in a small town, law officers know best. While Smokey Joe's and City Barbecue were fine, Lexington #1 was better.

The pork is served in the North Carolina way—shredded into piquant fibers and tiny crisp flecks of meat. It's peppery and vinegar scented—no need for a sprinkling of the assorted hot sauces on each table.

The Lexington "platter" is a small yellow cardboard boat, packed half-and-half with meat and very fresh, finely chopped slaw. On the side were some of the best hushpuppies we found anywhere in the state—their crunchy crusts cracked open to reveal still steaming yellow meal inside.

Lexington #1 is a modern rectangle with booths and a parking lot featuring carhop service if you don't want to budge. It's a hot spot in the summer and on weekends, but when we dined here off hours, things were slow. The waitresses were clustered in a corner, engaged in an animated discussion about "Elephant Man disease" and lymph nodes. It was most educational and informative, at least as good as listening to Mel Tillis on the jukebox.

Melton's Barbecue

631 Ridge St., Rocky Mount, N.C.   Take Melton Drive off 301
(919) 446-8513

Tues.–Thurs. 8:30 a.m.–8 p.m., Fri. & Sat. 8:30 a.m.–9 p.m.

$5 or less

Colonel Bob Melton, who started barbecuing over fifty years ago, now belongs to the ages; but in eastern Carolina, his name is mythic. For years he was known hereabouts (with insouciance unique to regional food chauvinists) as the Barbecue King of the South. Melton's restaurant, now run by Pattie Smith, widow of Colonel Bob's partner, Add Smith, is a shrine to the gastronomic tradition Carolinians hold dear.

"We can't cook in an open pit anymore," Mrs. Smith lamented. "The health people outlawed that. So we use gas, with hickory chips to flavor it. It's not what it used to be."

Perhaps not, but Melton's barbecue is mighty good: uniquely North Carolina-style pork, served chopped up into a motley heap. It is lean, considerably drier than the greasy stuff preferred west of Raleigh, but rich and savory nonetheless. Each table is set with hot sauce, pickled peppers, Tabasco, vinegar, and ketchup; make your own sauce to moisten the meat.

Before the barbecue, waitresses bring every table a bowl of slaw—bright mustard-yellow, very pickley. With the meal comes a basket of hushpuppies. Pork plates are sided by Brunswick stew made of beans and sweet corn, plus boiled potatoes (an odd barbecue accoutrement unique to the small region between Rocky Mount and Fayetteville).

If you order iced tea, you get a medium-sized glass and a large pitcher for refills.

Groups can eat family-style, for which the table is set with platters of barbecue and all the fixins, plus fried chicken.

Melton's is a white house in a residential neighborhood, shaded by full leafy trees. Inside, the long all-wood dining room is set with neat rows of tables and chairs; fans turn overhead; through picture windows, you can see the Tar River below, slow and muddy. Even when it's crowded and noisy and rocking with pig pickers having a great time, there is something almost hallowed about this majestic restaurant.

Nu-Wray Inn

Burnsville, N.C.   On the square
(704) 682-2329

Daily breakfast & dinner 8:30 a.m. & 6:30 p.m. sharp, Sun. supper at noon (occasional 2nd servings at 2 p.m.)   No meals served Dec.–April Reservations advised

$10 or less

When Rush Wray rings the gong at 8 a.m., you've got a half hour to get downstairs for breakfast. Set out on long white-clothed tables in the Nu-Wray dining room are platters of pancakes and pitchers of warm syrup, country ham, grits and red-eye gravy, hot buttermilk biscuits, sourwood honey, apple butter, baked apples, cornbread, and blackberry jam. Elbow-to-elbow with other guests and travelers who have come for the meal, you help yourself. There's always plenty.

After breakfast, we had a ball exploring the music room, drawing room, and antique-furnished crannies of this well-worn inn. We then lounged in the lobby by the great stone fireplace (it gets chilly here in the mountains), and addressed Nu-Wray postcards to friends. The cards are ancient sepias, our favorite depicting Will, the old chef, toting hams from the smokehouse. The Nu-Wray is a piece of the past; its kitchen is tradition incarnate. "I'm a cookbook fiend," Rush Wray told us, and his friend, Miss Jelly, seated in a rocker to his side, nodded in agreement. "But what we serve here is simply good southern country cooking."

For dinner, that means chicken fried in ham drippings in great iron skillets, served with cream gravy and steamed rice; dressing made with Nu-Wray's wonderful cornbread; spicy yellow-eye baked beans; Mis' Sallie's candied yams; lettuce wilted down with hot bacon dressing; berry custard pie; bully pudding (laced with chopped pecans and dates); and tipsy cake (a cake and custard tower drenched with wine). It all comes family-style, in the old-fashioned blue dining room.

"We used to buy hundreds of green hams," Rush Wray told us. "Smoked and cured them all ourselves. Now the government won't allow that, so we have a man who does it, up in the mountains. Time was when we served three meals a day, seven days a week, three hundred and sixty-five days a year, no matter what. That's the way an inn ought to be . . . but we can't afford to do it in the winter anymore. I regret that, I really do."

Rush Wray may have had to modify things to suit changing times and government ham inspectors, but the meals served by the Nu-Wray kitchen are still southern cooking at its very best. "If it is anywhere near mealtime, pull up a chair with the rest of the boarders," Duncan Hines wrote about the Nu-Wray Inn in 1936, around the time it passed from the second to the third generation of Wray innkeepers. "They will treat you like one of the family, and you'll like it." What he said then still holds true.

(A double room at the Nu-Wray Inn runs about $30.)

TENNESSEE

Belle Meade Buffet

In the Belle Meade Plaza on West End, Nashville, Tenn.
(615) 298-5571

Lunch & dinner daily

$5–$10

Four-color transparencies of gorgeous, cornucopian platters decorate the lobby. Along the mazelike passageway leading to the cafeteria line, signs implore customers to STUDY MENUS AND MAKE SELECTIONS AS QUICKLY AS POSSIBLE. Not an easy chore, as there are well over one hundred different things to eat.

But you do choose fast, and the tray is carried quickly to a table by a member of the Belle Meade staff. And you eat fast, too.

The dining rooms, with their big chandeliers, are lit more than any other restaurant we know. They are crowded with families and singles, friends and lovers.

And yet, for all the speed and noise and bright lights, the Belle Meade, like all large southern cafeterias, is immensely soothing. The dining experience, stripped of restaurant folderol, is *yours*. Pick your own meal, eat at your own pace. Nobody bothers you, no waiters intrude on conversations. On a recent three-day trip to Nashville, although we ate breakfast and lunch all over town, we returned to the Belle Meade every night for supper, where we knew we could relax over some fine-tasting southern food.

There are all kinds of good entrees, like fried chicken, catfish, turkey (sliced off the breast as you watch), ribeye steak, roast beef, etc. But we like to glide straight to the vegetable sector of the line, where there is a choice of eighteen, including crisp fried okra, fresh turnip greens, vanilla-flavored yams streaked with marshmallows, yellow squash with a buttercrumb top, fiesta rice, pinto beans, butter beans, and real mashed potatoes. Side that with a wedge of lush, kernel-dotted jalapeno cornbread, and top it off with fudge pie or chess pie or one of the tallest lemon meringue pies in Tennessee (on a sensational graham cracker crust).

Your whole dinner's on the table five minutes after you walk in the door. Thirty minutes later, you are dispatching the last of the pie and coffee. And if it's 7:45, the Belle Meade Buffet will be readying to close. Cafeteria dinner is served early, for working people who have to get up in the morning.

Bobby Q's Barbeque & Catfish

1070 N. Washington Ave., Cookeville, Tenn.
(615) 526-1024

Mon.–Sat. lunch & dinner

$3–$8

"Every day our dessert chef surprises us with some heavenly confection," beams the Bobby Q menu. "It's well worth saving room for." A clipping from the local paper, framed in the entryway, raves about Bobby Q's chocolate pie and another legendary specialty of the dessert chef, called "better than sex lemon pie." Neither was on the menu the day we stopped in. But that was fine, because the day's surprise was banana pudding, which in our opinion is almost always better than sex.

Streaked white with billows of whipped cream, crumbling vanilla wafer lumps in a silken yellow custard that has a brown-sugar flavor verging on butterscotch, it is a culinary lullaby, soft and sweet.

Should you wish to eat a meal before dessert, Bobby Q's will serve you well. The pork barbecue is hacked into large shreds with crusty tips and ends, moist meat with a subtle smoke flavor that blossoms when you pour on the hot sauce that comes alongside. Barbecued beef is lean, too thin; even a liberal dose of sauce doesn't compensate for its dryness.

With the Q, we recommend a side dish of beans and an order of "pool room slaw," listed on the menu as an "80-year-old recipe," given to Bobby Q's chef by a retired barbecue man from Nashville. Hot stuff, the spicy cabbage doused with red sauce.

Two whole catfish come on a platter. They are mild beasts, grain-fed, pond-raised, with clean white meat beneath their sandy breading. They are accompanied by two perfectly round red-gold hushpuppies with steamy cornmeal insides.

Nice touches: lemonade is made from squeezed lemons, water and sugar; iced tea is freshly brewed, served in mason jars.

A modern cafe, parked in the lot of a small shopping center several miles from the interstate, Bobby Q's is so strictly local that the waitress couldn't resist asking, "How did you find us?" We told her that a lady at a nearby flea market had recommended Bobby Q's as the best food for miles around. "True," the waitress grinned ingenuously. "I eat here all the time."

Buntyn Restaurant

3070 Southern Ave., Memphis, Tenn.
(901) 458-8776

Mon.–Fri. 11 a.m.–8 p.m.

$5 or less

The shocking thing about a visit to Buntyn is the way its customers behave. We mean the regulars; city people who come every day for lunch. Here they sit, at booth or table, carrying on calm conversations, placid expressions on their faces. How do they do it? How can they possibly be so cool? How can sentient human beings eat a Buntyn lunch without dropping their fork in amazement at the flavor of the turnip greens; or crying out joyously at the texture of a yeast roll when they gently pull it into fluffy halves; or weeping with contentment at the sight of the banana pudding, heaped so high with meringue and wafers and banana slices?

For those of us who cannot come here every weekday of the year, as many Memphians do, this two-room cafe by the tracks, next to a seed and feed store, is no ordinary place to eat. Buntyn is simply Plate Lunch Heaven, the Assumption of Meat-and-3-Veg.

The well air-conditioned dining rooms are painted pea green, fitted with Formica tables worn smooth by nearly forty years of good food on sturdy plates. It is crowded throughout the lunch hour; meals are fast and service is friendly.

To start with, the bread basket holds those enormous rectangular yeast rolls, risen high, with tender tan crusts. And there are moist pie-shaped cornbread wedges, butter-yellow.

Fried chicken is astoundingly juicy—luscious dark meat, steamy white breasts, both with a brittle crust impregnated with pepper and spice. You can order chicken and dumplings, blue-plate meat loaf, or catfish steaks, three at a time. And all are exemplary . . . but it is not for the entrees that we have returned to Buntyn every day we spend in Memphis. It is for the "vegetable choice" on the menu—two or three with each main course, or a plate of four:

Vibrant turnip greens, resonating hambone zest; powerfully spiced sweet potato soufflé, streaked with semi-melted miniature marshmallows and raisins; whole kernel corn; black-eyed peas; green beans; creamed potatoes; tempura-light fried eggplant fingers; Waldorf salad with raisins, apples, mini-'mallows again, but no nuts; and the revelation among them, listed innocuously as "fresh squash." And that *is* what it is—chunks, baked and buttered, lightly seasoned. Why, then, is it so rich and delicious?

Now, about that banana pudding: it's a jumbo bowl of mushed-up custard, banana slices, moist meringue, and broken vanilla wafers. What puts it over the top is its warmth. It isn't hot, just tepid—the exact temperature of baby formula; and it is guaranteed to reduce the most eloquent epicure to cries of "num num goo goo."

Every day there is a cobbler—peach, strawberry, cherry, or apple, but if for any reason we want something other than 'nanner pudding, we order coconut pie, a sturdy wedge of filling topped with meringue that seems more air than egg white, liberally sprinkled with shreds of toasted coconut.

Our first time here, we had to know: Mrs. Wiggins, please, could you give us recipes? "Oh, dear," she chuckled, having been asked the same question a thousand times. "We have no recipes here. You know what it's like—a pinch of this, a handful of that." But the truth is that even if we watched them in the kitchen, observing every move and measurement, there would be no way to imitate such food with mere ingredients and cooking techniques. It is transcendent, and it is Buntyn's alone.

Charlie Vergos Rendezvous

*52 S. Second St., Memphis, Tenn.   In Gen. Washburn Alley
(901) 523-2746*

Tues.–Fri. 11:30 a.m.–1 a.m., Sat. 3:30 p.m.–1 a.m.

$5–$10

We woke up in Memphis and turned on the TV just in time to hear the host of a local talk show sign off by saying, "Have a nice day . . . and don't eat too many ribs." Memphians are rib-crazed people, a condition due in part to the Rendezvous, which for the last twenty years has been making something known here as dry ribs.

They're weird, these ribs. They're not like any baked or barbecued ribs you will get anywhere else. There is no sauce on them at all, no ketchup or tomato. But there is a lot of taste; oh, God, is there a lot of taste! Charlie Vergos's ribs are covered, completely blanketed, with a layer of dry seasoning that tastes exactly like dry onion soup. "Flavorful" is not nearly a strong enough word for these ribs. You could have a stroke from so much flavor.

They are really quite beautiful, their crust red-brown; and they are the leanest ribs we have ever seen, without so much as a vein of fat: nothing but crisp, chewy pork, with a strong charcoal taste peeking out from under the spray of dry spice.

Don't go anywhere you can't drink a lot after eating them. Here, people consume beer by the pitcher; kegs of beer are stored everywhere, in and out of sight.

The Rendezvous is underground—a raffish, impolite place; but very popular. The stairway leading down is plastered with thousands of calling cards.

Ribs are pretty much the story, except to say that if you have to wait for a table (likely), get one of the appetizer plates—good cheese and sausage or ham with sour pickles.

Coletta's

1063 S. Parkway East, Memphis, Tenn.
(901) 948-7652

Mon.–Fri. 11 a.m.–11 p.m., Sat. & Sun. 4 p.m.–11 p.m.

$5–$10

We thought we'd seen barbecued *everything* in our travels across the country, but barbecue pizza was a new one on us. Coletta's, a dark Italian restaurant in business since 1923, has been making barbecue pizza for as long as anyone in town could remember.

"I think it was invented in Chicago or someplace like that," the girl at the cash register surmised. We doubt it. If it had to happen, Memphis is the right place; no city is more barbecue-happy.

So, barbecue pizza: chewy crust, nice stringy cheese topping, and mounds of shredded barbecued pork in a sugar and spice tomato sauce. It's a heterodox but pleasing combination, sweeter than pizza, less porcine than straight barbecue.

It hasn't exactly caught on (Coletta's is the only place we know that does it), but it's a local anomaly we recommend to those with an experimental nature.

Elliston Place Soda Shop

2111 Elliston Place, Nashville, Tenn.
(615) 327-1091

Mon.–Sat. 6 a.m.–9 p.m.

$5 or less

Every Thursday, for the last 2,500 weeks, the lunch special has been turkey and dressing with candied yams and cranberries. Six days a week, Tennessee country ham is on the menu. The booths and chairs are done in shades of burgundy and yellow that have ceased to exist in the world outside. The floor is made of tiny hexagonal tiles that somehow haven't aged at all since the Elliston Place Soda Shop opened for business in 1939.

To call it a relic makes it sound hoary; but the Elliston Place Soda Shop seems *new*, as clean and neat as the day it opened. And that means the old-fashioned plate lunches and soda fountain specialties are all the better—the exact food we would hope to find if a time machine deposited us in Nashville, fifty years ago.

Southern fried chicken, liver and onions, baked or country ham, roast beef and gravy, fish filets on Friday: a standard cafe repertoire, everything made by good cooks (the same ones who were here in the 1940s), without any shortcuts or convenience products. And of course, since this is Tennessee, every entree is accompanied by three vegetables.

Southern vegetables, seasoned with brio. Choose from well over a dozen, including whole okra, black-eyed peas, baked squash, blue lake green beans, whipped potatoes, and turnip greens. Also on the list of candidates are non-vegetable side dishes like creole spaghetti, baked pears and peaches, and candied apples.

The homemade chess pie is great, as is the Dixie-sweet lemon icebox, but you don't want to eat a meal here, not even breakfast (ham, biscuits, red-eye or cream gravy) without a taste of the authentic soda fountain. There is no more wonderful way to learn about America's true gastronomic history than firsthand research into Elliston Place's three-dip banana split; or pine-apple soda; or hot fudge sundae topped with whipped cream, nuts, and a cherry; or foamy chocolate malt.

Four Way Grill

998 Mississippi Ave., Memphis, Tenn.
(901) 775-2351

Daily 7 a.m.–11 p.m.

$5 or under

It is said that the Mississippi delta begins in the lobby of Memphis's Peabody Hotel. We love the Peabody; it's a grand old place. But for us, the delta begins in a booth at the Four Way Grill—the sweetest soul-food restaurant in the south.

Soul food often means a scary place or a dump for which excuses must be made. Not so here. The Four Way is a humble storefront, but it is neat and nice. When we first stopped in, one blazing hot summer day, the air conditioner had the place cooled down to nearly 50 degrees; *Flipper* was playing on the counter television. Hanging on the pale green wall was a sign advising NO LOITERING; NO SOLICITING; NO PROFANITY.

We were attended by a white-uniformed waitress, who carefully con-structed each place setting. First she put down a paper napkin, then set worn cafe silverware on top of that, then covered the silver with another napkin. It is always done that way, at every place setting. However plain the mate-rials, the Four Way Grill does everything with a distinct style.

And that, after all, is what soul food is all about: the resourceful transformation of unpromising ingredients into good food; the turning of a sow's ear into . . . in this case, sow's ears—boiled to tangy delectability in a strong vinegar gravy. There are ham hocks, too, and pickled pig's feet with brown sugar gravy, and chitlins, steamed or fried—everything, the old saying goes, except the squeal.

It is possible to eat higher on the pigmeat food chain at the Four Way. Pork chops are done to perfection, dramatically seasoned, hot and tangy. Get them sided by collard greens, flavored with fatback and a dash of hot pepper. At breakfast, there is strong resilient ham, served with ham-drippin gravy, dotted with bits of cracklin (morsels of pork skin, like tough bacon); you can even order eggs and pork brains.

Sunday food is the kitchen's forte: beautiful baked ham, or duck and dressing, served with buttered rice and spicy stewed apples; or turkey and dressing, with candied yams and sweet corn. Follow any of these with banana pudding or the Four Way's chunky peach cobbler, and you will have enjoyed an exemplary southern feast.

Gridley's

4101 Summer Ave., Memphis, Tenn.
(901) 452-4057

Sun.–Thurs. 6 a.m.–11 p.m., Fri. & Sat. 6 a.m.–midnight

$5–$10

Gridley's and Charlie Vergos Rendezvous are the twin stars of the Memphis rib scene, each with its own advocates and detractors. The ribs served at the two places are polar opposites. Charlie Vergos's are "dry." Gridley's are "wet"—sticky gooey messy wet, glazed with a fruity red sauce. Since the sauce is applied as the ribs cook (not after), it bakes on—and into—the meat, turning the slab rusty red, tipped with crisp charcoal. Although very lean, they are juicy and dripping with flavor; the meat pulls off the bones easily in long luscious strips. Gridley's waiters are prepared with supplies of wet-naps and boxes of toothpicks.

Memphis is the northernmost corner of the Mississippi delta, and Memphians share with their neighbors to the south a passion for shrimp, or, in the delta accent, "swimp." Gridley's barbecue shrimp come in their shells (u-peel-em). They are firm and full and buttery, and they are sided by a zesty tomato/pepper sauce for dipping. The shrimp and the sauce together are an exquisite combination that sets taste buds ringing.

You will want to avail yourself of that loaf of bread that comes to the table with the shrimp. It is made here (from scratch, not from one of those half-baked loaves lazy restaurants get from Pepperidge Farm); it is sturdy enough to mop up plenty of sauce and stay chewy, with a fine toasty crust.

Nor should the cumin-spiked pork and beans be overlooked; or the phenomenal seafood gumbo (weekends only); or breakfast (6 a.m.–11 a.m. only), where you serve yourself, cafeteria-style, to hot biscuits and sausage made from the trimmings of Gridley's pork.

Good desserts, too—only two varieties, both Mrs. Gridley's recipes: lemon icebox or pecan pie. The lemon pie is small and unspectacular-looking, but it is creamy with an endearing lemony piquance; the crust is masterful, light and crisp. The pecan pie is thick with nutmeats and syrupy sweet; too rich, probably, for anyone who's preceded it with a slab of ribs.

Never mind that it's in a ho-hum shopping center in East Memphis; when you enter Gridley's, you are walking into the pantheon of American eats.

Hap Townes

493 Humphreys St., Nashville, Tenn.   At Chestnut, near Greer Stadium
(615) 251-9648

Breakfast and lunch Mon.–Fri.

Under $5

On the outskirts of Nashville, Hap Townes' stone-walled cottage looks like a tiny castle, with metal awnings and glass brick windows in the vestibule. Through the seafoam-green entryway, the dining room is hardly bigger than a mobile home, wood paneled, with a counter along one wall and a half-dozen tables. As you enter, a waitress—one of five in the minuscule road-house—asks what you want to drink. You tell her tea or coffee or Coke, then step up to the stainless steel counter at one end of the room.

Here is Hap Townes, ready to describe the menu for the day and prepare each customer's lunch from the steam table. Hap is a strikingly handsome silver-haired Tennessean, six and a half feet tall, thin as a post, with a hypnotically mellifluous voice.

"Nice soft roast beef . . . good old butter beans . . . oh, these stewed tomatoes are sweet. . . ." The impassioned commentary continues as he assembles and carefully arranges each plate. "I'll get you a nice hot piece of country steak from the bottom of the pan . . . Don't forget to take your cornbread—there it is, off the grill with butter."

When the plate is full, Hap carefully circles the edge with his towel and hands it over, announcing "Meat and Three." You turn around and spot your waitress, who is setting drinks at a table. Now dig into some down-home vittles.

We lunched at Hap Townes on a Thursday, which meant country fried steak (breaded) or roast beef, cut and chipped. Both were served with stick-to-the ribs gravy. The vegetable choices included cottage cheese and slaw, assertively porky butter beans, crowder peas, limp braised cabbage with chunks of ham, sweet stewed tomatoes, and stewed raisins.

Meat-and-three, vegetables only—however you organize your lunch, it is accompanied by wondrous cornbread. This mid-south "bread" is skillet-fried, light-textured and steamy, served with melting pats of butter on top. Cobbler is the dessert of choice.

Dining at Hap's is hardly like being in a restaurant. One morning we arrived at six, but it was winter, and so Hap wasn't planning to open until seven. But he let us in, right along with Dugger the Tater Man (delivering whole spuds from his van). Ever gracious, Hap offered to fix us breakfast. He gave us sausage and eggs, and a morning paper to read. As soon as we were set, he sat down at the counter to have his own morning bowl of cereal.

In the summer of 1985, Hap Townes wrote to us saying he had hung up his skillet and apron. His successors, he assured us, would maintain everything as it has been for the last forty years, when Hap began.

John Wills Bar-B-Que Pit

2450 Central Ave., Memphis, Tenn.
(901) 274-8000

Daily lunch & dinner

$4–$8

A few years ago, *Memphis* magazine decided to settle, once and for all, the question of who made the best barbecue in town—a significant undertaking, given the fact that Memphis is the pork capital of America. There are more barbecue parlors here than hamburger joints; and there are better ones than in Kansas City, Birmingham, or Little Rock. "Wet ribs," "dry ribs," chopped, sliced, on pizza or with a plate of spaghetti, barbecue is everywhere, in every form.

The jury decided to focus only on sandwiches, and spent four months eating 500 of them, consuming an estimated quarter million calories. ("We did not want to be accused of being hasty, reckless, or shoddy in our work.")

The sandwich they liked best was John Wills'. Being Gridley's partisans (Gridley's sandwich earned sixth place), we hastened to Memphis to see about this piggy-come-lately. John Wills, we learned, opened his restaurant after winning the 1980 and 1981 International Barbecue Cooking Contests (held, natch, in Memphis). His restaurant is clean and modern, with none of the funky panache of the old-time pits, its wood-paneled walls decorated with handsome portraits of cows and pigs. But all is well, it is not so sanitized that you don't smell the hickory smoke when you enter.

As we watched in amazement, two dainty white-haired ladies at the next table gnawed with gusto on slabs of pork ribs, with side orders of gigantic, four-inch-across onion rings. We ordered pork and beef sandwich plates.

The pork is bathed with sauce, served on a bun pre-spread with pickly slaw. Wonderful, but it stops short of being the "ambrosia" that made *Memphis* magazine swoon. For us, the sauce is a little too . . . Carolinian, with more vinegar tang than one wants in Memphis. The meat itself, however, is unsurpassed—creamy chunks of shoulder, faintly smoky.

Brisket is even smokier, with a sharp wood-fire bite, spread out in thick, melting tender slices. On the side of a sandwich plate you get barbecue beans.

We followed the white-haired ladies' lead and ordered apple cobbler for dessert. Another giant-size dish, strips of crust spread over the hypersweet fruit, with vanilla ice cream melting fast on top.

We still like Gridley's sandwich better, but we would never kick John Wills' off the plate. Second best in Memphis, after all, would be blue-ribbon fare in any other town. (And if the truth be told, Memphis ribs are so much better than its sandwiches, than any other ribs, possibly than any other food on earth, that when we come to town we order sandwiches only as a chaser.)

The Little Tea Shop

69 Monroe, Memphis, Tenn.
(901) 525-6000

Lunch Mon.–Fri.

$5 or less

The Little Tea Shop, established 1918, is one of at least three restaurants claiming to be Memphis's oldest. It is an inexpensive lunchroom, yet the men and women who eat here are dressed in clothes that would fit in at a $100-a-plate New York power lunch. Not a pastel leisure suit or synthetic dress in the house. Of course not; The Little Tea Shop is right around the corner from Cotton Row, and still maintains an informal "Cotton Table" for traders and executives. Tables are Formica, but napkins are the softest white cloth.

The menu features three different turnip greens plates (with salt pork, onions, or baked ham) and specials like country fried steak (Monday) or catfish and chicken pan pie (Friday). The Lacey Special (named after C. A. Lacey, a famous cotton broker) is available every day: chicken breast and corn sticks topped with gravy, with rice and apple jelly on the side.

This is the only restaurant we know other than Mary Mac's in Atlanta where pot likker is always on the menu. It is a viscous brown-green brew, essence of boiled vegetables, its tonic potency perfectly balanced by the crunch and fluff of the sweet corn sticks that come with it.

The pork chop, a Thursday special, is fried to a soulful crisp; we got ours with a cheese-enriched soufflé called broccoli puffs. As is customary in southern lunchrooms, the menu features an all-vegetable plate: your choice of four from among the six or eight prepared that day. We loved the sliced yams, tender and festively spiced; the whole-leaf collard greens; and the fresh cabbage slaw with carrots and scallions.

For dessert, there is pie. Banana cream pie, a frequent special, is a flaky-crusted masterpiece, its tender custard decorated with sliced bananas. And there is fruit cobbler—a rich mélange of crust and fruit goo, insanely sweet, topped with thick whipped cream.

Memphians, even the foodniks among them, take The Little Tea Shop for granted. For the rest of us, it is both a fascinating glimpse of the classy, conservatively dressed cotton brokers, and a taste of southern cooking, equally untouched by fashion's whim.

Loveless Motel & Restaurant

*Hwy. 100, near exit 201 off I-40, about fifteen miles west of Nashville, Tenn.
(615) 646-9700*

Tues–Sat 8 a.m.–2 p.m. & 5 p.m.–9 p.m., Sun 8 a.m.–9 p.m.
Reservations advised

$10 or less

A "visitor's guide" in our motel room boasted that Nashville's restaurants have managed to attain a degree of culinary sophistication second only to Atlanta's. One soigné bistro advertised "continental services"; another touted its year-round selection of frozen fish from the many corners of the world.

It's fun to chuckle at the silly culinary culture-mongering, because we've got a secret. That secret is the Loveless Motel & Restaurant. While others dine on frozen fluke and have continental services performed over their food, we suggest you drive out to the Loveless, where you will have the best meal in town, at one of the great undiscovered restaurants of the south.

The food is pure Tennessee, without the pomp of nouveau Nashville. The Loveless is to southern cooking what the Grand Old Opry was to country music—before it became Opryland.

When you call to make a reservation, you will probably be asked if you are coming for fried chicken (a traditional summertime breakfast in Tennessee), so they know to prepare enough and have it ready for your arrival. The fried chicken is a superlative, light-crusted, juicy bird; but the best thing on the Loveless menu is the country ham. It is grand ham, ham you take seriously just by the way it looks: aged to a venerable brownish red, gently fried so the piping of fat around the edge turns the color of honey. It is chewy, bursting with flavor—food to be savored slowly, during a long, thoughtful meal.

The Loveless provides all the accoutrements for savoring. Along with the ham comes a bowl of red-eye gravy, a fetching blend of ham drippings and coffee. To keep the gravy warm, a plate is put on top of the bowl; and on this plate you will find biscuits—tiny round ones, still hot. Dunk them in the red-eye.

Or spread a biscuit with the sorghum syrup set on each table; better yet, try Loveless's preserves. There is peach—sun-colored, with chunks of fruit; and there is a spectacular berry preserve, made from glistening caviar-sized local blackberries. It is puckeringly tart, its intense flavor underlayed with a taste of smoke so distinct that it conjures up images of country women boiling down the fruit in big copper pots outside their mountain cabins. We bought three jars to take home, and used it to top morning toast and evening ice cream; and when the third jar was getting low, we simply took to spooning it up plain, no excuses needed.

The Loveless is a neat roadhouse perfectly preserved from the 1940s, a small wood-paneled cafe with checked tablecloths and fast, friendly waitresses who are happy to explain the difference between country ham and city ham, and who positively blush with pride when complimented on the deliciousness of a meal.

As we were finishing a Loveless dinner one night, we saw a flashy private motor coach pull up outside. Out of it stepped a troup of musicians who, the waitress whispered to us, were performing at Opryland that week. They filed into the cafe and gathered around a back table, where they always sit when they come here—which they always do when they're in town. On the way out, we noticed a clipping from the local paper tacked up in the cafe's vestibule. It was headlined "Funky Cafe Attracts Celebrities."

So you see, we lied when we said the Loveless Motel & Restaurant was our little secret. Actually, it's a favorite haunt of many country-music stars when they come to Nashville. They think it's their little secret. They know they won't be treated like royalty here—nobody is; and they know the food, like a country song, is honest and good.

(There is a motel behind the cafe, where rooms are cheap—about $20— but we didn't much like its looks.)

Mamie's

219 Madison, Memphis, Tenn.
(901) 526-2063

Mon.–Fri. 11 a.m.–3 p.m.

$5 or less

The day we ate at Mamie's, her son Charles was putting up the awning on her all-new lunchroom. It's fresh and clean and tidy, but Mamie Gammon is not a newcomer to the restaurant business. For years she ran a basement cafeteria just down the street, a favorite lunch haunt for downtown businessmen. Her mother, Lydia O'Kelly, used to sell hot meals out of a chuck wagon in a laundry on Beale Street. "People would come to us with empty plates, and we'd fill 'em up," Mamie told us.

Mamie is the kind of person you want filling up your plate. A cheery white-haired black lady in a starched white dress, she exudes cooking skill. As a restaurateur, Mamie is known best for fresh vegetables, fried pies, and low prices. Many of the recipes are her mother's: the candied yams, for instance, which she told us are cooked in a casserole without a separate glaze. "You save a pot that way," Mamie explained as we polished off the beautiful cinnamon-scented potatoes.

Turnip greens with pot likker and cornbread are on Mamie's menu almost every day. There are always hot rolls and corn muffins. Entrees are standards like fried chicken in giblet gravy, baked ham with pineapple sauce (real ham, not canned, the pineapple mixed with bits of parsley), meat loaf with mushroom gravy, or catfish. For a couple of dollars, you can make a lunch of three vegetables—greens, carrots, yams, beets in orange sauce, steamed rice, whatever Mamie can get fresh—plus banana pudding, strawberry shortcake, or fried pie for dessert.

Almost any Memphian can tell you about Mamie's fried pies. As a caterer, her pie-making skills are much in demand about town. At the restaurant she serves apple, peach, or sweet potato, the soft fillings encased in a crescent of lard crust, fried to a gold-flake brown. The frying crisps the crust, making it easy to hold. Fried pie, unique to Tennessee and Arkansas, is one of the best portable sweets there is.

Ridgewood Restaurant

Rte. 19E, south of Bluff City, Tenn.
(615) 538-7543

Tues.–Thurs. 11:30 a.m.–7:30 p.m., Fri. & Sat. 11:30 a.m.–2:45 p.m. &
4:30 p.m.–8:30 p.m., Sun. 11:30 a.m.–2:45 p.m. & 4:30 p.m.–7:30 p.m.

About $5

We have found perfection, and its name is the Ridgewood Restaurant.

It all started when we received a tantalizing letter signed "Bill Yankee," in which the author wrote, "As an avid Roadfooder, I've eaten a lot of bar-b-que, but the Ridgewood Restaurant in east Tennessee is the best. In fact, if you try it, and don't rate it four stars, send me your bill and I'll pay for your meal."

It was a no-lose proposition—we'd either eat great barbecue or get free lunch. There was only one hitch: Yankee's letter had no return address!

Still, the gauntlet had been thrown. We headed for the Tennessee Mountains in search of greatness . . . and now, Mr. Bill Yankee, Mr. Wherever You Are, we want *you* to have your next meal at the Ridgewood on us! Thanks for pointing the way to America's best barbecue restaurant. For this place, four stars hardly seem adequate.

The barbecue (or, as it's spelled here, "bar-b-que") is pit-cooked ham, hand-sliced into pieces of varying thickness. Some are soft and fall into juicy shreds as they are lifted by finger or fork; others, more resilient, yield their flavor slowly. Slices are rimmed with crunchy blackened edges singed by hickory smoke. Over the ham is ladled a glistening spicy red sauce, a sauce to take your breath away.

As you eat this barbecue, the taste comes on stronger. You eat faster; the flavors amplify, the sauce's mysteries deepen, and you are far away in a hickory-perfumed haze. This is barbecue to make strong men weep, mystical eats, a pig epiphany. Midway through the meal we looked up from our plates for the first time, staring weakly at each other, dazed and confused, in a stunning neural trance.

Mrs. Proffitt, who runs the parlor, knows how disabling this barbecue can be, because alongside it is served a mound of the best cole slaw we have ever eaten. Sparkling green and fresh, it is the smoke-pit fancier's sorbet, perfect for refreshing the palate between bouts with a mighty barbecue.

Also on the plate are great, droopy french fries, freshly cut and fried in clean oil, husky enough to have the satisfying, earthy taste of a good potato.

As if this were not enough, Mrs. Proffitt recently added barbecued beans to her menu, beans that give a whole new dimension to that humble legume. They come in a crock, in a broth laced with strips of ham, bits of sweet onion, and—the secret of their greatness—a dollop of Mrs. Proffitt's sauce.

A wonderful bonus, almost overlooked in our barbecue stupor: oven-hot Parker House rolls.

The Ridgewood's excellence in all things has been perfected over thirty-eight years. Every morning Mrs. Proffitt brews twelve to sixteen gallons of sauce. ("You can't do it in advance," she explained. "It's no good if it stands too long.") All week, her pitmasters work the pork over smouldering green hickory wood.

A comfortable restaurant, with a lovely dark wood slat ceiling, and a line of booths that provide a view of the grill and the waitresses at work. Mrs. Proffitt's veteran staff has changed little since 1948, when, she told us, "I used to have to drive up and down through the hollers to pick them up for work each day." They're an earnest group, these big old gals, most of whom echo Mrs. Proffitt's queenly proportions. They don't kibbitz or joke around; but there's nobody who can tote platters of barbecue with their aplomb.

The Satsuma Tea Room

417 Union St., Nashville, Tenn.
(615) 256-5211

Lunch only Mon.–Fri.

$5 or less

"Food can give such pleasure to life—comfort in sorrow, relief from tension." So begins *More Fun for the Cook*, a recipe pamphlet issued by The Satsuma Tea Room, where that philosophy reigns. Here is a thriving example of a style of downtown gastronomy in which the midday meal is known not as lunch, but luncheon—meaning not merely nutrition, but a civilized interlude.

The pleasure begins as you wait for a table in the vestibule, lined with an appetizing display of baked goods for sale: chess pies and lemon cakes, dinner rolls and cinnamon buns. Take what you want now. By the end of luncheon hour, they will likely be gone.

Downstairs is bustling. The upstairs dining rooms are quieter. Wherever you sit, luncheon at The Satsuma is a palliative hour of ladylike southern food.

Look over the menu, and write your own order on a small pad set upon the table. We love this system; not speaking the order frees us to list many more things than we would if we had to call them out. The waitress, in white uniform and red apron, looks over the list and doesn't even blink at four desserts for the two of us.

Fluffy cupcake-shaped rolls and corn sticks accompany meals such as turkey ala king (made with fresh mushrooms) served *en timbale*, or shrimp salad in a tomato. A vegetable luncheon of turnip greens, zucchini and to-matoes is spread upon a bed of warm noodles topped with poppyseeds. You can get a nice hot lunch like a pork chop, mashed potatoes, gravy, and a crabapple pickle, or filet of sole amandine with head lettuce salad; and there is a long list of cottage cheese salads, turkey, and tuna.

Wonderful frozen salads, whipped up from cranberry sauce and cream and cheese, then chilled until firm and served with fresh mayonnaise.

Satsuma's caramel custard is a soft pale pile of the meekest pap. Lemon cake is gentle, too. Prune cake is spicy, laced with shredded prunes. Chocolate pie, with its hovering meringue cloud and crunchy nut crust, is a stylish *coup de grâce.* There are fresh berry shortcakes and cheesecakes, but the single great dessert at Satsuma is ice cream: coffee-sherry or eggnog-sherry, pale and served nearly soup-soft, a sweet, comforting taste that summarizes everything good about tea-room dining.

Southern Grill

3553 Broadway, Knoxville, Tenn.
(615) 688-3600

Daily 6 a.m.–3 p.m.

$5 or less

Here is red-eye gravy to reckon with: cayenne-red, nearly orange, with a strong smoky bite. Spoon it up, touch it, and you feel how slippery it is—pure and delicious oil of oink. It's just about the best thing in the world to go with country ham and biscuits and a cup of coffee in the morning.

And how about these Southern Grill biscuits, with their broad golden top and white insides, ready to get dunked! Or pull one apart and insert a thin slice of brick-red country ham. It is salty meat with a good hard chaw to it, but fleshy enough to yield the most fetching nut-sweet flavor, especially in concert with the steamy-textured biscuits.

Or if you're in need of extra calories, dip the biscuits in a bowl of heavy cream gravy, flecked with pepper.

Traditional Tennessee mountain food, all of it, including morning prunes, served *warm*, like all good southern side dishes, and lunch specials such as pork tenderloin and chicken with dressing, creamed potatoes, and fried okra.

The Southern Grill is a large, air-conditioned rectangle with a few retro decorator's touches. Above our booth hung a bold impressionistic painting of a Spanish galleon, its impasto as thick as cream gravy. And next to that, in a variation of the maritime motif, was a stuffed catfish.

VIRGINIA

Brooks Restaurant

Rte. 11, Verona, Va.
(703) 248-1722

Daily 7 a.m.–dinner

About $5

Brooks makes a deliciously deviant ham biscuit called a "famous ham bun." They do away with the small powdery biscuit usually served with ham in these parts and replace it with a large, light bun made with eggy dough liberally saturated with butter. Like challah bread, the bun is sweet—a good balance to the salty ham, which is sliced thin and layered in the cushion of bread: a simple change from tradition, and a good one.

Whoever wrote the Brooks menu guarded his adjectives with quotation marks: "homemade" fruit cobbler, "fresh" strawberry pie, "our own" pecan pie . . . Do the quotes belie disbelief in the fact that such good home cooking still exists? It's a worrisome problem for mobile gourmands, but you can be sure that the food at Brooks is the real thing—beautiful cobblers made from scratch, exemplary pies, and that justly "famous" ham bun. No quotes are necessary.

Earl's Restaurant

Rte. 301, Port Royal, Va.
(804) 742-5769

Wed.–Sun. 11 a.m.–8 p.m.

Under $10

Earl's is the place that put Port Royal on the map . . . as the dominion of Pork Royal. A red brick highway cafe with a sow-shaped sign outside, Miss Piggy mannequin overlooking the dining room, and sizzling hickory aroma, it is an ode to barbecue. If you are heading south from Maryland on 301, it makes a grand appetizer to the state of Virginia.

Thirteen years of pork cookery are enshrined above the boomerang-pattern Formica booths: clippings touting the food alongside local news of all variety, the time a roving reporter on the trail of odd beer cans stopped to eat, Gene Autry's autograph on a pad from the Hotel Mayflower in Washington. These time-weathered pale green walls are a scrapbook of the lives of Earl and Eula Agee, who live in the trailer out back, behind their cafe.

Their pork is exemplary—coarsely chopped, infused with the smoke of the wood fire, bathed in a keen red sauce, sold as a plate lunch or a sandwich on a warm seeded roll, by the meal or pound. There is a full menu, too, of baked ham, liver and onions, and a highly recommended bean and pork soup; but the fact is that nobody comes to Earl's for anything but barbecue . . . occasionally barbecued beef, which isn't nearly as succulent as the pork.

Earl built himself a new pit recently, and he supervises all the cooking and makes the sauce himself—a demanding schedule, especially when no-show employees leave him and Eula all alone . . . as happened one Wednesday when we stopped by for lunch and found Earl's door locked. "If it can't be done right," he announced as he stepped from his trailer, eyes glowing like the coals in a stoked pit, "I close up."

The next day he was open, and crowded with loyal Port Royal lunchers who know him as the King of Q. If you are planning a special trip, call ahead.

Landmark Crab House

Landmark Plaza, Chincoteague Island, Va.
(804) 336-5552

Mon.–Sat. 5 p.m.–9 p.m., Sun. 1 p.m.–9 p.m.   Closed Mon. in winter

$10–$15

The view from the dining room is picture-perfect: the docks of Chincoteague Bay, oyster boats parked for the night. Around the Landmark is a deck for strolling and breathing sea air. Dining tables are highly varnished old wooden planks taken from fishing craft. The salad bar is a converted crab float; next to it sits an antique stove set with crackers. On the ceiling, a clam boat is suspended upside down. Very atmospheric, very "now," the kind of place referred to by people less grouchy than we as "fun."

What we find fun is good food, which the Landmark Crab House has in abundance. The first reason to come here is Chincoteague oysters, which, contrary to myth, always "R" in season. It's just that in the R-less months, they are thinner and more anemic, and generally aren't worth shipping out of town. In season, these are princes among oysters: beautiful giants, glistening gray laced with black; cool and tender. When they arrive on their bed of ice, you smell the sea. No oyster has as breathtaking a saltwater taste as the Chincoteague.

You can get them steamed, too, in a bucket, with a tub of melted butter and a slew of crackers—a simple preparation that tastes like rich man's food.

The Landmark's crab dinners are exemplary Norfolk-style seafood, sauteed and dripping with butter. Crab imperial blends crabmeat into a mild white sauce, studded with pimiento and green pepper, browned in a ceramic shell. You can also get fresh lump crabmeat sauteed with nuggets of strong Smithfield ham, served in a cast-iron skillet with four toast points. The salty ham and tender crabmeat are an incomparable combo. These excellent dinners were sided by a silly loaf of "home-baked" bread, the kind that chefs buy half-baked because it saves them the trouble of doing it themselves.

This is not our idea of a perfect restaurant. It is too popular, popular with tourists. Being perpetual tourists ourselves, we prefer the kind of place that makes one feel less like one of "them" and more like a townie, with all the rights and privileges thereof.

Tourists and bad bread notwithstanding, the Landmark's crab and oyster dishes are recommended.

Lockhart's of Norfolk

8440 Tidewater Dr., Norfolk, Va.
(804) 588-0405

Daily from 5 p.m.   Reservations advised

$15–$30

Up and down the mid-Atlantic coast, menus boast of Norfolk-style seafood; yet here we were, cruising Norfolk/Hampton/Virginia Beach one fine evening, unable to scrounge up anything better than deep-fried mystery fish, and giant eating barns full of vulgar vacationers. We gave up and headed for the highway, passing a windowless brown building with a small sign that said GOURMET SEAFOOD. Oh oh. "Gourmet": there's a word that's been on the skids for years, its pejoration absolute as soon as Tom Carvel applied it to his ice cream.

But we were hungry; gourmets we'd be this night. Leaving our *Roadfood/ Goodfood* notebook in the car, we entered.

Funny, Lockhart's doesn't *look* like a gourmet restaurant. It doesn't look like anything but itself, a culinary anomaly. Past wine- and beer-cooling cabinets, you enter one of several dining rooms with Formica tables, paper placemats, and cloth napkins. The rooms are dark and clubby, one decorated with nautical pictures, another with paintings of Rimbaud and Ezra Pound.

The menu is voluminous, eight pages (plus dessert, wine, and a ninety-brand beer list), including the history of the Lockhart Clan from 1329 (nearly everyone who works here is a Lockhart), a seasonal roll call of local seafood, and a sidebar called "Story of the Lockhart Steak." Each item is numbered, so that the waiters, boys in plaid vests, don't get flummoxed.

Crab Norfolk is just what we wanted: a ceramic dish filled with hot, sweet back-fin crabmeat, dripping butter. Simple and unsurpassable.

Equally elementary is flounder with crabmeat, a hill of fish that is poached, split, and stuffed, then broiled so the sweet slivers of crab are crusty brown on top (but moist inside). The flounder gets crisped by the broiler, too; its meat is firm and heavy.

Oysters Ghent is a wet, salty meal, heaps of buttery spinach topped with slivers of country ham, with tender oysters buried underneath. Under a menu heading called "Cloud-Light Frying" you will find crab cakes, tender beauties, mild and moist, dotted with green pepper.

Lockhart's won us over with its basic Tidewater repertoire, but who could resist sampling a dish called Super Sauton Picasso, "dedicated to the late Pablo Picasso, a work of art." It is a combo of crab, oyster, shrimp, and scallops in a wine sauce with mushrooms, pimiento, and the Lockhart's favorite cooking medium, "golden vegetron," the juices, according to the menu, "BLENDED AU NATUREL . . . not only for great taste but also for color, which stimulates the taste buds."

With each meal, you choose vegetables from an array of ten, including cinnamon-spiked stewed apples, pickled beets with fresh mint (from the garden behind the parking lot), tomatoes or creamed spinach, and, also in a tart shell, creamed corn that is so custard-like you could eat it for dessert.

Except for a billowy chocolate mousse, desserts are immemorial: brandied peaches, ginger pears, berries and cream, or a cup of hot wassail.

We still haven't quite figured out this eccentric place. We wonder about soft crab nouvelle, Paris bouillabaisse à la Johnny "served in a flaming pot," and the Scottish beer they were temporarily out of that night. Even if it does try hard to be fancy, Lockhart's has too much real character to follow the path of gourmet pedantry.

The Owl

Rte. 13, Parksley, Va.   North of Accomac
(804) 665-5191

Daily 7 a.m.–9 p.m.

$5–$10

We break our own rules—but not often. At The Owl, the rule about restaurants attached to motels went right out the window. The Owl would be a great place if it was attached to Ronald McDonald's shoe.

The Owl has been run by the Roache family for thirty-five years, with the same cook and much of the same staff for most of that time—long enough to earn them quite a local reputation as the place to find Tidewater cooking in a homey atmosphere.

To see what we mean by homey, direct your attention to the hand-tinted picture of the Roaches' sons over the counter, near the clock that says "Chevrolet time" on the dial. It's a mid-fifties shot of two kids with baldie haircuts wearing their best Roy Rogers suits. The cute boys grew up and now manage the place, no doubt keeping things just as they remember from childhood.

The food, like the atmo, is genuine old Virginia: sensational crab cakes, intense country ham, chicken, either deep-fried or, if requested, pan-fried. Pan-fried, the traditional country way, is better, raising a grand crust on the steamy bird. Chincoteague oysters, caught just miles away, are served fried in summer, and in an oyster stew when the weather gets cold.

The Owl claims to have invented french fried sweet potatoes. They are an autumnal dish, a refreshing change from the clichéed sweet glaze normally applied to yams.

Spoonbread is made nightly to be served with seafood; The Owl's formidable reputation is based in part on this luxurious, well-cooked grain. Although it's a traditional southern dish, spoonbread is a rarity. It requires a lot of trouble in the kitchen. The Owl's cooks eat trouble for breakfast— and serve great spoonbread for dinner.

We were alerted to The Owl by Virginian Edith Rosenthal, who told us we "would not believe" the chocolate rum pie. This is a confection you would expect to find in a much flossier place, not a motel restaurant. The chocolate filling is intensely rich yet not a bit gummy; it rests on a thin meringue, a lovely white-sugar crust that melts together with the chocolate as it's broken with a fork. Edith, we believe!

The kitchen produces a more-than-adequate sweet potato pie that is a pillowy pale orange and makes a nice if unorthodox breakfast along with coffee.

Even though it's next to the Roache motel, this kitchen's prowess with Virginia food is unimpeachable; The Owl is a restaurant to treasure.

Rowe's Family Restaurant

Rte. 250, two and a half miles east of Staunton, Va.
Exit 57 from I-81
(703) 886-1833

Mon.–Sat. 6:30 a.m.–9 p.m.

$3–$8

Staunton is the birthplace of Woodrow Wilson and the Statler Brothers, but we prefer to think of it as home to America's premier banana pudding. What a masterwork it is: crunchy meringue wed to a bed of moist banana cake, its custard lumpy with bananas. This is the definitive banana pudding of the south—soothing food for grown-up babies, food that assures you all is well with the world.

If there's no banana pudding on the day's menu at Rowe's Family Restaurant, perhaps—if fortune smiles—there will be mince pie, a fragrant fancy Mrs. Rowe makes when the weather is cool. Mrs. Rowe is a crackerjack cook, a wizard, a pie prodigy; her mincemeat is made from the best ingredients, including lean sirloin tips, local Johnson or York apples, and fresh-pressed cider. Topped with hot butter rum sauce, this magnificent dessert has no pie peers.

Although Rowe's is an efficient roadhouse where it is entirely possible to eat cheap and beat it, we suggest a long lunch. Before you get to the pudding and pies, backtrack and sample Rowe's expert version of the Virginia favorite, pan-fried chicken. It is breaded and laid in a cast-iron skillet when ordered. It takes a half hour, and is worth the wait.

One of the best dishes you can get at Rowe's is pork chops with baked apples. The chops don't look special; in fact, they're rather small and not too thick. But they are as juicy as pork can be, mounded high with slivers of baked Virginia apples. On the side, try the whipped potatoes. Dotted with tiny nuggets of potato yet unmashed, rich with cream and butter, these spuds belong in the *Roadfood and Goodfood* gallery of honor—perhaps next to the banana pudding, in the Hall of Comforting Foods.

There are lots of nice little extras about a meal at Rowe's: like warm chewy dinner rolls; or iced tea served in a carafe, "so you have enough to last through lunch," the waitress explained.

We could go on, dish by dish, but suffice it to say that anything you order at Rowe's will be good regional fare prepared with culinary skill close to genius.

Not long ago we heard a true story about a very pregnant woman who came to Rowe's, placed her order, then promptly went into labor. "I'm not leaving until I have fried chicken and mince pie," the woman declared. Her husband finally convinced her to go to the hospital, but not before Mrs. Rowe promised to bring her a plate of chicken after the baby was born.

Sally Bell's Kitchen

708 W. Grace St., Richmond, Va.
(804) 644-2838

Mon.–Fri. 8:30 a.m.–4 p.m.

Under $5

Our first books, about truckdrivers and roadside diners, got us a reputation as trenchermen on the prowl for heavyweight grub. Sure, on a cold winter day we like the blue plates piled high with meat loaf and mashed potatoes; but if our nerves are feeling delicate, if the world is brutish, if it becomes necessary to revert to our primal needy selves, what we really want is box lunch.

There is only one place to get it: Sally Bell's of Richmond, established 1926, originally called Sara Lee's, until the big guys made them change their name. You cannot eat in Sally Bell's; it's strictly take-out, bakery goods or the house special box lunch—a meal the likes of which all but vanished from the land about the time Mamie Eisenhower left the White House.

Inside your white cardboard box, inscribed with a Sally Bell silhouette, you will find a single sandwich on thinly sliced bread; a cup of tomato aspic or potato salad; a half a deviled egg, wrapped in wax paper; a crisp cheese wafer (no bigger than a quarter) with a pecan exactly in its center; and a cupcake or fruit tart.

The sandwich bread is white, crustless, elegant of crumb; fillings are demure portions of chicken salad or salty Smithfield ham, or arcane tea-time spreads like pimiento-cheese, cream cheese and nut, or olive-mayonnaise. We love the potato salad with its cucumber and onion crunch, and the sweet deviled egg that ineluctably conjures images of picnics long ago, but the cheese wafer makes us cry. So delicate, sadly out of fashion, with no place in the world outside this outré bakery, two little bites and it is gone; and you get only one in a box—a souvenir token of your visit to another era.

Lovely upside-down cupcakes, sides and bottoms glazed, but top bare: devil's food with mocha icing, or yellow cake with chocolate. Fruit tarts are made in fragile patty shells, dusted with powdered sugar.

While we itinerants confine ourselves to box lunch, people with homes come to buy gorgeous whole lemon chess or sweet potato pies, and (on special order) Lady Baltimore cake. Sally Bell's also makes beaten biscuits— crisp tan rounds with nine fork-prong marks forming a perfect square across their silky tops.

Southern Kitchen

Rte. 11, New Market, Va.
(703) 740-3514

Mon.–Sat. 6:30 a.m.–11 p.m., Sun. 7 a.m.–10 p.m.

$10 or less

It was at the Southern Kitchen we first tasted Virginia peanut soup. Now we were curious, many bowls later, to see if our beginners' enthusiasm over this modest cafe version of the venerable southern appetizer was justified. The problem was that we arrived in New Market at breakfast time. Appended to our orders of country ham and eggs was a plea to the waitress to see if she could convince the ladies in the kitchen to scare up an early morning bowl of the house specialty for a couple of peanut-crazy northerners.

The ham came first, and it was good: high-flavored, but not a bit dry or burned by its salt cure. We noted a cluster of hams casually hung up like coats on a standing rack near the door.

Mid-ham, the soup arrived, trailing a faint cloud of toasted nut fragrance. What is amazing about Southern Kitchen peanut soup is how light it is, how easy to eat. Make no mistake: it's a substantial bisque, enriched with plenty of butter; but it isn't thick; it doesn't weigh you down or bury your appetite for half a day. Velvet smooth and sweetened with bits of onion, this peanut soup is an elixir, still the best we've tasted.

If you try the soup when it is usually served, before lunch or dinner, you'll find what follows to be a medley of Virginia fare: ham in raisin sauce, pan-fried trout from the James River, fried chicken, and apple pie.

It could have been the friendly vibes of this small-town cafe or the soothing qualities of the peanut soup, but it wasn't easy for us to leave our pale green booth. We might have stayed till lunch if we weren't eager to get to the nearby Luray Caverns to buy postcards of our favorite tourist attractions —the Wall of Petrified Fried Eggs and the Mighty Stalacpipe Organ.

The Surrey House

Va. 10, Surry, Va.
(804) 294-9655

Daily 6 a.m.–9 p.m.

$5–$10 lunch & dinner, breakfast less

The menu at The Surrey House explains that "Peanuts are to Surry County what honey is to bees—our greatest crop!" The indigenous legume parades from the kitchen on salads, on desserts and in vegetables, and as peanut soup —in more guises than a Mr. Peanut fashion show.

Surrey House peanut soup is quite brothy, not nearly as butter-thick as the bisques found farther west. Garnished with chopped peanuts, it has a toasty taste, an appealing tan hue; it may remind you more of chicken soup than nuts.

A good follow-up to the soup is ham—pretty pink, scalloped with a thin ring of translucent fat around the edge. Because this ham has been aged only six months, a relatively short period for country ham, it retains its moistness and tastes a bit more like city ham than the scarlet jerky preferred by hard-core ham-o-philes.

Ham comes as a lone entree or with turkey and cornbread dressing; on a trio of yeast rolls; or with fried chicken. At breakfast, it is served with fried apples, or as the meat of eggs benedict.

Meals at The Surrey House are served with vegetables that are honestly garden-fresh, many pulled in fact from owner Owen Gwaltney's garden. Our waitress boasted that "Uncle" Owen had just harvested some fresh kale. She also told us that the kitchen had made apple fritters (small slices of apple deep-fried in a light crust, then sprinkled with powdered sugar). As we ate our ham, fresh kale, and fritters, a portrait of Uncle Owen smiled down beatifically.

For dessert, we returned to peanutville via peanut raisin pie. It was not unlike a pecan pie with a different nut, plus raisins, which lend it a red-brown hue. The brown sugar, the nuts, and the raisins were a stupefying combination—delicious, but nearly enough to induce insulin shock.

The Surrey's lemon chess pie is a slice of creamy egg and sugar filling finessed with a hint of citrus flavor. The crusts on both pies were not as light as they should have been, so we scooped out the excellent fillings, leaving two sad pale V's of dough behind.

The Surrey House is country comfortable: knotty pine paneling, blue and russet banquettes, brass railings, and bentwood chairs. We found the service solicitous, the waitress fretting over our abandoned pie bottoms.

PS: If you think peanuts belong only in peanut butter, The Surrey House will fix you up with the paragon of peanut butter sandwiches. It's a do-it-yourself affair with jelly, raisins, apple slices, cheese, a banana, bacon, honey, two kinds of bread, a jar of peanut butter, plus a small workbench cum cutting board on which to construct your own.

Virginia Diner

Hwy. 460, Wakefield, Va.
(804) 899-3106

Daily 6 a.m.–9 p.m.   Winter weekdays until 7:30 p.m.

$10 or less

For those with a romantic affinity for the American road as it used to be, this wood-sided diner is a vision. Casually arranged red-checked tables, stacks of souvenirs to take home from your visit to the "Peanut Capital of the World"; signs along Route 460 counting down, 12, 10, 8 MILES TO GO, and finally the glow of neon outside the dining room: all are talismans of a roadside culture that vanished long ago.

A waitress confides that the Virginia Diner—not the town of Wakefield —but this very diner, is the Peanut Capital of the World: "We were peanuts long before Jimmy Carter." Although superior nuts are sold in bulk and nutty souvenirs in abundance, the printed menu doesn't list a single nut dish available to be eaten here. But there *is* one, a doozy, the class act in this country cafe—peanut pie.

In concept it is like pecan pie—nuts and Karo syrup amber goo. The filling is sweet and gentle, sticky but not murderously gummy, a cushion for the nearly explosive crunch of the nuts. They are large, whole, toasty, resonating glorious goober flavor.

And there are more good things to eat: Virginia country cooking such as pepper-coated ham and fluffy biscuits, served with strong-flavored greens and a blimp of a candied yam; or fried chicken, the kind no northern cook, however skillful, can hope to make, its toasty moist meat encased within a crust of golden skin. And lamblike banana pudding, so much meeker than the pie, with crumbling wafer crumbs among the custard.

It's hard to leave without at least one bag of nuts for the road: shelled water-blanched beauties, butter toasted, salted in the shells, unsalted in the shells, or candied peanut brittle. Next to the cash register, customers help themselves to water-blanched jumbos as they pay their check.

These remarkable specimens make you think you have never before tasted a peanut. Each skinless tan seed is large and long, shatteringly brittle; but as you chew it, and as the earthy flavor blooms, the granularity turns to peanut butter . . . and so you toss down another handful, to relish that wicked crunch again.

Virginia House Restaurant

Rte. 11, Lexington, Va.
(703) 463-3643

Daily 9 a.m.–2 p.m. & 5 p.m.–8:30 p.m.

$10 or less

We had been on a pleasant regimen of fried chicken, spoonbread, and peanut soup when we sat down at a linen-covered table in this comfortable cafe. We noticed a tell-your-fortune scale in the vestibule. Michael put in a penny and the wheels spun round. What the future was, neither of us remembers; because the scale revealed that the man aboard had gained thirty-one pounds since leaving home, one week before. "I refuse to get on a scale that is obviously defective," Jane proclaimed, and so we never discovered what a week of Virginia's best had done to her. Nonetheless, it was clear a dash of moderation was in order.

We vowed to do as sensible professional tasters do, and merely touch ham biscuits to tongue. No need to eat four of them apiece to see how good they are! But, oh, these Virginia House ones *were* good—small, irregularly shaped biscuits sandwiching strong country ham; ham that struck a perfect balance between salt and sweet; ham with crisp ridges where it had fried on the grill and soft, juicy marbled streaks.

After finishing the ham, we concentrated on vegetables—always a good way to watch the waistline . . . except in the Southland. Our baked yams were succulent finger food, served without sauce, just buttery discs of sweet potato. Corn pudding was creamy and sweet and sprinkled with cinnamon, as were the tender baked apples.

Of course we had to order dessert; after all, it's our job to sample the Virginia House's versions of lemon chess pie and chocolate pecan. The latter was unusually moist, with a layer of grainy chocolate over the filling, and only a few token pecans on top. Chess pie is virtually unheard of in the north: a very southern combination of cream, sugar, eggs, and a little cornmeal, the result something close to hard sauce in a crust. Virginia House lemon chess pie was, like the chocolate pecan, extraordinarily juicy, the consistency of lemon sponge pudding with a macaroon crust. (Out of deference to our new diets, we ordered only one slice of each, and split them—just another sacrifice one must make for one's art.)

Deep South

War Eagle Mill
WAR EAGLE

Apple Village Restaurant
GREEN FOREST

Coy's Place
FAYETTEVILLE

Jim Lewis Cafeteria
FORT SMITH

Ozark Folk Center
MOUNTAIN VIEW

Catfish 'N'
DARDANELLE

Craig's Bar-B-Q
Family Pie Shop
DE VALLS BLUFF

The Hollywood Cafe
ROBINSONVILLE (5 mi, N. of H'wood)

Ruth 'N' Jimmie's
ABBEVILLE

Smitty's
OXFORD

Stubby's Hik-Ry Pit Bar-B-Q
HOT SPRINGS

Abe's
CLARKSDALE

Taylor Gro. & Restaur
TAYLOR

Uncle Mo
JA

ARKANSAS

Lusco's
GREENWOOD

Doe's Eat Place
GREENVILLE

Bob Sykes Bar
B

MISSISSIPPI

Stub's
YAZOO CITY

Waysider Restaurant
TUSCALOOSA

Weidmann's Restaurant
MERIDIAN

ALA

Lasyone's Meat Pie Kitchen
NATCHITOCHES

The White House
JACKSON

Bayless Restaurar
BAY SPRINGS

Mendenhall Hotel
MENDENHALL

The Dinner Bell
McCOMB

Mack's Fish Camp
HATTIESBURG

Cock of the Walk
NATCHEZ

LOUISIANA

Mosca's
WAGGAMAN

Wintzell's
Oyster House
MOBILE

Robin's
HENDERSON

Middendorf's
AKERS

Buster Holmes
Casamento's
Central Grocery
Chez Helene
Eddie's Restaurant
Galatoire's
NEW ORLEANS

Hop
Boar
H
PENSA

Boudin King
JENNINGS

The Cabin
BURNSIDE

Le Boeuf's
LAFAYETTE

Chez Marceaux
AMELIA

Morning Call Coffee Stand
METAIRIE

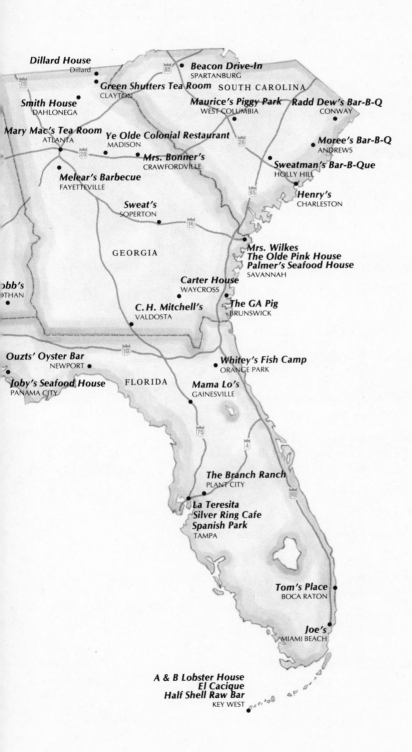

Dillard House
Dillard

Beacon Drive-In
SPARTANBURG

Green Shutters Tea Room   SOUTH CAROLINA
CLAYTON

Smith House
DAHLONEGA

Maurice's Piggy Park   Radd Dew's Bar-B-Q
WEST COLUMBIA   CONWAY

Mary Mac's Tea Room   Ye Olde Colonial Restaurant
ATLANTA   MADISON

Moree's Bar-B-Q
ANDREWS

Mrs. Bonner's
CRAWFORDVILLE

Sweatman's Bar-B-Que
HOLLY HILL

Melear's Barbecue
FAYETTEVILLE

Henry's
CHARLESTON

Sweat's
SOPERTON

GEORGIA

Mrs. Wilkes
The Olde Pink House
Palmer's Seafood House
SAVANNAH

Carter House
WAYCROSS

obb's
THAN

C. H. Mitchell's
VALDOSTA

The GA Pig
BRUNSWICK

Ouzts' Oyster Bar
NEWPORT

Whitey's Fish Camp
ORANGE PARK

Joby's Seafood House   FLORIDA   Mama Lo's
PANAMA CITY   GAINESVILLE

The Branch Ranch
PLANT CITY

La Teresita
Silver Ring Cafe
Spanish Park
TAMPA

Tom's Place
BOCA RATON

Joe's
MIAMI BEACH

A & B Lobster House
El Cacique
Half Shell Raw Bar
KEY WEST

Deep South Specialties

Where we list several places, we have starred the one we think best.

Banana Pudding

Hopkins Boarding House (Pensacola, FL)   228
★ Mrs. Wilkes (Savannah, GA)   245
Lasyone's Meat Pie Kitchen (Natchitoches, LA)   261

Barbecued Beans

★ Coy's Place (Fayetteville, AR)   218
Craig's Bar-B-Q (De Valls Bluff, AR)   219
Stubby's Hik-Ry Pit Bar-B-Q (Hot Springs, AR)   223
The GA Pig (Brunswick, GA)   240

Barbecue Salad—Lettuce salad topped with barbecued pork and sauce

Coy's Place (Fayetteville, AR)   218

Beignets—New Orleans' traditional breakfast pastry

Morning Call Coffee Stand (Metairie, LA)   264

Boudin—Creole sausage made of rice, pork, hot pepper, and in the case of boudin rouge, blood

Boudin King (Jennings, LA)   252
The Cabin (Burnside, LA)   254
★ Le Boeuf's (Lafayette, LA)   262

Bourbon Pie

Weidmann's Restaurant (Meridian, MS)   280

Brunswick Stew—A soulful brew of vegetables and pig meat, often accompanying barbecue

Dobb's (Dothan, AL)   212
C. H. Mitchell's (Valdosta, GA)   237
★ Melear's Barbecue (Fayetteville, GA)   243
Smith House (Dahlonega, GA)   249
Sweat's (Soperton, GA)   250

Catfish

Chess Pie—Elemental sugar and egg pie

Cobbler—Baked fruit dessert

Conch Chowder—The meat of the Floridian mollusk stewed with tomatoes and salt pork into a thick soup

Conch Salad—Like seviche; marinated raw conch

Cornbread

Fried Crawfish

    Boudin King (Jennings, LA)   252
    Chez Marceaux (Amelia, LA)   257
★ Robin's (Henderson, LA)   265

Fried Dill Pickles—A Mississippi delta specialty

    Cock of the Walk (Natchez, MS)   268
★ The Hollywood (Robinsonville, MS)   272

Fried Pie—Fruit filling in a fried pocket of dough

    Apple Village Restaurant (Green Forest, AR)   216
★ Family Pie Shop (De Valls Bluff, AR)   220
    Ozark Folk Center (Mountain View, AR)   222
    Boudin King (Jennings, LA)   252

Greens—Turnip, collard, or mustard leaves slow simmered with a hambone

    Ozark Folk Center (Mountain View, AR)   222
    Mama Lo's (Gainesville, FL)   231
    Tom's Place (Boca Raton, FL)   236
    C. H. Mitchell's (Valdosta, GA)   237
    Dillard House (Dillard, GA)   239
★ Mary Mac's Tea Room (Atlanta, GA)   242
    Smith House (Dahlonega, GA)   249
    Ye Olde Colonial Restaurant (Madison, GA)   250
    Buster Holmes (New Orleans, LA)   253
    Chez Helene (New Orleans, LA)   256
    Lasyone's Meat Pie Kitchen (Natchitoches, LA)   261
    Cock of the Walk (Natchez, MS)   268
    Mendenhall Hotel (Mendenhall, MS)   275
    Ruth 'N' Jimmie's (Abbeville, MS)   277
    Smitty's (Oxford, MS)   278

Gumbo—Creole stew thickened with okra and file powder

    Wintzell's Oyster House (Mobile, AL)   215
    The Olde Pink House (Savannah, GA)   246
    Boudin King (Jennings, LA)   252
    Chez Helene (New Orleans, LA)   256
★ Eddie's Restaurant (New Orleans, LA)   258
    Middendorf's (Akers, LA)   263
    Robin's (Henderson, LA)   265
    Weidmann's Restaurant (Meridian, MS)   280

Hushpuppies—Small deep-fried cornmeal balls

 ★ Catfish 'N' (Dardanelle, AR)   217
   Tom's Place (Boca Raton, FL)   236
   Whitey's Fish Camp (Orange Park, FL)   236
   Middendorf's (Akers, LA)   263
   Cock of the Walk (Natchez, MS)   268
   Mack's Fish Camp (Hattiesburg, MS)   274

Jambalaya—A Spanish-ancestored Creole stew

   The Cabin (Burnside, LA)   254

Louisiana Meat Pie—A large meat-stuffed crescent of dough

   Lasyone's Meat Pie Kitchen (Natchitoches, LA)   261

Mississippi Delta Tamales

   Doe's Eat Place (Greenville, MS)   270

Muffuletta—A huge circular Creole/Italian sandwich

   Central Grocery (New Orleans, LA)   256

Ogeechee Mull—A Carolina jambalaya served on rice

   The Olde Pink House (Savannah, GA)   246

Oyster Loaves and Po Boys—New Orleans–style hero sandwiches

   Wintzell's Oyster House (Mobile, AL)   215
   The Cabin (Burnside, LA)   254
 ★ Casamento's (New Orleans, LA)   255
   Chez Marceaux (Amelia, LA)   257

Oysters Bienville—Oysters richly sauced with shrimp, mushrooms, and wine

   Chez Helene (New Orleans, LA)   256
 ★ Galatoire's (New Orleans, LA)   259
   Weidmann's Restaurant (Meridian, MS)   280

Oysters Rockefeller—Oysters baked under a Pernod-flavored spinach sauce

 ★ Chez Helene (New Orleans, LA)   256
   Galatoire's (New Orleans, LA)   259

Pecan Pie

* ★ Family Pie Shop (De Valls Bluff, AR)   220
  Jim Lewis Cafeteria (Fort Smith, AR)   221
  Sweat's (Soperton, GA)   250

Picadillo—A Cuban meat hash seasoned with rice and olives

  El Cacique (Key West, FL)   227
* ★ Spanish Park (Tampa, FL)   234

Pork Skin—Fried and eaten like a giant potato chip

  Maurice's Piggy Park (West Columbia, SC)   284
* ★ Moree's Bar-B-Q (Andrews, SC)   285
  Sweatman's Bar-B-Que (Holly Hill, SC)   287

Pot Likker—Broth retrieved from long-simmered greens

  Mary Mac's Tea Room (Atlanta, GA)   242

Red Beans and Rice—New Orleans' traditional Monday meal

* ★ Buster Holmes (New Orleans, LA)   253
  The Cabin (Burnside, LA)   254
  Chez Helene (New Orleans, LA)   256
  Eddie's Restaurant (New Orleans, LA)   258

Red-Eye Gravy—Gravy made from ham drippings and coffee

  Uncle Mort's (Jasper, AL)   213
* ★ Waysider Restaurant (Tuscaloosa, AL)   214
  Carter House (Waycross, GA)   238
  Mrs. Wilkes (Savannah, GA)   245
  Smitty's (Oxford, MS)   278
  Stub's (Yazoo City, MS)   278

Red Rice—A low-country tomato, ham, and rice dish

* ★ Mrs. Wilkes (Savannah, GA)   245
  The Olde Pink House (Savannah, GA)   246

Rock Shrimp—Craggy-shelled Florida shrimp

* ★ Half Shell Raw Bar (Key West, FL)   228
  Palmer's Seafood House (Savannah, GA)   248

Shrimp Remoulade—Shrimp in a piquant sauce brewed from horseradish, ketchup, and spices

Chez Helene (New Orleans, LA)   256
★ Galatoire's (New Orleans, LA)   259
Weidmann's Restaurant (Meridian, MS)   280

Smoked Mullet

Ouzts' Oyster Bar (Newport, FL)   232

South Carolina Barbecue—Hickory-smoked pork, doused in a vinegar or mustard sauce, customarily served with rice and hash (a pig meat stew)

Beacon Drive-In (Spartanburg, SC)   282
Maurice's Piggy Park (West Columbia, SC)   284
Moree's Bar-B-Q (Andrews, SC)   285
Radd Dew's Bar-B-Q (Conway, SC)   286
★ Sweatman's Bar-B-Que (Holly Hill, SC)   287

Southern Barbecue—Smoked pork, usually basted with a sweet, pungent tomato sauce

Bob Sykes Bar-B-Que (Bessemer, AL)   211
Dobb's (Dothan, AL)   212
Coy's Place (Fayetteville, AR)   218
★ Craig's Bar-B-Q (De Valls Bluff, AR)   219
Stubby's Hik-Ry Pit Bar-B-Q (Hot Springs, AR)   223
C. H. Mitchell's (Valdosta, GA)   237
The GA Pig (Brunswick, GA)   240
Melear's Barbecue (Fayetteville, GA)   243
Sweat's (Soperton, GA)   250
Ye Olde Colonial Restaurant (Madison, GA)   250
Abe's (Clarksdale, MS)   267
Beacon Drive-In (Spartanburg, SC)   282

Stone Crabs—Florida crabs, claws only

A & B Lobster House (Key West, FL)   225
★ Joe's (Miami Beach, FL)   230
Ouzts' Oyster Bar (Newport, FL)   232

Streak o' Lean—Thickly sliced country-cured bacon

Waysider Restaurant (Tuscaloosa, AL)   214
★ Melear's Barbecue (Fayetteville, GA)   243

Stuffed Crabs—A Mobile specialty; crabmeat, bread, eggs, hot sauce, and peppers

Wintzell's Oyster House (Mobile, AL)   215

Sweet Tater Pie

Family Pie Shop (De Valls Bluff, AR)   220
C. H. Mitchell's (Valdosta, GA)   237
★ Mrs. Bonner's (Crawfordville, GA)   244
Mrs. Wilkes (Savannah, GA)   245
Buster Holmes (New Orleans, LA)   253

Trifle—A multi-layered dessert of pound cake, jam, and cream

The Olde Pink House (Savannah, GA)   246

Trout Marguery—A mélange of trout, shrimp, truffles, and mushrooms in a rich hollandaise-like sauce

Chez Helene (New Orleans, LA)   256
★ Galatoire's (New Orleans, LA)   259

West Indies Salad—Marinated crabmeat salad

Wintzell's Oyster House (Mobile, AL)   215

Types of Deep South Restaurants

Boarding Houses

Hopkins Boarding House (Pensacola, FL)   228
Mrs. Wilkes (Savannah, GA)   245
The White House (Jackson, MS)   281

Cafeterias

Jim Lewis Cafeteria (Fort Smith, AR)   221
Carter House (Waycross, GA)   238
Ye Olde Colonial Restaurant (Madison, GA)   250

Drive-Ins

Beacon Drive-In (Spartanburg, SC)   282
Maurice's Piggy Park (West Columbia, SC)   284

Family-Style All-You-Can-Eat (see also Round Table Dining and Boarding Houses)

The Branch Ranch (Plant City, FL)   226
Dillard House (Dillard, GA)   239
Mack's Fish Camp (Hattiesburg, MS)   274

Fish Camps and Catfish Parlors

Catfish 'N' (Dardanelle, AR)   217
Whitey's Fish Camp (Orange Park, FL)   236
Cock of the Walk (Natchez, MS)   268
Mack's Fish Camp (Hattiesburg, MS)   274
Taylor Gro. & Restaurant (Taylor, MS)   279

Grist Mill

War Eagle Mill (War Eagle, AR)   224

Grocery Store Dining Rooms

Central Grocery (New Orleans, LA)   256
Le Boeuf's (Lafayette, LA)   262
Doe's Eat Place (Greenville, MS)   270
Lusco's (Greenwood, MS)   273
Ruth 'N' Jimmie's (Abbeville, MS)   277
Taylor Gro. & Restaurant (Taylor, MS)   279

Hotels

Dillard House (Dillard, GA)   239
Smith House (Dahlonega, GA)   249
Mendenhall Hotel (Mendenhall, MS)   275

Oyster Bars

Wintzell's Oyster House (Mobile, AL)   215
Half Shell Raw Bar (Key West, FL)   228
Joby's Seafood House (Panama City, FL)   229
Ouzts' Oyster Bar (Newport, FL)   232
Casamento's (New Orleans, LA)   255

Pig Pickin Buffets

Round Table Dining

ALABAMA

Bob Sykes Bar-B-Que

1724 9th Ave., Bessemer, Ala.   Rte. 11
(205) 426-1400

Mon.–Thurs. 10 a.m.–10 p.m., Fri. & Sat. 10 a.m.–11 p.m.

$3–$10

We had polished off one slab of Bob Sykes's ribs and returned to the counter for more. "Honey," said the waitress, "ribs is like popcorn. Once you start eating them, you can't ever stop!" When the ribs in question are Bob Sykes's, truer words were never spoken. Ever since we first ate here in 1975, these ribs have set a standard against which we have measured all others.

When you walk into Bob Sykes, you can see the slabs of ribs, along with pork shoulders, roasting on the grate to the right of the order counter. They are mopped with sauce as they cook; the sauce glistens and turns to russet glaze. The meat is forked off the grate to be carved, still sizzling, its edges and tips blackened by the fire. When the ribs are cut or the shoulders carved, the pork yields wisps of sweet steam into the air; the smell inside Bob Sykes could drive a man wild with desire.

The ribs are southern-style, which means they are big and juicy and served drenched with red sauce. The slow cooking process results in a "skin": a tough, spicy crust that you can pull off the ribs in shreds. These shreds have a delicious crunch, but they are only the beginning; for beneath the skin, the meat of the ribs is drippingly succulent, with a sharp taste that is perfectly balanced by the sweetness of the sauce.

The flavors are intense; this is the kind of barbecue that builds in flavor as you eat it. At first it is very good; then soon you realize you have increased eating speed, and you are licking sauce off your fingers and worrying each bone more thoroughly than a happy dog. When you are finished, the taste of Bob Sykes barbecue lingers like the afterglow of great sex.

If ribs were all there was to Bob Sykes, we would choose it as one of the restaurants we'd want with us if we were marooned on a desert island. But there is more. First, there is sliced pork—available as "inside" meat (meaning just the soft, pale interior of the smoked shoulder) or "outside" (meaning lots of spicier crisp hunks from the part that has been brushed with sauce and touched by fire). Second, and maybe best of all, there is Mrs. Sykes's lemon meringue pie.

Yes, we know we gushed shamelessly about the ribs, but please believe us when we tell you this lemon meringue pie is one of the best in the pie-happy south. With its two-inch-tall unbelievably airy meringue, its tart filling as clean and pure as a fresh-cut lemon, its crust a bed of moist gingersnap crumbs, the pie is a perfect conclusion to a Bob Sykes meal—a soft, mellow variation of the sugar and spice theme set by the grand ribs.

Dobb's

Rte. 231 south of circle, Dothan, Ala.
(205) 794-5195

Tues.–Thurs. 10 a.m.–11 p.m., Fri. & Sat. to midnight,
Sun. 10 a.m.–11 p.m.

About $5

If you are in a hurry, Dobb's is the place to stop for barbecue. From 4 p.m. Tuesday through Friday and all day Saturday and Sunday, all you need do is pull into the parking lot and honk your horn. "Can I hep you?" drawls the carhop, at your window in a flash. And within minutes, you've got a carload of Q.

Table service is nice, too. It's a wood-paneled room with a few fish and antlers on the wall and baseball trophies above the booths. You can get barbecued beef, chicken, or pork. The pork is our recommendation, accompanied by french fries and finely chopped cole slaw, preceded by a bowl of camp stew. A Dobb's specialty, the lusty stew is a delicious variation of Brunswick stew, made from corn kernels, minced pork barbecue, and sweet tomato sauce.

The one dessert worth knowing about is strawberry shortcake, made on the spot in Dobb's kitchen. The pies, bought elsewhere, are no big deal.

Uncle Mort's

Hwy. 78, six miles east of Jasper, Ala.
(205) 483-7614

Mon.–Sat. 5:30 a.m.–10 p.m., Sun. 6:30 a.m.–10 p.m.

$5 or less

Breakfast has a bad reputation among travelers as a perfunctory meal: How do you want your eggs? Bacon or sausage? Ho hum.

But breakfast doesn't have to be a bore. At a place like Uncle Mort's, breakfast ("served anytime") is the best meal of the day.

As soon as you are seated in your ladderback chair in one of Mort's rustic dining rooms, it starts coming: hot coffee, sorghum syrup in little crockery pitchers, a bowl of red-eye gravy with its distinctive sweet-sour aroma, and a basket filled with large steamy biscuits. All this is the beginning of an "Uncle Mort's Special," which also gets you eggs and grits and hash browns (the least interesting parts of the meal) and a choice of bacon, fresh sausage, country ham, smoked pork chops, or smoked pork tenderloin.

Uncle Mort smokes his own. His pork chops are mild and juicy, the tenderloin ever so sweet. The country ham was pretty coral pink and tender, although not as strongly flavored as we prefer; those who find traditional salt-cured hams too powerful may find this one just right.

As you plow through breakfast at Uncle Mort's, coffee cups are constantly refilled, the biscuit basket replenished. You *will* go through biscuits. They are tall fluffy ones, with a crisp browned disc of crust at top and bottom, and airy centers just right for sopping up red-eye gravy and/or sorghum syrup.

It is unlikely you will be inclined to order dessert after an Uncle Mort's breakfast, so ask the waitress to wrap up a slice of peanut butter pie for later. It's made here, and it is delicious.

Uncle Mort's also serves normal lunch and dinner food like steaks, catfish, barbecue, and fried chicken. We've never tried any of it, and we don't know anyone who has.

Waysider Restaurant

1512 Greensboro Ave., Tuscaloosa, Ala.
(205) 345-8239

Tues.–Fri. 5:30 a.m.–11 a.m., Sat. 5:30 a.m.–noon, Sun. 6:30 a.m.–
1 p.m.   Dinner Tues.–Sun.

About $5

The Waysider is a pretty cafe in a little red house on the outskirts of Tuscaloosa. "Home cooked food served in a pleasant atmosphere" is the motto on
the menu. Breakfast is the specialty of the house; and in the south, breakfast
is always more than just a bowl of Total or a doughnut eaten on the run. It's
a big, hot, sit-down meal with ham and biscuits and gravy and grits and a
few cups of coffee. And it's a lot of conversation, too.

At the Waysider you won't find the customers hurriedly slurping coffee
as they rev up to start the day. Soft music plays on the radio. The cop over
in the corner, with his Electra-Glide parked outside, he's chatting with the
businessman in short sleeves and bowtie. Under the framed pictures of Bear
Bryant and the U. of Alabama football team are the Professor and his wife,
getting a second helping of biscuits to go with their third cup of coffee.
College kids and workmen saunter out the door, toothpicks peeking from
their mouths, satiated, calm, ready to take anything in stride.

A southern breakfast will do that to you; it's better than morning meditation or a five-mile run for lowering the pulse to near-lizard levels.

There is no breakfast more traditionally southern than streak o' lean, a
specialty of the Waysider seldom found outside home kitchens. It is four
strips of pork, each about the length and width of a slice of bacon, but cut a
quarter-inch thick. The slices are crisp, impossible to eat with utensils, so
you pick one up and take a chew. Unlike bacon, streak o' lean has a quirkily
diverse consistency. Each piece has veins of translucent, marbled fat that
melt away immediately; along the fat are streaks of lean, chewy pork, some
soft and juicy, others as hard as dried jerky. Streak o' lean is served with
brown gravy and—of course—biscuits.

No matter what you order at the Waysider, you will get biscuits: teeny
demure little fluffs of flour, light enough to be bench-pressed by a butterfly.
When you finish the biscuits (easy to do), more will be brought to you. There
will be a pitcher of honey on the table to go with them; and if you order
country ham, it comes with red-eye gravy (made from ham drippings and
coffee), perfect for biscuit-dunking.

Waysider country ham is the genuine article—dark and firm, with a
powerful lingering taste of the salt cure. For those with more delicate taste
buds, the menu offers sugar-cured ham, which is pinker and more tender
than its country cousin.

De rigueur in the south, and an automatic side dish on almost every

Waysider breakfast, are (or *is*, if you're a real southerner) grits, the coarse hot corn cereal onto which you put butter, gravy, or—as we saw one co-ed do here—sugar to bring them up to taste.

About the only thing that disappointed us at the Waysider was the cup of hot tea we ordered with breakfast. You see, down here people drink coffee. If you order tea, you get iced tea. Hot tea is an alien beverage. Our entire meals came to the table with admirable efficiency and speed, but the tea came in three parts, throughout breakfast—first an empty cup, then a pitcher of hot water . . . then, at last, a tea bag in a little dish.

Wintzell's Oyster House

605 Dauphin St., Mobile, Ala.
(205) 433-1004

Mon.–Sat. 11 a.m.–9:45 p.m.

$5–$10

Wintzell's is a restaurant for aficionados of bad taste and good Gulf seafood. You've got to like both to eat here. Even before you enter, you know you are in for something . . . different. DUNCAN HINES NEVER ATE HERE, a sign proclaims. EMILY POST FAINTED HERE, says another. And across the front of the restaurant are painted cartoons of three oysters—fried, stewed, and nude: the first in a frying pan, fanning himself from the heat; another in a bowl, holding a bottle marked "XXX"; the third standing in a shell, looking embarrassed and trying to cover up his private parts.

Inside, it gets much worse. Wintzell's is a pandemonium of little signs everywhere, over ten thousand of them, like IF YOU WANT HOME COOKING, STAY HOME, and I FEEL ABOUT DIETS THE WAY I FEEL ABOUT AIRPLANES. THEY ARE WONDERFUL THINGS FOR OTHER PEOPLE TO GO ON. Et cetera. Even the menu is covered with Mr. Wintzell's bons mots, such as:

The service, though it's slow and crude here,
It's slightly better than the food here.

Till now you've felt dismayed and beaten,
But you'll feel worse when you have eaten!

Dumb gags notwithstanding, Wintzell's food is tops. Oysters are opened fresh when ordered at the bar (where the stools have little signs saying THIS IS GOVERNOR WALLACE'S FAVORITE STOOL and FULBRIGHT CAN SIT ON A TACK and SPIRO AGNEW CAN HAVE THIS STOOL). On the half-shell, they are silky silver-gray beauties, served with ice sprinkled on and around them—a messy but delicious plate. (If, by the way, you break the record of nineteen dozen oysters eaten in twenty-five minutes, set in 1975, the oysters are free, plus you get $25.)

You can get a good West Indies salad (marinated lump crabmeat—a dish originated in Mobile), delicious little breaded crab claws, catfish (fileted) and hushpuppies, and a variety of excellent broiled fish. Wintzell's oyster loaf is a jumbo length of bread spread with mayo and relish, bursting with some of the best fried oysters you will find anywhere (including New Orleans). Gumbo is another regionally accented specialty, filled with oysters, rich and thick, speckled with rice. We also highly recommend the baked crabs—devilishly seasoned fresh crabmeat stuffed back in the shell.

Hung up among the silly signs is a clothesline with copies of Wintzell's two books (for sale, $2.50 each), *Oysters and Politics* and *Bits of Wit and Wisdom.* Mr. Wintzell himself passed away a few years ago, but the two long-standing (since 1938) Wintzell traditions of painful jocularity and the freshest oysters have both been meticulously maintained.

ARKANSAS

Apple Village Restaurant

Rte. 62 west of Green Forest, Ark.
(501) 438-5278

April–Dec. Mon.–Sat. 9 a.m.–6:30 p.m., Sun. noon–6:30 p.m.

Under $5

Apple, peach, and pear trees thrive in the idyllic rolling forest land of northwest Arkansas. Our favorite orchard is Norris Farms' 100-acre spread, where in the midst of the trees there is a restaurant specializing in apple dumplings, fried apple pies, and ham cured the old-fashioned mountain way with honey and sorghum.

The Apple Village Restaurant smells wonderful. It's a combination of apples cooking, beans baking, and the sweet scent of the curing ham, which you can see hung up in a smoky room, through a glass wall. It is a modern place, with paintings of apples on the wall and pretty country curtains, and a shop next door where you can buy an assortment of apple-themed gifts, as well as jugs of fresh pressed cider and, of course, bushels of apples.

There is a small regionally accented menu, including smoked ham and turkey sandwiches, and barbecue. But the best item is the apple dumpling, the specialty of the house, a rich compote of apples and spice and crust, served hot in a small bowl. You can get it topped with either melted cheese or ice cream.

Apple Village fried pies are unusually delicate, so limp they cannot be held in one hand (as is traditional with fried pies), but must be eaten with a fork. What they lack in portability is made up for by their delicacy. They are packed with dried-here apples mashed into a spicy sweet filling, a kind of Ozark blintz.

Catfish 'N'

Dardanelle Dam Rd., Dardanelle, Ark.
(501) 229-3321

Tues.–Sat. 4 p.m.–9 p.m., Sun. 11 a.m.–9 p.m.

About $5

The catfish is delicious—hearty steaks with a good snap to the breading, their meat luscious, gamey in an agreeable way, but absolutely fresh—like you'd just caught it yourself; but it is the 'N' at Catfish 'N' that makes it worth a detour off I-40.

For instance: hushpuppies, the traditional catfish companion. The ones at Catfish 'N' are moist and oniony, made of coarse cornmeal, so that when they are deep-fried, the outside of each hushpup toughens into a chewy skin with a sandy texture: sturdy food, downright audible when bitten into—a perfect partner for the country flavor of the fish.

French fries are special, too—thick cuts of potato fried only long enough to turn them tender, still tasting clean, like real potatoes, not grease. The sparkling cole slaw is just the ticket when you need a breather from the flavors of the fried food.

One of the nicest 'N's at Catfish 'N' is the setting. It is a tidy wood-shingle building overlooking the Arkansas River, with a view afforded by picture windows all along one wall. It is a functional restaurant, with Formica tables lined up in rows, and a buffet line where you help yourself to catfish and fixins, or fried chicken. A sign invites patrons to TAKE ALL YOU CAN EAT, but implores, PLEASE EAT ALL YOU TAKE, then warns, WE CHARGE EXTRA FOR WASTING FOOD. Catfish 'N' goes through more than a ton of catfish every month.

On weekends the lines to get into Catfish 'N' run onto the grass outside, which would be an easy, lovely place to linger if it weren't for the tantalizing odor of fresh fried catfish that emanates from inside.

Coy's Place

2601 N. College (Business 71), Fayetteville, Ark.
(501) 442-9664

Weekdays 11 a.m.–9:30 p.m., later on weekends

Lunch about $5, dinner $8–$15

We first came across one of the weirdest variations of American barbecue at Coy's Place. It is the Arkansan dish called barbecue salad: a chef's salad with lettuce, tomatoes, a few cold cuts, etc., covered with strips of barbecued beef or pork (your choice), then topped with either barbecue sauce or salad dressing (again your choice). We couldn't resist.

What arrived at the table is not the kind of salad fashion models eat to keep slim. On a large oval plate were plenty of greens and healthy stuff, covered with neat white slices of pork, the pork in turn completely covered with approximately two pounds of mayonnaise-rich Thousand Island dressing. This was not merely a large salad; it was one of the heaviest dishes of any kind we have encountered west of Pennsylvania Dutch country. We nibbled, then quit without making more than a short foray into the Thousand Islands. We wanted to have an appetite for Coy's non-salad barbecue, which is some of the best in Arkansas and the south.

Among America's myriad styles of barbecue—smoked over mesquite or black jack oak, doused with tomato or mustard sauce or no sauce at all—Arkansas's is the heartiest. It is mountain vittles, heavily spiced hickory-smoked pork, drenched in deep red opaque sauce, usually accompanied by pit-baked potatoes or sweet potatoes cooked right in among the coals.

And there are always barbecued beans; Coy's are exemplary—sweet and smoky, generously laced with chunks of ham and sausage and bits of jalapeno pepper, with a special brilliant verve that is unique to mountain cooking.

Coy's beans accompany enormous ribs, redolent of the green hickory wood over which they've been smoked, heavy with thick ribbons of meat on both sides of the bone. They are slightly fatty, the way folks around here like them. Another rich meat is Coy's sausage—bursting with juice, hot like a Texas link. For a leaner entree, we recommend the sliced pork. It is very mild, best garnished with an application of one of Coy's two barbecue sauces, both brought to the table in Grolsch beer bottles; the one with the rubber band around its neck's the hot one.

We tried a bit of everything on Coy's variety plate, and only the barbecued beef disappointed—too dry. Ours was a lunch meal, and although you can still order barbecue at dinner, the menu gets fancier at night, with offerings like hickory smoked prime rib and (with three hours' notice) quail wrapped in bacon, served on medallions of beef, topped with béarnaise sauce.

Coy's is a clubby place, somewhat labyrinthine without a view outside. Decor consists of walls lined with dozens of bottles of rare beer from around the world (orderable with your meal).

Craig's Bar-B-Q

Rte. 70, De Valls Bluff, Ark.
(501) 998-2616

Daily 9 a.m.–10 p.m.

$5 or less

"How do you want it?" we were asked when we stepped up to the counter at Craig's and ordered a plate of sliced pork and a sandwich. We didn't know how to answer until the waitress prompted us, "Mild, medium, or hot?" We chose a medium plate and a hot sandwich, and sat down at a table. It was lunchtime. Into Craig's streamed fellows in overalls, big pink farm boys, a couple hundred pounds each, ordering "extra hots," to go.

Craig's smells like great barbecue. Hickory smoke wafts through the gravel parking lot outside and permeates the air in the small white cafe. There is a distinct *feel* of great barbecue about the place, too—nothing mystical or abstract, this feel; it is simply the residue of the smoke pit clinging to the tables and chairs, making the marbelized linoleum floor slippery. Only Arthur Bryant's in Kansas City has a slipperier floor than Craig's.

Almost all the big guys sitting at the mismatched tables and chairs are waiting for carry-out; even if you want to eat here, your sandwich comes from the kitchen wrapped in wax paper and held together with a toothpick. Full plates, with slaw and beans, come in white pie boxes.

How the boys in overalls can take theirs extra hot, we don't know. Our sandwich—ordered merely hot—was lip-burning barbecue. It comes topped with slaw, which in this case is a good idea, a built-in balm that provides a cool balance to the fire.

Heat and all, the barbecue is delicious—lean slices of pork, well-spiced even before the pepper-hot sauce is applied. The sauce is lovely—granular, red-orange; at its best, we felt, in the medium incarnation. Although tomato-based, it is not at all sweet. Sweetness is provided by the barbecue beans that come on a plate—silky beauties with a pork flavor, the kind of great beans you get only in Arkansas.

For dessert, drive fifty yards across the road to the Family Pie Shop, which, in concert with Craig's, makes De Valls Bluff quite a culinary landmark in Arkansas, and a beacon for anyone traveling I-40 through the south.

Family Pie Shop

Rte. 70, De Valls Bluff, Ark.
(501) 998-2279

Daily 9 a.m.–dinnertime

About $5 per pie, 80¢ a slice

We have eaten Key lime pies in Florida and wild blackberry pies in Oregon, blueberry pies in Maine, and sour cream raisin pies in Iowa. But the place we like eating pies best is the south, where love of sweets vies with love of car and coondog as a regional obsession. (Only in the south could you find a candy bar called Goo Goo Clusters, advertised by the happy hedonistic slogan, "Don't say candy; say Goo Goo.")

Among the pie lodes of the south, Arkansas is the richest; and of all the great pie shops in the state, Mary's place—formally known as the Family Pie Shop—is without doubt the best. It is a humble setting for culinary grandeur, a converted tool shop behind Mary Thomas's house. Discarded furniture and kids' toys are strewn about the lawn. Except for a couple of rickety tables, there really isn't any place to eat inside—just enough room for a couple of ovens and some shelves to hold the pies. Most business is take-out.

Mary starts baking about 6 a.m., and by mid-morning, the pickup trucks and chauffeur-driven Cadillacs begin pulling into the scrubby driveway, most of the former buying by the slice, the latter by the whole pie.

Mary's pies are masterpieces, their white, toasty-crusted meringues artfully decorated with little swirling gridmarks made by the tines of a fork. The crust on the coconut, egg, or lemon pies is the lightest imaginable, a *mille-feuille* you would gladly eat by itself as a pastry.

We have never had a sweet potato pie quite so creamy, so perfectly spiced, with such a beautiful dark brown crust rising up high in a neat circle, taller than the filling.

By late morning, Mary also has the deep-fryers going to make the old-fashioned mid-southern specialty, fried pies—apple or peach.

If you order ahead, Mary will make a special pie she calls Karo-nut, a dark pecan pie made with Karo syrup. It is not available by the slice, and she doesn't make it regularly, she explained, "because the nuts are so expensive, I'd have to sell it for a dollar a slice." It's $5.50 for a whole pie—a fair price, we'd say, for America's best.

Jim Lewis Cafeteria

3400 Rogers Ave., Fort Smith, Ark.   In Park Plaza Shopping Center
(501) 783-4569

Mon.–Sat. 11 a.m.–2 p.m., 4:30 p.m.–8 p.m., Sun. 11 a.m.–3 p.m.

About $5

Many of us who grew up in the north had our only cafeteria experiences in the school lunch line, where the offerings were little more than cheese sandwiches or sliced turkey roll. But in the south, cafeteria-style dining reaches gluttonous heights. Take, for instance, the Jim Lewis Cafeteria. One pass through this line of foods is enough to make anyone who loves to eat weep for joy.

The first thing in line is salad—make that plural: salads. More salads than we ever knew existed: fruit salad; watermelon salad; spinach salad; salads made from cottage cheese, Jell-O, carrots, macaroni, and potatoes; three or four kinds of slaw; salads with little marshmallows on top.

After the salads come the entrees. Fried chicken is what we like best. Its dark crust is crackling thin; the meat tender. You buy it by the piece, whatever you like. Hickory-smoked steaks are a Jim Lewis specialty. The line moves fast, and the turnover is so quick that nothing seems to suffer the limpness of too long a stay on a steam table. The steaks are branded with crisp lines of black from the grill. The chicken-fried steak at Jim Lewis is a wide bubbly patty, customarily served with Texas potatoes—floppy cross-sections of potato, fried with onions until the onions turn into crisp little squiggles.

We won't even begin to enumerate all the kinds of fresh vegetables, boiled greens, sweet potatoes, and stuffings that you can get for side dishes, except to say: Get the fried okra. It is fresh and firm, with a cornmeal crust —a southwestern specialty done to perfection at Jim Lewis.

Next come the breads: wheat rolls, white rolls, corn muffins or sticks shaped like miniature ears of corn, enormous cinnamon twirls, irregularly shaped powder biscuits; or choose a whole miniature loaf of pineapple bread or jalapeno cornbread.

Unless you have a servant to tote a second tray for you, the only logical way to fit dessert among everything else is to return for it at the end of the meal. The one dessert that must not be missed at Jim Lewis is the Arkansas favorite, buttermilk chess pie. It is thick and creamy, like a translucent cheesecake, its sweetness offset slightly by a sour buttermilk tingle.

We also recommend the German chocolate pie, an incredibly rich concoction with a chewy top of toasted coconut and pecans. And don't miss the classics: pecan and mince pie, or the peach cobbler. We haven't yet tried Jim Lewis's chocolate icebox cake, or the apple pie, or cherry delight, or strawberry shortcake with whipped cream, or any of the puddings. Nor have we been inclined to sample the dieter's dessert—a tumbler of fresh strawberries, with a glass of Arkansas buttermilk on the side.

Ozark Folk Center

Just off Ark. 14, Mountain View, Ark.
(501) 264-3139   Main number: 269-3851

Summer daily 7 a.m.–9 p.m.   Shorter hours in fall and spring.
Closed Nov.–March

About $5

If we describe the Ozark Folk Center as a museum of mountain culture, don't get the idea that it is a dreary place filled with lifeless displays of the way things used to be. There are few museums more lively than this. Carved out of a hillside in the lush White River Valley, the Ozark Folk Center is an ongoing festival of folk music and dance and cabin crafts—including lots of country cooking.

The place is set up for visitors to wander the grounds and "stop in" at various rustic cabins where mountain folks are hard at work quilting, dulcimer-making, gunsmithing, canning, or baking. It's all quite informal, and as the lady at the woodstove finishes up her pot of greens and pulls the cornbread from the oven, she offers samples all around. One day you might get a taste of ham hocks and beans; another time burgoo or persimmon pudding; and there are almost always newly put-up preserves of peach butter or muscadine jelly for sale by the jar.

Outside the cooking cabin is a stand that sells traditional fried pies, either peach or apple.

There is also a restaurant at the Folk Center where it is possible to eat mountain cuisine such as chicken and dumplings, catfish, or ham and white beans and turnip greens. Some of the food here is exemplary. The cornbread that sides each meal is great hearty mountain eats; the white beans are nicely seasoned. Unfortunately, the mashed potatoes are bogus, some of the entrees little better than truck-stop chow, the morning biscuits only so-so.

One area in which the kitchen doesn't fail is pies. We tried a peanut butter pie that was sensuously creamy with the lightest possible crust. The meringue atop the coconut cream pie jiggled precariously as the waitress carried it to our table, and completely collapsed into an amorphous cloud of pure white as soon as it was touched with a fork.

After dinner, there is always lots of mountain music to listen to—concerts, shows, performances by young novices and old-timers, local people with rough rustic voices and famous country singers revisiting their roots. If you are a folk musician or would-be clog dancer, you will love the Center and the town of Mountain View. Most of the shows and concerts that seem to always be under way in these parts are so folksy that strangers are often asked to join in the pickin.

Stubby's Hik-Ry Pit Bar-B-Q

1000 Park Ave., Hot Springs, Ark.
(501) 624-9323

Daily 10 a.m.–8:45 p.m.

About $5

We like Stubby's style. When you walk along the cafeteria line, things get done fast, and they get done big. It is not possible to come to Stubby's and eat moderately; nor would anyone who loves great barbecue want to.

The line forms at the door. Ahead are the pit and the work area, lit by wire-covered work lights, the kind used by mechanics. Here, beef and pork are sliced, ribs chopped, all of Stubby's distinguished side dishes prepared.

The beef, on a sandwich or in a cardboard basket, is lean, moist, and strewn with "brownies"—the crunchy morsels of sauce-drenched meat from the outside of the brisket that singe over the hickory fire as the inside absorbs a fainter dose of smoke.

Stubby's ribs are nearly blackened by fire. They are crisp and chewy; you can pull long ribbons of pork from the bone—a tad dry as is, but perfect when dipped in Stubby's sauce, which is a fierce red brew, inadequately described on the label of take-home bottles as "catsup, vinegar, heavy spices."

There is nothing on Stubby's menu more definitively Arkansan than the ham and beans, which come in a prehistoric-looking stone crock. The ham is diced into crusty cubes, the beans long simmered in sweet molasses.

The baked potato epitomizes all that is good about Stubby's. For one thing, it's gigantic. For another, it's cooked in the pit, untouched by the hateful foil plague. What happens when a potato is cooked in this slow way is the skin absorbs all the smoke and turns tough. If you don't fancy potato skins, you won't like it. But if you enjoy a good flavorful chaw, it's a memorable delicacy. The inside of this spud is pure white creamy fluff. And finally, the corker—Stubby's knockout punch: the server cuts open the potato, and as steam escapes, he dollops on two full-sized ice cream scoops' worth of butter.

War Eagle Mill

Off Hwy. 12, War Eagle, Ark.   Thirteen miles east of Rogers
(501) 789-5343

Daily 9 a.m.–5 p.m.   Shorter hours in winter, Sat. & Sun. only in Jan. & Feb.

$5 or less

"Bring your corn and wheat to the mill just as your ancestors might have done 150 years ago," suggests the War Eagle catalogue of buhrstone-ground cereals, local honey, and preserves. Powered by an eighteen-foot redwood waterwheel, the mill is a picturesque restoration of a place that was once the focal point for the farmers on the War Eagle River. It is a peaceful scene, surrounded by fields with grazing cows, the river dotted with canoeists, swimmers, and fishermen.

Unlike our ancestors, those of us who visit the mill today can sit down to a good meal while our grain is ground. Above the old country store that now occupies the first two levels of the mill is a pleasant dining room, decorated with quilts and rag rugs and graniteware plates and platters (all for sale). The food is traditional fare, surprisingly homey considering that a majority of the customers are in fact tourists rather than farmers with sacks of corn to be ground.

Especially good are the breakfast buckwheat cakes, large discs with a heady country aroma reminiscent of Sunday mornings around a fireplace in a woodsy cabin. There are fine biscuits, too, covered with sausage gravy—a real rib-sticking meal.

The breakfast menu is discontinued at ten-thirty, replaced by lunches of smoked ham sandwiches on whole-wheat bread, beans served with triangles of moist yellow cornbread, fresh slaw, and oatmeal apple-sauce tarts or some other country-style baked goody for dessert.

The good food is presented on charming blue spatter-patterned graniteware dishes; iced tea, scented with sprigs of fresh mint, is served in mason jars.

FLORIDA

A & B Lobster House

700 Front St., Key West, Fla.
(305) 294-2536

Mon.–Sat. 5 p.m.–10 p.m.   Closed in Sept.

$10–$15

The A & B Lobster House is a genuine conch restaurant, meaning not only that the menu features dishes made from that tough mollusk that grazes in the coral reefs off the Florida Keys, but that it is run by Conchs—the name native-born Key Westers call themselves, presumably to identify with the tough character of the conch. In this case, the Conchs are the Felton family, who have run the A & B since 1947, and also operate the seafood market underneath the restaurant.

Conchs (the animals) are resilient bivalves reminiscent of their tough New England relatives, quahogs; and like the big downeast clams, they are best known as the main ingredient in a hearty tomato and salt pork chowder.

The choicest way to taste conch is to try the A & B's conch salad—a regional specialty unique to Key West. It is a tart marinade of raw conch in lime juice, with a few bits of sweet onion: an exhilarating dish, one to make you fall in love with—or swear off—conch forever.

You can get a less intense taste of conch in conch fritters—the Florida Key version of southern hushpuppies—for which the meat is chopped into a flour and egg batter and deep fried.

Another local treat featured on the A & B menu is yellowtail, a member of the snapper family. It is served here either broiled or fried, and while the fry cook has a light touch, we recommend you get it broiled, with a few almonds sprinkled on top. Yellowtail is one of the mildest fish in the ocean, clean and lean.

The A & B also serves stone crabs, boiled, either hot or cold, with the customary butter and mustard sauce condiments. Hot stone crabs are sumptuous food, especially if dipped in butter. Most people get them cold. Of course, you only get the crab claws, one per crab. The remainder of the animal is still in the south Florida waters, regenerating a replacement.

We'll admit that as New Englanders with a passion for the Maine variety of lobster, we at first had a hard time dealing with the Florida lobster, an overgrown crawfish totally lacking claws—and the soft meat contained therein. But we were quickly won over by the spiny lobster's taste. All you eat is the tail meat; it is not nearly as sweet as a Maine lobster, but it has a fetching oceanic succulence all its own. The A & B will boil it, broil it, sautee it, or smother it in au gratin sauce. We got ours broiled, which seemed not to toughen the meat at all.

To go with all this native food, the A & B offers its patrons a gargantuan fourteen-foot salad boat (for real) plus an unmatched view of the bay, shrimp boats and all, through picture windows on three sides of the dining room.

The Branch Ranch

Branch-Forbes exit off I-4, Plant City, Fla.
(813) 752-1957

Tues.–Sun. 11:30 a.m.–9:30 p.m.   Reservations advised

$7–$15

The great moment is the arrival of the tower of vegetables, five hot pans stacked nearly two feet high, set upon the table and explained by the waitress, one by one: baked yams, scalloped eggplant, yellow squash, chicken pot pie, and pole beans with ham and white potatoes.

In a separate basket, already on the table, are little golden biscuit rounds, warm and chewy. And to accompany the biscuits, orange marmalade, wonderfully bitter, with a powerful citrus flavor; plus strawberry preserves, packed with whole soft-textured berries, picked from local bushes. There is a salad tray, too, with genuine tomatoes, and there are pickled beets and crunchy bread and butter pickles, put up with lots of garlic and an alluring spice bouquet.

Everybody who eats at The Branch Ranch gets all of these things, as much as they want; plus, if you are so inclined, a slab of country ham or baked ham, or prime rib or fried chicken. Ourselves, we don't mind sidestepping entrees altogether (ordering the low-cost "vegetable plate"), although the chicken *is* good, so's the ham; but it's all the goodies on the side that have made The Branch Ranch a legendary groaning board.

Simple cooking, plain and good. The baked squash is just that—a big yellow squash baked whole in a pool of butter and milk: soft, comforting food. The yams are gigantic, fibrous, orange blimps. The chicken pot pie is a sunny casserole, shreds of meat and vegetables in milk gravy, topped with powdery biscuits.

The way the vegetable stack comes to the table, it is natural for one person to stand and dole out portions, just like at some mythical American Sunday dinner, the way it probably used to be in the 1950s when The Branch Ranch was Mary Branch's home, and she used to invite friends and neighbors in to share her bounty. Mary's reputation spread fast, and the Ranch grew, and now it's a huge place with many dining rooms and tourists and a million calling cards from around the country tacked onto every bit of wall in the entryway.

But it remains a lovely place to visit, a brief detour off the highway into a scenic countryside of orange groves and grazing cattle. And despite its size, it is an apotheosis of farm cooking, an honest country meal impossible to find anywhere else in Florida, a rare and genuine taste of the state bounty that somehow manages to get shipped everywhere else in the nation but to local restaurants.

El Cacique

125 Duvall St., Key West, Fla.
(305) 294-4000

Mon.–Sat. 11 a.m.–9 p.m.

$5–$10, Cuban mix sandwiches less

El Cacique is a cozy little joint with paintings of Cuba on the wall, hanging plants everywhere, and a menu of local seafood and Cuban specialties.

For a couple of dollars you can order one of the best Cuban mixes any-where—that distinctive latino variation of the hero sandwich. It is a wedge of toasty pressed bread packed with salami, cheese, ham, sliced pork, and pickles. On the side, try fried plantains, either ripe or green. To us, green plantains, a favorite Caribbean dish, are rather pointless; the ripe ones, on the other hand, are dark and sorghum-sweet, a good companion to whatever else is ordered.

El Cacique makes a sturdy conch chowder, the conch ground finely with bits of salt pork and small cubes of potato in a thick bay-leaf-accented to-mato stock. The fried yellowtail we sampled was sweet and flavorful, flake-apart fresh. Other local fish regularly available include red snapper and (are you ready?) jewfish steak—a lean white-fleshed member of the grouper fam-ily. With all dinners, you get what Cubans call Moors and Christians (black beans and rice). To add more variety to your plate, try *picadillo*, the Cuban version of chili, made with highly seasoned ground meat and olives.

If you call an hour in advance, El Cacique will put together a paella for two, which we are told by El Cacique regulars is the best dish in the house.

And for a beverage, although many here drink beer, we can never resist one of the creamy El Cacique fruit shakes—mango, guanabana, pineapple, or baby-pink mamey.

Bread pudding and balmy flan are the choice desserts.

Half Shell Raw Bar

#1 Lands End Village, at Caroline & Margaret, Key West, Fla.
(305) 294-7496

Daily 11 a.m.–11 p.m.

$5–$10

Here is the plainest of settings in which to sample the finest of southern Florida's specialties, the conch. Conch connoisseurs will tell you that the best way to savor meat from the hornlike mollusks that inhabit Key West's coral reefs is in conch chowder, a feisty brew of finely chopped conch, sizzled salt pork, and tomatoes. Steaming hot and briny with the taste of the sea, the Half Shell's chowder is the best we found along the Keys. It is chocked with conch sharing space with small potato cubes, a few grains of rice, and plenty of garlic. On the side, have conch fritters, in which bits of conch meat are mixed into a flour and egg batter and deep-fried.

During World War II, the Navy, on maneuvers off the Florida coast, picked up strange beeps on their sonar. The beeps turned out to be heavy concentrations of pink shrimp—known now as Key West shrimp, a heretofore untapped species of seafood. Shrimping became a big industry in the waters off Key West, and the Half Shell is the best place we know to taste its fruits. Rock shrimp, with their craggy shells, are a Florida specialty, more like crawfish or tiny lobsters: rich and buttery, much more luscious than ordinary shrimp.

Clams and oysters are always in season in Key West, sold at the Half Shell, on the half-shell, 365 days a year.

There are fancier restaurants on the island that serve native fare; but somehow the Half Shell Raw Bar seems like the right place to soak up Key West's raffish air while enjoying its unbeatable and unique seafood.

Hopkins Boarding House

900 N. Spring St., Pensacola, Fla.
(904) 438-3979

Tues.–Sat. breakfast, lunch, & dinner, Sun. breakfast & lunch only

$5 or less

One of your dining companions at Hopkins Boarding House will likely be a man who has stayed, and eaten, here for thirty-one years. If you are interested in a shorter visit than that, you can room by the week for $50, meals included (shorter stays are discouraged); or you can drop by any mealtime and enjoy an authentic southern boarding-house feast.

Hopkins is a grand old place in Pensacola's historic district, with tall ceilings and chandeliers and a few well-weathered great tables that accommodate a dozen at a time, with room in the center for large serving platters.

At breakfast, the serving dishes are filled with eggs done in various ways, ham, bacon, and sausage, bowls of grits, and baskets of warm biscuits. The turnover is fast; as soon as any platter starts looking sad, it gets whisked away in favor of hot-from-the kitchen replacements. If you want a limited breakfast, you can order a la carte, but where's the fun in that?

Vegetables are the featured attraction at lunch and dinner, a stunning array of fresh peas, corn, turnip greens, pole beans, squash casseroles, rutabaga, cabbage, rice and gravy, slaws, and salads. Toasty fried chicken is almost always the main entree, with a rotating selection of roasts, turkey, and barbecue as a second choice. Desserts are especially good: cobblers made with fresh blackberries or peaches; banana pudding; demure and delicious apple pie.

Lest you spend all your time passing things back and forth, a boarding-house reach is quite proper.

After dining at Hopkins, avail yourself of the preferred post-boarding-house-meal activity: find a rocker on the long front porch and while away some time.

Joby's Seafood House

1213 W. 15th St., Panama City, Fla.
(904) 785-2041

Daily 11 a.m.–10 p.m.

$10 or less

The specialty of the house at Joby's is oysters on the half-shell; you will find none along the Gulf that are fresher, cheaper, or more fun to eat. For oyster fanciers, each of Joby's tables is set with a pile of small paper cups and a lazy susan, laden with every sauce, spice, oil, condiment, pepper, and pickle known to man. Take a paper cup and concoct your own sauce while your oysters are being shucked. The dozens carried forth to your table are always immaculate—plump, sparkling baubles that hardly call for the mixological pyrotechnics encouraged by the condiment chemistry set.

The best thing at Joby's, other than the oysters, is mullet, prepared here the way Floridians on the Gulf Coast prefer—smoked. It is a rich, savory fish, and the smoking accents its flavor perfectly; you can get the mullet broiled or fried. The menu is all Gulf seafood: shrimp and snapper are specialties. Dinners come with hushpuppies, french fries, and cole slaw.

Joby's is an old place, casual in the extreme, and decorated to the hilt with thousands of special-edition Jim Beam liquor bottles. It has been a Panama City favorite for many years.

Joe's

227 Biscayne St., Miami Beach, Fla.
(305) 673-0365

Mid-Oct.–mid-May, Mon.–Fri. 11:30 a.m.–2 p.m. & 5 p.m.–10 p.m., Sat.–Sun. 5 p.m.–10 p.m. only   Reservations required

About $15

Miami is a city of extravagant restaurants: the fanciest French palaces, pricey Italian pavilions, boisterous Jewish delicatessens, plus Cuban places so Miamian that no gastronomic trip here would be complete without an excursion to Little Havana.

But what about indigenous Florida food in a restaurant with a Florida feel to it? For that, there is one place to go in Miami: Joe's, a.k.a. Joe's Stone Crab, named for its specialty, the uniquely Floridian stone crab claws.

Stone crabs are abundant in this part of the Atlantic, but they are hard to catch. They are mean, nippy creatures, and they use their considerable might to burrow deep into mud. When they are caught, only one claw is broken off; the crab is then thrown back in the water, where it will grow a new claw in about two seasons' time. All of this means that stone crabs are expensive—about $15 an order (five or six claws) at last taste. Joe's are the best.

Stone crabs are served cool, their tough shells cracked in the kitchen. They are pretty things, pinkish white with ebony pincer tips. A long fork is used to pull out the meat, which is sweet and rather lobstery in texture. There are two condiments: hot butter and cold mustard sauce. If you lean on the waiter, you can get hot stone crabs, more luscious, but somehow not as festive as the coldies.

On the side, get Joe's cottage-fried sweet potatoes or hash browns; and beyond crabs, there is an array of fresh Florida fish, plainly broiled: yellowtail, pompano, red snapper. For dessert, nearly everyone orders Key lime pie —too sweet for our tastes.

The purely regional menu is authenticated by Joe's old Florida atmosphere. On the southernmost tip of Miami Beach, Joe's is a grand old don of a restaurant that still manages the amenities that prevailed down here back in the 1930s, including a staff attired in tuxedos.

La Teresita

3202 W. Columbus Dr., Tampa, Fla.
(813) 879-4909

Daily breakfast, lunch, & dinner

$5 or less

Columbus Drive is known as Boliche Boulevard, an avenue of restaurants and grocery stores. The hot spot among them is La Teresita, a brickface cafe across the street from La Teresita Grocery and Fish Market. It is a bustling business, with a lot of razzle-dazzle going on behind and in front of its three horseshoe counters. Much of the commotion arises as the occupants of stools juggle back and forth so that large parties can all sit in a row. The chatter is in Spanish, and although a fair number of Anglos eat here, you will have trouble making yourself understood to the waiters if you don't know how to order your coffee "con leche."

If you don't get it "con leche" (half brew, half steamed, sweetened milk), you get a teeny-weeny cup of espresso "strong enough to make the rooster crow," according to a coffee hound sitting next to us. In the morning, La Teresita regulars come for double doses of killer coffee sided by lengths of toasted and buttered Cuban bread. For lunch, the Latin-flavored menu lists *carne asada* (pot roast), *ropa vieja* (flank steak), Chinese fried rice, and a new one on us, *trucha a la russa*, subtitled "trout in Russian sauce."

We were here for breakfast, but 9 a.m. wasn't too early to get a fine Cuban sandwich, hot and crusty, packed with pork, ham, salami, and a single slice of limp but not-quite-melted Swiss cheese.

As we left, we passed several small groups of men holding court in the parking lot, talking politics and smoking fat cigars.

Mama Lo's

618 NW 6th St., Gainesville, Fla.
(904) 372-3034

Mon.–Sat. lunch & dinner

Under $5

Mama Lo's cafe is a taste of the other, real Florida, neither the coast nor the Keys, but a tradition-soaked place where foodways are rooted in the deep-south soul-food kitchen. Although the cuisine and the staff are black, the restaurant is a favorite among both blacks and whites, students and townies, whole families who come for Sunday dinner six days a week.

It's a clean, whitewashed building with two small wood-paneled dining rooms, one with a pool table. There are only a few menus, to be shared among the clientele, because each is painstakingly hand-written (in ball point, on blue-lined notebook paper), and although this is a tiny place with a home-size kitchen, the menu is long.

One day last summer, the itemized list of vegetables included: collard greens, steamed squash, steamed cabbage, candied yams, string beans, broccoli casserole, baked apple ring, buttered carrots, okra and tomatoes, macaroni and cheese, baby lima beans, black-eye peas, mashed potatoes, whole white potatoes, fried corn, steamed rice, cucumber salad, diced watermelon, sliced peaches, corn on the cob, fruit cocktail, and tossed salad.

Each vegetable is served in a separate little dish, alongside a choice from a list of about a half-dozen entrees such as pork chops, baked chicken, chicken and yellow rice, smoked sausage and yams, chitlins, barbecued chicken. Every meal comes with a square of cornbread.

The pork chop arrives sizzling, dripping natural onion gravy, atop a mound of dressing. The chop is chewy and succulent; the dressing astounding, a peppery mélange of white bread, gravy, and spice, magically transformed into something delicious. You begin to think about the notion of an intangible "cook's touch," about how we could get the recipe for this dressing and make it and it would taste like wet white bread; but Mama Lo has the touch, and it is spectacular.

Smoked sausage packs a garlic haymaker, softened only a little by the sweet, spicy yams on its side. Chicken and yellow rice is a simple dish, but even so, it fairly oozes flavor. They don't call this stuff soul food for nothing.

No *al dente* vegetables here; as per southern custom, these greens, most of them from the farm market rather than a can, are *cooked*, then served awash in their cooking juices: pungent ham-flavored gravy for the collards; okra mixed with falling-apart tomatoes and corn kernels; silken lima beans in a salty broth; and glorious broccoli casserole, laced with yellow cheese.

The dessert we like is pound cake, a bland relief after the fire and spice of the meal. Coconut cake is good too, a big three-tiered slab with lots of gooey white icing. Peach shortcake suffers from spray-on topping, but at $3 for the otherwise impeccable feast, who's complaining?

Ouzts' Oyster Bar

U.S. 98 E, Newport, Fla.   At St. Marks River Bridge
(904) 925-6448

Daily 9 a.m.–9 p.m., Fri. & Sat. until 10 p.m.

$5 or less

A pint-size snack shack in a shady grove by the side of the highway, Ouzts' is our choice as the nicest place in Florida. Not necessarily the best restaurant, although there is no smoked mullet more delicious than what you'll get here; certainly not the most interesting menu, since mullet, plus shrimp and oysters, is all there is; but the kindest, the one we remember with the fondest memories, the one we most want to visit again. It's the sort of cafe that makes us happy to be on the road, experiencing places and people and food we would never know back home.

For atmosphere, you can't beat chickens and roosters pecking their way around the parking lot; or a dining room that is nothing more than a five-stool bar and two tables (set with hot sauce, crackers, toothpicks, and paper napkins), with good country music on the radio.

It was a dramatic day when we first stopped by. Four people at the counter and a couple at one of the tables were all filthy, covered with mud. But it was no reflection on their—or Ouzts'—hygiene. The foursome, all locals, had just pulled the couple's car out of a muddy ditch into which it had skidded; and everyone had come back here for beer and oysters, and to enjoy the glow of the good deed.

Mr. Ouzts himself soon appeared, an ancient mariner as gnarled as the shell of an Appalachicola oyster; and when we asked about the mullet, he told us he's been perfecting his smoke technique for years. "Bay wood and oak," he said. "They give your best flavor. Two woods I don't like—hickory and pine. They'll blacken the fish."

The chunk of mullet you are served (on a paper plate) appears dry. But as soon as you begin pulling pieces from the bone, you realize that the dryness is merely the smoky crust of fish. Its meat is sultry, not quite juicy but immensely flavorful, its natural soul powerfully augmented by the peppery tang of the wood fire. Sensational!

Oysters (at $1.75 a dozen) are fresh from the Bay, held in a small cooler chest until ordered, then swiftly opened and served on the half shell, aswim in their briny liquor. The other item on the menu is shrimp, either boiled or broiled, wrapped in bacon and brushed with garlic butter.

Beer and soda are sold by the can; and, as Ouzts' manager Sally Wagoner warned us, "Don't drink the water unless you like sulfur."

We ordered oysters by the dozen, and a chunk of mullet now and then, joining in the communal conversation (the place is too small not to), and stayed on for hours. It was the end of a long day on the road, and we had been tired, but by the time we left, we were totally revived by Outzs' food and hospitality.

Silver Ring Cafe

1831 E. 7th Ave., Tampa, Fla.
(813) 248-2549

Mon.–Sat. 8 a.m.–5 p.m.   Closed in July

$5 or less

Take a slender torpedo of chewy white bread, slice it lengthwise, stuff it with ham, salami, pork, and Swiss cheese, then toast it to a crisp. The result: a Cuban sandwich, known in Tampa as "a sandwich" (is there any other kind?) or "a Cuban."

A hundred shops in Ybor City, Tampa's cigar- and coffee-scented enclave of Cuban life, specialize in sandwiches; Angelo's Silver Ring Cafe has been making them since 1936, which is probably when the seafoam-green walls in the weathered luncheonette were last painted. The front is decorated with two bigger-than-life illustrations, one of an overstuffed sandwich, the other of a fat deviled crab. The enthusiasm of the artist for the astounding girth of both delicacies makes them look identical. Above the painted sandwich, in the storefront window, is Angelo's meat slicing machine. Here, throughout the day, you can stand on the sidewalk and watch the sandwiches assembled.

Next door is the Maniscalco Cigar Company (manufacturers of "El Coloso" cigars), and at 1815 East 7th Avenue is the Continental Deli, a slightly tidier sandwich shop (wood-paneled walls, matching orange molded plastic chairs and Formica tables) that makes its sandwiches with *baked*, not boiled, ham, and stuffs in about twice as much pork. Anyone intent on comparing all the Cuban sandwiches in Tampa probably ought to set their benchmark at the Silver Ring, but the Continental Deli cannot be ignored.

Spanish Park

3517 E. 7th Ave. at 36th St., Tampa, Fla.   In Ybor City
(813) 248-6138

Daily 11 a.m.–11 p.m.   Reservations advised

$10–$20

Walk along the street in Ybor City, and you will hear more Spanish spoken than English. You will smell cigar factories where stogies are still hand-rolled and coffee shops where the brew is so thick and black and strong that it perfumes the air. You will find a hundred small cafes serving the layered hero sandwich called a Cuban mix, or black bean soup with rice and onions, and dozens of good restaurants featuring Spanish food.

Our favorite place to savor Ybor City's foreign flavors is Spanish Park, where the Mediterranean kitchen does wonders with Gulf seafood. The menu is large, with nearly every native fish available, as well as Cuban standards like *picadillo* and the Tampa-Spanish specialty, chicken and yellow rice—a bird sauteed in olive oil, peppers, and garlic, then baked with rice and chablis.

The one dish that gets you the most different things all at once is paella, a jamboree of Florida lobster, snapper, stone crabs, and scallops, mixed with chicken and pork, and baked with rice, onions, pimientos, and peppers. It's good paella—completely local ingredients with a distinct foreign flavor—but you can do better here.

The best thing on the Spanish Park menu is actually the plainest—broiled pompano. To be any good at all, pompano must be utterly fresh; and here it is: broiled quickly, its flesh is nearly as firm as Dover sole. It is a classy fish, with a faintly sweet sea flavor. They skin it and bone it for you by your table, and serve it with lemon and butter sauce. Price varies with size.

You won't get the full ethnic flavor of Spanish Park by ordering broiled fish, but there are few restaurants that do it as well: grouper steak, red snapper, or a simple Florida lobster are all impeccable.

Shrimp Valdez, named after the family that has run the restaurant since the early 1930s, is a muscular dish: large Gulf shrimp are split and stuffed with ham and piquant Spanish sausage, then wrapped with bacon and deep-fried. Another invention of the house is Chicken Breasts Landeta, stuffed with sausage and baked in a tomato and wine sauce.

If you want to really eat ethnic, start with Spanish bean soup, thick with pieces of spicy chorizo sausage, then move on to the Cuban specialty called *picadillo*, a hash of ground steak, onions, olives, capers, and peppers baked in wine. On the side come fried plantains. Be sure to accompany your meal with sangría. At Spanish Park, they make it with the usual trio of wine, brandy, and triple sec, but use fresh orange and lime juice, and virtually no sugar. For dessert, get that soothing mild caramel custard called flan, or a good *arroz con leche* (rice pudding).

Spanish Park is a fairly fancy-looking place, with a Moorish tiled roof outside and arched colonnades in the dining room. Service is expert in a polished European way. It isn't cheap, but for a taste of Tampa's specialties, it is tops.

Tom's Place

1198 N. Dixie Hwy., Boca Raton, Fla.
(305) 368-3502

Wed.–Fri. 11:30 a.m.–10 p.m., Sat. noon–10 p.m.

$5 or less

Of course Florida's regional cuisine is mostly seafood—pompano, stone crab, conch, and the like—but it is also a very southern state, with some grand deep-south soul food, as found at Tom's Place.

Pit-cooked spare ribs are Tom's pièces de résistance: falling-off-the-bone tender, bright with a zesty mustard sauce. The sliced pork is good too, drenched with the vivid sauce, sweet and succulent. Get a dinner of either and it comes with french fries or eggy potato salad, and some of the best-seasoned collard greens you will find anywhere, powerfully flavored by a hambone in the boiling pot, then bathed in a peppery vinegar dressing. There are also black-eyed peas, buttered corn on the cob, or oniony hushpuppies.

Tom makes barbecued chicken, flavored with the same sauce used on the pork; and there is also a traditional catfish and hushpuppy dinner. On Friday and Saturday nights conch fritters are offered as an oceanic side dish. Tom doesn't bother making dessert.

Tom's is a plain bunkerlike place, a little difficult to spot. It's painted white; you'll find it just across the road from Florida Atlantic University.

Whitey's Fish Camp

2032 State Road 220, Orange Park, Fla.
(904) 264-9198

Daily lunch & dinner

$10 or less

Floridians call this style of food "cracker cooking" to distinguish it from the culinary antics brought to the state by northern retirees, vacationers, and Caribbean immigrants. A cracker is a down-home Florida native, what in other parts of the south might be a redneck or a coon ass; and a cracker's food is basically what he catches in the ocean, Gulf, rivers, and lakes.

For instance, turtle meat, small veallike chunks that are deep fried and served with cole slaw and hushpuppies; or 'gator tail, from the once endangered, now prodigal beast, also cut into bite-size chunks, tough and swampy-tasting.

Unlike frog legs in the other forty-nine states, almost all of which are withered little limbs imported from the Third World, the ones you are served at Whitey's are the actual legs of Florida frogs, big pairs of leapers with lots of succulent, tender meat. The catfish, too, is local and wild, its heavy meat fairly dripping flavor; none of those farm-raised, grain-fed blandies for these good old boys. Whitey's specialty is an "all U can eat" catfish dinner, with fries, slaw, and hushpuppies.

There is more familiar seafood on the menu, like shrimp, scallops, and oysters, all breaded and fried; or a length of broiled snapper; it is also possible to get a sandwich or hamburger; or to simply stop in for a Coke or beer.

Whitey's is a comfortable base of operations for the fishermen who moor and launch their boats outside and buy bait from the shed at the other side of the dusty parking lot. The interior, with adjoining bar and dining room, and molded plastic chairs at oilcloth-covered tables, is decorated in a style that might be called Winnebago Waterman, its focal point a large and some-what weatherbeaten trophy case display of especially large fish. On the walls are various stuffed whole creatures, fur and feather-bearing, even an ugly boar's head.

GEORGIA

C. H. Mitchell's

515 S. Ashley, Valdosta, Ga.
(912) 244-2684

Mon.–Sat. 8:30 a.m.–11 p.m., Sun. 3 p.m.–midnight

$10 or less

C. H. Mitchell's is a black-run place in a funky southern city, a magnet for street people, farm boys, and all Valdostans—black and white—who love great southern soul food.

Ribs are the specialty of the house, slathered with an opaque red sauce that comes on sweet and mild at first, then gains verve, until by the end of the meal your taste buds are ringing. The ribs are big bats, with plenty of juicy meat to worry over. You can buy them (or sliced pork or beef) by the pound, or on a dinner plate with rice, onto which a couple of spoons of hot Brunswick stew are ladled. On the side you will get rutabaga or a mound of greens, heavy in a pool of natural pot likker. Supplementing the barbecue on the menu is fried chicken; and for dessert choose peach or sweet potato pie.

On a steamy weekend night in the summer, the scene in and around this little restaurant is exhilarating—a lot of commotion, a lot of R & B music and neighborhood parties.

In the center of the hubbub is Mrs. Mitchell, a soft-spoken little lady who stands behind the carry-out counter, ruling over her helpers and a dozing pitmaster in back. Since most of the business is take-out, by the pound, there are only four Formica tables in the restaurant, but for dining ambience, there is no place with a more authentic south Georgia beat.

Should you want to take some of that great barbecue sauce with you, Mrs. Mitchell is always happy to rustle up an old juice or wine bottle, fill it up, and set a price.

Carter House

514 Mary St., Waycross, Ga.
(912) 283-1348

Breakfast Mon.–Sat. 5 a.m.–10 a.m., lunch daily 11:30 a.m.–2:30 p.m., dinner Mon.–Fri. 5:30 p.m.–8:30 p.m.

$5 or less

Carter House was the answer to a prayer, the prayer being that somewhere between Savannah and Valdosta we'd find something to eat. It was Sunday, and we were hungry enough so that just about anything decent would do; we didn't dare hope for that glory of southern gastronomy, a Sunday cafeteria line.

We almost passed Carter House right by. It scarcely looks like a restaurant—a big old white house with a front porch and a perfunctory sign that really isn't needed, since everybody who eats here knows where it is anyway. But we must have been living right that day, because something drew us inside—maybe it was the smell of hot apple cobbler or biscuits coming out of the oven. We entered through a hallway, and there it was before us: a buffet stocked with everything that small-town Georgians eat for Sunday supper after church.

It certainly isn't fancy. Honestly, it isn't even superlative food. There is better fried chicken at Mary Mac's, and if you look hard enough, you'll find fluffier biscuits; and we once had tastier fried okra at a cafe in Arkansas . . . but it is all good, prepared by people to whom cooking comes naturally.

We loaded up on fried chicken, and chicken and dumplings, and vegetables along the buffet line—black-eyed peas, macaroni and cheese, potato salad, crisp okra—and apple cobbler. As we reached for rolls, the lady behind us whispered, "Wait," and, figuring she had some good reason for doing so, we abstained. At the end of the line we paid the prix fixe for one trayful and found a place at one of the plain Formica tables-for-eight set out in the front porch (there are other tables in other rooms).

As soon as we were seated we discovered why we had been dissuaded from the rolls in the buffet line. Into the dining room walked a man in an apron with a basket offering chewy biscuits fresh from the kitchen; and he returned several times throughout the meal with a new hot batch. Our dining companions included an old man in his blue serge church suit, a mother and her baby, and an 18-year-old Georgia cop whose chivalrous table manners would have put Emily Post in the shade.

There was a lot of table-hopping going on at Carter House, people show-ing other people snapshots and making plans for later in the day or week; the tone was less like a restaurant than a big family reunion. Everybody knew everybody else, and the two of us—perfect strangers—were made to feel right at home. There is nothing like Sunday in the south, the day to gab and eat hearty.

Dillard House

Hwy. 441, Dillard, Ga.
(404) 746-5349

Mon.–Sat. 7 a.m.–9:30 a.m., 11:30 a.m.–3 p.m., 5 p.m.–8 p.m., Sun. 11:30 a.m.–8 p.m.

$10 or less

A madhouse, the vestibule jammed with southerners waiting for their num-ber to be called. When it's time, you are seated in the boisterous dining room, and the food is set upon the shared wood table. You didn't order this food; nobody *orders* food at Dillard House. You get what the kitchen has cooked, itemized on a blackboard list that changes almost hourly, as dishes are eaten up and new ones prepared.

We came late one summer evening, and so had a table all to ourselves. Here's what we got: crisp-crusted fried chicken; slabs of country ham; pork barbecue hand-hewn into luscious chunks, some crusty with pungent baked-on sauce, others limp and moist; rice and gravy; creamed corn; stewed apples; astounding acorn squash soufflé, laced with coconut and raisins; peppery steamed cabbage with a strange, almost dry, piggy texture; green beans, sliced tomatoes; biscuits; dinner rolls; and peach cobbler with ice cream. Iced tea was served in mason jars. $8.95 prix fixe, all you can eat.

In another setting, the take-a-number atmosphere would feel too insti-tutional; but here the big feed is fun, like going back to summer camp in the mountains, except the food is delicious, especially the changing array of soulful vegetables. When the serving platters come, everybody at the table digs in at once. Plates fly, and as soon as they are empty, waitresses refill them. You can't help but get in the spirit.

Visitors are prepped to enjoy this rustic meal by the drive to Dillard, a speck of a town in the north Georgia mountains. The miles around it are a little-known American landscape of winding cliffside roads and small wood cabins, waterfalls, and Appalachian hiking trails.

In fact, it is so picturesque that movie companies often stay here to shoot locations. Burt Reynolds' picture is on the wall to prove it; and Loni Anderson's, too. This place has been discovered, and tourists of every stripe come to enjoy the inn, motel, petting zoo, and horse stables. But don't be scared by the commotion; Dillard House food is real country cooking, no matter how much of it they dish out.

(Room rates are between $25 and $50, depending on whether you stay in the inn or a motel unit.)

The GA Pig

I-95 and U.S. 17 south, Brunswick, Ga.   Exit 6
(912) 264-6664

Daily 9 a.m.–9 p.m.

$5 or less

The setting is backwoods Georgia: a wood frame shack in a grove of sweet-smelling pines, a rail fence lining a walkway of cypress bark shavings, a handsplit wood shingle roof over a wide front porch. The GA Pig is as rustic a restaurant as you will find anywhere, yet it is only a few hundred yards from the Interstate, next to a gas station. HAVE THEM FILL UP YOUR CAR WHILE YOU EAT, says a sign inside.

The primitive atmosphere of The GA Pig is absolutely authentic, even if deliberate. Owner Ed Powers lists himself as "Franchisor" on his calling cards, but when we asked Mrs. Powers how many Pigs had been franchised so far, she told us "Two . . . but they both went out of business. Barbecue is a lot of hard work. You can't take any shortcuts."

Here at the one and only GA Pig, pork is cooked slowly over a fire of oak and hickory logs and brushed with a sauce developed by pitmaster Lawrence Williams. Because it is cooked in a brick oven rather than an open pit, the meat absorbs more smoke and develops a delicious nip. It is torn off the bone in big hunks, then doused again in the tangy tomato sauce, resulting in a just-about-perfect confluence of mild pork, sharp smoke, and sweet sauce, tender inside meat and crusty outside strips. We prefer GA Pig barbecue in this form—chipped on a platter with molasses-heavy baked beans, or on a sesame bun sandwich. You can also get ribs, which were not, to our taste, as luscious.

Dine at picnic tables inside or on the front porch.

Green Shutters Tea Room

Old Hwy. 441, Clayton, Ga.
(404) 782-3342

June 1 to mid–Oct., breakfast, lunch, & dinner daily except Sun. night and all day Mon.

$5 or less

It is a quiet wood house, painted white with bright green shutters, on a back road in the north Georgia hills. A split log fence runs along a meadow where horses and mules frolic. At the back of the house, a screened porch overlooks the meadow, and in the early morning, you can see the soft grass glisten with a halo of mountain dew.

Outside, a rooster crows, and hot biscuits arrive in a basket, each top browned crisp, insides all fluffy steam; with the biscuits, honey, taken from the hive just a week ago.

A breeze wafts through the porch: mountain air, carrying a wisp of sizzling country ham and hickory perfume from the wood stove on which everything at Green Shutters is cooked.

No, we didn't make it up; we wouldn't dare be so corny; it's all real. Biscuits and grits and country ham in the morning; family-style meals of fried chicken and cornbread and bowls full of fresh vegetables and fruit cobbler at lunch and dinner.

You can dine on the porch, with a panoramic view of the meadow, or in an inside room, its handful of tables covered with green-checked cloths. The room has a fireplace, which blazes in October when the air gets cool, making this a perfect biscuit stop for those who come to view the turning autumn leaves. Above the restaurant is a small antique store, and outside the dining room, a lovely little garden, which is a surreal mixture of real and silk flowering plants.

Built in 1934 as an apple stand, Green Shutters has an endearing home-spun personality. We especially liked our waiter, a shy lad who although he tried to walk as tall as a grown man, blushed terribly when his voice cracked.

Mary Mac's Tea Room

228 Ponce de Leon Ave., NE, Atlanta, Ga.
(404) 875-4337

Mon.–Fri. 11:30 a.m.–2 p.m. & 5 p.m.–8 p.m.

Lunch $5 or less, dinner $5–$10

Mary Mac's is a model of modern eat-and-run efficiency that serves some of the best oldfangled southern cooking in the state of Georgia. It is one of two restaurants we know where you can get the Dixie soul soup called pot likker, a virile spruce-green brew dredged from the bottom of the pot after greens are cooked with a cracked hambone. Pot likker is strong stuff: a brew to make you feel like Popeye the Sailor.

With hot corn muffins on the side (pot likker is always served with cornbread), a bowl of Mary Mac's pot likker is practically a health-food meal in itself. But we'd recommend you get only a cup. There are about twenty other great dishes on Mary Mac's menu that deserve a try.

The best among them is fried chicken—giant meaty pieces enveloped in dark gold crust. In all the south, there are no breasts more tender, no legs and thighs more succulent, no crust a more ideal balance between crunch and chew.

If you don't like your chicken fried, you can get chicken pan pie jambalaya, or chicken and dumplings with dressing, black-eyed peas, and okra. There are other genres of entree—country ham, snapper, steaks, and stews —but chicken, in all its many southern ways, is Mary Mac's forte.

What would a true southern meal be without plenty of vegetables? Mary Mac's menu lists about two dozen. A vegetarian could feast here; in fact, one of the choices always on the menu is a lunch or dinner consisting of four selections from the vegetable roster. Three vegetables come with any dinner entree, and for an extra 50¢, you can get a fourth. Be sure to pick sweet potato soufflé or corn soufflé; and try the fresh turnip greens. These are not what we get in diners up north when the meal comes with a perfunctory dish of some utterly boring good-for-you limp seaweed. They are vigorous, well-seasoned greens—like the pot likker, a genuine tonic. Navy beans cooked with hambone are another delicious surprise for folks not familiar with the glory of southern vegetables.

For dessert, choose from a familiar array of peach or cherry cobblers, apple brown Betty, rum-and-raisin pudding, or an item called Carter Custard, a velvety peanut butter concoction invented at Mary Mac's to honor the Georgia peanut farmer who made good.

Parties of five or more who come to Mary Mac's for dinner can save themselves the dilemma of choosing from the vast menu by ordering a country dinner. Everybody gets pot likker and cornbread, and the table is set with capacious platters of fried chicken, steak, country ham and red-eye gravy, hot breads, and a mess of vegetables. You are still required to select dessert.

At lunch, Mary Mac's—with a seating capacity of several hundred—is always crowded. There is a line, but the line moves fast. When you reach its head, you are led to a table in one of the enormous dining rooms. After making your selection from the pastel-colored menu, you write down your own order, which a waitress nabs without so much as a kindly "Hi y'all." She is back soon with lunch. The menu says, "Mary Mac's is the place for good food—for fast service. Mary Mac's is NOT the place for a leisurely luncheon."

The bustling new Atlanta that is Mary Mac's at noontime gives way to a slower pace at dinner. And while it's probably true that this food is best savored in the most relaxed setting, there is something ingratiating about the lunch hustle. Perhaps it's the utter lack of pretense. In some of Atlanta's more preciously southern restaurants, it is necessary to suffer endless Disneyesque dinner theater in order to get the "genuine olde timey Dixie cookin'." At Mary Mac's, there's not a bit of pomp. The food's the thing.

Melear's Barbecue

Ga. 85 (not the Interstate), south of Fayetteville, Ga.
(404) 461-7180

Mon.–Thurs. 6 a.m.–9 p.m., Fri. & Sat. 6 a.m.–10 p.m., Sun. 10 a.m.–10 p.m.

$5 or less

Our friends who have never traveled through the south think we are a bit nutty when we begin to rhapsodize about that wonderful southern specialty, iced tea. Tea (no need for the word *iced;* it's always served that way) is to southerners what wine is to the Frenchman, or Coors to a Coloradan. No meal, no lazy afternoon is complete without it.

The best place we know to gain an appreciation of tea at southern tables is Melear's Barbecue. The barbecue is A-1 regional food, and we'll get to that straight away, but first gaze upon a glass of Melear's tea. Yes, it is over one foot tall and a full six inches wide at the mouth. It contains ice and one quart of tea. Unless you specify differently, the tea is presweetened, intensely sugary. (Remember, Coca-Cola's home, Atlanta, is only a few miles north.) The menu, you will note, says "all you can drink"; and sure enough, all around you, as the men and women of Fayetteville eat their barbecue and Brunswick stew, they are getting refills: second and third quarts of tea!

There is nothing exotic about the way this tea tastes. You could make it at home; although, at home, you'd never have the nerve to sugar it so heavily —nor would you have the mammoth one-quart tubs; and to pour this tea into a six- or eight- or ten-ounce glass, well, that's about as gauche as serving champagne in a Dixie Cup.

The point is that, like the favored local soft drinks, Coke and Mr. Pibb, tea's sweetness goes perfectly with southern weather, southern food, and the syrupy tempo of traditional southern dining—all of which you will find in great abundance at Melear's Barbecue.

The barbecue is pork or beef smoked over hickory wood (with just a bit of oak thrown in for bite, according to Mr. Melear). It is served on trays in portioned plates along with chips, pickles, bread, and Brunswick stew. You can also get a sandwich, or what the menu lists simply as "bowl of pork." The Q is very mild; it is up to you to sprinkle on sauce, of which Melear's makes two varieties: sweet and hot. The latter is feverish orange, speckled with pepper, and has a vinegar snap.

After a couple of late-day barbecue meals, we stopped in one early morning for an equally classic southern breakfast of hot biscuits and sausage patties. The sausage was delicious—ground here by Kenneth Melear when he takes time out from tending the pit. The menu also features streak o' lean, pork strips that made us think of industrial-strength bacon—oinky thick and chewy.

The Melear family has been barbecuing for sixty-eight years. Kenneth Melear learned how to do it when he was 8 years old, and his place in Fayetteville is about as comfortable a restaurant as you will find for tasting what three generations of barbecue expertise can do to a pig. It is a neat rustic pork parlor with high-backed wooden chairs and aged wood tables, a counter, and a "Kiwanis Club Annex" off to one side. Next to the counter, right out in the open, is owner Kenneth Melear's desk, a command post from which he talks on the phone, oversees his restaurant, and holds forth on the mysteries of the pit. "I guess by now I've got barbecue sauce in my veins instead of blood," he told us.

Mrs. Bonner's

Monument St., Crawfordville, Ga.
(404) 456-2347

Mon.–Sat. 6 a.m.–9 p.m. usually, but call to make sure

$5 or less

Mrs. Bonner's is the closest thing we know to a time machine. Step inside and you are walking into small-town Georgia, circa 1926. That's when she opened her cafe (she was 19 years old) and that's when she started making the best sweet tater pie in the world.

What you eat here before the exalted pie depends on what Mrs. Bonner has cooked that day. It is absolutely traditional small-town cafe food, probably the same repertoire she had fifty-seven years ago: baked ham, fried chicken, roast beef, barbecue. There is always a slew of vegetables, depending on what the market has plenty of, cheap and fresh: field peas, pole beans, greens, corn, yams. At breakfast, most days, there are lovely little biscuits— unless Mrs. Bonner wasn't in the mood to make them.

It's homey, as loose and informal as can be. In fact, we recommend calling ahead if you plan to dine at Mrs. Bonner's, to make sure she's open and to see what she has prepared that day. Tell her you're coming, and if you are a large group, she'll serve it family style.

One thing Mrs. Bonner always has is sweet tater pie. You get a thin slice, barely an inch tall, atop a smooth light crust. The filling is autumn orange, beautiful and tender, with a wisp of smoke laced through a cloud of vanilla-scented sweet potatoes. There is a food writer in New Orleans who calls paradigmatic dishes "Platonic," meaning they are the best imaginable version. Mrs. Bonner's pie is indeed Platonic—although we doubt if even Plato's mom made it this good.

Mrs. Bonner's place is a tall single room with tables, booths and a counter, overhead fans, and a sign outside that says simply, CAFE. If you are a stranger in town, ask anybody where it is; when you enter, Mrs. B. will draw a bead on you; and if you're relatively well-dressed and well-mannered, she might tell you, as she told us, "You're mighty nice-looking people." From that point on, you're in fat city.

Mrs. Wilkes

107 W. Jones St., Savannah, Ga.
(912) 236-9816

Mon.–Fri. lunch

About $5

There is no sign at all outside Mrs. Wilkes's restaurant. Yet if you walk along West Jones Street a little past eleven any day of the week, you will have no trouble picking out which of the stately brick houses is hers. It's the one with the line outside, the line of Savannah cognoscenti and a few informed travelers who all happen to know—through word of mouth only—that Mrs. Wilkes serves the best lunch in town, one of the most bedrock southern meals in all the south.

Mrs. Wilkes's place is famous in an underground kind of way. She has published a cookbook, and in it are testimonials from the various likes of Richard Chamberlain, David Brinkley, and Lorne Greene. Even exalted food writer Roy Andries de Groot ate at Mrs. Wilkes and declared, "One could hardly praise the food too highly." Despite the accolades and the daily lines outside, success hasn't changed Mrs. Wilkes's place one bit.

When she rings the dinner bell at 11:30 a.m., diners are ushered in to one of several large oval tables and seated, boarding-house style, with strangers. (Before her reputation spread, Mrs. Wilkes's place was a boarding house, serving roomers only.) Mrs. Wilkes says grace, and then it's time to dig in. To the tables are brought platters of fried chicken, cornbread dressing, sweet potato soufflé, snap beans, black-eyed peas, okra gumbo, and what Monsieur de Groot called "the best homemade corn muffins and hot biscuits I have ever tasted."

There are always at least half a dozen vegetables; a few of our favorites with a distinct regional flavor include candied yams with lemon and raisins, green rice (with cheese and broccoli), brown rice (with bacon drippings and green onions), and that low-country standby, red rice (with tomatoes, onions, peppers, crumbled bacon, and parmesan cheese). The repertoire of entrees varies; in addition to fried chicken, standards include pork sausages with brown gravy served with hot peppered rice. Another time your choice might include chipped roast beef hash or country-style steaks, smothered in onion gravy, or a low-country crab stew spiked with sherry. So many of Mrs. Wilkes's customers are regulars, she has to vary the menu from day to day.

When Mrs. Wilkes sees that everybody at the table has eaten his fill, out come the dessert trays: fruit cobbler, banana pudding, sour lemon meringue pie, sweet potato pie, a delicious Boston cream pie.

The only restriction to a meal at Mrs. Wilkes is time. You cannot sit down at eleven-thirty and eat all day. In order to accommodate those waiting outside, there is an unwritten rule of the house that limits lunch to about thirty minutes. That way everybody has a chance.

When we asked her why she never put up a sign outside, Mrs. Wilkes said, "It would spoil the nice-looking street; this way it's more like home . . . don't you think?" No, it's more than that. It is a living sampler of the south's culinary heritage, one of the most authentically regional eating experiences we know.

The Olde Pink House

23 Abercorn St., Savannah, Ga.
(912) 232-4286

Mon.–Sat. 11:30 a.m.–2:30 p.m. & 6 p.m.–11 p.m.   Reservations advised

Lunch: $5–$10, dinner $15–$25

We had to make a choice. There was time and appetite enough for only one dinner in Savannah before we left. We had been to Mrs. Wilkes for lunch, and the night before we had driven out to Wilmington Island for a seafood feast at Palmer's. We had "done" Savannah well, except we still hadn't had a grand old south meal; where to go for low-country cuisine like Savannah red rice and okra gumbo, Georgia ham, or shrimp in Creole sauce? Or that favorite deep south dessert, trifle. In a city like Savannah, at least one fancy meal was a must.

Using other people's recommendations and our own goodfood-seeking radar, the choice was narrowed down to two: the Pirate's House and The Olde Pink House. The Pirate's House is the more famous of the two, and we arrived to find buses disgorging tourists into a souvenir shop clogged with people waiting to be called in to dinner. We had a drink in an upstairs lounge where water actually dribbles down from the ceiling (yes, on purpose!) accompanied by the recorded sound effect of thunder, simulating a storm at sea; we looked at a menu that featured cordon bleu and kabobs along with a few token regional offerings—and we went to The Olde Pink House for dinner.

Here at Reynolds Square was a real Savannah tableau: an eighteenth-century Georgian mansion, Jamaica pink, with a front porch on which gentlemen in rumpled white suits were rocking off their meals. We sat down in a dining room furnished with antiques, hurricane lamps, and portraits of colonial Savannahns. And we feasted our eyes on a menu that offered gumbo, salmagundi (salad), Savannah deviled crabs, and most of the classic coastal food we sought.

Dinner began with turtle bean soup, made not with turtle meat, but with firm, tasty "black-turtle" beans, cooked with ham hock, onions, and garlic, then seasoned liberally with lemon juice and cumin powder, and finally garnished with chopped hard-boiled egg, parsley, and a lemon slice. It takes the better part of a day to make this dense soup, perfected years ago by one of The Olde Pink House's veteran cooks; it is always on the dinner menu. We also tried riverfront gumbo, an explosively peppery okra-dominated mélange cooked with ham, chicken, and beef marrow bones. It came topped with crunchy colonial benne bit (sesame seed) croutons.

Following the soup came a recreation of Thomas Jefferson's favorite salmagundi (salad)—bibb, romaine, and spinach leaves mixed with sliced mushrooms and topped with a wine-accented cream dressing.

For one entree, we chose crab Savannah, a rich cheese and lump crabmeat casserole topped with mayonnaise and egg-white meringue. The other dinner was a combo platter, called "Georgian supper" on the menu—half-and-half baked ham and turkey in orange sauce, sided by a baked deviled crab cake. Other choices on the menu include steaks, "veal Thomas Jefferson," and "breast of chicken Queen Anne."

(The lunch menu is less grand, with sandwiches, a shrimp Creole dish called Ogeechee Mull, crab cakes, and meal-size gumbos.)

Along with lunch or dinner come puffy hot rolls, so aromatically yeasty you could get drunk just sniffing one; the dinners also included carrots in mustard sauce, yellow rice cooked in chicken stock, and what's listed on the menu as "mystery fried vegetable." We asked our waiter if it was rutabaga;

he looked shocked and told us we were right. But we won no prize for our correct guess.

There were only two desserts available. Both were wonderful. Ann's peanut butter pie is custard and peanut butter layered into a pastry crust, topped with whipped cream and crumbled sugary peanuts. Pink House trifle is the famous colonial cake and custard and whipped cream concoction, veined with raspberry preserves and flavored with sherry.

After polishing off this feast, we went out and took our places on the front porch, enjoying the afterglow of a genuine Savannah meal, rocking lazily in the warm summer night. We had found just what we were looking for.

Palmer's Seafood House

80 Wilmington Island Rd., Savannah, Ga.
(912) 897-2611

Sun. noon–9 p.m., Mon. 5 p.m.–10 p.m., Tues.–Sat. noon–10 p.m.

$5–$10

The good news is that since Watson's Crab House changed its name to Palmer's back in 1978, it has gotten much better. The new restaurant serves not only the well-spiced steamed blue crabs that made its predecessor famous, but also grand platters of rock shrimp, oysters, clams, scallops, deviled crabs, and stone crab claws.

The bad news is that Palmer's is hideously crowded at any hour that could possibly be thought of as meal-time. And they don't take reservations. Lunch isn't bad if you're here at noon sharp, and dinner at four is fine. Any other time, prepare for a good long wait. There is a pleasant patio outside, but even this fills up on weekends, and the overflow crowd lounges in the dusty parking lot, watching people try to squeeze their cars into a space. Actually, if you are not an impatient type, the marina where Palmer's is situated is a pleasant place to linger.

Once inside, you find a restaurant that offers seafood in a sleeves-up setting. Tables are covered with traditional crab feast nappery—daily newspapers, changed for each new group of diners. There are plenty of picks and mallets and nutcrackers to go around for extracting seafood from its shell. Like most eat-in-the-rough seafood houses, Palmer's is a boisterous place; and in keeping with its tone of largesse, platters are enormous.

We like the "shellfish combination" of hard crabs, shrimp, stone crab claws, clams, and oysters—a fine way to sample some of everything in its freshest form, without fancy flourishes; but even the fried seafood combo, which includes shrimp, oysters, deviled crab, flounder, scallops, hushpuppies, french fries, corn on the cob, and salad, has the snap of freshness. It is rare to find fried seafood so expertly breaded and so distinctive in its varying flavors. Palmer's tartar sauce is an especially good piquant condiment on the side.

Desserts are for gluttons only: huge hot fudge sundaes, banana splits, or hot apple pie a la mode, and the "coupe de goo"—hot fudge cake, a barge of cake and ice cream and whipped cream topped with nuts and cherries. When it comes to the table, heads turn; other diners laugh and point.

Smith House

202 S. Chestatee, Dahlonega, Ga.
(404) 864-3566

Tues.–Sun. 11:30 a.m.–7:30 p.m.

$10 or less

Dahlonega was the site of America's first gold rush in 1828, and there is a rumor that the Smith House was built atop an untapped vein. But it is not to strike it rich that people trek here from Atlanta every Sunday (there *is* a tourist attraction in town where you can pan for gold); they come to pig out, southern-style.

At the Smith House you eat your fill seated at a long wooden table with your family and with strangers. You all spend a lot of time passing platters and bowls back and forth, because the kitchen continues to bring out food as long as anyone at the table keeps eating. The Smith House began as an inn, and true to that bed-and-board heritage, there is no menu. You get whatever the kitchen has decided to prepare that day.

Even finicky people needn't worry. There is always a considerable choice. If you don't like the fried chicken with its buttery crust, perhaps Brunswick stew or pork chops with wild rice will appeal. The kitchen's strong suits include "cola roast" (yup, beef basted in Coke, a favorite trick of southern cooks ever since Coke was invented), buttermilk-baked chicken, ham and dumplings, and (on Fridays only) whole catfish and hushpuppies.

Constellations of vegetable bowls circle each table. The very best of them (and one that is almost always on the menu) is chestnut soufflé, a brandy-scented confection sprinkled with powdered sugar. Candied yams are another regular item, as are turnip greens, hominy, and fried okra. Pumpkin fritters are served with a choice of syrup or honey.

As far back as the 1940s, Smith House was known for its angel biscuits, small buttermilky circles with a slightly sour undertaste. If they are not on that day's agenda, perhaps there will be sweet potato biscuits, or cracklin cornbread or blueberry lemon muffins. Yeast rolls are always on the table.

Cobblers, made from apples in the fall, strawberries in the summer, are a traditional southern dessert, and the peach cobbler we had at Smith House was rich and satisfying—although one fellow at our table would not shut up about the great fried bananas he had been served here the week before.

Smith House is legendary for its feasts, and Dahlonega's gold is quite a magnet for tourists, so the crowds can be discouraging, especially on weekends. (No reservations are accepted: it's first come, first served.)

There is cafeteria service during the week for those who prefer portioned meals over infinite ones. Should you be unable to ambulate after whaling down a Smith House dinner, the hotel upstairs has some charming rustic rooms available for between $25 and $50.

Sweat's

I-16 at GA 29, Soperton, Ga.
(912) 529-3637

Mon.–Sat. 10:30 a.m.–9 p.m., Sun. 3 p.m.–9 p.m.

$5 or less

The Sweat's name means barbecue in Soperton, and the fact that the once-ramshackle smoke shack is now a modern cinderblock rectangle near the highway, with Formica tables and wood paneling and a salad bar for those who come for steak or shrimp, doesn't in any way diminish the deserved renown of the barbecue.

The partitioned plate comes piled high with pork, lean zesty shreds, lots of outside pieces permeated with smoke flavor. Each table has a rack of sauce and spices to customize it to your liking. The second third of the plate will contain an ice cream scoop of good slaw or potato salad; and the last indentation holds Brunswick stew—carrots, peas, chunks of meat, little nubbins of potato in a peppery sauce. White bread comes on the side.

Sweat's pecan pie is shockingly thin, not more than a half inch tall; but it's dynamite, powerfully rich and southern, heaps of chopped pecans atop the sticky amber filling, a fine flaky crust below.

Ye Olde Colonial Restaurant

108 E. Washington St., Madison, Ga.
(404) 342-2211

Mon.–Sat. breakfast, lunch, & dinner

$5 or less

Some restaurants cry out to be sampled; other less likely-looking spots are passed word-of-mouth among cognoscenti. Then there are the places that look like nothing, that nobody has ever heard of, that a person accidentally wanders into because there is no place else to go. If one of these turns out good, we feel like a dowser who's just hit water, and get all smug about our wonderful and mysterious *Roadfood and Goodfood* radar.

So it happened in Madison, Georgia, a speck of a town we had known previously only for its offbeat religious art environment called Space View, "the park that promises you a future."

As New Englanders who have seen our share of Ye Olde Colonialoid Eating Emporia, we were doubly dubious about the gothic-lettered sign on the town square. But the moment we entered, we knew we had hit paydirt.

Here is the nice place in town, where good people get in the cafeteria line and load up their trays with wonderful southern cafe food like pork chops and cornbread and all kinds of vegetable casseroles. It is a large, two-room place, the main dining room a former bank, with fine wood paneling, red flocked wallpaper, and high arched windows looking out on the street. There are some booths, and several large round tables in the center of the room, shared by customers, all of whom know each other.

We passed the fried fish filets and baked chicken, stopping in line for a mound of pork barbecue, torn into shreds and doused with a pungent sauce. On the side we got corn sticks, pencil-thin and crunchy, and collard greens drenched in pot likker, dotted with salty bits of ham. There was a fine squash casserole, of custard consistency; smoky yams; and a major rutabaga casserole—strong and spicy, with an alluring sour undertaste. Dessert is thick fruit cobbler, either apple or strawberry. Pitchers of iced tea, presweetened of course, are on every table.

Pay at the cash register on the way out. Behind the cashier are bins full of yams, squash, onions, and the like—still farm-dirty, ready to be carried back to the kitchen.

LOUISIANA

Boudin King

906 W. Division St., Jennings, La.
(318) 824-6593

Mon.–Sat. 8 a.m.–9 p.m.

$5 or less

Descendant of boudin blanc, the sausage that Frenchmen eat on Christmas Eve and other festive occasions, Cajun boudin has gained considerable zest in its long gastronomic journey from France to Acadie (now called Nova Scotia) to the Louisiana bayous. While the French progenitor is customarily made from a bland amalgam of chicken, cream, and a little pork, the Cajun version is a cayenne and black pepper bomb of pork, liver, kidneys, heart, and Louisiana rice.

"Nowhere else in America, except perhaps where the Mexicans live, is food properly spiced," Ellis Cormier declared. Cormier is the owner/chef of Boudin King, one of Louisiana's oddest restaurants. His boudin comes either mild or hot, but you must realize that the Cajun scale of hotness starts several notches higher than anywhere other than New Mexico. It is steamed and served warm, by the link, like kielbasa: a lusty taste of Cajun soul.

The peculiar thing about Boudin King is that it operates like a fast-food hamburger joint, complete with plastic plates, drive-through window, and separate order and pick-up areas. Yet the boudin is absolutely authentic— you can see them stuffing it behind the counter—and the rest of Boudin King's menu is a sampler of well-made Cajun specialties. Only in Louisiana would you find such a happy marriage of complex cuisine and customer management technology.

Hog's head cheese is sold by the pound; there are fried crawfish tails in the spring; Cormier's chicken and sausage gumbo is a smoky marvel, subtle and sophisticated—plastic spoon notwithstanding. Even the patented and elsewhere franchised "Cajunway" fried chicken is extraordinary.

Finish off your meal with dark roasted Cajun coffee (in a throwaway cup of course) and a fried peach pie.

Buster Holmes

Burgundy & Orleans, New Orleans, La.
(504) 524-5234

Mon.–Sat. 9 a.m.–7:30 p.m., Sun. noon–5 p.m.

$5 or less

Never what you'd call a *fancy* restaurant, Buster's beanery is every bit as dilapidated as it always was, and the clientele now seems more seedy than Bohemian; but a meal here is still a colorful experience unique to the French Quarter.

"May I have some butter for my cornbread?" asks the man at the bar.

"What you think this is, a fancy restaurant?" retorts the lady behind the counter, spinning off into a stream of curses in an indecipherable patois as she hacks a big square of butter from a one-pound brick for the man's cornbread.

Buster's is not the place to come for gracious dining or polite service. The jukebox is loud; the place is a mess. But the cuisine, even if it's slipped a little since the halcyon 75¢-a-plate red-beans-and-rice days, is still good, cheap New Orleans soul food.

The best dish at Buster Holmes is his hot sausage, a jumbo length of dense cayenne-red pork, finely chopped, thick with garlic. It comes with French bread, rice, and red beans. Buster's beans, simmered with ham hock and garlic and onions, are a miracle—legumes transcendent.

The fried pork chops are meaty things, served glistening with dark sauce. You can get a platter of turnip greens and rice with cornbread on the side. The greens—all the vegetables—are bought at the French Market at the edge of the Vieux Carre.

Fried chicken, once Buster Holmes's glory, disappointed us on our last visit. The crust was a little too . . . soulful: oily instead of crisp, without the zesty garlic flavor we remembered.

Dessert at Buster Holmes is simple and good: sweet potato pie, bread pudding, or apple dumplings. "I always like something sweet," Buster says.

You'd never know it by looking at the place, with its sign outside advertising SOFE DRINKS GOOD SERVED, but Buster Holmes is famous and successful, a much-in-demand caterer about town. Buster Holmes T-shirts are sold behind the bar, as is a cookbook of "hand made" food that advises the reader that Satchmo used to eat red beans and rice at Buster's all the time.

Buster Holmes has opened in a second location, at 620 Decatur. The above telephone number is for the Decatur store.

The Cabin

Junction of Hwys. 44 & 22, Burnside, La.
(504) 473-3007

Mon.–Wed. 11 a.m.–3 p.m., Thurs. & Fri. until 9 p.m., Sat. until 10 p.m.,
Sun. until 6 p.m.

$5–$10

One hundred fifty years ago, The Cabin was a slave quarters on the nearby
Monroe Plantation. The people who lived in it probably ate a lot of Creole
gumbo, stewed rabbit, and hot boudin sausage.

The renovated Cabin of today serves pretty much the same thing—slave
food, if you will—with the patrician addition of mint juleps and martinis.
Actually, what you get is something much more than slave food. It is the
indigenous food of the people of Louisiana; blacks and whites, Frenchmen,
Africans, Spaniards—all of whom added something to the jambalaya melting pot that is Creole cuisine.

The Cabin is frequented by many locals, and there are always off-the-
menu specials. Some of the pot luck choices are jambalaya, shrimp Creole,
fried chicken, and pork chops. White beans and rice are a popular side dish.

The Cajuns' favorite Monday meal—red beans and rice—is available
every day, as is an intriguing local dish called the pirogue, named for the
silent bayou canoes made from cypress trees, light enough to glide over the
swamps. The Cabin's pirogue is the best dish in the house, a typically festive
Louisianan conglomeration that is anything but light. It does bear a resemblance to Cajun canoes in that it is made from a loaf of bread hollowed out
like a cypress log. Into the loaf is stuffed a large school of fried fish, oysters,
and shrimp: a hearty variation of the New Orleans po boy. As if you needed
ballast, red beans and rice come alongside.

Creole bread pudding, capped with a sharp rum sauce, is top choice for
dessert; or choose a more Dixie-accented buttermilk pie, sweet and fluffy.

If you come to The Cabin on a chilly winter night, you can warm up with
that old southern favorite, a hot toddy—bourbon made medicinally good for
you by mixing it with hot lemon juice and honey.

There are two dining rooms: the slave cabin, with its old cypress roof
still intact, and the *garçonnière*, built to resemble the quarters in which
gentlemen were housed overnight when they came calling on plantation
ladies.

Casamento's

4330 Magazine, New Orleans, La.
(504) 895-9761

Tues.–Sun. 11:45 a.m.–1:30 p.m. & 5:30 p.m.–9 p.m.
Closed June–mid-Sept.

$4–$10

Casamento's is a neighborhood oyster bar, far from the French Quarter and the seedier aspects of New Orleans street life. It is a decidedly *nice* place—upright, clean, pleasant. Very old-fashioned: walls done in white and pale green Spanish tiles, a timeworn oyster bar, and slickly tonsured oyster shuckers (the Casamentos) whose demeanor and appearance are an instant flash of 1940s nostalgia.

To watch them work is hypnotic. They stand behind the bar, using a miniature pitchfork to pull oysters out of a cooler box to their left, then opening the shells fast—not too fast, though—just fast enough to keep up with the oyster eaters at the bar and orders from the tables. They assemble dozens with supreme artistry—each broad icy white plate is a knockout, crowned with a dozen shimmering silver-gray Louisiana oysters. Breathtaking oysters they are, small gusts of edible ocean air. Mix your own sauce from a selection of vinegar peppers, hot sauces, horseradish, etc.

Beyond oysters, the menu is a short one: Italian spaghetti served with either meatballs or daube (Creole roast), fried shrimp, tenderloined trout, fried soft-shell crabs in season.

Casamento's makes the best oyster loaf in New Orleans. Fresh-shucked oysters are fried, then stuffed into a loaf of pan bread—actually a whole loaf of unsliced white bread, cut lengthwise and toasted, with a smooth buttery flavor that complements the salty golden oysters: a formidable sandwich, enough for two.

Don't let the nonchalance of Casamento's lull you into thinking it is anything but a great and rare restaurant, one of the city's jewels.

Central Grocery

923 Decatur St., New Orleans, La.
(504) 523-1620

Mon.–Sat. 9 a.m.–5:30 p.m.

$5 or less

New Orleans is the home of two distinctly different versions of the hero sandwich—the po boy and the muffuletta (say *moof-uh-lah-tah*). The Central Grocery, which opened for business in the early 1900s, is where the muffuletta was invented. It is an Italian sandwich made on a large round loaf of chewy bread dotted with sesame seeds. The bread is sprinkled with olive oil, then layered with thin slices of salami, ham, cheese, mortadella, and a salad made from broken olives and pickled vegetables.

The muffuletta is a relatively neat, easy-to-eat sandwich, which is a good thing, since there is no place to sit down at the Central Grocery. It *is* a grocery, a fascinating one at that, stocked with exotic imported foodstuffs, smelling of garlic and sausage and Italian cheeses, with yellowing travel posters on weathered walls. The man who makes the muffuletta does his work behind a tall counter, where at first it seems he is out of sight; but then you realize that a mirror has been positioned above him, enabling you to watch from the center of the store as the sandwich is built. It is a painstaking process; muffulettas are not slapped together.

You can eat while strolling along the French Market, or take the sandwich to the river with a bottle of Dixie beer; either way has been a tradition for decades.

Chez Helene

1540 N. Robertson St., New Orleans, La.
(504) 947-9155

Always open

$5–$15

Damn! There once was a time when we would say without qualification that Chez Helene was the best soul/Creole restaurant in the world. But like any creative person, a chef has his ups and downs; and the last time we dined here, chef Austin Leslie (Helene's nephew) was definitely down.

We had a good meal—a very good meal, one of the best in town. But the corn muffins . . . didn't they taste a little too much like the ones you make from a boxed mix? The stuffed pepper was still quite all right, but could no longer be said to transcend the plain nature of its humble ingredients.

Enough complaining. Our oysters Rockefeller were as wonderful as ever, inelegantly presented on a throwaway foil pie plate filled with rock salt. The oysters were cooked briefly enough to stay tender, with a fresh, briny flavor; their spinach topping was formidable army green, hot and spicy: potent food!

Chez Helene's fried chicken didn't make us swoon with delight as it has done in the past, but was just on the far side of paradise—meltingly soulful crust enveloping luscious meat that takes little coaxing to fall from the bone. Greens that come on the side are startlingly pungent, dripping pot likker and dotted with soft cubes of turnip. Smoky sweet potatoes are spiced to take your breath away.

Chez Helene's menu is extensive, with a range from soul to haute Creole that would make us dubious if we haven't had great red beans and rice and hot sausage one day, then come back the next for equally excellent oysters Bienville and filet of trout Marguery.

Whether you choose funky food or fancy, follow it with bread pudding. This is a Creole standard—dense and chocked with raisins, seasoned heavily with cinnamon and nutmeg, topped with a heavy dollop of whiskey hard sauce.

It is easy to forgive a slump at Chez Helene because the restaurant—a small cafe in the black part of town—is so unpretentious. The modest dining room is set with about a dozen tables and a few booths; a jukebox plays soul music in the corner; and there is a tavern adjacent where the staff sometimes sits at the bar, peeling shrimp for Creole gumbo.

The fact is that even on a bad day, the kitchen at Chez Helene can cook rings around all but the very best chefs.

Chez Marceaux

Hwy. 90 east, Amelia, La.
(504) 631-9843

Mon.–Thurs. 9 a.m.–3 p.m., Fri. 9 a.m.–10 p.m.

$5–$10

On the wall of Chez Marceaux there is a dandy clock in the shape of an oil rig, a dramatic tableau complete with the rig's twinkling lights. Amelia is on the lower Atchafalaya River—oil country; and Chez Marceaux is patronized by men in hard hats who work heavy construction jobs all morning, then come in for lunch of crawfish etouffee.

A workingman's cafe; gourmet food. Chez Marceaux's étouffée is a triumph—made with crawfish tails and thickened with their fat, spiked with pepper and an enigmatic vein of herbs, served over white rice. You can also get nine-inch plates mounded high with either boiled crawfish or shrimp (peel 'em yourself), served cold, as is customary everywhere else, or still warm, the way they like it in bayou country.

Even Chez Marceaux's fried crawfish are savory little morsels—without the oceanic zip of clams or shrimp, just the rich flavor of the crawdad, accented by a delicate breading.

Our turtle piquante was less successful, the chunks of turtle meat a bit too thick and fatty for our taste, although the brown sauce in which it came had an agreeable Tabasco tang.

Chez Marceaux's oyster po boys are good, made on toasted loaves of French bread, spread with mayo, lettuce, tomatoes, and pickles; but we counted only six oysters on our twelve-inch loaf. They were big and delicious, so we piled them all onto half the length of bread and had ourselves a rightly apportioned sandwich.

Chez Marceaux is a cinderblock-walled roadhouse with bright yellow tables and chairs, and strong air conditioning. Aside from the clock, the "atmosphere" in the place is totally natural—workmen sitting over Dixie beers, conversing with each other and the waitresses in Cajun French.

Eddie's Restaurant

2119 Law, New Orleans, La.
(504) 945-2207

Mon.–Thurs. 11 a.m.–midnight, Fri. & Sat. 11 a.m.–2 a.m.

$5–$10

Eddie's is the mythical great undiscovered hole in the wall. In fact, when you finally find Law Street and locate 2119 (Eddie's is 2 blocks off Elysian Fields), you will be sure it *is* mythical. Where is everybody?

Look closely. There's the sign: EDDIE'S: HOME OF NEW ORLEANS COOKING. Yes, Eddie's is real. There is *nothing* more real than the red beans and rice Eddie makes—each bean a small pillow of creamy silk sitting gently atop the rice, which is fluffy enough to absorb the soulful garlicky flavor of this perfectly seasoned dish. New Orleanians make a big deal out of red beans and rice, a passion out-of-towners find difficult to fathom. Eddie's version turns skeptics into believers.

Experts say you can get better gumbo out in Cajun swampland, but we have never found a bowl that can hold a candle to Eddie's—neither in the bayous or at New Orleans's famed (and good) Gumbo Shop. Made from an extraordinarily smoky roux, ebullient with a fierce array of spice that, if somehow separated, might form a complete catalogue of Creole cookery,

Eddie's bowl of gumbo is mesmerizing. Spoon into its depths and find shrimp, oysters, chicken, ham, two varieties of sausage—mild smoked and hot, and bits of beef and pork. At the last moment of preparation it has been thickened with file powder, which not only turns the stock into gravy but also imparts a delicate flavor that reminds some people of thyme, but is more fragrant, headier. Inhale the cloud of steam above a bowl of Eddie's gumbo; inhale and swoon. "I like to think I make the best gumbo in town," the chef told us. We know he does.

Only slightly less boggling is a pork chop with oyster stuffing. "I don't stuff the chop," he said; "you don't want the stuffing and the chop together until they go on the plate." The chop is a beaut—large, moist, faintly sweet. The stuffing is rich and luxurious, food for kings and noblemen, yet utterly honest. It arrives in a mound on top of the pork chop: one of the best meals in town.

Oyster stuffing is available separately, so why not try it on the side of fried chicken, chicken with a crust so firm it is audible when crunched into. Please note that this is Creole fried chicken, not mild and mellow Kentucky or Virginia fried chicken, but highly spiced, soulful food; it is chicken like Buster Holmes used to make.

For dessert, choose the Creole standard, bread pudding, a dish created by New Orleans chefs as a thrifty way to use day-old French bread. Eddie soaks his bread in milk, mixes it with raisins, eggs, sugar, vanilla, and who-knows-what-else, then bakes. While it's baking, a buttery, whiskey hard sauce is made. The pudding is served hot. It is nothing like the bland bread puddings served outside of Louisiana. It is strong, powerfully flavored food: food with personality—like everything at Eddie's Restaurant.

Galatoire's

209 Bourbon St., New Orleans, La.
(504) 525-2021

Tues.–Sat. 11:30 a.m.–9 p.m., Sun. noon–9 p.m.

$15–$30

Most visitors to New Orleans want to have at least one grand and fancy meal. If it is Creole food in a classic setting you want, Galatoire's is the only place to go. Yes, there is Le Ruth's, but that's really more French than Creole, actually more original than French—in any case, it's not the place for famous New Orleans specialties. There is Antoine's, too, where oysters Rockefeller were invented, but it's impossible; good service requires currying the favor of a "personal" waiter. We've had too many bad breakfasts at Brennan's; and the Court of Two Sisters is strictly for the tour bus set.

Galatoire's has its problems, too. A democratic policy of no reservations means long lines any time other than between three and five in the afternoon; and when full, the small dining room can be menacingly loud. Still, for our money, Galatoire's is *the* great New Orleans restaurant.

Here is where to set new standards for oysters Rockefeller (baked, topped with vivid anise-flavored spinach or something that resembles spinach; the recipe is a guarded secret) and oysters en brochette (fried with bacon, served with meunière sauce). There is no shrimp remoulade more breathtaking than Galatoire's, a tingly chilled salad of shrimp dressed with a sauce of Creole mustard and horseradish.

Nor can you go wrong starting with crawfish bisque. It is a dark, thick brew, enriched with crawfish fat, afloat with stuffed crawfish heads.

Some Orleanians swear by Galatoire's gumbos; they are hearty, less delicate than the rest of the kitchen's work, but a wonderful meal—especially with this restaurant's incomparable French bread.

The menu goes on forever; you could write a book describing Galatoire's brilliant realizations of all the Creole classics, many of which have become classic precisely because of Galatoire's consistency with them—since 1905. If you stick to seafood, it is impossible to go wrong. Two suggestions: trout amandine, tenderloined, dabbed in flour, and fried, covered with a shower of toasted almonds; and trout Marguery, the most famous dish in the house, shrimp on top of speckled trout filets, blanketed with a heady hollandaise sauce. This is Galatoire's unique hollandaise, here enriched by the truffle- and scallion-laced liquid in which the fish has been poached.

You'll find hollandaise also on the New Orleans specialty called eggs Sardou (that's poached, with creamed spinach), and on fresh vegetables: asparagus, broccoli, artichokes.

Dessert: get the princess cup, an infantile confection of fruit cocktail and ice cream that has made strong men and strict food critics weep for joy. Crêpes maison are a more sophisticated choice; the airy pancakes are rolled around currant jelly, then topped with slivered almonds, orange and lemon peel, and Curaçao. Have coffee; Galatoire's serves New Orleans's best, thick and strong.

In an odd, old-fashioned way, Galatoire's is beautiful. Its mirrored walls are lined functionally with brass hooks for overcoats, the floor is finished in clean, plain tile. It reminds us of New York's Gage and Tollner, fancy in the way we imagine Delmonico's used to be: bold and brightly lit; very bourgeois; very American.

Lasyone's Meat Pie Kitchen

622 2nd St., Natchitoches, La.
(318) 352-3353

Mon.–Sat. 7 a.m.–7 p.m.

$5 or less

Natchitoches is an ancient town on the Cane River, settled by the French in 1714. While the cooking here is heavily flavored with Cajun spice, the French flair is tempered by Natchitoches's affinity to the deep south. This is catfish country more than crawfish; morning coffee will likely be sided by biscuits rather than beignets.

There is one culinary specialty unique to Natchitoches, and nearly as old—the Louisiana meat pie. Since the eighteenth century, it has been a popular lunch item in Cane River country homes, but there is only one restaurant in town that prepares it—Lasyone's.

The Natchitoches meat pie is a local variation of Italian ravioli, Chinese wonton, and Polish pirogen: the pocket of dough stuffed with meat. Its formidable size and hearty flavor most resemble the Cornish variation, pasties, found on Michigan's Upper Peninsula, but it is deep-fried, and the filling is zestier: ground pork and beef (heavier on the pork), lots of chopped onions and parsley, cooked up in a roux of shortening and flour. The filling is then chilled overnight, and the next day a pastry crust is rolled very thin, folded over the filling into a half circle, crimped with a fork at the edge, and fried until it turns golden brown.

The meat pie is unique, but the rest of Lasyone's menu is a repertoire of southern and Acadian classics, such as the excellent plate lunch we sampled on our last visit: chicken and dumplings with mustard greens, black-eyed peas, and blocks of dense cornbread, followed by a Dixie-tender banana pudding. Lasyone makes an incongruous but quite spectacular Boston cream pie out of gingerbread and custard: unique, de rigueur for traveling pie fanciers.

From the Cajun side of the kitchen, we enjoyed a platter of stout sausage sided by red beans that had been simmered to silken perfection with a cracked hambone. The beans and sausage were served with the hurricane country favorite, "dirty rice," so named because it is cooked with—and stained by—chopped chicken giblets. It is rich, swampy, intensely aromatic: perfectly Louisianan in character.

Lasyone's is a casual village cafe, easy to spot as you drive along Second Street: look for the storefront with the large papier-mâché meat pie hanging in the window.

Le Boeuf's

3450 W. Pinhook Rd., Lafayette, La.   North of Broussard
(318) 837-9856

Mon.–Fri. 9 a.m.–6 p.m.   Boudin is usually ready by noon

Under $5

At first glance, Le Boeuf's looks like any ordinary supermarket in a suburban town. But why are those workmen lined up in back at the meat counter? And who is the small black man in galoshes, blue baseball cap, and blood-spattered apron?

We stopped in Le Boeuf's, not to buy groceries, but because Raymond Sokolov had written about it as one of the rare places (if not the only place) in Louisiana that still makes boudin rouge—Cajun blood pudding. The black man in the apron is Jacques Benjamin, *le boucher;* and the workmen are waiting for their lunch—lengths of boudin blanc and boudin rouge.

When Monsieur Benjamin has finished his work, the sausage is put in two large pots next to the otherwise unremarkable butcher counter. Made with pork and rice, boudin is, with a bottle of Dixie beer, a meal in itself. Twisted into sausages of varying length, it is sold by the pound and wrapped in butcher paper—to be eaten outside on a stoop or in the cab of your truck.

The boudin rouge is an alarming sight: thick and dark red, nearly purple. Lots of cayenne pepper is used to give it a severe nip. It is packed with finely ground pork moistened by veal blood and an extra helping of fat. This is strong stuff, its visceral nature undisguised, not for the faint of heart.

Le Boeuf's boudin blanc seems coarse-ground, with more rice than the red. It is pale mottled brown in color; and to our taste it is more flavorful than the awesome boudin rouge, seasoned with garlic and salt and not as much hot pepper. Both types of sausage are stuffed into tough casings, making it easy to squeeze out the insides as you eat.

Having arrived at Le Boeuf's early, before the sausage was completed, we went sightseeing along the aisles. With the exception of restaurants and pharmacies, supermarkets are our favorite places to explore when in a strange locale. And we have found none more fascinating than this. As we eavesdropped and tried to understand shoppers chatting with each other in Cajun French, we filled a basket with Luzianne Coffee, Savoie's Roux, Cajun Power Concentrated Chili Sauce, and a range of exotic condiments the likes of which you could never find outside the bayous.

Middendorf's

U.S. 55 & 51 at Pass Manchac on Lake Maurepas, Akers, La.
(504) 386-6666

Mon.–Sat. 11 a.m.–9:30 p.m. Sun. 11 a.m.–9 p.m.

About $10

Middendorf's specializes in catfish, served two ways: thick or thin. "Thick" is what might elsewhere be called tenderloin catfish—that is, meaty cross-sections of the fish, still with a few stray bones, deep-fried. This is the catfish connoisseur's choice: agreeably gamey, rich and flavorful. More timid souls, or catfish novices, will want to order their catfish "thin." These are curly boneless filets, also fried, with a well-seasoned crust, but not nearly as lusciously catfishy. Either comes with french fries, hushpups, and cole slaw salad.

Since this is southern Louisiana, it ought not to come as any surprise that the rest of Middendorf's menu is pretty sensational. Raw oysters or boiled shrimp or crawfish are as fresh and clean as you can get, served with an empty cocktail cup for patrons to brew their own sauce from an assortment of lemon, ketchup, Worcestershire, et al. on the table. On the side get that New Orleans favorite, the Italian salad, packed with olives and heavily showered with oregano.

There is good gumbo, too, made from crab, shrimp, or a combination of the two; it's a delicate gumbo, not as murky or intense as the kind made by Creole chefs in New Orleans. Soft-shell crabs at Middendorf's are delicious —you can get them fried, with the thinnest of crusts, or plainly broiled. On our last visit, a man sitting at the next table ordered three fried soft-shells and made himself a breathtakingly big soft-shell po boy with the French bread that comes in a basket with every meal.

Middendorf's is big and noisy. A favorite weekend eatery-in-the-sticks for nearly fifty years, it has recently become so crowded that a whole new restaurant was added next door to handle the multitudes. It has the same menu and the same no-frills ambience that seafood fanciers prefer. About the only decoration at all in Middendorf's are the functional coat hooks along the walls, made from shiny cypress knees, the funny-looking knobs at the bottom of the trees that grow in nearby swamps.

Morning Call Coffee Stand

3325 Severn Ave., Metairie, La.   In Jefferson Parish
(504) 885-4068

Always open

Under $5

Coffee is *the* New Orleans drink—a dark roast, enriched with chicory. Thick and black, this strong stuff is a revelation, robust enough to pack a punch even when cut with hot milk to become café au lait, as it is customarily served in New Orleans coffee houses.

The Morning Call was one of New Orleans's two celebrated French Market coffee houses, at the opposite end of the Market from Cafe du Monde. Not long ago, it was moved, fixture by fixture, to Metairie, to an imitation French Quarter called Fat City. The surroundings aren't much fun, and the muddy morning breezes from the Mississippi are missing, but the café au lait is unsurpassed.

And Morning Call beignets are the quintessential version of that famous Creole pastry—golden squares of fried, sweetened dough, showered with powdered sugar. Unlike the too chewy beignets still sold back in the French Market, these are crisp-skinned and fluffy, perfectly delicious.

To hell with breakfast at Brennan's. For about one-tenth the cost, we prefer chicory coffee and Creole doughnuts at the Morning Call. There is no simpler, more spiritually envigorating way to start a day . . . or end a night . . . in New Orleans.

Mosca's

Rte. 90, Waggaman, La.   About 15 miles west of New Orleans
(504) 436-9942

Tues.–Sat. 5:30 p.m.–9:30 p.m.   Reservations required

$10–$20

In a region with dozens of inventive great restaurants, Mosca's has been conspicuously inspired and consistently great for more than thirty years. Creator of a unique Italian-Creole cuisine, it is an original; it would have to be to stay in business where it is, as it is: a ramshackle white roadhouse way out over the skinny Huey P. Long Bridge, a half hour from the city, and from anyplace anyone would ever want to be.

But people do come; they flock. The only bad thing we have to say about Mosca's is that usually you have to make a reservation several days in advance; and even with a reservation, you have to expect to hang around at the bar awhile before you get to eat. This is especially maddening because, while you are waiting, the smell of garlic and olive oil wafts through the restaurant. The delay is exquisite torture.

Nearly everybody who comes to Mosca's begins with Italian crab salad, a piquant marinade available in the shell (hard work) or already picked. It is a dish that shouldn't be missed. But then again, there is *nothing* this place makes that should be missed. Pity the diners who come to Mosca's only in pairs. Servings are prodigious; there is no way two—or four—people can hope to sample it all.

Be sure to try the oysters Italian-style, a baked casserole of oysters in a strong garlic and oil sauce topped with breadcrumbs: a legendary dish. Split an order of Mosca's spaghetti bordelaise, the noodles glistening and slip-sliding in a buttery herbed sauce (also fortified with garlic). The supple strands of spaghetti are themselves remarkable, thoroughly cooked, yet still retaining a toothsome body. Mosca's skilled staff of waitresses manages to get it to the table in this perfect *al dente* form every time. The kitchen also makes ravioli.

What else? Shrimp Mosca (similar to the oyster casserole), chicken cacciatore sauteed with tomatoes and great olive oil, Italian sausage and roasted potatoes, beautifully grilled steaks, quails and squabs and cornish hens.

Two desserts: cheesecake and pineapple fluff. The cheesecake is genuine "New York cheesecake," made according to a recipe the Mosca family secured from Lindy's before it bit the dust. It is a monumental wedge, thick and polished, not as heavy as it appears—and yet too much after a meal here. More appropriate is the pineapple fluff, an audacious confection made with melted marshmallows; like Galatoire's princess cup, it is an example of how the great New Orleans chefs transcend the silliest ingredients with impunity.

But the working of such miracles is only a parenthesis to Mosca's story. Magic isn't necessary in a kitchen where artistry prevails.

Robin's

Hwy. 352, Henderson, La.   Exit 115 off I-10
(318) 228-2725

Daily 10 a.m.–10 p.m.   Reservations advised

$10–$15

We found Robin's while in a deep depression over the demise of Thelma's in nearby Breaux Bridge, the crawfish capital of Louisiana. Thelma had run one of America's great roadside restaurants; no one made crawfish better than she.

"Thelma never seasoned anything correctly," Lionel Robin said without disapprobation in his voice. To him, this was a plain fact. "She knew how to cook, certainly, but she did not know how to season. That is something you either have or you do not have. I have been a chef since I was a boy. *I* know how to do it right."

Too bad Thelma's isn't still around for a Cajun cook-off between her and Robin; what a *fais dodo* that would be! Robin's braggadocio cannot be dismissed as hot air. The fact is, in his words, he "has it." He has the skill, genius, artistry—whatever it is that turns groceries into great food.

Lionel Robin's restaurant has a full Cajun menu, including a wide variety of gumbos, shrimp and oyster dishes, catfish court bouillon and catfish filets, soft-shell crabs and frog legs, but like Thelma's (*pardon*, Robin!), his glory is crawfish, prepared ten different ways.

For the traveler who plans to stop here but once, there is what's called a crawfish dinner, which gives you a little bit of most preparations—but could leave you frustrated without enough of the one you like most. After a salad, you get crawfish bisque, a smoky roux-based soup afloat with stuffed crawfish heads. Then come crawfish étouffée (a tingly crawfish and vegetable stew), crawfish-stuffed bell pepper, crawfish pie (the traditional garlicky crawfish and vegetable dish baked in a paper-thin pie dough), fried crawfish (with lots of pink peeking out through the tender golden breading), and crawfish boulettes (small meatballs made from crawfish meat, onions, red peppers, and breadcrumbs).

It is possible to do so many different things with crawfish because it is a mild crustacean, without the snap of shrimp or even lobster. In its simplest preparations—boiled or fried in Robin's delicate batter—the crawfish has a melting sweet flavor. In étouffée, the taste is punched up with cayenne pepper; it is enriched in the bisque by the addition of crawfish fat. Whatever wonders Robin works in his kitchen, he does nothing to smother or diminish the crawfish's uniquely rich taste; nor is its gentle texture meddled with.

You don't get any gumbo with the crawfish dinner, so why not order a small bowl on the side. The crawfish gumbo is good, thick with crawdaddies; but you might like Robin's shrimp and okra gumbo better. It is a good companion to the crawfish dishes on the menu.

Robin's is immensely successful, patronized by locals and the same New Orleans gourmets who used to drive out to Thelma's between November and June, when the crawfish are at their tender best. It is a modern place, with comfortable understated decor, tables covered with thick white cloths, and a great selection of Cajun zydeco records for sale near the cash register.

"A reviewer from New Orleans said I was as great a chef as Paul Bocuse," Robin told us. "Can you imagine? To compare the simple crawfish with *la grande cuisine?* This," he scoffed, gesturing to a platter of fried crawfish we munched on as we talked, "this is nothing. I cook for a group of men

—Cajuns—we meet every Thursday . . . just to eat. We have met seventy-two Thursdays and never once eaten the same thing. Now I am preparing frog legs étouffée. I looked two years for these frog legs.

"My restaurant grew quickly to three hundred seats. Too big. To hell with that, I said; where is the joy? So I cut back. I cook because I love to cook. My father cooked before me. My wife, she is almost as great a chef as I am. You see, we are Cajun; and here, my friends, you must understand that people live to eat!"

MISSISSIPPI

Abe's

616 State St., Clarksdale, Miss.
(601) 624-9211

Daily 9 a.m.–9 p.m.

$5 or less

We still haven't figured out how tamales got to be the specialty of so many restaurants and street-corner vendors in the delta, but here they are at a sixty-year-old barbecue house named Abe's. Abe's has modernized in recent years and is now a nondescript Formica rectangle, with one handsome mural inside showing a smoke shack and a happy pig playing a violin.

No frills. Plastic utensils, fast service, and hot tamales, three to an order, moist and grainy-flavored, either plain or topped with chili.

The tamales are fine, but the stand-out at Abe's is hickory-smoked barbecue, sweet and porcine, sliced thin with lots of fire-flavored crunchy edges. Two outsized jugs of dark red sauce are brought with the meal; the mild one is liquid silk, the other, amplified with peppers, is tongue-tingling hot. With the meat you get a dollop of thick, porky beans flavored with sauce, and a simple slaw of pickled cabbage . . . also spritzed with sauce!

Bayless Restaurant

Hwy. 15, Bay Springs, Miss.
(601) 764-6914

Mon.–Fri. 6 a.m.–9 p.m., Sat. 6 a.m.–2 p.m.

$5 or less

A traveler through Bay Springs would never suspect that lurking behind the simple facade of the Bayless Restaurant are some of the best pies in America. It looks like so many southern cafes: cinderblock walls painted landlord green, tables and booths and a TV set (on) behind the counter. You could even look at the menu, a plastic laminated job printed in some faraway place, and still never guess that you were about to learn a thing or two about pie making.

We began to wonder if this was no ordinary cafe when we peeked into the kitchen and saw a crew of ladies that looked like they might be posing for a *Life* magazine article entitled "Great Cooks of the Deep South." They were large black women, their substantial middles tied with crisp white aprons, their heads wrapped with bandanas, their hands coated with flour.

First came a coconut pie the likes of which we have never seen. A good inch and a half of custard was bursting with the taste of coconut—not sticky sweet coconut like what comes out of an instant pudding box; but soft and tender, painfully delicious. It was resting on the lightest flake crust imaginable; and it was topped with a three-inch meringue cloud, so fluffy it ought to have been tied down with a tether rope. The meringue was sweet but not too sweet, and not a grain of unincorporated sugar shone forth from the egg fluff. The top was coated with shreds of toasted coconut.

Then came blueberry pie, minutes out of the oven. The purple fruit was contained in a crust of countless buttery layers. We took the prongs of a fork and probed the crust, marveling at how different this spectacular multi-layered piece of pastry was from our own homemade version that we had always considered pretty decent.

Cock of the Walk

Under-the-Hill at the end of Silver St., Natchez, Miss.
(601) 446-8920

Mon.–Sat. 6 p.m.–10 p.m.

$5–$10

In the last century, Mississippi boatmen earned a reputation as rough-and-tumble guys; and the meanest one on each boat was dubbed the Cock of the

Walk. Overlooking the Mississippi from the banks where fleets of keelboats and flatboats used to dock, the Cock of the Walk Restaurant pretty much reverses the meaning of the term. It is the nicest, most genteel place we know to sample a food that is generally found at its best in rougher surroundings.

Catfish is the only entree on the menu—catfish filets, so you don't have to worry about bones. They are toasty, breaded with a highly seasoned crust; the thin filets of fish are flaky and pure white. In fact, we almost hate to say it, inclined as we are to champion a funky out-of-the-way catfish parlor as more *appropriate* to the nature of the dish, but Cock of the Walk serves some of the best catfish in Mississippi.

Our reluctance stems from the fact that this restaurant caters to lots of tourists; the menu is written in cute southernisms ("sumpin' sweet" means dessert); the rough-hewn interior leans a little toward being decorator-rustic. And what's worse is that this original Cock of the Walk has franchised throughout the south. But damned if the food isn't delicious; and damned again if the riverboat theme doesn't work—well.

The moment you sit down (there can be a wait on weekend nights), young Fess Parker, in open shirt and hairy chest, sets an iron skillet of warm cornbread on the table. Brilliant cornbread: heavy and buttery, sharply laced with bits of jalapeno pepper.

You find your utensils in a little bucket on the table; food comes on dented (but clean) tin plates; ice water in a metal cup—an atmospheric touch that works, offering a pleasant cooling sensation each time you pick it up. Service is virile and fast.

Side dishes are impeccably regional in character. Mustard greens, dotted with melting bits of fatback, come in a cast-iron pot. Hushpuppies are light, crisp, and easy to eat—the perfect companion for catfish. You can even order that delta oddity, fried dill pickles.

The Dinner Bell

229 5th Ave., McComb, Miss.
(601) 684-4883

May–Oct. Tues.–Sun. 11 a.m.–2 p.m. & 5:30 p.m.–8 p.m.
Lunch only in winter

Under $10

McComb is a town of old homes and tree-shaded streets, and a romantic custom of illuminating the fragrant azaleas when they blossom in the spring. The Dinner Bell is the best—the *only*—place in town to eat if you want a Mississippi meal to match McComb's antebellum character.

The food is pure deep-south cookery: fried chicken, chicken and dumplings, at least half a dozen fresh vegetables every day, including turnips, black-eyed peas, speckled butter beans and baby limas, and yam casserole with melted marshmallows. There are hot dinner rolls and sticks of corn-bread baked to look like little ears of corn; and for dessert there is shortcake topped with fresh strawberries, or pistachio nut cake, or bread pudding.

The nice thing is that you can taste it all, and eat all you want of what-ever you like, because The Dinner Bell is a revolving-table restaurant, a uniquely southern—primarily Mississippian—style of feasting. All the food is set out on a lazy susan in the center of a table-for-eighteen. The center can be spun for easy access to anything, and eighteen tablemates keep on helping themselves while the kitchen staff replenishes the serving platters.

Round-table dining was invented in 1915 (see Mississippi's Mendenhall Hotel), but when The Dinner Bell began as a boarding house in the early 1940s, it had ordinary rectangular tables. Boarders spent a lot of time reach-ing and passing things back and forth and otherwise groping for their meal, so when The Dinner Bell moved down the street in 1961 to this location, four round tables were installed to expedite eating. Just two years ago, The Din-ner Bell got new owners—John and Carolyn Lopinto. They spiffed up their antique home (they live upstairs) with lace curtains and colonial decor, but they kept the round tables—and the regional food.

By all means, try some of everything. The fried chicken and throng of vegetables are always on the lazy susan. But allow us to direct you to a few daily specials. On Thursday, you can dig into stewed rabbit with a Cajun-accented shower of spice; Sunday is the biggest day of the week, when the ordinarily groaning board gains the added weight of ham or turkey with all the trimmings, as well as a half dozen additional vegetables—that is, a half dozen more than the half dozen that are always on the table. Catfish is Fridays only—boneless filets; Saturday is western-flavored, with barbecued ribs, smoked sausage, and Mexican cornbread.

Every day, there is fried okra on the table; in all the south you will find none better. And save room for dessert. Mrs. Lopinto's pies and cakes—especially the old-fashioned pound cake—are memorable.

Doe's Eat Place

502 Nelson, Greenville, Miss.
(601) 334-3315

Mon.–Sat. dinner   Tamales available earlier in the day

Steak dinners about $25, tamales $4 per dozen

Doe's is the Willie Nelson of restaurants; despite its fame and exalted repu-tation among *cognoscenti* of great American eats, it hasn't gone uptown one bit. It is still just a few ramshackle dining rooms in the back of a dilapidated ex-grocery store in a crummy part of town.

We walked in the front door on our last visit, and there relaxing in easy chairs near the grocery counter were two black men sipping out of mason jars. In the kitchen in back, where one can eat at tables in sight of the stove and counter, there were the same letters and Christmas greeting cards taped to the wall that we had seen three years earlier on a previous visit.

When we sat down to eat and told the waitress we wanted medium T-bones, she went to the refrigerator and selected a couple of raw cuts to display to us on their butcher paper. They were gorgeous; and a short while later, when they returned to our table, nearly blackened by flame, fibrous and bursting with juice, with skillet-cooked french fries on the side, it didn't take long for us to feel certain that what we claimed in 1978 is still true: this is the best steak dinner in America.

What makes Doe's memorable, in addition to the quality of the meat and the skill with which it is cooked, is the *character* of the operation. At a time when institutionalized restaurant decor has reached new levels of sleek style, there is something especially wonderful about Doe's pale green walls with shelves of miscellaneous pitchers, baskets, glasses, and plates, lined up for diners to see. It is a pleasure to dine in the kitchen and watch the waitresses mix serving bowls of salad from which your individual bowl will be scooped; to see the french fries sizzling in a skillet on an ordinary kitchen stove. How nice it is to hear a waitress boast with genuine awe that "The man from 'As the World Turns' was here last week," then run off to bring you his autographed picture.

Doe's is such a great place that we would figure out some justification to put it in any book about good food, but there is no need to bend the rules to list it here. One of the most unlikely regional specialties found in the area around Greenville and north to Memphis is tamales. All along the Mississippi River, every little town has its tamale stands. Why? What are they doing here? We've consulted experts in southern foodways, and nobody has a credible explanation of how the tamale found its way from Mexico to Mississippi.

However it migrated, here it is, and Doe's makes some of the best, sold by the dozen, packed in old coffee cans to take home. You can get them as an appetizer before dinner, or earlier in the day, to go. On a plate, you can peel away the husk and eat tamales in a civilized manner, but we much prefer the messy way, squeezing the hot, soulfully spiced cornmeal out of the husk while strolling down the street.

The only problem is that Doe's tamales are so good, it's easy to pack away a dozen before dinner. Try facing a 2½-pound sirloin after that!

The Hollywood

Just off Rte. 61, Robinsonville, Miss.
(601) 363-1126

Fri. & Sat. dinner only   Reservations advised

About $10

We've dined on some pretty peculiar regional food, but of all the odd local specialties we found eating our way across America, none was odder or more surprising than that Mississippi delta curiosity, the fried dill pickle. We first saw it on a menu in Natchez and thought it was just an anomaly, the whim of a homesick kosher chef who found himself marooned in a land of deep-fried catfish. But as we wound our way up past Vicksburg, fried dill pickles appeared on menus with disconcerting regularity.

It wasn't until we got to the Center for Southern Folklore in Memphis that Judy Peiser, Center director and fried-pie authority, informed us that local folklorists had located the birth of the fried dill pickle at The Hollywood, only a half hour south of Memphis on legendary Route 61.

We later returned to the historic site and discovered that The Great Moment occurred years ago when, on one particularly busy weekend night, The Hollywood *ran out of food!* No more steaks, no more pork chops, no more shrimp or catfish. And so the inventive cook took a jar of dill pickles, sliced them, breaded the slices, and threw them in the hot oil. If you like dill pickles, and if you like southern fried food, you will probably like the result. If you don't like either one, stay away from fried dill pickles.

But there is a lot more to The Hollywood than that. Since the birth of the fried dill pickle, they have not, to our knowledge, run out of good thick steaks and pork chops. You can get frog legs dinners and a strange dish that might be called good old nouvelle boy cuisine—marinated catfish. Catfish, which is of course customarily fried, is in this case fileted, soaked in a marinade of soy and Worcestershire and pepper, then cooked on the grill. It is lighter than the fried version, and the marinade is tasty; but it is a dish for catfish lovers only. For dessert, most people choose "the Hollywood dessert," a concoction of liquor and ice cream resembling a brandy Alexander.

The Hollywood is a big brick and plaster-walled roadhouse with a bandstand, making it possible to grab a dance or two in the time between your salad and T-bone, or between the fried shrimp and dessert. People come from far away to dine and dance here, and it is, despite the fairly loose roadside ambience, a pretty toney place; your pickle-munching companions will more likely be socialites from Memphis than cotton pickers from Eudora.

Lusco's

722 Carrollton, Greenwood, Miss.
(601) 453-5365

Dinner Mon.–Sat.   Reservations advised

$15–$20

No, this *cannot* be the place—a tattered grocery store on the wrong side of the tracks. You enter and see no tables, just a big room with a counter, a random easy chair and couch, a few shelves stocked with dusty cans of food with labels so old a collector of ephemera would covet them. This cannot be the place that native Mississippians tell you serves the finest food in the state.

But if you know the delta, then you know that this *must* be the place; a gastronomic reliquary where tradition is so enshrined that it would be sacrilegious to alter even the smallest detail; to scrape the ceiling, which has been peeling for decades; to paint the pale green walls or varnish the creaky wood floors, or move the men's room from the outdoor breezeway to the inside.

This is how it works: you bide your time in the front room, admiring the stuffed ducks on the wall, or placing a call from the indoor pay phone booth, then, when they are ready for you, a waiter comes out and leads you back, down a hallway to your own private dining room, a small cubicle veiled by a chintz curtain.

The room is dingy, faded green, partitioned from the others by a wall that doesn't reach the tin ceiling. There is no getting around the fact that this is a dump, but willfully and eccentrically so. Remember, though, you are in cotton country—and so each table is set with fine white cloths and napkins.

Sitting in utter seclusion, in the back of this run-down grocery store, you have severed all ties with modern life as the rest of the world knows it. You have penetrated to the heart of the Mississippi delta; and suddenly, you understand William Faulkner and B. B. King, and the utterly incongruous affinity between them.

The waiter, a tall black man in a white apron, draws the curtain, leans in, and calls off the menu (or, if you wish, hands you one to read). He has eyes the color of the grocery store's walls, and his gold tooth gleams as he tells you that the boneless sirloin strip steak is "as tender as a mother's love."

With the first slice of the knife, you recognize the texture as the highest-quality beef, fibrous and heavy with juice. It is gently grilled, served with fresh-cut french fries on an oval plate ringed with a magnolia pattern. A grand dinner, equal to any steak in America, but more special, thanks to the induplicable cachet of its raffish backroom setting.

Lusco's most outstanding dish is pompano. One week a few years ago, when fresh pompano could not be found, the men's room was marked with the graffiti, THE GREAT DEPRESSION OF '84. LUSCO'S HAS NO POMPANO.) The flavor of the fish is unutterably delicate, its flesh firm and clean, and it is gilded with piquant butter and lemon sauce. To perfectly balance its elegance, get an order of batter-wrapped onion rings.

Beyond steak and pompano, the menu is limited: broiled shrimp in a hot pepper red sauce, oysters on the half shell or baked with bacon, fried or broiled chicken. You can also get pasta with meat sauce—a reminder of the 1930s, when Papa Lusco built the private booths to serve home brew and spaghetti to local cotton kings.

Full and happy after dinner, we pushed back from the table, pressed a button to summon the waiter, and gazed up at the green ribbons threatening to fall off the ceiling. Oh, if peeling paint could talk, imagine the Prohibition stories, the tales of celebrating soldiers whose troop trains stopped across the street during World War II, the times Bob Mitchum and Steve McQueen hung out here while filming *The Reivers*.

Our reveries broke off when we saw the butter pats stuck on the ceiling among the paint chips, flipped up who-knows-when. "I see you looking at the ceiling," intoned the waiter, peering in through the curtain. "But you would be surprised, the people that come from around the world to eat in here." No, we wouldn't be surprised at all. Lusco's is an American original, always the same, changing only as it ages. You can be sure that the way it is is how it always will be. And that is why Mississippians love it so.

Mack's Fish Camp

Off Hwy. 49, six miles north of Hattiesburg, Miss.
(601) 582-5101

Daily 11 a.m.–9 p.m.

$5–$10

Mack's is for serious chowhounds. As long as you keep eating, they keep bringing platters piled with catfish, hushpuppies, french fries, and slaw. Even tea (iced, of course) comes in titanic glasses, about a quart's worth, barely graspable in one normal-sized hand. "Did you have plenty to eat?" asks the lady at the cash register. How could anyone say no?

Itinerant gourmets Rob and Jeanne Goldfarb directed us to Mack's, off the beaten path in cricket-chirping countryside north of Hattiesburg, where they said they had found a real Mississippi meal that made them weep for joy.

We followed their lead to a clean wood-paneled hall designed for eating in bulk: wide communal tables covered with blue checked cloths, broad-beamed ladderback chairs, overhead fans to cool things down. It's been southeastern Mississippi's premier catfish parlor since 1960, when Odell "Mack" McLaurin decided to combine the boarding-house all-you-can-eat principle with the menu of a fish camp. "Mack started selling fish before they ever figured out how to raise them," says Earl Shoemaker, Mack's son-in-law. "Now they're fed pure grain, on the farm, just like a cow or chicken."

But Earl admits, "I'd rather have a river fish. You pick him up and he's firm, he's swimming against that current all the time." On the other hand, the ones he serves here are lean and clean, sweet, moist, fresh—far less gamy than the river fish he prefers. They are fried in a thin gold jacket of fine-grained, sandy crust, served headless. Catfish skeletons are virtually monadic, making whole fish easy to eat; but lazy folks can order filets for a few dollars extra.

The hushpuppies are sweet, onion-flecked little balls; the slaw has a lot of zest, and it plays a part in the meal like tartar sauce, enhancing the flavor of the fish.

No beer or liquor is served, in order to safeguard the restaurant's wholesomeness. It is a family operation, Earl in the kitchen, Helen Shoemaker at the cash register, sons Jesse, Mark, Randy, and Randy's wife Rhonda in the kitchen. And Mack still comes in from time to time for a plate of catfish.

Mendenhall Hotel

Rte. 49, Mendenhall, Miss.
(601) 847-3113

Mon.–Sat. 11 a.m.–2 p.m. & 6 p.m.–7:30 p.m., Sun. 11 a.m.–2 p.m.

$10 or less

Round-table dining is a uniquely southern way to eat. In the center of a big circular table is a lazy susan, where the meal is laid out in bowls and on platters. Around the edge of the table sit ten to twenty people, usually strangers. When you want something from the lazy susan, you spin it and grab. The center keeps spinning, and you keep eating, until you are too stuffed to do anything but surrender your seat at the table to another diner.

With three round tables and a front porch just right for rocking when the meal is through, the Mendenhall Hotel is one of the finest places we know to sample this Dixie-style meal. In fact, it was here, in 1915, that round-table dining was invented by the hotel's owners—the Morgan family. The wheels of good food have been spinning ever since.

At the door, Fred Morgan greets everyone who enters. Perhaps *greets* is the wrong word; it's more like scrutinizes. Mr. Morgan runs his hotel like the captain of the tightest ship in the fleet. No hippy, no vagabond, no dirty-nail type has ever gotten a foot past the front door.

Once he decides you are fittingly clean and well-mannered enough to join the crew, you are ushered into the dining room and shown to a seat at one of the round oak tables built by Fred's grandfather. The walls are bedecked with souvenir plates, and in the center of the lazy susan there is a bouquet of plastic flowers.

Your tablemates will likely include old skinny-tie Mendenhall regulars with accents so thick and slow any northerner will need Berlitz to keep up a conversation; there will be clean-cut jocks in football jerseys, nice ladies who look like local secretaries in tan pantyhose and white sandals, and a few travelers from up in Jackson, which in Mendenhall practically makes them Yankees.

Iced tea is already on the table, so all that's left to do is dig in. The dinner plates are trimmed with magnolias; enjoy them when you first sit down—it isn't likely you will see the tops of the plates again for quite some time. On the lazy susan circle platters of fried chicken, chicken and dumplings, smoked sausage, and spaghetti; also beets, rice, mounds of black-eyed peas, turnip greens, squash casserole, green beans, candied yams, boiled okra, creamed corn, cornbread and biscuits, four kinds of relishes, and bowls of hot gravy for the chicken.

Strangers sometimes have a bit of trouble getting the knack of round-table dining; we were helped considerably by a friendly gent who noticed that our boarding-house reach simply wasn't fast enough to hook the fried chicken when it spun past. "When that plate you want comes your way," he said, "just grab the whole thing. Help yourself, then put it back in any empty spot that circles past." We learned quickly. Our other concern was that it would be uncouth to take too much. But in the world of round-table dining, there is no such thing. The minute a plate starts looking empty, the quick-on-their-feet kitchen staff replace it with a full one.

The table seemed to always spin clockwise. We wondered what Emily Post would have to say about the boob who decided to turn it from right to left.

When you start slowing down, a small individual fruit cobbler is brought to your place. Nobody really goes to a round table for dessert, although this cobbler was mighty good—perhaps better than we have any right to comment on, since by this time we were full to bursting.

Rooms are still available at the Mendenhall—plain, clean quarters that go for $12 to $18 a night. It's a homey place to stay, just the ticket for a heap of deep south ambience, complete with old coots in rocking chairs, a lazy dog snoozing on the porch, and a bulletin board with newspaper clippings of "Miss Southern Hospitality"—a native of Mendenhall.

Ruth 'N' Jimmie's

Rte. 7, Abbeville, Miss.
(601) 234-4312

Daily lunch

$5 or less

In his introduction to the tantalizing book, *A Cook's Tour of Mississippi*, Willie Morris wrote, "In Lafayette County, which some know as Yoknapatawpha, I have found . . . a strange colorful place . . . which made me forget the martini business lunches in Manhattan at the Four Seasons or the Oak Room of the Plaza."

It didn't take much detective work when we arrived in Oxford to find the place to which he was referring. Ole Miss historian Charles Wilson told us to head up to Abbeville, near the Tallahatchie River, and look for Ruth 'N' Jimmie's.

The Four Seasons it isn't. Mississippi it is: a large grocery store shaped like a shotgun house, with a long counter and stools in the back and a slate on which the day's menu is written. By no stretch of the imagination a fine or fancy restaurant, and certainly no home of sophisticated cuisine, it is a place only for people who want to sample the cooking of the rural south, served in authentically regional surroundings.

How authentic? Well, you have to walk past the gas pumps out front, then past the tub of live bait, then into the store among shelves of tools and hard goods and groceries. It's a dark place, with wood slat walls and ceiling —cool on a hot summer's day.

Everything served here is made here. Vegetables are pulled from nearby gardens. No shortcuts are taken. Nearly all of Ruth 'N' Jimmie's customers are regulars, and they just wouldn't allow the quality of the cooking to slip.

The day we dined at the long counter, the blackboard listed chicken-fried steak and ham; side dishes were black-eyed peas, greens, creamed potatoes, and cooked apples. For dessert there was a choice of peach cobbler or a heavy, granular dark fudge pie. We relished our steaks, mopping up the delicious grainy brown gravy with cornbread. The fudge pie was sensational —a definitive conclusion to an enchanting country meal.

For a silly moment, we imagined the clientele of the Four Seasons dining at Ruth 'N' Jimmie's lunch counter, then buying a bucket of live bait to take back to New York to go catfishing in the Four Seasons' pool room between martinis.

Smitty's

208 S. Lamar, Oxford, Miss.
(601) 234-9111

Mon.–Sat. 5:30 a.m.–9 p.m.

About $5

Just off the town square in Oxford, Smitty's is a citadel of southern cafe cuisine. It's the place to come for greens and hog jowl and cornbread, ham hock and beans, or country-style smothered steaks. We agreed to meet here for breakfast one morning with our friend Ella King Torrey, a folklorist who scours the deep south in search of quilts and catfish suppers.

We arrived first and found a table. Mrs. Smith brought us coffee and biscuits while we waited, along with butter and some convenience bubble-packs of "mixed fruit" jelly.

Ella soon arrived, and when Mrs. Smith saw that we were with one of her regulars, out came her own homemade muscadine jelly and pear preserves—the kind of thick, homey spreads that take first prize at county fairs.

Breakfast was terrific. Ella came with a couple of friends, and the five of us spent the better part of the morning laying waste to baskets full of big oval biscuits and platters of dark red country ham. We dipped the biscuits in red-eye gravy, covered them with molasses or Mrs. Smith's blue-ribbon preserves, sampled them smothered in heavy sawmill gravy.

On our way out, in deference to our responsibilities as writers of this book, we asked Mrs. Smith how a person who isn't a regular or a friend of one can get her private stock preserves instead of the bubble-packs of yukky jelly.

"Just ask," she said, as if there were actually some customers who would just as soon have the mixed fruit. So, if you stop at Smitty's, be sure to ask for the good stuff. And if that doesn't work, tell her you're a friend of a friend of Ella King Torrey's.

Stub's

Hwy. 49E, Yazoo City, Miss.
(601) 746-1204

Daily 4:30 a.m.–10 p.m.

$10 or less

In a small glass case next to the cash register, bathed in the amber glow of a warming light, is the primary reason Stub's has become a beacon in the southern delta: chocolate chess pie. It arrives at the table just barely warm, like heavy cocoa pudding, with a thin, pale sheet of dry chocolate "crust" on top. What is wonderful about this pie is how old-fashioned it is, how it makes you suddenly remember a time before chocolate became sinful and decadent, when it used to be nice.

But retro pie is not Stub's sole glory. Nor would we base our *apologia* on Stub's lip-smacking breakfast of hot biscuits, country ham, and red-eye gravy. No, what puts this roadhouse in the pantheon is hot lunch.

Sandwiches and fast food seem so barbarian compared to this civilized —yet informal—midday meal. The waitress puts her card on the table, inscribed, "Hello, my name is Debbie," then you get your tea, presweetened or not, and start things off with a crusty-topped corn muffin or butter-enriched dinner roll from the basket. Now comes the daily special.

The chicken pot pie is a bountiful meal, spilling beyond its boundaries on its sectioned plate, broken crust and peppery gravy and little chunks of hard-boiled egg mingling with the liquor of strong collard greens in the adjoining section. The third item on the plate is an endearing doot listed on the menu as a "pear salad"—a half a canned pear, with a dab of mayonnaise on top.

Stuffed shrimp are vigorously spiced, a mere two of them, with lots of peppers in the breading, accompanied by intensely sweet yams in syrup and English peas in cream sauce.

The thermometer read 113 degrees when we stopped by at noon, but it was sweater-cool inside. Here sat the respectable people of Yazoo City, men with clean fingernails, ladies with white shoes and matching purses (not a single pair of jeans in the house), and on this blistering hot day, to a man and woman, they were all eating hot lunch and warm chocolate chess pie for dessert.

Taylor Gro. & Restaurant

Taylor, Miss.   Next to the post office
(601) 236-1716

Thurs.–Sun. dinner

About $5

Doe's Eat Place, Ruth 'N' Jimmie's, and Taylor Gro. & Restaurant: some of the best Mississippi food is served in the backs of grocery stores. Taylor Gro. is the most atmospheric of the three, situated in the tiny village where Faulkner's *Sanctuary* took place, up a raised wooden sidewalk next to the post office. It is a weather-worn store with wood ceiling and floors and five mismatched dining tables in back. The plaster walls are covered with graffiti written by exuberant Ole Miss students, who have made it a custom to drive out to Taylor for catfish on the night before a big football game.

You get one utensil—a fork wrapped in a paper napkin; you get a basket of saltines; and you choose between catfish filets or the complete (headless) fiddler. We recommend that even inexperienced catfish eaters go for the unsevered whole. Catfish skeletons are sturdy, well-bonded structures; it is easy to insert the fork and perform a complete osteotomy in one neat operation, or to scrape the meat off as you go without fear of stray bones.

The fish is pure country, mild and juicy, encased in a thick crust. It comes with hushpuppies, french fries, slaw, and a scallion. Fried apple pies are served for dessert. There are huge glasses of iced tea, but to make this a completely traditional Mississippi meal, bring your own beer. Mrs. Hudson will refrigerate it for you.

Weidmann's Restaurant

208 22nd Ave., Meridian, Miss.
(601) 693-1751

Daily 6 a.m.–10:00 p.m.

$5–$15

In 1860, Meridian, Mississippi, was incorporated as a town. Ten years later, the Weidmann family opened a restaurant. Generations of Meridianites have made a habit of Weidmann's, especially on Saturday nights; and no visitor should leave town without a meal here. Weidmann's history is as intertwined with Meridian's as a willow tree wrapped with kudzu vines.

Felix Weidmann, who came from Zurich, began with a counter and four stools. It is a huge place now, all dark wood and casement windows, an idiosyncratic Alpine enclave in the heart of Dixie.

High above, old-fashioned ceiling fans churn slowly. The main dining room is separated from the long counter by a burnished brass rail as thick as a prize-fighter's arm. On the walls are some of the most elaborate antler-bedecked cuckoo clocks this side of Bavaria. Stuffed animal heads and fish, brown with age, hang on the walls of the three dining rooms, along with at least a thousand 8 x 10 photos of people dear to the heart of Meridian: the boys who marched off to fight World War II, Miss Orange Bowl 1935, Jimmy Rodgers (a native son), pugilist Primo Carnera, Skeeter Davis (another of Meridian's own), baseball players, pilots, ladies in flying goggles, men in business suits, men in overalls . . .

A meal at Weidmann's can be as down-home as ham and red-eye gravy and turnip greens simmered with ham hock, or as fancy as oysters Bienville or prime rib. When Weidmann's makes chicken-fried steak, they use choice round steak. The traditional topping of cream gravy is speckled with mushrooms, and there are good stewed apples on the side.

Mississippians love seafood, and the menu is heavy with oysters, crabs, trout, and Gulf shrimp. For a sampling of Weidmann's best, we ordered a half dozen appetizers for dinner, including stacked shrimp ravigotte, Gulf shrimp remoulade, and a "one dozen" oyster stew in milk. We were lucky; it was Friday, when the specialty is Creole gumbo, a colorful bouillabaisse of fresh seafood and bright Louisiana-accented spice.

Dinner and lunch come with hot rolls and a small crock of peanut butter. The peanut butter began during World War II, when butter was in short supply. Customers grew to like peanut butter for their crackers and bread; and the tradition has stayed on.

Our favorite Weidmann's tradition is black-bottom pie, a lofty fantasy of brandy- and bourbon-spiked chiffon sitting on a thin vein of bittersweet chocolate and a crunchy gingersnap crust.

Weidmann's traditions were explained to us by Miss Billy Mahoney, who has been at Weidmann's for forty-five years, making sure everything runs correctly, as it always has. She is a lady of a certain age, with delicately veined hands, a slightly deflated blond hairdo, a string of pearls, and a tiny whispery voice that positively drips southern charm.

Miss Billy filled us in on the history of Weidmann's from when it was just a twinkle in Felix's eye. "When Mr. Felix died, his son took over, then *his* son, Mr. Henry. Mr. Henry was the last male Weidmann. He had no sons, only three daughters. His son-in-law took over; that would be Mr. Mac-Williams, who goes by the name of Shorty and married the second Weidmann daughter; and now they've had four daughters . . ."

On and on Miss Billy went as we continued eating. Southerners love tradition—and we love Weidmann's.

The White House

848 North St., Jackson, Miss.
(601) 352-0664

Lunch daily; dinner Thurs., Fri., & Sat.; breakfast for boarders only

$5 or less

The White House seems like a living museum, a hands-on exhibition that the Smithsonian might mount, titled "The American Boarding House." For the price of a meal, you sit shoulder to shoulder with genuine boarders at a genuine boarding house, and as the lazy susan round tables offer up their cornucopic bounty, you become part of a vanished way of life.

Over the front porch, a sign announces OUTSIDE MEALS. Inside, fading family portraits hang on fading wallpaper. A cast-iron stove keeps pans of biscuits warm.

Boarding-house food: fried chicken and cream gravy, collard or turnip greens, sweet peas, hominy corn, baked and candied yams, fruit cobbler and banana pudding. It is not superlative cuisine—merely good down-home cooking.

The White House is not the place to splurge or celebrate a special occasion. It's quieter, more subtle than that. You may find, as we did, that you tend to speak in hushed tones when you sit at the round tables for the first time. After all, we are strangers, joining folks who eat here every day. Of course, they're used to that, and like any newcomer to the boarding house, you will be helped along by either the staff or residents, or regular "outside" diners. They take their meal and its absolutely authentic surroundings for granted; they don't know they are part of an extraordinary exhibit of southern folklife.

SOUTH CAROLINA

Beacon Drive-In

255 Reidville Rd., Spartanburg, S.C.
(803) 585-9387

Mon.–Sat. 7 a.m.–11:30 p.m.

$5 or less

There are only a few grand drive-ins left in the world, places with soul and charm, where the service is every bit as fast as the franchises (faster, actually), but the food is good. The Beacon Drive-In is the best of them, opened in 1947 by John White, and still run by White and sons; it is one of America's most American eateries.

At the Beacon, you will forget all about junk-food franchised clowns and service reminiscent of waiting in line at a government welfare office. Here is fast food at its fastest—and finest. Here is the paradigm of drive-ins.

It is possible to dine in your car at the Beacon; curb attendants await. But the real fun is inside.

Be ready to think fast when you enter. There seems to be little logic about who gets served first. What happens is you step up to the order counter and *instantly* a server makes eye contact with you. You tell him what you want, and he calls it back to the immense visible kitchen, where dozens of white-clad cooks are chopping and frying and assembling hundreds of orders. You wonder: Is it possible in all the din and commotion that anyone heard him call out yours? You move down the line, getting your drink or dessert (this takes maybe thirty seconds), and bingo—your food appears, brought to you by the man who shouted it out.

Overhead signs say J.C. SAYS IT'S FINE TO PASS IN LINE and J.B. SAYS LET'S

DON'T BOOGIE JIVE; LET'S MERCHANDISE! J.C. and J.B. are two of the mercurial order-takers.

Another sign, proudly displayed, is the Lipton Award, to THE WORLD'S LARGEST USER OF LIPTON'S TEA. That's not hard to believe if you order a glass. It is titanic. It is also shockingly sweet, just the way they like it in the south. In this age of diet mania, there was something wonderfully outré about the way the man behind the counter boasted to us that "We use two tons of sugar each and every week to sweeten our tea."

There are probably one hundred different sandwiches on the Beacon menu, ranging from a plain tomato sandwich to a double chili cheeseburger with bacon; but most people, when face-to-face with J.C. or J.B., call out "Slice!" or "Outside!" That refers to the Beacon's excellent barbecue, *outside* meaning the exterior cuts of the meat, which absorb more seasoning as they cook—and yield a more savory flavor as they are chewed. A *sliced* plate or sandwich gets you the inside meat—mild, leaner slices. Both come topped with a vinegar-tomato sauce scented with cloves and nutmeg. The Beacon roasts about a ton and a half of pork per week.

The Beacon also specializes in such Carolina regional favorites as hash (a stewlike dish made from minced beef) and barbecue slaw (a sweet relish to accompany barbecue). Be sure to try the fried onion rings. And don't forget dessert. It's not just an add-on at the Beacon. There are good icebox or pecan pies, and a selection of sundaes that range from hot fudge and banana boats to the startling flagship of the ice cream fleet, a $5 "pig's dinner."

The Beacon is truly a landmark. Across the street, there is a helicopter pad for drop-in patrons. On weekends, the gigantic parking lot is Times Square, New Year's Eve. Once a year, the tone changes from exuberant to solemn, when the Beacon holds its "Annual Worship in the Parking Lot."

"There is only *one* Beacon!" boasts the menu. No aficionado of roadside America can afford to miss it.

Henry's

48-54 Market St., Charleston, S.C.
(803) 723-4363

Daily noon–10:30 p.m.

About $10

She-crab soup, made with the meat and roe of the female blue crab, is Charleston's most renowned delicacy. We know few out-of-towners who like it at first taste. "Lacking in zip," our dining companion (a Baltimorean) proclaimed one night. "That's just the point," replied the resident she-crab expert across the table. "Pour in all that pepper and you kill the crab-meat. Only those with jaded palates don't like she-crab soup, especially here."

The debate between he- and she-crab boosters took place over a table at

Henry's, Charleston's grand old seafood house. Henry's soup is indeed bland by comparison to the peppery orange crab soup served up north around the Chesapeake Bay. It is a frail cream dotted with a few onions, flavored with mace and Worcestershire sauce and only a pinch of cayenne pepper. The mild white crabmeat is underscored by a shot of sherry; the pale orange roe imparts a fine silky texture.

(Although the natural spawning season for the blue crab runs from April through early autumn, she-crab soup is always available at Henry's. A man in the kitchen swore to us that he gets she-crabs with eggs year-round, but admitted that in the spring, there is more—and better-tasting—roe in each. We've never had the opportunity to sample winter she-crab soup here. If we did, we'd look for telltale bits of hard-boiled egg yolk—customarily used by Charleston cooks to substitute for roe out of season.)

Whatever your reaction to she-crab soup, Henry's is worth visiting for a variety of coastal seafood: flounder stuffed with small local shrimp and sherry-marinated crabmeat; red snapper baked in white wine, topped with a shrimp and oyster sauce; delicious (and not a bit bland) deviled crabs; terrific oyster dishes, broiled or stewed in milk or cream.

As is the Carolina wont, there are fried seafood platters on the menu: scallops, mini-shrimp, oysters, nameless fish. Only the cole slaw impressed us; the fried stuff was insipid, unworthy of Henry's.

In lieu of dessert, have your waiter bring some corn muffins—great with a glass of buttermilk on the side.

Maurice's Piggy Park

1600 Charleston Hwy., West Columbia, S.C.
(803) 796-0220

Mon.–Sat. 10 a.m.–10:30 p.m.

$5 or less

Where to begin describing Maurice's Piggy Park? With the largest American flag in South Carolina, flying overhead? With the Lighthouse Mission and Religious Meeting Hall at the edge of the parking lot? With the lightning-fast curb-service operation that guarantees three-minute service? Perhaps we should begin with Maurice Bessinger himself, a legendary name in Carolina cuisine ever since he and his brother Melvin opened their first barbecue stand in a converted Zesto drive-in thirty years ago.

We have never seen him in person, but his personality permeates the restaurant like smoke in a closed pit. A drawing of the Great Man on the bottled barbecue sauce sold at Piggy Park depicts him as a large free-floating head with charismatic eyes, a gleaming smile, and skin that glows sauce-red. On the order board in each parking space is his signed testimonial about how everything is done the old-fashioned way, hogs cooked eighteen to twenty-four hours over hickory coals, basted with the "million dollar secret sauce" that has been in his family for years. In addition to overseeing the Piggy Park, he directs the religious mission next door, promising "free Bibles, counseling, and refreshments" to all who enter. Mister Bessinger is a dynamo.

His barbecue is a style unique to the small area around Columbia, bathed neither in vinegar pepper marinade nor red ketchupy dressing, but rather in a yellow mustard sauce, tingling with apple cider and a sprinkle of spice. In a sandwich or on a "Q-pork plate," it is lean and crusty, agreeably sweet. Side dishes include beautiful multihued fried pork skin; and pork hash on rice, the hash made from the jowls and liver. There are also delicious sauce-drenched ribs, and a large variety of sandwiches—from a foot-long dog to a beefalo burger.

Whether you employ a curb attendant or eat in one of the comfortably rustic dining rooms inside, service, by waitresses in red-and-white checked shirts and blue skirts, is fast and friendly.

Maurice's Piggy Park is a one-stop southern experience. Here, you get it all: church next door, the flag overhead, and barbecue to eat in your car.

Moree's Bar-B-Q

Hwy. 527, north of Andrews, S.C.   Off Rte. 41
(803) 221-5643

Fri. & Sat. 5 p.m.–10 p.m.   Closed first two weeks in July

About $5

It was thanks to Allie Patricia Wall and Ron L. Layne, authors of *Hog Heaven*, a terrific book about South Carolina barbecue, that we found Moree's. They called it "some of the best in South Carolina," and they are absolutely right, our only caveat being that Carolina barbecue (North and South) is peculiar stuff, nothing like the sweet and sloppy barbecue you get in midwestern cities or the deeper south. In the Carolinas, they don't much like tomato-based sauce; they do like vinegar. Most pit-cooked pig is presented fairly nude: pale chunks of pork in a peppery vinegar sauce.

At Moree's, the big shreds of meat are very lean and smoky, available either medium or hot. You can try a little of each, since service here is in the traditional South Carolina barbecue manner, along a help-yourself buffet line. Also along the line are barbecued chicken and ribs which, unlike the chopped pork, are covered with a red sauce that we, being partial to that tomato tang, prefer.

The accompaniments at Moree's are without peer; Carolina classics like rice and hog-drippin gravy; rich pork hash; sweet potatoes; and two different kinds of pig skin, one fried honeycomb light, the other stripped off the pit-cooked pig, tough and redolent of the vinegar sauce with which the meat was basted over oak logs on the open pit. Moree-made chocolate cake completes the meal.

What makes Moree's important, in addition to the plain fact that it serves quintessentially regional food, is that it offers a completely authentic performance of an ancient gastronomic ceremony. Note that Moree's is open only on Friday and Saturday nights. That is because the cooking process is a long one, beginning on Wednesday, when the hogs are put onto the pit. Two centuries ago, smoke from just such an open pit would be a signal to all around that a weekend feast, a "pig pickin," was about to happen; and when Friday night rolled around and the hogs were ready, it was time to celebrate. At Moree's, as in the 1700s, virtually all of the hog is utilized—the ribs, the butt and shoulder for chopped barbecue, the rest for hash and gravy, even the skin.

And at Moree's, as in older times, the hogs are Moree hogs, raised here. They are corn-fed, with Moree corn, grown here. What you see when you walk along the buffet line is home cooked *and* home grown.

After you fill a tray, there are two dining rooms in which to sit, each with a couple of long tables, shared by friends and strangers. You may find there is a wait. Moree's has been a busy place for more than a dozen years. In a state where there is barbecue on every block and along nearly every county road, the popularity is testimony to its excellence and to the enduring strength of an obsolete culinary ritual.

Radd Dew's Bar-B-Q

Hwy. 701, south of Conway, S.C.
(803) 397-3453

Fri. & Sat. 5 p.m.–9 p.m.

$5 or less

In the parking area outside Radd Dew's are delivery trucks to take barbecue to restaurants and stores up and down the coast from Calabash to Georgetown. It's famous stuff, this barbecue; and although the red-label brand that goes elsewhere is efficiently made in an electric cooker, all of what's served *here* is done the painstaking old way, on an open pit over smouldering hickory and black jack oak wood.

The dining room at Radd Dew's is a pleasant place, with green tile floors, white walls, and a small assortment of Formica and wood tables. As is the Carolina custom at weekend-only barbecue parlors, where it makes no sense to have a lot of hired help, you serve yourself at a buffet line. Lean chopped pork from Boston butts, bathed in the family-recipe sauce of vinegar and peppers; candied yams; hushpuppies; green beans; rice and liver hash; cole slaw; and iced tea: a pure and authentic South Carolina weekend feast.

Sweatman's Bar-B-Que

Rte. 453 north of Holly Hill, S.C.
no phone

Fri. & Sat. 11:30 a.m.–10:30 p.m.

$5 or less

Sweatman's takes the prize as the south's most beautiful barbecue parlor. The downstairs rooms of this gracious shingled farmhouse retain their original wood walls, stained dark with age, now set with comfortable rustic tables. There are tall ceilings and working fireplaces, and patchwork curtains at the windows; large ovals of cut glass decorate the doors. Outside, the broad porch is shaded by pecan trees: a sweet nostalgic scene that probably hasn't changed much at all since 1900, which is when the Sweatman family began a tradition of weekend barbecues in the fertile farmland north of Holly Hill.

The weekly pig pickins used to be just for friends, but the word spread; and now, on a good weekend, Bub Sweatman will cook two dozen hogs over oak coals in his open pit.

You enter Sweatman's through a wide hallway and proceed to the back room and along a buffet line that features first-rate South Carolina barbecue in all its forms: jumbo chunks of fall-apart tender pork, pale and juicy with a slight vinegar/mustard taste; ribs—lean and dry, smoky, virtually all "brownies," real pig pickin meat, easy and fun to tear off the bone; pungent, tomatoey hash on rice; and pig skins—fried light, with an oily crunch. There are two sauces to ladle on whatever you choose—a yellow mustardy one and another with a hot pepper tang, but go easy with either. You will want to savor Sweatman's barbecue au naturel.

For dessert, we had bread pudding with raisins, topped with vanilla sauce.

The way things usually work, customers pay the prix fixe, which entitles them to go through the line once, taking all of whatever they want. When the girl at the cash register saw us knit our brows over the various offerings, debating about who should take what, she asked if it was our first time here. When we admitted that it was, she said, "Don't you fuss or worry. Just take what looks good now, and you're welcome to come back for more." We did. And we will again.

Midwest

MINNESOTA

Crabtree's Kitchen
MARINE ON ST. CROIX

The Village Smithy
GLENCOE
The Indian Trail
WINNETKA
Leikam's Tavern
HALF DAY
Walker Brothers
Original Pancake House
WILMETTE
Carmen's
EVANSTON
Carson's
SKOKIE

White Gull Inn
FISH CREEK

Norske Nook
OSSEO

Anderson House
WABASHA

WISCONSIN

Gosse's
Schulz's Restaurant
SHEBOYGAN

Edie's
FAIRMONT

Boder's on the River
MEQUON

The Pantry Cafe
LeMARS

IOWA

Jack Pandl's
Three Brothers
Watts Tea Shop
MILWAUKEE

Green Gables
SIOUX CITY

Quivey's Grove
MADISON

Iowa Beef Steak House
DES MOINES

Mary's Cafe
CASEY

Ronneberg Restaurant
AMANA

Hamburg Inn No. 2
IOWA CITY

Strawtown Inn
PELLA

Oberweis Dairy
AURORA

Al's
The Berghoff
Connie's
Edith's Bar-B-Q
Edwardo's
Giordano's
Ideal Candies
Lou Mitchell's
Morton's
Mr. Beef
Pizzeria Uno
CHICAGO

The Gardens
WALNUT

The Coffee Cup Cafe
SULLY

The White Way
DURANT

The White Mill
MONMOUTH

Big John's
PEORIA

K.C. Cafe
FAIRFIELD

MISSOURI

Wilton Candy Kitchen
WILTON

Chief Mahaska Restaurant
OSKALOOSA

Flo's Family Restaurant
MARSEILLES

ILLINOIS

Arthur Bryant
Boots & Coats
Jess & Jim's Annex
Granny's
Richard's Barbecue
Smokestack Bar-B-Que
Snead's Corner Bar-B-Q
Stroud's
KANSAS CITY

Finn Inn
GRAFTON

Richards Farm
CASEY

Busch's Grove
C & K B-B-Q
China Chop Suey Restaurant
The Haven
Lou Boccardi's
Miss Hulling's
Mr. Austin's Bar-B-Q
The Q King
Ted Drewes Custard
ST. LOUIS

Hale's Restaurant
GRAND TOWER

Mary Lou's
CARBONDALE

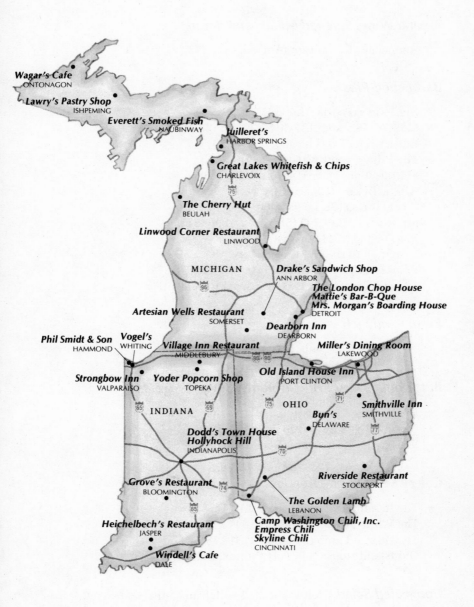

Wagar's Cafe
ONTONAGON

Lawry's Pastry Shop
ISHPEMING

Everett's Smoked Fish
NAUBINWAY

Juilleret's
HARBOR SPRINGS

Great Lakes Whitefish & Chips
CHARLEVOIX

The Cherry Hut
BEULAH

Linwood Corner Restaurant
LINWOOD

MICHIGAN

Drake's Sandwich Shop
ANN ARBOR

The London Chop House
Mattie's Bar-B-Que
Mrs. Morgan's Boarding House
DETROIT

Artesian Wells Restaurant
SOMERSET

Dearborn Inn
DEARBORN

Phil Smidt & Son
HAMMOND

Vogel's
WHITING

Village Inn Restaurant
MIDDLEBURY

Miller's Dining Room
LAKEWOOD

Strongbow Inn
VALPARAISO

Yoder Popcorn Shop
TOPEKA

Old Island House Inn
PORT CLINTON

INDIANA

OHIO

Bun's
DELAWARE

Smithville Inn
SMITHVILLE

Dodd's Town House
Hollyhock Hill
INDIANAPOLIS

Grove's Restaurant
BLOOMINGTON

Riverside Restaurant
STOCKPORT

The Golden Lamb
LEBANON

Heichelbech's Restaurant
JASPER

Camp Washington Chili, Inc.
Empress Chili
Skyline Chili
CINCINNATI

Windell's Cafe
DALE

Midwest Specialties

Where we list several places, we have starred the one we think best.

Amana Wine, Smoked Meats, and Bread

Ronneberg Restaurant (Amana, IA)   342

Barbecued Ribs

Big John's (Peoria, IL)   302
★ Carson's (Skokie, IL)   304
Edith's Bar-B-Q (Chicago, IL)   306
The Village Smithy (Glencoe, IL)   320
Mattie's Bar-B-Que (Detroit, MI)   356
Arthur Bryant (Kansas City, MO)   362
C & K B-B-Q (St. Louis, MO)   365
Mr. Austin's Bar-B-Q (St. Louis, MO)   372
The Q King (St. Louis, MO)   373
Richard's Barbecue (Kansas City, MO)   374
Smokestack Bar-B-Que (Kansas City, MO)   374
Snead's Corner Bar-B-Q (Kansas City, MO)   375

Brain Sandwich

The Haven (St. Louis, MO)   368

Buttermilk Pie or Old-Fashioned Sugar Cream Pie

Dodd's Town House (Indianapolis, IN)   323
★ Groves' Restaurant (Bloomington, IN)   324
Village Inn Restaurant (Middlebury, IN)   329

Celery Seed Salad Dressing

★ The Indian Trail (Winnetka, IL)   311
The White Way (Durant, IA)   344
The Golden Lamb (Lebanon, OH)   381
Old Island House Inn (Port Clinton, OH)   383

Congealed Salad—Jell-O chocked with fruits, nuts, and sweets

The Indian Trail (Winnetka, IL)   311
Richards Farm (Casey, IL)   319
Groves' Restaurant (Bloomington, IN)   324

Cream Torte

Deep-Dish, Stuffed, and Double-Crust Pizza—All variations of pan-cooked pizza, a Chicago-area specialty

Door County Fish Boil—A traditional fish feast originated by Wisconsin's Icelandic settlers

Dubois County Turtle Soup

Dutch Lettuce

Five-Way Chili—A uniquely Cincinnatian concoction of seasoned ground meat, beans, spaghetti, onions, and cheese

German Pancake

Gold Brick Sundae—Praline-laced chocolate syrup on ice cream

★ Carson's (Skokie, IL)   304
The Village Smithy (Glencoe, IL)   320
The London Chop House (Detroit, MI)   355

Gooseberry Pie

Richards Farm (Casey, IL)   319
★ Phil Smidt & Son (Hammond, IN)   327
Mary's Cafe (Casey, IA)   340

Italian Beef—Shaved beef on a hero roll, topped with peppers

Al's (Chicago, IL)   300
Connie's (Chicago, IL)   305
★ Mr. Beef (Chicago, IL)   316

Michigan Cherry Pie

★ The Cherry Hut (Beulah, MI)   347
Dearborn Inn (Dearborn, MI)   348

Milwaukee Rye Bread

Jack Pandl's (Milwaukee, WI)   389
★ Three Brothers (Milwaukee, WI)   392

Pan Fried Chicken

Dodd's Town House (Indianapolis, IN)   323
Groves' Restaurant (Bloomington, IN)   324
Hollyhock Hill (Indianapolis, IN)   326
Boots and Coats (Kansas City, MO)   363
Granny's (Kansas City, MO)   367
Snead's Corner Bar-B-Q (Kansas City, MO)   375
★ Stroud's (Kansas City, MO)   376
The Golden Lamb (Lebanon, OH)   381

Pasties—Beef stew in a dough pouch

Finlandia Restaurant and Bakery (Marquette, MI)   350
★ Lawry's Pasty Shop (Ishpeming, MI)   353
Wagar's Cafe (Ontonagon, MI)   358

Pea Salad

Richards Farm (Casey, IL)   319
K.C. Cafe (Fairfield, IA)   339
★ The White Way (Durant, IA)   344
Dearborn Inn (Dearborn, MI)   348
Juilleret's (Harbor Springs, MI)   352

Perch

The Berghoff (Chicago, IL)   301
The Village Smithy (Glencoe, IL)   320
★ Phil Smidt & Son (Hammond, IN)   327
Vogel's (Whiting, IN)   330
Dearborn Inn (Dearborn, MI)   348
The London Chop House (Detroit, MI)   355
Old Island House Inn (Port Clinton, OH)   383

Persimmon Pudding

Richards Farm (Casey, IL)   319

Pheasant and Wild Rice

Anderson House (Wabasha, MN)   358

Pickerel

Dearborn Inn (Dearborn, MI)   348
★ Old Island House Inn (Port Clinton, OH)   383

Pork Tenderloins (on a bun)

★ Flo's Family Restaurant (Marseilles, IL)   308
The White Mill (Monmouth, IL)   322
Chief Mahaska Restaurant (Oskaloosa, IA)   333
The Coffee Cup Cafe (Sully, IA)   334
Hamburg Inn No. 2 (Iowa City, IA)   337
K.C. Cafe (Fairfield, IA)   339
Mary's Cafe (Casey, IA)   340
The Pantry Cafe (LeMars, IA)   341
The White Way (Durant, IA)   344
Gosse's (Sheboygan, WI)   388
Schulz's Restaurant (Sheboygan, WI)   392

St. Paul—A St. Louis egg foo yung sandwich

China Chop Suey Restaurant (St. Louis, MO)   366

Schaum Torte—A meringue-based pie filled with fruit or ice cream

★ Boder's on the River (Mequon, WI)   387
  Jack Pandl's (Milwaukee, WI)   389

Shaker Lemon Pìe

The Golden Lamb (Lebanon, OH)   381

Sheboygan Brat—Charcoal-grilled wurst served on a bun

★ Gosse's (Sheboygan, WI)   388
  Schulz's Restaurant (Sheboygan, WI)   392

Smoked Lake Fish

★ Everett's Smoked Fish (Naubinway, MI)   349
  The London Chop House (Detroit, MI)   355
  Smokestack Bar-B-Que (Kansas City, MO)   374

Snoots—Pig snouts, St. Louis soul food style

★ C & K B-B-Q (St. Louis, MO)   365
  Mr. Austin's Bar-B-Q (St. Louis, MO)   372

Sour Cream Raisin Pie

Chief Mahaska Restaurant (Oskaloosa, IA)   333
The Coffee Cup Cafe (Sully, IA)   334
Mary's Cafe (Casey, IA)   340
Ronneberg Restaurant (Amana, IA)   342
The White Way (Durant, IA)   344
Anderson House (Wabasha, MN)   358
Edie's (Fairmont, MN)   361
★ Norske Nook (Osseo, WI)   390

Stack Pie—Delicate layers of pastry separated by sweet filling

The Golden Lamb (Lebanon, OH)   381

Steak

The Berghoff (Chicago, IL)   301
Carson's (Skokie, IL)   304

Toasted Ravioli—Deep-fried ravioli, unique to St. Louis

Walleye Pike

Whitefish

Wisconsin Duckling

Types of Midwestern Restaurants

Bakeries

Finlandia Restaurant and Bakery (Marquette, MI)   350
Bun's (Delaware, OH)   378
Boder's on the River (Mequon, WI)   387

Barbecues

Big John's (Peoria, IL)   302
Edith's Bar-B-Q (Chicago, IL)   306
Mattie's Bar-B-Que (Detroit, MI)   356
Arthur Bryant (Kansas City, MO)   362
C & K B-B-Q (St. Louis, MO)   365
Mr. Austin's Bar-B-Q (St. Louis, MO)   372
The Q King (St. Louis, MO)   373
Richard's Barbecue (Kansas City, MO)   374
Smokestack Bar-B-Que (Kansas City, MO)   374
Snead's Corner Bar-B-Q (Kansas City, MO)   375

Cherry Hut

The Cherry Hut (Beulah, MI)   347

Chicken Dinner Restaurants

Hale's Restaurant (Grand Tower, IL)   310
Hollyhock Hill (Indianapolis, IN)   326
Boots and Coats (Kansas City, MO)   363
Granny's (Kansas City, MO)   367
Stroud's (Kansas City, MO)   376
Smithville Inn (Smithville, OH)   386

Cincinnati Chili Parlors

Camp Washington Chili, Inc. (Cincinnati, OH)   379
Empress Chili (Cincinnati, OH)   379
Skyline Chili (Cincinnati, OH)   385

Farm Restaurant

Richards Farm (Casey, IL)   319

Inns

Strawtown Inn (Pella, IA)   343
Dearborn Inn (Dearborn, MI)   348
The Golden Lamb (Lebanon, OH)   381
Old Island House Inn (Port Clinton, OH)   383
White Gull Inn (Fish Creek, WI)   395

Noodle Parlor

China Chop Suey Restaurant (St. Louis, MO)   366

Pizzerias

Carmen's (Evanston, IL)   303
Edwardo's (Chicago, IL)   306
Giordano's (Chicago, IL)   309
Pizzeria Uno (Chicago, IL)   318
The Coffee Cup Cafe [Friday only] (Sully, IA)   334

Small Town Cafes

Flo's Family Restaurant (Marseilles, IL)   308
The White Mill (Monmouth, IL)   322
Village Inn Restaurant (Middlebury, IN)   329
Chief Mahaska Restaurant (Oskaloosa, IA)   333
The Coffee Cup Cafe (Sully, IA)   334
Mary's Cafe (Casey, IA)   340
The Pantry Cafe (LeMars, IA)   341
Wagar's Cafe (Ontonagon, MI)   358
Edie's (Fairmont, MN)   361
Bun's (Delaware, OH)   378
Norske Nook (Osseo, WI)   390

Smoke House

Everett's Smoked Fish (Naubinway, MI)   349

Soda Fountains

Ideal Candies (Chicago, IL)   311
Oberweis Dairy (Aurora, IL)   317
Green Gables (Sioux City, IA)   336
Wilton Candy Kitchen (Wilton, IA)   345
Juilleret's (Harbor Springs, MI)   352
Drake's Sandwich Shop (Ann Arbor, MI)   349
Ted Drewes Custard (St. Louis, MO)   377

Steak Houses

Morton's (Chicago, IL)   315
The Gardens (Walnut, IA)   335
Iowa Beef Steak House (Des Moines, IA)   338
Jess and Jim's Annex (Kansas City, MO)   369

Taverns

Leikam's Tavern (Half Day, IL)   312
The Haven (St. Louis, MO)   368
Three Brothers (Milwaukee, WI)   392

. . . in the Tea-Room Tradition

The Indian Trail (Winnetka, IL)   311
Groves' Restaurant (Bloomington, IN)   324
Miller's Dining Room (Lakewood, OH)   382
Boder's on the River (Mequon, WI)   387
Watts Tea Shop (Milwaukee, WI)   394

ILLINOIS

Al's

1079 W. Taylor, Chicago, Ill.
(312) 226-4017

Mon.–Sat. 9 a.m.–1 a.m.

$5 or less

An Italian beef sandwich is a pile of highly spiced, shaved roast beef inserted into a length of Italian bread and topped with either sweet peppers or *giardiniera* (an oily medley of hot peppers, carrots, olives, and onions). Like its Philadelphia cousin, the cheese steak, it is street food: messy, cheap, fun to eat, and addictive.

Aside from the fact that most of its vendors are of Italian descent, there isn't much of the old country about it. It is a specialty unique to America, to the city of Chicago; and it is sold at hundreds of stand-up huts throughout the city.

Al's, an open wood-sided stand in a small Italian enclave on Chicago's West Side, is the ideal place to savor an Italian beef sandwich. Its patrons are the most discriminating Italian beef eaters—neighborhood folks and Chicago cops (there were four squad cars in the parking lot when we pulled in). The counter is run by brash Italians who keep up a patter with customers, and occasionally throw stale bread out the back door for pigeons.

Beef for the sandwich is forked out of a trough of gravy. It is lean, paper-thin meat, so tender it seems on the verge of becoming hash—but it doesn't; it retains its fine sliced character, and that is one of the secrets of a superior Italian beef sandwich. The beef is spiced with pepper and awash in gloriously garlicked gravy, but we feel Al's lacks a certain zip until it is topped with the vaguely sour *giardiniera*. Al's bread is exemplary: fresh but tough, tough enough to stay intact even when sopped with beef and gravy.

It is also possible to get a combo sandwich—Italian beef nestled in bread along with a crackling tube of sausage that Al's roasts over charcoal briquettes.

For a drink, go across the street to Mario's Italian lemonade stand, where slushy ices are made with real peaches, watermelon, cantaloupe, etc., in sizes ranging from a 25¢ eyecup to a $1.50 vat.

At Al's, you eat standing up in the street or leaning against your car in the parking lot.

The Berghoff

17 W. Adams St., Chicago, Ill.
(312) 427-3170

Lunch & dinner Mon.–Sat.

$5–$10

Pot roast and buttered noodles; roast turkey with dressing and mashed potatoes; lamb stew; pork shank; corned beef and cabbage; bread pudding, rice pudding, and caramel custard for dessert: nowhere in America will you find food so *normal* . . . at prices that are abnormally low. You cannot spend more than $10 for dinner; many plate lunches are well under $5.

The Berghoff is a relic, a fine old restaurant opened in 1898, where they still serve their own brand of beer, and where everybody waits in line for a table. The turnover is fast, because the pace of a Berghoff meal is of pre–expense account days, when lunch meant an hour's worth of good food, then back to work. Here come shoppers loaded down with packages, and businessmen in pinstripe suits who tuck napkins into starched white collars.

What a grand place, with its high ceiling and solemn portraits of the Berghoff family and chandeliers stocked with lightbulbs that look like Edison originals, their filaments glowing above the dark wood dining hall.

The menu is large and innocent, advising that "escargots" are imported French snails and suggesting "there is nothing finer than a Berghoff steak."

Meat-and-potatoes meals, but with a distinct German accent: you can get sauerbraten with potato pancakes or Alpen ragout or knackwurst or homemade sausage cakes. You can also get good southern fried chicken and Boston scrod and that garlic-drenched Chicagoland specialty, shrimp de Jonghe. Among the plate-lunch specials, there is moist corned beef hash, browned in a skillet, topped with a poached egg. The turkey and dressing and mashed potatoes are the real thing. Broiled whitefish is fresh from Lake Superior.

It is pot roast that won our hearts: fall-apart tender, served with fat limp noodles glistening with butter, sided by a mountain of zesty creamed spinach. All meals are accompanied by a basket of good sour rye bread. Drinks, including Coke and root beer, are served in beer steins.

Lots of desserts, from apricot *rouladen* and strudel to chocolate mousse and flourless chocolate mint cake. Bread pudding is served as a hot crusty-topped block with heaps of warm, vanilla sauce. Amazingly, it is studded with caraway seeds along with raisins, and although it doesn't look dark, you swear it is made from the house rye bread . . . a strange and wonderful counterpoint to the sweetness of the custard sauce on top.

Big John's

719 N. Monson St., Peoria, Ill.   At 7th & Kumpf
Next to U.I. Medical School
(309) 674-4158

Sun. & Tues.–Thurs. 10 a.m.–midnight, Fri. & Sat. to 1 a.m.

$10 or less

Big John Robinson is a black man who learned to cook ribs in Mississippi. He brought his recipe to the rib-crazed state of Illinois, where for more than thirty years his Peoria soul shack (it really was a shack—exactly thirty-two square feet) served a far-flung clientele of whites and blacks of every social stratum.

Fans had a scare a few years ago, when it looked like Big John's joint was going to get torn down to make way for the new medical center, but John moved to modern quarters, where despite the fact that the smell of the pit is kept out of the dining room by a glass partition, he still sells fine slabs of bone.

John's ribs are crusted with strips of glazed pork, served with a squeeze bottle of tart red-orange sauce. On the side are french fries, crisp and speckled with shreds of skin. A plate of white bread is served as a mop for sauce. Two people will do well ordering the "P & P," which is a pitcher of beer and a platter of ribs.

Big John also hickory-smokes brisket—tender meat edged with a burnt crust, a little dry au naturel, luscious with a few squeezes of the sultry sauce. On four hours' notice, it is possible to get a barbecued chicken.

As we mentioned, this is a *modern* place. You can see the pit men working behind glass, but other than that, the setting is all wood-grain Formica, with soul Muzak piped in to aid digestion.

As we paid our bill (with an American Express card!), two Peorians stopped in to pick up ten pounds of ribs. They were driving to California, they explained, and didn't want to go ribless.

Carmen's

1600 Orrington Ave., Evanston, Ill.   At Fountain Sq.
(312) 328-6131

Sun.–Thurs. 11 a.m.–midnight, Fri. & Sat. to 1:30 a.m.

$10 or less

Like the vent of a volcano, Carmen's stuffed pizza bubbles furiously when it arrives at the table. It has a smooth circumference of crust, the image of a springform pan made of golden toast, a full two inches high. Inside the crust is filling—nearly as tall, a flow of molten mozzarella cheese topped with a layer of tomato sauce.

Afloat in the resilient cheese are the ingredients of the pizza: powerfully spiced sausage, or mushrooms, or sauteed green peppers or onions.

Slice into the circle, remove a wedge, and what you have is a triangle of *cheese pie*, descendant of Chicago's famous deep-dish pizza, but so much deeper, so profoundly cheesier, so overstuffed, that it has evolved into another food altogether.

Because its shocking dimensions make it nearly impossible to eat with the hands, a stuffed pizza a la Carmen's is not messy. Eaten with knife and fork, in small increments, it is, for pizza, quite civilized.

Nor is stuffed pizza, like its déclassé forebears, greasy or gross. The ingredients are top quality—the cheese buttery, the peppers and mushrooms fresh, the tomato sauce lumpy with savory little bits of red, the chunk sausage lean. And the crust is absolutely greaseless, hard and toasty. It keeps its crunch on the sides and the bottom, but at the *top* of the bottom layer, where it is weighed down by cheese, it softens, deliciously so, to a consistency reminiscent of *al dente* pasta.

Carmen's pizza has a healthy, if immeasurably robust, quality. It is real, not junk food. The menu lists vegetarian pizza; and for the extremely health-conscious, a stuffed spinach pie made with four kinds of cheese. This is a tour de force, with real spinach taste, but we missed Carmen's Italian sausage.

Because of their depth, stuffed pizzas take a full half hour to cook, which will give you plenty of time to soak up the atmosphere. Carmen's is a happy place with a jukebox, a few ferns, and purchasable art on the walls. The waitresses are pretty Evanstonians; the pizza-makers ogle girls from Northwestern University sitting outside in Fountain Square.

Carson's

8617 Niles Center Rd., Skokie, Ill.
(312) 675-6800

Mon.–Thurs. 4 p.m.–midnight, Fri. & Sat. 4 p.m.–1 a.m.,
Sun. 2 p.m.–11 p.m.   No reservations.

$10–$20

When *Chicago*, America's most food-savvy regional magazine, declared Carson's ribs the best in the city, we were shocked. We look for great midwestern barbecued ribs in funky shacks like The Q King in St. Louis. Ribs are, after all, soul food, traditionally the province of black chefs. And Carson's is, with the exception of the valets who park your car, a white man's restaurant, located in the very Jewish suburb of Skokie, Illinois.

Midway through our first slab of Carson's barbecued baby back ribs, skepticism dissolved. Here are the best in the land: sensuously sticky with dark baked-on sauce, a sauce brilliantly poised between molasses sweetness and spicy tang. The ribs are just a wee bit smoky, lean with only the meagerest necessary veins of lubricating fat—the meatiest ribs imaginable, their sweet pork taste accentuated, but not overwhelmed, by the sauce or the hickory smoke. A full slab runs on for about eighteen inches; it's an enormous amount of food.

There is something definitively Skokiean about the lavishness of Carson's. Inside it is dark and well air-conditioned; the booths are overstuffed; everything is designed to keep big eaters in a state of maximum comfort. If you must wait for a table in the bar (and you usually must), there are blocks of chopped liver with rye bread to feast on. Once seated, you are brought a basket of fabulous breadstuffs, rather unorthodox offerings for a rib joint:

bagels, poppy seed rolls, challah bread, deliciously odorous onion rolls. An ice cream scoop of creamy butter accompanies.

Before the ribs comes a hill of salad with anchovy sour cream dressing. It's iceberg lettuce, the only lettuce with enough body and cold crunch to balance the cream dressing. Along with the ribs come potatoes—fries, baked, skins (too dry), or a nice-sized casserole of au gratins: cheddary, blackened on top, really delicious and yet—because of all the vast quantities of other great food—often neglected.

Before we get to the peerless Gold Brick sundae, we must tell you that, in addition to the world's best ribs, Carson's serves a truly great steak, the kind of steak Chicago was once famous for when the stockyards were running full steam. It is called a Giant New York Sirloin, a boneless prime-graded, dry-aged strip steak, over an inch thick. It comes on a plate unadorned but for a scrap of lettuce leaf and a slice of tomato, and it is stunning in its black mantle of char. (The waitress will ask if you want a "char crust." This means a coating of salty dry seasoning. Without the artificial crust, a Carson's steak is perfectly charred.)

If you wish, the kitchen will top your steak with chopped garlic as it cooks. Each bit of bud turns crisp under the flame, but like the steak it tops, the garlic is not weakened by the fire. It tastes like what it is—fresh garlic edged with flame, adding a nip to the kingly slab of beef. The steak is tender, yet fibrous enough to yield a grand, faintly gamey aged flavor.

Gold Brick sundae, a midwest favorite, is vanilla ice cream topped with Gold Brick sauce—chocolate with little bits of praline and bigger bits of pecan. The sauce hardens on the ice cream into a sheath of milk chocolate, then melts and crumbles delicately in your mouth.

(There are other Carson's in Chicago, at 612 N. Wells, 5970 N. Ridge, 400 E. Roosevelt in Lombard, and 5050 N. Harlem in Harwood Heights.)

Connie's

6266 W. North Ave., Chicago, Ill.
(312) 237-3994

Mon.–Fri. 10 a.m.–8 p.m., Sat. & Sun. 10 a.m.–7 p.m.

Under $5

"A real gem and an absolute must for enthusiasts," raved Rich Bowen and Dick Fay in their indispensable *Hot Dog Chicago*, a 180-page book devoted exclusively to the evaluation of restaurants in Chicago that specialize in hot dogs, Polish sausages, Gyros, and Italian beef sandwiches.

A tiny brick-face storefront on the west side, Connie's roasts its own beef, serving it up thinly sliced, hot and aromatic, natural garlicky juices sopping into the soft insides of its chewy Italian roll. Doll it up if you wish with a splash of gentle-flavored marinated peppers.

Fabulous, but there is more: tubes of pork sausage, made right here, grilled to crackling succulence on a charcoal fire. Alone in a bun, or in concert with the elegant Italian beef, this is street food nonpareil, Chicago-style.

Edith's Bar-B-Q

1863 N. Clybourn Ave., Chicago, Ill.
(312) 327-5160

Mon.–Thurs. 11 a.m.–10:30 p.m., Fri. to 1:30 a.m., Sat. 3:30 p.m.–12:30 a.m.

$3–$10

Edith is a kindly black lady with her hair in a snood who hickory-smokes beautiful spare ribs. Her restaurant isn't much more than a storefront, with a counter and a few tables, and she does the smoking right here, so you are hit with the appetizing perfume of pork and burning hickory as soon as you enter.

Edith's are russet-glazed ribs, with crisp edges and plenty of tender, hickory-flavored meat: the kind of great midwest city food we would kill for when marooned in the ribless northeast. Edith puts the ribs in a basket on top of fries and Wonder bread, then uses a paintbrush to apply a translucent, syrupy sauce, redolent of cider vinegar. There is a hotter version, not as good.

A lovely little restaurant, painted orange and black, each table adorned with a white vase with little plastic flowers—a shipshape soul shack.

Edwardo's

1212 N. Dearborn, Chicago, Ill.
(312) 337-4490

Mon.–Thurs. 5:30 p.m.–11:30 p.m., Fri. & Sat. 6 p.m.–11 p.m.

$10 or less

Edwardo's is the leading wave in Chicago's ever-rolling tide of pizza progress.

First there was deep-dish pizza, invented by Ike Sewell at Pizzeria Uno in 1943. For years, that was the regional specialty known as Chicago pizza.

Then about ten years ago (this has yet to be historically documented; if only culinary students studied really important subjects like pizza history instead of portion control!) a new kind of pizza appeared on the scene: stuffed pizza, twice as thick as deep dish. Stuffed pizza begat double-crust pizza. And now, at Edwardo's, double-crust pizza has begot the pizza soufflé.

It nearly does have the consistency of a lumpish soufflé: a puff of airy cheese laced with flakes of spinach, capped with a layer of tomato sauce, bubbling inside the crispest, tallest hard crust in town; a lush pizza with a haunting aroma.

Where will it end? How far toward healthy food can the Chicago deep-dish pizzerias go before they lose contact with the earthy roots of junky pizza pie, as we in the rest of the country know it? The latest wrinkle at Edwardo's is the pesto pizza, made with basil grown in in-house hydroponic planters! (The basil is also put to good use in a fresh basil salad.) The pizza menu even offers wholewheat crust, boasting that it's "high in fiber"!

There are two other Edwardo pizzerias in Chicago: at 1937 West Howard Street; and on the South Side, at 1321 East Fifty-seventh.

Finn Inn

Rte. 100, Grafton, Ill.
(618) 786-2030

Mon.–Thurs. & Sun. 11:30 a.m.–8 p.m., Fri. & Sat. to 8:30 p.m.

$10 or less

We are suckers for aberrations of proportion. We have screeched off the road to view miniature replicas of Mount Vernon, giant coffee cups, bibles no bigger than a sugar cube, and "the largest cheese in the history of mankind." And so we were lured off the southern Illinois pork tenderloin trail by the Finn Inn's sign that boasted of a 2,000-gallon aquarium.

The aquarium runs the width of the restaurant, and is partitioned to provide each booth a private view. The wall of glass is framed in cemented-together stones (echoing the stone motif of the rock garden outside and the stone walls of the aquarium). The underwater population is a heterogeneous group of fish and turtles, swimming casually . . . until someone drops a dime in the "feed the fish" box at the table. Then they all shoot to the surface and start gobbling.

It's amusing, the point apparently being to pique customers' appetites for Finn Inn food, which is almost entirely freshwater fish. Grafton, you see, is a river town, where the Illinois River joins the Mississippi. Although the Finn Inn is just across the road from the water, the inside is sequestered, too far for an outside view. Hence, the fish tank to stimulate thoughts of seafood.

(Actually, we were relieved when the waitress explained that residents of the aquarium are pets, not the evening's menu.)

Decorated with captioned pictures of at least a dozen fish, the menu lists carp and buffalo fish in various-sized filets as well as bite-size fritters; but we chose catfish. Both filets and the whole fish were fried in a sandy crust and served with onion-spangled hushpuppies. The whole ones come on a pallet of white bread, filets arrive curled up crisp and crunchy on the plate. Either way, the meat is clean and flaky, with a sweet succulence unique to good catfish. It was a little weird to gobble it up in view of the merrily swimming school to our side, but there was no denying its goodness.

Friday and Saturday nights, Finn Inn offers all-you-can-eat catfish fries for under $10.

Flo's Family Restaurant

329 Main, Marseilles, Ill.
(815) 795-4422

Mon.–Fri. 5 a.m.–8 p.m., Sat. 6 a.m.–5 p.m., Sun. 6 a.m.–3 p.m.

$5 or less

We like Flo's motto: "If I can't eat it, I won't serve it." We also like Flo's sobriquet: "Home of jumbo tenderloins."

Jumbo? You will find none larger. One tenderloin was a twelve-inch diameter disc, deep fried until golden. The crust is rough, highly seasoned, and pulls away from the pounded-thin pork within. It is so much broader than the bun on which it is served that it is impossible, unless you have immense fingers, to grip the bun with one hand. "Start on the outside," our waitress instructed, "then work your way to the middle. That's the fun part."

If you are an aficionado of cafe cuisine, you will find a lot to like about this storefront hash house with its red-checked oilcloths and short back counter. It is a slice of blue-plate Americana, with lunch specials that include Polish sausage and fried cabbage, baked chicken and dressing, and good old tuna-noodle casserole.

At breakfast there are soft frosted cinnamon rolls, and plates of pork chops and eggs with hashed brown potatoes that have the pungent greasy flavor of the grill. Or you can get biscuits blanketed with high-viscosity cream gravy.

Pies are literally homemade, brought in to the cafe, including rhubarb in the spring and summer, when the pie cook can get it fresh. We had rhubarb custard, an eggy balance of sweet and tart in a sturdy crust, and Dutch apple, strewn with heaps of buttery crumbs.

For us, there was something nostalgic about eating at Flo's. The food and ambience evoked that mythical time when truckers *did* know all the good places to eat. Indeed, the street outside was nothing but vans, wreckers, and pickups.

When the waitress got too busy to refill coffee cups, a customer circled through the dining room helping out. As he poured the coffee, his wife explained, "He's retired," and he joked back, "Now I work only for tips." All through our meal, we eavesdropped on a conversation at a nearby men's table, where one 18-year-old boy sat mesmerized as older truckers told tales of brakeline freeze-ups in Montana and hair-raising curves at Fancy Gap, Virginia.

Giordano's

747 N. Rush St., Chicago, Ill.
(312) 951-0747

Mon.–Thurs. 11 a.m.–midnight, Fri. & Sat. to 1 a.m., Sun. noon–midnight

About $5

Two, three . . . could it be *four* inches high? This is the tallest pizza in America, a casserole formed out of a trough of dense, rugged dough that holds pounds of mozzarella, Parmesan, and Romano cheese, plus fennel sausage, plus a top crust brushed with red sauce. A monumental pizza pie—the heftiest, creamiest in town.

It is known as stuffed pizza, and it first came to Chicago in 1974, nearly thirty years after Pizzeria Uno fashioned its first deep-dish pizza, the single-crusted extravaganza known nationwide as Chicago-style. Although many second-city pizzerias now serve stuffed pizza, it was Giordano's that introduced it, upping the ante in the local pizza sweepstakes. The restaurant was named after Joe and Efren Boglio's mother, who was famous in Turin, Italy, for her Easter pizza—deep-dish, double-crusted, stuffed with ricotta.

The closest to this old-country specialty you can get at Giordano's is the one called "stuffed spinach special"—gobs of cheese laced with oily spinach and mushrooms. There is a terrific "Vegi'ordano" pie that adds peppers and onions to the formula. A fine idea, but we would never pass up the good garlicky sausage, strewn in abundance along with vegetables throughout the Giordano special.

In addition to a full repertoire of stuffed pan pizzas, the menu lists thin pizzas and a few sandwiches, plus a trademarked item called "Pop-A Giordano's," which is a half-baked stuffed pizza ready to be popped into a home oven. It works!

Ambience at Giordano's? Pure urban pizza parlor: functional booths, plastic laminate materials, bits and pieces of Mediterranean decor. You would call it gloomy place if it weren't for the smell of the mighty double-crusters, fresh out of the oven, bringing happiness to tablesful of second-city pizza hounds.

(There are other Giordano's locations around the city at 5311 S. Blackstone, 3214 W. 63rd, 201 Plainfield Road in Willowbrook, and 14325 S. LaGrange Road in Orland Park.)

Hale's Restaurant

Across from the red caboose
Grand Tower, Ill.
(618) 565-8384

Tues.–Sun. 11 a.m.–7 p.m.

Under $10

Back in the 1940s, a woman called Ma Hale began serving meals to outsiders in the dining room of her home. Her skillet-fried ham and chicken dinners became a southern Illinois legend, and on Sundays especially, people from Marion and Carbondale, Cape Girardeau and even St. Louis would travel to the tiny river town of Grand Tower for her family feasts.

Ma Hale died twelve years ago, but people still journey to Hale's Restaurant, now run by Esther Cripps, for dinner in this nice old house just off the main street of town.

The food is country cooking, served in bowls to which everybody at the table helps themselves. There are green beans, mashed potatoes and gravy, dumplings, cole slaw, buttery hominy corn, and warm dinner rolls. Not everything is as farm-fresh as one would want in this rustic restaurant; our beans were limp; the potatoes were powdery. But the hominy was sweet and the rolls fresh and yeasty.

We liked the fried chicken main course; the country ham was sliced too thickly for our taste, although it had a pleasant flavor. On Sunday, these two regular entrees are supplemented by a third, most often turkey and dressing. For dessert, we had some fine apple pie.

Hale's is very literally a homey restaurant, with some of Ma's old pictures still hung on the walls and long tables you will likely share with strangers during the crowded noonday meal.

Ideal Candies

3311 N. Clark, Chicago, Ill.
(312) 327-2880

Wed.–Sat. 11 a.m.–9:30 p.m., Sun. 11 a.m.–5 p.m.

Under $5

EST. 1937, says the sign outside, on a Chi-town main drag that has seen at least a half dozen changings of the guard in the fifty years since Ideal Candies dipped its first chocolate bonbons. Whatever tongue is spoken on the street (Korean seems to prevail today), the lingo of the soda fountain reigns supreme inside this living antique.

Order your malt regular, extra heavy, or super. Get your limeade floated with a scoop of vanilla ice cream. Have a phosphate or an egg cream; a black cow or a butterscotch split. Cokes are drawn from a classic round-edged bomb-shaped dispenser.

An argument could be made for Clark Street as America's caramel apple boulevard, as it is home to both Ideal Candies and the Affy Tapple factory (where "broken sticks," factory seconds, and otherwise slightly blemished specimens are sold to passersby). Between September and December, when apples are at their best, Ideal makes its own superb caramel-dipped apples, crisp and fresh and weighted all around with creamy tan gunk, with or without nuts.

All these blasts from the confectionery past are dished out in a setting that is truly *ideal:* at the soda fountain counter (on chrome and leather stools), in dark wooden booths, or at marble-topped wrought-iron tables. Along the wall, Ideal's own candies are displayed in mahogany fixtures, and in the window, gift boxes share the pen with a nurseryful of cute, fuzzy animals.

The Indian Trail

507 Chestnut St., Winnetka, Ill.
(312) 446-1703

Tues.–Sat. lunch & dinner, Sun. 11:30 a.m.–7:30 p.m.

Lunch about $5, dinner $10 or less

Many people on the North Shore think of The Indian Trail as a tea room. It is a soothing kind of place, and there's no denying it's a favorite of Winnetka's blue-haired ladies and their gents. But "tea room" implies wimpy fare, and that's not right, because The Indian Trail's meals, while never gross, are always satisfying. No surprises; no pretensions, no funny business—just good food.

Credit belongs to the Klingeman family, who for decades have refused to compromise quality with institutional restaurant shortcuts. The mashed potatoes are mashed potatoes, not reconstituted flakes; the lovely apple-scented sweet rolls and dinner rolls are baked fresh each day. Classic American desserts like apple pan dowdy and cherry tarts are topped with real whipped cream, not spray-on foam.

When Winnetka voted to allow liquor sales in town (just five years ago), The Indian Trail grew sleeker, adding a beer garden and a menu full of prose, but the dependable kitchen never changed. It still turns out square food like roast loin of pork sided by green bean succotash and creamed spinach in a tiny crock; broiled whitefish—a true taste of the Great Lakes; and our long-time favorite, fricassee of turkey breast.

You can still get an unfashionable wedge of iceberg lettuce dripping with honey-spiked celery seed dressing—a greatly unappreciated specialty of many midwestern restaurants; and you can still begin a meal with a fresh rhubarb and raspberry cup or chunked turkey salad with walnuts and capers and a peeled tomato wedge, served with an itty-bitty fork.

In the summer, there are always half a dozen desserts made with fresh fruit, either plain or with sour cream and brown sugar, or with whipped cream in a flaky lard crust.

The Indian Trail is tradition, a place to take your old aunt—or your kids —for a "nice" dinner: a multigenerational restaurant that continues to be a bastion of all things good about American family dining.

Leikam's Tavern

Rte. 45, Half Day, Ill.
(312) 634-3468

9 a.m.–2 a.m.   Kitchen closes at 7 p.m.

About $5

"Home cooking and a brew or two," is the way Chicagoland food sleuth Debby Hartz described Leikam's charms, insisting that we check it out the next time we headed west by northwest. "It's your kind of place," she grinned knowingly.

Our kind of place? It is in fact a roadside tavern favored by the wide-load crowd. But Debby was right. Leikam's is a taste of true farmland cooking.

The house-special hamburgers look normal in the beefy hands of this bar's patrons; but when we scrawny under 200-pound types pick one up, we are bowled over. The juice-dripping behemoth is over one half pound of red meat heaped with cheese, bacon, mushrooms, onions, and—in the summer —thick slices of farm-fresh tomatoes. The french fries are hand-cut; cole slaw, speckled with carrots and green pepper, is made from an old family recipe; briny-sweet pickles are put up by Betty Leikam and her daughter Cindy.

In the morning, omelettes are made with eggs from a farmer in nearby Lake Geneva. Sweet corn, eggplant, and zucchini are pulled from the Leikam's own vegetable garden. Betty cooks a motherly pot roast; and there is always homemade soup.

It isn't all pastoral cuisine. These patrons eat their share of beef jerky and Whippo pie, right alongside the impeccable farm-fresh produce. And in a way, that is what we like about Leikam's. The food served here is an expression not of culinary purism, but of the way real people live.

Lou Mitchell's

560 W. Jackson Blvd., Chicago, Ill.
(312) 939-3111

Mon.–Fri. 5:30 a.m.–4 p.m., Sat. 5:30 a.m.–2 p.m.

$5 or less

Although there are several logical reasons to favor Lou Mitchell's restaurant, none exactly or fully explains why Chicagoans (and Jane and Michael Stern) love it so.

WORLD'S FINEST CUP OF COFFEE, proclaims the sign outside. Oh, it's excellent java all right—served with a pitcher of thick cream, but honestly, it's not the finest in the world.

Jeff Lyons, who first led us to the unpretentious coffee shop on the west side of the loop, said he liked it for the double-yolk eggs. Quite amazing— order two sunnyside up, and you'll see double. The four eyes arrive sizzling in their skillet, along with potatoes and good ham and plenty of butter. The waitress plops the pan on a wooden trivet, and you dig in, fighting for elbow room with the strangers seated next to you at the long communal tables (there are some booths, too). Terrific eggs, accompanied by thick-cut "Greek toast" . . . but eggs, however wonderful, will never cause us to fall in love.

The side dishes are pretty terrific: clove-scented prunes, tart homemade marmalade, freshly squeezed orange juice. "Dear Treasured Customer," Lou writes on his menu. "Every effort is made . . . to buy the freshest and best All American Fruit on a daily basis." But it's not the high-quality extra goodies that make us love this place.

Nor is it the luscious spinach and feta cheese omelette, or the malted milk waffles or pancakes served with stewed fruit and sour cream.

What we really love is walking in the door. To the right is a bank of aquaria, big ones without fish, filled with furiously bubbling green-tinted, fluorescent-lit water. TRIPLE FILTERED WATER, according to the sign. Is this the secret of Lou's "gold cup award coffee"? It would seem so, but how does this Martian-colored water get into the coffee pots? We don't want to know.

Straight ahead, behind the water, is Lou Mitchell himself, a mischievous septuagenarian whose eyes light up with glee when a coed couple enters. "Oh, gorgeous woman," he tells each lady, passing her a small complimentary box of Milk Duds as he leads her to a table.

Who could resist a breakfast of double-yolk eggs, gold-cup coffee, and Milk Duds?

Mary Lou's

114 S. Illinois, Carbondale, Ill.
(618) 457-5084

Mon.–Sat. 7 a.m.–3 p.m.

$5 or less

When Mary Lou's was just a diner, with a few stools along a counter, she was known among Southern Illinois University students as a soft touch, a tough bird with a heart of gold, who, if she knew you were down on your luck, would mix up a batch of "poor boy" chocolate pudding or a plate of biscuits on the house. Her new restaurant is bigger now, with a real kitchen in back, and a dining room, and thirty-two stools at the counter; but it hasn't gotten away from her. This is still Mary Lou Trammel's domain, a beanery with a vivid personality.

Nothing Mary Lou makes is likely to find its way into the pages of *Gourmet* magazine; her repertoire, with the exception of the omelettes that still get whipped up with considerable savoir faire, is a lumpish cuisine. It is biscuits smothered with thick country gravy in the morning. Or salty ham and stacks of griddle cakes. And waterfalls of coffee, for the regulars.

At lunch Mary Lou's specialty is chicken and dumplings, a fortifying, motherly dish; or there is that southern midwestern favorite, ham and beans, accompanied by a side of warm cornbread suitable for crumbling atop the bulky meal; there are jumbo pork steaks, the likes of which you don't see in any other part of the country; turkey and dressing, smothered steaks, and meat loaf.

For dessert, Mary Lou's serves traditional cream pies and cobblers, and occasionally, her special invention, poor boy pudding made with devil's-food cake.

You can't miss Mary Lou. She's the one kibbitzing at the cash register with her regular customers, some of whom eat here six days a week, and have for years.

Morton's

1050 N. State, Chicago, Ill.   Downstairs at Newberry Plaza
(312) 266-4820

Mon.–Fri. 5 p.m.–11:30 p.m., Sat. to 1 a.m.   Reservations required

$15–$40

"This is the menu for tonight," says the white-aproned waiter as he rolls up a cart topped with various raw cuts of meat. He picks up each Saran-Wrapped steak for you to inspect; each is a looker, deeply marbled the way you *never* see meat in a supermarket.

Chicago is an eater's paradise, with a staggering variety of plain and exotic foods, but there is nothing better, no food more grandly Chicagoan than these steaks on the Morton's cart.

Also displayed are a live lobster, chicken oregano, veal chops, and the largest unbaked potato in the western world. There is no menu; it is all show and tell, each dish described by the waiter in as much detail as you request —even the price, if you are interested. Near the open, stainless-steel kitchen, where the chefs work at the red-hot grill, there is a tiny blackboard listing everything, including prices; but if you are watching your budget, don't come here. Morton's is for splurging: devil-may-care dining for big appetites.

At our table of four, we ordered an estimated seventy-five ounces of meat. The best cut is the "New York sirloin," a foot-long, two-inch-thick leviathan almost totally trimmed of fat. But this is the primest of prime, so even without its rim of amber, the steak is savory. It is thick enough so that the inside is brilliant scarlet, even when the crust is charred. It is served with watercress, on a warm plate.

The filet mignon, a mere fourteen ounces, is also devoid of fat; unbelievably tender.

Cuts of prime rib are not immense, but they are ample, bursting with natural juice and unsurpassed flavor. Morton's garnish, shredded white radish, adds a brilliant sting.

About that baked potato on the "menu cart": the one we received was, if anything, bigger than the demo model: nearly football-sized, with a tough, clean skin. But this was not some freakish tasteless specimen from the back of a seed catalogue. It was absolutely delicious, with the purest potato taste imaginable. A thin, crisp pancake of hashed browns is also available, the kind of shredded spuds sometimes called haystack potatoes in lower Illinois. They have a delicate flavor which has a hard time holding its own at this bullish meal.

Salads are copious. The Caesar salad is surprisingly mild; the spinach salad sparkles with bits of avocado and crisp bacon. Only the beefsteak tomato and onion salad disappointed. It was the height of tomato season, and yet the thick slices of tomato were just not good enough.

A Morton's meal begins with a loaf of warm, eggy bread, topped with squiggles of burnt onion. It ends with good cheesecake, or a soufflé. The soufflé is a steamy cloud of bittersweet chocolate, dotted with bits of cocoa, served with wine-laced *crème fraîche*.

Morton's is strong and masculine, yet preeminently comfortable—a truly luxurious place, without airs. Service, by confident men and women with no chips on their shoulders, is fast and helpful. The appointments are modern, decor consisting of fresh flowers and handsome charcoal drawings of Illinois celebrities.

Chicago has long outgrown its reputation as a steak-only city, but if you want that great mythical heartland steak, this is the place.

Mr. Beef

666 N. Orleans, Chicago, Ill.
(312) 337-8500

Mon.–Fri. 7 a.m.–6 p.m.

$5 or less

Many of Mr. Beef's patrons are men from Scala Beef Packers across the street, where *all* of Chicago's good Italian beef originates; so one suspects the sandwiches here will rank high. They are, in fact, the best Italian beefs in the city.

A simmering garlic and beef aroma wafts upward when you unwrap a Mr. Beef sandwich. The bread is crusty with plenty of oomph, retaining its chewy character to the last bite; the beef, totally lean, occasionally even rare in spots, is savory, highly spiced, full of sass and character, just oozing juice. It tastes good, and leaves a satisfying tang of an aftertaste. If you want to see why Chicagoans are Italian beef crazed, a Mr. Beef sandwich will explain it.

There are two choices for a garnish. We thought Mr. Beef's sandwich was better with a single firm slice of sweet pepper than with the hot, and somewhat overwhelming, *giardiniera*.

Mr. Beef also serves the best combo sandwich we had in Chicago—beef and Italian sausage (also from Scala)—a doozy of a sandwich, in which the plumpness of the round sausage and the leanness of the limp shreds of beef balance perfectly, especially if interknit with a few lengths of crunchy sweet roasted pepper.

There is an eating area outside that resembles a loading dock set with a couple of long picnic tables, offering a view of the parking lot.

Although it is humble food, Italian beef knows no social bounds. At our picnic table, at lunch, we saw as many briefcases and pinstriped suits as meatpacker's overalls and hard hats.

Oberweis Dairy

945 N. Lake St., Aurora, Ill.
(312) 897-0512

Mon.–Sat. 9 a.m.–10 p.m., Sun. 10 a.m.–1 p.m.

Under $5

It is hardly a bucolic setting, nestled next to a dry cleaner, down the road from McDonald's; but Oberweis Dairy is a pure taste of farmland Illinois. It is a genuine dairy store, with ice cream packed in back (watch it flow into cartons through a wall of glass) and a steady stream of customers returning empty milk bottles—made of glass!—and leaving with fresh milk.

Oberweis's heavy cream is legendary. High butterfat, straight from the farm, it is sweetened and flavored and frozen to make superior ice cream—which is then turned into sundaes, malts, and sodas in this small ice cream parlor with a handful of tables (sorry, no counter and stools).

Vanilla ice cream is pure silky white, a solid foundation for a "turtle candy sundae," made with caramel sauce and hot fudge and a liberal sprinkle of eye-openingly crisp roasted pecans. The nut-and-ice-cream theme is also expressed in classic tin roof sundaes—chocolate topping and salty Spanish peanuts, no whipped cream. For serious pig-outs, there is a stupefying banana royal made with three flavors of ice cream, pineapple, strawberries, bananas, pecans, and gobs of hot fudge.

Caramel sauce is king in this part of the midwest, at least as popular as fudge, and you can order it not only as an ice cream topping, but as the primary flavoring in malts, shakes, and sodas. "Creamy caramel" is its name on the menu; it is a magical amber fusion of sugar and cream.

Caramel and fudge are gooey and strong-flavored, demanding a clear chaser. "Fresh chilled water from our own well is available at the water cooler," advises the menu. Help yourself, with a small paper cup.

Pizzeria Uno

29 E. Ohio, Chicago, Ill.
(312) 321-1000

Tues.–Fri. 11:30 a.m.–1 a.m., Sat. to 2 a.m.

$10 or less

THIS IS WHERE IT ALL BEGAN! exclaims a plaque outside Pizzeria Uno. For many years, Uno's, the creator of Chicago-style pizza, was unique in Chicago and the world. But during the last decade, pizza evolution has speeded up. Extrapolating from Uno's deep-dish concept, Chicago's culinary experimenters have invented stuffed pizza, double-crust pizza, even pizza soufflés. They are all interesting, and most are very good; no question—Chicago is more a pizza town than Naples or New Haven, or anywhere.

But to us, no variation on the deep-dish theme has the essential pizzaness of an Uno original. (None of the "Chicago-style" pizzerias that have opened in other cities even resemble it.) There is still only one pure and authentic Chicago pizza, and Uno's is it.

It is a genuine pizza *pie,* cooked in a pan, about an inch high. The circumference of crust is uneven, thick-and-thin, rising above a landscape of tomatoes and cheese and, preferably, sausage. Uno's sausage is a kick—sweet, coarse-ground pork, wide patties covering whole slices, most buried under drifts of superior cheese and great mottled clots of deep red tomato (not tomato sauce). The crust is thick but not doughy; a geological terrain of little shelves and small savory mounds, all with a wicked, oily crunch.

The evolutionary forms of this pizza—Carmen's stuffed double-crusters, Edwardo's spinachy fantasies—however excellent they may be, lack the *balls* of Uno's primeval pie, lack the brutishness that is, we contend, a necessary quality of pizza. Without it, you've got quiche.

Since opening in 1943, Uno's has sold more than 25 million pizzas, a fact attested to by former Mayor Byrne, who saw fit to commend Uno's pie as "a great American tradition."

Uno's is a raffish grotto with graffiti on the walls and red Naugahyde tablecloths. An annex, Due's, just down the street at 619 North Wabash, is also cavelike, but has classical busts and mosaics instead of graffiti. Due's is open later at night, and on Sunday and Monday. The number there is 943-2400. The menus at both places are the same, the pizzas equal. The pizzas sold at Uno's franchises in other cities are second rate.

Richards Farm

Rural Rte. 1, Casey, Ill.
(217) 932-5300

Sun.–Fri. lunch, daily dinner

$10 or less

We who live in the northeast are hog-deprived: no ribs or barbecue; no sausages or hams of any merit. And no one-pound pork chops, as served at Richards Farm, in the pig-rich state of Illinois. It looks like a beef steak, this mighty chop, but the taste is pure clean pork: not oozing like beef, nor as dense, and yet every bit as succulent. It is baked, then broiled in a tangy red sauce. Sided by pan-fried potatoes, vegetables from the garden (by way of the salad bar), and a slab of hot bread with apple butter, this is a vision of farm food to be found nowhere else in America.

Better still, you eat it in a barn. Mind you, the animals have been evacuated—the place is quite modern and clean; but it's still a two-story hip-roof building, and you can still dine in the renovated hayloft on top, or downstairs, where the feedway cuts down the center. Somewhere else, eating in a barn might seem too gimmicky. Here, it is right. This was the Richards Farm barn when Richards Farm was a farm, not a restaurant.

And although it is a big restaurant, there is nothing institutional about the food. One-pound pork chops are not something sold by your average meat distributor. They are cut here from whole loins. All the pork is processed here: ham steaks are cut; the tenderloins are cut and hammered and breaded to make the tenderest tenderloin sandwich in the midwest; the bones are cooked and stripped of meat to make barbecue, and then they are thrown in the stock pot for vegetable soup.

The salad bar is pure heartland, too. It's not just lettuce and greens and croutons and bacon bits, like the paltry excuses for salad bars in other parts of the country. You *can* make an ordinary green salad, but there are about eight or ten already-made salads at this bar: slaws, puddings, fruit Jell-Os, bean salads, potato salads, and—in summer—fresh melons.

This meal would not be complete without an appropriately rustic dessert, and if you peek into Richards Farm's kitchen early in the day you will see ladies filling feathery crusts with tart rhubarb or gooseberries. Or, if it is autumn, you may be lucky—persimmon pudding can be yours.

Persimmon pudding! In all our travels, we had found only one place to get this traditional—and yet virtually extinct—midwestern specialty; and a few years back, when we drove to that place, in Gnaw Bone, Indiana, we found a For Sale sign on its shutters. Would we ever taste persimmon pudding again? Probably not—the fruit industry, which imports larger but less flavorful persimmons from Asia (and has transplanted them to California), doesn't bother with American persimmons. But Richards Farm *does* bother. Just after the southern midwest's first frost, when the small fragile orbs begin to turn from puckery green to fragrant, plummy fruits, Richards pays schoolchildren to gather them, then makes persimmon pudding for dessert.

It's a pretty dish, as red-orange as autumn, baked in a cake pan and then sliced. Its consistency is firm like bread pudding, and the flavor is unique— strong, but no longer tart; the tannic bitterness of the unripened persimmon has turned exquisitely sweet.

A one-pound pork chop and wild persimmon pudding for dessert: God bless America.

The Village Smithy

368 Park Ave., Glencoe, Ill.
(312) 835-0220

Mon.–Sat. lunch & dinner, Sun. dinner   Reservations advised

Lunch about $5, dinner $10

Glencoe is the kind of well-to-do suburban community where the clientele at the good restaurant sports a pewter-haired, Brooks Brothers look. This is not meant to imply that The Village Smithy is stuffy. In fact, it serves what might be called glorified home cooking, distinctively American, mostly midwestern.

Dinner began with tiny cornbread and blueberry muffins, hot from the oven, and large powdery rolls with steamy white insides. The butter is whipped, the bread plate made of pewter.

Smithy baby back ribs, similar in style and taste to those you will get in Chicago's most elite ribberies, are slathered in a mahogany glaze, falling-off-the-bone tender: superior pork.

Ask for duckling extra crisp, and that's what you get. The meat is fatless, still moist; the skin has a delectable melting crunch. Duck is served with a triumvirate of sauces—pear, apple, and peach—suitable for dipping.

There is almost always a fresh lake fish or two on the menu—perch, whitefish, walleye pike, as well as some seafood imported from the oceans; you can get a modest slab of ham steak, a few vegetarian casseroles; and chicken is barbecued on an outdoor patio over oak logs every Thursday.

Dinners come with a choice of salads, the best of which is spinach, served with an eggy dressing and a generous sprinkle of real bacon. Vegetables were the only silly part of our meal: a side plate with two discs of crisply sauteed zucchini and a microdot of whipped potato. It looked like dolls' food.

(The good ribs are available in a half-slab size at lunch, plus there are salads and sandwiches, including the midwestern favorite, pork loin sandwich, served with cottage-fried potatoes.)

Desserts: our chocolate chip pecan pie oozed warm chocolate with every bite, the dark veins counterpointed by a brown-sugar nut crust. The Chicagoland dessert called Gold Brick sundae was a modest scoop of vanilla ice cream with a cap of praline-studded milk chocolate. Indian pudding, molasses-rich cornmeal with a dollop of ice cream on top, was dowdy enough to please the fussiest New Englander.

The Henry Wadsworth Longfellow *hommage* derives from The Village Smithy's setting, in a building that was once a blacksmith's shop. The walls are raw brick, hung with a few black-and-white photos of the old shop; there is even a spreading chestnut tree overhanging the pleasant outdoor patio. But the theme is not overwhelming; just a pleasant complement to the food.

Walker Brothers Original Pancake House

153 Green Bay, Wilmette, Ill.
(312) 251-6000

Sun.–Thurs. 7 a.m.–10 p.m., Fri. & Sat. 7 a.m.–midnight

$5 or less

When a Walker Brothers apple pancake is paraded toward the table, trailing wisps of cinnamon steam, the pancake is all you see. Yes, there is a plate beneath it—a full twelve-incher—but the plate is covered edge to edge. The pancake is a dark sizzling mound, its dough heaped high with apples. The limp slices and slivers that blanket the cake are so caramelized that it is impossible to see exactly where the stewed fruit ends and the pancake edge rises up at the circumference.

Sugary pools of cinnamon and butter weigh upon the dough, and the mahogany puff begins to settle as you work your way into the landscape-sized breakfast.

It is a meal fit for two, or three, or maybe even four to share. And it is so good, it is practically the only thing we ever eat at Walker Brothers . . . even though the German pancake is gorgeous (it's the same high-rise eggy batter, without fruit) and the Palestine pancakes, wrapped around Cointreau cream, melt in the mouth. The problem of choosing what to eat at Walker Brothers is that everything on the menu is superb, of infinitely higher quality than you will get in any other pancake house between New Hampshire and Kansas: thick-cut bacon, onion-perfumed hash browns, wide sourdough pancakes, strong coffee—offered constantly through the meal, heavy cream on the side. No wonder the lines to get in often reach out onto Green Bay Road.

And there is the place itself. Decor is carved and polished wood and panels of spectacular stained and beveled glass. You would never guess, looking at it from the outside, that it was anything special. But the decoration tips you off that something wonderful is going on; and when that apple pancake hits the table, you know you've struck paydirt—one of America's great breakfasts . . . or lunches . . . or suppers.

The White Mill

S. Main & W. 6th Ave., Monmouth, Ill.
(309) 734-6519

Mon.–Fri. 10 a.m.–8 p.m., Sat. 10 a.m.–6 p.m.

$5 or less

Look carefully when you cruise down Main Street in Monmouth. Heading south, The White Mill is on the left, marked on both sides by a sign. The problem is that the sign reads HOME OF WYATT EARP. Nothing outside says that this is The White Mill.

But the lady standing behind the small cafeteria line assured us it was The White Mill, and mentioned that, yes, she has heard that Wyatt Earp was born in Monmouth, and that's all she knows about the sign. She was much more interested in reciting the inventory of her steam table. Lifting lids off the day's array, one by one, she enumerated "roast beef, ham, pepper steak, mashed potatoes, peas, greens . . ."

But Ort Carlton, the traveling trencherman of Athens, Georgia, had not directed us to The White Mill for steam-table chow. Our grail in Monmouth was The White Mill's tenderloin sandwich. "Must be seen to be believed," Ort had written. Tenderloins are ordered from a second lady behind the counter. You get whatever salad or Jell-O you want and carry it to one of the front room's grand total of three booths (or to the annex dining room in back).

As our tenderloins fried, we perused the menu, noting an entry called "sandy mash," which the steam table lady explained was a beef, ham, tenderloin, or hamburger sandwich cut in half, separated by a mound of mashed potatoes, then blanketed, edge to edge, with gravy. "Some call it a Manhattan," she explained. The menu also boasted "Pie—a great variety," but the pies we tasted from the cafeteria line—lemon, pumpkin, apple—were nothing to rave about.

The tenderloin, on the other hand, is a vision. In Illinois and Iowa, where tenderloins reign as the sandwich supreme, the competition among cafes is for both breadth and brittleness. This one scores at the top on both counts. Crackling crisp, its thin golden crust bound inextricably to the pounded-thin pork cutlet it encloses, it is at least twice as wide as its bun. You eat half a meal before you hit bread—a frustrating situation for those of us who like our tenderloins with condiments, which are spread only on the bun.

Although the tenderloin is the culinary attraction of The White Mill, there is an irresistible charm about the tiny unmarked—or oddly marked—cafe. It is worn but tidy, decorated with little crocheted dolls and advertisements for invisible hearing aids.

And for a post-tenderloin treat, if Wyatt Earp's hometown doesn't get your blood racing, head sixteen miles west to Oquawka, Illinois, site of "The Grave of Norma Jean Elephant," whose marker declares she was killed by lightning. What the elephant was doing in Oquawka the sign doesn't say.

INDIANA

Dodd's Town House

5694 N. Meridian, Indianapolis, Ind.
(317) 255-0872

Tues.–Sun. dinner only   Reservations advised

$8–$15

Indiana calls itself "The main street of the midwest." Like its two celebrity offspring, David Letterman and Jane Pauley, it is unabashedly American. So you can understand why Dodd's Town House is Indianapolis's most enduringly popular place to dine. It's a nice restaurant, where nice people go to eat nice food.

That means meat or, on occasion, fried chicken. There are seven different cuts of steak on the menu, from the "ladies steak" (a small ribeye) to hefty porterhouses and sirloin strips.

Most of Dodd's clientele has been coming here forever. An old gent to our right was expounding on how he had eaten at "Betty Dodd's" for well nigh twenty-five years. Like the rest of the regulars, he didn't bother to look at the menu; just sang out "Chicken" as the waitress approached—and she turned on her heel and was off to the kitchen without another word being spoken.

The chicken is fried in a skillet and has a country crunch. The steaks are also pan-fried, which means they have a crusty surface sealing in plenty of unadulterated juices. With dinner come potatoes, either baked, with a pleasant tough skin, or french fries—long toasty gold sticks. Also iceberg lettuce salad with a sweet and sour garlic dressing, or creamy cole slaw.

If we seem to be rushing through the meal, you have to understand that many diners rush through their meals at Dodd's—to get to dessert. The Town

House is famous for pies. The buttermilk pie, a blissfully bland yellow custard with a blush of tartness, is a nutmeg-sprinkled masterpiece. The pale pastry crust is a fragile shell that pulls apart into the thinnest possible flakes. Blueberry pie, a wide messy slab oozing tart fruit, is served hot, usually under a melting scoop of ice cream.

We noticed that the ladies to our left, who looked like retired instructors of poise and charm, made a complete meal out of sour-cream-filled baked potatoes and two pieces of pie apiece. If you're a card-carrying nice person, you can get away with murder.

Groves' Restaurant

1008 N. Walnut, Bloomington, Ind.
(812) 336-3679

Tues.–Fri. 11 a.m.–1:30 p.m. & 4:30 p.m.–8 p.m., Sat. 4:30 p.m.–8 p.m., Sun. 11 a.m.–7:30 p.m.

Lunch $5 or less, dinner $5–$10

Sitting in a quiet booth at Groves', with paintings of rural life hung on the paneled walls, you would never know there is a college town outside, its streets lined with pizza parlors, wicker bars, and "eating emporia" that serve potato skins. Groves' is the most unchic place in town. There is no booze, no smoking, not even any soda water. Just coffee, tea, or milk—and country cooking to bring nostalgic tears to the eyes of the most jaded urban food faddist.

The white-haired lady who greets guests is soft-spoken in a grandmotherly way; we bet she's been here as long as Groves' has—thirty-six years. The waitresses do not seem like U. of Indiana part-timers; more like farm girls, wearing nursey uniforms and white shoes.

Dinner begins with a choice of individual Jell-O mold or pale green creamy cole slaw. Both are little promises from the kitchen that nothing served at Groves' will be scary or weird. The Jell-O was heart-shaped, a corny red valentine on a dainty plate. Square dinner rolls come four at a time in a silver bowl. They are the best of their kind—artful yeast rolls that are intoxicating when pulled apart, without need of any butter or condiment.

The chicken is pan-fried and enveloped in a crust with just the right amount of crunch, sided by angelic mashed potatoes, both blanketed with pan giblet gravy. Pork tenderloin is served with slivered and cinnamon-scented fried apples. You can get creamed chicken in a patty shell, or a demure "petite filet mignon." Every Sunday—of course—Groves' makes roast turkey dinner with all the fixins.

The pie selection varies. If sugar cream is on the menu, grab it. You may shrug when you see it; to look at this pie is nothing special. It is small and thin; and in fact, even at first bite, it isn't amazing. But then it begins to dawn on you that this is the Platonic ideal of piehood: plain sugar and egg and cream; elemental, nourishing food; you could feed it to a small baby— and the baby would grow up strong and build America.

Other good dessert bets: strawberry tart, topped with a cloud of whipped cream, made from firm, immensely flavorful strawberries and a flake crust; raisin pie; cheesecake topped with the same remarkable strawberries; tart rhubarb pie.

Groves' is a little hard to spot, except on Sunday when whole large families surround the place for their turkey dinners. It is red brick, with flower boxes out front—across the road from Burger King and Taco Tico.

Heichelbech's Restaurant

12th and Mill, Jasper, Ind.
(812) 482-4050

Mon.–Sat. lunch & dinner

$5–$15

The people of Dubois County, Indiana, spend summer Sundays at church picnics. As at any southern midwest church picnic, they raffle quilts, barbe- cue chicken, and compete in foot races and horse pulls. They also cook up enormous kettles full of turtle soup, a gastronomic rite unique to the tiny area south of Jasper and north of Ferdinand.

Why turtle soup? Dubois County is heavily German Catholic, and turtle was a way of circumventing the no-meat-on-Friday rule. Beyond that, no one knows why.

"We used to serve turtle every which way," Mrs. Heichelbech told us. "Did you ever have it deep-fried? That was *good.*" Mrs. Heichelbech has made turtle soup for the last thirty-five years; and if you can't spoon into a kettle at a Sunday picnic, hers is the place to try it.

Turtle soup is a slumgullion of corn kernels, peas, noodles, green beans, carrots, et al. in a thick, peppery tomato stock. What it most resembles is Kentucky burgoo, served in cafes just the other side of the Ohio River; but here gamey chunks of mutton are replaced by more savory filaments of turtle meat, making for a luscious brew. Mrs. Heichelbech's soup is dark red and heavy; there is little room for the thick soup in the interstices between the vegetables and turtle meat. We ordered one more portion for the road. It came in a full quart container, enough for eight.

The rest of the menu is "international": Italian stromboli, schnitzels, chicken and dumplings, steaks.

Heichelbech's is a small-town eatery, with pictures of the high school football players on the wall in the entryway. The German flair is apparent in the beer stein decor and Black Forest cool of the dark dining room. Comfortable and clubby, it is split half and half between a tavern for the men from the Indiana Desk Company across the street, and a restaurant for the same men when they come for dinner with their families.

Hollyhock Hill

8110 N. College Ave., Indianapolis, Ind.
(317) 251-2294

Tues.–Sat. dinner, Sun. noon–7:30 p.m. Reservations required on weekends

$10 or less

In 1928, M. D. Vincent opened a restaurant that offered a menu limited to chicken dinners. You had to drive into the country to get there: a Sunday excursion to a beautiful cottage surrounded by hollyhocks. Inspired by Vincent's concept, and by a traditional Hoosier affection for fried chicken, Indianapolis is today a city of chicken dinners, with several family-style restaurants offering nearly identical menus.

While no longer "country," Hollyhock Hill is in an elegant part of town, on a boulevard of mansions. It is a white building surrounded by colorful foliage, but the gardeny ambience is stronger still inside. An equal mix of real and plastic plantings, Hollyhock's interior is all white and pale green and lavender; benches and trellises are pastel wrought iron; murals of hollyhocks bedeck the walls. What a ladylike world! It looks like a faery cake you'd serve at tea.

There are tables of all sizes, some extra-large round ones with lazy susans in the center for parties and big families. No matter where you sit, the meal is always the same: first, pickled beets and cottage cheese and relish; then iceberg lettuce salad with sweet and sour dressing; heavy white bread that pulls apart only a little reluctantly into thick slices. Now comes the big game—platters of pan-fried chicken, blanketed with a toasty crust; mashed potatoes and chickeny pan-drippin gravy; green beans and buttered corn.

The corn and beans are not interesting, and the potatoes, to our chagrin, tasted more instant than authentic. But there is no denying the excellence of the chicken, or the bread, or the gravy.

Dessert is a simple matter: chewy brownies, ice cream (peppermint is the Indiana favorite), and a choice of toppings to make your own sundae.

Phil Smidt & Son

1205 N. Calumet Ave., Hammond, Ind.
(219) 659-0025 In Chicago: (312) 768-6686

Mon.–Thurs. 11:15 a.m.–9:30 p.m., Fri. & Sat. to 10:30 p.m.

$10 or less

Hammond, Indiana, is a WPA mural come to life, a city of muscle, sweat, and steel. At the end of the road, across from an especially bleak industrial tableau, is the fabled Phil Smidt & Son. It has been here for seventy-three years, predating most of the factories, originally a small tavern where fishermen would bring Phil their catch and he would cook it up for them to enjoy with their beers.

Today it is a large restaurant, but it still has a small menu, featuring the lake perch and frog legs on which its reputation was based.

The bar offers a striking vista: freight trains heading west into the sunset. There are three dining rooms, but you want the Rose Room. It is one of America's ravishing eating places, a visual blockbuster. Two walls are painted a soft rose hue; another bears gargantuan rose murals in high-gloss paint on a shiny black background. There are rose-colored linen napkins, white tablecloths with pink borders, water glasses embossed with roses. Light filters in through blocks of "aquarium" glass. Even when every seat in the room is occupied, there is an eerie quiet, as if the sounds of mere people are swallowed by the grand design.

Nothing in this enchanted room is accidental. You have stepped into a primitive painting of the utmost formality—a sweet-sixteen party decorated by the foreman at United States Steel.

The waitresses, dressed in black, their jet-black name pins festooned with roses and rhinestones, are fast and friendly. They greet you with a number of bowls of appetizers: heavily egged potato salad; kidney bean marinade; shredded cabbage in a mild dressing; beets; cottage cheese; and rolls in a silver basket—on a pink napkin. Five serving spoons are set in a row for diners to help themselves.

You can get Smidt's celebrated frog legs either sauteed or fried; they are plump little limbs, juicy and easy to eat, but to our mind, boring. There was a time when baby frog legs were a regional specialty hereabouts, drawn from the shore around Lake Michigan. Today, Smidt's legs, like most frog legs served in most American restaurants, come from Bangladesh. The menu also offers fileted walleye pike, broiled or fried, or half a chicken.

But lake perch is the reason for Smidt's repute. It is sold either whole or boned, buttered or unbuttered. Two men sitting nearby, obviously old pros, easily deboned their fish; but if you're new to it, pay the extra buck and a half and have the kitchen do the work. Boned and buttered, that's the ticket. You get a pile of extraordinarily firm filets, their skins crisp, flesh sweet and flaky, swimming in a dish of butter: an exquisite plate of food.

People will rave about Phil Smidt's pecan pie; but, spoiled by the ambrosial deep southern versions we've sampled, we found it disappointing—a skinny wedge of no particular pedigree. Gooseberry is a better choice, served warm under ice cream.

After the outré luxury of Phil Smidt, it is staggering to find yourself back on the streets of Hammond again, facing smokestacks. But in fact, Smidt's riveting style could exist nowhere else in America. It's the soul of the city of steel.

Strongbow Inn

U.S. Hwy. 30, Valparaiso, Ind.
(219) 462-3311

Wed.–Mon. lunch & dinner

Lunch about $5, dinner about $10

If you asked us how we liked the food at the Strongbow Inn, we would answer, "Yedl, yedl, yedl." That, according to the family who has run the Inn since the 1940s, is what turkeys say when they want to communicate to each other that "the food's great."

We had heard about Strongbow for years, heard that eating here was like year-round Thanksgiving. As eaters to whom no holiday is complete without a bird and all the trimmings, we were dubious, and approached with critical faculties in a fierce state of tune. Surely, no one could make dressing as good as our Aunt Liz's; or cranberry relish like our next-door neighbor's; or roast turkey as succulent as (excuse us for this one) ours. But we were wrong. Strongbow surpassed its legend.

The delights began immediately, with turkey soup. It is nothing but broth, essence of bird, laced with broad homemade noodles and a sprinkling of parsley. Turkey paté was a shocker, more robust than that made from chicken, loud and gamey, topped with bits of chopped onion.

The waitress, dressed in a neat black-and-white-striped uniform reminiscent of Schrafft's in its heyday, then brought a basket of celestial yeast rolls—fluffy buns that perfumed the air with their eggy smell, served with a quarter stick of butter. If the meal had stopped right here, we wouldn't have been disappointed.

But of course we chose a sliced roast turkey dinner: white and dark pieces of freshly roasted meat atop a mound of sage-scented dressing, the lightest, most flavorful dressing imaginable. On the side were good mashed potatoes, giblet gravy, and a dish of lively cranberry sauce, chocked with tart fruit.

We also got a turkey pie—a six-inch circle of hand-formed crust filled to the brim with hunks of turkey, no vegetables, very little gravy. It resembled a coarse turkey hash, with each morsel retaining its individuality—some light, some dark, some tender, crisp, moist, dry . . . With a little gravy poured on one side of the pie and a bank of the zippy relish on the other, we were in heaven.

The menu also lists turkey wings, a whole drumstick, and turkey salad. Thursday at lunch, the kitchen makes Potawatomie roll-ups, named for a local Indian tribe: crepes filled with turkey meat, topped with cranberry relish.

What's good for dessert after turkey? Apple pie, natch. Strongbow's is a hot and spicy classic. The lemon meringue pie is good, too—fall-apart sweet, with a masterful brittle crust. But our favorite dessert is the cup custard, as wholesome as the turkey that preceded it. In the fall, Strongbow does a landoffice business in pumpkin pies.

After dinner, we bought Strongbow's book, *Turkey Always and All Ways*, and read that the Strongbow turkey farm used to herd their turkeys like cattle in turkey marches that "incurred the wrath of motorists as birds balked, stampeded or took to the air." We also learned that Ben Franklin proposed replacing the bald eagle ("a bird of bad moral character") with the turkey as the official U.S. bird. The turkey, he contended, is a "respectable bird, a true native of America."

Village Inn Restaurant

104 S. Main St., Middlebury, Ind.
(219) 825-2043

Mon.–Sat. 5 a.m.–9 p.m.

$5 or less

Outside of Lancaster County, northern Indiana has the largest settlement of Amish people in America; and like their Pennsylvania brethren, the midwestern Amish have just about perfected the craft of pie-making. You can sample their expertise at the Village Inn, a little lunchroom in a town where horse-drawn buggies are as common as cars.

Among the customers will be austere Amish men with long beards, come to town to buy dry goods at the shop next door: pants with buttons instead of zippers, high-topped shoes, broad-brimmed hats.

The staff at the Village Inn are mostly Mennonite girls in organdy caps. For breakfast, they carry a lot of cornmeal mush and head cheese to the tables—calorific horrors that fuel a farmer to work the fields all day without benefit of machines. Lunch is ponderous too: chicken and noodles, meat loaf, baked steak.

But the pies take flight. Our nomination for the most outstanding is the "old-fashioned" cream. It's a double-size wedge of dark-skinned custard, pure cream and brown sugar. It's slightly jiggly, and it came to our table (at noon) still warm from the oven. Its lovely scored crust broke easily into flakes when touched with the prong of a fork.

A close runner-up to the O.F. pie is the gooey raisin, with a light crust of little dough windows, like a minimalist's lattice top. The raisins had plumped to grape size; but as rich as this pie was, it did not cloy.

There are six to a dozen kinds of pie each day, including cherry custard, peach, pineapple, banana cream, and (local) blueberry. You can buy them by the slice, or order whole pies in advance, to go.

Vogel's

1250 Indianapolis Blvd., Whiting, Ind.
(219) 659-1250

Tues.–Thurs. 11 a.m.–10:30 p.m., Fri. & Sat. 11 a.m.–midnight, Sun. 11 a.m.–10 p.m.   Reservations advised

$10–$20

It was dusk when we coasted off the Toll Road onto the streets of Steel City. The sky was smoky orange; the air smelled of sulphur and petroleum. Calumet Boulevard runs past rows of oil storage tanks and lots lined up with idle trucks shut down for the weekend. Convenience store signs began to shine through the ashy air: SPECIAL—MILK, WORK GLOVES . . . WEEKEND BUY—ICE CREAM AND WORK GLOVES.

Saturday night; Hammond, Indiana! We had driven straight through from Connecticut to have it like this. Delirious from fifteen hours on the road, we plunged through the gray city landscape, adrenalin pumping, until we parked in Vogel's lot, walked inside, and had heart attacks. Not exactly cardial infarctions, but something that intense—visceral and muscular. Vogel's is the most astounding eating environment we have ever seen.

First, the lobby, a cavern that could have been designed by cartoonist Bruce McCall, with two hostesses—tiny little figures at the far distant end. You trek to them, and halfway across the carpet you notice that their stature is significantly augmented by their hair—great sculpted structures with billow, pile, and puff held in laquered perfection.

The one who speaks to us sees that we are not regulars, and so offers to lead us to the lounge, with the semi-classical pianist ("You know it as *Sheherazade*, actually, it's Rimsky-Korsakov").

Oh, no, we don't want the lounge. We have glimpsed to the left. The Crown Room. This is where Vogel's is truest to itself. The Crown Room is approximately the size of a football field, populated with tables and what the waitress calls booths. Each "booth" is a free-standing banquette large enough for two giants, set at a table opposite two chairs. Banquettes and chairs are upholstered in Naugahyde, vivid orange stripped from the set of a Jerry Lewis movie. The orange throbs in contrast to a brindle-green rug and scarlet drapes.

The ceiling appears thirty feet high, hung with five octopus-armed chandeliers that might have been designed by Edvard Munch if he had lived in Hammond and gone into lamps instead of painting. Periodically during dinner, the lights flicker and dim. Major power drains from the refineries?

There are steaks and chops on the menu—thick slabs of beef, milady's tenderest filet (wrapped in bacon), surf 'n' turf for big spenders. But the thing to eat at Vogel's, the ritualized meal unique to the Calumet region south of Chicago, home of America's *cuisine industrielle*, is perch.

Perch, boned and buttered: nine strips of boneless fish arrive hot in a pool of butter. They slice easily with the edge of a fork. The meat is firm, sweet, freshwater mild. The fish has been pan-fried to a crisp. When you finish the nine small filets, more are carried to the table.

Northern Indiana ritual demands that perch be preceded by relishes— exactly five: beets, slaw, potato salad, kidney bean salad, and cottage cheese.

The meal is precisely the meal served at Phil Smidt, around the corner in Hammond; but the experience is completely different. Smidt draws crowds from all of Chicagoland. Its steelman style is so polished, it's practically hip. The word in Chicago is that after a long decline, Phil Smidt has revived.

Not so at Vogel's. Vogel's hasn't revived. Its gargantuan decor, although not the least bit threadbare, is hammeringly out of fashion. With funeral-home formality, it continues to embody its original style the way resin holds a fly.

Exit, and you stand across from the Lever Brothers' wall: beige bricks, not a window in sight, looming over Vogel's like a stone sky.

Windell's Cafe

6 West Metcalf, Dale, Ind.
(812) 937-4253

Daily 5 a.m.–8 p.m.

$5 or less

We discovered Windell's on the trail of southern Indiana turtle soup. "Yuk," said our waitress, a Mariel Hemingway look-alike. "They eat that up north, not here." ("Up north" is approximately five miles away.) Mariel's comrade, an older lady, advised us that the town of Dale does *not* do anything with turtles . . . although she admitted that her son caught one the other day and gave it to the neighbors to dress.

We did enjoy two very good plate lunches at Windell's. We suggest you stop in here if you want pan-fried chicken or pork tenderloin with whipped potatoes and corn niblets; come if you want fabulous coconut pie with lots of toasty meringue on top, or strawberry shortcake, or peach pie baked that morning at four, when the Kissells (who own Windell's) start work in the kitchen.

Just don't come for turtle soup. Yuk.

Yoder Popcorn Shop

C.R. 2005, just off S.R. 5, Topeka, Ind.   Four mi. south of Shipshewana *(219) 768-4051*

April–Dec. Mon.–Fri. 8 a.m.–5 p.m., Sat. 8 a.m.–4 p.m.; Jan–March only until noon on Sat.

Under $5

You must drive carefully in this part of Indiana, since the narrow country roads are used by Amish people in horse-drawn buggies. Drive too fast, and you will miss bake sales in front of farm houses, where ladies in bonnets sit by tables laden with huckleberry pies, sticky buns, and angelic angel cakes. It was May when we meandered through, and the barnyards were populated with newborn animals, our favorite being a one-day-old workhorse, still unsure about how to walk on its great knobby legs.

Not far from the colt, on Country Road 2005, four miles south of the Shipshewana flea market (another lure to this unspoiled land), is a popcorn farm called Yoder's. Down a long driveway, behind the house and opposite the barn and corn cribs is a one-room showroom where you can buy popcorn straight from the farm. Get it popped or unpopped, white or yellow, regular-size or what Yoder's calls "T.T.," meaning tiny tender kernels from the tip of the ear. There is caramel corn, too, as well as small jars of farmy things like pumpkin butter and preserves. They even sell black-hulled popcorn as a novelty item.

As we perused the selection, a girl in an organdy bonnet working at a desk offered us a small bag of corn to munch. This was T.T. corn, popped into morsels so feathery they seemed weightless. Despite the rustic setting, the inventory in the small room is modern, including microwave packs, gift packages, and flavored salts. After we bought some corn to take home, we noticed the girl return to a ledger book, to do the accounts by hand.

(For mail order information, write Yoder's, RR 1, Topeka, IN 46571.)

IOWA

Chief Mahaska Restaurant

112 1st Ave., Oskaloosa, Iowa
(515) 673-9032

Mon.–Sat. 6 a.m.–4 p.m., Sun. 6 a.m.–2 p.m.

$5 or less

"Who's Chief Mahaska?" we asked the waitress.

"He's the Indian chief," she explained. "You know, the one named for the county."

His portrait, plus other *objets* of Indian and western art, decorates the first floor dining room of this cafe on the square in Oskaloosa.

Upstairs, where the salad bar is located at lunch, the walls carry a more contemporary theme: the work of a local photo studio, including an impressive array of soft-focus babies, little girls with their teddy bears, and handsome lads almost ready for their first shave.

We ordered hot lunch (pork tenderloin) and helped ourselves at the salad bar. The array was a good one: sweet and sour carrots, pistachio Jell-O, orange and marshmallow ambrosia, potato salad, tuna salad, slaw with celery seed dressing, and a most amazing pasta salad.

If we're not mistaken, it wasn't too long ago that pasta salad was chic. Now it's commonplace, but even so, there has always been something svelte about it in our minds . . . until we tasted Chief Mahaska's and gained a whole new perspective on the possibilities of cold noodles. The chief's salad is made with shells, but the shells are combined with crushed canned pineapple and vast quantities of halved maraschino cherries. Sweet? You don't know the meaning of the word until you've dipped into this red and yellow screamer.

Next to the salad bar are the day's pies. The one that cried out to be tasted was rhubarb, tightly packed into a lard crust. This was pie mastery, as subtle as the pasta salad was loud, the tart flavor of the rhubarb deftly sugared but not overwhelmed.

Back at the table, as we plunged through salads, the pork tenderloin arrived. Wow! It was a mammoth meal, the cutlets overwhelming a large dinner plate. Sandy-crusted, nearly greaseless, with a thick center of meat in proportion to the breading, it was classy pork loin, for plates instead of sandwiches.

As we polished it off, and surveyed the emptied plates on the table, it occurred to us that this meal—broad pork tenderloin, pull-all-stops salad bar, and wizardly rhubarb pie—was a veritable definition of heartland cafe cookery.

The Coffee Cup Cafe

On the town square, Sully, Iowa
(515) 594-3765

Mon.–Thurs. 6 a.m.–4:45 p.m., Fri. 6 a.m.–10 p.m., Sat. 6 a.m.–1 p.m.

$5 or less

"I am sure we do have a street address," Coffee Cup owner Linda Zylstra told us. "But I don't know it." A postman, who was finishing his morning banana bread, didn't know it either. "On the square," Linda suggested. On the square, indeed it is.

Ah, small-town Iowa! Here is the best of it—a cozy cafe with a coffee-cup motif (clock and coat hooks are cup-shaped), where the people of Sully come to breakfast on the day's homemade sweet bread, or on pecan rolls with sticky amber outsides. Or pancakes, made from scratch with a feather-weight batter, fried until pale gold and crisp; so fragrant and gentle-tasting, you don't want any syrup. You *do* want sausage. It is coarse-grained, made for the cafe from freshly butchered hogs, peppered with a bright shot of spice.

We came too early for lunch, which was a special of meat loaf, peas, and deviled eggs; but there was one piece of yesterday's pie to sample: whole sweet strawberries packed tightly together on a flaky lard crust, topped with whipped cream. It was the height of rhubarb season, but the rhubarb pie, for which The Coffee Cup is best known, was not yet ready.

We did manage to plow into a wonderful specialty of the house known as Dutch lettuce (many of the people who live in this part of Iowa are Dutch-ancestored). It's an iceberg lettuce salad smothered with warm celery-seed-and-mustard dressing, and topped with bacon bits and hard-boiled eggs.

As we bought a few homemade cookies from the canister behind the counter, Linda invited us to return on a Friday night, the only night of the week The Coffee Cup is open—for pizza. The dough is made from scratch, as are sausage and all other toppings. By Friday, we would be back east. We drove away from this cafe on the square, through the contoured fields of farmland Iowa, dreaming of the next time.

The Gardens

Pearl and Atlantic Sts., Walnut, Iowa
(712) 784-3559

Thurs., Fri., & Sat. 5:30 p.m.–10 p.m.   Reservations advised

$10–$15

Every real man or woman has his or her favorite steak house. Ours happens to be in Walnut, Iowa—a dot of a town surrounded by acres of the richest farmland in the world.

The Gardens is open only three nights a week. You will know it's one of those nights by the ring of cars and pickup trucks at the front door. Outside, you hear strains of a jukebox playing country songs; in the door, the convivial chatter of Iowa gentry out for a night on the town.

You are seated at a plain Formica table in a booth, and as your eyes adjust to the low light, the decor becomes visible—beautiful murals of western towns, like primitive dioramas in this comfortable grotto. At one side of the dining room is the small bar, ringed by old-fashioned metal barstools and lamps with shades made, inexplicably, from sheeps' pelts.

Like the priciest New York steak joints, The Gardens has no menu. The waitress recites what's available: steak, sirloin, filet, or ribeye. That's all. Choose the cut, the size, the degree of doneness.

"Potato?" she asks. Baked, french fries, or hash browns. We recommend the hash browns, a buttery cake of shredded spuds under a crust of gold.

"Garlic toast?" Don't bother—double-size slabs of white bread spread with garlic butter.

"Onion rings?" Definitely. The rings come early, while the steak cooks. They are dark, irregularly sized circles, the breading well-seasoned, the onion crisp and sweet.

"Beer?" The waitress ticks off the brands. They are all domestic, not an import in the lot.

After a small iceberg lettuce salad, the steak arrives, alone on an oval plate. It is blackened on the outside, glistening. Even the large one is not huge, but it is butter-knife tender; intensely flavorful, dense with natural juices.

There is no dessert, but our waitress suggests that the bar could whip up a pink squirrel or a gold Cadillac, both kitschy ice cream and booze concoctions that seem a fitting end to this all-American meal.

When we ask to send our compliments to the chef, we are escorted back into the smallest kitchen this side of a houseboat's galley. There stands Russ Lenhardt, chef and owner, hard at work over his griddle, where the hash browns and steaks are cooked.

"Great steaks, Russ," we compliment him. And he replies with a monologue on the difficulty of getting genuine prime beef, which is all he will serve. "Sometimes I don't offer sirloin, because I can't get the quality I want," he says as he sears a richly marbled cut on the griddle.

We guarantee that as long as there is The Gardens, and as long as there is a Russ, there will be prime Iowa corn-fed beef on your plate, perfectly cooked, and served in one of the simplest and best restaurants in this land.

Green Gables

1800 Pierce St., Sioux City, Iowa
(712) 255-7604

Daily 11 a.m.–midnight, Sat. until 1 a.m.

$10 or less

A bright, happy restaurant where families come to partake of what is, in other parts of the country, a rare culinary honesty. In Siouxland, such good food seems to happen naturally, and Green Gables packs them in simply by doing what it's been doing for the last fifty-seven years.

Beneath a backlit mural of Sioux City at night, we wrote our own ticket on the pad provided, advised by a uniformed waitress who seemed quite amused at our unfamiliarity with how things work. Most people who eat at Green Gables *always* eat at Green Gables.

The meal began with a basket of nice warm rolls, both dark and light, brought to the table covered with Saran Wrap. Lemonade, made not from a mix but from the juice of lemons and sugar, was decorated with half a maraschino cherry and served with a Flexi-straw.

Food is wheeled out of the kitchen on rolling carts: mostly steaks and chops, a few fish (including filet of walleye pike that the waitress assured us was her favorite, and roughy filet that she also recommended but couldn't describe), and Gables' specialties like smoked barbecue ribs, puffy-crusted fried chicken, and "oriental chicken chow mein."

How could we resist chow mein in Sioux City? Piled onto crisp noodles, it was powerfully salty, layered with whole slices of moist, fresh chicken, and skinny strips of omelette across the top. Bravo! The barbecued ribs were winners, too, their meat tumbling off the bone at the slightest prodding, the rich pork glazed with sweet red sauce. We noticed that approximately half the men in the house were digging into another Gable specialty—broiled ground beefsteak, smothered in onions. It looked great.

Dinner, of course, includes dessert: a small square of iced marble cake served alongside ice cream, sherbet, or Jell-O. Very nice, but since we knew we wouldn't be returning soon, we ordered more from the long list of ice cream sodas and sundaes.

After dinner Green Gables gradually shifts toward a soda-fountain spirit, and becomes the place people go for old-fogy favorites like a goshawful gooey (vanilla ice cream, orange sherbet, marshmallow sauce), a harem share'm (three ice cream flavors, chocolate syrup, and a flaming banana), or an H-bomb. An H-bomb is a superlush soda, loaded with whipped cream and extra ice cream.

Hot fudge sundaes made our day. Peppermint stick ice cream came topped with whipped cream, but the fudge was on the side, in a small pitcher. This is an ingenious system that allows the sundae eater to maintain the warmth of the fudge and to control the ice-cream-to-fudge ratio all the way to the bottom of the glass.

Hamburg Inn No. 2

214 Linn St., Iowa City, Iowa
(319) 337-5512

Mon.–Fri. 5 a.m.–11 p.m., Sat. 5 a.m.–midnight, Sun. 6 a.m.–11 p.m.

$5 or less

"I've traveled in 48 states," wrote Gary Sanders, a Roadfooder from Iowa City, "and the Hamburg Inn No. 2 is the best restaurant of its type I know. I urge you to sample the breakfast."

We had eggs over easy, bacon on the side: fine, but the pièces de résistance were American fried potatoes. Big chunky spuds heaped on the grill, a cup an order, sprinkled with grease, and fried until crusty. Delicious! Egg aficionados can wallow in a repertoire of sixty omelettes.

Breakfast is served all day long, but we were warned not to try to eat here Saturday or Sunday morning, when the place is packed. Our tipster also recommended we return for lunch to try a terrific hamburger ("Get grilled onions only," were his specific instructions). But the day we want to return is Sunday, when the Hamburg Inn specialty is chicken dinner with all the fixins.

In fact it's not the chicken dinner or fried potatoes, probably not even the hamburger, however wonderful it may be, that makes this college-town cafe seem special. We like it for the camaraderie, for the blackboard menus hanging on the wall, and the way the waitresses write orders on a big sheet of wax paper for the grill man to read. It is the type of place whose honest grub helps collegians act blue collar; and so it seems perfectly natural, even for strangers, to heed the sign above the grill that requests PLEASE SHARE BOOTHS DURING RUSH HOUR.

(The Hamburg Inn No. 1, by the way, went out of business in the late 1970s.)

Iowa Beef Steak House

1201 E. Euclid, Des Moines, Iowa
(319) 262-1138

Sun.–Thurs. 5 p.m.–10 p.m., Fri. & Sat. 5 p.m.–11 p.m.

$10–$15

Meat and potato, salad bar on the side: here is an Iowa meal reduced to its essentials. True to steak-house tradition, there is no printed menu, just a blackboard at the front door listing available cuts of meat in ascending order from fourteen-ounce filet mignon to twenty-eight-ounce T-bone. Or you can get two pork chops, one pound each. Everything costs the same. With the meat comes a potato, baked, and toast brushed with butter and sprinkled with garlic salt. Help yourself to a salad bar.

The fun comes when it is time to order. The waiter reminds you what's available, then advises, "We will cook it for you, or for a dollar less, you can cook it yourself." And he points you to a giant pit at the front of the restaurant, where the house chef toils with tongs over a furiously smoking bed of coals. To his sides, also tweaking, poking, and prodding steaks, are customers.

Although hands-on food preparation was a real treat for us after weeks on the road away from a kitchen, what lured us to the fire was that if you cook your own, you get to choose your own. To the side of the grill, surrounded by bags of charcoal, is a refrigerated case stocked with all the raw slabs of meat. What a handsome display: strip steaks two inches tall and a foot long; filets even deeper than that, wrapped with bacon; pound-and-a-half sirloins broader than any dish in the house. Take a pair of tongs, grab the piece you want, and throw it on the fire.

Then, just like on the patio at home, you tend it. Salt and pepper are provided; also seasoned salt, garlic salt, and melted butter with a long-handled brush. As the meat grills, you can take presliced bread and toast it on the fire, too, brushing it with butter and sprinkling on garlic. When happy with the meat's doneness, select a foil-wrapped baked potato from the tray in which they're stored at the center of the grill.

The potato is okay. The bread, if you've buttered and salted it right, is fine. The steak (like all steaks you cook yourself) is fantastic. Lean, but rimmed with enough fat to stay juicy, the sirloin and the ribeye each develop a crusty char on this furious fire. If you cook them medium-rare, as we did ours, they are perfectly resilient, tender but not *too* tender, yielding plenty of juice to drizzle into the baked potato. Just like home, only better, because someone else cleans the grill and washes the dishes.

K.C. Cafe

502 W. Burlington, Fairfield, Iowa
(515) 472-4613

Mon.–Fri. 5:30 a.m.–3 p.m., Sat. 5:30 a.m.–2 p.m., Sun. 6:30 a.m.–
2 p.m.

$5 or less

"You must visit K.C. Cafe, Fairfield, Iowa, for breaded pork tenderloin," said
the postcard from Sylvia Carter, a midwestern expatriate who makes the
best pie crust in the east. The card was postmarked Missouri, just south of
Fairfield, so as we headed southeast from Des Moines, we retraced Sylvia's
path.

The K.C. is an old-fashioned roadside diner with counter and booths and
stainless steel walls. Flip-cards of local businesses rotate adjacent to the
clock. Lunchtime wisecracks batted back and forth when we walked in. "I
haven't thrown anyone out today . . . yet," said the waitress as she set a cup
of vegetable soup before a customer.

The menu is good reading, offering vegetable soup (in season), chili
(winter only) that is "tastefully seasoned," breakfast ("served all day!"), and
king-sized Danish rolls. And Sylvia's favorite, listed simply as "giant loin on
a bun."

It was a beaut of a tenderloin, brittle and well-seasoned, a perfect ratio
of pork to crust, spilling beyond the bun, which was stuffed with lettuce,
tomato, and Russian dressing. Mustard came on the side, in a little paper
cup. It was large, but not the midwest's largest loin; you can still manage it
with two hands.

In this ramshackle diner, the handwritten list of daily specials included
such Iowa exotica as rhubarb pudding (profoundly sweet), pea salad (pale
green and pickly), and five-cup salad (made with whipped cream instead of
sour cream!—surely the most fattening food on earth).

On the way out, we asked for a king-size Danish roll. "There are no more
king-size Danishes," lamented the waitress. "But we do have cinnamon
rolls." It turned out to be gigantic, prince-size at least, a big frosted square
of soft, sweetened dough veined with cinnamon.

Mary's Cafe

Main St., Casey, Iowa
(515) 746-2721

Mon.–Sat. 7 a.m.–8 p.m., Sun. 8 a.m.–2 p.m.

$5 or less

Mary's Cafe sits on the corner in a town that looks like a stage set for a play about small-town life. Men in faded overalls stroll arm in arm with ladies in sun-washed housecoats: pristine Americana, a scene from Iowa artist Grant Wood's sketchbook.

Mary's is where the overall crowd takes breakfast and "dinner" (as the noon meal is called)—an ancient cafe with dark wood fixtures and an ornate silver cash register, high-backed booths and slow-spinning overhead fans. We arrived at 7 a.m., but a handful of geezers had beaten us to it. As we found a booth, one called out to the waitress, "Better switch on your headlights, girl," as she fumbled her way toward us in the morning's dim light.

The fluorescents blinked, and Mary's slowly came to life. Dave Berlau, who took over from Mary when she retired several years ago, smothered a pan of freshly baked doughnuts with a hot vanilla glaze. The cinnamon rolls, finished rising, were put into the oven. The crusts for the pies were ready for their fillings—sour cream raisin (the house specialty), rhubarb, gooseberry, and occasionally, peanut butter cream.

"Home cooking" is an abused term; but that is what you get here—assuming, of course, your home was an Iowa farm and your mom regularly won blue ribbons at the state fair. There are some silly items like "cheddar crisps" and fish shapes, but those are for the children of tourists. The overalled gents eat dinners of Iowa beef and real mashed potatoes, and creamy sweet cole slaw, made from Mary's original top-secret recipe. "We had a fella from England came in here once to eat," Dave told us. "And he begged me for that slaw recipe." "Did you give it to him?" we asked. "Nope. And I never will. I promised Mary."

Mary's also makes its own tenderloins, a flattened patty of pork served in a sandwich. Tenderloins are found all over the plains states; most are nothing much. This one is exquisite.

Casey, Iowa, calls itself "the sparkling jewel in Guthrie County's crown." With its old-fashioned high sidewalks, its population of wise and weathered farmers, and the unshakable continuity of Mary's Cafe, it is red, white, and blue royalty.

The Pantry Cafe

Central Ave. & 1st St., LeMars, Iowa
(712) 546-6800

Mon.–Sat. 5 a.m.–8 p.m., Sun. 5 a.m.–1:30 p.m.

$5 or less

We never would have wandered into LeMars if Marcia and Richard Poole of Sioux City hadn't tipped us off to The Pantry. "Genuine" was their word to describe it when they recommended we stop in for breakfast on our way north.

It was early Sunday morning. At the corner of 1st and Central, we spotted a group of old men in Sunday suits and ladies holding down their white hair to protect it from the spring winds. Church bells were ringing, and they were on their way . . . after cinnamon rolls and coffee at The Pantry.

The rolls, referred to by the waitress as "sticky rolls," are enormous: four inches square, two inches high, great puffs of dough topped with amber caramelized sugar. They are to Iowa what muffins are to Maine or biscuits to Tennessee: the essential stuff for breakfast, made fresh at The Pantry every morning.

Most of the menu is just as true a taste of Iowa: grilled pork chops on toast, pork tenderloin sandwiches, beef stew, and navy bean soup. There is a long list of outré-sounding sandwiches, including a club house sandwich, a deviled egg sandwich, and a "busy man special" (baked ham on rye with a cup of soup).

The place is a relic, with its antique wooden booths and burl-pattern brown-and-white tables rimmed with silver bands. The floor is tiny six-sided black and white tiles. Uniformed waitresses are pros. Ours volunteered an apology when she served coffee whitener instead of cream.

Eating here is not a pristine experience. The menu also lists yukky-sounding patty melts; and on one wall hangs a four-color portrait of a happy broasted-chicken loving family, eating it from a take-out bag. But we don't mind ignoring them and their feed bag, not so long as the cinnamon rolls are real.

Ronneberg Restaurant

Amana, Iowa
(319) 622-3641

Daily lunch & dinner

$10 or less

Lutheran Separatists began the Amana Colonies in 1854 as an experiment in communal living and farming—one of America's many mid-nineteenth-century utopias. In 1932, communism was abandoned, but the seven villages continue to practice some of the crafts that made them famous, including meat-smoking, bread-baking, and grape-pressing.

The Amanans were Germans, and most of the restaurants in this popular tourist area advertise that they serve German cuisine; but we realized at Ronneberg that the food is as much Iowan as German. It is the cooking of immigrant farmers who brought some recipes with them, but whose expertise was in making the best of the Iowa farmland's yield.

The pickled ham, for instance, listed as an appetizer: nothing you will ever see or taste is more purely midwestern in spirit—a big bowl full of half-inch cubes of pale pink ham and chunks of crunchy onion. It's a dish for which every Iowa farm wife must have a hand-me-down recipe.

We began our meal with glasses of Amana wine. The varieties include rhubarb, grape, cherry, cranberry, blackberry, and more. We chose cranberry, which was rich and fruity, like Manischewitz. The rhubarb tasted like raw home brew made from caraway seeds—definitely an acquired taste.

Dinner was preceded by cottage cheese mixed with scallions and buttermilk: creamy country food. The main courses were pork: Amana smoked chops, juicy with a deep smoke flavor; and a monstrous length of zesty sausage. In side dishes came pickled sauerkraut, corn in butter sauce, some first-rate bread dumplings topped with toasted breadcrumbs, a mound of variegated hash-brown potatoes, and brown gravy.

The meal was so purely Iowan that we had forgotten the German side of Amana until a chap in lederhosen and Tyrolean hat wandered in with an accordion and started to serenade us with the Disneyland anthem, "It's a Small World After All." We were jostled back to the reality of tourist dining.

But dessert made it easy to regain our rustic reveries. Ronneberg pies are baked by a rotating team of ladies, each of whom has her own specialties. There is one who makes sour cream raisin, another whose forte is butterscotch chess with nuts and raisins, another known for rhubarb custard. For this meal, the one who makes homemade sponge cake with wine sauce was on duty, and let us tell you, she can cook. The wine sauce, made from Amana wines (the good ones, not that rhubarb stuff) was mixed with raisins that had stewed in the wine long enough to plump back up to grape size. This sprightly gelatin is cascaded over the lightest of sponge cakes, creating a homely but eloquent farmland dessert.

Strawtown Inn

1111 Washington, Pella, Iowa
(515) 628-4043

Mon.–Sat. 11:30 a.m.–1:30 p.m., Tues.–Thurs. 5 p.m.–10 p.m., Fri. & Sat. 5 p.m.–11 p.m.   Reservations suggested for dinner

Lunch $5 or less, dinner $10–$20

Thanks to Garrietta Jackson of Des Moines for directing us off the highway to the town of Pella, where Dutch-ancestored Iowans celebrate tulip time every May, and where a small hotel called the Strawtown Inn serves spiced beef for dinner.

What a savory meal this beef is, cooked until fall-apart tender, presented wallowing in its own highly seasoned juices, with plenty of rice to sop it up. With the beef comes moist apple bread, and before it you get salad, soup, and barbecued meatballs.

There are other things to order at the Strawtown Inn. In the heart of the heartland, stuffed pork chops are practically *cuisine ordinaire*, on every menu. But few are as good as Strawtown's, tall and tender, served with apple walnut dressing in mushroom wine sauce.

Most of the rest of the repertoire is basic fancy-food fare: stuffed Cornish hen, chicken cordon bleu, fried shrimp, pheasant under glass (one day's notice required), and a spectacular-looking chateaubriand (one day's notice). At lunch, there are sandwiches, some typically Iowan (pork tenderloin, roast beef au jus), some definitively Dutch (spiced beef, roast beef or ham with sunnyside-up eggs). Each item on the menu is listed by its Dutch name.

Next time, we intend to stay at the Strawtown Inn. It is an Old World place, clean and charming in that lacy Dutch way. And the hotel brochure promises guests "a delightful Dutch breakfast of cold meat, Dutch cheeses, breads, coffee or tea, and always a boiled egg!"

The White Way

8th Ave. (Rte. 6), Durant, Iowa
(319) 785-6202

Tues.–Sat. 11 a.m.–8 p.m., Sun. to 7 p.m.

$10 or less

We arrived at The White Way for dinner at a quarter to six on Saturday night and were ushered to the last remaining table. By six-fifteen, the restaurant had half-emptied; by seven, we were dining alone. This is the heartland, farmer country. Dinner hour is 5 p.m.

The White Way is not white; it's brown. And it looks like the last place you would think to stop for dinner. Not that it's especially ugly or run-down; it's just blah, another slab-sided building that looks utterly ordinary. It is not.

The pulse of The White Way is its salad bar—a dozen bowls buried up to their rims in a cooler. It is not your standard bacon-bit-and-crouton iceberg-lettuce salad bar—not by a country mile. It is what you would expect to find at a church picnic.

The pea salad sent us off the map into uncharted areas of bliss, the garden nubbins of peas buried in salad dressing, enriched with bits of chopped egg. Next to it were two other golden egg concoctions—German potato salad and macaroni salad. In another bowl was an eccentric cold bean salad mixed with bits of crumbled tortilla chips which, instead of turning unpleasantly soggy, absorbed a maximum amount of chili flavor and floated happily in the cumin-spiked tomato binder.

A bracing sweet and sour cucumber salad was next—then, heaven again, in the form of an "ambrosia" mixture of miniature marshmallows, pineapple chunks, tiny mandarin oranges, and grated coconut. What fun! It is not, admittedly, a sophisticated dish. But let sophisticates go elsewhere and get a rash eating red peppercorns. We'll take White Way ambrosia every time.

Other salad bar items: pickled beets in clove-scented marinade, three-bean salad, carrot slaw, cabbage slaw, a variety of relishes, and bowls of spinach, lettuce, and other customary salad fixings. The lettuce is worth taking—so you can drench it in The White Way's celery seed dressing.

We could live happily ever after on the salad bar, but grudgingly, we ordered dinner. Almost everyone in the house was eating Iowa pork, either the tender smoked chop, baked and smothered in mushroom gravy, or the thinner grilled chops, bearing nice black score marks across the lean flesh. We liked baked better. It was pot roast tender, sweet and rich.

Less delicious was roast beef, which the menu describes as "the best you've ever eaten." The menu is wrong. Some shameful shortcuts are taken here. Whipped potatoes are not the McCoy; baked potatoes are sheathed in foil; hash browns are only so-so.

Dessert, however, takes us back to Olympian levels of cookery. Sour cream raisin pie, a specialty of the tri-state dairy belt of Wisconsin, Minnesota, and Iowa, is peerless at The White Way, its meringue top floating on a layer of the creamiest imaginable blend of cream and vanilla custard, studded with swollen raisins, all hefted into a thin pastry shell.

Unfortunately, as we sat down to dinner, The White Way sold its last piece of raisin cream pie. We sulked and tried to bribe the old man in overalls at the next table out of his piece, but we failed—and were forced to order apple crumb pie.

Apple crumb is not normally a favorite, but with this piece, it took on new dimensions. It was a monumental triangle, its ragged crust atop a thick yet ungummy mélange of apples, butter, and sugar. We asked the waitress if there was sour cream in it as well, but she shrugged her shoulders impishly and pleaded ignorance.

As we left The White Way, knowing it would be maybe a couple of years before we could get back, we wished we had become Iowa pig farmers instead of writers.

Wilton Candy Kitchen

Cedar Street, Wilton, Iowa
(319) 732-9278

Daily 6 a.m.–10:30 p.m.

Under $5

When nineteen-year-old Gus Napoulos froze his first quart of ice cream in 1910, the original ice cream sundae, invented north of here in Two Rivers, Wisconsin, was only thirteen years old. Until he died at age 92, Gus continued to specialize in sundaes. And now his son and grandson continue the tradition, serving up sundaes, green rivers, phosphates, sodas, and double chocolate malts.

Their ice-cream parlor, the Wilton Candy Kitchen, is one of the great surviving soda fountains in the midwest, just a short hop off the highway in a gentle town with a wide main street that looks like it hasn't changed much either. The "Kitchen" is a flat-fronted brick building with a striped green awning and two simple neon signs in the window announcing LUNCH and SODA.

Lunch isn't much more than sandwiches. But the soda fountain is extraordinary—homemade ice cream and a vast variety of syrups, blended in every conceivable combination with soda, candy sprinkles, and various mystery ingredients to yield a repertoire of nostalgic sweets. "What's a dipsy doodle?" we asked George Napoulos as he wiped the marble counter with his towel. "A little bit of everything; not too much of anything," he replied with a wink.

What better way to relieve the hammering tedium of Interstate 80 than with a dish of George's special maple walnut ice cream or a tutti fruitti sundae?

MICHIGAN

Artesian Wells Restaurant

U.S. 127 & 12, Somerset, Mich.
(517) 547-6575

Daily 11 a.m.–10 p.m.

$5 or less

It is thanks to Ann Arbor's Connie Crump, whose calling card identifies her as a Pleasure Food Specialist, that we hit upon the Artesian Wells Restaurant, known to regulars by its former sign FOOD-BAR. As the moniker suggests, Food-Bar is not exactly a temple of haute cuisine; but each Friday, starting before noon, it is the dining place of choice in lower Michigan for aficionados of the traditional all-you-can-eat midwestern fish fry.

Whitefish from the Great Lakes—silken, meaty, deliciously moist—is dished out in multitudes, encased in crisp golden batter. (Ocean perch is also available, by itself or in combination with whitefish.) On the side come tartar sauce, french fries, finely shredded slaw, a roll and a pat of butter. None of this stuff, except the fish, is served on an all-you-can-eat basis. The beverage preferred by fish-fry hounds is, of course, beer on tap; an alternative might be Artesian Well water from the fountain on the wall. Dessert? Nobody around here seems ever to have heard of it.

Few tourists or strangers are lured by the hunkering look of this place from the outside, but it is a friendly kind of eatery, with decor that Connie called "'50s Formica, down-home and comfortable." We found the hospitality ingenuous, our waitress relentlessly cajoling us to second and third helpings, even though the restaurant was packed, as it always is by early evening every Friday.

The Cherry Hut

Rte. 31, Beulah, Mich.
(616) 882-4431

Summer daily 7 a.m.–10 p.m.   Shorter hours Sept.–Oct.
Closed in winter

$2–$7

From July 4th through mid-August, when you drive through Mason and Benzie Counties, you pass dozens of little roadside stands with hand-painted signs advertising washed cherries (i.e. clean and ready to eat). The cherries are nearly black, with glistening taut skin that cracks open when you bite it, bursting dark liquory juices and yielding a mouthful of sweet firm cherry meat: one of the midwest's most delectable crops.

Scenic places, these roadside stands, surrounded by farmland, often decorated with multicolored pennants or imaginatively anthropomorphic portraits of cherries. Their provender is cherries, tomatoes, or apricots, occasionally small pieces of handmade fudge.

In 1922, The Cherry Hut was such a stand, selling not much more than cherry pies, into whose crusts were cut the face of Cherry Jerry, a dead ringer for the Happy Face (a.k.a. Smiley Face); in fact, we suspect Jerry was the *original* Happy Face, before he turned jaundice yellow.

Be that as it may, in sixty years The Cherry Hut has become a summer tradition in Beulah, Michigan; and although it's expanded into a chalet-style restaurant serving real meals, it is still a happy informal place, under the smiling sign of Cherry Jerry. There are umbrella'd picnic tables outside, some booths and a counter inside. The waitresses are friendly schoolgirls, dressed in red and white.

You can get all kinds of sandwiches for lunch, roast pork and baked chicken and (on Fridays) fresh lake trout and whitefish for dinner. With every meal comes a tender cinnamon roll. But we were here to sample cherries: a Cherry Ade float—squeezed cherries with a scoop of vanilla ice cream; a sundae, dolloped with syrupy whole-fruit sauce; and pie, a classic, with a great tart filling, cherries spilling out the sides of the slice like molten marbles. The top crust is light and crumbly, a wee salty—a counterpoint to the sweet/tart cherries. Coffee comes in a large thermos pitcher, from which you help yourself.

Pies, cherry sundae sauce, jellies, jams, preserves, and conserves are all available to take home.

Dearborn Inn

20301 Oakwood Blvd., Dearborn, Mich.
(313) 271-2700

Daily breakfast, lunch, & dinner   Reservations advised

Breakfast about $5, lunch about $10, dinner $20 or less

Built by Ford to house and feed visiting executives, the Dearborn Inn is a colonial brick hotel furnished in what might be called haute WASP taste: stenciled walls, sconces, bobeches, swags, ginger-jar lamps, and a solemn portrait of Mr. Ford gazing down from above the fireplace. It is a masculine place; we'd guess 90 percent of the guests are men.

The food served in the dining room of the Dearborn Inn is midwestern man food: prime ribs, lamb chops, roast leg of pork. The Inn still bothers to *plank* beef on occasion, an old-fashioned American way to appreciate the splendor of a meal, laying it all out on a warm inch-thick wooden board— the steak, vegetables, and a wall of piped potatoes all around.

Great Lakes fish look especially good when served this way. Last August, the Inn's menu (which changes each month) offered Lake Superior trout on a plank. It was a luscious, oily platter of fish, its meat vaguely pink, surrounded by gardeny vegetables and a phalanx of deliciously seasoned Duchess potatoes.

Dearborn kitchens prepare a considerable amount of local fish in season: pickerel, perch, whitefish . . . plus lobsters et al. flown in from the east.

One recent meal at the Dearborn Inn was highlighted by a fascinating scene at a nearby table, where a Ford exec was hosting a dinner party for a dozen unsmiling Red Chinese. As this representative of American auto muscle tried to charm his Oriental wards, we asked our waitress to bring us an assortment from the salad bar. We didn't want to miss a word.

It was the first time we had ever let the waitress decide, because this salad bar (actually an elegant, white-clothed table, *sans* sneeze guard) is, for us, the best part of a Dearborn Inn meal, laden with the freshest produce from Michigan's farms. Dinner-size chilled plates are provided.

As we neared the end of dinner, the Chinese rose en masse, leaving the American alone at the table. No deal, apparently. At the next table, another solo diner, a gray-suited executive type, was being told by the hostess that quiche is "a sort of bacon and egg pie." There's a real man for you!

(Rooms at the Dearborn Inn are $50 to $100.)

Drake's Sandwich Shop

709 N. University, Ann Arbor, Mich.
(313) 668-8853

Mon.–Thurs. 10 a.m.–10:45 p.m., Fri. & Sat. until 11:45 p.m.

$5 or less

The last time we dined at Drake's, on cucumber sandwiches and fresh-squeezed limeade, we ate in a high-backed wooden booth on the main floor: wonderfully atmospheric, but let us tell you it was no Martian Room. The Martian Room is upstairs, a relic from the 1950s based on the boomerang shapes that were then evocative of modernity. The booths downstairs have boomerangs in their Formica, too, but they are reminiscent of a much earlier time—of 1924, when Drake's opened for business.

Write your own lunch ticket after studying a menu of museum-quality antiquity. Dagwood sandwiches have names like the Harvard and the Cornell; there is a full array of soda-fountain specialties; and each day one freshly baked twin-layer frosted cake is set upon a pedestal for dessert. Varieties include chocolate, banana, and spice cake, their surfaces festooned with a swirling complementary-colored frosting. In the morning, everybody's favorite meal is Drake's pecan roll, a sticky-sweet behemoth that is fine *au naturel*, although many prefer it twice-cooked—toasted on the grill. Should you be in dire need of coddling, Drake's makes nursery-right milktoast.

And across from the soda fountain, feast your eyes on a spectacular array of candy jars filled with licorice whips and pretty bonbons.

Everett's Smoked Fish

Rte. 2, Naubinway, Mich.
No phone

Late June–Dec. 1   Hours vary

Priced per pound: under $5 for a good snack

Everett's isn't a restaurant, just a small general store with a sparse selection of canned coffee, pretty pieces of driftwood, and used paperback books for sale—sundries for hunters who roam this awesome unspoiled woodland on Michigan's Upper Peninsula.

"Would you like to see the fish?" asked a pleasant white-haired lady behind the counter as we entered. Not knowing what she was talking about, we said "Sure," and as she went into the back, we noticed a residue of smoke in the room.

Out she came with three unwieldy cardboard boxes in her arms. She set them on the counter in a row; then, with the care and gentleness that might be used by a salesperson in Tiffany's displaying valuable jewels, she lifted up several choice pieces of smoked fish for us to examine. We were facing three boxes of the Upper Peninsula's catch—smoked daily, the lady told us, over apple and maple wood.

Each box held a different variety: salmon—big dark orange chunks; whitefish—both whole and sectioned; menominee—small round whitefish, sold whole.

We chose one of each. They were wrapped separately in white butcher's paper and tied with string. Down the road we bought some Stroh's beer, and as we headed north, had ourselves quite a feast of finger food.

Of the three varieties, we liked menominee best. All that's necessary to enjoy it is to peel back the skin. The meat, clean and dry, pulls easily off the bones. The whitefish was oilier, juicier, with a deeper sting of wood smoke. Salmon is the richest of the three, with the heaviest meat and strongest fish flavor—not for newcomers to Great Lakes smoked fish.

Everett Snyder has run his roadside smokehouse for a third of a century. If you are traveling around the Great Lakes, it's a regional delicacy not to be missed.

Finlandia Restaurant and Bakery

119 S. Front St., Marquette, Mich.
(906) 228-9708

Mon.–Fri. 6 a.m.–5 p.m. (until 5:30 for pasty pick-up), Sat. to 2 p.m.

$5 or less

"A real cream and butter place with quality service" is how Finlandia describes itself on the menu; and we agree. But *Finlandia?* In a book about American food? Absolutely—because the house specialty is Cornish pasties.

If you haven't been to Michigan's Upper Peninsula, this may not make much sense, so allow us to explain. A little over a hundred years ago, Cornishmen came to work the iron mines of the Menominee Range. They brought with them a dish called the pasty (say *pass-tee*), a large sealed pocket of pastry filled with stew. It was favored by miners because it was portable, and because it retained its warmth for hours.

Later, when large groups of Finnish people came to the northern woods, they took to this cold-weather food as naturally as the Pilgrims took to Indian corn. And now, in the U.P., pasties are as Finnish a dish as they are Cornish; which is to say they are, in a manner characteristic of the midwestern melting pot, American.

Although it would be possible to eat one of Finlandia's pasties with the hands, as was the original purpose of the self-contained meat pie, it is served here on a plate (a pretty one, in fact, speckled and rimmed in blue) with knife and fork. Unlike the crescent-shaped pasties sold at a hundred stands and stores between St. Ignace and Marquette, it is a smooth neat oval. The dough is thinner, more sophisticated than we imagine the miners' pasties were a century ago—but, of course, few people need to carry these pasties around in their pockets for half a day.

Inside the crust is a mixture of shredded beef and pork, sweet onions, and small cubes of potato and carrot. It is dry enough so it doesn't ooze, but it has a lush buttery taste; its aroma is that of the best warm pot roast.

Beyond the pasty, Finlandia's repertoire is mainstream American: burgers, French dip, etc. The menu says "lemonade in season," and sure enough, the glass we got last summer was squeezed fresh from lemons, not too sweet. The promise about "quality service" was kept, too. A waitress was at our booth before we were settled, pouring coffee. And our cups were kept full throughout the meal.

Finlandia is as plain as crockery, a hospitable cafe of booths and tables and a small bakery case up front. Here you will find some very American doughnuts and sticky buns, and loaves of Finnish cardamom bread.

Great Lakes Whitefish & Chips

411 Bridge St., Charlevoix, Mich.
(616) 547-4374

May–Oct. Mon.–Sat. 11:30 a.m.–9 p.m., Sun. noon–9 p.m.

$5 or less

The fish is fresh lake whitefish, falling into flakes, its heady moistness sealed inside crisp batter. This snowy meat could easily be turned to mush by gross or greasy frying; but Great Lakes Whitefish & Chips' oil is clean, its batter nicely seasoned and a little chewy, but light—always complementary to the purity of the fish.

For a dollar and a half more, it is possible to get walleye instead of whitefish. Walleye meat is richer and heavier. When battered and fried, it is stouter food.

Unfortunately, the chips to go with these good fish are not good; but there are some other side dishes to know about. Spears of fried zucchini, served with horseradish sauce, have a fresh snap. Great Lakes fish chowder, a thin milky potato broth, is weighted with large hunks of fish. It's salty, reminiscent more of the sea than the lakes. And there's cheesecake for dessert.

A spin-off of a fishmarket around the corner, Great Lakes Whitefish &

Chips is a pleasant informal cafe on the main street of town. There are checked tables indoors and a few on the sidewalk for alfresco dining and people watching.

Juilleret's

130 State, Harbor Springs, Mich.
(616) 526-2821

May–Oct. daily 9 a.m.–11 p.m.

About $10, less for sandwiches

Juilleret's is a historic soda fountain in a well-heeled resort community. Aside from the fact that the fox trot "Sleepy Time Gal" was written here in 1923, two things put it on our map: ice cream and planked whitefish.

What a sight, to see the wooden boards of whitefish carried forth from Juilleret's kitchen—some of them small, for two people, others immense, with enough fish for eight or ten. The broiled filets are speckled orange with black crisped edges, moist ivory white inside. They are piled in the center of the plank, strewn with slices of lemon and tomato; and all around the plank's circumference is a rippling ridge of piped potatoes. The spuds are encased in a fragile crust that develops as they are grilled on the plank. In addition to being delicious and pretty, they serve a higher purpose—to shore in the buttery juices of the fish.

Along with the plank comes a loaf of freshly baked bread. The salad bar is copiously stocked with midwestern goodies such as ambrosia salad with teeny-weeny marshmallows, pea salad with walnuts, carrot salad, and a superior spinach salad of glossy dark leaves already dressed in a sweet and sour vinaigrette, dotted with real bacon.

Planked whitefish is a luxurious platter of food that no aficionado of regional cookery ought to miss. It is Juilleret's specialty, supplemented on the menu, for the sake of those who eat here all the time, by pan-fried lake perch, steak, and on Friday and Saturday, planked prime rib. There is a long list of sandwiches and burgers.

From Juilleret's soda fountain come sundaes, sodas, banana splits, tin roofs, cream puffs, coolers, and rainbows galore. The ice cream and the toppings are made here. For a "velvet," the soda jerks handblend vanilla ice cream, bittersweet chocolate sauce, and marshmallow cream, creating a custard that resembles a milk shake, but is thicker. It is icy cold with a cocoa taste, and a few pleasant lumps of unblended vanilla ice cream. You eat it with a spoon. The other famous dessert is called a thundercloud, for which the same ingredients are layered rather than blended, and topped with chopped nuts.

Juilleret's is one of the most boisterous places you will ever eat in, bubbling with the noise of people having a great time, eating vacation food.

Conversations are loud, sometimes jumping tables to include friends or summer neighbors or strangers; babies cry; teenagers court and flirt.

Generations of vacationing Michiganders have made this a favorite town gathering spot. It's been open every season for eighty-eight years, and no one we know can remember a night when it wasn't jammed. With that kind of record, many restaurateurs would raise the tariff and put on airs. Yet nearly a century of success hasn't spoiled Juilleret's a bit. It's still the town lunchroom, and loads of fun.

(There are two other restaurants called Juilleret's, in Charlevoix and Petoskey, run by relatives of the Harbor Springs original. We cannot recommend either one.)

Lawry's Pasty Shop

2381 U.S. 41 west   Four miles west of Ishpeming, Mich.
(906) 485-5589

Summer daily 8 a.m.–9 p.m., winter daily 8 a.m.–7 p.m.

$5 or less

Many delicious-tasting things smell wonderful; some look gorgeous; but Nancy Lawry's pasties *feel* good—not on the tongue (although they're just fine there), but in the hands. What a pleasure it is to feel the smooth tan skin of pliant dough around this Michigan meat pie, to grasp its pillowy weight, soft and heavy and warm as a puppy. And yet it is a sturdy thing—hand food, to be eaten without utensils, and without mess.

Pasties are *the* specialty along the shore of Lake Superior, more popular than burgers or buckets of chicken. They have been the region's dish for more than a hundred years, introduced by Cornishmen who carried them in their pockets down to the iron mines.

You understand their popularity in the cold north woods when you take possession of a Lawry's pasty. Just to hold this big piece of food imparts a feeling of security.

As pasties are supposed to do, it stays warm for hours. The crust is so good you could eat it alone; and inside is a peppery mélange of beef (no pork), suet, onions, and potatoes.

Lawry's used to be Madelyne's, long renowned for pasty prowess. If anything, the new regime has made it better. It's a pretty little place, with colorful impatiens planted all around, and bleeding hearts hanging near the door. The inside is tiny, just a counter and a couple of tables, with a kitchen bigger than the dining room.

Back there you see Nancy and her help rolling out the pasty dough, and mixing up the filling, all by hand. Lawry's has never heard of convenience products. Everything that's done here is done with fresh ingredients, old recipes, and a heap of talent. At breakfast there are yeasty cinnamon rolls.

For after pasties, at lunch, a Dutch apple pie made of the thinnest apple slivers, topped with a homely layer of buttercrumbs.

Lawry's also makes whole pork pies and whole tea rings, to go. Most of the business is take-out, especially pasties, which were born to roam, and can easily be eaten with one hand while you steer your car with the other.

But don't rush away from Lawry's, at least not without some cookies. You'll see them along the counter, in clear glass jars: pure golden sugar cookies, painfully brittle, not much more than a perfect blend of sugar and butter; and gingersnaps, molasses dark, with just exactly the right amount of *bend* before they snap. These are without question some of the plainest, and most delicious, cookies in America.

Linwood Corner Restaurant

44 N. Huron Rd., Linwood, Mich.
(517) 697-5141

Daily 5 a.m.–8 p.m.

$3–$8

"Good morning, neighbor!" says the menu. "Have a hearty breakfast . . . and a pleasant day!" How can you help feeling chipper gazing over platters of just-baked donuts and cinnamon rolls, French toast made with homemade bread and sided by freshly ground pork sausage, and a "fisherman's breakfast" of steak and eggs and American fried potatoes, cut from peeled-here spuds?

When the Linwood Corner Restaurant moved to bigger quarters and installed twin salad bars, we feared the new digs might mean an end to the simple but always excellent food we had learned to count on when heading up I-75—hale breakfasts, bakery goods, and Great Lakes fish dinners.

But it's the same; better—those salad bars are farmland feasts in themselves. The kitchen still peels potatoes (a ton a week) and fries superior hash browns; bread and pies and sweet rolls are baked every morning; and fresh lake perch is on the menu every day. Whitefish, snowier and more delicate than the compact meat of the perch, is served "in season," generally summer into fall.

As much as Michigan abounds in freshwater fish, it is, like all the heartland, pork country; and the pig meat served at Linwood Corner is outstanding. There are pork chops, either grilled or smoked and smothered, sliced pork, baked ham, breakfast sausage and chewy smoked bacon, and a sleeper —Polish sausage. Made here, it's a crisp-skinned tube steak, served smothered in kraut or topped with Linwood's zesty "Coney Island sauce."

Linwood's repertoire extends beyond local fish and midwestern pork. We especially recommend the homey chicken soup, afloat with irregularly shaped noodles as soft as dumplings. We have yet to sample the stupendous-looking steak sandwich—on freshly baked Italian bread, topped with cheese and sauce, nor have we tried fried rabbit, listed inconspicuously on the menu between the T-bone and liver and onions.

The London Chop House

155 W. Congress, Detroit, Mich.
(313) 962-0277

Mon.–Thurs. 11:30 a.m.–midnight, Fri. & Sat. until 2 a.m.
Reservations advised

Lunch $10–$20, dinner $20–$30

The London Chop House looks like money and power. It is the one undisputably great restaurant in the Motor City—a dark club where families with cars named after them have regular tables. For the rest of us, it is a place to put on the dog. The wine list is monumental; the food is the best of the midwest, with a smidgen of fancier stuff thrown in.

Luncheon and dinner menus are three feet tall, a foot and a half wide, heavy paper sheets printed every day, wines on one side, food on the obverse. The type is small; to read the entire thing, especially in this dim light, would take an hour.

The item listed on the menu as "a mess of Lake Erie perch" is not the Chop House being coy. Although "a mess of . . ." sounds like the way the Beverly Hillbillies order dinner, it is in fact the correct term, like a gaggle of geese, or a knot of toads. This mess of perch is a pile of small, buttery filets, one of the Lake's richest foods, and the best uniquely regional dish on the menu.

LCH will sautee pickerel from Lake Erie, too; or better yet, grill the long, tender filets with fragrant sprigs of fennel.

There is a vast selection of hors d'oeuvres. We especially recommend the green fettucini with fresh basil and mushrooms and parmesan cheese. Or for a more Michiganian flavor, smoked Lake Superior trout, a gusty piece of fish, gilded with a cream horseradish sauce.

Steaks are dry-aged prime beef, broiled over charcoal.

Lamb is a strong suit, especially—no surprise—chops. Double-thick baby lamb chops with bacon are perfectly charred on the outside, soft pink inside, exactly as ordered. The lamb is mild and tender, yet with a satisfying depth of character.

Salads include arugula with cherry tomatoes and mimosa, spinach salad with hot bacon dressing, tossed greens, endive and watercress, but we like the ragtag "kitchen salad" best. It's bibb lettuce, watercress, avocados, and mushrooms, topped preferably with house-made creamy garlic dressing. We could dive into a bowl of dressing alone, and happily forget about greens altogether.

Terrific potatoes: German-fried, shoestrings, hashed browns, lyonnaise, and grilled skins. Get the skins with sour cream.

If you are a minimalist, or a strict regionalist, you can have a bowl of Michigan blueberries for dessert. There is, of course, much more: frozen hazelnut soufflé with pralines, bittersweet hot fudge sundaes, the uniquely midwestern Gold Brick sundae (vanilla ice cream capped with a sheath of milk-chocolate praline sauce), magnificent Lundi Gras chocolate chestnut cake, and an off-the-map hot raspberry soufflé.

To put a point on this meal, you want Café Diablo Flambé. By its light, observe that the matchbooks at your table have been imprinted with your name (assuming you gave your real name when making a reservation). The Chop House sure knows how to make a person feel like a swell!

Mattie's Bar-B-Que

11728 Dexter, Detroit, Mich.
(313) 869-6331

Daily 7 a.m.–11 p.m.

$10 or less

Motown is crazy for ribs. Yet it wasn't easy to find good ones here. During a week-long stay, we hit a disappointing string of soulless bone shacks, then finally stopped in Mattie's. It's an unprepossessing cafe between a beauty shop and barber shop, not much more than a counter and a few tables, with a little fruit stand outside. For excellent barbecued ribs, as well as a repertoire of classic urban soul-food meals, it's tops in Detroit.

The barbecued spare ribs served at Mattie's come in slabs or half-slabs, or occasionally as tips—hacked up ends that are a godawful, fingerlicking mess to eat. They are zesty high-spiced bones, glazed with what tastes like a brown-sugar and pepper sauce, with perhaps a bit less meat than we'd like; but what meat there is exudes flavor.

If you prefer to eat with knife and fork, try Mattie's chicken and dumplings—simple warming food, served with likker-dripping turnip greens and candied sweet potatoes on the side. We were told that the kitchen regularly makes ham hocks, and roasted pigs' feet. The rest of the menu is authoritative blue-plate cooking: short ribs, meat loaf, smothered steak, peppery chicken dressing; melting-soft candied sweet potatoes, crisp fried chicken, even luscious macaroni and cheese. Not much dessert, other than a sticky-sweet peach cobbler.

There is a fetching aroma in this friendly, family restaurant; it's like a kitchen at home, with pots bubbling on the stove and the oven going full steam. In fact, it isn't much more than that.

Mrs. Morgan's Boarding House

2590 Puritan, Detroit, Mich.
(313) 341-8286

Lunch & dinner Wed.–Sun.

$8–$15

A black-run restaurant near the University of Detroit, Mrs. Morgan's is a rare opportunity to sample the unsung cuisine of the urban midwest. It is southern-style food, but like the blues when they migrated from Mississippi to St. Louis and Chicago, country eating gained a certain nostalgic poignancy when it came into northern cities, far from home. These 1930s dining rooms are a conscious evocation of what Mrs. Morgan calls "the Old World foods."

As the pianist croons gentle jazz in the background, you can go back home again (even if you've never been there) with bracing plates of ham and red-eye gravy, catfish and grits, chicken and dumplings every Sunday, biscuits on Wednesday, and side dishes of collard greens, candied yams, cornbread dressing, and fresh squash casserole.

Mrs. Morgan's is in a residential area, and has the feel of a private home circa 1935. Service is boarding-house style to the degree that vegetables are served in platters and bowls shared by everyone at the table. However, each party gets a private table of their own, and in addition to the nightly soul-food specials, the menu lists a full array of middle-class, non–boarding-house fare such as shrimp, steaks, and crab legs.

The decor is patchwork plain, as it ought to be, simple surroundings suitable for contemplating food as an expression of soul.

Wagar's Cafe

227 River St., Ontonagon, Mich.
(906) 884-4475

Daily 5:30 a.m.–10 p.m. until 11 p.m. in summer   Closed for
vacation two weeks in Oct., one week in May

$5 or less

Since 1937, Anna Wagar's Cafe has been famous for its pancakes. Made from
scratch each morning, they arrive steaming from the grill to nearly everyone
who comes for breakfast. It is rare to find pancakes this good—buttery crisp
around the edges, light and fork tender. Buy them three at a time, bacon on
the side.

If you don't want pancakes, Audrey Basto—Anna Wagar's culinary heir
—will set you up just fine with a homemade sweet roll or fruit turnover. Or
you can do some serious chowing down on a farmer's omelette.

After breakfast, everything else is authentic small-town cafe cuisine:
fresh-baked bread, lake trout, pasties every Saturday, and comfort meals
like meat loaf or creamed turkey nestled by a hill of mashed potatoes. Locals
come in for nothing fancier than sandwiches, with real french fries on the
side.

For dessert, a majority of Wagar's patrons dig into tart lemon pie, a
house specialty for decades.

MINNESOTA

Anderson House

333 W. Main St., Wabasha, Minn.
(612) 565-4524

Daily breakfast, lunch, & dinner   Reservations advised

Breakfast & lunch $5 or less, dinner $10 or less

Breakfast, lunch, dinner, and ice cream snacks are all pretty terrific at Anderson House, but there is one dish, served only on weekends, that is the
hotel's pièce de résistance: pheasant on wild rice. You get half a bird, but-

tered and braised, then simmered in a wine and mushroom gravy. Pheasant can be stringy if dry-cooked, but the buttering and the cream sauce moisten the meat. This pheasant is lush and elegant, high-flavored; in contrast, domesticated fowl tastes neutered.

To accompany this game meat you need a starch with guts and body. That of course is wild rice, which is, like pheasant, indigenous to the north-central states. Anderson House serves a blend of wild and brown rice, but the brown isn't much more than an extender for the chewy dearer grains harvested from northern lakes.

Follow the pheasant and wild rice with a slice of superior sour cream raisin pie, and you will have a meal that is the best of the northern midwest: game, grain, and cream.

This is pork country, too: Anderson House turns out heartland meals of pork chops with red cabbage; roast pork loin with sauerkraut; and barbecued ribs basted in an unbelievably luxurious sauce made from stock that is retrieved when the ribs are boiled—before they are baked. Beef roll is another house specialty, a thin steak rolled around mustard, bacon, and burger meat, cooked in mushroom gravy. For chicken and dumplings, the dumplings are made here—as are noodles for soup and *ten different kinds of bread*, every day.

The best bread thing is the cinnamon bun served at breakfast—the Colossus of Rolls, measuring six inches across and three inches high—freshly baked each morning. The roll is more than an adequate meal, and it can be had alone; but it is also available—there is something really swell about starting the day in style, isn't there?—as part of a "Giant's Breakfast," which includes the 100-cubic-inch roll, plus a steak, plus eggs, grits, and fried cornmeal mush.

Fortunately, it is possible to book lodging at Anderson House, eliminating any necessity of locomoting immediately after a meal. It is a country hotel, 125 years old, run by the same family for four generations. Rooms ($25 to $50) are furnished with four-posters and antique quilts.

Crabtree's Kitchen

19173 Quinell Ave. N (Hwy. 95), Marine on St. Croix, Minn.
(612) 433-2455

Tues.–Sun. 9 a.m.–8 p.m.

$3–$10

There is virtually no Scandinavian food sold in Minnesota restaurants. The culinary talents of the Swedes and Norskis who settled here are limited to private homes. Because of that, unless you are a fisherman or a hunter, or unless you get in a canoe and harvest your own wild rice (of which Minnesota has an abundance), there are precious few opportunities to have a uniquely Minnesotan meal.

Crabtree's Kitchen is a real North Star restaurant. The repertoire is mostly all-American food like steaks and seafood, roasted chicken and pork tenderloin, short ribs with kraut and dumplings; but the kitchen also makes spunky Swedish meatballs, and during the winter, *lutefisk* and *lefse*.

Lutefisk is a rarity almost never on menus (because it is customarily made at home). It is an arcane dish, made obsolete by modern food processing and refrigeration methods, treasured in the north as part of the Viking heritage.

The elaborate preparation begins with air-dried cod, pieces of fish so devoid of moisture they resemble driftwood. (Originally, the drying was a method of preservation.) The fish is reconstituted by a good long soak in a solution of birch ashes and lye, then fresh water, by which point it has almost no taste at all—just a trembly tough texture. The flavor of *lutefisk* comes from the pork drippings in which it is bathed, the boiled potatoes and yellow peas that always nestle with it on the plate, and chewy discs of *lefse* bread. *Lutefisk* and *lefse* are the specialties of the house at Crabtree's Kitchen during the winter holidays.

Any time of year other than the holidays, it's the fancy pastries and desserts at Crabtree's Kitchen that are a distinct reminder of Minnesota's deep ethnic roots. Of all the sweets, our favorite is the "raw apple dessert," a cake laced with apple slivers and served with sticky butterscotch sauce. There is a sour cream chocolate cake that comes drenched with fudge; strawberry shortcake on nice light biscuits; and in the fall, hot apple dumplings with cream.

On weekends, the kitchen whips up a lumberjack-style "Crabtree breakfast" of hotcakes, eggs, toast and homemade jelly, American fried potatoes, and Swedish sausage. The big feed is served family-style on pretty, rustic platters.

No convenience foods are used at Crabtree's. Potatoes are peeled and mashed here; gravy for the roast beef is made from the drippings of the meat; even the butterscotch and hot fudge are from scratch.

In the middle of nowhere on the St. Croix River, but just a short drive up from the Twin Cities, Crabtree's Kitchen is in a weathered 100-year-old building full of antique tools and furniture. It is a comfortable spot to sample the country cooking of the northern midwest—both ethnic-edged and mainline American.

Edie's

110 W. 1st, Fairmont, Minn.
(612) 235-5700

Mon.–Fri. 5 a.m.–7:30 p.m., Sat. 5 a.m.–2:30 p.m., Sun. 6 a.m.–2 p.m.

$5 or less

Edie's calls itself "a restaurant even mom would approve of." The day we ate there, it was packed with moms. In fact, it was the best possible day of the year to eat at Edie's: Mother's Day. Every mom in the house was wearing a corsage, and "Happy Mother's Day" echoed through this large town lunchroom as greetings were exchanged across the tables.

In their ruffle-neck blouses, sling-back shoes, and large-lens, low-ride glasses, the Minnesota moms swarmed in on the arms of their sons and husbands to sit back and enjoy a non–home-cooked meal.

Edie's is nothing fancy, with its green plaster walls, stamped tin ceiling, plastic and Formica booths, and paper placemats. But there is a touch of class about it: an individual sconce to illuminate each booth; pastoral pictures along the wall.

The meals we ate were mom's cooking, midwestern-style. Roast turkey, sliced from a plump tender bird, was served on top of sage-scented giblet dressing, beneath a blanket of sunny gravy. Baked chicken was moist, with a crusty, high-seasoned skin. Both were accompanied by an item called "pistachio salad," which, for devotees of heartland cookery, is a quivering taste of heaven. It is a cool green block of gelatin, pale and opaque, more the color than the flavor of pistachio nuts. What you taste, other than the sweetness, are crushed pineapple and itty-bitty micro-marshmallows.

Nearly everyone in the house was eating turkey or chicken, except for a few gents nearby cooing over their fried walleye pike. Good food, except for the mashed potatoes, which seemed ersatz.

Pies were mom-level good, especially the buttery-textured rhubarb pie, so heavy it fell to pieces when it was hefted from pan to plate. We also liked the fresh strawberry pie, made on a graham cracker crust with whole berries packed into clear red goo.

MISSOURI

Arthur Bryant

1727 Brooklyn, Kansas City, Mo.
(816) BE 1-1123

Mon.–Sat. 10 a.m.–11 p.m.   Closed in Jan.

About $5, more for slabs of ribs

With the possible exception of Jerry Lewis's endorsements of Brown's Hotel, no restaurant has ever had a more effective publicity agent than Arthur Bryant's barbecue does in Calvin Trillin. Since he began declaring it the best restaurant in the world, thousands of people from ribless America have made pilgrimages to Kansas City to get their taste of *New Yorker*-approved Americana. Even the K.C. tourist magazine, the kind that you find in hotel rooms and that always lists the most *ersatz* eateries in town, directs visitors to Bryant's "unpretentious" restaurant.

Unpretentious? If a floor strewn with shreds of beef and old french fries and wadded-up napkins from the last two hundred customers is unpretentious, you would definitely say that Arthur Bryant's is unpretentious. Amazingly—indeed, perhaps admirably—Arthur Bryant's celebrity never altered the winning formula one iota. Until his death in 1982, the place was always a dump . . . as it remains today.

And the ribs, the beef, the french fries, most of all, the sauce—are still extraordinary.

Service is cafeteria-style, and that's some of the fun of this place—watching the pit men fork ribs off the fire, smear sauce on slabs with a housepainter's brush, pile up mounds of thin-sliced ham and brisket. Since Mr. Bryant died, the one significant change has been the addition of a beef slicing machine—meaning uniform slices instead of the variety of thicknesses that used to fill a sandwich. But the sandwich man still presses down hard just before he cuts it, leaving a perfect imprint of his hand in the soft Wonder bread.

Bryant's ribs have a beautiful crisp glaze, with blackened burnt edges all around, lots of chewy meat within. They are "soulful" ribs, a complimentary euphemism for greasy. The most popular item in the house is beef brisket, mellow and a little dry—until you pour on the sauce.

It is the sauce that stays with you after a visit to Arthur Bryant. The ribs, the brisket, the tender honey-colored french fries, they're all excellent, but all admit competition. There is, however, nothing on earth like Arthur Bryant's powerhouse sauce: opaque red-orange, hot but not fiery, more tart than sweet, a muffled explosion of cayenne, tomato, curry, and a thousand other sparks of flavor.

Boots and Coats

905 W. 103rd St., west of Wornall, Kansas City, Mo.
(816) 942-9910

Mon.–Sat. lunch & dinner   Chicken at dinner only

$10 or less

More than any other place in America, Kansas City is a fried-chicken town. Passion for fried chicken supports at least a dozen restaurants that serve virtually nothing else. There is a theogony among chicken devotees, including, in the pantheon of chef-gods, a woman known as "Chicken Betty" (Betty Lucas). Her legendary skills with batter and bird have been plied at most of the city's foremost chicken joints. But once the fried chicken is elevated into the stratosphere, Betty always moves on, like the hired gun in a western movie, to some other kitchen that needs her.

One of Chicken Betty's first triumphs was Boots and Coats, which remains today one of the city's triumvirate of great fried-chicken houses. Named for its owners, Boots Boutross and Al Coates, B & C serves a basic dinner: half a bird, slow-cooked in an iron skillet, cottage-fried potatoes, country gravy, and steamy white biscuits. The batter on the chicken is out of this world—thin and flaky, tweaked with pepper, hugging close to the plump meat. Gravy, made from pan drippings and milk, is suitable for pouring on the chicken, the biscuits, or the likeably oily cottage fries.

Boots and Coats is small and dark, snug as a neighborhood bar. On weekends at dinner, you'll have a hard time getting a seat; but once you do, the chicken comes fast. Because it is the only thing anybody ever orders for dinner, the kitchen can keep skilletsful bubbling all the time.

Busch's Grove

9160 Clayton Rd., St. Louis, Mo.
(314) 993-0011

Tues.–Thurs. 11:30 a.m.–11:30 p.m., Fri. & Sat. until midnight
Reservations advised

$20–$30

Having spent three days in St. Louis tracking down soul-food snoots, noodle-parlor chop suey, toasted ravioli on the hill, concrete custards at Ted Drewes, and fried-brain sandwiches in taverns all over town, we were pooped. We wanted a nice dinner of respectable things to eat. So we went to Busch's Grove, a white frame roadhouse where St. Louis society has gathered since the 1890s to eat first-class food.

Next to us, a lady was complaining that her private plane doesn't hold enough people. Nearly every person who walked into the dining room stopped at tables to greet friends. It was a club, where everyone was known to all, except for us. That was okay; we were treated fine.

We asked the waiter, a kingly red-jacketed black man, if he had mint juleps. "This is the place," he bellowed. When he brought them, he intoned, "From a man's bar—Butch's Grove." And he wasn't kidding. Topped with parasols and fresh mint leaves, served in proper silver tumblers, these juleps are dynamite.

The waiter fairly orated the menu, repeating each major item twice, in cadence, for emphasis. There were few surprises, no "inventive cuisine." Only entrenched favorites: slabs of prime rib, genteel barbecued ribs, calves liver and onions. We had steaks—tender beef running rivers of natural juice. And in homage to St. Louis custom, we started with toasted ravioli, tiny deep-fried pasta pockets sprinkled heavily with sharp cheese, served with meaty red sauce on the side.

We especially like Busch's Grove's salads, including the spinach laden with bacon, eggs, and sweet and sour dressing, with the spinach so finely chopped up it is almost like limp slaw. "Russ's salad" is another happy hodgepodge chef's salad topped with a garlicky cream dressing loaded with crumbled hard-boiled eggs.

For dessert, we went the pillowy route with peanut butter cream pie and coconut cream pie, both just fine.

Busch's Grove is a kick in the summer, when you can dine in an outdoor "cage" behind the restaurant. Screened-in, fan-cooled gazebos range from romantic tables-for-two to large-party size. A mint julep sipped in one of these jungle huts seems like the ultimate in recherché libations.

C & K B-B-Q

1512 Goodfellow, St. Louis, Mo.
(314) 385-5740

Mon.–Sat. 10 a.m.–2:30 a.m., Sun. 10 a.m.–1 a.m.

$10 or less

Mister Austin, across the street at 1511 Goodfellow, was out of snoots. But we are not ones to visit St. Louis and leave without at least one snoot sandwich, so after rib dinners and triple-layer cake sitting in the car outside Mr. A (there is no table service), we coasted fifty yards to the C & K parking lot, stepped out of the car, and inhaled.

Our noses told us we were on a good trail. The lot was enveloped in smoke that seemed equal parts hickory and pork. Inside, the menu (all take-out again) listed ribs, tips, links . . . and snoots—the St. Louis soul-food term for deep-fried slabs of pig snout.

We watched our snoot sandwich assembled. A whole hog's nose worth, at least half a dozen jumbo chunks, were piled atop a slice of white bread, completely dwarfing the pitiful spongey pallet. Spicy red sauce was drizzled onto the snoots through a strainer. On another slice of bread, the sandwich maker plopped a scoop of potato salad. Then the two halves were slapped together and wrapped.

The monstrous package is impossible to eat neatly. Sauce dissolves the bread, snoot sections tumble out from between your fingers . . . and you better be wearing jeans or a smock.

These snoots are worth the dry-cleaning bills. Crusty, porous, light-bodied, yet as rich as deep-fried fat, there is nothing nasal about the way they chew. They're more like the fine fried skin at a southern pig pickin, luscious, glazed with sauce.

Desserts at C & K aren't quite as spectacular-looking as Mr. Austin's (mere two-layer cakes instead of three), but don't leave without a pecan pie. Made as an individual five-inch circle (but enough for two), one of these glistening amber pies is the Cadillac of soul-food desserts.

China Chop Suey Restaurant

6165 W. Florissant, St. Louis, Mo.
(314) 382-1819

Mon.–Thurs. 11 a.m.–11:30 p.m., Fri. 11 a.m.–1 a.m., Sat. noon–12:30 a.m.

$5 or less

Years ago, at the end of a grueling day in Arizona, we had a brilliant idea for dinner. Why not go to a local Chinese restaurant and get chop suey? We were in a town where many Chinese had settled when they built the railroads; and so we reasoned that maybe the Chinese food would be special. Were we ever wrong!

In 1985, while traveling through the southern midwest, we realized that our earlier inspiration had been a good one. The only problem was, we had had it in the wrong place. St. Louis, Missouri, was the place to eat chop suey.

St. Louis has a chop suey culture all its own. Noodle shops, as they are known hereabouts, are more numerous than chili parlors in Cincinnati or barbecues in Kansas City. We counted 100, then gave up counting. Chop suey is everywhere.

St. Louisian Howard Wong told us that it began as a strictly ghetto dish, served to blacks by Chinese, from storefront dives equipped with nothing more than a chopping block and wok. The noodle shops proliferated, and while they never went upscale, they did gain an air of what Mr. Wong called "semi-respectability."

One of the nicest such places we visited was the China Chop Suey Restaurant, a take-out operation (like most noodle shops) with a full menu of chop suey, fried rice, fried noodles, egg foo yung, and the only-in-St.-Louis oddity known as "St. Paul."

A St. Paul, which you will find on virtually every Chinese menu in town, is an individual-sized egg foo yung, served without rice or gravy between two pieces of bread: a Chinaman's sandwich! We ordered shrimp St. Paul for a buck-and-a-half. It was crisp, golden crusted, the oily fried egg laced with sprouts, diced pepper and onion, and little pink nuggets of shrimp. It came on white bread, garnished with pickle slices and onion. A weird combo, but not bad at all.

As we chomped our St. Paul, we watched through the order window as the man made chop suey. From scratch! Celery, onion, and fresh mushrooms were sliced. Chicken shreds and sprouts were quick-fried in a wok. The vegetables were added, then water, seasoning, and plenty of cornstarch. The result, poured into a white quart carton, was simply the heaviest container of Chinese food we have ever toted. And it stayed hot for hours.

For all the hand chopping and fresh ingredients, the result was basic chop suey—beige, soupy, salty, and simple. Nothing like the sophisticated

Chinese food we have all come to know in the last ten or fifteen years. But we liked it—a lot; so much so that when we returned home, we went to our local Cantonese restaurant for chop suey. And you know what? It was awful! That is why we offer St. Louis as the chop suey capital of America.

Granny's

1803 Baltimore, Kansas City, Mo.
(816) 421-1100

Mon.–Fri. 6 a.m.–10 p.m., Sat. 5 p.m.–10 p.m., Sun. 4 p.m.–9 p.m.

$10 or less

Usually, when restaurant reviewers go out to eat, everybody orders something different, to maximize the tasting possibilities. We went to Granny's as a party of five. Four people ordered pan-fried chicken; one person ordered pan-fried chicken, all white meat.

We *do* hear that Granny's steak is excellent, ditto the catfish, pork chops, and liver-gizzard combo. But all five of us were very aware of wanting a definitive *Kansas City* dinner; that being the case, only fried chicken would do.

Granny's sells a ritualized meal of all the requisite Kansas City elements, including an appetizer of soup. We scoffed at soup when the waitress said it came with the meal, but we ate our words when it arrived. The chicken noodle soup was packed with gigantic noodles, more like dumplings, floating in a fantastic peppery broth. The vegetable soup was loaded with real vegetables. We're still not convinced that these rib-stickers are what one wants before digging into fried chicken, but they sure are good.

Blue-cheese salad dressing commands a 55¢ premium. Pebbles of stinging-strong cheese come to the table floating in a bowl of garlicky orange oil: pour it on yourself. It's worth the extra cash.

The chicken sections are enveloped in a ragged crust that is so much a separate entity that you can pull huge strips of it away from the meat. Yet there is always more. This is crust-lover's chicken, fried in lard with a strong pepper seasoning that permeates the steamy depths of the moist white meat.

The potato choice includes mashed (real), french fried (fresh cut), pan fried, or American fried. The latter are brittle tile circles, like potato chips. We liked pan fried best, especially when ordered with onions and green peppers (another 55¢). A bowl of gravy was set down next to the person who ordered the mashed potatoes, and although the rest of the table contended that the gravy was for all of us to share, the mashed-potato–eater staked them as her own, saying there was only enough for her spuds.

Kansas City custom is saluted with a basket of cinnamon rolls to accompany the meal. They are homely yeast spirals almost as good as Stroud's.

Granny's ambience is interesting: a chicken house with a raised consciousness. Pictures of grannies hang all over the walls, and customers are invited to bring their own granny pictures to join them. The proprietors (who identify themselves as "Granny Darby" and "Granny Schanzer" on the menu) seem tongue-in-cheek about the notion of granny's old-fashioned food. It's all good fun. But there is nothing silly about the meals they serve, which are some of the best chicken dinners in town.

The Haven

6625 Morgan Ford, St. Louis, Mo.
(314) 353-7350

Food served Mon.–Sat. noon–11 p.m.

$5 or less

"I don't eat anybody else's brains," explained Gordon Beck, the man behind the bar at The Haven. "I don't even eat my own. I clean them. That's enough, if you know what I mean."

We were discussing brains, fried, on rye (with pickles and onions) with Mr. Beck because his is one of a handful of tavern restaurants in St. Louis that specialize in them. Fried brain sandwiches: yet another idiosyncratic St. Louis specialty.

"Some of the other places chop them up and make patties," he told us with disdain. "That's the easy way. I devein them one by one; and when you get a brain sandwich here, there is half a brain on it, nothing less. That's why I call it the 'Old Tyme' brain sandwich."

And so it is listed on the menu, among an otherwise ordinary assortment of sandwiches. It comes between squared-off pullman-style slices of rye; it is golden brown, sandy crusted like any other deep-fried patty. But look closely, and sure enough, you see the brain in there. Take a bite and your teeth slide easily into the convoluted gray meat, mild and tender, and rich to a numbing extreme.

Gordon told us that even though he came in second in a recent citywide brain-cooking contest (Dieckmeyer's Tavern on South Broadway was number one), he felt these were the best. Although we haven't yet had the opportunity to taste Dieckmeyer's brains, we thought the Haven sandwich was excellent. And we told Gordon so. At that point, a patron at the bar warned us that we better stop complimenting Gordon on his brains, or his head would start to swell.

Jess and Jim's Annex

13035 Holmes Rd., Kansas City, Mo.
(816) 942-7454

Daily lunch & dinner

$8–$15

This has got to be the best-sounding steak in America: "Jess and Jim's Kansas City Playboy Strip," carried from the kitchen, sizzling furiously on a metal tray. It looks good, too: two inches high, a foot long, edged with a thick ribbon of fat; its charred crust glistens black. Slice into it; the knife moves easily, but not *too* easily. Fork up a thick triangle of scarlet meat, heavy with juice.

Here is the hunk of beef for which Kansas City is renowned—rich and deliciously tart, a more spritely steak than the deeply aged cuts served in the fancy steak houses of Chicago and the east.

Get Jess and Jim's baked potato on the side. It too is gigantic, arriving at the table split open and buttered, with a chewy skin that seems also to have been basted. Cottage fries are available as well; they're a Kansas City favorite: oily cross-sections of potato, best ordered well-done, so they crisp up.

Before all this you'll get a bowl of salad at the table to dole out yourself. Nothing much: less-than-sparkling iceberg lettuce, a bit of cabbage, shredded carrots, and some cukes. Four bottles of truly awful supermarket salad dressing are lined up on each table.

Steak and potatoes, stick with that. There are seven different cuts of meat listed on the menu, which is one of those laminated jobs with pictures of laminated-looking food. One of the pictures shows a piece of apple pie. But there is none. There is no dessert at all. Like we said, steak and potatoes.

You would never drive by Jess and Jim's Annex and think, *Say, there's an interesting restaurant.* It's a loungy looking place in a shingle-roof shopping center. A peek inside does little to inspire confidence: red and gold Mediterranean-style wallpaper, packets of sugar on the table emblazoned, mysteriously, with the Holiday Inn trademark. But then you hear a Playboy Strip come hissing out of the kitchen—and you know you are in Kansas City's great steak house.

(The original Jess and Jim's, just around the corner at 517 East 135th Street, serves the same food, but is open shorter hours.)

Lou Boccardi's

5424 Magnolia Ave., St. Louis, Mo.
(314) 647-1151

Mon.–Fri. lunch & dinner, Sat. dinner only   Reservations advised on weekends

$5–$10

St. Louis is a bonanza for aficionados of Italian food. At Cunetto House of Pasta (across from Lou Boccardi's, at 5453 Magnolia Avenue), and at a score of other restaurants on "the Hill," St. Louisians line up early in the evening for great inexpensive meals of fresh pasta and inventive sauces of vegetables or seafood.

Many of these restaurants list an appetizer that sounds Italian, and is definitely of Italian extraction—but is distinctly American, unique to St. Louis: toasted ravioli.

What a swell invention! Take some raviolis filled with spicy ground beef, and instead of merely boiling them in water, fry them in oil. After being submerged a few moments, they turn into golden squares, nice and crisp, with a chewy, almost tough consistency. They are, to say the least, well-built pieces of food—*deep-fried*, meat-stuffed pasta, after all. But they're fun to eat, and, as served at Lou Boccardi's, with a zesty red sauce, delicious. We can't understand why toasted ravioli never made it outside St. Louis.

We recommend Lou Boccardi's for toasted ravioli because the food is good and because, unlike many of the Hill's restaurants, you *can* make a reservation here. Also, there is an unspoiled, undiscovered feel about it; Lou's is the classic neighborhood Italian joint.

Whereas the city's more fashionably decorated pasta palaces play down the St. Louis ravioli in favor of more elegant fare, the ambience of Lou Boccardi's says toasted ravioli loud and clear. It's a three-story townhouse, but each story isn't much more than one room, noisy with local patrons. Decor is baroque—ritzy red and gold wallpaper, mirrors with swirls of gold, and sentimental paintings-on-velvet.

In the barroom downstairs, we watched a table of four mammoth men consume four full plates of toasted ravioli between them—an appetizer before their spaghetti-and-meatball meal.

Miss Hulling's

1105 Locust St., St. Louis, Mo.
(314) 436-0840

Mon.–Sat. breakfast, lunch, & dinner

$5 or less

Toasted ravioli notwithstanding, St. Louis has always been for us a city of tea cakes and soda-fountain treats. It was here the first ice cream cone was constructed, at the World's Fair of 1904. Planter's punch, peanut butter, iced tea, and angel food cake are all claimed as local inventions.

The best place we know to taste that marshmallowy heritage—and then some—is Miss Hulling's, a cafeteria that embodies the pretty half of St. Louis's culinary spirit.

You are met at the door by vintage portraits of Miss Hulling and her family. Inside, everything is cotton-candy pink—linen, napkins, servers' uniforms. One wall is dominated by a striking mural of hobnobbing dandies and belles—Cafe Society of a vanished era.

We have never seen such an array of desserts as here: cakes and pies and puddings and fruit cups, lined up in a resplendent floral-hued display. There is classic St. Louis angel food cake—plain, airy, and moist. There is angel food swirl, angel food with strawberries on top, mocha angel food.

The prettiest of all desserts is "ribbon cake"—layers of pink and white and chocolate cake, separated by dark red jam, with cherry-colored frosting. To coronate the cake, choose an orb of peppermint ice cream, made here.

Should you wish to precede your sweets with a meal, the choices are nearly as comely and every bit as copious. Entrees include a hefty pink roast beef, from which slices are cut to order by a dignified man in a *toque blanche*. We opted for ladies'-lunch fare—chicken fricassee and pot pie. From two dozen possible side dishes, we chose mashed potatoes—the best thick spuds imaginable, a twice-baked potato filled with cheese—and butternut squash mixed with cornflakes, brown sugar, butter, and apple chunks—a textural triumph of crunch, crisp, and filamentous squash.

Breads, rolls, biscuits, fritters, muffins (including one called Queen of Muffins, dotted with chopped sour red cherries) are all made here, in Miss Hulling's bakery. There was simply no room on our trays for salad, not even one of the festively colored individual Jell-O molds, or a single deviled egg.

Mr. Austin's Bar-B-Q

1511 Goodfellow, St. Louis, Mo.
(314) 385-4122

Mon.–Sat. 10 a.m.–2:30 a.m., Sun. until 1 a.m.

$10 or less

Nearly every St. Louis soul-food restaurant serves tripe alongside its barbecued ribs and hot links. Mr. Austin's is the best we've tried. Several broad
slices, deep fried to a dark frizzled crisp, are layered between white bread
with pickle slices, mustard, and onion, and doused with sauce.

Like all soul-food sandwiches, it is a total mess, made even more ridiculous by the resilient texture of the tripe, which pulls away in long cheesy
strings as you try to bite it. For aficionados of viscera, it is a magnificent
challenge.

For squeamish types, we recommend Mr. Austin's excellent barbecue,
especially the expensive whole rib slab. This is a soul-stirring feast, to be
eaten with gusto and plenty of napkins. The pork is smoky, tender, glazed
with sauce, and striated with fat. You don't get ribs like this outside the
midwest.

Ribs, rib tips (economical hacked-up ends), and hot-link dinners are
served with what the menu calls "St. Louis style potato salad." It looks like
mashed potatoes, completely smooth, but sweetened with mayo. A delicious
counterpoint to hot-spiced pork. Also on the side comes a reminder of St.
Louis's ethnic variety—a cup of spaghetti!

When you place your order at the small-slit window, you cannot help
but view what would be, in any other urban soul-food restaurant, an anomaly—dessert. A showstopper selection! Only in St. Louis do rib eaters continue on to cakes like this. Tall triple-layer behemoths, dark or light, heavily
iced, moist and sweet, they would do any bakery proud.

Even better than the cakes is Mr. Austin's sweet potato pie, made (as per
St. Louis soul-food custom) in single-serving circles, each pie vivid orange,
smooth, and heavy as caramel. They're a little lumpy, and no two are quite
alike. It's a homemade assortment; like everything else about Mr. A, an
expression of St. Louis' thriving street-eats culture.

(Mr. Austin has another location: 4408 Lee, phone: 381-0093)

The Q King

2909 N. Kingshighway, St. Louis, Mo.
(314) 361-9364

Daily 11 a.m.–3 a.m.

$5 or less

The Q King is a restaurant with humble charm and grand barbecue. It's little more than a kitchen with a single room in front, where red-checked cloths decorate the half dozen tables, and pretty pink and blue tiles cover the floor—but most business is take-out, through the window in the vestibule on the side.

The menu is classic lower-midwestern barbecue: lamb, ribs, pork, ham, and hot links, smoked leisurely over hickory wood. The ribs are heavily spiced, with plenty of meat. Crisp but not burnt, they are glazed with a powerful grainy sauce, full of pepper and . . . is it horseradish? A full slab (about $10) is a feast for two: serious eating, major ribs.

Lamb fares well over pitmaster Henry Thomas's fire. The tang of the ewe is perfectly mellowed by hickory smoke, complemented—but not over-whelmed—by the strong sauce. Ham was our only disappointment; it seemed too dense to take on any of the character imparted by the pit, and it simply shed sauce.

Q's hot links are crisp red sausages needled with pepper, slit down the middle for a sandwich. This is your basic soul sandwich, on the blandest, softest white bread obtainable. The link is doused with sauce. The sandwich is therefore impossible to eat with two hands before the bread dissolves like a wet napkin, leaving you with handfuls of link and sauce. A delicious mess.

In fact, it is possible, for under a dollar, to get simply an order of "bread and sauce." Now that's for barbecue purists!

On our last visit to The Q King, we called out an order to the lady behind the take-out window, who replied to us in an unfamiliar tongue. "Huh?" said we, completely perplexed.

"Let me," said a younger black woman waiting behind us. She gave our order to the serving person, and translated the serving person's words to us. It was the first time we have required a translator from Connecticutese to St. Louis black English.

Richard's Barbecue

6201 Blue Hwy., Kansas City, Mo.
(816) 921-9330

Mon.–Thurs. 11 a.m.–1 a.m., Fri. & Sat. 11 a.m.–3 a.m.,
Sun. noon–1 a.m.

$10 or less

"The true inheritor of Arthur Bryant," is how Art Siemering of the Kansas City *Times* described Richard's Barbecue on the east side of town. Richard cooked at Bryant's place for years, and when the old man died in 1982, Richard set up his own pit, with meats and sauce that almost exactly replicate the grandeur of KC's most famous barbecue.

The sauce is a ringer for Bryant's: gritty orange, aggressively salty, complex, and long-lasting *hot*. And the beef is like Bryant's before the automatic slicer was installed. Irregularly carved into hunks, chunks, slabs, curls, flaps, and fibers, it is heavily smoked and laced with crusty charred outside meat. And if you want more of that blackened edge, Richard has it—known as "brownies"—by the trayful. Just ask.

French fries are amazing. They actually taste like potatoes—starchy white inside, their skins a hodgepodge of amber softness and frizzled brittle strips.

For big spenders there are racks of ribs, nearly fatless; and there are ham, pork, and sausage, as well as fried catfish and chicken. But it is the beef brisket sandwich, piled so high it is impossible to eat, fries on the side, that is the classic Kansas City pit-cooked meal.

Smokestack Bar-B-Que

135th & Holmes, Kansas City, Mo.   In Martin City
(816) 942-9141

Mon.–Thurs. 11 a.m.–10 p.m., Fri. 11 a.m.–10:30 p.m., Sat. 11:30 a.m.–10:30 p.m., Sun. 11:30 a.m.–10 p.m.

$10 or less

Although many of the midwest's fine barbecues are dumps, it isn't necessary to go slumming to eat well. This happy house of good eats in the fertile gastronomic land south of Kansas City is a respectable place. It is casual (you wouldn't want your Q any other way), but a lot of effort has been made to create atmosphere. Decor is an assortment of old west and new west memorabilia, hanging plants, and stained glass. The menu even includes seafood (oh, that hickory-smoked trout!), spinach salad, and vegetable kabob.

Pretty window dressing in no way diminishes the serious intent of the barbecue. Beef, ham, lamb ribs, pork ribs, and sausage: it's a full smokehouse repertoire, with sides of curlicue french fries and out-of-this-world "pit beans" (lots of meat shreds among them).

Smokestack sandwiches are gigantic, and although it is barbecue heresy, they come on French loaves instead of blah bread. The quality bread is wonderful for soaking up maximum quantities of sauce.

Our favorite Smokestack meal is a burnt-end dinner, the low-concept name for all the well-done crisp-crusted shreds and scraps of beef, pork, and ham after the tender gentle pieces have been cut away. The ends are big rugged chunks with anvil impact. Beef ends get especially chewy, dark, and tough; and one inevitably remembers, as one chews and chews, that Kansas City is the culinary gateway to the west.

Tough chow! And delicious, if a smoky chaw is your idea of good eating. If not, simply order falling-off-the-bone lamb ribs, or center-cut sliced pork. There's nothing mellower. The Smokestack has something for everyone who cherishes the taste of wood smoke.

Snead's Corner Bar-B-Q

171st and Holmes, Kansas City, Mo.   In Martin City
(816) 331-9858

Wed., Thurs., & Sun. 11 a.m.–9 p.m., Fri. & Sat. 11 a.m.–10 p.m.

$10 or less

Brownies, listed on Snead's menu at about a dollar a pound less than beef, pork, or ham, are the pièces de résistance. Beef brownies, ham brownies, or a combination thereof arrive as a mountain of crusty chunks—ends, tips, strips, a few soft fibers joined to blackened crust, all the less-than-prime cuts off the barbecued meat.

Each piece resonates with smoke. Most beef brownies demand a vigorous workout, like princely jerky; a few fall into moist strips, having been basted for hours by the brisket's natural striations of fat. Ham brownies are firm, glistening scarlet, saltier than beef, and denser. The tight-fibered ham absorbs a sharp hickory bite that is nearly alarming compared to the meek beef. They are all large pieces, twin-bite size, their concentrated flavor an exhausting and induplicable smoke-pit eating experience.

Now the best part: Snead's sauce. Peppery orange, granular, salty, like Arthur Bryant's but not as rough, it comes regular and hot. We like the latter, which although not scorching, sets one's tongue aglow.

And so to salve the palate, there is sweet, finely chopped slaw; and there are profoundly lush barbecued beans. Back and forth—sauced meat to slaw to beans, and into the meat again. A Snead's meal teases the tongue, soothes it, excites it again. It just gets better and better until you can't eat anymore.

Other highlights from the menu: pan-fried chicken among K.C.'s finest; barbecued pork (not brownies); and "log" sandwiches on small or long buns. A log is a crumbly mixture of minced beef, pork, and ham, somewhere near the texture of a Maid-Rite sandwich. It lacks the savory impact of brownies.

Snead's is way way out, a pink-walled roadhouse south of Kansas City, next to a service station and nothing else. When we stopped by, a sign outside announced, BILL SNEAD IS COOKING AGAIN. Indeed he is; and while he is, this is the place we'll go for the best barbecue in or out of town. Snead's is worth the trip—from Kansas City, or from New York or the moon.

Stroud's

1015 E. 85th St., Kansas City, Mo.
(816) 333-2132

Mon.–Thurs. 4 p.m.–10 p.m., Fri. & Sat. 11 a.m.–10:30 p.m., Sun. 11 a.m.–10 p.m.   A wait is likely, especially on weekends

$10 or less

The fried-chicken belt: a wide band that stretches like a cummerbund across the middle of America, including *southern* fried chicken, *Hoosier* fried chicken, *Kentucky* fried chicken (the real thing, not the Colonel's slime-in-a-bucket), and *Kansas* fried chicken.

We'll cut away all the confusion and direct you to the best fried chicken in America—at Stroud's. It is fried in a heavy iron skillet—the most beautiful burnished gold you will ever see, the thin breading crusty, but with a succulent body all its own. You crunch easily into the meat, and once that fragile envelope is broken through, juices flow freely down hands and chin. It is not merely the crust on this bird that is superior; the meat itself has an undeniably *fresh* flavor—a revelation.

Along with the chicken, Stroud's serves a bowl of feathery mashed potatoes (better than any of the cottage fries more commonly dished out in Kansas City chicken joints); thick pan-dripping gravy with a pepper punch; and big swirling sweet rolls. The rolls are a stroke of genius, more cinnamon than sweet, with just a tease of caramelized cinnamon butter around the base: the perfect companion for the chicken.

You dine in a big open room with a bar at one end, overseen by a deer's head sporting a bandana and 3-D viewing glasses. At the red-checked tables, strewn with no apparent design across the wood floor, boisterous diners plow through bowls of food with party-time exuberance. Stroud's *is* a party, a joyous place to feast at an informal banquet that is one of the culinary triumphs of America's heartland.

Stroud's recently opened a somewhat more gracious branch—Stroud's Oak Ridge Manor, at 5410 NE Oak Ridge Road, in Oak Ridge—with a menu of fried chicken, catfish, and steaks.

Ted Drewes Custard

6726 Chippewa Ave., St. Louis, Mo.
(314) 481-2652

Late March–early Nov. daily 11 a.m.–12:30 a.m., until 11:30 p.m. in March, April, & May

Under $5

Mid-May, Wednesday afternoon, 2 p.m. There is a long line at Ted Drewes Custard, a twenty-minute wait. It is mostly kids playing hookey and retirees (everyone else is at work). They all seem positively *thrilled*, deliriously happy with anticipation of what they are about to eat: genuine ice cream custard, as thick as . . . well, as thick as concrete, which is what most of them will order.

Concrete is Ted Drewes' term for a "milk shake" made with whole-egg custard. We put the term in quotes because a concrete is like no other shake. We reached the head of the line and ordered a hot fudge concrete and a strawberry chocolate chip concrete. When the server handed them over, he turned both cups upside down momentarily, and sure enough, the milk shakes stayed in their cups, not dripping a bit—a dramatic demonstration of just how the concrete gets its name. Into the heavy cup the server plunged a plastic spoon and a straw. The straw is merely an ornament. An Electrolux couldn't suck this stuff up that skinny tube.

The custard, sold plain as well as mixed into concretes, is liquid alabaster, modestly sweet, a taste of focused dairy goodness that no flavored, doctored-up ice cream can provide. In fact, as we slurped into our concretes in Ted Drewes' parking lot on this jubilant May afternoon, sharing one of St. Louis' most special treats with locals young and old, we noticed that across the street there was a Baskin-Robbins store. It was empty, not a customer in sight, and the girl who worked there was standing at the window, staring longingly at Ted's.

OHIO

Bun's

10 W. Winter St., Delaware, Ohio
(614) 363-3731

Tues.–Sun. lunch & dinner   Sometimes closed two weeks in July

Lunch about $5, dinner $10 or less

Yes, Bun's does bake buns; but the name comes from George "Bun" Hoffman, grandson of the patriarch Hoffman who came to Delaware, Ohio, from Germany in 1863 and opened a bakery. When the bakery was passed down to Bun, he expanded it into a small restaurant. Bun's son Biscuit continued the expansion, and today his son (another George) runs the place, with plans for passing it on to a fifth generation.

Bun's still has the feel of a small-town bake shop; and it has a kitchen where old-fashioned cooking is taken seriously. When you order roast turkey with dressing and mashed potatoes, you get slices of meat from a freshly roasted bird; dressing made from bakery bread; real mashed potatoes. Pork, the most popular meat of the midwest, is always on the menu: roast pork; spare ribs in a dark, rich sauce; grilled pork chops; baked ham; and the "Bunwich"—ham and cheese grilled on wholewheat.

"Let us help you build a salad," suggests the menu atop a list of twelve different ingredients, each individually priced: chunks of chicken (65¢), a hard-boiled egg (45¢), croutons (20¢), one ounce of Gulf shrimp (90¢), etc. Salads come with rolls hot from the bakery—white and dark rye.

You walk into Bun's through the bakery, so it's likely dessert will be on your mind throughout the meal. The outstanding bakery item is that brick-like rectangle frosted with dark chocolate—Bun's fudge cake, a chocoholic's devilish dream.

Bun's does not serve breakfast, but it's a Delaware tradition to stop in for a cup of self-service coffee in the morning, and choose from a showcase of pecan rings, pecan loafs, butterscotch twists, and Danish pull-aparts. Customers are welcome to make themselves comfortable at a table.

You will have no trouble finding Bun's in this little town where Ohio Wesleyan College sets the pace of life. The cafe sign dangles from a tall arch that curves over Winter Street like a metal rainbow, pointing to the old brick building that has stood in the same place for a century.

Camp Washington Chili, Inc.

Colerain & Hopple, Cincinnati, Ohio
(513) 541-0061

Always open except 3:30 a.m. Sun.–5 a.m. Mon.

Under $5

Camp Washington Chili has been in business since 1940, but unlike the Empress and Skyline chili chains, it never multiplied. There is only one Camp Washington, and of the ninety-seven Cincinnati restaurants that specialize in five-way chili, it is the best.

The meatiest chili in town: finely ground choice beef, spiced with peppers, with a dash less of the nutmeg kick unique to Cincinnati chili. There is more cinnamon here—and clove and mustard and ginger and cumin. It is a thick brew, dark red, lean and hearty, prodigiously ladled onto a bed of spaghetti noodles, topped with beans and onions, and crowned with a fluffy layer of shredded Wisconsin cheddar. It's the same configuration as all genuine Cincinnati chilies, but no other version is as poised as this: an architectonic stratification of texture and wildly diverse tastes.

The chef is John Johnson, a Greek (all Cincinnati chili men are Greek; many Americanize their names). His finesse with five-way has made his parlor a mecca for chiliheads. "Some people come in every day of the week," explained our waitress, Lucy. "They're hooked."

Lucy is another reason we like Camp Washington. She's been here twenty years; she works the counter and booths with devastating savoir faire. She also makes the waitresses' gingham aprons.

Formica tables and booths, a blue and white tile floor, baseball trophies above the counter: a very 1940s-looking place, like the city's other chili parlors, but cleaner and with personality.

(Camp Washington also specializes in Cincinnati "double-deckers," Dagwood sandwiches similar in concept to layered five-way chili.)

Empress Chili

Cincinnati, Ohio   Locations all over town

Hours vary at different locations, but most are open about
11 a.m.–midnight or later

Under $5

Like many regional dishes, Cincinnati five-way chili comes out of the melting pot. It was invented by Athanas Kiradjieff, a Macedonian immigrant who arrived in New York in 1920, then spent two years selling hot dogs in lower Manhattan. To spice up the wieners, which to his ethnic palate seemed too bland, he began experimenting with a chili-sauce topping.

In 1922, after moving to Cincinnati and opening a hot-dog stand called the Empress, Kiradjieff had a brainstorm that would make him a Zeus among the gods of Cincinnati gastronomy. What kind of genius inspired him to discard the hot dogs (which Kiradjieff had renamed Coney Islands in homage to his first home in America) and replace them with spaghetti? Onto the spaghetti he heaped chili and cheese and onions—traditional Coney Island condiments. But how on earth did this man conceive the fifth layer of kidney beans?

Food historians speculate the beans were a customer's suggestion. But what customer? Who would know that the polymorphous plate of noodles, meat sauce, cheese, and onions needed a layer of kidney beans to draw the whole mess together into perfect consonance? Perhaps popularity of beans in Macedonian cooking was his source. Perhaps ancient astronauts heaved a plate of five-way from their ship as they rocketed away from the Queen City. There is simply no logic that explains the utter eccentricity of five-way chili.

Athanas Kiradjieff's Empress chili parlor was the cornerstone for a chili empire in Cincinnati; competitors with their own subtle variations on the recipe swept into town. Cincinnati became—and remains—chili-crazed.

The quirky manner in which five-way chili is assembled is the same at all Empress parlors. Onto a bed of spaghetti on an oval platter is ladled the Kiradjieff family secret-recipe chili (brewed in a basement three times a week). It is a nutmeggy red-brown meat sauce, comparatively mild, a tad soupy. Next, the onions and the beans; then the bright yellow shredded cheese, mounded by hand into a five-way Superdome.

Need we say that this monstrous meal is not the kind of food one eats off linen tablecloths? Chili parlors are—let us be kind—humble cafes. Most of the Empress joints have all the charm of a subway station: white tiles, fluorescent lights, institutional napkin dispensers, and sullen teenage countermen. In other words, suitable surroundings for a great raunchy meal.

It is a tribute to the intestinal fortitude of Cincinnati chiliheads that the traditional side dishes for a plate of five-way are a couple of cheese Coneys (four-inch franks heaped with shredded cheddar) and a bowl of oyster crackers.

The Golden Lamb

27 S. Broadway, Lebanon, Ohio
(513) 932-5065

Mon.–Thurs. 11 a.m.–3 p.m. & 5 p.m.–9 p.m., Fri. & Sat. until 10 p.m.,
Sun. 8 a.m.–10 a.m. & noon–8 p.m.   Reservations advised

Dinner $10–$15, lunch & breakfast less

Shaker museum, historical tavern where ten Presidents have stayed, meeting place for the Kiwanis, the inn known as The Golden Lamb is also a very midwestern restaurant. Roast pork, turkey and dressing, leg of lamb, celery seed dressing, and Shaker lemon pie: Ohio's culinary heritage is plain and plenteous.

We began with an appetizer of sauerkraut balls, deep-fried rounds of finely ground pork and ham and kraut. They are gold-crusted, juicy with a spritz of pickled flavor. It was easy to eat the ten crusty spheres on our plate; but difficult to finish dinner afterward. They are richer than they seem. Beware.

The Golden Lamb relish tray is a rustic spread of strongly dilled vegetables, corn relish, and egg salad.

Next, salad: lots of iceberg lettuce heaped with dressing, either sweet translucent celery seed or creamy pepper herb. Along with the salad came a basket of hot dinner rolls—big aromatic puffs, impossible for bread-lovers to resist.

The kitchen does well with the basic foodstuffs; the best dish in the house: Butler County turkey dinner, served with a mound of sage-scented dressing. Whipped potatoes, buttered zucchini, and spinach come on the side.

The fried chicken was excellent, too, its crust buttery and crisp. It is served awash in country gravy. But the biscuit alongside the bird disappointed. It was dry, a perfunctory piece of bread.

At a second Golden Lamb dinner, we had leg of lamb served in its natural gravy, and pork loin with the same herb dressing. Both were unfashionable and good.

The Shaker lemon pie offered for dessert is nearly pure sugar—dark brown, nutmeggy, with a layer of sticky molasses between the filling and the crumbling crust. There is "stack pie," too, a twin wedge with a crust in the middle (like a Cincinnati double-decker sandwich), and lots of real lemon peel in the curd. Both pies are rare and good, but the simplest dessert is the best: vanilla meringue filled with ice cream and fresh strawberries. What could be more middle-of-America than that?

Room rates are under $50.

Miller's Dining Room

16707 Detroit Ave., Lakewood, Ohio   Just west of Cleveland
(216) 221-5811

Mon.–Sat. 11 a.m.–8 p.m., Sun. 11:30 a.m.–7:30 p.m.
Reservations advised on weekends

Lunch $5 or less, dinner $10 or less

Cleveland is an interesting eating town. Its two strong suits are ethnic food (with one of the largest Hungarian populations outside Budapest, and the exceptional Balaton Restaurant to prove it) and Stouffer's. Yes, Stouffer's, which was not always synonymous with toaster-oven cookery. In earlier days, there really was a Mother Stouffer, and she ran a restaurant that turned out tea-room cuisine of great charm and imagination.

Today, however, in what was the original Stouffer's Restaurant, the "Smiling Stouffer Girl" in her starched pastel apron has been replaced by khaki-trousered wait-persons; and the menu has turned from tea-room fancies to "eclectic" continental fare. Mother Stouffer's glory has been relegated to a small glass case in a Shaker Heights motel run by the company. Vintage menus and a life-size cutout of the Stouffer Girl, smiling like mad, are enough to make you want to book passage on the first time machine heading back to 1938.

But there isn't any need to travel farther than Detroit Avenue in Lakewood, where Miller's Dining Room holds Cleveland's escutcheon of wholesome food high. No Smiling Stouffer Girl here, but that's okay. Meet Miller's Roll Girl. She has the delightful job of circulating with a battered silver tray of rolls fresh from the oven: hot messy sticky buns, neat cloverleaf yeast rolls, sticks of cornbread, tiny gems of bran and blueberry. Each time she returns throughout the meal, her tray is newly stocked.

Then comes the Smiling Salad Girl to lean a tray in your direction. It is a vision out of a 1940s ladies' magazine: Jell-O salads in every color of the rainbow, shimmering mounds of ambrosia whipped and filled with fresh fruits, nuts, and miniature marshmallows. There are cabbage and carrot slaws, rings of pineapple, and miniature Waldorfs. The summer fruit salad (available also as an appetizer) was nothing but the freshest cuts of cantaloupe, nectarine, peach, honeydew melon, grapes, oranges, and raisins—as pretty as a new Easter hat.

Mother Stouffer's cooking was characterized not only by its wholesomeness, but by its playful, cream-sauced combinations of comforting American (but vaguely foreign-sounding) food, such as chicken divan or turkey tetrazzini. At Miller's the showstopper is chicken-a-la-king-in-a-basket. The basket is a nest of potato slivers fried crisp, like the best hash browns. Into it is dolloped a creamy mound of large chunks of white meat, *fresh* mushrooms, peas, and a few festive ribbons of pimiento. All accompanying vegetables are from the garden, not the can: beets bathed in orange sauce, snapping string beans, great mashed potatoes.

Miller's has a long menu, and it's the chicken basket that is truest to form; but we have also enjoyed unbeatable roast tom turkey with the works, ham puffs with escalloped apples, and braised lamb shank with vegetable gravy. It is all what you might call *honest* food, or maybe even *innocent* food: pure, quality ingredients, handled expertly by the kitchen, and presented not with solemn ceremony but in a spirit of guileless panache.

Perfection continues into dessert: sour cream apple pie topped with freshly whipped cream; crisscross lattice-topped cherry pie, apple silk cheese pie, sundaes, parfaits, and rainbow sherbets. Miller's baked date pudding must be what God eats for dessert. It is simply the richest, and at the same time healthiest-tasting, sweet thing in creation.

There is liquor and wine, but the proper drinks to accompany this fantasy food should probably be selected from the list of "Citrus Isle Mocktails" —glamorous adult versions of the Shirley Temple, with names like Pink Mist, Golden Surf, and The Tradewind ("a Planter's Punch that leaves you on your feet").

Miller's could pass as an Ethan Allen showroom: it is all muted shades of blue and cream, with a few columnar accents along the walls, and fresh flowers on the tables.

After dinner, one last Smiling Miller's Girl approaches the table to bring finger bowls—not an affectation; just a seemly end to a truly decent meal.

There are a few—maybe four or five—restaurants in the world that we like as much as Miller's Dining Room. Often, at home, we conjure up memories of favorite places, and the conjuring induces monstrous hunger. But when we think about Miller's, it's not just the outré food we long for. It is the style and taste of the place, so suave that it appears totally casual. And it *is* casual, but that does not mean sloppy. Miller's is an impeccable restaurant. Mother Stouffer would be proud.

Old Island House Inn

102 Madison St., Port Clinton, Ohio
(419) 734-2166

Mon.–Thurs. 6:30 a.m.–9 p.m., Fri. & Sat. to 10 p.m.,
Sun. 7:30 a.m.–8 p.m.

$8–$20

For years a rumor circulated that Lake Erie was dead, and would remain so for eons. Miraculously, it has been reborn and is now a fisherman's paradise, jumping with walleye. Restaurants from Detroit to Buffalo serve perch and pickerel drawn from the lake, but none is quite as appropriate a place to savor these freshwater fish as the Old Island House.

It's a 100-year-old (but modernized) hotel on the corner, downtown in the bustling vacation community of Port Clinton, just a short walk from the water.

The kitchen makes a specialty of lake fish, whatever's the current catch. Perch is usually available. You can get it deep-fried, which isn't bad—the fish is not overwhelmed by its batter; or you can get it broiled, an even better preparation that accentuates the fish's firmness and buttery flavor. Pickerel, a needlenosed variety of pike, is sold, too, whole or as a mess of filets. Even in the filets there can be intermuscular bones, although frying softens—or dissolves—these enough to make them edible.

Meals begin with one of a repertoire of substantial soups made of barley, bean, or potato, then a salad cart piled with seasonal greens and a number of homemade dressings. Ohio, from Cincinnati to Sandusky, is famous for its celery seed dressing. The Island House's version is among the very best.

Hot rolls and most desserts are baked daily. The wine list includes a number of Ohio wines. On Sunday, the Old Island House features "Harvest Dinners" of ham or turkey and all the fixings, served family-style to groups of two or more.

(Rooms at the Old Island House Inn range between $20 and $60, depending on the season. It's a swell jumping-off place for a Great Lakes vacation.)

Riverside Restaurant

Water St., Stockport, Ohio
(614) 559-2210

Daily 9 a.m.–9 p.m.   May be closed in Jan. & Feb.

$5 or less

Here is a restaurant serving food that is truly indigenous. Take, for instance, the dark honeyish elderberry pie you get for dessert. That feathery crust is rolled out here; the filling is cooked here; the berries in the filling are gathered from bushes in owner Frances Brandon's fields.

Most of the salad bar is picked from the family garden: they're not fancy things—just lettuce, tomatoes, cucumbers, green peppers, etc.—but they are as fresh as vegetables can be, picked yesterday, or maybe even this morning.

As for the roast beef, Frances's daughter Sarah Moody has a farm. She raises cattle. She is also co-owner of the restaurant. Her cows are slaughtered, inspected, and butchered, and roasts and steaks from them are served right here.

The pork and barbecued spare ribs, as we understand it, come from farther west. There isn't much more to the menu than that. The Riverside is a meat and potatoes kind of place.

There is not, to our knowledge, a potato garden out back either, but Frances and Sarah make better potatoes than you'll ever get in Idaho. "Real potatoes," the menu says, "cooked the way you like them." All the dinner rolls and breads are baked here, from Frances's grandmother's recipes.

At breakfast there are always biscuits. They're served with eggs that come from the hens on the family farm.

The Riverside Restaurant is a big old barn of a place, paneled in hickory and ash. From the dining room you can see the Muskingum River, where livestock and produce were once barged up to be sold in this building, which years ago was the local farmers' exchange.

Our only regret is that we've never dined here on a Sunday. "That," says Frances, "is something special." We don't doubt it.

Skyline Chili

Cincinnati, Ohio   Locations all over town

Hours vary at different locations, but most are open about 11 a.m.– midnight or later

Under $5

It was the Empress that first served five-way chili, and for decades the Empress and Skyline chains have been the Hertz and Avis of the Cincinnati chili world. The last time we were in Cincinnati, our chili connection there took us first to an Empress parlor, then to the Skyline at 106 East Sixth Street. He wanted to prove that Skyline, even if it isn't the original, is the best.

We'll confess that after one plate of five-way chili we are in no condition to make subtle value judgments; and frankly, with the exception of Camp Washington's clearly superior plate of five-way, most Cincinnati chilies taste pretty much the same to us. Perhaps only natives develop the capacity to distinguish the fine differences.

Yes, Skyline's was more substantial, meatier than the Empress mix; and yes, it did seem that there might be a subtle hint of chocolate (what a stroke of genius!) in among the bay leaves, cumin, cinnamon, nutmeg, curry, oregano, cloves, basil, and cayenne—all of which it is rumored the Lambrinides family uses in their secret recipe.

On the other hand, maybe we hit the Skyline at just the right moment, when the chili was at its peak. Some students of Queen City chili culture maintain that freshly brewed chili needs eight to twelve hours to age properly, time for the disparate ingredients to harmonize.

We are only dilettantes, and although our hearts are with the Empress parlors—where Cincinnati chili was invented—perhaps Skyline does try harder.

Smithville Inn

109 W. Main, Smithville, Ohio
(216) 669-2641

Tues.–Fri. & Sun. 11:30 a.m.–7:30 p.m., Sat. until 8 p.m., closed Mon.

About $5

The Smithfield Inn is an 1818-vintage stage stop that has been serving family-style chicken dinners since 1929. Its dining rooms reminded us of a cheery farmhouse: white tablecloths, ceramic chickens roosting on the windowsills, a few built-in china cabinets, and chairs and tables made of cherry wood.

Some fish and chops are on the menu . . . next to the Inn logo, a crowned bird declaring "Smithfield Inn—Where Chicken Is King!" A word to the wise.

The chicken is buttery soft (not breaded and deep fried), served with broad noodles, whipped potatoes, dressing, slaw, biscuits, and apple butter. Creamed chicken over biscuits is good comfort food; likewise gravy on a hot chicken sandwich. Comfort is what the Smithfield Inn is about; no surprises; no fancy or scary food; no one person's check much more than $5.

Lots of homemade pies for dessert, but the corker is the Inn specialty: custard chiffon egg nog.

WISCONSIN

Boder's on the River

11919 N. River Rd. (Rte. 43W), Mequon, Wis.
(414) 242-0335

Tues.–Sun. lunch & dinner   Reservations advised

Lunch about $10, dinner $15–$20

All around America restaurants call themselves "family-style," but there is none so familial as Boder's. Boder's sells a cookbook, forty-five pages long; twenty-seven of those pages are about the Boders themselves—snapshots, genealogy, stories about funny pets. And the clientele—with the exception of groups of ladies who come up for luncheon (it used to be a tea room)—is all families; midwesterners dressed in white shoes, women with white purses, men in white belts. You've seen them before, in the audience of the Phil Donahue show before it moved east.

They're on to a good thing, these solid citizens. Boder's, whose recipe book is introduced by the homily, "Good Food Is Good Health," has a bakery that turns out blue-ribbon goods: softball-size corn fritters, dripping rich, studded with kernels of corn, served hot with maple syrup; blueberry and black cherry muffins with a dusting of sandy cinnamon-sugar; pecan rolls; baking-powder biscuits.

A tray of old-fashioned relishes comes with dinner: carrot or zucchini relish, creamy kidney bean salad, a classic macaroni salad livened up with bits of pineapple. The fruit plate we had at the height of the summer fruit season was flawless. For congealed salads (Jell-O), or for chicken or shrimp salad, Boder's makes its own mayonnaise.

Desserts are stunning. Only in the midwest, perhaps only in the Dairy State of Wisconsin, will you find so lavish a use of butter and eggs and whipping cream. There is no sweet thing in the world with a more sensuous texture than Boder's schaum torte, a melting-sweet, just-barely-chewy meringue that is filled with raspberries and topped with whipped cream. Schaum torte is on many menus around Lake Michigan; none we have sampled compares to this elementally perfect version.

Butter Brickle pie, also meringuey in texture, is flavored with graham cracker crumbs and chopped walnuts, served with local butter brickle ice cream. The repertoire of sweets includes such deliciously unfashionable items as Hershey torte, tropical ice cream pie, sunny silver lemon torte, and peanut swirl ice cream pie.

As for what comes between the breads and relishes and dessert, there is half a crisped roast duck sold at dinner (which the menu calls Wisconsin premium duckling), available with wild rice; there is baked filet of whitefish "from the cold waters of Lake Superior"; there are steaks and chops and African rock lobster tails . . . but it's the fore- and after- play that makes Boder's an outstanding restaurant. And the management knows it. That is why, at both lunch and dinner, it is possible to order from a section of the menu entitled "Not Hungry?" This gets you all the extras—muffins, relishes, soup, a corn fritter, and dessert—without the burden of an entree. Even if you *are* hungry, it will suffice.

You will get lost trying to find Boder's. It is off in what was once the country, but is now the suburbs, still a lovely riverside setting, surrounded by well-tended flowers and manicured lawns, with outdoor wrought-iron benches to sit on.

Gosse's

1637 Geele Ave., Sheboygan, Wis.   At Calumet Dr.
(414) 458-1147

Mon.–Sat. 5 a.m.–7 p.m., Sun. 7 a.m.–noon

$5 or less

Wisconsin is a land of sausage and wurst; in Sheboygan, they've got a brat-wurst all their own—the "Sheboygan brat." It's a plump tube of pork cut-tings with crackling crisp skin, customarily served on a hard roll with butter and grilled onions. The sausage has a strong garlic flavor tempered by the taste of charcoal.

Sheboygan brats are people's food, mostly eaten at picnics, but you can taste some superior brat sausages at Gosse's restaurant, a clean working-man's cafe with kitchen wallpaper, a short counter, and about a half dozen tables.

When we told our waitress that these local brats were new to us, she explained how she does hers at home, steeping them in onions and beer first, always cooking them over charcoal. She told us we could get a single or double brat sandwich, with or without onions. Ours arrived at the table wrapped in paper and stuck with toothpicks, *sans* plates.

We would point the way to Gosse's for this regional specialty alone, but there is more of Wisconsin's flavor to be savored here.

"I won't tell you to enjoy it, because I know you will," our waitress said when she brought us tortes for dessert. Tortes are the Wisconsin dessert-lover's choice, even more than cream pies. Each serving of a Gosse's torte was a square hunk, a thick layer of cheesecake atop a crumb bottom, with an almost perfunctory spread of blueberries on top. The heart of it is the center of white cream, pure fresh essence of dairyland, a block of solid moo.

Jack Pandl's

1319 E. Henry Clay, Whitefish Bay, Wis.   At Lake Dr.
Northern Milwaukee
(414) 964-3800

Mon.–Sat. lunch & dinner   Reservations advised

$10–$15

There may be two or three weeks in the dead of winter, when all the lakes are frozen over, when Jack Pandl's serves no whitefish. The rest of the year it is always on the menu: expertly broiled so that the most fragile paprika-dusted "crust" forms on the boneless filet. This is a simple dish, fresh and clean and pure, a great specialty of the Great Lakes.

Beyond the whitefish, there is a strong German accent to Jack Pandl's menu, as at so many of the city's restaurants; but unlike Karl Ratzsch and Mader's, Pandl's is not, in spirit, German. Milwaukeean is more like it—friendly, informal, an especially comfortable place to eat.

It is all dark wood, but with plenty of windows for looking out over the elegant Lake Drive on which it resides. Beer steins are displayed behind glass. The waitresses wear dirndl skirts. At lunch, you eat off paper mats on functional steel-banded tables; for dinner, the tables are covered with white cloths.

Meals begin with baskets of rolls and crisps of toast soaked with butter and garlic. Our farina dumpling soup was blissful, its broth flecked with parsley and bits of onion, the dumpling just a frail puff of starch. Spinach salad came drenched in hot bacon dressing.

Pandl's bar, as you might expect, offers a variety of beers, local and German. We accompanied our feast with sweet May wine prettied up with a strawberry, and half-liter steins of foamy Pschorr-bräu.

Along with the whitefish, we ordered one of Pandl's German pancakes—a deep-dish shape of baked eggy batter, brown and crisp along its topmost edges, soft yellow inside and at the bottom of the trough. It's not unlike Yorkshire pudding, but it is served with powdered sugar and lemon, both of which you apply yourself, creating a squeaky syrup. What an immense plate of food!

Duty demanded we sample Pandl's schaum torte, a favorite Wisconsin dessert. It is a crisp meringue with a semicaramelized top, dolloped with freshly made ice cream. When the waitress told us this would be soft-serve ice cream, we expected Carvel-style shaving cream—obviously forgetting we were in the official Dairy State. (The menu reluctantly informs that "margerine is available . . . for cholesterol watchers only.") The homemade soft-serve ice cream was just about the creamiest, thickest thing imaginable, a jolting reminder that ice cream came to America two centuries ago, as, simply, sweetened and iced cream.

It isn't necessary to go whole hog at Pandl's. For lunch, you can get a julienne salad made with Wisconsin Swiss cheese, or a Reuben sandwich made with same, and stunning dark red corned beef, on sour Milwaukee rye bread. On Saturday night only, the kitchen roasts Wisconsin duckling.

Norske Nook

7th and Harmony Sts., Osseo, Wis.
(715) 597-3069

Mon.–Sat. 5:30 a.m.–9:30 p.m.

$5 or less

Last year a man called the Norske Nook from Florida and pleaded with owner Helen Myhre to send him a pie, the kind he remembered eating there when he passed through: mincemeat with rum sauce. She obliged. "I suppose the liquor preserved it," she laughed. A week later he called again to thank her—and order more.

The Norske Nook is not a mail-order house, but if we could figure out a way to ship our favorite varieties of Helen Myhre's pies, we'd have a standing request for about three a week. What would they be? First, the Dairy State special: sour cream raisin—tall, thick, and creamy, packed with plump raisins, and topped with a lofty meringue—never found outside the midwest. Then classic strawberry pie: not much more than large sugared berries, just barely cooked, mounded into a thin crust. Maybe we'd choose raspberry or blueberry glaze, or tart rhubarb. Or carrot cake, laced with fine shreds of carrot. Or apple turnovers. Or caramel rolls, or hermits, or date bars.

Every day in this tiny cafe, there are at least that many varieties of cakes, pies, and cookies. They are homey pastries—sugar-dusted crusts rolled out by hand, ungainly fillings that don't quite hold together when a wedge of pie is cut, cookies the size of small dinner plates. This is farm cooking, literally; Helen is a farm wife who decided to open a restaurant after years of being told by guests how wonderful it was to visit the Myhres' for coffee and baked goodies.

The Nook is a pie stop. Unless you come in October, when the kitchen goes all-out with *lutefisk* and *lefse* suppers and *rollepolse* and Norwegian cheeses and meatballs, the repertoire of entrees is burgers-plus.

But the problem of which pies to sample is complicated by the fact that each serving is titanic; and the best in the house, sour cream raisin pie—basically, eggs, sugar, raisins, and sour cream—is not light food. You can enjoy one piece, maybe two, before appetite is only a memory.

But you can always get more to go, for later. Take something with you, at least a snapshot of the day's pies laid out on newspapers on the counter. Once you leave the Norske Nook, you will not find pies like these again.

Quivey's Grove

6261 Nesbitt Rd., Madison, Wis.
(608) 273-4900

Lunch Tues.–Fri., dinner daily   Reservations for dinner advised

$10 or less

Each dinner at Quivey's Grove has a name: Lamb Doty, Pork Brigham, Chicken Randall. Doty was a mid-nineteenth-century farmer; Colonel Ebeneezer Brigham was an early justice of the peace; Alexander Randall was Wisconsin's Civil War governor. Get it? Quivey's Grove is a homage to history, a culinary ode to 1855, the year in which the mansion that now houses the restaurant was built.

It isn't only the names of the food that harken back to another time. The tastes are nostalgic, too: like Brigham's pork loin, marinated in cider, sided by sweet and sour cabbage and a mess of mashed potatoes; or fish Phoenix (named after a steamer that sank in Lake Michigan in 1847), two firm rainbow trout filets, fried in butter and garnished with walnuts. Steamy, sugar-crusted muffins (apple, cranberry-orange, or strawberry) come with every meal.

All the recipes, according to Mr. and Mrs. Gregg Burmeister, the Madisonians who clued us in to Quivey's Grove, reflect generations of German, Swiss, Norwegian, and English ancestors. Which is not to say that everything is historically authentic. You can come here for lunch and eat a chef's salad, an omelette, or a stuffed popover; or you can start dinner with mundane stuffed mushrooms ("Mushrooms Madison," named after the president after whom the city was named).

But even many of the modern-seeming foods are regional in character. The sausage appetizer, for instance, is rolled with local Gouda cheese, honey, and pepper. A "Riley" sandwich is an assortment of only-in-Wisconsin wursts and brats on pumpernickel. In the summer, an all-vegetable item called "Garden Bouquet" evidences the real farm flavor of fresh tomatoes, peppers, eggplant, and squash.

The kitchen's strivings are authenticated by the setting, a great field-stone building, its five dining rooms decorated to evoke nineteenth-century Wisconsin. A tunnel leads to the stable, now a taproom featuring beer from small local breweries.

It is all scrupulously planned, suitable for dinner *à deux* or a formal wedding reception. Not exactly pristine Americana, but a very successful re-creation. We like the Quivey's Grove motto: "Other restaurants are in Wisconsin, Quivey's IS Wisconsin."

Schulz's Restaurant

1644 Calumet Dr., Sheboygan, Wis.
(414) 452-1880

Mon.–Sat. 11 a.m.–7 p.m.

$5 or less

Schulz's version of the Sheboygan bratwurst is a thin patty, cooked, like all Sheboygan brats, over charcoal. These skinless sausages are quite delicious, rich and garlicky, absorbing more char than the cased variety; but we miss the plumpness, the snap when tooth breaks taut skin, the burst of flavor characteristic of the more common tube steak. Schulz's brat—either single or double—does make a neater sandwich, and it is served on an excellent crusty hard roll, with lots of pure butter and onions.

Another favorite sandwich in eastern Wisconsin is what's called a butterfly pork chop, a boneless pat of pig, pounded flat, like a cube steak, seasoned with plenty of pepper, and cooked alongside the brats over a charcoal fire. It is not reconstituted pork, like the odious McRib, but a real chop, with some very tender areas, a few streaks of fat, and a sweet, undoctored flavor. It, too, comes on a tough-crusted hard roll.

You can get good American potato salad as a side dish, but for dessert we recommend a trip up the street to Gosse's for one of the sensational cream tortes.

All the grilling is done in the open at Schulz's, at a fire visible from every seat at the double horseshoe counter and the few wall booths. The grill man uses an interesting technique, stoking up the flame high enough to engulf the brats and butterflies, then reaching for a handy shower head and squirting out a spray of water to tamp things down and prevent his work from burning.

Three Brothers

2414 S. St. Clair St., Milwaukee, Wis.   East of I-94
(414) 481-7530

Tues.–Sun. dinner   Reservations advised

$10–$15

We'll say it: Three Brothers is a Serbian restaurant. Why include it in a book about indigenous American food? First, you have to understand that Milwaukee is a city of corner taverns. We didn't write about the sensational Hungarian cafes in Cleveland or the little Czech joints we found in Chicago, because they might just as easily be in Europe. But Three Brothers you could find *only* in Milwaukee. It is a mom-and-pop neighborhood saloon that gives a better feel for the city than any of its "American" restaurants.

In fact, Three Brothers is a registered national landmark—as the best remaining example of a brewery-owned tavern (of which the Beer City once had dozens). Designed in 1897 as a Schlitz outlet, it still has the company globe atop its roof—the only one in the midwest, according to owner Branko Radicevic.

We could also justify Three Brothers' inclusion on the basis of the wild game they serve—Wisconsin duck and goose, both long-time local favorites. We might even point to whitefish and walleye pike on the menu; they are, after all, regional. But we won't do that. Hardly anybody, except for the Serbs who eat here all the time, orders fish from the Great Lakes, which is listed under "Other Entrees."

No, while Three Brothers is in every way a genuinely Milwaukee-flavored *place*, the food you want to eat here is purely ethnic. So sue us. For a restaurant this good, rules should be bent.

We won't go into detail about the various exotica the kitchen prepares, since we frankly don't know what we're talking about when it comes to *chevapchichi* or *raznjici*. We do know that the Serbian salad at the start of our meal was a colorful plate of finely chopped fresh tomatoes, peppers, and onions covered with a delicious goat's cheese milder than Greek feta. Rye bread (that's *Milwaukee* rye bread, mind you, dense and sour) is served with a spread called *kajmak*, a butter derived from goat's, rather than cow's, milk.

For a main course, we chose the house specialty, a *burek*, a large double-crust pie of the thinnest imaginable pastry leaves, filled with steamy tart cheese and spinach. Also roast goose—headily aromatic, juicy but not fat, served with sweet-pepper dressing and pickled cabbage.

This is peasant food, satisfying to the body and the soul—at its best accompanied by a few half-liter bottles of the malty Bip beer that Three Brothers imports from Yugoslavia, or by any one of a number of Serbian wines that you are invited to taste before ordering.

After supper there are eight-layer walnut and cream tortes, *palachinka* pancakes filled with fruit preserve, sweet mocha-enriched Serbian coffee, and glasses of *slivovitz* (plum brandy) or *kruskovac* (pear liqueur).

During dinner, you can watch an old jukebox select records from its repertoire, which ranges from Gladys Knight to Lepa Lukig, the latter sounding just right for crying into beer or smashing glasses on the floor. At the back table at the end of the bar in the large, convivial dining room sits 84-year-old Mama Radicevic, enjoying the sight of people enjoying her food.

Watts Tea Shop

761 N. Jefferson St., Milwaukee, Wis.
(414) 276-6352

Lunch Mon.–Sat. 11 a.m.–2:30 p.m., tea Mon.–Sat. 2:30 p.m.–4 p.m.

About $5

Shopping is hard work; after madame has spent her morning picking out wedding gifts and china and crystal and Steuben glass, she needs a midday refresher before she returns to the aisles to select that certain *objet d'art* or silver salver to complete her collection.

George Watts & Son, serving Milwaukee for 115 years, offers two large floors showcasing all of the above, more fancy *tchachkes* than we ever knew existed. What drew us here, however, was not the Wisconsin-wide bridal registry, but the tea shop upstairs.

Here is a dining room that serves food perfectly in keeping with the finery in the showcases: high-quality, genteel, ladylike lunch.

Waitresses in crisp black-and-white uniforms carry iced tea, *fresh* lemonade, or "Russian chocolate" (coffee, chocolate, and whipped cream) to tables that provide lunchers with a second-story view of East Town, Milwaukee's elegant shopping district. The walls are pale blue. Easy music filters in to aid digestion. The menu, printed every day, is small, homemade, dainty, and delicious.

All the sandwich breads, including puffy English muffins, are made daily. A bisque is always on the menu—vegetable, spinach (enriched with chicken fat), tomato. There are sandwiches of chicken salad (tiny, bite-size chunks), or ham and cheese; salads are whipped up with homemade mayonnaise and stuffed into tomatoes; there is always one substantial hot lunch.

The day we lunched at Watts, the featured entree was shrimp Newburg —pretty pink crescents in a pale cream sauce, served atop whole wheat toast. It was a mild dish, but we spiced it up with Gaylord Hauser–recommended seasonings, Vegit and Spike, provided on every table.

Desserts are displayed on a little cart in the vestibule. We tried the spicy apple cake and a banana tart, topped with plenty of whipped cream. But dessert #3 was the corker, a Watts tradition—filled sunshine cake. It is layered made-this-morning sponge cake alternating with thick ribbons of custard-rich buttercream. The yellow wedge is swirled with seven-minute frosting threaded with strands of orange peel. At noon, the moist cake and its sugary frosting were both still slightly warm.

White Gull Inn

Fish Creek, Wis.
(414) 868-3517

Dinner Wed.–Mon., lunch summer only; fish boils on Wed., Fri.,
Sat., & Sun. in summer, Sat. only in winter   Reservations required
well in advance

$10 or less

It is the easiest recipe in the world: into a cauldron of boiling water throw
scrubbed potatoes; a few minutes later, add onions; then add fish steaks and
more salt (the salt keeps the fish firm, and raises the boiling point of the
water). Wait until the aroma of wood smoke and simmering fish piques your
appetite (about ten minutes); remove and serve, under a wash of butter.

This is the legendary Door County fish boil, a joyous outdoor feast
around an open fire—a ritual invented by Icelandic lumbermen, unique to
Wisconsin. In the summer, on the finger of land bounded by Green Bay and
the lake, you will see a score of signs pointing the ways to evening fish boils,
some of them informal picnics by the water, others organized affairs for
which reservations are needed.

At every fish boil, the cooking style is the same. A roaring wood fire, a
boiling cauldron, the dramatic flame of the "afterboil" when it's over—all
essential parts of the ceremony. And the menu never changes. A fish-boil
dinner consists of white fish steaks, potatoes and onions, cole slaw, bread,
and a piece of cherry pie.

We had our fish boil at the White Gull Inn, a comfortable clapboard
building in the quaint Green Bay village called Fish Creek. Let us warn you
that Door County is a tourist-trod area, and in the middle of the summer it
is necessary to make a reservation *weeks in advance* for a White Gull fish
boil. But if you are a plan-ahead type, this is the place to experience the
famous feast in all its raucous joviality.

The White Gull Inn makes its own bread and cole slaw; the fish is fresh,
flaking into large, delicately flavored hunks; and the atmosphere around the
twin bubbling cauldrons is suitably merry, reminiscent of overnight camp
picnics. After the last boil of the evening, there was even a man with an
accordion who led a ragged group sing-along.

On Monday and Thursday nights in the summer, the White Gull serves
a buffet featuring colonial American food like clam pies, baked beans, and
glazed ham. Rooms at the inn run between $35 and $50.

Southwest

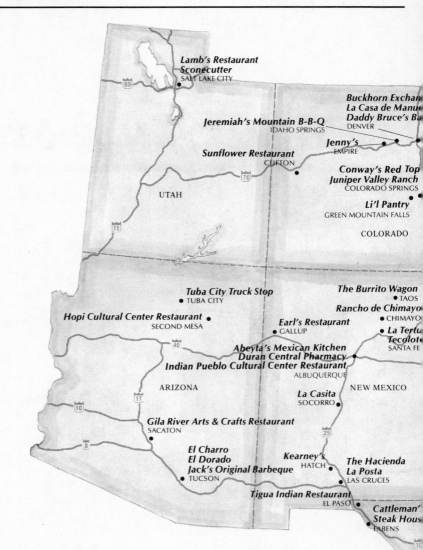

Lamb's Restaurant
Sconecutter
SALT LAKE CITY

Buckhorn Excha
La Casa de Manue
Daddy Bruce's Ba
DENVER

Jeremiah's Mountain B-B-Q
IDAHO SPRINGS

Jenny's
EMPIRE

Sunflower Restaurant
CLIFTON

Conway's Red Top
Juniper Valley Ranch
COLORADO SPRINGS

UTAH

Li'l Pantry
GREEN MOUNTAIN FALLS

COLORADO

Tuba City Truck Stop
TUBA CITY

The Burrito Wagon
TAOS

Rancho de Chimayo
CHIMAYO

Hopi Cultural Center Restaurant
SECOND MESA

Earl's Restaurant
GALLUP

La Tertu
Tecolote
SANTA FE

Abeyta's Mexican Kitchen
Duran Central Pharmacy
Indian Pueblo Cultural Center Restaurant
ALBUQUERQUE

ARIZONA

NEW MEXICO

La Casita
SOCORRO

Gila River Arts & Crafts Restaurant
SACATON

El Charro
El Dorado
Jack's Original Barbeque
TUCSON

Kearney's
HATCH

The Hacienda
La Posta
LAS CRUCES

Tigua Indian Restaurant
EL PASO

Cattleman'
Steak Hous
FABENS

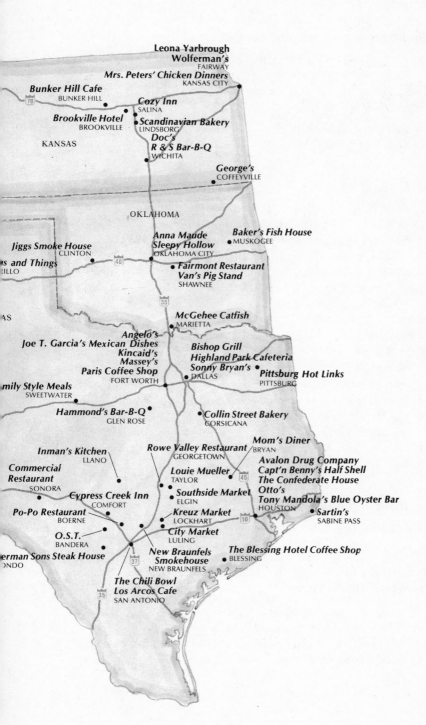

Leona Yarbrough
Wolferman's
FAIRWAY
Mrs. Peters' Chicken Dinners
KANSAS CITY

Bunker Hill Cafe
BUNKER HILL

Cozy Inn
SALINA

Brookville Hotel
BROOKVILLE

Scandinavian Bakery
LINDSBORG

Doc's
R & S Bar-B-Q
WICHITA

KANSAS

George's
COFFEYVILLE

OKLAHOMA

Jiggs Smoke House
CLINTON

s and Things
ILLO

Anna Maude
Sleepy Hollow
OKLAHOMA CITY

Baker's Fish House
MUSKOGEE

Fairmont Restaurant
Van's Pig Stand
SHAWNEE

McGehee Catfish
MARIETTA

AS

Angelo's
Joe T. Garcia's Mexican Dishes
Kincaid's
Massey's
Paris Coffee Shop
FORT WORTH

Bishop Grill
Highland Park Cafeteria
Sonny Bryan's
DALLAS

Pittsburg Hot Links
PITTSBURG

mily Style Meals
SWEETWATER

Hammond's Bar-B-Q
GLEN ROSE

Collin Street Bakery
CORSICANA

Mom's Diner
BRYAN

Inman's Kitchen
LLANO

Rowe Valley Restaurant
GEORGETOWN

Avalon Drug Company
Capt'n Benny's Half Shell
The Confederate House
Otto's
Tony Mandola's Blue Oyster Bar
HOUSTON

Commercial
Restaurant
SONORA

Louie Mueller
TAYLOR

Cypress Creek Inn
COMFORT

Southside Market
ELGIN

Po-Po Restaurant
BOERNE

Kreuz Market
LOCKHART

Sartin's
SABINE PASS

O.S.T.
BANDERA

City Market
LULING

rman Sons Steak House
NDO

New Braunfels
Smokehouse
NEW BRAUNFELS

The Blessing Hotel Coffee Shop
BLESSING

The Chili Bowl
Los Arcos Cafe
SAN ANTONIO

Southwest Specialties

Where we list several places, we have starred the one we think best.

Albóndingas Soup—chili and meatballs

El Dorado (Tucson, AZ)   410

Arizona-Mexican Food

★ El Charro (Tucson, AZ)   408
El Dorado (Tucson, AZ)   410

Barbecue

Jack's Original Barbeque (Tucson, AZ)   413
Daddy Bruce's Bar-B-Q (Denver, CO)   417
Jeremiah's Mountain Bar-B-Q (Idaho Springs, CO)   417
Sunflower Restaurant (Clifton, CO)   422
R & S Bar-B-Q (Wichita, KS)   430
Jiggs Smoke House (Clinton, OK)   446
Van's Pig Stand (Shawnee, OK)   449
Angelo's (Fort Worth, TX)   451
Beans and Things (Amarillo, TX)   452
City Market (Luling, TX)   458
Hammond's Bar-B-Q (Glen Rose, TX)   463
Inman's Kitchen (Llano, TX)   466
Kreuz Market (Lockhart, TX)   468
★ Louie Mueller (Taylor, TX)   470
Otto's (Houston, TX)   474
Pittsburg Hot Links (Pittsburg, TX)   476
Sonny Bryan's (Dallas, TX)   479

Black Bean and Jalapeño Soup

La Tertulia (Santa Fe, NM)   439

Blue Corn Enchilada—chilies, meat, beans, or cheese layered on a tortilla made with blue maize

Abeyta's Mexican Kitchen (Albuquerque, NM)   432
The Hacienda (Las Cruces, NM)   435
Indian Pueblo Cultural Center Restaurant (Albuquerque, NM)   436
★ La Tertulia (Santa Fe, NM)   439

Blue Corn Piki Bread—a strudel-like pastry made with blue maize

Buffalo

Burritos—spicy meat or vegetable filling in a flour tortilla

Capirotada—southwestern bread pudding

Carne Adovada—pork marinated in chilies

Casuela—soup made with dried beef and chilies

Catfish

Chicharrónes—bits of rendered pork

Chicken-Fried Steak—thin steak dipped in flour and fried

Chili

Chil-il Ou Gya Va—Hopi chili

Chili Rellenos—Batter-fried chili peppers stuffed with cheese

Chimichangas—Flour tortillas filled with chilies and cheese and deep fried

★ El Dorado (Tucson, AZ)   410
   The Hacienda (Las Cruces, NM)   435

Fajitas—Sizzling grilled beef in a flour tortilla

   Joe T. Garcia's Mexican Dishes (Fort Worth, TX)   467

Flautas—Deep-fried tortillas rolled around spicy filling

★ Rancho de Chimayo (Chimayo, NM)   441
   Joe T. Garcia's Mexican Dishes (Fort Worth, TX)   467
   Tigua Indian Restaurant (El Paso, TX)   481

Fried Chicken

   Juniper Valley Ranch (Colorado Springs, CO)   419
   Brookville Hotel (Brookville, KS)   423
   Leona Yarbrough (Fairway, KS)   428
   Mrs. Peters' Chicken Dinners (Kansas City, KS)   429
   Anna Maude (Oklahoma City, OK)   443
   Fairmont Restaurant (Shawnee, OK)   445
★ Sleepy Hollow (Oklahoma City, OK)   447
   Allen's Family Style Meals (Sweetwater, TX)   450
   The Blessing Hotel Coffee Shop (Blessing, TX)   455
   Cypress Creek Inn (Comfort, TX)   462
   Highland Park Cafeteria (Dallas, TX)   465
   Paris Coffee Shop (Fort Worth, TX)   475
   Po-Po Restaurant (Boerne, TX)   476
   Lamb's Restaurant (Salt Lake City, UT)   483

Gorditas—Cornmeal pockets stuffed with chili

   Tigua Indian Restaurant (El Paso, TX)   481

Gulf Seafood

   Capt'n Benny's Half Shell (Houston, TX)   456
   Sartin's (Sabine Pass, TX)   478
★ Tony Mandola's Blue Oyster Bar (Houston, TX)   482

Hot Links—Barbecued Texas sausage

   Angelo's (Fort Worth, TX)   451
   City Market (Luling, TX)   458
   Louie Mueller (Taylor, TX)   470
   Pittsburg Hot Links (Pittsburg, TX)   476
★ Southside Market (Elgin, TX)   480

Huevos Rancheros—Traditional southwestern breakfast of eggs, beans, and chili on a corn or flour tortilla

    Abeyta's Mexican Kitchen (Albuquerque, NM)   432
★ Duran Central Pharmacy (Albuquerque, NM)   433
    Earl's Restaurant (Gallup, NM)   434
    Indian Pueblo Cultural Center Restaurant (Albuquerque, NM)   436
    Tecolote Cafe (Santa Fe, NM)   442

Indian Fry Bread—A flat disc of skillet-cooked bread

★ Gila River Arts and Crafts Restaurant (Sacaton, AZ)   411
    Hopi Cultural Center Restaurant (Second Mesa, AZ)   412
    Indian Pueblo Cultural Center Restaurant (Albuquerque, NM)   436

Indian Tacos—Fry bread topped with chili and cheese

★ Hopi Cultural Center Restaurant (Second Mesa, AZ)   412
    Tuba City Truck Stop (Tuba City, AZ)   414
    The Hacienda (Las Cruces, NM)   435
    Indian Pueblo Cultural Center Restaurant (Albuquerque, NM)   436

Jerky Meat—Air-dried beef

★ Jiggs Smoke House (Clinton, OK)   446
    New Braunfels Smokehouse (New Braunfels, TX)   472

Menudo—Tripe and hominy stew

    El Dorado (Tucson, AZ)   410
★ Abeyta's Mexican Kitchen (Albuquerque, NM)   432
    Los Arcos Cafe (San Antonio, TX)   469
    O.S.T. (Bandera, TX)   473
    Tigua Indian Restaurant (El Paso, TX)   481

Mesquite-Smoked Barbecue

★ Jack's Original Barbeque (Tucson, AZ)   413
    The Hacienda (Las Cruces, NM)   435
    Cattleman's Steak House (Fabens, TX)   457

New Mexican Food

    Abeyta's Mexican Kitchen (Albuquerque, NM)   432
    Duran Central Pharmacy (Albuquerque, NM)   433
    The Hacienda (Las Cruces, NM)   435
    La Casita (Socorro, NM)   437

Nok Qui Vi—Stew of mutton and hominy corn

Pecan Pastries

Posole—Hominy corn soaked in lime until soft

Rocky Mountain Oysters—deep-fried bull's testicles

Scones—stuffed, fried bread

Sopaipillas—Quick-fried hot bread served with honey

Steak

★ Cattleman's Steak House (Fabens, TX)   457
Herman Sons Steak House (Hondo, TX)   464
Po-Po Restaurant (Boerne, TX)   476
Rowe Valley Restaurant (Georgetown, TX)   477

Texas Hill Country Sausage

Cypress Creek Inn (Comfort, TX)   462
★ Inman's Kitchen (Llano, TX)   466
New Braunfels Smokehouse (New Braunfels, TX)   472

Tex-Mex Food

Commercial Restaurant (Sonora, TX)   460
Herman Sons Steak House (Hondo, TX)   464
★ Joe T. Garcia's Mexican Dishes (Fort Worth, TX)   467
O.S.T. (Bandera, TX)   473

Topopo Salad—A pyramid-shaped salad made with chicken or beef and steamed vegetables

El Charro (Tucson, AZ)   408

Tostadas—Large thin tortillas topped pizza-like with cheese, chili, or meat

★ El Charro (Tucson, AZ)   408
El Dorado (Tucson, AZ)   410

Tostadas Compuestas—Cup-shaped corn tortillas filled with spicy meat and beans, topped with hot sauce and cheese

★ La Posta (Las Cruces, NM)   438
Tecolote Cafe (Santa Fe, NM)   442

Types of Southwestern Restaurants

Barbecue Pits

Jack's Original Barbeque (Tucson, AZ)   413
Jeremiah's Mountain Bar-B-Q (Idaho Springs, CO)   419
R & S Bar-B-Q (Wichita, KS)   430
Jiggs Smoke House (Clinton, OK)   446

Van's Pig Stand (Shawnee, OK)   449
Angelo's (Fort Worth, TX)   451
Beans and Things (Amarillo, TX)   452
Hammond's Bar-B-Q (Glen Rose, TX)   463
Louie Mueller (Taylor, TX)   470
Sonny Bryan's (Dallas, TX)   479

Boarding Houses and Hotels

Brookville Hotel (Brookville, KS)   423
Allen's Family Style Meals (Sweetwater, TX)   450
The Blessing Hotel Coffee Shop (Blessing, TX)   455
Mom's Diner (Bryan, TX)   472

Burger Shops

Conway's Red Top (Colorado Springs, CO)   416
Cozy Inn (Salina, KS)   425
Kincaid's (Fort Worth, TX)   468

Cafeterias

Anna Maude (Oklahoma City, OK)   443
Highland Park Cafeteria (Dallas, TX)   465

Catfish Parlors

Baker's Fish House (Muskogee, OK)   444
McGehee Catfish (Marietta, OK)   447

Indian Reservations

Gila River Arts and Crafts Restaurant (Sacaton, AZ)   411
Hopi Cultural Center Restaurant (Second Mesa, AZ)   412
Tuba City Truck Stop (Tuba City, AZ)   414
Indian Pueblo Cultural Center Restaurant (Albuquerque, NM)   436
Tigua Indian Restaurant (El Paso, TX)   481

Meat Market Barbecues

City Market (Luling, TX)   458
Kreuz Market (Lockhart, TX)   468
Southside Market (Elgin, TX)   480

Pharmacy Lunch Counters

Duran Central Pharmacy (Albuquerque, NM)   433
Avalon Drug Company (Houston, TX)   452

Smoke Houses

Jiggs Smoke House (Clinton, OK)   446
Inman's Kitchen (Llano, TX)   466
New Braunfels Smokehouse (New Braunfels, TX)   472
Pittsburg Hot Links (Pittsburg, TX)   476

Steak Houses

Buckhorn Exchange (Denver, CO)   415
Bunker Hill Cafe (Bunker Hill, KS)   424
Doc's (Wichita, KS)   426
Sleepy Hollow (Oklahoma City, OK)   447
Cattleman's Steak House (Fabens, TX)   457
Herman Sons Steak House (Hondo, TX)   464
Po-Po Restaurant (Boerne, TX)   476
Rowe Valley Restaurant (Georgetown, TX)   477

ARIZONA

El Charro

311 N. Court Ave., Tucson, Ariz.   Two blocks west of stone underpass
(602) 622-5465

Mon.–Thurs. 11 a.m.–9 p.m., Fri. 11 a.m.–10 p.m., Sat. 4 p.m.–10 p.m.,
Sun. 11 a.m.–9 p.m.

$4–$10

El Charro is the kind of place one dreams about when miles away from good
Mexican food. In fact, our reminiscing began as Tucson faded from sight in
the rearview mirror. "Wasn't that *topopo* salad grand?" we moaned; "and

the *carne seca flautas* . . . and the *chimichangas* . . ." On and on we went, fighting the urge to turn the car around 180 degrees and start the meal all over again.

El Charro's cuisine is Arizona-Mexican, meaning that large thin flour tortillas are favored over those made of corn; and the sauces won't be as blistering hot as in neighboring New Mexico. Arizonians are inventive Mexican chefs, known for devising new combinations of traditional ingredients to wrap in soft tortillas. Most typically Arizona-Mexican dishes are delightfully messy—oozing warm cheese and *salsa*, overstuffed with chili con carne, *carne seca* (dried beef), or *frijoles* (beans).

For starters at El Charro, we recommend you order a pitcher of sangría, a red fruit-spiked wine punch that bears no resemblance to the sticky-sweet stuff that comes in bottles. You will be brought a dish of salty tortilla chips and hot red *salsa* to dip them in.

A favorite appetizer is what Tucson restaurants call a Mexican pizza, listed on the El Charro menu simply as a tostada. It arrives "en pedestal," an enormous crisp corn tortilla, topped with melted cheese and your choice of beans, guacamole, shredded chicken, or *carne seca*. The tortilla base is wafer-thin, and has a faint ashy taste that perfectly complements the bite of the cheese.

The *pieza de resistencia* at El Charro is *topopo* salad, a mini-Mayan pyramid of cool lettuce shreds dotted with hot peas and cubed carrots. Columns of cheese and cold shredded chicken run up the side of the mound, and a ring of avocado slices encircles the bottom. It is all piled atop a warm base of refried beans on a soft tortilla: an unbelievably complex combination of varying temperatures and textures, in which each ingredient retains its own character.

Vegetarians can have a field day at El Charro, where the menu features meatless entrees like squash or *chili rellenos*, a variety of salads, and burros (large soft tortillas) stuffed with cheese or beans.

Desserts are icing on the El Charro cake. Try the *almendrado*, a square of tri-colored meringue designed to look like a Mexican flag: broad stripes of red, white, and green, the tri-colored fluff topped with a velvety almond-scented vanilla sauce. The *pastelito de fruta* is also a winner—a deep-fried fruit twist (ours was apple filled) topped with whipped cream.

El Charro has been open since 1922—ten years after Arizona became a state. It was created by Monica Flin, who in the early days used to take a customer's order and then run out to the grocery store to buy the necessary ingredients. When Ms. Flin died about eight years ago, the business was taken over by her grandniece, Carlotta Dunn Flores, and her husband.

It is a picturesque little building in the old part of Tucson, with a small terrace for alfresco dining, decorated with hanging plants and Mexican pottery. Inside, the walls are choc-a-bloc with all manner of Mexican paraphernalia, most prominently, El Charro calendars going back to 1946 when Monica Flin began a tradition of giving them to customers.

Big deal, you say? Every gas station gives out calendars, no? No, not like El Charro's. You see, the part with the months is a throwaway; what's wonderful is the art: big four-color paintings done in a style best described as Aztec Confidential. Heroic sun gods with bulging muscles and'unpronounceable names carry their dead but still beautiful mistresses up ancient pyramids; the dramatis personae include sultry-eyed maidens in mantillas, sultry-eyed caballeros serenading them, and sultry-eyed horses with roses twined in their hair.

El Dorado

1949 S. 4th Ave., Tucson, Ariz.
(602) 622-9171

Sun.–Tues. 11 a.m.–11 p.m., Thurs. 11 a.m.–11 p.m., Fri. & Sat. 11 a.m.–midnight

$5 or less

We have a confession: We used to think all Mexican food was the same—a plate full of flattened red and brown things covered with cheese, so hot you needed an asbestos tongue shield. But anyone who travels through the southwest soon learns there are at least three distinct kinds of "Mexican" food in the U.S.A.—Tex-Mex, New Mex–Mex, and Arizona-Mex. These bear little resemblance to the classic cuisine of Mexico; in fact, all three are best known for gringo dishes you will never find south of the border.

Witness the *chimichanga*, a soft flour tortilla wrapped around chili (green or red) or beans and dried meat and deep-fried so that it resembles an enormous blintz or egg roll: the definitive Arizona-Mexican dish, invented in Tucson in the 1950s, served by nearly every Mexican restaurant in town.

After extensive *chimichanga* eating all across Tucson, we like to think we found the best at a restaurant called El Dorado.

At El Dorado, you can eat a *chimichanga* (Spanish for "thingamajig") in an atmosphere of paintings-on-velvet, Naugahyde booths, and a wall rug onto which are woven the faces of the murdered Kennedy brothers. But don't let the kitsch decor get you down. We have learned that in this part of the country, the food with the best taste is often served in places done up in the worst taste.

El Dorado's *chimichanga* is shockingly large, a majestic log spread liberally with sour cream and melting shreds of cheese. The tortilla was as flaky as strudel, packed full with meat and chili sauce. Since it was the height of chili season (late summer), when most green chili is scorching, we stuck with red. It was fresh and full-bodied, and plenty hot for all but pyromaniacal chiliheads.

One *chimichanga* at El Dorado is a full meal and then some, but you don't want to eat here and not sample the grandiose cheese tostada. It is served on what looks like a pizza pedestal, and in fact resembles a very delicate pizza—a wide paper-thin tortilla, spread with cheese onto which is added your choice of chilies, guacamole, or *carne seca* (dried beef). The El Dorado menu is a long one, listing southwestern food like *topopo* salad, *albóndigas* soup (Mexican meatballs), and *menudo* (tripe stew) by the bowl or to take out, by the gallon.

It was apparent as we looked around at the booths crowded with Mexican-American families that people come to El Dorado to feast. Most meals are so large they are pushed out of the kitchen on rolling carts. Service is a little on the slow side; the jukebox is hot, the food is not: an authentic taste of Tucson.

Gila River Arts and Crafts Restaurant

Exit 175, Casa Blanca Rd., off I-10, Sacaton, Ariz.
(602) 562-9901

Mon.–Fri. 8 a.m.–5 p.m., Sat. & Sun. 9 a.m.–5 p.m.

$5 or less

The Gila River Indian Center resembles an adobe Guggenheim Museum, a handsome nautilus-shell shape that contains a place to eat native American food cooked by the Pima tribe. The Center also sports a museum of Indian life and a shop that sells Papago baskets, rugs, and hand-tooled silver belts. Palo Verde trees surround an interior courtyard with a gurgling fountain, and bigger-than-a-man cacti ring the outside of the building. It is a quiet oasis in the desert, an island of pure air and ancient crafts—including the craft of Indian fry-bread making.

Fry bread resembles Arabic pita bread, but is puffier and larger—a full eight inches across. At its best, and here it *is* at its best, it is clean, sandy brown, with a thin not-quite-crisp crust. Tear it open and the inside is steaming hot. If you are a bread lover, fry bread is a dream come true, because you don't have to pretend to use the bread as a mere side dish to other things. Here, it is all.

The limited menu at the Gila River Coffee Shop features little more than fry bread topped with beans, or with red or green chili, or as an Indian taco, covered with the works—beans, meat, shredded cheese, and hot chili sauce. Or, for a purer taste of the chewy Indian specialty, you can ask them to hold the beans and chili, and sprinkle the fresh-from-the-skillet bread with powdered sugar or honey.

Hopi Cultural Center Restaurant

Rte. 264, Second Mesa, Ariz.   Five miles west of State Rd. 87
(602) 734-2401

Daily breakfast, lunch, & dinner

About $5

The Hopi's finest culinary treat is piki bread, a tissue-thin sheaf of cornbread rolled into a multi-layered spiral. It is a startling slate blue, made from genetically mutated blue corn; to Hopis, it is almost sacred, a symbol of the continuity of their culture.

The blue piki bread served at the Hopi Cultural Center Restaurant is still made in the centuries-old way, on smooth piki stones, heirlooms passed down from mother to daughter. The stones are heated and greased with sheep's brains until they are slick; then the finely ground blue cornmeal is laid on. It cooks like a crepe, and is peeled off the stone and rolled into a cylinder. The taste and texture are extraordinarily fine, as delicate as strudel pastry.

Munching on our piki bread, we looked around to see who we were dining with at this isolated restaurant in Second Mesa, what the Hopis call the Center of the Universe. The clientele was a mixture of native Americans and tourists; some people read the *Navajo Times* as they ate, others snapped pictures of each other posed next to Indian artifacts on display.

The wilderness for miles around the small Hopi reservation (surrounded by Navajo land) probably looks the same as it did a thousand years ago; we were encouraged by the barrenness of the drive from Tuba City to the Center of the Universe to expect the most unadulterated Hopi meal when we arrived. It was disconcerting to find the restaurant just past a bland motel desk (there are adobe rooms for tourists to rent), and to find BLTs and fried shrimp on the menu—right along with *Nok Qui Vi* and *Chil-il Ou Gya Va*. But what can you do? There was no denying the authenticity—or the rarity—of the piki bread we savored, or of the native American food that followed.

We followed the lead of the man at the next table—an old Hopi with long braided hair—and ordered a bowl of stew, called *Nok Qui Vi*. It is a Hopi dish made with lamb and corn, sided by baked green chilies and triangles of fry bread nearly as airy as New Mexican *sopaipillas*. Our enjoyment of the dish was scarcely diminished by the fact that the fry bread's traditional garnish, honey, was served in little plastic bubble-packs.

The menu's listing of *Chil-il Ou Gya Va* proved to be Hopi chili—beans and ground beef in red sauce, also accompanied by fry bread and a honey-pak.

Having recently driven out of New Mexico, we were surprised by the relative mildness of the native food. The tastes are less of fire than of the earth—cornmeal and hominy and mutton.

We would love to return to the Hopi Restaurant for *Tala'Vai-Nova* (breakfast). The menu lists pancakes made with blue cornmeal, and a blue cornmeal omelette as well. But if the truth be told, the one thing that will probably bring us back to the Center of the Universe is blue corn-flakes.

Jack's Original Barbeque

5250 E. 22nd, Tucson, Ariz.
(602) 790-2351

Mon.–Sat. 11 a.m.–8 p.m., Sun. noon–8 p.m.

$5 or less

When people ask how we discover good restaurants in an unfamiliar city, we never tell them one of our best methods because it makes us sound like Jeanne Dixon and The Amazing Kreskin. The fact is that over the years we have developed what we like to think is well-honed psychic radar for reading Yellow Pages. It was in this way that we discovered Jack's, a southwestern barbecue par excellence.

When we let our fingers do the walking, they often stop at a place with an ad like Jack's: "Thirty-one years in Tucson," it says, opposite a photo of Jack himself, a smiling black man in a tall chef's hat, pointing at his own motto: PUTS THE CONFIDENCE BACK IN GOOD EATING. Looking for a boost in confidence, we exited our Holiday Inn room in search of Jack's.

It proved to be a pleasant drive-in stand with three picnic tables out front painted blue and yellow, like concrete crocuses. Inside, Jack's was shiny clean, and the scent of the pit-cooked food was instantly appetizing. A sweet lady behind the counter took pity on us as we stumbled in, carrying notepads, cameras, pencils, and a look of general confusion. "Have you eaten here before?" she asked, and when we said no she started slicing a snippet of beef and a pair of ribs for us to taste before deciding.

Jack's serves southwestern soul food. Like most barbecue west of San Antonio, his beef is mesquite-smoked brisket. It is ridged with crust, mild and mellow, sided (if you order a dinner) by hot chili-flavored beans: a genuine western combination if ever there was one. But with a nod to the Southland, Jack ladles his sliced or chopped brisket with a spicy tomato-based sauce that has a hint of sweetness you'd never find in traditional Texas or Arizona barbecues.

The ribs were even more soulful, bathed in the peppery red brew that is Jack's secret. They were glazed a deep mahogany brown, lean but wonderfully juicy; their uniformity reminded us of Oriental spare ribs. Jack also smokes hot link sausages and hams.

Do not leave this place without tasting a piece of sweet potato pie or peach cobbler. They are classic soul-food desserts, a swell finale to the smoky meat.

Tuba City Truck Stop

Junction of Rtes. 160 & 264, Tuba City, Ariz.
No phone

Daily 6 a.m.–9 p.m.

$5 or less

The best Navajo taco in the southwest is served at the very unfancy tables and booths of the Tuba City Truck Stop.

We were set on the trail of this place by an old friend who wrote us a postcard covered with exclamation marks and splattered with red sauce. She told us to go to the town cafe, where we would get the Navajo taco of our dreams: a giant piece of freshly made fry bread, topped pizzalike with red bean and meat chili, shredded cheese, chopped lettuce and tomatoes, and crowned with a marinated pepper on top, like the cherry on a sundae.

When we arrived in Tuba City (a tiny town on the Navajo reservation surrounded by miles of cactus and not much else) we had little trouble finding the cafe—and even less trouble seeing that it was boarded up, closed, out of business . . . *finito.*

An old Indian woman in a dusty velvet skirt and a Fort Knox worth of turquoise around her wrinkled neck was walking by. In broken English she pointed toward the outskirts of town. "Tuck sop," she said, her necklaces waving in the hot Arizona breeze.

The yellow cinderblock truck stop was the new home of the old cafe. We were the only non-Indians in the place, except for a blond waitress who took our order. The rest of the menu was uninteresting: truck-stop grub like eggs and burgers. But the Navajo taco made our trip worthwhile. It is a majestic dish, enough for two—even two piggy sorts like us. In a part of the country where good food is hard to find, we couldn't have been happier.

COLORADO

Buckhorn Exchange

1000 Osage St., Denver, Colo.
(303) 534-9505

Mon.–Fri. lunch, daily dinner

Lunch $5 or less, dinner $10–$25

"What animals do you have steaks of?" asks Steve Martin in a comedy routine. They're all here, the heads of them anyway, every animal it is possible to make a steak of, and then some: five hundred trophies total, a hundred antique guns and rifles, a carved white oak bar, matching poker tables and bentwood chairs, plus photos of former owner Shorty Zietz's deer, buffalo, and elk hunts.

The thicket of Wild West artifacts is legit; the Buckhorn Exchange, in an out-of-the-way neighborhood across from a train yard, is the oldest restaurant in Colorado, holder of state liquor license #1.

Of all the kitchen's work, none packs as direct a frontier punch as the ham and bean soup: chuck-wagon grub. You can get it at lunch, but most of the midday menu is ordinary: burgers, salads, and sandwiches. The highlight is a buffalo Reuben, the extremely lean meat shaved thin, piled high on dark pumpernickel. The buffalo is smoked and highly spiced, its natural dryness offset by a buttery layer of cheese.

At dinner, the menu is more western: 24-ounce T-bones, some smaller steaks, trout done in various ways, split quails, and buffalo steaks. You can begin with Rocky Mountain oysters (bull's testicles), sliced thin and deep-fried, served with horseradish; or try the well-spiced buffalo sausage, topped with cheddar cheese. The buffalo steak reminded us of horsemeat, hardly marbled at all: a curiosity, no more than that, truly inferior to steaks made from cows. If you get it cooked one whit more than rare, the meat is stringy. Even black and blue, it lacks the savor of good beef. It was no accident that cows, rather than buffalos, became our primary domestic meat animal.

On the other hand, the Buckhorn's large T-bone is a beauty—broiled, or if you request, pan-fried. Pan frying tastes better because the thick steak gets a crust that pockets its juices inside. Dinners come with soup and either a baked potato or crunchy cottage fries ("Saratoga chips" on the menu).

For dessert, choose the expensive but excellent "old-fashioned" apple pie, with a sweet butter-crumb top, served with cinnamon hard sauce.

Conway's Red Top

1520 S. Nevada, Colorado Springs, Colo.
(303) 633-2444

Mon.–Thurs. 11 a.m.–9 p.m., Fri. & Sat. 11 a.m.–10 p.m.,
Sun. noon–9 p.m.

$5 or less

"One's a meal" is the Red Top motto, referring to the largest hamburger
west of . . . west of everywhere we've ever been. Six inches in diameter,
served inside a bun specially baked to match, these behemoth burgers are
the fast food of choice in Colorado Springs.

Everything's big at Red Top except the place itself, which is a generic
cinderblock bunker with no more than two dozen tables. Large sodas arrive
in a pitcher like a wine carafe. Beef stew, whether ordered by the cup or
bowl, *seems* large because the hunks of meat and potato are so much bigger
than a mouthful. And what good stew it is—spiced with authority, long-
simmered so the meat is tender and the flavors sing harmony. We agree with
its menu subtitle: "delicious, nutritious, and healthy."

They don't write menus like this one anymore. Who could not love the
innocent enthusiasm of Red Top's cheeseburger description: "topped with a
generous serving of Velveeta cheese." And let us assure you that Velveeta is
the perfect complement to these jumbo burgers and their great steamy buns.

You can get fancier, too, with a Señor Red Top, with jalapeño cheese, or
a Hickory Dickery Top, which somehow gets infused with smoke flavor and
is topped with onions. In our not so humble opinion, such folderol does not
become the basic Red Top formula for greatness.

On the other hand, you'd be a fool not to accompany a giant burger with
french fries. These are real potatoes, sliced thin and irregularly sized, with
lots of crisp shriveled tips, great for crunching.

Service at Red Top is faster than any fast-food restaurant. In true
burger-house style, the waitresses leave your check with the food. And when
you pay the bill at the cash register, the lady there offers an after-dinner
mint.

Daddy Bruce's Bar-B-Q

1629 E. 34th Ave., Denver, Colo.
(303) 295-9115

Tues.–Thurs. 11 a.m.–midnight, Fri. & Sat. to 1 a.m.,
Sun. 4 p.m.–midnight

$5–$10

Southwestern soul-food barbecue: a cuisine of peppers and beans, meaty ribs in mean smoky sauce, plump hot links, and sweet tater pie. Daddy Bruce Randolph's funky shack in the wrong part of town is the place to taste it all.

The exterior whitewashed walls are decorated with crudely painted biblical quotations, advertisements for fresh catfish from Pine Bluff, Arkansas, and a notice saying "God loves you." When we pulled up, a fistfight had just erupted into the street from the bar across the way. As we waited in our car to see what would happen, the door to Daddy Bruce's opened, and we were beckoned inside by a bemused employee who had obviously had to deal with cautious strangers before.

The interior of Daddy Bruce's isn't much prettier than the outside, but it's clean and safe. There are only a few tables in a small dining room to the right; most of Daddy Bruce's business is take-out, over the counter just inside the door.

Crusty charred ribs, served in a wash of powerful sauce, are the house specialty, a fine mess to eat; after running out of napkins, we resorted to white bread (the blah slices traditional with barbecue) to wipe our sauce-stained faces. The sting of the ribs is balanced by thick-cut cabbage slaw and starchy beans.

Daddy Bruce's hot links, copiously dotted with fierce pepper seeds, pack a wallop. A link sandwich is even messier than the ribs, the link cut into four spears, falling out of its casing, precariously contained in two slices of soft white bread made even softer by a dose of the mighty sauce.

Sweet tater pie is the only possible way to end a Daddy Bruce meal; even it is strong food: glowing orange, highly spiced with cloves, unblended nuggets of sweet potato laced into the filling. The definitive soul-food dessert.

Jenny's

4 W. Park, Empire, Colo.
(303) 569-2570

Wed.–Mon. 11:15 a.m.–9 p.m., breakfast Sat. & Sun.

$5 or less

One of the strangest entries in our log of regional proclivities yet uninvesti-
gated is Colorado's passion for eggs. There are at least a half-dozen egg
restaurants in Denver, more in Colorado Springs. And how, parenthetically,
did the Denver omelette get its name?

While we have no answers, not even a catalogue of egg fancy in these
parts, we do offer one restaurant we discovered thanks to Colorado egg
mania: Jenny's, in the mountain village of Empire.

Breakfast Now Served (WITH EGGS!) read a sign on the door. Who could
resist such a strange boast? We ordered ours over easy. Guess what? They
were plain ol' eggs, nice eggs, cooked to order in a panful of butter . . . but
hardly something to make a sign about. Thick sliced bacon on the side was
good, as was a sweet roll that tasted like it was made with yellow cake mix,
pecans, and extra veins of cinnamon and sugar.

An okay breakfast, but we especially liked the place itself, with its wood-
burning stove and old wooden bar, calico tablecloths, and panoply of antiques across the walls—everything from souvenir coffee cups to oldie
records.

The lunch menu listed items that were definitely more interesting than
eggs; so we returned for the largest ribeye sandwich we have ever seen, the
steak as big as an extra heavy slab of prime rib, overhanging the plate,
accompanied by fantastic steak fries sliced as thin as potato chips. And our
half-pound buffalo burger was lean, with a hearty western chaw, almost as
tasty as cow meat.

Cauliflower-mushroom soup was lava-thick, topped with shreds of
cheese and parsley, served in a rough-textured pottery cup. Desserts were of
the stick-to-your-ribs school, too, most notably a wedge of "sweet German
chocolate pie"—granular, gooey, with a nut and butter flavor augmenting
the translucent chocolate gunk. If you like undercooked cookies, this one's
for you.

Jenny's—need we say it?—is not for fastidious epicures. The food is big
and crude; the place is shambling; the service, although kindly, is hardly
suave. In other words, it's a real taste of unlicked frontier grub.

Jeremiah's Mountain Bar-B-Q

15th & Miner Sts., Idaho Springs, Colo.
(303) 567-2589

Wed.–Mon. 11 a.m.–9 p.m.

$5–$15

Where we live, places that affect the ambience of a western saloon are so common, and their food is so uniformly bad, that we did a double-take before appreciating that Jeremiah's was not just another theme restaurant. It *is* a western saloon (beer only), the real thing, with a geographical prerogative to call its food vittles and grub. If you doubt its authenticity, read the menu —a short sweet list of meat, meat, or meat.

Ribs are the house specialty: big, coarse-fibered beef ribs; spare ribs; baby back ribs by the "Miner's Slab" (over two feet long), the "Mountaineer's Platter" (about a foot), or the "Rib Tickler" (about a half dozen).

The pork ribs are stubby, heavy with meat to which Jeremiah's particulate sauce easily adheres. It is this spicy red sauce that makes the ribs so good; it's a tonic to the tongue, encouraging appetite and extra pitchers of beer.

There are sandwiches, too, sliced-thin pork or beef, both of which are quite fatty, and without the satisfying succulence of meat yanked by tooth from bone.

With all meals, Jeremiah's allows one trip to a fixins bar: good cole slaw, eggy potato salad, pork and beans (which are vastly improved by a ladleful of that powerful sauce).

The dining room is appropriately rough-hewn. Timber wall panels are hung with a few semiprimitive paintings of local scenery, plus a rib chart that marks the progress of contestants in an ongoing monthly rib-eating contest. The sign outside is painted in such a way that it reads *Jeremiah's Bar-B-Q Mountain.*

Juniper Valley Ranch

Rte. 115, south of Colorado Springs, Colo.   Midway to Penrose
(303) 576-0741

Wed.–Sat. 5 p.m.–8:30 p.m., Sun. 4 p.m.–7:30 p.m., June–early Sept. only   Reservations advised

$10 or less

When we told friends who have spent some summers in Colorado Springs about *Roadfood and Goodfood,* they told us there was one restaurant that we had to include. "Juniper Valley is just the kind of place you're looking for. The only problem is occasional cannon fire outside, or a tank rumbling by as you approach."

Surrounded by Fort Carson (where the military maneuvers are practiced) and a lot of beautiful rocks, Juniper Valley Ranch is a low pueblo house that serves rustic Colorado meals. It is a picturesque location, even with the occasional tank or cannon fire. An utterly simple restaurant: no drinks, no entertainment—nothing but good food.

There isn't even a long menu from which to choose. Everyone begins with either curried consommé or spiced apple cider. For a main course, choose skillet-cooked chicken or ham baked—and served—in an oval casserole dish. On the side you will get a brace of tiny hot biscuits and apple butter, thick pan-flavored chicken gravy, fresh cole slaw, a country stew of okra, tomatoes, and onions, and a wonderful dish called riced potatoes— spuds that have been boiled, then, instead of mashed, run through a ricer to give them a fluffier texture.

You eat this homey chow in one of three comfortably small dining rooms furnished with old tools and western artifacts, and a bit of Mexican decor. Tablecloths are faded calico, stitched together from different colored bolts of fabric. The iced-tea spoons are handmade, of wood.

La Casa de Manuel

2010 Larimer St., Denver, Colo.
(303) 295-1752

Tues.–Thurs. 11:30 a.m.–8:30 p.m., Fri. 11:30 a.m.–11:30 p.m., Sat. noon–11:30 p.m.

$10 or less

Colorado has some of the best southwestern-style Mexican food in the country; but the places that serve it are usually dumps. That's what we thought as we pulled up to La Casa de Manuel, a small storefront on a street of pawn shops and bars: the end of the line. But it wasn't bums who were streaming into Manuel's place for lunch; it was a sharp crowd: yes, a few burnt-out hippies, but smart folks too—well-dressed ladies and gentlemen, gainfully employed types who looked as though they might return to useful, even interesting professions after lunch.

The point is that if you can read these words, you will feel comfortable once you step inside Casa de Manuel. It is not, by any stretch of the imagination, a middle-class dining environment. The lighting is overhead neon tubes; the chairs are kitchen-style chrome; the walls are hung with stunning, actually beautiful folk art renderings of cock fights, street dances, and other scenes of Mexican village life. The murals are signed, *"Pintado exclusiva-mente para La Casa de Manuel por Castillo."* In these surroundings, you know the food is going to be, at least, authentic.

It is better than that. The *carnitas,* for instance, crusty cubes of pork with a fabulous roasted texture and sweet taste, are just about the best we've found. They are served on a platter with guacamole and a paste of refried beans. Manuel's *menudo* (tripe stew) is also superior: soothing food, just the opposite of all the hot-pepper Mexican clichés.

The green chili will be a shocker for anyone who hasn't tasted real southwestern chili. It is stew, with big hunks of meat, no beans or noodles or any of those starchy fillers. It is very spicy but, oddly, not hot. Fire-eaters will want to dab on some of the powerful red and green chili sauce that accompanies chips to the table at the beginning of the meal. You can get the green chili as a main dish, with dry rice and refried beans, or as a topping for enchiladas or burritos.

Manuel's *barbacoa* tacos are a grungy, satisfying Tex-Mex kind of dish: three soft corn tortillas packed with oily shredded meat, sided by a mound of killer chopped onions, lettuce, and strong Chinese parsley. This is heavy, meaty, American frontier food; it bears little resemblance to anything you would get in a Mexican restaurant in Mexico.

There is no dessert at La Casa de Manuel, but our waitress directed us next door to a Mexican bakery that makes empanadas and cinnamon crisps. If you are so directed, we suggest you ignore the advice. The pastries we got were bad.

Li'l Pantry

6980 Lake St., Green Mountain Falls, Colo.
(303) 684-9018

Daily 7 a.m.–9 p.m.   Sometimes closed on Wed.

$5–$10

Breakfast cinnamon rolls here are eight inches across, as thick as a mountain man's flapjack pile. Each roll arrives warm, oozing butter, frosted with a dark layer of moistened cinnamon sugar spread clear across the top. You would never consider hefting such a monumental mass of dough in your hands, so you plow into it with knife and fork, and finish off three full cups of coffee before the roll is dispatched.

Pies are a specialty of the Li'l Pantry: fruit and cream, Hershey and "Hershey Mint." We thought we'd sample apple pie. One slice, please: a fifth of the entire pie is set before us, approximately two pounds' worth, wider than the plate, a hot triangular brick of apple chunk mosaic in a sturdy crust. Any ordinary cafe would divide this wedge into two servings, maybe three.

"Is this really *one* scoop of ice cream?" asks the lady down the counter when approximately a half-pint is presented to her in a large glass bowl.

Everything is gigantic. Variations of eggs benedict (avocado, crabmeat, broccoli, even eggless with broccoli, ham, and turkey) are blanketed completely with thick yellow cheese sauce. Omelettes are all made with three eggs, and come loaded with ingredients—especially if you order "Matt's Omelette," which the menu describes as "everything you can imagine." Our inventory listed two cheeses, ham, turkey, broccoli, mushrooms, onions, and peppers. On the side came cinnamon raisin toast, the homemade loaf cleaved into inch-thick slabs.

None of this, you can be sure, is elegant fare. Delicacy is unheard of in the Li'l Pantry kitchen; so we advise a visit when you are very hungry and in the mood for western-style grub served with campfire enthusiasm. Most of it is darn good. We only wish the cook would throw away the aerated whipped topping (on the pie); nor do we recommend the glutinous hot fruit compotes. But for a big-feed breakfast or a bloated (design your own topping) burger at lunch, the Li'l Pantry is sure to satisfy.

It is a charmer, across a parking lot from Green Mountain Falls' Victorian gazebo, at the edge of a peninsula in a small lake. Seats in the dining room provide a view of the restaurant's sunflower garden and an aviary's worth of birds who peck at fallen seeds. We were met outside the door by a young dog who instead of a collar wore the garb of counterculture canines everywhere—a red bandana.

Sunflower Restaurant

201 2nd St., Clifton, Colo.
(303) 434-5140

Mon.–Fri. 11 a.m.–10 p.m., Sat. & Sun. 8 a.m.–10 p.m.

$10 or less

Although the beef ribs are excellent—meaty bats sticky with tingly sweet sauce—it is not merely for local cuisine that we like the Sunflower Restaurant. In fact, a lot of the menu isn't local in character at all; there are burgers and fettucini, seafood from far away, even surf and turf. Along with charcoal portraits of John Wayne, a few (not too many) ferns are hung in this carefully restored bank building. It is all pleasantly hip, an antidote to the raw cowboy land and bad roadside cafes that surround it for hundreds of miles.

The ribs, "specialty of the house," says the menu, are served with what is, for western grub, high style—on a bed of lettuce, sided by watermelon wedges, rice, and slices of squash. Unlike the stark offerings of other barbecue joints of the southwest, Sunflower ribs are part of a full meal, preceded by a nice gardeny salad and accompanied by wholewheat rolls. Dessert was very cute: zucchini walnut bars and dainty cupcakes, the selection presented under a glass dome. Both were freshly made, not too sweet, very healthy-tasting.

On Saturday and Sunday, the Sunflower Restaurant features brunch: "Good grain things," says the menu, including hotcakes, French toast, even fruit blintzes and granola.

So it's not a strictly regional restaurant. Maybe we were won over as much by the intelligent waitress, who actually spoke entire English sentences, as much as by the good ribs. We suspect a lot of travelers in the food-barren wasteland of western Colorado may find the Sunflower Restaurant just as welcome a taste of counterculture as we did.

KANSAS

Brookville Hotel

Brookville, Kans.   15 miles west of Salina on KS 140
(913) 225-6666

Tues.–Sat. dinner   Reservations advised

$10 or less

We were told about the Brookville Hotel by a lawyer who used to live in Wichita. He thought nothing of making the 200-mile round trip for a meal; in fact, we have been told that some people come from Kansas City—three hours away—for Sunday chicken dinners, then drive home. The Brookville Hotel is a special-occasion restaurant.

Here in the middle of Kansas, in the middle of America, the special-occasion food is chicken, country-style—fried in a skillet until its crust is crunchy dark brown, the inside still moist and tender. The fixins for this squarest of square meals are served bountifully on platters or in bowls, so everyone at the table can help themselves to all they want. When the bowls near empty, more food is brought.

Side dishes include sweet and sour cole slaw, cottage cheese mixed from dry curds and heavy cream, hot baking-powder biscuits with whipped butter and strawberry preserves, creamed corn, mashed potatoes, and chicken gravy. Everything except, alas, the potatoes, is made here from scratch.

The Brookville is genuinely western, with Victorian wallpaper in one of the dining rooms, red-checked tables in another, a "bank dining room," which was, in fact, the bank when Brookville was the roundhouse town for the Central Pacific Railroad. If you want to drink with dinner, Kansas liquor laws require your joining a private club, here called the Ironhorse Club. Membership requirements are lax.

Built in 1870 as the railroad hotel for the Union Pacific crew, the Brookville has been run by four generations of the same family since 1897. There are no accommodations now, but the town is great for browsing. After dinner, we wandered into an old general store and bought a fifty-year-old etiquette book from a bearded frontierman who apparently had no use for it anymore.

Bunker Hill Cafe

Downtown Bunker Hill, Kans.   Eight miles east of Russell
(913) 483-6544

Mon.–Sat. lunch & dinner   Open Mother's Day & Father's Day

$10–$25

From David Kershaw of Kershaw Ready-Mix Concrete and Sand Co. we received a letter announcing that the Bunker Hill Cafe served him "the best steak I've had since Louie Keck (of Keck's Steak House, Manhattan, Kansas) was killed in an accident ten years ago." We took the rave seriously, as Mr. Kershaw has been a fount of good-eats tips over the years, including Cozy burgers in Salina and Chicken Annie's in Frontenac.

You know this restaurant means business as soon as you peruse the Bunker Hill menu. No adjectives here, just the facts. Under each cut of steak are four to six listings, as follows: 4 oz., 6 oz., 8 oz., 10 oz., etc. Sirloins range from four to sixteen ounces, filets from four to twelve ("plus bacon"). A 24–28-ounce T-bone dinner (including salad, potato, corn on the cob, raisin bread, and a drink) is $23.50; should you wish to split it, that'll be $28.25 for two, $33.00 for three, etc. Degrees of doneness from "real rare" to "burnt" are described exactly.

Details, details! No one could ever complain that they don't know what to expect when they order dinner at the Bunker Hill Cafe. Even non-steak entrees are sold by weight: from two to ten ounces of shrimp, fried or boiled; four-to-twelve-ounce charcoal-grilled salmon filets; various-sized whole catfish and boneless filets. If that isn't specific enough for you, the side orders include sliced sirloin, in one-ounce increments, stuffed shrimp at $2 a head, and salmon by the quarter pound.

Such an inventory-style menu signals a culinary style somewhat lacking in panache. That's okay, because the quality of the food is first-rate. We second Mr. Kershaw's recommendation of sirloin steak, a full pound, center cut, broiled so its faintly crusty skin pockets some delicious juice. The catfish —boneless filets, encased in a fine sandy breading—is perfectly moist. Hamburgers (five ounces) are served on whole wheat buns. The outstanding freshly baked raisin bread that accompanies dinner is available to take home, listed at $1.75 per loaf . . . or $1.25 for loaves that are one-day old.

Fifty cents buys dessert: a single scoop of Schwan's ice cream.

Cozy Inn

108 N. 7th, Salina, Kans.
(913) 825-9407

Mon.–Sat. 9:30 a.m.–11 p.m.

Under $5

On the great family tree of hamburger genealogy, just fifteen years after Louis Lassen gave birth to the burger and long before it was a gleam in the McDonald brothers' eyes, is the Cozy burger of Salina, Kansas.

1922. Bob Kinkel bought a place on 7th Street called the Cozy Inn. He flattened patties of ground beef to the thickness of a nickle, fried them with onions on a griddle, and served them forth at 5¢ apiece.

The price of a Cozy has octupled (or you can buy a half-dozen for $2.28), but veteran Salinians assure us that it hasn't changed a wink. It is still the same bitty burger on a bun, garnished with pickle slices and mustard and/or ketchup. Cheeseburgers (invented at Kaelin's Restaurant in Louisville, Kentucky) are not available. If you know White Castle burgers, the Cozy will look familiar, although this Kansas patty isn't nearly as pulpy.

Most people get 'em to go, by the dozen; there is inside seating, too—six stools, where connoisseurs savor Cozies hot off the griddle, where a hundred fry at once. And if you develop a taste for the little devils when you visit, but cannot get back to Salina quick enough, don't worry: the Cozy Inn is accustomed to shipping Cozies, packed in dry ice, to homesick Kansans all over the globe.

Doc's

1515 N. Broadway, Wichita, Kans.
(316) 264-4735

Mon.–Thurs. 11 a.m.–10 p.m., Fri. 11 a.m.–11 p.m., Sat. 4 p.m.–11 p.m.

$10 or less

Doc's is a steak house with a stern personality. In the entryway, a sign says OUR STEAKS HAVE NOT BEEN FROZEN, TENDERIZED, MARINATED, OR ADULTERATED IN ANY MANNER. Skeptical? Doc's current meat suppliers are listed just below.

Doc's has the strictest menu in the west: "NO split orders (defined as more than one person, adults or children, sharing the same meal. If the customer proceeds to split the meal there will be an 85¢ charge and no plate furnished.)" Furthermore, "Only certain substitutions are permitted," and "We do not replace steaks ordered well done." Doc's also "reserves the right to treat children preferentially."

The point of the rules is "to provide a quality-quantity meal for a reasonable price, expecting a reasonable profit from each customer rather than an excess profit from some customers and no profit from others."

The get-tough policy works. Doc's serves choice steaks at low prices. The large T-bone we ordered had a pleasing texture, with just enough chew to work out an honest—if not deeply aged—flavor. Our thinly breaded chicken-fried steak was fair, served without gravy or mashed potatoes.

French fries or baked (actually steamed-in-foil) potatoes come on the side; but the meal's surprising pièce de résistance was the salad, a locally famous thing called garlic salad, a scoop of intensely garlicked creamy cole slaw, finely chopped, atop a leaf of iceberg lettuce—an extraordinary confluence of diverse, yet strangely complementary flavors. It is possible to order double garlic salad, which we would recommend so long as you have no social engagements for the next three days.

The menu is divided into various categories: "Our Most Complete Meals," which lists the steaks, catfish, and some chops; "Children Only"; "For the Baby"; and our favorite heading, "Meager Meals for the Meager Appetite." Drinks are extra, and there is no dessert.

Service, by nylon-uniformed waitresses, is fast, befitting a no-frills meal. But we must make it clear that Doc's is not in any conceivable way a *plain* restaurant. What it is, is purely Kansan. We have always maintained that Kansas is easily the most eccentric state in the Union. California craziness is child's play by comparison. Doc's harping menu gives just a small hint of the feverish peculiarity of this landbound rectangle; but Doc's decor, one of the most quietly unsettling restaurant environments you will ever see, is truly essence-of-weird.

From the outside, it's stone and wood, like a Polynesian luau palace. There are no windows; all lighting is indirect. Once inside, you are detached

from familiar shapes, sounds, and colors. In the front dining room, a canti-
levered wall tilts outward at a dramatic angle, like a fun house, and it is
implanted with fixtures that glow a phosphorescent color you'd have to call
Martian blue. High-backed booths separate each table in this room from all
other patrons. No alcoholic drinks are served at Doc's, but the unearthliness
of the setting made us woozy.

Steak and garlic slaw in limbo: a true Kansas meal.

George's

228 W. 9th St., Coffeyville, Kans.
(316) 251-5690

Mon.–Sat. lunch & dinner, Sun. midday meal only

About $5

Years ago, we circled Coffeyville on our Kansas map because we heard there
was a farmer there named Oral Watts, who had a collection of three
thousand telephones. We found the collection, and it was great—crank-ups,
Princesses, wooden phones, plastic phones. We also found George's
cafeteria-style restaurant, and it has since eclipsed Oral's telephones, even
Wendell Willkie's mementos in the local museum, as a good reason to route
a trip west through this lunchbucket burg on the Oklahoma border.

There are two lines at George's: one for "light" meals, meaning soups,
sandwiches, and salads; and a line for serious "hot" meals—worth walking
through if only to feast one's eyes on the lavish selection. Look at even a
small category, like potatoes. George's offers baked potatoes, mashed potatoes, cubed sweet potatoes, twice-baked potatoes, crisp or floppy potatoes,
and two or three kinds of fried potatoes. Breads are all made here, every day:
cinnamon rolls, dinner rolls, hot biscuits, garlic toast, cornbread.

At George's, "salad" is interpreted in its most catholic sense, including
not just lettuce and garden vegetables, but all manner of carrot and cabbage
slaw, salads with raisins, nuts, and fruits, a rainbow of Jell-O, and one especially confectionery salad made from cranberries, nuts, whipped cream, and
marshmallows.

The sides are fancy, but George's entrees are plain breadbasket cuisine:
chicken, either smothered or deep-fried; roast beef; steaks cooked to order;
lamb shanks; turkey and dressing on Sunday.

Dessert? Loganberry, boysenberry, or Dutch apple pie. Icebox pies. Meringue pies. German chocolate cake, carrot cake, white cake, devil's food
cake. A dozen puddings. And a dessert called Oh-So-Good—walnuts, pecans,
egg whites, and whipped cream, blended together to form one of the richest
pies in history.

Leona Yarbrough

2800 W. 53rd, Fairway, Kans.
(913) 722-4800

Tues.–Sat. 11 a.m.–8 p.m., Sun. 11 a.m.–7 p.m.

$5 or less

There are certain *soigné* people, from the Missouri side of Kansas City, who poked fun at us when we trooped to Leona Yarbrough's for lunch. We were in the company of Alan McDermott and Donna Martin, Leona aficionados whose only fault as far as we were concerned was that both of them insisted on ordering the same thing, which they both always order when they lunch here: egg salad sandwiches, on whole wheat toast.

Leona's is the type of restaurant that inspires such steady habits. It is a temple of normal food, from egg salad to turkey divan to lattice-crust apple pie. It is the antithesis of chic, a comfortable haven for the blue-haired set as well as whippersnappers who appreciate a sense of culinary security.

Although thrill seekers won't find excitement in the seafood tetrazzini or braised lamb shank with mint jelly, such forthrightness makes our hearts throb. Nothing expresses Leona Yarbrough's cuisine better than a few choice listings from her menu (mimeographed daily): whipped potato, browned potato, parslied potato . . . molded salad, cucumbers in sour cream, pickled beets . . . blackberry cobbler, prune whip, fresh apple cake. A small order-pad and pencil are provided for customers to write their own ticket—a discreet system that allows diners to converse among themselves instead of bellowing orders to a waitress.

The thing about Leona's is—as any menu connoisseur could tell you—everything is absolutely fresh, from scratch, homemade. It is portioned out modestly, in pretty floral patterned plates. And it tastes like it should, because Leona, whose reputation has made her the definitive Kansas City square-meals chef in the thirty-seven years she has run the kitchen, is a master.

Look at this baked tenderloin, a dainty oval with a gentle crust, the meat so tender it slices easily with a little pressure from the edge of a fork. It is garnished with cream gravy, sided by whipped potatoes and buttered corn. Boring? You bet. Delicious? We cleaned our plates.

The lunch menu has a lot of sandwiches, like that famous egg salad, which is the plainest-tasting egg salad you will ever eat, served on fragrant, fine-crumbed slices of Leona's whole wheat. Ham salad comes on homemade rye. Spinach salad, topped with warm sweet and sour dressing, is sided by a block of high-flavored cornbread, the secret of which, Leona confided, is chicken fat in the batter.

"We cook a lot of hens," she explained, "and we render and chill the fat. It goes into muffins, too." And she told us how her nine-year-old grandson's peanut-butter cookies were improved, at her suggestion, with a little chicken fat. Now the boy makes them regularly—for one of Leona's steady customers.

Dinner is on a slightly larger scale than lunch, but it's the same idea: corned beef and cabbage, roast beef and gravy, chicken fried in an iron skillet, liver and onions, turkey divan on an English muffin.

Now, about dessert: lattice-top pies, made with the flakiest lard crusts; rice custard, which is like rice pudding but with the custard part layered on top of rice; prune whip, an old-fashioned froth of shredded prunes suspended in sweetened whipped egg whites; and—hold on to your hat—fruit Jell-O, orange sherbet, or vanilla ice cream. If you want to make the vanilla ice cream into a chocolate sundae, Leona charges 10¢ extra.

Mrs. Peters' Chicken Dinners

4960 State Ave., Kansas City, Kans.
(913) 287-7711

Tues.–Sat. 5 p.m.–9 p.m., Sun. noon–8 p.m.   Reservations advised

$10 or less

Chicken-shaped things are everywhere. Cheery blue gingham curtains hang in the windows. Gingerbread moldings and country tools are part of what might be called a "decorator farmhouse" look. On Sunday, most tables are sixes, or tens, or twelves.

Although pork chops and country-fried steak are available, nearly all those big tables of jumbo Kansas City families are sitting down to plates piled with fried chicken, four crunchy golden pieces each, plus bowls full of mashed potatoes and gravy, biscuits and honey butter, cole slaw, corn, and marinated vegetable salad. A real country feed.

Lemonade and coffee are the drinks of choice. For dessert, there is homemade vanilla ice cream, peach cobbler, or Dutch apple pie.

When we spotted Mrs. Peters', after hearing about it in glowing terms from local food mavens, we admit to a pinch of disappointment. At first glance, it could pass as a redecorated Howard Johnson's, and we had expected a rural farmhouse. Inside, it is clean, downright sanitary; but that's where any resemblance to institutionalized food service ends. Unlike some of the midwest's overwhelmingly huge chicken-dinner houses, where patrons are processed like so many fresh-laid eggs, Mrs. Peters' is a friendly, happy place, a restaurant with a personality so distinct you can practically hear it cackle.

R & S Bar-B-Q

1918 E. 13th St., Wichita, Kans.
(316) 265-1465

Tues.–Fri. 11 a.m.–3 p.m.   Closed two weeks in Aug.

About $5

R & S's truncated hours of operation are possible because it is the most popular place in Wichita. The people who run it simply do all the business they want four days a week, at lunch only.

It's an ugly building made of tin, painted white and mustard, with only a few tall skinny windows to let in light. If there is a mob of cars in the gravel parking lot and a smell of hickory smoke blowing down Thirteenth Street for blocks, you know it's open. Service is cafeteria-style, by some of the fastest countermen in the west.

Superior southwestern beef brisket can be bought by the sandwich, plate, or pound; and R & S's hot links have a savory pepper punch, but the thing to eat here is ribs—pork spare ribs with hot sauce. These are quality bones, a great gnaw of chewy pork electrified by the sauce, which, in its hot form, perfectly needles the taste buds to all the better appreciate the subtleties of the hickory-laced meat. Mild or mixed sauces are also available, but they lack the necessary kick.

Cole slaw and baked beans can be had on the side, as can extra bread at 4¢ a slice. The ribs always come with a few slices of white bread, which is eminently suitable for absorbing sauce like an edible sponge.

Scandinavian Bakery

107 N. Main, Lindsborg, Kans.
(913) 227-3525

Mon.–Sat. 7 a.m.–4 p.m.

Under $5

We're bending our rules including the Scandinavian Bakery in a book about great American food, but the Jayhawker State is known for its pancakes (they even match Olney, England's annual pancake race with one of their own); and this small bakery/pancake parlor in the town that calls itself "Little Sweden, USA" is the place to eat them.

Although you can get good sandwiches on Swedish limpa (cardamom) bread, most people come for pancakes, thin Swedish roll-ups, served with lingonberries or blueberries and sour cream. There are "American Griddle

Cakes," too—thick plate-size patties available as a stack (3), short stack (2), or single.

A pot of good coffee is located in the back of the cafe, next to the table of overalled farmers and town gents who come here to gossip over their wheat-cakes.

When you leave, buy a loaf of Swedish rye or delicious limpa bread with dried fruit in the middle.

Wolferman's

2820 W. 53rd, Fairway, Kans.
(913) 432-6131

Breakfast Mon.–Fri. 7 a.m.–10 a.m., Sat. 9 a.m.–11 a.m., lunch Mon.–Fri. 11 a.m.–2:30 p.m., Sat. 11:30 a.m.–3 p.m., brunch Sun.

$10 or less

Once you have sunk your teeth into a Wolferman's high-rise English muffin, you can never go back to the scrubby little discs you used to think were pretty swell. Twice as tall as normal, Wolferman's muffins are made only in Kansas City, where they have been a local favorite since Louis Wolferman created them in 1888.

The place to eat them (other than home) is Wolferman's store, on a second-story balcony that specializes in breakfast and lunch. As you watch people on the floor below shop for "good things to eat" (the house motto), you are served by waitresses whose black uniforms suggest a time, many years ago, when Wolferman's ran a full-scale tea room.

The menu is reminiscent of those days: welsh rarebit (on a muffin), eggs dijon (a tomato stuffed with a poached egg), and salads topped with essence-of-heartland poppy-seed dressing. Ladylike cuisine, most of it served with or poured over muffins.

Ordered alone, a muffin arrives hewn into jagged halves, each side a mountain range of peaks and valleys (and we were once content with mere nooks and crannies!). Flowing across this hot pot-holed terrain is melting butter, faintly flavored with apricot and honey. The muffin's thickness allows for a sweeping variety of textures, from the crisp-crusted surface, down into doughy, barely toasted furrows, to the sandy meal-imprinted bottom. On the side comes a plastic cup of tart marmalade.

Muffins are available plain-flavored, light wheat, cheddar cheese, or cinnamon raisin.

The best way to doll up a muffin is by turning it into eggs benedict—which Wolferman's offers at every meal. The halves are layered with Canadian bacon, poached eggs, and Hollandaise sauce. As far as we're concerned, that's the best breakfast in town.

NEW MEXICO

Abeyta's Mexican Kitchen

2805 San Mateo, NE, Albuquerque, N. Mex.
(505) 881-5314

Mon.–Sat. 10 a.m.–9 p.m.

$5 or less

Menudo is not always easy to find in the southwest. It is a weekend dish, customarily served the morning after to sooth frizzled nerves. In Albuquerque, you can treat a hangover six days a week at the eatery called Abeyta's, where the mimeographed menu promises *menudo* made fresh every day.

Understand that making *menudo* requires long hours as well as skill, because tripe must be simmered until it is tender—so tender it slithers off a spoon. Sharing space in the broth with the gelatinous patches of tripe is *posole*—also known as hominy corn—which must itself be softened with a bath of lye until it puffs up as tender as a bite of spoonbread. The combination has a pacific corn fragrance, its textural reticence a comfort even if you aren't hung over.

Those unaccustomed to southwest-Mex food may find that *chicharrónes* take even more getting used to than *menudo*. They are the ultimate bacon—small cubes of pork with plenty of fat, fried until crisp, served as an appetizer with corn tortillas. Or you can get a *chicharróne* burrito, loaded with beans interspersed with the luxurious pork nuggets.

Like hot food? Order *carne adovada*—rugged hunks of pork marinated in a fierce puree of red chili peppers. For a milder taste of New Mexico, we recommend *chili rellenos*—less aggressive peppers stuffed with cheese, their flavor amplified by red or green chili sauce.

Dinners are accompanied by warm flour tortillas—freshly made, flaky, a fine mop for the rice, beans, chili, lettuce, and tomato that accompany entrees.

Also in the category of home cooking, New Mexican style, are Abeyta tamales—fat tubes of hot cornmeal and spiced meat wrapped in cornhusks. And guacamole that tastes of fresh avocados and plenty of garlic. And chewy blue corn tortillas. And dynamite salsa speckled with pepper seeds, served with chips at the beginning of the meal. And jiggly *natilla* pudding (for tapioca lovers only).

Honest eats, served fast and cheap: to those who live in Albuquerque and have access to New Mexican cooking all the time, Abeyta's might seem like just another cafe. To those of us from regions of America where "Mexican food" is synonymous with Ken-l Ration, it is a special place precisely because it is so casual, entirely authentic. This is where real people come to eat —off slightly disheveled tablecloths, to the tunes of a city radio station, in the company of friendly help who radiate neighborly cheer. In the next room, at Abeyta's take-out desk, locals line up to buy tamales by the dozen, *chicharrónes* and *menudo* by the quart.

The Burrito Wagon

Taos, N. Mex.   Next to the county courthouse
No phone

Mon.–Sat. 11 a.m.–4 p.m.

Under $5

When in Taos, keep an all-points lookout for The Burrito Wagon, a humble van parked near the courthouse in the supermarket parking lot. It's a mobile eatery that dispenses what natives of this arty town generally agree are the best burritos you can get.

Run by Leonard Padilla and his wife Deela, the Wagon sells five different varieties, all sharing the basic burrito configuration: a flour tortilla folded into a tight tube around your choice of pinto beans, ground beef, red or green chili sauce, and grated cheese. Around the tube is wrapped wax paper, conveniently folded at the bottom so nothing leaks out as you saunter around the Taos Plaza, eating it like an ice cream cone: an ideal portable meal.

The tortillas are made fresh each morning by Leonard's mother at home, but each burrito is assembled when ordered inside the truck. Among the five varieties are a vegetarian model and a super-jumbo deluxe burrito for those who find their appetites enhanced by the high altitude.

The only other item on the abbreviated menu is Leonard's mother's homemade tamales—warm sticks of moist cornmeal laced with spiced chopped meat and held together in a corn husk—equally portable, equally delicious.

Duran Central Pharmacy

1815 Central, NW, Albuquerque, N. Mex.
(505) 247-4141

Mon.–Fri. 9 a.m.–6:30 p.m., Sat. 9 a.m.–2 p.m.

$5 or less

From outside, it looks like any ordinary pharmacy. Enter, and it looks that way, too: shelves well stocked with modern liniments and patent medicines, household sundries and personal hygiene enhancers. It smells like a pharmacy, of alcohol and soap. But as much as we do love America's drug stores —and recommend them to any traveler in search of local color—it is not for the gum or candy that we rank Duran among Albuquerque's culinary highlights.

Head left toward the back of the store and you find a small gateway that leads to one of the most remarkable drug-store lunch counters in America. It isn't large, and like all pharmacy cafes, it has only an open kitchen—a grill, a counter, a few coffee makers and pop-up toasters.

Four ladies do all the work. One of them seems to have a single task: making tortillas. On a two-by-two-foot counter with nothing more elaborate than a short wooden dowel, she rolls out a ball of flour into an eight-inch circle. She lifts the dough pancake and turns toward the grill. As she turns she tosses the circle back and forth between her hands, stretching it further, then slaps it down to fry. Hardly any oil is used, so in fact it *bakes* as much as fries. The result is a quarter-inch-thin round of bread, crisped in mottled patches on its skin, soft and warm inside. It is brushed with melted butter just before it is served. Since almost every meal at Duran is accompanied by a tortilla, the tortilla maker always has a couple going on the grill, which holds no more than two at a time.

Red chili, by the bowl, is mild, a soupy stew of ground meat and beans, redolent of starchy corn odor. Green chili is hotter, translucent, terrific as a topping for *huevos rancheros*.

Not much more to the menu: tacos, burritos, and enchiladas, burgers served on tortillas with green chili topping, a torpedo (tortilla-wrapped potatoes, chili, and cheese), *carne adovada* on Thursday, and stuffed *sopaipillas* on Wednesday and Friday.

Naturally, as this is a true drug-store lunch counter, you can accompany the authentic New Mexican cuisine with an all-American chocolate milk shake.

Earl's Restaurant

1321 E. Rte. 66, Gallup, N. Mex.
(505) 863-4201

Mon.–Sat. 6 a.m.–10 p.m., Sun. 7 a.m.–9 p.m.

$5 or less

Earl's does the kind of cooking best described as haute truck stop—like Mom might have done if she had been a man. And so we list it here because among the many things New Mexico is famous for are its truck drivers. Yes, that's right; along with chili peppers, adobe haciendas, and Georgia O'Keeffe, this state is home to an incredible number of men who drive the big rigs; and it was a few years back, while writing a book about the habits of the cowboys on eighteen wheels, that we were clued by one of them to Earl's.

Earl's isn't really a truck stop, but it has the feel of one: not much to look at, a modern mansard-roofed rectangle is all; a roomy place inside, with booths and tables all set in advance with enormous pitchers of ice water.

Most of the food is made from scratch: biscuits, cornbread, *sopaipillas* with honey, chicken with cornbread dressing, and homemade pies. Everything seems to be double-sized. One wedge of pie is enough for two; pancakes hang over the edge of their plate; coffee comes in big thermos pitchers that allow you to keep refilling your cup.

The cuisine is a mix of Mexican and downhome American chow—green chili omelettes, Virginia ham, tacos (soft or crisp), roast turkey and giblet gravy. Either side of the border you choose, the food is hearty fare.

We wouldn't travel out of our way for a meal at Earl's, but along this food-barren highway, it's an oasis.

The Hacienda

2605 S. Espina, Las Cruces, N. Mex.
(505) 522-6380

Mon.–Sat. 11 a.m.–2 p.m. & 5 p.m.–9 p.m., Fri. & Sat. until 10 p.m.

$10 or less

Created out of ingredients taken from Mexico and the southwest, with a dash of spice from Spain and a few borrowings from the Indians, New Mexican cookery is America's most colorful cuisine; and The Hacienda is one of the best places we know to admire its polychromatic beauty: fire-red chilies, golden *posole*, *salsas* in red and bright green, and blue corn tortillas.

Start your meal with homemade *sopaipillas*—airy puffs of fried hot bread that are unique to New Mexican kitchens. The Hacienda's are ethereal, elegant, the color of champagne.

Although blue corn (a genetic anomaly) doesn't taste any different than yellow, it is an ancient Indian favorite, enjoyed for its aesthetic value, perhaps for its resemblance to the sky or to turquoise, or perhaps just because it is weird. The Hacienda's owners buy their blue corn in bulk and have it made into tortillas by a Las Cruces tortilla factory.

The thin cornmeal circles are slate blue, like no other food—especially attractive as tacos, when filled with meat, shreds of lettuce, and small cubes of tomato. Blue corn enchiladas, dripping with yellow jack cheese, can be ordered topped with red or green chili sauce: another stunning composition.

Red or green, both *salsas* are freshly made at The Hacienda, from peppers bought at chili farms in the Mesilla valley. The difference in taste between red and green varies with chili season. By the end of August, when the chili plants are fully mature, they produce the maximum amount of heat. At that time, green sauce—made from unripened chilies—is scorching hot; red is milder, having had time to mellow out in the sun. The rest of the year, the difference is more subtle.

One of the best dishes at The Hacienda is the *chili rellenos:* two green "big Jim" chilies, each nearly a foot long, stuffed with cheese, batter-dipped and deep-fried—hot stuff, mouth-watering good.

A Hacienda specialty of different colors is the Indian fry bread *compuesta*—like a *sopaipilla*, but larger, and made without lard so it stays flat rather than puffing up. You can get it topped with beef or chicken, beans, and cheese: a meal of earth tones and heavier textures.

For dessert, the color is chocolate brown, in a spectacularly delicious dish called *sopaipillas y champura*. It is made from a recipe that has been in co-owner Evelyn Snyder's family for years: a simple dish—strips of freshly fried *sopaipilla* blanketed with a warm just-barely-sweet chocolate sauce.

The setting for this bouquet of New Mexican food is a pretty one. The Hacienda is relaxed and cheery, with a ranch house feel about the dining rooms, and a garden area for taking in the clean Las Cruces air. It's a big adobe house on a residential street. There are prickly-pear cacti out front and chili *ristras* hung along its walls. You'll know it by the mission bell at the entrance.

Indian Pueblo Cultural Center Restaurant

2401 Twelfth St., NW, Albuquerque, N. Mex.
(505) 843-7270

Tues.–Sat. 7 a.m.–9 p.m., Sun. & Mon. 7 a.m.–3 p.m.

$10 or less

A fifteen-inch circle of sweet dough quickly fried in hot oil until it bubbles into crisp pockets above a soft chewy base is slathered with butter and sprinkled with cinnamon sugar. That is breakfast at the Indian Pueblo Cultural Center Restaurant, a serving of fry bread known as *The Zia*, after one of the tribes that are banded together in this enclave of desert culture surrounded by the city of Albuquerque.

You can also breakfast on toast made from bread baked in clay ovens; or eggs scrambled with spicy chopped *chorizo* sausage; or a breakfast burrito —bacon and eggs and chili wrapped in a soft flour burrito; or French toast; or cold cereal.

This pueblo kitchen is not purely native American, not even purely southwestern. BLTs and tuna fish sandwiches share the lunch menu with blue cornmeal enchiladas and green chili stew. For dinner, choose between trout amandine and *carne adovada*. The dining room is tasteful and modern, its booths separated by adobe-style step dividers, and it has a sanitary salad bar.

We are suckers for fry bread, sweet or savory, so any time other than breakfast *Tiwa Tacos* are our dish: sandwiches of beans, cheese, chili (red or green), lettuce, and tomatoes layered between two discs of fry bread. Such a taco is not quite edible by hand; and utensils are nearly useless; it's a mess either way.

Easier to eat—but harder on the tongue—is green chili stew, a thick brew of pork chunks and potatoes in green chili laced with onions and a few tomatoes. It isn't four-alarm hot, but you definitely want a slice of clay-oven bread on the side to soothe your mouth.

La Casita

519 Central Ave., Socorro, N. Mex.
(505) 835-0821

Mon.–Thurs. 11 a.m.–9 p.m., Fri.–Sun. 11 a.m.–10 p.m.

$3–$12

Juanita Martinez is a wisp of a lady who has been cooking New Mexican food since she was a child. We wouldn't dare to ask her age, but she is far from young; and the skills she has honed since the age of 11 have found a happy home at La Casita.

Juanita is one of those gifted natural artists who transforms simple ingredients into outstanding food. *Sopaipillas*, for instance. We watched her make them one day in the modern kitchen of the restaurant. She used a simple wooden dowel to roll the dough flat, then—zip, zip—the dough was cut into squares and folded over. She eased the squares into a pan of sizzling oil. Like helium balloons, they puffed with air and seemed to float out of the pan on her spoon as she drained them for a second on a sheet of absorbent paper. These *sopaipillas* are so thin that the honey we poured into them threatened to tear their delicate shells.

Having seen Juanita do it, we tried to reproduce her *sopaipillas* at home. We made the dough just right—flour, water, baking powder, a dash of oil and salt—and we fried them in good clean oil like she does. The results made us even more appreciative of her art.

La Casita has expanded from a sparse cafe to a relatively fancy joint, complete with salad bar and liquor license (try the seventeen-ounce "Margarita supergrande"); and there are now steaks and seafood on the menu; but the soul of the place is still 100 percent New Mexican. Owner Maimie Trujillo is a fussy lady, and she travels south regularly to select just the right chili peppers from Salem or Hatch. When she finds ones that suit her, they are ground here in the restaurant with a coarse stone. Likewise, La Casita grinds its own corn for meal.

You will find a full array of New Mexican specialties on the La Casita menu, including *chili rellenos*, red and green chili, *sopa de arroz* (a tomato-based rice dish often called Spanish rice), and best of all, Juanita Martinez's divine *sopaipillas*.

La Posta

In the village of Mesilla, one mile south of Las Cruces, N. Mex.
(505) 524-3524

Tues.–Sun. 11 a.m.–9:30 p.m.   Reservations advised

$10 or less

The most beautiful sunset we have ever seen was in Las Cruces, New Mexico. Fading rays turned the whole town the color of hammered gold in front of a jagged backdrop of indigo mountains. As soon as the spectacle passed, we regained our power of speech and croaked out the words, "Let's eat." Then we trotted off to La Posta.

The restaurant is a low adobe building more than 150 years old, a stopping place for infamous southwesterners like Billy the Kid, Kit Carson, and Pancho Villa. After waiting in a vestibule under a translucent ceiling, filled with a jungle of vines and parrots squawking like mad, you are led from the tropical rain forest to a table in one of several dining rooms.

Like all restaurants that flaunt the native cuisine of New Mexico, La Posta pays homage to the chili pepper. The menu even offers a dab of history, informing diners that the chili is a New World vegetable brought back to Europe by Christopher Columbus, who touted it as "a pepper more pungent than that from the Caucasus." (A hundred years after Columbus, the chili was brought north by Spanish explorers to what is now New Mexico.)

About 350 years after that (1939 to be exact), La Posta invented a dish that has become a New Mexican standard—tostadas *compuestas*. It is a corn tortilla formed into a cup while frying. Into the cup is placed chili con carne with *frijoles* (beans), and that is topped with lettuce, diced tomatoes, and grated cheese. You can order this as a main course (you get three), or as part of a combination meal ("La Posta Chica"), which gets you one *compuestas* cup, plus a *chili relleno* (a deep-fried, cheese-stuffed pepper), a taco, and a lovely fresh guacamole salad. All dinners come with hot corn tortillas, served in a basket shaped like a Mexican hat.

A La Posta combination for big eaters is the "banquette elegante." It starts off simply with tortilla chips and green *salsa* for dipping, then picks up gastronomic speed with *carne adovada* (pork marinated in chili sauce, about which the menu notes, "Caramba!"), refried beans, and chili.

Be sure to order *sopaipillas* on the side. La Posta's are delicious, quick-fried when ordered, so they puff up with air, served hot with a pitcher of honey to pour inside. Food historians speculate that *sopaipillas* are New Mexican descendants of Navajo fry bread, which makes sense, since like the Indian bread, people eat them before a meal, as appetizers; during, in lieu of bread; and after, for dessert.

For dessert, we recommend a mince empanada, a rolled and fried pocket of dough stuffed with fruit, served hot and topped with melting ice cream.

La Posta is a mixed blessing of a restaurant. The service can be uneven, the diners a mix of locals and tourists, and the tropical decor a bit too much like a Florida parrot jungle/souvenir shop. But despite all that, La Posta's food bears the signs of a kitchen staff that cares about good eating and is expert in the ways of New Mexican cookery.

La Tertulia

416 Agua Fria, Santa Fe, N. Mex.
(505) 988-2769

Tues.–Sun. 11:30 a.m.–2 p.m., 5 p.m.–9 p.m.   Reservations advised

$5–$12

La Tertulia is what all other restaurants of its genre aspire to be. But the food here bears absolutely no resemblance to the hammered-down red and brown gruel that passes for Mexican cooking in the other forty-nine states.

Despite its urban locale, La Tertulia has a laid-back elegance that is uniquely Santa Fe. The customers are an interesting mix of sun-streaked *Town and Country* types draped with turquoise jewelry, native New Mexicans with their dusky skins and seal-dark hair, and young arriviste artistes.

The building is beautiful: an old convent with thick adobe walls. Rugged beams run across the ceiling; a fading mural decorates the tile-floored garden room; a radiant outdoor patio is opened up for summer dining. Prices are moderate, but La Tertulia feels expensive.

We settled in with a pitcher of sangría, and with the tortilla chips and *salsa* that take the place of rolls and butter in New Mexican restaurants. We could tell from the fresh bite of the red sauce that La Tertulia had a few serious hands at work in the kitchen. So we decided to order a lot.

The meal began with black bean and jalapeño soup, a thick rust-red brew with lots of tiny shreds of chili pod and seeds of the fiery jalapeño. The first taste was of bean, rich and delicious, then *pow*—an aftershock courtesy of the peppers. It was a formidable combination, the beans offsetting the heat, and jalapeno peppers energizing the dowdy bean.

From there we moved to enchiladas, a common food in the southwest—spectacular at La Tertulia. They begin with blue corn tortillas—not robin's-egg blue like soda pop, but murky volcanic blue, ground from New Mexican blue maize. The red chili that topped the blue tortilla wove shreds of meat into a blazing hot sauce that made our foreheads moist and our eyes bright. The enchilada was further topped with shredded cheese and refried beans, all on a peculiar double-tiered plate that kept it as hot in temperature as in spice.

Next came a *chalupa* plate, a corn tortilla topped with chicken, cheese, sour cream, and warm guacamole—a layering of textures and rivulets of warm and cool foods. On the side was delicious *posole*, nuggets of hominy corn soaked in lime until they puff up, served firm and buttery—a nice rest from the fire of the other dishes.

Sopaipillas are served with every meal, soft pastries into which one customarily pours warm honey. La Tertulia's were not the most delicate we have tasted, but the lapse in perfection was almost made up for by the cup of honey butter that came alongside.

Our lace tablecloth was embarrassingly obscured by the enormous meal we had ordered, so we finished, paid our bill, and returned the next day to start again. We asked our waiter what the *carne adovada* was like. He rolled his eyes. "Unbelievably hot," he said in a voice we took as a challenge. "We'll have that, and bring us an order of *chili rellenos* and *camarones con pimientas y tomates.*"

He was right. The *carne adovada* was so hot we clutched the edge of the table after the first bite. For those who relish hot food, it is a fabulous dish: cubed pork marinated to fork tenderness in chili sauce.

The *chili rellenos* and *camarones* proved milder. The *rellenos* platter was two large chilies, stuffed with cheese, dipped in light batter, and fried. The *camarones* are shrimp, split open and cooked in a sauce of green peppers, tomatoes, and flecks of onions. Served on Spanish rice and garnished with slices of avocado, it is a refreshing and unusual New Mexican mélange.

Capirotada is a traditional Mexican bread pudding, here cooked in its cup. The bread cubes were drenched in sweet syrup, spiced with cinnamon, and topped oddly with yellow cheese. In the baking, the cheese chars, and is a perfect textural balance to the moist bread and puffy raisins below. *Natilla* is New Mexican custard, a creamy bland balm unfortunately topped with less-than-perfect whipped cream. We didn't try the New Mexican praline, but from what we saw of it on neighboring tables, we wish we had.

Rancho de Chimayo

Rte. 520, off Rte. 76, Chimayo, N. Mex.   North of Santa Fe
(505) 351-4444

Tues.–Sun. noon–9 p.m.   Closed in Jan.   Reservations advised

$10 or less

Rancho de Chimayo serves native New Mexican cuisine in the most picturesque setting imaginable. The narrow road leading to the 400-year-old village of Chimayo winds through the lush upper Rio Grande valley, past tiny
roadside stands selling chili *ristras* (vines of dried red chili peppers) and
native apples. Adobe houses are painted pink and baby blue; the golden
mountain light brings everything into vivid focus.

You will know you have arrived at Rancho de Chimayo when you spot a
big adobe ranch house, its front draped with red chili *ristras*, the driveway
crowded with scores of cars. Despite its isolation, Rancho de Chimayo is one
of New Mexico's favorite eating places.

The restaurant is the Jaramillo family home, a nineteenth-century ranch
with wide wood plank floors, fireplaces, and hammered tin chandeliers hanging from low-beamed ceilings. The Jaramillo family has lived in Chimayo
since the 1700s, and are descendants of the Spanish colonists who settled in
this Tewa Indian village called Tsimajo ("good quality stone") in the 1600s.
Their lineage alone ought to suggest they know a thing or two about native
New Mexican cuisine.

If you aren't impressed by family trees, crack open the menu and order
just about any dish you see. It's easy to fall in love with the cooking here.
There is no restaurant we know that gives a better feeling for the uniqueness
of New Mexican cookery, in which the traditional Spanish/Mexican repertoire is woven with Indian-accented foods like *posole* and piñon nuts.

Yes, this food is hot; after all, New Mexico's state vegetable is the chili
pepper. But it is much more than hot. After the initial wave of fire fades on
the tongue, a Rancho de Chimayo meal will be a stunning spectrum of subtle
and loud flavors, and textures that range from ethereal *sopaipillas* to earthy
wheat-flour tortillas.

All this is a way of getting to our favorite dish, which is also the hottest
—*carne adovada*. Although the menu doesn't bear a warning next to its description of "pork cutlets marinated, cooked in a red chili sauce, served with
posole," we will give it to you straight: *carne adovada* is a killer—but what a
way to go. The pork is glistening dark red, marinated to fall-apart tenderness
in Chimayo-grown chilies, which have a unique rich flavor beneath their veil
of heat. It's so hot it hurts; but it is so good you fork up some mild *posole* to
tamp it down, have a swig of your frozen margarita, maybe a forkful of
cooling avocado guacamole; and by then your taste buds are begging for
another masochistic taste of the luscious pork.

Carne adovada is an addiction—perhaps quite literally. A report in *The Johns Hopkins Magazine* on the work of Professor Paul Rozin, a psychologist specializing in "the acquisition of likes and dislikes for food," theorizes that "Chili eating provides a painful stimulus, true—and the body responds by producing the opposite effect, secreting endorphins—natural morphine." No wonder!

If you don't want to start with the hard stuff, there are terrific milder dishes, too. *Sopaipilla rellena* is a triangular hot bread stuffed with beef, beans, tomato, and Spanish rice. Over this fat popover is ladled red or green chili; and on the side you get the soothing citrus-spiked guacamole. *Flautas* (Spanish for "flutes") are rolled corn tortillas filled with chicken or pork, then fried until crisp. We love them topped with sour cream, but you may be satisfied to have them merely topped with the Jaramillos' red chili sauce.

A first-timer at Rancho de Chimayo can get a combination plate called *combinación picante* (that means hot, folks), which has the *carne adovada*, a tamale, a rolled enchilada, refried beans, *posole*, and red chili.

Frozen margaritas are the drink of choice among most Rancho de Chimayo patrons, but another way to put out the fire is a cooler called the Chimayo cocktail, made from tequila and apple juice. A great nonalcoholic way to sooth the palate is simply *cidro de manzana* (native Chimayo apple cider).

Rancho de Chimayo is a place to linger—especially in warm weather, when you can eat on the outdoor patio by candlelight. Despite its gourmet status, Rancho de Chimayo is characteristically New Mexican—informal and hospitable. Yes, there are a disproportionate number of Mercedes parked outside, but you will not find stuffy service or uptight patrons here— just crowds of people having fun while eating first-rate food.

Tecolote Cafe

1203 Cerrillos Rd., Santa Fe, N. Mex.
(505) 988-1362

Wed.–Sun. 7 a.m.–2 p.m., dinner Fri.–Sun. only

About $5

Look up *tecolote* in a Spanish dictionary and you will discover it means "owl"; it also means the best breakfast in Santa Fe, and for miles around.

To Bill and Alice Jennison, who run this comfortable multi-room cafe, breakfast is a calling. Their menu explains how they started in business because they felt that breakfast is "a meal too often neglected." To remedy that situation, they devised a repertoire of morning food that combines traditional American breakfast fare with the best southwestern specialties.

Everything at Tecolote Cafe is made fresh, from the best ingredients available; a blackboard always lists the seasonal fruits that are featured in salads and as garnishes for meals. Coffee is freshly ground; orange juice freshly squeezed; and biscuits and muffins spend little time between the oven and your plate.

While it is possible to put together an excellent nonregional breakfast of ham and eggs or pancakes and bacon, we prefer the zesty local offerings, like Tecolote's breakfast burrito. It's a large homemade flour tortilla rolled around eggs that have been scrambled with chunks of ham or sausage, then topped with meat-speckled green or red chili, drizzled with shredded cheese, and served with either refried beans or *posole* (puffy hominy corn kernels).

Tecolote's *huevos rancheros* are resplendent: fried eggs atop a corn tortilla, smothered with red or green chili, sided by *posole* and served with either warm soft tortillas or delicious little biscuits.

Lunch at Tecolote consists of good New Mexican standards like burritos, green chili stew, tacos, and a large tostada *compuesta*—a fried corn tortilla mounded with beans, cheese, chili, assorted salad ingredients, and guacamole.

OKLAHOMA

Anna Maude

1867 Penn Square, Oklahoma City, Okla.
(405) 840-2174

Mon.–Fri. 11 a.m.–7:30 p.m.

About $5

If you love a great cafeteria, or if, like us, you revert to happy baby gurgles while dining on tea-room cuisine like chicken pie and orange-pineapple-carrot gelatin salad and whiter-than-white angel food cake, Anna Maude is a restaurant that will make you think you've died and gone to heaven and you are sitting down with all the angels for ladies' lunch.

Meat-and-potato eaters needn't worry that Anna Maude is all nursery food. Oklahomans like to eat hearty: favorites are smothered steaks and fried chicken—both glorious. But it is the variety and excellence of the side dishes that takes one's breath away—good fresh vegetables, some regional favorites like black-eyed peas, escalloped squash, mustard greens, and buttered turnips, plus venerable cafeteria fare like creamy mashed potatoes or macaroni and cheese.

There are a dozen gelatin salads: apple celery nut, royal Ann cherry, tomato savory, tropical fruit, and a variety of aspics.

The breads and rolls are baked each morning: cornbread, plank bread, gingerbread, cheese bread, honey almond rolls, wholewheat rolls, bran muffins, cinnamon rolls, pecan rolls, orange nut muffins, apple muffins, and the best white dinner rolls.

There is never enough room on a tray for all the desserts one wants to sample. Which cake will you choose: caramel nut? . . . red devil's food? . . . sour cream chocolate? . . . orange date nut? . . . or the one cake no one must ever leave Anna Maude without sampling—the burnt-sugar chiffon? There are cookies, too, and brownies, and pies with hand-rolled crusts, filled with peeled-that-morning apples, or boysenberries, or rhubarb; plus about a dozen other pies and cakes that we were too stunned to remember to write down on our notepad.

"An unusual variety of well-prepared, appetizing-looking foods, attractively displayed" is how Duncan Hines described Anna Maude in *Adventures in Good Eating*, first published in 1936. "I believe you will like it here even if you don't love cafeterias." In Oklahoma City, it is apparent the citizens do love cafeterias. July 11th is Anna Maude Day, by order of the mayor.

Baker's Fish House

Rte. 69, seven miles north of Muskogee, Okla.
(918) 682-2367

Mon.–Sat. 11 a.m.–10 p.m., Sun. noon–9 p.m.

$10 or less

In eastern Oklahoma, when you've got a hankering for wild catfish steaks with all the fixins, there is only one place to go—Baker's Fish House. Although it moved to its current modern location only ten years ago, the old Baker's was a favorite catfish parlor in these parts for at least a couple dozen years before that. The new digs are north of Muskogee, up near the catfish-rich Arkansas River. Muskogeeans make a habit out of Baker's, and on Sunday you may have to wait for a table.

The menu is small and distinctively Oklahoman—limited to catfish and charcoal-grilled steaks. Whatever you choose, get onion rings on the side. They're the thick kind, dipped in batter and flour, made from large Bermuda onions peeled and sliced here. Each order is fried fresh, so the circles of sweet onion retain a pleasing crunch beneath their crusts.

You get three good-sized catfish steaks on a platter. They are deep-fried, with a rugged skin of breading enveloping the fish. The meat is luscious, nutty-rich; each steak is a cross-section with a few bones yet to be extracted. On the side come french fries, green salad or slaw, and oven-hot corn dodgers —small cylinders of grainy cornbread that are a dandy complement to the fish.

Fairmont Restaurant

4900 N. Harrison, Shawnee, Okla.   At I-40
(405) 275-0740

Daily 6 a.m.–10 p.m.

$3–$10

Anyone who's traveled America has seen the Fairmont menu a thousand times. It's the mass-produced laminated one, with unreal photos of happy fried eggs and bubbling oatmeal, or meat patties from Central Casting "nestled" on beds of crisp lettuce. We had come to Shawnee to eat at Van's Pig Stand, but we were too early, so we found the Fairmont, looked at the bill of fare, and resigned ourselves to a blah egg breakfast.

How wrong we were! What emerged from the Fairmont kitchen bore no resemblance to the pictures in the dull-witted menu. It was real down-home food, beginning with the morning specialty, a cinnamon roll—not even listed. But everyone in the restaurant had one, so we joined the crowd and asked the waitress for "whatever it is they're all eating." The roll came hot from the kitchen, a tender flat spiral, steamy and sweet, so affixed to its small plate by a deluge of cinnamon-sugar glaze that it was necessary to slice and pull it up bite by bite. The omelette we ordered was literally a square meal, the eggs folded around the cheese in a perfect geometrical shape, sided by little round biscuits.

When we saw the hairnetted ladies exit the kitchen for their morning coffee break, toting a parade of meringue pies they had just baked for lunch, we vowed to return once the pies had cooled.

Lunch at the Fairmont is Oklahoma favorites at their best: pan-fried chicken, dark and crusty, served with cornbread, pinto beans, and deep-fried okra; chicken-fried steak; catfish; and a large assortment of steaks ranging from a small sirloin to a giant T-bone.

Fairmont pies included peach, apricot, chocolate, raisin, coconut, and Dutch apple. Crowned with the tallest and airiest meringue, sprinkled with crunchy shreds of toasted coconut, the coconut cream pie had us swooning at first bite. The dark crumbly Dutch apple was, as pro wrestler Fred Blassie says, "the piece of resistance."

Despite its location near the Interstate, the Fairmont has a strong local feel about it. And despite its vast interior proportions that resemble the hangars in which 747s are built (it is so large that the architect fitted a shingled mansard roof *indoors*, over the counter), it is rather quaint. Note the glass case by the door as you exit; it contains an impressive collection of souvenir dolls, ash trays, bronze poodles, and ceramic shoes.

Jiggs Smoke House

Clinton, Okla.   Exit 62 off I-40
(405) 323-5641

Mon.–Sat. 10 a.m.–6 p.m.

$5 or less

Jiggs is a smokehouse and barbecue parlor with a limited menu and a lot of soul. The fading billboards announcing its presence look like they've been around since Bobby Troup wrote "Route 66" thirty-five years ago, long before this famous highway's name got changed to I-40. At the end of a dirt access road you'll find it: an antique log cabin, dark and balmy with the sweet residue of smoke.

The counter is stacked with jars of Jiggs chow-chow and tomato relish in varying degrees of hotness. In a freezer to the side are frozen calf and turkey fries (testicles) to take home for supper. A butcher case is filled with smoked turkeys, pork and beef sausage, hog jowls, and pepper ham.

If you don't have ready access to a kitchen, the best you can do with a lot of this stuff is admire how pretty the smoke-imparted reddish glaze is; but there are cold cuts and barbecue suitable for eating on the spot at Jiggs's single spool table or in your car as you bomb down the highway.

The barbecue sandwich you get here is immense, filling up a double-size hamburger bun. It is good barbecue, too—the meat a variety of juicy inside hunks and blackened shreds from the outside of the cut, topped with a sharp tomato sauce. On the side try some cheese, very dry and powerfully smoky. And don't forget that southwestern favorite, jerky—flavorful strands of deep red air-dried beef, only a bit more tender than a rawhide rope.

The ambience of Jiggs is just right for a country snack. When we stopped by, a few friendly regulars sat at the spool table sipping coffee; we perused a bulletin board covered with hundreds of calling cards and found an article from a local paper proudly noting that Jiggs has been patronized by the likes of such down-home celebrities as Pearl Bailey, Chill Wills, and Goober, from the TV show "Mayberry, RFD."

McGehee Catfish

Marietta, Okla.   Off I-35 (take Hwy. 32 one and a half miles west, then turn south; follow signs)
(405) 276-2751

Mon.–Fri. 5 p.m.–10 p.m., Sat. & Sun. 1 p.m.–10 p.m.

$10 or less

Catfish is queer. At its best, it is more savory than carp or northern pike or any other freshwater fish you can think of. Channel catfish, on the other hand, spawned in muddy river bottoms, can have a flavor reminiscent of . . . muddy river bottoms. That's why, for a taste of this southern delicacy at its sweetest, you should make a pilgrimage to McGehee Catfish.

For one thing, it's a lovely restaurant, perched high above the Red River, with a working fireplace and a handsome display of frontier implements set about for decor. The panoramic scenery outside includes a view of McGehee's catfish ponds, and therein lies the main reason we direct you here.

McGehee catfish are raised on special feed in the clearest waters. Crack apart the crusty breading on one of McGehee's catfish steaks and you will see the purest, firmest, whitest flesh. It's flavorful as only catfish can be, but not the least bit fishy.

When you buy dinner, you get all the catfish steaks you can eat. These are cross-sections of the fish (with a few bones), breaded in cornmeal and deepfried. The side dishes are the traditional accoutrements: french fries, cole slaw, and excellent hushpuppies. For dessert, have a sweet cherry tart, served hot. It is a uniquely southern meal, and a memorable one.

Sleepy Hollow

1101 NE 50th St., Oklahoma City, Okla.
(405) 424-1614

Wed.–Mon. 5:30 p.m.–11 p.m.   Reservations advised

$10–$15

If we were exiled to another country for a long spell, Sleepy Hollow might well be the restaurant we'd choose for our coming-home meal. It is meat-and-potatoes America at its finest: very 1950s, straight out of *The Saturday Evening Post,* a *nice* place, where Oklahoma City's solid citizens come for Friday supper. The chairs are comfortable, the tables broad, covered with soft white nappery. There is a romantic glow in Sleepy Hollow's low beamed-ceiling dining room, generated by subdued wall sconces—low lighting, yes, but lighting straightforward enough to let you see what's on your plate.

There is no menu, and a choice of only three entrees: steak, chicken, or shrimp. The chicken is fried—succulent, golden-crusted, an Oklahoma specialty not done better anywhere else in the state. There are two sizes of steak: the ten-ounce club and, as the waitresses call it, the "sixteen-ounce KC." We ordered the big boy. Its crust was blackened by flame, deliciously seasoned, and it willingly split open to yield a burst of rare red juicy beef. This is a steak that will make any meat eater want to stand up and pledge allegiance to the flag of the United States of America.

Ignore the shrimp. This is, after all, Oklahoma, where fried chicken and steak are practically revered, and where any shrimp you come across are necessarily aliens from at least five hundred miles away.

Before the entree comes, there is a small salad—iceberg lettuce (what else? . . . this is the U.S. of A., pal) drenched in sweet and sour dressing. Side dishes are served family-style in big bowls. No surprises here, either: mashed potatoes, peas, and little biscuits so fresh and light we imagine them coming out of the ovens continuously, all night. Seconds and thirds of everything, as you need it, are supplied as long as you wish. Waitresses tote big pitchers of iced tea. For dessert everybody gets a little dish of pineapple sherbet.

This is about as easy a meal as anyone could hope for—with one exception. And that is getting a drink. You see, Oklahoma law doesn't permit restaurants to serve liquor. But private clubs *can* serve liquor. So when you sit down and ask your waitress can you get a drink, she will point you to a door leading to a lower level of Sleepy Hollow.

We headed downstairs and found ourselves among a large group of festive folks gathered around a table set with open liquor bottles. Assuming this is where the upstairs waitress had directed us, we helped ourselves to a couple of generous drinks—and got some rather funny looks from the revelers. It then dawned on us: this was *not* the bar, but a private party.

After sheepishly retreating, we took a different turn, and located the "private club" of Sleepy Hollow. Here, when we asked the barmaid for a drink, she said she'd first have to see our business cards; this to "prove" to her that we were not members of the ABC (Alcoholic Beverage Control). Fortunately, we did have some old business cards (what happens to people who don't?), and from that point on, we drank all we wanted.

Apparently, once you've gone downstairs a couple of times for your drinks or wine, the barmaid learns to trust you, because by our third round, she came upstairs and served us, just like in a state with normal liquor laws. Somehow, all the convolutions over booze seemed mighty American, too.

Van's Pig Stand

717 E. Highland, Shawnee, Okla.
(405) 273-8704

Mon.–Sat. 11 a.m.–9 p.m., Sun. 11:30 a.m.–3 p.m.

$5 or less

"We use nothing but hickory wood in that big old pit out back," the waitress volunteered. "Don't you know, there are some who cook their pigs with gas. They don't think it matters. But I can tell you what's a gas-cooked pig with one sniff. It'll stay on your meat no matter how you try to cover it. Gas just makes everything taste like . . . well, like gas. So, what'll you folks have?"

We tried some of everything cooked in Van's genuine hickory pit: beef, pork ribs, and what the menu simply calls "pig"—pork shoulders, chopped into bite-size hunks. There are sandwiches of pig and beef (with good tangy sauce), which you can get alone or "Vanized," which means accompanied by Susie Q's (the thin curls of fried potato that are found only in the southern midwest). The ribs here are real midwestern, too—crusty, moistened with a sweet sauce. If you order a rib dinner, you'll have to choose between the excellent Susie Q's and a Vanized baked potato (here the term signifies that the spud is cut open and spread with garlic butter).

As almost anyone in Shawnee can tell you, Van's Pig Stand is the progeny of Van's father's many pig stands in Oklahoma years ago. Today, more than fifty years since it opened, Van's is a comfortable restaurant, with a well-appointed dining room, pretty iron trelliswork, and a handsome row of tall pine trees in back—scarcely a "stand" anymore.

If you like good middle-of-America barbecue, Van's will make you very happy. Everything on the menu—officially Vanized or not—is prepared with the assured skills of an experienced pitmaster.

TEXAS

Allen's Family Style Meals

1301 E. Broadway, Sweetwater, Tex.
(915) 235-2060

Lunch only Tues.–Sun.   Closed the first two weeks in Aug.

$5 or less

Here is a feast for the eyes, the soul, and, not least, the stomach. The view of Business Route 80 isn't much, but look in back at Mrs. Allen breading and frying chicken in the open kitchen. About twenty minutes after it gets dropped in the sizzling oil, it's on its way to your plate, sided by cream gravy. The tables, which are shared by strangers, are an amazing view— tons of food, set out in big help-yourself platters.

Dig into red beans, green beans, buttered squash, cabbage slaw, maca- roni salad, pea salad, corn niblets, pickled beets, rolls and butter. And if you get tired of crunching into chicken, there is a plate of brisket, too, or hope- lessly gray roast beef.

It is the chicken that has kept Mrs. Allen's on the good-eats map since she opened up the one-room restaurant in 1940. Each piece is audibly crisp with a smooth, nutty flavor, greaseless on the outside but endlessly moist once you crack through its crust.

It is impossible not to pig out. When's the next time you will find fried chicken this good? But we advise you to save a shred of appetite for dessert. There is only one dessert at Mrs. Allen's, the same every day: four-star peach cobbler. It is hunky wads of pastry wallowing in dizzyingly sweet fruit com- pote. Really uncouth stuff, but it doesn't take more than a couple of spoon- fuls to adjust to the sudden sugar shock. After it, nothing will ever taste quite as sweet again.

Angelo's

2533 White Settlement Rd., Fort Worth, Tex.
(817) 332-0357

Mon.–Sat. 11 a.m.–10 p.m.

$5 or less

The first time we visited Angelo's, the floor of the big eating hall was covered with sawdust. "It humidifies the air and tones down the noise," explained a bartender as he drew an icy oversized glass of beer from the tap. The sawdust also smelled great, especially in combination with the odor of burning hickory that emanates from Angelo's barbecue pit.

The next time we stopped in, the doleful moose head and stuffed bear still gazed at us as we walked in the front door, the barbecue was delicious as usual, and the atmosphere was as familiar and hospitable as ever; but the sawdust was gone, outlawed by city health inspectors.

Oh well, it's not for the sawdust that we loved Angelo's. Even without it, the place has a western feel you just don't get anywhere else. At lunchtime, the joint jumps with cattlemen and businessmen who come for beef sandwiches, pit-cooked ham, and crackly-skinned Polish sausage—and always big glasses of beer. It's a real treat to watch the countermen whip together sandwiches and the barkeeps draw the beers, and to listen to the raucous bustle of Fort Worth. This is cowboy country, the beginning of West Texas. Dallas—fashionable and sunbelt chic—is only a half hour's drive, but at Angelo's, at noon, it seems a thousand miles away.

Dinner is a little quieter because that's when people start eating Angelo's pork ribs, and ribs—especially ribs this succulent—encourage a more meditative ambience. You can see it happen: as diners work their way along their line of meaty bones, conversations fall off as words give way to grunts of pleasure; the whole world is reduced to a simple matter of thoroughly denuding each and every delicious bone.

Hold the wire. . . . We hear the sawdust has come back again. It doesn't really matter. Whether you get sawdust or bare floors, Angelo's is a Fort Worth experience that no fancier of cowboy cuisine can afford to miss.

Avalon Drug Company

2518 Kirby, Houston, Tex.
(713) 529-9136

Mon.–Fri. 6:30 a.m.–6 p.m., Sat. 8 a.m.–4 p.m., Sun. 8:30 a.m.–1:30 p.m.

$5 or less

When Houston food authority Tessie Fruge set out on a hunt for the perfect Texas hamburger, she divided her findings into two categories, thick and thin. At the top of the list of great thin burgers was that served up at the counter of this forty-year-old drug store. Thin but still juicy, gray through and through, flavored with the inimitable tang of a long-aged griddle, it comes on a soft lightly toasted bun, with or without cheese. You can't beat it.

The Avalon is an essential stop for all connoisseurs of drug-store cuisine. At counter or table, the air is perfumed with that magic mingled smell of pharmacy and short-order cooking, of liniments and baking waffles.

You can get plate lunches with aggressively cooked southern vegetables, breakfast omelettes, pancake-flat grilled cheese sandwiches, and fine soda-fountain treats. But it's the basic burger, served in a classic 1940s environment, that will bring us back every time.

Beans and Things

1700 Amarillo Blvd. East, Amarillo, Tex.
(806) 373-7383

Mon.–Sat. 11 a.m.–7 p.m.

$5 or less

Barbecue sauce gets people's hackles up. The argument over who makes the best turns normal folks into Hatfields and McCoys. There are those who worship at the smoky altar of Arthur Bryant in Kansas City; others who carry home quarts of sauce from Stubby's in Hot Springs with a reverence usually reserved for holy water. Let the lines be drawn and the chips get knocked off shoulders other than our own, because while aficionados battle it out over big-name barbecues, Jane and Michael Stern will be happily setting up their shrine at a place that no out-of-towners know about, a place we guarantee has the best barbecue sauce in America.

The name is Beans and Things, and it was purely by accident that we discovered it one spring day as we hightailed through Amarillo, heading east, looking for one last taste of southwestern barbecue. We stopped at a small shingled building with a plaster cow staring grouchily down at us from the roof.

Our hopes weren't high when we entered; but then the olfactory radar started buzzing from the scent of hickory-smoked Texas beef—just what we were after. We ordered a plate to go, and encouraged by a hand-lettered sign announcing 2-ALARM CHILI TODAY, put in for a bowl of red on the side. The rest of the menu was a short one, featuring pork ribs and cowboy favorites such as cornbread and beans or beef stew.

While the waitress gathered our order, we watched owner and pitmaster Wiley Alexander chat with a buddy who looked for sure like a fellow ex-Marine. There's no mistaking Mr. Alexander's allegiance to the Corps: the walls of Beans and Things are plastered with mementos of his leatherneck days—insignias, photos, even a handsome picture of Duke Wayne from *Sands of Iwo Jima*. There's also a rugged display of various types of barbed wire. The message is clear: this is a man's barbecue joint. Why, even the salad bar in the middle of the room lacks any frilly leafy stuff. It's mostly jalapeno peppers, strong pickles, and hot sauces.

We ate in the car, heading east. The chopped brisket had been cut into large one-inch pieces. The meat was soft and rich, nearly buttery-tasting, each piece trimmed with an edge of dark crust. On the side was fresh cole slaw, some equally nice potato salad, and rather plebeian beans. But it was the sauce that covered the meat that moved us to new heights of barbecue adoration. It was deep red, grainy, full of pepper and spice; the kind of sauce that is delicious on first taste, but with an intensity that grows for an hour afterwards; the kind of sauce that feels like it is glowing in your mouth with an afterplay of taste that allows you to continue savoring the flavor, long after it is past. It will remind the connoisseur of Arthur Bryant, except it is undeniably better, smoother, sexier: like twenty-year-old whiskey compared to twelve.

Confronted by a sauce of such dimension, we felt our veneer of civilized behavior begin to crumble. Unsteadily, we pulled the car off the road and tried to write notes as we ate, but the writing pad turned into a soggy napkin and our pen was only able to scribble out such pathetic expletives as "yum yum" and four feeble-looking stars. Like Ray Milland in *The Lost Weekend*, we were reduced to turning the extra container of sauce Wiley Alexander had provided upside down, licking out the last few remaining drops.

It would be anticlimactic to launch into raves over the excellence of the chili made at Beans and Things. Leave it to say that it is authentic southwestern stuff, spiked well with cumin and small cubes of beef. Similarly, the pork ribs were great, but we could have been given xylophone keys slathered with the wondrous sauce and been happy. It isn't often one finds a diamond in the rough; but when it happens, it is cause for celebration. Long live Wiley Alexander! Long live his sauce!

Bishop Grill

308 N. Bishop Ave., Dallas, Tex.
(214) 946-1752

Mon.–Fri. lunch

$5 or less

"Being from New York, y'all probably won't know what I mean when I say there are places in this town that are dumps, but serve great food," explained Gus Hudson, the man who runs the Bishop Grill. We do know what he means, and we don't think he would be the least bit insulted if we included his little lunchroom in that category.

Gus's grandmother Gennie started the Grill, then his mother Rose Marie took over, and now Gus does all the menu planning and the cooking, and he has kept it as down-home as they come.

For decor you will find little more than a slew of business cards tacked on the wall, and a few write-ups of Gennie's by newspaper people as happy about their discovery as we were. Oh, yes, there's a picture of the Dallas Cowboys, too—which Gus hoped didn't offend our eastern sensibilities.

Forget the decor, or lack of it, and line up at the steam counter for what the Bishop Grill does best: chicken-fried steak. Always on the menu, it is a broad, hearty affair, nicely matched to the mountainous mashed potatoes just down the line. You can also pile the plate with vegetables like acorn squash, cauliflower, baked spinach, turnip greens, and the Texas favorite, pinto beans; take a couple of those hot rolls, too.

Gus barbecues chicken and makes pepper steaks, liver, and some other entrees, but if you are going to eat here once, take the chicken-fried steak. It is exemplary, and with the spuds and good vegetables, it makes for a hearty, warming plate of food—a taste of both the southern and western character of Dallas.

For dessert, do not miss the oozingly rich peanut butter pie or balmy nanner pudding.

There are only eleven tables at the Grill, so you should expect a wait, and you should expect to dine elbow-to-elbow with a raft of hungry Texans nearly as formidable as the Cowboys on the wall.

The Blessing Hotel Coffee Shop

Ranch Rd. 616, at the caution light, Blessing, Tex.   Southwest of Houston
via U.S. 59 & 71
(512) 588-6623

Daily 6 a.m.–2 p.m.

$5 or less

"It's just like Christmas and Thanksgiving!" one enthusiastic eater declared as she rose from her table at The Blessing Hotel to fetch second helpings of turkey and dressing and sweet potatoes and creamed corn and squash and black-eyed peas and hot dinner rolls.

It is a two-hour drive from Houston to Blessing, but look around the dining room on any Sunday, and you will see pilgrims who have come from the city for one of Texas's best family-style meals—a bounty of pure country cooking.

The Coffee Shop is located in what was once The Blessing Hotel ballroom. Only a few years ago, customers were encouraged to simply walk into the kitchen and help themselves to whatever was cooking in the cast-iron pots on the stove. The health inspector decided that wouldn't do, so a couple of wood-stoves have been set up in the dining room, and now you serve yourself from these toasty mantels. It's still a lot of fun, but not as personal as getting advice about what's good straight from the cook in her own kitchen.

The Coffee Shop menu is different for each day of the week, although you can always count on there being homemade rolls and cornbread, a variety of vegetables including turnip or mustard greens, and cake for dessert: tall, classic layer cake—chocolate, yellow, or white. Sunday is the big meal of the week, featuring turkey and ham. The rest of the week's offerings include roast beef, chicken-fried steak, fried chicken, and something called roast hash—a delicious scramble made from the previous day's roast, potatoes, and onions.

"Whenever I serve chicken," chef Helen Feldhousen told us, "I have to have something else on the menu, too, for my regulars who won't eat it. A lot of them are cattle men, and they insist on meat. And you know I have to serve rice every day. There's a lot of rice farmers who come in. On Saturday I make rice pudding. They love that."

At breakfast, you will see these local men gathered over Mrs. Feldhousen's hot cinnamon rolls and coffee, gossiping or talking shop about feed prices and the weather.

The Blessing Hotel was built in 1907 from native cypress wood. It fell into some disrepair over the years, but was recently refurbished, and is now maintained by the Blessing Historical Foundation. The dining room still has its old hardwood floor and red-and-white checked tablecloths. The rooms upstairs have been tidied up, and for $15 ($17.50 with private bath), you can stay the night.

Capt'n Benny's Half Shell

7409 S. Main, Houston, Tex.
(713) 795-9051

Mon.–Sat. 11 a.m.–11 p.m.

About $5

There is only one problem at Capt'n Benny's: you can't get in. At any normal lunch or dinner hour, the half dozen stools are occupied, as is every cubic yard of space in the minuscule restaurant. However, if you don't mind elbowing your way through throngs toward the counter, or if you come between, say, two and four o'clock in the afternoon, you will be rewarded with Houston's best seafood—in the rough, in the very, very rough.

Benny's is actually ship-shaped, a jaunty trawler painted red, white, and green, that somehow ran aground in a neighborhood where its harbormates include some of the city's more "colorful" bars and peep shows. Inside, there's hardly any room for decor; if there is any, we haven't seen it, being too busy trying to zero in on a plate of oysters on the half-shell or an order of boiled shrimp.

This is Gulf seafood at its freshest. The oysters, taken from beds in Matagorda Bay south of Houston, are formidable creatures, plump and briny, yet with delicious frail bodies. The shrimp are simply boiled, served cold, snapping fresh.

You can also get fried seafood at Capt'n Benny's, and it is quite good, the impeccable oysters and shrimp never overwhelmed by their breading. There is gumbo on the menu, and fried catfish that *Texas* magazine once described as the best in town, and that's all. No salads and side dishes, no mixed drinks (only beer or soda), no decor, no seats, no service—just good food.

(Three other Capt'n Benny's have opened in Houston, on Katy Freeway, Wilcrest, and FM 1960 West.)

Cattleman's Steak House

*Indian Cliffs Ranch, Fabens, Tex.   Twenty miles east of El Paso
(take Fabens Exit off I-10 and head north four miles)
(915) 764-2283*

Tues.–Sat. 5 p.m.–10 p.m., Sun. noon–9 p.m.   Reservations advised

$10–$20

Our search for the perfect Texas steak house reached its happy ending here: a great piece of mesquite-charred beef served in what has to be the ultimate Lone Star setting.

Cattleman's is more than just a restaurant. It is part of the Indian Cliffs Ranch, which besides feeding steak-hungry people, rents horses for trail rides, arranges picnics and hayrides, and provides all manner of genuine western fun. It is at the end of a long road that cuts across the desert east of El Paso—a completely unspoiled place; just acre upon acre of saguaro cacti, blowing tumbleweeds, and scooting roadrunners. The ranch is a handsome adobe fort atop a small mesa, and from the windows of its restaurant you look out over the stables, and beyond them, the Texas wilderness.

Inside, there is wood paneling and wagon-wheel lighting fixtures—the kind of decor that would look hokey anywhere else; but at Cattleman's . . . well, it's just about perfect.

We suggest you rent a horse, take a long ride to work up a fierce appetite, then order the top-of-the-line $17.85 T-bone, cooked over mesquite in the traditional West Texas manner, splashed with sweet vermouth to offset the bite from the fire. This glorious steak has not been tenderized. Not that it's tough, not at all, just that here is a hunk of steak for meat eaters who know that texture is every bit as important as taste; in fact, the texture makes the taste: it's in the chewing that the pleasure of a good Texas steak is savored.

Along with the steak come cole slaw and beans in cast-iron pots; also corn or rice. There are smaller cuts of meat, too, but we noticed that several couples ordered the two-pounder between them and paid $3 for an extra plate with the fixins. Somehow it doesn't seem right to come to Cattleman's and order a small steak. The spacious dining room, the vast landscape outside, and the general feeling of expansive goodwill about this place all make you want to do things in a big way.

The Chili Bowl

220 Fredericksburg Rd., San Antonio, Tex.
(512) 732-0406

Mon.–Fri. 7 a.m.–5 p.m., Sat. 8 a.m.–4 p.m.

$5 or less

One order of chili is, as chef Lupe Fischer calls it, "a bowl full of meat." Nothing else. No beans. No soup. It is not a large bowl, but it contains over a half-pound of coarsely ground beef that has been simmered in a pot of ferocious cumin-dominated spice until it is heavy with the savory chili juices. "There are some, from up your way, who say it's too hot," Lupe told us. "They add ketchup to the chili! But my regular customers, they like to add this sauce I make." She showed us a jalapeno pepper sauce that, honest to God, sizzled when we touched it to our tongues.

A dash of the hot sauce does liven up this meaty food, but even without the jalapenos, it has a strong ting, the kind of earthy pepper bite that no chili outside the southwest can match. It is served with your choice of saltines or white bread—both excellent salves if you take too much of the hot sauce.

It is also possible, if you want to cut the intensity of your "bowl full of meat," to get chili with beans, a half-and-half mixture, both cooked separately. The rest of the menu is short and spicy: homemade enchiladas, burgers topped with chili meat, and, in cooler months, superior hand-rolled tamales—warm tubes of peppery coarse cornmeal.

This small cafe has been known as San Antonio's premier chili parlor for more than forty years, and although the original owner, Louis Kuykendall, sold it to Lupe Fischer five years ago (after which the name changed from Kuykendall's to The Chili Bowl), the chili recipe used today is the original. With its stunning opaque hue and a sexy aroma that must, in all candor, be compared to a good honest sweat, this is one of the few authentic and great restaurant chilies still to be had in Texas.

City Market

633 Davis, Luling, Tex.
(512) 875-9019

Mon.–Sat. 7 a.m.–6 p.m.

$5 or less

Texas's great barbecue parlors began as adjuncts to the butcher's counter in grocery stores—economical outlets for unsold cuts of meat. Almost every

Texas town used to have one. Now there are only a handful of market/barbecue emporia left. In Luling, home of the Watermelon Thump, an annual festival in honor of same, you will find the City Market, the best of the last grocery store/barbecues, a delicious taste of Texas in a classic setting that hasn't changed in twenty years.

The market is a vast space, brightly lit, with a row of knotty pine booths hugging each wall. Up front at the cash register is a counter where necessary provisions are dispensed: soda, beans, potato salad, and utility towel napkins.

Everything about the market looked right when we entered, except for one thing. Where was the barbecue pit? A woman leaned against the cash register talking to a farmer about the cost of fertilizer. "Looking for something?" she asked, noticing our confusion.

"The pit," we stammered. She smiled and pointed to a door at the back of the eating hall. Through the door was a room-within-a-room, an inner sanctum. Here the air was dark, so smoky we imagined it turning even the toughest food critic into a tender butt. Our eyes teared as the pitmaster speared a hunk of brisket and carved us half a pound. Each piece was a perfect cross-section with a thin ribbon of fat dividing the lean lower meat from the fattier top. Each was rimmed with a crunchy black crust, keen with the taste of smoke. The hot links we got on the side burst open at the touch of a knife; they too were perfumed by the pit. There is a good sweet mustard sauce dotted with peppers, but neither the links or brisket require it.

All this is served in the traditional way—on red butcher's paper, which the server bunches up around the meat so it's easy to carry to a table. It was 8 a.m. when we toted our hot links and pound of brisket to a booth, but others had preceded us. Four Mexicans were feasting happily on pork ribs and links at one table. At another table, a lone Texas cowboy sat pensively over five Coors and three pounds of beef.

Collin Street Bakery

W. 7th Ave. & S. 14th St., Corsicana, Tex.
(214) 872-3951

Mon.–Fri. 9:30 a.m.–5:30 p.m.

Under $5

Corsicana, Texas, is the heart of the pecan belt; it is also the home of the Deluxe Fruitcake, the world's most popular Christmas gift, a fruitcake so famous that the bakery has been declared an Official Landmark by the Texas Historical Commission.

Founded in 1896, the Collin Street Bakery has grown from a little place into a factory large enough to keep a long list of mail-order customers happy —customers that include (the bakery brag sheet notes) Mr. and Mrs. Zubin Mehta, Laverne and Shirley, and the Sincere Company of Hong Kong.

But what about the hungry traveler who stumbles into the sun-streaked town of Corsicana looking for a pecan goodie? Do you have to buy a post office box and wait longingly until the celebrity roster has been serviced? No indeed! In fact, the Collin Street Bakery runs a cute little shop on the premises where you can purchase not only the Deluxe Fruitcake, but an assortment of other pecan delicacies that Laverne and Shirley and Zubin Mehta don't even know exist!

In the lobby, where a Bunn-O-Matic dispenses coffee at a dime a cup, there is one small table with two chairs. Here you can sit and sample delicious pecan rolls, pecan strudel, pecan coffee cake, and pecan danishes, not to mention the wonderful (though pecanless) apple fritters—dark, knobby sweet rolls glazed with sugar and packed with little slivers of apple. There are also German chocolate cakes with enough chopped pecans on top to satisfy the most nut-hungry traveler.

The item that made us happiest was the pecan brittle. Like peanut brittle, this confection consists of little more than molten brown sugar and butter washed, lavalike, over a bounty of nuts. Collin Street Bakery's pecan brittle is the most awesomely rich we have tasted, due in large part to the meatiness of the fresh pecans. After one taste we bought three more boxes and threw them in the trunk of the car to use as gifts for friends and relatives we would be seeing in California. By the time we reached the coast, there wasn't a scrap of brittle left.

Commercial Restaurant

Glassok and Plum Sts., Sonora, Tex.
(915) 387-9928

Tues.–Sat. 11 a.m.–2:30 p.m. & 5 p.m.–9 p.m.

About $5

West Texas is not a culinary bonanza for the traveler. It is a long way between little towns on I-10, and most of the food is bad. Bad chicken-fried steaks, bad tacos, bad beef jerky. That is why we treasure the Commercial Restaurant.

"One hundred percent Tex-Mex," is how the Commercial's owner, Lemuel Lopez, described his kitchen. "We do it all from scratch. Look here." He took us to a cauldron on a stove. There boiled a vivid red and green portion of chilies, tomatoes, onions, and spices destined to become the Commercial's *salsa ranchera*, the hot sauce used as a dip for tortilla chips and to flavor main courses like the enchiladas.

The Commercial is an unpretentious cafe in the Mexican part of town. It's clean and air-conditioned with plain booths and tables and minimal decor. It has been *the* Mexican restaurant in Sonora since 1921.

The best way to begin a meal here is with supernachos, a characteristically inventive Tex-Mex fancy that piles refried beans, grated cheese, avocado, hot sauce, and jalapeño pepper atop tortilla chips. On the lighter side, the guacamole dip is a refreshing verdant green. For a main course, the *chili rellenos*—big deep-fried peppers stuffed with cheese—are outstanding. In a place like this where everything is made from scratch, it's not a bad idea to spring for the Commercial "Special Dinner," which provides you a sample of just about everything, including the *chili rellenos*, a taco, an enchilada, refried beans, Mexican rice, etc.

The food at the Commercial Restaurant is hot, although not as fiery or as complex as the cooking farther west in the neighboring state of New Mexico. It is simply good Texas-style home cooking. There are no gastronomic surprises, but in this barren part of the southwest, it's surprise enough to find a place that bothers to do so good a job preparing Tex-Mex cuisine.

The Confederate House

4007 Westheimer, Houston, Tex.
(713) 622-1936

Daily 11:30 a.m.–2:30 p.m. & 6 p.m.–10 p.m.   Reservations advised, dress for dinner

About $20

While Dallas is definitely the west, Houston is a city with strong ties to the south; and if there is one restaurant that epitomizes Houston cuisine, it is The Confederate House. It began life as a private club some thirty-five years ago during a "dry" period in the city's history. Wealthy Houstonians came for drinks while they dined, but the food was so good that even when local prohibition was lifted, The Confederate House remained as popular as ever.

While no longer a private club, it is still quiet, decorous, genteel. From crystal chandeliers to portraits of Jefferson Davis and Robert E. Lee on tasteful dark blue walls, this is definitely "Old South." So are the serving staff, a troop of faithful waiters whose expertise and measured charm have not diminished over the years.

The kitchen is a bastion of regional cooking. Not a trace of nouvelle nonsense here: local red snapper broiled to a turn, fried oysters from the Texas Gulf just a few miles away, Gulf shrimp—fried or hickory-smoked and deliciously salted, prime ribs, lamb chops, a brace of quail, and, of course, grilled steaks. Side dishes are faultless: the freshest vegetables, cheesy au gratin potatoes, baked-here rolls—and tall, cooling southern drinks, too.

We were disappointed the last time we ate Confederate dessert: fudge pie like cookie dough, and the once-classic chess pie was wan.

At lunch, the menu is a downscale version of dinner, but with the happy addition of a fresh fruit salad bathed in poppy-seed dressing—a sweet combination that adds just the right touch of southern sugar to the restaurant's charms.

The Confederate House is frequented by regulars who started eating here long ago. But do not fret if you are a first-timer; southern hospitality will insure you don't feel like a stranger for long.

Cypress Creek Inn

Just off Route 10, Comfort, Tex.
(512) 995-3977

Tues.–Sat. 11:30 a.m.–2:30 p.m., 5:30 p.m.–8:30 p.m., Sun. 11:30 a.m.–
2:30 p.m.   Closed first week in Aug.

$5 or less

When colonists settled near the spring-fed Guadalupe River in the 1850s, they thought the land so beautiful they called it "The Hills of God." It soon became known as Camp Comfort, a place of pure water and lush greenery. People still come here to fish, camp, and hunt . . . and to eat at the Cypress Creek Inn, a homey restaurant that's been around for more than thirty years.

The Cypress Creek Inn serves what is best described as Texas country cooking. On Sunday that will be baked ham with raisin sauce, roast beef, or a grilled T-bone. During the week, it's liver and onions, smoked German sausage, or barbecued chicken.

Our favorite is the chicken-fried steak, on the menu Tuesday through Saturday. A tender cutlet is dipped in egg and milk and bread crumbs, then fried crisp and served with cream gravy spiked with pan drippings. At the Cypress Creek Inn, there are always plenty of vegetables—we especially adore the mashed potatoes, speckled with bits of skin and running with little rivers of butter; and the very special creamed cabbage that has been Mrs. Charlotte Holmes' specialty for years. Hot rolls accompany dinner. And for dessert, Mrs. Holmes bakes apple pie and a good Boston cream.

The Cypress Creek Inn has always been the simplest of eateries. "We're not elegant," Mrs. Holmes said, "but I like to think it's neat. You know, you can't eat atmosphere." Such as it is, atmosphere consists of little more than a few old pictures and newspapers on the wall . . . and the aroma of good cooking that wafts from the kitchen.

Hammond's Bar-B-Q

On the Coyote Strip, nine miles west of Glen Rose, Tex.   Off Rte. 67
(817) 897-2324

Fri. 5 p.m.–9 p.m., Sat. 11 a.m.–9 p.m., Sun. 11 a.m.–8 p.m.
Closed last week in Dec. until April

$10 or less

Hammond's Bar-B-Q is located at the end of a long winding road that is so intensely Texan that you have to blink your eyes and shake your head periodically to remind yourself that what you are seeing isn't being brought to you in VistaVision. Past acres of grazing cattle and beautiful farmlands, you finally reach Hammond's: a red tin building surrounded by western-style fences hung with bleached cattle skulls and well-worn saddles.

Follow the trail of old bones (now white with age from basking in the sun) that have been tossed casually about the yard by people who savored them when they were Hammond's barbecued ribs.

Inside, there are long calico-oilcloth-covered tables and benches; there is sawdust on the floor; and the walls are covered with the scribbled musings of the people who make a regular habit of eating Hammond's barbecue.

From all over Texas they come to savor the ribs or beef brisket. The latter is our favorite, cooked slowly over hickory coals—tender, with a smoky piquance, perfect without a drop of sauce. It comes chopped or sliced, on a sandwich or a plate, with or without pinto beans on the side. We like it with the beans, which are a good moist balance to the meat, making a complete meal that is the apotheosis of chuck-wagon chow. If the weather is nice, you can take your plate of food outside to one of the picnic tables set around the property. Listen to the distant mooing of the shorthorn cattle as you eat, and we guarantee you will leave here speaking with a Texas accent.

Oh, yes, one final reminder. Enjoy the barbecue, and enjoy the scenery, but make sure you save room for a slice of Mrs. Hammond's peanut butter pie. It's a tawny wedge of velvet that perfectly tamps down the barbecue you just ate, and sets you up perfectly for that long trek back down the Coyote Strip.

(A second Hammond's, in Glen Rose, is open Wednesday through Sunday, year-round.)

Herman Sons Steak House

Hwy. 90, one mile east of Hondo, Tex.
(512) 426-2220

Tues.–Sun. 11 a.m.–9 p.m.

$10 or less

Herman Sons is famous around these parts for a cheeseburger steak layered with jalapeño peppers, served in degrees ranging from mild to hot. Cheeseburgers aren't talked about much in this, the land of T-bones, so you know that for Herman Sons to make a reputation on them, they've got to be something special. We ordered ours hot, and at first bite were disappointed: good burger, good taste, but no jalapeno kick. We nibbled more, and four or five bites later we were reaching for the beer, the ice water, anything to tamp down the fire blazing on the backs of our tongues. Sneaky devil this steak, but mighty good, served with jumbo Texas steak fries.

As in any good steak house, it is possible to get a T-bone or ribeye. They are real Lone Star cuts, tender but with still plenty of chew to work the flavor from the beef. Order a guacamole appetizer to start. It's a real eye-catcher, served with bright red tortilla chips. We don't know how Herman Sons gets them the color of a distress flag, but they certainly do look festive against the soothing guacamole green.

Hondo, Texas, is a small town surrounded by lots of giant ranch spreads. Herman Sons fits right in. It's a wide-open restaurant with well-worn hardwood floors and plenty of elbow room between tables. It's friendly, too. When we asked the good-looking cowboy type who runs the place about another nearby restaurant whose name we couldn't recall, he fussed and fretted and finally handed us what has to be the skinniest Yellow Pages in the United States. We were then taken under the wing of several other diners, who wouldn't let us leave until they devised a scenic tour that would show off their home state to its best advantage. And that, folks, is another reason we love Texas.

Highland Park Cafeteria

4611 Cole St., Dallas, Tex.   At Knox
(214) 526-3801

Mon.–Sat. 11 a.m.–8 p.m.

About $5

It is said there are residents of the exclusive Highland Park part of Dallas who have had lunch at the Highland Park Cafeteria every weekday for the last ten years. When we visited friends who lived in a less ritzy part of town, the HPC was where they took us. Never mind the museum or the zoo or the Cotton Bowl; put Sonny Bryan's barbecue on hold. The first thing we had to do was lunch at the Highland Park Cafeteria.

Local millionaires and famous Texans like Van Cliburn and Stanley Marcus arrive in limousines. Other less glamorous types come in battered pickup trucks. Once the ladies behind the steam tables get to know you, they'll have a platter of your favorite food waiting when you move down the line, or they'll tell you what's especially good.

It isn't necessary to be a regular customer to adore the Highland Park Cafeteria. All that's required is that you be . . . FULLY ATTIRED AND APPROPRIATELY DRESSED FOR A FAMILY DINING ROOM. Once you've passed that sign at the door, you have entered the queen of American cafeterias, a Valhalla of victuals.

The most striking thing about the HPC, before you spy the line of food, is the subdued tone of the place. It's big and crowded, and everyone from the Hunt brothers to cowboy-booted workmen has to wait in line, but it's quiet in here; everybody's on his best behavior. Pictures of American Presidents decorate the serving line. Oriental rugs hang on the wall. Royal Doulton china is displayed in cupboards. Propriety reigns.

Like the decorous appointments, the food bespeaks concern for quality. No shortcuts are taken in the kitchen; fresh ingredients and a repertoire of tried-and-true house recipes prevail. It isn't easy to know exactly what to recommend, since there are always three dozen different kinds of salad at the head of the line, ten or fifteen entrees, a couple dozen vegetables, and a large bakery's worth of pies and cakes at the end of the line. The cuisine is Texan with a strong southern accent: lots of good cream gravies, plenty of greens flavored with ham drippings.

Some of the best dishes we have eaten here are classic regional specialties: fried chicken, chicken and dumplings, smothered steak, and a celestial buttermilk pie. Much of the food is what you'd call standard cafeteria fare, —like the HPC's macaroni and cheese, the Platonic ideal to which Kraft Dinner and all other lower forms of macaroni aspire—but there is no cafeteria that does it better. Other offerings are more inventive: like the creamy baked eggplant casserole; zucchini muffins; and "millionaire pie," a specialty of the house that blends chunks of pineapple with whipped cream and nuts.

A meal at the Highland Park Cafeteria is a reassuring retreat to a world that preexisted both fast food and food fads.

Inman's Kitchen

300 E. Young, Llano, Tex.
(915) 247-5257

Daily 7 a.m.–8 p.m.   Closed Sun. Jan.–Oct.

$5 or less

Smoked sausage and smoked turkey are favorite foods in the Texas hill country, and few make them better than Inman's Kitchen. It is also the self-proclaimed Home of the Turkey Sausage, a German-style wurst stuffed in a hog casing and slow-smoked over post oak wood.

Turkey sausage is a wonderful invention; the turkey meat is leaner than pork, and its taste gentle enough to showcase the subtle variety of flavors imparted by the smoking process. For those who crave more zip in their sausage, there is a variation made with bits of jalapeno pepper and laced with Swiss cheese.

A lot of Inman's business is take-out, but it's fun to eat here. The "Kitchen" is actually an old house, set with checked-cloth tables and tractor seats instead of chairs. The menu is branded onto boards hung on the wall, and there is a woodstove in the dining room where pinto beans and tangy barbecue sauce are set out for diners to help themselves. Dinners of sausage, turkey, ham, or beef brisket come with slaw, pickles, onions, and thick slices of made-here white or wheat bread.

For dessert, choose pecan pie made from Texas pecans; or peach pie from Texas peaches. Either is a definitive denouement.

Joe T. Garcia's Mexican Dishes

2201 N. Commerce, Fort Worth, Tex.

Lunch Mon.–Sat. 11 a.m.–2 p.m., dinner Mon.–Sat. 5 p.m.–10:30 p.m., Sun. 2 p.m.–10 p.m.

$10 or less

In a ragtag neighborhood on the north side of Fort Worth, where the stock-yards once perfumed all of cowtown, there is a white house, trimmed in green, that looks like it is about to cave in. The house has been expanded relentlessly—big party rooms in back, patio and pool outdoors. This is Joe T. Garcia's, the southwest's most celebrated Mexican restaurant. Although its fame has spread since it opened in 1935 as Joe's Barbecue and Mexican Dishes, the formula for success has remained simple: plenty of old-fashioned Tex-Mex chow.

"Dinners?" asks the waiter as soon as you get your beer or frozen margaritas. If you say yes, he is gone, and the food starts arriving right away. First—crisp tortilla chips, with red salsa. Then a plate of *quesidillas*—small tortillas topped with melted cheese and diced jalapeño peppers, hot enough to snap your taste buds to attention.

Now comes dinner, dished out family style. Bubbling enchiladas, trailing yellow strings of molten cheese, are slid off the platter onto each person's plate. Help yourself to gruesomely purple refried beans that happen to be the most luscious, porky beans we have ever tasted; spoon out some seasoned rice; grab a couple tacos from the serving tray; dip into *real* guacamole, thick with avocado chunks and bits of garlic; and soothe your tastebuds with steamy soft corn tortillas, spread with butter. If you want to put a sweet point on the meal, grab a couple of cinnamon-sugar dusted *bunuelos* (deep-fried bread discs) by the cash register on your way out.

It is also possible to order a la carte dishes such as *chili rellenos, fajitas,* and *flautas;* but what we like about Joe T's is the happy mindlessness of getting just plain *dinner*—the usual—no menu to worry about, no questions asked.

The food comes fast. Everybody eats fast and drinks plenty. If you are sitting in the front room of the original house, there is a great neighborhood feel about the place, despite the press of crowds waiting to get in. In back, the atmosphere is more like a Mexican mess hall. But it doesn't matter. Wherever you eat, the food is tasty and the experience impeccably authentic.

Kincaid's

4901 Camp Bowie, Fort Worth, Tex.
(817) 732-2881

Mon.–Sat. 10 a.m.–6 p.m.

$5 or less

A half pound of beef, grilled to perfection, just the way you want it, crusty and well-seasoned, lean yet juicy, sandwiched between thick halves of a big warm bun, dripping onions and tomato and lettuce, and all the condiments you dare: this is why Kincaid's sells at least a thousand burgers every day.

Kincaid's is a grocery store, where the burgers are served forth from grills lined up behind the meat counter. It is possible to get a very nice plate lunch of other items, too, such as steam-table meat loaf or catfish, with southern-style vegetables and yummy banana pudding to go along with them. There are no chairs or tables, so you find a place along one of the long shelves (formerly doors) that top the low-slung racks of groceries. Dangling from above are plastic yellow happy faces, humanoid hot dogs, and similar amusing critters, and the shelves are scattered with year-old magazines to read. Ideal ambience for scarfing down what may be the best burger in the west.

Kreuz Market

208 S. Commerce, Lockhart, Tex.
(512) 398-2361

Mon.–Fri. 7 a.m.–6 p.m., Sat. 7 a.m.–6:30 p.m.

$5 or less

Fanciers of Texas barbecue, when debating the relative excellence of favorite places, play with what some might consider inverted rules. The plainer the place, the better it is. If there are amenities like tablecloths and plates, forget it. If utensils are more elaborate than a single knife chained to a post and shared by everyone, it's too soigné for the real connoisseur. If there is anything on the menu other than beef, it's not the real thing. As Texan Max Apple wrote, "In the Texas pits, barbecue is not on the menu: it *is* the menu."

The Kreuz Market will satisfy the purest of purists. Here, they don't cotton to fancy stuff. After eighty years in the business of smoking beef, they figure they've got it just about right, which is why they don't even bother making any sauce or side dishes. When you walk past the market to the U-shaped pit in back and order a pound, you get sliced beef on red butcher's paper. The server gathers the paper around the beef and you carry it to a table. There's a bar for buying a whole onion, a whole avocado, a whole jalapeno pepper, or a whole tomato. To cut any of these things into dainty slices is definitely not the Kreuz style. You eat them, quite simply, by taking a chaw between bites of barbecue.

Grab the chained knife and slice into the meat: here is the crème de la cow, the quiddity of Q—lean shoulder cuts that have been enveloped in the smoke of oak wood until beef turns ambrosial. The outsides are charred and chewy; the center of each slice mild, only faintly imprinted with smoke.

In the old part of the Kreuz Market, where the pit is, the walls themselves have been smoked to the color of a hot link sausage. This is the part with the wood benches and chained knife—an inspiring place to enjoy Texas tradition.

To the side there is a new dining room, no doubt horrifying to the faithful purists. It is air-conditioned, and the tables are Formica-topped, and the knives on long chains have given way to plastic. Even here, though, the menu —or lack of menu—is exactly the same as it has been since Kreuz started barbecuing in 1900.

Los Arcos Cafe

502 S. Zarzamora, San Antonio, Tex.   At Durango
(512) 432-9035

Sun., Wed., & Thurs. 6:15 a.m.–midnight, Fri. to 2 a.m., Sat. to 3 a.m.

$5 or less

In its original Mexican form, we are told that Sonoran *menudo* is a spicy dish, peppered with green chilies and mint. Texan *menudo*, exemplary bowls of which are served at Los Arcos Cafe, is a peaceful stew of tripe and hominy, one of the most comforting foods you can eat.

Menudo is not ordinarily listed on the Los Arcos menu, simply because everyone who eats here knows it is always available. It is the most popular dish in the house—especially late at night, for its supposedly curative powers after too much partying. Simply inhaling the earthy aroma atop a steaming bowl works miracles. If chicken soup is "Jewish penicillin," this is the Tex-Mex equivalent.

At lunch, Los Arcos features *caldo de rez,* a hearty beef soup chocked with firm vegetables; and there are always a couple of unusual Tex-Mex specialties: tongue, for instance, breaded and fried, served in a piquant "Spanish sauce"; or *cabrito asado* (barbecued kid); or calf's head enchiladas.

Los Arcos Cafe is one of the best places we know to sample genuine Tex-Mex cuisine, to which San Antonio is the eastern gateway. In addition to *menudo* and the exotic lunch specials, all the familiar Texican dishes are on the menu, including tacos, enchiladas, chili, *carne guisada* (beef stew), guacamole, rice, and beans; and all that we have sampled are excellent, made from good ingredients, with corn and flour tortillas rolled on the premises.

Louie Mueller

206 W. 2nd St., Taylor, Tex.
(512) 352-6206

Mon.–Sat. 7 a.m.–6:30 p.m.

$5 or less

If you want to know why Texans make such a fuss over barbecue, go to Taylor, Texas, for the answer. A quick foray through the phone book yields more barbecue pits and smokehouses in this sleepy hamlet of ten thousand than there are fast-food franchises in Orlando. Here in Taylor, around the corner from the town square, is a place called Louie Mueller, the quintessential Texas barbecue parlor.

Built as a gymnasium in 1906, Louie Mueller is still one voluminous room with the original wood floor, its green plaster walls darkened to the color of mahogany by twenty-three years of barbecue smoke. The stamped tin ceiling has been smoked dark, too, and although there is a skylight above, the room is dim, quiet—cathedral-like. It is divided into two areas by a counter. In the front of the room are square wooden tables and chairs and a small service counter with help-yourself tea and coffee. Behind the counter is the sanctum sanctorum—the pit—where the briskets sit beneath a metal cover on a grate over burning post oak, hickory, and blackjack wood, a low fire vigilantly maintained by Louie Mueller's pitmaster Fred Fountaine.

Beginning before dawn, and continuously throughout the day, Mr. Fountaine tugs a pulleyed rope to raise the metal lid so he can inspect and adjust the fire underneath his briskets. When he's happy with the mixture of wood —just enough green so it smoulders and doesn't burn too hot, he turns his attention to the barbecue sauce—a simple translucent brew of bouillon, onions, and spices.

You order barbecue by the pound. A brisket is forked out of the pit and several thick slices are lopped off and laid on a sheet of butcher's wrapping paper on a cafeteria tray. You can get potato salad or cole slaw or a slice of white bread to go with it, but none of that matters because the meat on the tray you take to a table needs nothing more than the spacious hush of the barbecue parlor to carry you to a smoky epiphany.

This is elemental food—the perfect melding of beef and fire and smoke. Each slice is unbelievably tender, the cross-sections halved by a glistening ribbon of fat. Below that line, the beef is lean and dense; above it, more voluptuous, striated and juicy. All around the edge runs a thick blackened crust, musky with the taste of smouldering wood. There is no better Texas barbecue.

Another regional specialty we'd recommend at Louie Mueller—the traditional handmaiden to barbecued brisket—is the hot link sausages. They're made three times a week by Bobby Mueller, Louie's son. In the summer he uses what he calls "bull meat and brisket"; in the winter, pork. The links are hung in the pit to smoke until they are a deep reddish brown. They emerge plump but muscular, with a resistance to the tooth that Texans consider just about perfect. Cut into one and it cracks open to reveal coarsely textured sausage meat. It's strong, with more bite than the mild brisket.

We ate well at Louie Mueller, then lingered over our iced tea. We knew it would be a long time before we'd be in a place like this again. There is certainly nothing like it outside Texas, and even here the great pits seem to be on the endangered list. Pitmasters retire, and health department bureaucrats demand pits be as clean as the neighborhood McDonald's, when in fact one of the secrets of great barbecue is the patina of grease that accumulates on the grill and keeps the brisket from getting singed. Besides, as Fred Fountaine rhetorically asked one reporter, "Who's going to get up at four in the morning to cook with wood when you can leave the gas on all night and come in at eight? Fifty years from now there won't be any more pit barbecue. Maybe twenty."

For a distinctive taste of America, run to Louie Mueller—while you still can.

Massey's

1805 8th Ave., Fort Worth, Tex.
(817) 924-8242

Daily 6:30 a.m.–10 p.m.

$10 or less

There is no southwestern food more down-home than a chicken-fried steak. The best chicken-fried steak, as any country boy will readily tell you, is made at home in a big cast-iron skillet. It's a slim cutlet, pounded skinny by loving hands, dipped in egg then flour, and fried . . . then covered with cream gravy. Sadly, the miserable greasy excuses for chicken-fried steak you find served in every truck stop from Tucumcari to Muskogee have given this regional specialty a bad name.

But at Massey's you will taste the real thing in all its country glory. They've been cooking chicken-fried steak here for more than forty years, and although the outside of the restaurant was fancied up with cedar wood last year, a vinyl-upholstered booth at Massey's is about as folksy a place as you will find for sampling a much-maligned cowboy favorite.

The chicken-fried steak is tender enough to cut easily with a fork, sheathed in a gold crust of breading that bubbles up from the meat in crisp puffs. It is awash in a river of rich cream gravy, and on the side, there are warm biscuits, fluffy but substantial enough for mopping up.

At lunch, the servings are big; at dinner, it takes a prodigious eater to polish off the two or three individual cutlets that come on a plate. This is rich food: the gravy laced with meat drippings, the biscuits, the savory breading on the steak; most people, our waitress confided when she saw us loosening our belts, leave a piece on their plates to take home with them for later.

Mom's Diner

1207 E. 25th, Bryan, Tex.
(409) 779-8600

Mon.–Fri. lunch and dinner, Sat. dinner

$5 or less

It is a measure of this restaurant's culinary innocence that its name refers to an actual, living mom: Mrs. R. E. Carlton. She ran the place for a half a century, until a few years ago when it was turned over to Don Mahan, who upholds her boarding-house all-you-can-eat tradition.

Two entrees are set upon the tables-for-six every day. They're Texas mom-type food like chicken-fried steak, meat loaf, pork chops, and on Saturday, enchiladas. On the side come a slew of vegetables, including great bowlsful of mashed potatoes, beans and corn, and home-grown greens. Iced tea (presweetened) is served in quart-size Mason jars. Dessert, doled out only one serving per customer, was a nice piece of chocolate cake the day we stopped in.

Mom's is in a residential neighborhood and is shaded by a big magnolia tree.

New Braunfels Smokehouse

Rte. 81, New Braunfels, Tex.   One block west of Exit 46 off I-35
(512) 625-2416

Sun.–Thurs. 7:30 a.m.–8 p.m., Fri. & Sat. 7:30 a.m.–9 p.m.

$3–$8

There is a European flavor to the cuisine of the Texas hill country, going back to the nineteenth century when Poles, Czechs, and Germans settled in the Republic of Texas. Here you will find blutwurst sided by jalapeño peppers and barbecue served on bulky rolls. Rare is the hill country town without a good bakery, smokehouse, and sausage factory.

A fine place to have a taste of the cultural mélange is the New Braunfels Smokehouse, where the menu features platters of bratwurst and sauerkraut, smoked chicken and German potato salad—as well as barbecue sandwiches, enchiladas, and good old southern sausage biscuits. Plus, to quote Texas food authority Frank X. Tolbert, "Canadian bacon unequaled by any other restaurant, even in Canada."

If you're going to stop in New Braunfels only once, the dish to order is the "Wunderbar" dinner, a platter of smoked beef, sausage, turkey, chicken, cheeses, and salads. For those not in a smoky mood, we'd recommend the chicken and dumplings, served with cranberry salad and thickly sliced bread. For a more Texan taste, there's something called Pot of Beans, in which the beans are accompanied by cornbread, sliced onion, and jalapeno.

Dessert is not to be missed. The bread pudding is more like a fluffy cake, served warm, dolloped with butter sauce. There is apple strudel, German chocolate cake, and brightly spiced apple dumplings.

If you are in a hurry, the Smokehouse has a "Brown Bag Lunch" ready to go—salami, crackers, turkey or ham sandwich, and a wedge of German chocolate cake. In the front of the restaurant is the gift shop and butchery, where meats and cheeses of all variety are sold in bulk. Here we sampled something not normally a favorite food of ours, but a real delicacy in these parts: beef jerky—rough and plenty chewy.

O.S.T.

Main St. (Rte. 173), Bandera, Tex.
(512) 796-3836

Mon.–Thurs. 6 a.m.–11 p.m., Fri. 6 a.m.–1:30 a.m., Sat. 6 a.m.–2:30 a.m., Sun. 8 a.m.–10 p.m.

About $5

Bandera is a picturesque Texas town known for the dude ranches that surround it. Main Street is crowded with dudes and cowboys, and at lunchtime you will see both in the O.S.T. restaurant, where the ranch hands come to take a break from teaching greenhorns how to not fall off a horse, and where the greenhorns come to soak up the atmosphere of a real Tex-Mex cafe—and where both of them enjoy some of the best chicken-fried steaks in Texas.

With its long communal picnic tables covered in checked oilcloth, the restaurant has a boisterous tone that reminded us of a ranch mess hall. On the walls are fading Kodachromes of pretty cowgirls, rodeo champions, and (need we even say it) John Wayne. Big overhead fans tousle your hair, and the heavy western accents you hear will be punctuated by the electronic pings of a game room off to one side of the dining area.

The menu is pure Tex-Mex, featuring steaks, enchiladas, *menudo* (tripe stew), *chorizo mexicano* (sausage), chili, and the house specialty, that terrific chicken-fried steak.

There are many bad chicken-fried steaks in Texas, rubbery whoppers that give the real McCoy a bad name; but at the O.S.T. it is easy to see why the humble dish has become such a cult item to lovers of down-home cuisine. It is a thin slab of beef that has been pounded even thinner before being dipped in flour and fried to a crisp in fresh oil. The crust puffs away from the meat in big brown bubbles of delicate batter. Over the steak is a ladleful of delicious pepper-flecked cream gravy. On the side come thick-cut french fries and double-size hunks of "Texas toast."

O.S.T. stands for the Old Spanish Trail, which ran through Bandera. If you are just passing through, it's a great town for window shopping; the stores display a passel of Tony Llama boots for rich dudes.

Otto's

5502 Memorial Dr., Houston, Tex.
(713) 864-8526   For barbecue call 864-2573

Mon.–Fri. 9 a.m.–midnight, Sat. 9 a.m.–6 p.m.

$5 or less

Otto's is actually two restaurants in one, both of them very Houstonian. In back is the barbecue, where brisket is served in the old-fashioned tote-it-yourself manner. It's the kind of barbecue that West Texans abhor but southerners—and East Texans—favor: tender and mild meat, covered with pungent red sauce. Regional polemics aside, we love Otto's. It's messy, sweet, sleeves-up eats; the best barbecue in town.

Houston is hamburger-mad, and we'll admit we had a hard time choosing between the enormous double burgers at the Old Bayou Inn, the cheddar cheeseburger at Zeke's, and Ouisie's Table's burger, served with garlic mayonnaise, piquante sauce, and baby Swiss cheese. But above all these fine and fancy patties, we like Otto's best. Here you will find a modest hamburger of quiet virtue, the kind you savor long after all the more fashionable burgers have faded from memory.

In the front of the barbecue restaurant is Otto's burger bar, where for thirty-eight years, thin patties have been hand-formed from meat ground fresh every day. Let us make it clear—these are not gourmet burgers. They are not tarted up with French mustard or chopped garlic or breadcrumbs or fancy cheese. They are meat, grilled, period. The patties are thin, cooked throughout, served on soft store-bought buns (lightly toasted): classic burgers, pharmacy-counter burgers, the burger you want when you are in the mood for an old favorite. On the side you get potato chips.

Paris Coffee Shop

704 W. Magnolia, Fort Worth, Tex.
(817) 335-2041

Mon.–Fri. 6 a.m.–3 p.m., Sat. until 11 a.m.

$5 or less

John Mariani, as fine a palate as ever hit the trail west, told us the Paris Coffee Shop was a "democratic luncheonette with society ladies and truckers side by side." He recommended we order the onion rings, which turned out to be singular circles of brittle oily batter around thick sweet onions. He called the enchilada perfect, which it was—a perfect Tex-Mex mess; and he also recommended the oily Texas chili.

"Terrible chicken-fried steak," John had warned; but damned if half the cowboys in the joint weren't eating it. We couldn't resist ordering a platter, with mashed potatoes and steamed cabbage on the side. Good grub, we thought. Inelegant in the extreme, in fact rather ignominious meat, but it had been pounded and beaten and cooked until tender, and smothered with thick white gravy, and although we know we should have higher, finer standards, like John, we kinda liked this funky version. It's authentic western cafe food; the real thing, if not the very best.

The same goes for the meal known hereabouts as an "Arkansas traveler": a hot roast beef sandwich on cornbread with mashed potatoes and pinto beans. How nice it is to find a homey, good-tasting meal so unabashedly calorific . . . with extra cornbread and biscuits on the side!

As you might guess in a coffee shop as archetypal as this, pies are outstanding. At 11 a.m., our coconut cream pie and egg custard pie were served faintly warm, their crusts flaky and light, toasty meringues standing tall above their sweet filling.

Pittsburg Hot Links

128 Marshall St., Pittsburg, Tex.
(214) 856-5765

Mon.–Sat. 9 a.m.–6 p.m.

$5 or less

Ever since 1897, when a local butcher named Charlie Hasselback hung some sausages over a smoke pit, Pittsburg has considered itself the hot-link capital of Texas, and therefore of the world. The links are all-beef sausages, loaded with pepper and spice, oozing savory grease as soon as you poke through the casing with a knife. But what we like best about hot links, Pittsburg-style, is the way they're served.

Place your order at the counter from a menu that lists one entree: links, buy 'em by the piece. For side dishes, choose from an assortment of pickles, peppers, and onions. And of course you'll want hot sauce, saltines, and a soda. End of menu.

The primeval meal is presented on a piece of butcher paper on a tray, with plastic picnic flatware. Tote it to a heavy wooden table, climb over the bench and get comfortable. Now dig in to a unique east Texas feast.

Po-Po Restaurant

Welfare exit off I-10, seven miles north of Boerne, Tex.
(512) 537-4399

Wed.–Sat. 5 p.m.–9:45 p.m., Sun. noon–9 p.m.

$10 or less

Today, when most restaurants zap their food with microwave death rays, it is a pleasure to find one so old-fashioned that it doesn't even have a freezer. At Po-Po, a freezer isn't needed. Since it opened up in 1947 and began serving food to the residents of the Texas hill country (the culinary heart of Texas), Po-Po's reputation has been won by the unimpeachable freshness of everything it serves.

The small menu is devoted to steak and seafood. The seafood—shrimp and oysters—is from the Texas Gulf, served in the locally popular way, fried. It's quite all right, but a better choice is one of Po-Po's steaks, ranging from the six-ounce filet to the one-pound T-bone. There's nothing fancy; they are simply broiled on a grill. But it's good juicy meat, with a savory singed crust.

Another good bet is fried chicken. It is coated with a toasty fissured crust through which savory juices leak as soon as fork or finger touches it. Try a side of cream gravy and an order of "dirty rice." To make dirty rice, the cook boils it with chicken gizzards and livers and a handful of spices until the rice is tender, and flecked with the chicken parts. It looks dirty but tastes delicious.

A Po-Po specialty, and one of the least expensive items on the menu, is the plate of sausage and kraut. The hill country is where the German immigrants settled, and the sausage bespeaks that history—plump, vividly spiced, served with firm steamed sauerkraut. To sip while you dine, do like the locals and order an Armadillo beer.

Unlike the rest of Texas, hill country people indulge their sweet teeth; Po-Po serves a fanciful little confection called Rum Tum Ditty, a piece of cake topped with pudding, then topped with soft strawberry topping. Also good is the Chocolate Delight à Po-Po, an extremely rich brownie weighted down with ice cream and syrup.

Po-Po is a clubby place that has hardly changed at all over the years. It is a cool stone building shaded by oak trees, with a sign outside announcing EATS.

Rowe Valley Restaurant

Off Rte. 29, twelve miles east of Georgetown, Tex.
(512) 352-9149

Tues.–Sat. 5 p.m.–10:30 p.m., Sun. noon–8:30 p.m.

$10 or less

When you are in Texas, looking for the best steak around, it isn't only a nice hunk of meat you want. You want home fries and thick-sliced Texas toast; you want a place ranchers and cowhands come for their T-bones; you want a real country steak house; you want the Rowe Valley Restaurant.

It's way out-of-the-way. To find it, follow the sign off Route 29 along a narrow road that leads to a lush pecan grove; and there in the shade of the trees is the Rowe Valley Restaurant, a low ranchlike building—just about the prettiest spot in Texas to dig into a Texas steak.

We've always thought it strange how some food writers can give separate ratings for food and atmosphere, as if you could go to a restaurant for food only, and forgo the atmosphere—or tell the waiter to bring a large bowl of atmosphere, easy on the food. Here at Rowe's, there is no need for schizo strategies. Food and atmo both earn top rating.

Inside, it's clean and easy: wood paneling, Formica tables, a bar off to one side. The menu is mostly steak—T-bones, filets, an excellent chicken-fried steak with cream gravy. The so-called K.C. strip is our recommendation if you want a genuine taste of Texas beef. It's a he-man cut, bloody and long on flavor. There's chicken on the menu, too, real country-style. There are even a few Mexican dishes, and Rowe Valley catfish. However, if you're coming here but once, get the steak. That's what this restaurant is all about.

Sartin's

Treemont & U.S. 87, Sabine Pass, Tex.
(409) 971-2158

Daily 11 a.m.–10 p.m., Sat. until 10:30 p.m.   Reservations advised for weekends

$10–$15

"From the outside," *Texas Monthly* commented, "Sartin's sounds like a gang of orthopedic surgeons at work." The cracking and hammering that issues forth from this restaurant is the sound of crabs splitting open as diners dig into one of the most bountiful seafood dinners on the Texas Gulf Coast.

The drive here, nearly an hour from Houston, is picturesque—through bayous and salt marshes, past rice fields, palm trees, and oil wells. The air smells of eucalyptus and seawater and petroleum. Sartin's is an ungraceful shed of a restaurant that began as a seafood market, an outlet for the catch of the Sartin family's shrimp boats.

You can dine one of two ways: sit at a small table and order a normal dinner with an entree and side dishes, or opt for "platter service." Unless you are on a diet or are a professional spoilsport, the latter is the only way to go. Platter service means that for $12 per person, you sit at a picnic table and all varieties of in-season seafood are carried to your table on platters for as long as you want. Platter service is a festival of excess, a glutton's dream.

The repertoire varies, but among the likely offerings will be crab claws, broiled snapper, fried snapper, stuffed crabs, frog legs, fried and/or boiled shrimp, crawfish (usually between January and June), plus french fries, cole slaw, and garlic bread. For an extra $2, you're also brought fried and raw oysters.

The best thing at Sartin's are the "Bar-B-Cue Crabs," which is actually a misnomer, since they are deep-fried rather than pit-cooked. Their secret's in the seasoning, a vivid blast of spice that seeps into the crabmeat while it fries and yields an incomparable flavor.

Almost everything on Sartin's menu is still caught by Sartin boats, just hours before it's served.

Sonny Bryan's

2202 Inwood Rd., Dallas, Tex.
(214) 357-7120

Mon.–Fri. 9 a.m.–about 5 p.m., Sat. 9 a.m.–3 p.m., Sun. 9 a.m.–2 p.m.

$5 or less

In the twenty-seven years Sonny Bryan has been cooking barbecue, he has made himself something of a legend in Dallas. But you could never say success has gone to Mr. Bryan's head. Stop in his tiny smokehouse in the middle of the dirt parking lot on Inwood and you will be privileged to see a master pit man at work. If it's morning, he will probably be poking at the fire, adjusting the stack of logs so the ham and pork ribs and beef briskets sizzle exactly right and absorb the correct amount of hickory haze to turn tender.

If it's noontime, the restaurant will be deluged with customers, and he will be wielding his knife, turning out beef sandwiches and plates of ribs lightning fast.

By mid-afternoon, Sonny Bryan's is quiet. After an especially busy day, all the barbecue will be gone, in which case the chef will simply close up and go home; but he'll always return early the next morning to stoke the fire.

Although the ham and pork ribs cannot be faulted, Sonny Bryan's brisket is his glory. It is thick-sliced and juicy, piled high on sandwich or platter, redolent of that most delectable Texas perfume, *eau de* pit. The sauce is sweet, struck with a hard jolt of vinegar for personality. This is the kind of barbecue sauce that simply cannot be made anywhere in the north: a Texas treasure; an unmitigated triumph.

On the side get french fries, onion rings, slaw, or delicious beans, dotted with bits of pork and onion.

A lot of Sonny Bryan's business is take-out, but patrons who prefer to dine here will find themselves cozy accommodations in one of the house seats —minuscule school desks for one.

Southside Market

109 Central, Elgin, Tex.
(512) 285-3883

Mon.–Sat. 7 a.m.–5:30 p.m.

$5 or less

Elgin is in the heart of Texas sausage country, the land north of Austin, settled by Germans when Texas was a republic in the middle of the last century. There isn't a self-respecting butcher shop in the area that doesn't make and smoke its own. Of the three sausage parlors in Elgin (pop. 4,500), the Southside Market—over a hundred years old—is the most colorful, and clearly the people's choice.

Walk through the meat market into the old dining room in back, where the pit smoulders, and seated at the long bench against the green-tiled wall, you will see farmers in overalls seated next to bank presidents in pinstripes, frail little ladies alongside leathery cowboys. They're all eating with their hands off crinkled butcher's paper; they're all pouring on hot sauce from whiskey bottles set along the counter; and they're all eating Elgin hot sausage.

"Lyndon Johnson came here one day when he was President," the counterman told us. "Sat right there. He was wearing work clothes, and everybody was so busy eating their sausage, no one even recognized him."

Elgin sausage has a bite. It is red with flecks of hot pepper, coarsely ground, plump and luscious. You get it at the pit along with a stack of saltines, then choose a seat either in the old dining room, where the air is heavy with smoke, or the new dining room, to the side, which is gussied up with wood paneling and tables and air conditioning. The floor in both rooms is spread with sawdust.

When the Southside Market is crowded (which it is at lunch), the room tone stays quiet; pit smoke has a way of calming nerves. Perhaps it is the simplicity of the food and the purely functional surroundings; no doubt about it, though—there is something wonderfully primeval about this place. Listen: the sound of people licking sauce off their fingers is louder than any conversation.

Even those who eat in the new room emerge aromatic, business suits and flowered dresses and jeans carrying forth the scent of the pit. That perfumey residue lasts a good part of the day, at first makes you smug, then wistful.

Tigua Indian Restaurant

Tigua Pueblo, 119 S. Old Pueblo Rd., El Paso, Tex.
(915) 859-3916

Wed.–Sat. 11 a.m.–9 p.m., Sun.–Tues. 11 a.m.–6 p.m.

$5 or less

Seekers of unusual cuisine won't find regional American food more esoteric than what's on the menu here. This is the only restaurant in the world that serves Tigua Indian chili in its traditional forms, both red and green. Either is stunning—to look at and to eat.

The red chili is the color of cinnabar, a glistening opaque brew thick with ground chili pods, cumin, tomato, coarsely cut beef, tiny chunks of potato, and a shower of spices. "Will bring tears to your eyes," says the Tigua menu. Will also pop beads of sweat on the forehead, cause lightheadedness, and stimulate yelps of pleasure.

Hot as it is, there is much more to this chili than the fire. The heat is just the first impression, "opening up" the taste buds, clearing the way for a volcanic flow of layered tastes: not just the hotness, but the *tastes* of chili peppers. It is rare to eat a dish that makes you aware that these red and green pods are vegetables; Tigua chili celebrates that fact, and helps you understand why people become chili fanatics.

Tigua green chili is hotter than red—probably hotter than anything we've been served in any restaurant, a real sinus drainer. It is monster-colored brownish green, dotted with pepper seeds and bits of mutton. The dominant tastes are *cominos* and garlic. Like the red chili, it is soupy; but there is a viscous texture to the broth, lent not so much by the meat, which is lean, but by the pepper pods that dominate the dish.

Both chilies are served with rice and refried beans on the side, and thick slices of sturdy Indian bread, baked in a clay oven. The bread is earthy, an excellent balm for the tongue between forays into your chili bowl.

Another soothing dish on the Tigua menu—in fact, it's the traditional southwestern cure for hangovers—is *menudo* (served only on Saturday and Sunday), a stew made with puffs of hominy corn and cubed honeycomb tripe.

A fabulous Tigua meal, suitable for non-fire eaters, is *gorditas*—soft pockets of flavorful cornmeal stuffed with beef, cheese, and lettuce, then fried to delicate crispness. We'd also recommend the *flautas*, flute-shaped rolled corn tortillas stuffed with shredded beef and served with sour cream and avocados.

Once a bare-bones cafeteria, the Tigua Indian Restaurant is now a wonderfully atmospheric place to eat, keyed in to tribal culture. Nothing fancy, but the Tiguas have made good use of their crafts, decorating the spacious restaurant area with pottery and rugs. The lighting is indirect and subtly dreamy, reminiscent of a natural history diorama. The dining area is all wood, shades of beige and brown, with a ceiling done in traditional stick and reed construction. In the background, Indian music plays softly.

The restaurant shares space with a store where crafts (and freshly baked Indian bread) are sold. Outside the restaurant, you can visit a pueblo and watch Tigua artisans and bakers and native dancers do their stuff: an appropriate appetizer—or conclusion—to a unique native American feast.

Tony Mandola's Blue Oyster Bar

1608 N. Shepherd, Houston, Tex.
(713) 864-0915

Mon.–Sat. 11 a.m.–10 p.m.

$10 or less

When she knew we were coming to town for just one night in the midst of a whirlwind cross-country trip, Houstonian Janice Shindeler gave some serious thought to where we ought to eat. Houston has a surfeit of fancy and funky eateries worth exploring but Janice figured that on our one night in town, what we really needed was comfort. So she and her husband Harry took us to *their* place, the joint they fall into whenever they need mothering. And they told us to order "mama's gumbo."

It really is Tony Mandola's mother's recipe, mud-colored thick, smelling of the sea and spice, crowded with seafood. We got a few bowlsful and a dozen oysters on the side; Harry advised us to slide a few of the raw oysters into the gumbo, and Janice spooned in hot peppers from the jar on the table, and let us tell you, we were home free, eating one of the great meals on the Gulf coast.

But that was just the beginning. Once the gumbo was polished off, we ordered red beans and rice, and crawfish étouffée. It's easy to eat a lot at Tony Mandola's. Order as you go, cups or bowls of everything, oysters by the dozen or half; and as soon as you've finished a course, the waiter asks what else you'd like. At Harry's suggestion, our multi-course meals were accompanied by long-neck bottles of Corona beer.

The red beans and rice are magnificent, dark and dense, packed with chunks of smoked sausage. Crawfish étouffée is hot enough to take your breath away, loaded with big pink chunks of sweet crawfish. Boiled crawfish is available in three-pound batches. We intend to come back on a Tuesday or Thursday, when the special is "Mama's Spaghetti" with shrimp and crabmeat sauce.

Tony's is an inconspicuous roadhouse, its prominent piece of decor a large service bar made of glass bricks, backlit all in blue. Outside, a sign advertises "Cajun food to geaux."

(Another—the original—Tony Mandola's is located at 8105 Gulf Freeway.)

UTAH

Lamb's Restaurant

169 S. Main St., Salt Lake City, Utah
(801) 364-7166

Mon.–Sat. 7 a.m.–9 p.m.

$10 or less

Because Mormons are encouraged to eat at home by their family-oriented religion, the restaurants of Salt Lake City are a paltry lot. We tried a few formal ones, and a handful of new ones in tourist-trod Trolley Square, then found Lamb's, the only place in town with good food and any real character. It's a sixty-year-old anomaly that we'd describe as a cross between a lunch counter and an old hotel dining room.

It isn't really either, although there is a long counter up front for single dining, mostly at breakfast and lunch. Beyond the counter is the nice part— a nearly hidden dining room where an old sign reads TROUT AND CHICKEN DINNERS SERVED DAILY. QUALITY—SERVICE—SANITATION.

There are tall, private booths, each with a silver light fixture in an old-fashioned futuristic mode. Waitresses wear white uniforms. Tables are covered with white linen. At dinner, soothing music is piped in. There is something heavenly, or at least dreamy, about this ambience of worn elegance, accentuated further by the genteel geriatric clientele.

Dinner began with slices of freshly baked sesame seed bread, followed by beef and barley soup. We chose trout, which our waitress expertly boned then put back together, carrying away only the head and skeleton. It smelled fabulous under a few strips of crisp bacon. Its skin was crackling, the flesh flaky with a good toasty flavor—although it was a bit greasy from its frying pan.

Trout is featured on Lamb's breakfast menu, too, along with other piscatoria such as finnan haddie and red snapper. There is a wide assortment of omelettes, fruits served with heavy cream, pancakes, waffles—even milk toast.

The chicken dinner touted on the sign proved to be a broiled half-bird with a baked-in-foil potato and some limp vegetables. A better choice was the "home-baked pork and beans en casserole." The pork was circles of Canadian bacon; the beans were soft and sweet.

It was August, and fresh fruits were available for dessert: Cranshaw melon, cantaloupe, strawberries and cream. The rice pudding described as "famous" on the menu was a rich homogenized paste with no detectable grains of rice at all, topped by a thick dusting of cinnamon. We couldn't resist ordering "Burgundy wine Jell-O," which was indeed Burgundian in color, but tasted identical to the black cherry gelatin we eat when we're ailing.

It is possible even in this teetotaling state of Utah to have a drink with dinner at Lamb's—if you fetch the mini-bottle yourself from a Cabinet of Shame. As you select, you confront a sign inside the cabinet's door, warning that alcohol consumption is dangerous both to oneself and to others.

Sconecutter

2040 S. State, Salt Lake City, Utah
(801) 485-9981

Always open

About $2

We always thought of scones as baked tea biscuits, powdery rolls that rich people eat in lieu of English muffins. Not in Utah. A Utah scone is a six-by-two-inch rectangle of dough that gets cooked by immersion in boiling oil. It turns all gold and puffy, and is then cut open and filled, like a hero roll.

We'd like to know how on earth the Scottish scone evolved into this grubby pastry, and why it took root in, of all places, Utah. But we weren't going to learn anything from the people at Sconecutter, because, you see, scones are fast food. Here, and at a few other cookshacks in the state, they are served with so little charm that they might as well be called McScones.

There is a dining room inside Sconecutter—all orange plastic and Formica; and a drive-through window. Although everything about this setup spells efficiency, it takes a surprising amount of time. Each scone is fried and stuffed to order.

Not bad grub, all things considered. We haven't tried the wheat-bread scones, or the "sloppy scones" (filled with chili meat), or the ham or beef and cheese scones so popular at lunch; but we did drive through and grab some breakfast scones on our way out of town: one filled with butter and honey, the other with butter and cinnamon.

We thought we'd eat them while driving. At first bite, the sticky filling spurted over the dashboard, steering wheel, and seats, and ran in rivers up to our elbows. How much honey and butter gets stuffed into these dough wallets? What a mess!

We wouldn't plan a special trip to Utah to eat scones, but next time we pass through, we'll give them another shot, either inside at a table or in the car, wearing a bib.

West

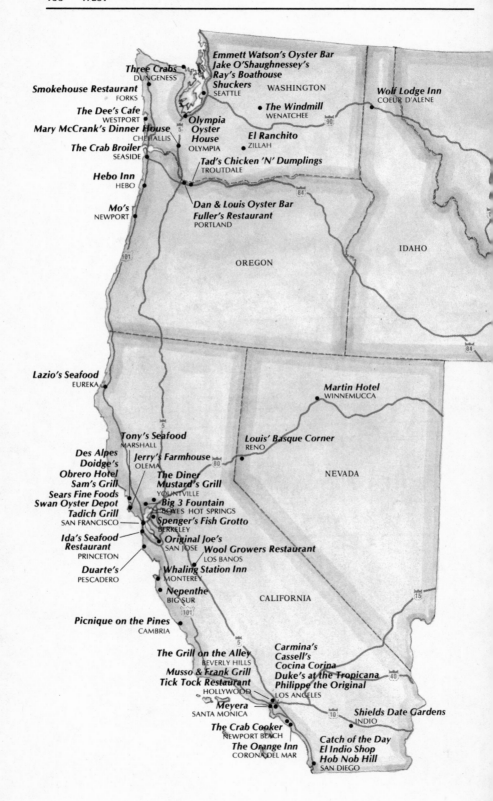

Three Crabs
DUNGENESS

Emmett Watson's Oyster Bar
Jake O'Shaughnessey's
Ray's Boathouse
Shuckers
SEATTLE   WASHINGTON

Wolf Lodge Inn
COEUR D'ALENE

Smokehouse Restaurant
FORKS

The Dee's Cafe
WESTPORT

Mary McCrank's Dinner House
CHEHALLIS

The Crab Broiler
SEASIDE

The Windmill
WENATCHEE

Olympia
Oyster
House
OLYMPIA

El Ranchito
ZILLAH

Tad's Chicken 'N' Dumplings
TROUTDALE

Hebo Inn
HEBO

Mo's
NEWPORT

Dan & Louis Oyster Bar
Fuller's Restaurant
PORTLAND

OREGON

IDAHO

Lazio's Seafood
EUREKA

Martin Hotel
WINNEMUCCA

Tony's Seafood
MARSHALL

Louis' Basque Corner
RENO

Des Alpes
Doidge's
Obrero Hotel
Sam's Grill
Sears Fine Foods
Swan Oyster Depot
Tadich Grill
SAN FRANCISCO

Jerry's Farmhouse
OLEMA

The Diner
Mustard's Grill
YOUNTVILLE

Big 3 Fountain
BOYES HOT SPRINGS

Spenger's Fish Grotto
BERKELEY

NEVADA

Ida's Seafood
Restaurant
PRINCETON

Original Joe's
SAN JOSE

Wool Growers Restaurant
LOS BANOS

Duarte's
PESCADERO

Whaling Station Inn
MONTEREY

Nepenthe
BIG SUR

CALIFORNIA

Picnique on the Pines
CAMBRIA

The Grill on the Alley
BEVERLY HILLS

Carmina's
Cassell's
Cocina Corina
Duke's at the Tropicana
Philippe the Original
LOS ANGELES

Musso & Frank Grill
Tick Tock Restaurant
HOLLYWOOD

Meyera
SANTA MONICA

Shields Date Gardens
INDIO

The Crab Cooker
NEWPORT BEACH

The Orange Inn
CORONA DEL MAR

Catch of the Day
El Indio Shop
Hob Nob Hill
SAN DIEGO

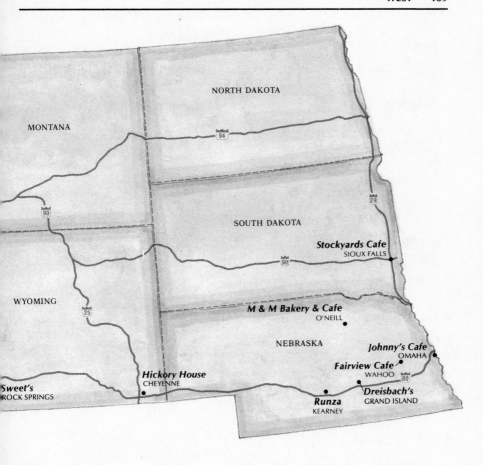

Western Specialties

Where we list several places, we have starred the one we think best.

Abalone Steak

★ Ida's Seafood Restaurant (Princeton, CA)   511
  Musso and Frank Grill (Hollywood, CA)   515

Alder-Smoked Salmon

  Smokehouse Restaurant (Forks, WA)   552

Artichoke Soup

★ Duarte's (Pescadero, CA)   506
  Whaling Station Inn (Monterey, CA)   529

Basque Dinners

★ Des Alpes (San Francisco, CA)   502
  Obrero Hotel (San Francisco, CA)   518
  Wool Growers Restaurant (Los Banos, CA)   530
  Louis' Basque Corner (Reno, NV)   537
  Martin Hotel (Winnemucca, NV)   538

Cal-Mex Cooking

  Carmina's (Los Angeles, CA)   498
  Cocina Corina (Los Angeles, CA)   501
  The Diner (Yountville, CA)   503
★ El Indio Shop (San Diego, CA)   508
  El Ranchito (Zillah, WA)   546

Chicken and Dumplings

  Hebo Inn (Hebo, OR)   541
★ Tad's Chicken 'N' Dumplings (Troutdale, OR)   543

Cioppino—California bouillabaisse

  Duarte's (Pescadero, CA)   506
  Lazio's Seafood (Eureka, CA)   513
  Spenger's Fish Grotto (Berkeley, CA)   525
★ Tadich Grill (San Francisco, CA)   527
  Tony's Seafood (Marshall, CA)   529
  Whaling Station Inn (Monterey, CA)   529

Clam Chowder, Oyster Stew

The Crab Cooker (Newport Beach, CA)   501
Ida's Seafood Restaurant (Princeton, CA)   511
Jerry's Farmhouse (Olema, CA)   512
Lazio's Seafood (Eureka, CA)   513
Sam's Grill (San Francisco, CA)   522
Spenger's Fish Grotto (Berkeley, CA)   525
Tadich Grill (San Francisco, CA)   527
Tony's Seafood (Marshall, CA)   529
Dan & Louis Oyster Bar (Portland, OR)   540
Hebo Inn (Hebo, OR)   541
★ Mo's (Newport, OR)   542
The Dee's Cafe (Westport, WA)   545
Emmett Watson's Oyster Bar (Seattle, WA)   546
Jake O'Shaughnessey's (Seattle, WA)   547
Olympia Oyster House (Olympia, WA)   549
Ray's Boathouse (Seattle, WA)   550
Shuckers (Seattle, WA)   551
Three Crabs (Dungeness, WA)   552

Cobb Salad

The Grill on the Alley (Beverly Hills, CA)   509

Crab or Shrimp Louie—Cold mayonnaise-based salad

Jerry's Farmhouse (Olema, CA)   512
Musso and Frank Grill (Hollywood, CA)   515
Picnique in the Pines (Cambria, CA)   522
Sam's Grill (San Francisco, CA)   522
Spenger's Fish Grotto (Berkeley, CA)   525
★ Swan Oyster Depot (San Francisco, CA)   526
Dan & Louis Oyster Bar (Portland, OR)   540
Olympia Oyster House (Olympia, WA)   549

Date Shakes

Duke's at the Tropicana (Los Angeles, CA)   507
The Orange Inn (Corona del Mar, CA)   519
★ Shields Date Gardens (Indio, CA)   524

Dungeness Crab

Catch of the Day (San Diego, CA)   499
The Crab Cooker (Newport Beach, CA)   501

French Dip—Roast beef sandwich *au jus*

Geoduck—An outsized northwest clam chopped for chowder or cut into steaks

Hamburgers

Hangtown Fry—Oysters and scrambled eggs

Idaho Potatoes

Monterey Prawns—Enormous roe-laden shrimp found only in Monterey Bay

New Joe Special—A mess of ground beef and spinach, unique to the Bay area

    Original Joe's (San Jose, CA)   520

Oysters—Drakes Bays, Olympias, Petits Points, Pigeon Points, Quilcenes, Tamales Bays, Yaquina Bays, etc.

    Duarte's (Pescadero, CA)   506
    Jerry's Farmhouse (Olema, CA)   512
    Lazio's Seafood (Eureka, CA)   513
    Spenger's Fish Grotto (Berkeley, CA)   525
★ Swan Oyster Depot (San Francisco, CA)   526
    Tadich Grill (San Francisco, CA)   527
    Tony's Seafood (Marshall, CA)   529
    The Crab Broiler (Seaside, OR)   539
    Dan & Louis Oyster Bar (Portland, OR)   540
    Mo's [Annex] (Newport, OR)   541
    Emmett Watson's Oyster Bar (Seattle, WA)   546
    Mary McCrank's Dinner House (Chehalis, WA)   548
    Olympia Oyster House (Olympia, WA)   549
    Shuckers (Seattle, WA)   551

Pacific Fish—Rex & petrale sole, sand dabs, ling cod, halibut, etc.

    Catch of the Day (San Diego, CA)   499
    The Crab Cooker (Newport Beach, CA)   501
    Duarte's (Pescadero, CA)   506
    The Grill on the Alley (Beverly Hills, CA)   509
    Ida's Seafood Restaurant (Princeton, CA)   511
    Jerry's Farmhouse (Olema, CA)   512
    Lazio's Seafood (Eureka, CA)   513
    Musso and Frank Grill (Hollywood, CA)   515
    Mustard's Grill (Yountville, CA)   516
    Sam's Grill (San Francisco, CA)   522
    Spenger's Fish Grotto (Berkeley, CA)   525
★ Tadich Grill (San Francisco, CA)   527
    Fuller's Restaurant (Portland, OR)   541
    Mo's (Newport, OR)   542
    The Dee's Cafe (Westport, WA)   545
    Olympia Oyster House (Olympia, WA)   549
    Ray's Boathouse (Seattle, WA)   550
    Shuckers (Seattle, WA)   551
    Smokehouse Restaurant (Forks, WA)   552
    Three Crabs (Dungeness, WA)   552

Pecan Waffles, Pancakes, Cakes, and Rolls

> ★ Hob Nob Hill (San Diego, CA)   510
>   Sears Fine Foods (San Francisco, CA)   523
>   M & M Bakery & Cafe (O'Neill, NE)   535

Razor Clams

>   The Crab Broiler (Seaside, OR)   539
> ★ Fuller's Restaurant (Portland, OR)   541
>   The Dee's Cafe (Westport, WA)   545

Rocky Mountain Oysters—Deep-fried bull's testicles

>   Wolf Lodge Inn (Coeur d'Alene, ID)   531

Runzas—Meat-and-cabbage-filled bread loaves

>   Runza (Kearney, NE)   536

Salmon—There are five species of Pacific salmon, served fresh as steaks and filets; also smoked and cured

>   The Crab Cooker (Newport Beach, CA)   501
>   The Grill on the Alley (Beverly Hills, CA)   509
>   Whaling Station Inn (Monterey, CA)   529
>   The Dee's Cafe (Westport, WA)   545
>   Jake O'Shaughnessey's (Seattle, WA)   547
> ★ Ray's Boathouse (Seattle, WA)   550
>   Shuckers (Seattle, WA)   551
>   Smokehouse Restaurant (Forks, WA)   552
>   Three Crabs (Dungeness, WA)   552

Shrimp Scatter—Small shrimp fried in a crisp crust

> ★ Spenger's Fish Grotto (Berkeley, CA)   525
>   Olympia Oyster House (Olympia, WA)   549

Sourdough Bread

>   Big 3 Fountain (Sonoma, CA)   497
>   Des Alpes (San Francisco, CA)   502
>   The Diner (Yountville, CA)   503
>   Doidge's (San Francisco, CA)   504
>   Duarte's (Pescadero, CA)   506
>   Musso and Frank Grill (Hollywood, CA)   515
> ★ Sam's Grill (San Francisco, CA)   522

Types of Western Restaurants

Boarding Houses

Emmett Watson's Oyster Bar (Seattle, WA)   546
Shuckers (Seattle, WA)   551

Smokehouse

Smokehouse Restaurant (Forks, WA)   552

Steak Houses

The Grill on the Alley (Beverly Hills, CA)   509
Wolf Lodge Inn (Coeur d'Alene, ID)   531
Dreisbach's (Grand Island, NE)   533
Johnny's Cafe (Omaha, NE)   534
Stockyards Cafe (Sioux Falls, SD)   544
The Windmill (Wenatchee, WA)   553

CALIFORNIA

Big 3 Fountain

Rte. 12, Boyes Hot Springs, Calif.   At the Sonoma Mission Inn
(707) 996-8132

Daily 7 a.m.–10 p.m.

The soda-fountain specialties are classic: black-and-white sundaes, banana splits, malts and floats and milk shakes (including fresh banana). There are sandwiches, too. But breakfast is the meal of the day.

Baked pancakes, large tawny puffs that look somewhere between a large omelette and a small soufflé, are the thing to get. Similar to the "German pancakes" found in parts of the midwest, they are served with powdered sugar and lemon that combine into tart syrup. You can get them plain (too dry), or filled with fresh fruit, or best of all, filled with baked apple slices, dark and caramelized.

French toast is pretty fine, too. It is sourdough French bread with a Grand Marnier tinge to its crust, also available with the luscious baked apples.

Each table at Big 3 has its own shiny toaster. "Most people who get eggs want their bread already toasted," says our waitress. "But for some people, it just isn't breakfast unless they can do it themselves."

Carmina's

2500 W. Pico, Los Angeles, Calif.   At Vermont
(213) 480-8184

Daily 8 a.m.–11:30 p.m.

$5 or less

It wasn't easy to pinpoint Los Angeles's own regional foods. One long-time Angeleno suggested we cover celebrity cuisine as the local contribution to American gastronomy. That might have been fun, but you have to be a celebrity, or behave like one, to get a table in the restaurants that serve it. That, as Sam Goldwyn said, includes us out.

Other than a burger at Cassell's, the one specialty every visitor to L.A. ought to try is Mexican food. Not fancy Mexican; the city is conspicuously lacking good fancy or middle-class Mexican restaurants. We're talking funky Mexican, street food, as served at corner burrito stands and luncheonettes like Carmina's.

Tostadas blanketed with molten cheese, meat-stuffed tacos, *quesadillas*, *carnitas*-laden burritos, chili *verde*, vegetable casserole soup (called *cosido*), fat tortillas made fresh every day, grilled to order and served warm: Carmina's kitchen turns out a full roster of Cal-Mex food.

It's an of-the-people cuisine that reminds us of Tex-Mex, minus chicken-fried steaks and jalapeno peppers, plus a lot of fresh tomatoes and chilies. The food served at Carmina's is milder than most southwestern cooking, but that peppery red and green *salsa* on the tables will set it on fire.

There is a dash of cookery from south of south of the border, too: Central American *pupusas*, like the tortillas, are handmade—stuffed with beef or cheese. They are chubbier than their Mexican counterparts, more for bread-lovers; and a Salvadorean dish called *guineos, frijoles y crema:* bananas (fried) with thinned sour cream and beans—an unlikely but delicious, rich meal.

A high-ceilinged booth-and-counter luncheonette, Carmina's is a natural —meaning it doesn't lay on any south-of-the-border schmaltz to authenticate its cooking.

Cassell's

3300 W. 6th St., Los Angeles, Calif.
(213) 480-8668

Mon.–Sat. 10 a.m.–3 p.m.

$5 or less

Los Angeles is a city of hamburger connoisseurs. Hot polemical debates have raged for years around issues such as The Thin Patty vs. The Thick Mound; Plain Hamburgers vs. Chiliburgers; and there are even corollary arguments about crinkle-cut or curved french-fries. (It is, of course, perfectly clear that the fervor is a form of atonement by a people overwhelmed with guilt for Southern California having been the birthplace of McDonald's, indeed, the cradle of fast food.)

You can get good burgers of every shape and class in this city, from Tommy's chili-doused street burgers (at the corner of Rampart and Beverly) to "Ra—the Untouchable Burger" at a place called Nucleus Nuance on Melrose Avenue, but the one undisputably great Los Angeles hamburger is Cassell's.

Prime beef, completely trimmed of fat, is ground each day to be formed into patties (1/3- and 2/3-pounders) and broiled under an open flame. A rare Cassell's burger—the large one—is a rosy puff of meat, a handsome aristocrat. Beware, though, of the thin patties: they are too lean to be cooked any longer than rare without drying out.

The burger is served on a large sesame bun, and augmented by an only-in-California condiment buffet that includes slices of beefsteak tomato, pickles, onions, and freshly made mayonnaise. The mayonnaise is also used in good potato salad. Lemons are squeezed here to make lemonade.

Cassell's is self-service, with plastic tables and folding chairs. Any other resemblance to fast food is strictly coincidental.

Catch of the Day

3760 Sports Arena Blvd., San Diego, Calif.   In Sports Arena Village
(619) 225-1111

Tues.–Fri. lunch, dinner daily   Reservations advised

$10 or less

This is what we'd call a dear place: tasteful print wallpaper, small tables covered with pale blue cloth and little bouquets of fresh flowers; even the sheet menu is pretty, detailed artistically with fish and tendrils of seaweed in pastel shades. Catch of the Day is an isle of quaintness in a modern California shopping center.

When a fish restaurant is as popular as this in an area as heavy with fish restaurants as San Diego, you suspect they must be doing something right. The formula for success is fresh seafood, simply prepared.

You won't find better scallops—broiled over charcoal, alternating with shrimp on a bamboo skewer, served with aïoli, a garlic mayonnaise. These scallops are large enough to char around the edges, but stay juicy and moist within. We also loved the flaky charcoal-grilled halibut, from Pacific waters.

Our meal had begun with seviche—chunks of fish marinated raw in lime juice and served in a cold glass bowl with green onions, tomato bits, celery, and shreds of parsley. When we ordered, we asked the waitress what kind of fish to expect. "Whatever is fresh," she answered. "Grouper and snapper today; a little later in the summer, swordfish."

The appetizer was followed by brandy pumpkin soup, a grainy orange bisque that was intensely pumpkiny, but not the slightest bit sweet, nothing like a bowl of Thanksgiving pie. A basket of tiny white and whole-wheat buns came with the soup, along with sweet butter in a silver scallop shell.

Main courses were sided by rice pilaf and a mound of fresh fruit—a sliver of honeydew melon, a piece of pineapple, a wedge of orange. On a second visit we sampled giant squid, served "abalone style," a San Diego specialty; that means the lengths of squid are breaded and fried, minimizing their resilience. Dungeness crabs (from farther up the coast, late fall and winter only) are steamed in the shell and served in a butter broth laced with dry white wine. There are never more than five or six different entrees on the Catch of the Day menu.

Portions are not enormous; you will have an appetite for dessert. It was a toss-up for us between Irish coffee pie and Amaretto Bavarian cream. We chose both. They were similar in looks—whipped cream fluffs scented with their respective liquors. Of the two, the Amaretto won by a nose; we were enthralled by its pale almond scent.

Catch of the Day is California casual. At both lunch and dinner, our fellow diners were clad in everything from jogging shorts to IBM-style business suits; and nobody looked askance at anybody else—except for the two of us, who were busily trying to figure out a way to steal the red rockfish filet in mushroom sauce from the diner at the next table. Oh, well, next time, for sure.

Cocina Corina

2040 W. Sunset Blvd., Los Angeles, Calif. In front of Sunset East Car Wash
No phone; car wash number is (213) 484-0821

Usually open

Under $5

We'd like to be more exact about Cocina Corina's hours of operation, but the folks at the stand would only tell us that they are "always open, usually." The guys who work in the car wash—regular patrons of this tiny *cocina*— said that yes, they bought tacos and burritos twenty-four hours a day. If you plan to come sample this California-Mexican meal-in-a-tortilla, we suggest calling the car wash and asking them to check out front to see what's what.

What you will get are some of the best burritos in a city where burritos are nearly as popular as burgers—overstuffed, sloppy rolled-up tubes oozing oily *carnitas*, pig stomach, tongue, or fierce chili *verde*, all garnished with breathy fresh cilantro.

A model Los Angeles street meal: while dining alfresco, standing on the sidewalk, you can watch your car getting clean.

The Crab Cooker

2200 Newport Blvd., Newport Beach, Calif.
(714) 673-0100

Daily 11 a.m.–9 p.m., later on weekend nights & in summer

$5–$15

The Crab Cooker is a *fun* restaurant, meaning the decor is a goof—a thirty-foot stuffed killer shark hanging from the ceiling; old street signs on the walls; a few nautical instruments. It is a former warehouse with its work-manlike air intact. You eat at picnic tables off plastic plates, with plastic utensils. *Fun* also means that you serve yourself, and that the cooks cook the food in the dining room with a fair degree of panache: like the famous Canlis Restaurant, without the high prices or maitre d'.

Surprise! Despite the fun, the food at The Crab Cooker is good. Simple seafood: filets of halibut and chinook salmon, white sea bass, rock cod. It is not all neighborhood fish. The restaurant's namesakes come from up the coast (Dungeness crabs) or Alaska (king crabs). Oysters are flown in from Long Island, littleneck clams from Massachusetts—but they survive the journey, and are plump and tender on their half-shells between October and April.

From the clams, The Crab Cooker makes a chowder touted as "the world's best." It isn't; but it is good—a California interpretation of Manhattan chowder, with plenty of vegetables and clam bits, but not nearly as stout as the definitive version at the Grand Central Oyster Bar.

From local waters comes rock cod, broiled over mesquite coals—firm and moist, breaking easily into thick flakes when prodded with a plastic fork. White sea bass is lean, its delicate flavor heightened by char-broiling. Chinook salmon (*chinook* is an Indian word for "spring," which is generally when it becomes available) is a fabulous dish when cooked over coal until the oily red meat sizzles.

Along with the broiled fish you get Romano potatoes (like mashed, with Romano cheese) or rice pilaf, slaw or fresh tomatoes.

That's about it, except to say that you enter through a fish market, and will probably have to wait in line (no reservations), and you shouldn't come if you want a quiet time. The Crab Cooker is a boisterous restaurant, the place to dine if you are in the mood for lots of local color—and Pacific seafood.

Des Alpes

732 Broadway, San Francisco, Calif.
(415) 788-9900

Tues.–Sun. dinner   Reservations advised

$10 or less

If you really love to eat, if eating is the point of visiting anywhere, San Francisco is a troublesome town. There is so much good stuff, and seldom enough time or appetite to get it all. Cioppino, sourdough bread, cracked Dungeness crab, petrale sole, hangtown fry, a New Joe Special: all are required eating. At the top of our list of uniquely San Franciscan dining pleasures is a meal in a North Beach boarding house, preferably Des Alpes.

Des Alpes no longer houses roomers, but the clientele includes a large number of Basque sheepherders who have come to town from the California hills. They are the hearty souls whose outdoor cookery was the inspiration for the now-famous boarding-house meals.

But Des Alpes is not a place for frontier chow. Unlike the lumpish Basque feeds served in the hotels and rooming houses of the mountains, Des Alpes refines the shepherds' cookery, serving meals that are notable as much for the excellence as for the abundance of the food.

Not that you shouldn't wear comfortable, loose-fitting clothes to dinner here; portions are staggering. First come split-pea soup and baskets of sour-dough bread. Next—here's where Des Alpes takes a higher road than its country cousins—green beans in a high-spirited mustard vinaigrette, laced with onions and hard-boiled eggs.

Now you are ready to eat. From a limited number of choices (usually two or three), you select an entree *and* a main course. The main course is almost always meat—roast lamb or roast beef, or for an extra couple of dollars, filet mignon. The beef, which we had on Saturday night, is expertly roasted, dripping with a flavorful pan gravy.

Before the meat, though, you get a "main course"—a giant portion of food that would happily serve any hungry person as a full dinner. This is the most distinctly Basque part of the meal. Our Saturday entree choices were sole and lamb. We chose lamb, a breathtaking stew in which the high flavor of the meat is buoyed even further by immoderate amounts of garlic and onion. Des Alpes' repertoire of main courses includes oxtail stew in wine sauce, steamed clams or trout with rice, lamb stew, sweetbreads, and tongue and mushroom casserole—traditional shepherd's dishes.

No one would call this food elegant; and in the hands of lesser cooks, it can be leaden. But at Des Alpes, despite the enormity, there is a logic to the meal, a graceful progression from the comfort of the soup to the lively beans to the high flavor point of the Basque stew, then the cushiony luxury of lamb or beef.

It is all followed by a tossed green salad, then coffee and spumoni ice cream.

Des Alpes is a robust place, decorated with pictures of Basque dancers, its table linen of the red-and-white checked variety. The smell of the food, the vigorous flavors, the cacophony of strangers breaking bread together all induce in us the nicest pastoral reveries about the simple life among out-doorsmen. These generous and forceful meals are food for the spirit, too.

The Diner

6476 Washington St., Yountville, Calif.
(707) 944-2626

Breakfast, lunch, & dinner daily

$5–$10

Yountville is fashionable wine country, with an abundance of culinary hot spots to match, but The Diner is something else. As the generic name implies, it is a conscious evocation of another culinary style. But please, purists, don't worry. It is not a camped-up art-deco palace serving imitation blue-plate food. It is not a defunct but now refunct hash house condemned to live again as a soulless diner zombie. It is a simple roadside eatery with real soul, and home cooking the likes of which few old diners ever knew.

Yes, there is a collection of pitchers, Fiestaware, etc., to look at behind the counter, but it seems quite modest because it is so simple. Actually, it's major.

Breakfast ("served all day") is why most people love the diner, with its choice of homemade wholegrain breads—potato, raisin-nut, wheat, or rye; its mammoth omelettes; the *chorizo* sausage-packed breakfast burrito. We like banana-walnut pancakes with real maple syrup; or finely shredded potato pancakes, speckled green with herbs from The Diner's backyard garden; or crisp corn cakes with boysenberry syrup.

But whatever else we get for breakfast, we always order seasoned potatoes: a great mound of buttery fried discs, skins on, laced with sauteed onions, blanketed with melted cheddar cheese. The cheese frizzles on the grill, so although the top is orange and runny, there are lush bottom shreds, browned and tensile, to chew along with the softened spuds.

At sunset, The Diner becomes El Diner, specializing in Cal-Mex cooking: great cheese crisps heaped with hot green peppers and sauce; creamy chicken and cheese enchiladas; shredded beef tacos; *huevos rancheros* atop corn tortillas. Guacamole is outstanding, at once smooth, yet chunky—essence of avocado heightened, but not tarted up, with a dose of fresh garlic.

Flan—pale, creamy, silk smooth—makes an appropriate denouement for the spicy food; but then again, you don't want to eat at The Diner without a few licks of Cassandra Mitchell's hot fudge sauce . . . which we saw her start to brew about 11 a.m. When we returned late that night for a couple of sundaes, our moans of pleasure as we spooned into the dark, grainy chocolate syrup were so exuberant that when we dispatched them (in record time), a lone milk-shake drinker at a nearby counter stool applauded with glee.

You can also get a chocolate, cherry, lemon, or vanilla Coke . . . or "a suicide," combining syrups. At breakfast, the favored beverage is a mimosa, made with fresh O.J. and locally bottled champagne.

Doidge's

2217 Union St., San Francisco, Calif.
(415) 921-2149

Mon.–Wed. 8:30 a.m.–2:30 p.m., Thurs.–Sun. 8:30 a.m.–9 p.m.
Reservations advised

$5–$10

If you've been around the USA, you know that certain meals are at their best in special places. New York is king of lunch; for family-style Sunday dinner, you can't beat the southern midwest; for after-church Sunday lunch, cafeterias in the deep south excel. And when it comes to sunny breakfasts, there is no place like California, from pecan waffles at Hob Nob Hill in San Diego to cocoa coffeecake at Cafe Beaujolais in Mendocino.

For years, every time we came to San Francisco, we breakfasted on Swedish pancakes and sourdough French toast at Sears Fine Foods, which was—and is, and always will be—beyond compare. But one morning in the wine country, as we lay waste to an avocado-and-sour-cream omelette at the premier breakfast place up there—The Diner in Yountville—chef/owner Cassandra Mitchell told us about Doidge's.

Take a look at Doidge's roast beef hash supreme: highly seasoned beef, coarsely cut, mixed with fresh mushrooms, flavored with onions and parsley and gobs of sour cream, its luxury sharpened by the taste of parmesan cheese, the whole heaping mess capped with a perfect poached egg. On the side are golden home-fried potatoes and a sourdough roll. This is breakfast!

But for those of us who have trouble choosing, Doidge's is murder. You like French toast? Great, how'll you have it? Made from white, whole wheat, light rye, dark rye, honey wheat, or raisin nut bread? Want it topped with fresh fruit, fruit and sour cream, or bananas, walnuts and cinnamon?

How about baked eggs, two bright-yolked cackles suspended inside kegs constructed from super-thick honey-cured bacon. Eggs Benedict or Florentine are topped with homemade hollandaise.

The omelette list is endless, including peach and walnut chutney, black olive and Monterey jack cheese, avocado and cream cheese, and all kinds of peppers.

Orange and grapefruit juice are, of course, freshly squeezed.

And do not overlook the possibility of dessert. In fact, if you sit at the counter, you *cannot* overlook it, because there they are in front of you: a German chocolate cake with white chocolate sails on top, and the most splendiforously tall, pure white coconut layer cake.

Doidge's is a cheerful, always crowded storefront, a counter in one room, a few pretty-clothed tables in the other. Doidge himself, in grey-blond bangs, cook's apron, and red bandana, is a natty man with a deep voice who sets up repartee behind the counter that his team of handsome young waiters then carries to the tables.

"We have attempted to provide our guests with an atmosphere that is warm, comfortable, and homey," says the menu. "Time's up!" jokes our waiter one crowded Saturday morning when we dally over choices instead of ordering immediately.

Duarte's

202 Stage Rd., Pescadero, Calif.
(415) 879-0464

Daily 7 a.m.–9 p.m., later on weekends   Reservations advised

$5–$15

To the west is the ocean, where fishermen gather rock cod, sand dabs, clams, oysters, and salmon. To the east is the most fertile farmland in the world, source of fresh tomatoes, corn, new potatoes, beans, lettuce, and artichokes. In the hills are wild berry bushes, orchards of apple and peach trees. And in the kitchen of Duarte's is Ronald Duarte, who regularly transforms the bounty all around into some of the best meals in California.

Square meals: pork chops with mashed potatoes and homemade applesauce (apples from Duarte trees); roast turkey and sage dressing. There is fancier fare, too, also local: rex sole, served with Duarte's tartar sauce; abalone steaks; Pigeon Point oysters (from a few miles away) baked with butter and garlic—a luscious dish to make oyster-lovers weep.

Every Friday and Saturday night, Duarte's makes laudable cioppino, as good as any we've had in San Francisco. It is a mild stew, easy on the garlic and onions, all the better to savor the prawns, clams, and chunks of crab. The tomato sauce in which this large population of shellfish resides is thickened in an ingenious way, with nearly imperceptible flakes of sole. As is customary with California fish stew, sourdough French bread (and salad) comes alongside. The bread is hot. Seconds of the cioppino are included in the price.

Duarte's artichoke soup is one of the most . . . what shall we call it . . . California-tasting dishes imaginable: farmy, good-for-you, and delicious. It is made from the hearts of artichokes. The artichokes are from the Duarte artichoke patch. (At breakfast, omelettes are made from same.)

With such produce, salads are lavish. They are *farm* salads, not elegant ones, made with fresh lettuce, carrots, beets, incomparable beefsteak tomatoes, dressed with tart vinegar and a little oil.

In May, wild Olallie berries are picked in the hills around Pescadero; from them, Emma makes wild berry pie. Later in the summer, the gardens sprout rhubarb; apricots and apples ripen on the trees. Duarte's pie crusts are plain, unsweetened lard pastry—feather light; and despite the spectacular freshness of the ingredients, the pies aren't showy. They are what you would want to be served in a farm wife's kitchen—maybe the best pies west of Arkansas.

The excellence of Duarte's is made more delicious by its lack of airs. It is today what it has been since 1894, when Frank Duarte opened for business: a small-town cafe. There are pine-paneled walls, mismatched tables and chairs, and a few counter seats. Most of the clientele are locals. When it's crowded, tables may be shared by strangers. You couldn't find a restaurant more American, in every good way.

Duke's at the Tropicana

8585 Santa Monica Blvd., Los Angeles, Calif.
(213) 652-9411

Mon.–Fri. 7 a.m.–9 p.m., Sat. & Sun. 8 a.m.–4 p.m.

$5 or less

Blintzes like this you don't even get at Nate and Al's in Beverly Hills: three pillowy crepes packed with cheese, heaped with grilled pineapples, fresh strawberries, or on one wonderful occasion, blackberries. French toast is extra-thick. Banana pancakes, small discs of fruit in feathery batter, sprinkled with cinnamon sugar, smell like heaven.

Three-egg omelettes are gargantuan, accompanied by buttery hash browns, filled with a Californioid ingredients like avocado and sour cream, spinach and ground beef (replicating the Bay Area's "New Joe Special"), fried oysters (hangtown fry), fresh fruit, Chinese vegetables, or a choice of a dozen kinds of cheese.

Orange juice, freshly squeezed and full of pulp, is sold in frosted mugs, or by the quart. Why is this California juice better than anywhere else in the USA?

Later in the day, Duke's offers a roster of two dozen hamburgers, French dip, three-deck sandwiches, "the duchess" (peanut butter, Boursin cheese, turkey, Canadian bacon, and cottage cheese!), "crusts" (sandwiches grilled on sourdough bread), and a whole range of southern California healthy eccentricities (such as a date shake).

But breakfast is the best time to come to Duke's, an only-in-L.A. dining experience. That is when the shared tables in the crowded coffee shop are elbow to elbow with geeks and pointy-haired pinheads and muscle boys, Hollywood agents, nervous lead guitarists, truck drivers reading *Billboard* and *Variety*, and stars coming back to search for their lost roots.

It is a genuine Hollywood hangout, located in the Tropicana Motel, where aspiring rock 'n' rollers stay. What a dump!

El Indio Shop

3695 India St., San Diego, Calif.   Sassafrass exit off I-5
(619) 299-0333

Mon.–Sat. 8 a.m.–8 p.m., until 7 p.m. in winter

$5 or less

El Indio is the tortilla factory that supplies the best Mexican restaurants in San Diego with chips and tortillas—and also uses its freshly made tortillas as the basis for some delicious take-out food. If you don't have anyplace to take the food to, don't worry: across the street is a fenced-in area El Indio provides for patrons, where you can spread your feast out under the warm San Diego sun on yellow cement picnic tables.

To order, step up to the counter under the portraits of a variety of Mayan gods: the god of war, the god of spring, of wind, of rain, and a new one on us —El Indio, the god of Mexican food. The cuisine is Sonoran-style, which means that you can eat it without fear of first-degree tongue burns.

Some specialties, like the hot corn tortillas, are available only when they are being made. (The machines are visible, behind the counter.) But given the specialization of El Indio's factory, the selection is broad: including *chimichangas, quesadillas,* tostadas of every kind, *nachos,* tamales, fruit burros, enchiladas, tacos, rice and beans, and dandy little items known diminutively as *taquitos.*

Meals come laid out in plastic take-out plates, the kind that look like giant Styrofoam clams. We pried our first plate open and found one of the most pulchritudinous *chimichangas* we've ever seen—a rolled flour tortilla oozing shreds of tender pot roast. It is deep-fried, then topped with guacamole and a blob of sour cream. Neatly arranged on the side were tomato slices and a cup of hot sauce to regulate the spice quotient.

Our *quesadilla* was even milder than the *chimi.* It too came in a flour tortilla casing, but one stab of the fork, and out flowed yellow cheese and peppers like slow lava.

El Indio's *taquitos* are small rolled-up tacos stuffed with browned meat and topped with finely grated cheese and lettuce. They are easy to eat— nothing falls out, as often happens with full-size tacos—and at less than 50¢ apiece, they're the best bargain in the place.

To complete this meal that consisted of three flour tubes filled with various things, we ordered a fourth, a fruit burro. This seductive whale must have weighed at least a pound—that is, a pound's worth of hot, somewhat gloppy fruit rolled and fried into a flour tortilla, then hit with a snowstorm of cinnamon sugar. It was a fried pie that looked like the original mother ship that all those pitiful fast-food fried pies try to emulate.

Perhaps when you visit El Indio, you will want to balance your meal better by choosing from the more than sixty non-tubular items on the menu.

But even if you go fried-tube happy as we did, you'll be eating some of San Diego's best Mexican food.

The Grill on the Alley

9560 Dayton Way, Beverly Hills, Calif.
(213) 276-0615

Mon.–Thurs. 11:30 a.m.–11 p.m., Fri. & Sat. until midnight
Reservations advised

$10–$40

It is hard to think of California, Beverly Hills in particular, as part of the great American west, but here it is—just off Rodeo Drive, behind Giorgio's boutique. The Grill serves square meals in strapping portions: meat and potatoes, fish and vegetables, even ham and eggs. The house motto, inscribed on every menu, reads "quality without compromise."

The dining room, aswarm with white-jacketed waiters, is comfortable, but nearly Spartan. You sit in a wide green booth at a table draped in heavy linen; you are surrounded by dark wood and mirrored walls; the scenery consists of other diners—the colorful people who live and work in the never-never land on the west side of Los Angeles.

In this glittering context, there is something affected about the less-is-more simplicity of The Grill; but the affect is all to the good. The bottom line is that the food, for what it is, has no peers anywhere in Southern California.

The menu (printed each day) is devoid of gastronomic braggadocio. It is a lucid, generic itemization that demands nothing beyond a rudimentary understanding of the English language and familiarity with the civilized eating habits of the western world. How delightful it is to find appetizers listed under a category called *appetizers*, soups under the heading *soups*, steaks and chops under *charcoal broiled meats*.

Our own personal favorite category is *potatoes and onions*, a glorious array that includes crunchy hashed browns; diced O'Briens mixed with onions, red and green peppers; a big baked spud; shoestrings; french fries; lyonnaise (with onions); and french-fried onions. The listing "fried potatoes and onions" is brittle shoestrings topped with ethereal onion rings so tender they fall apart as you grasp them. A single order, at $4, is enough for three or four normal appetites. The menu also lists an order for four, at $7. If three hippos will be joining you, it might be just the ticket.

You want regional specialties? Here is the best Cobb salad in the west: crisp smoky bacon, tender chunks of avocado, meaty turkey breast, powerful blue cheese, and a bunch of other things all chopped so fine you don't recognize them. This is what Cobb salad ought to be: cold, strong, pungent, a real kick in the rear, and a nice meal for the modest appetite.

Terrific steaks and chops: big, sizzling strips of charcoal-grilled beef, pork chops, double-cut lamb chops. The calves liver steak is a full inch thick, as soft as cream. You can get a baked half chicken or a broiled chicken imprinted with garlic. There is plenty of fish, too, grilled or sauteed. The charcoaled halibut we gobbled up was firm, white, juicy with a crusty zest along its edges.

The dessert list is delightfully retro: rice pudding, apple pie, berries and cream, ice cream, cake. The hot fudge sundae, made from pure (made-here) vanilla ice cream with a pitcher of spicy chocolate fudge on the side, is a drop-dead winner. Rice pudding is thick and plump and cheerfully plain. Only chocolate layer cake is not exactly true to form. It is—how shall we put it?—*gourmet* cake, sinful, too much like candy fudge and not enough like granny's (or Duncan Hines').

We are reminded, as we leave, that this restaurant is indeed in Beverly Hills. As the host seats a couple in a booth near the bar, we overhear him confiding, "You have the best table in the house." Hey, that's what he told us when he sat us in back!

Hob Nob Hill

2271 First Ave., San Diego, Calif.
(619) 239-8176

Sun.–Fri. 7 a.m.–9 p.m.

Breakfast $5 or less, lunch and dinner $4–$10

Hob Nob Hill is a gem. It has outstanding food, a homey atmosphere, and spectacularly good service. By good service, we do not mean that a waiter introduces himself to you by name; nor does the staff fawn. At Hob Nob Hill, you are served by professional waitresses, good old gals who favor big starched hankies worn on the bosom and white shoes with enough or-thopedic sole to lay rubber when they peel away from your table toward the kitchen. You do not have *a* waitress at Hob Nob Hill; you have several. They work as a team; and there is always one nearby to refill your coffee or anticipate your needs.

The service is matched by a kitchen that is a bastion of American food, prepared from scratch, presented in the most appetizing way possible. You couldn't go wrong if you ate here three times a day.

But if you are to dine at Hob Nob Hill only once, come for breakfast. Start with orange juice—pulpy, freshly squeezed; the coffee is top-quality brew; the maple syrup is hot. You are indulged in such niceties as fruit jelly served in a scooped-out orange half, garnished with mint. There are always at least a half dozen different Hob Nob Hill coffee cakes, sweet rolls, and muffins from which to choose.

The pecan waffle is our favorite breakfast—a golden confection with bits of nut in the batter and a shower of whole pecans on top. We also love eggs

Florentine—poached, on a bed of spinach, topped with cheddar cheese sauce. On the side of most breakfasts, you get a square of Hob Nob Hill coffee cake, a pineappley crumb-topped pastry. Or you can choose biscuits.

Hob Nob Hill's most extravagant breakfast is smoked pork chops and eggs. The chops are big, grilled to a reddish-brown crispness. "Three Musketeers" is another luxey platter—pancakes wrapped around ham or sausage and topped with sour cream.

At lunch and dinner, the Hob Nob Hill menu features warming food like chicken and dumplings, roast tom turkey with sage dressing and giblet gravy, and chicken-fried steak with cream gravy. You can get roast pork with an apple ring, ham and yams, or a set of well-stacked turkey croquettes.

Vegetables are fresh; applesauce is homemade, served warm; whipped potatoes are the McCoy.

Hob Nob Hill's desserts have such a good reputation in San Diego that many people buy whole pies and cakes to cart away and serve at home. You could eat here ten times and still not sample everything wonderful from the bakery, but we'd recommend the devilishly chocolatey individual bundt cakes, the German chocolate cake, and the lighter zucchini walnut loaf.

To whet your appetite, the cakes, loaves, and butter cream fancies are displayed in a glass case as you enter, along with Hob Nob Hill's single most delicious sweet—pecan rolls.

There is almost always a short line of people at the door, but don't let it dissuade you. It moves fast, and this restaurant is worth the wait. We cannot count the number of times, far away from San Diego, we have longed to be waiting in this line, about to enjoy the total excellence of Hob Nob Hill's food, and the probity of its style.

Ida's Seafood Restaurant

4230 Cabrillo Hwy., Princeton, Calif.   Northwest of El Granada
(415) 726-2822

Tues.–Sun. noon–8:30 p.m.   Shorter hours in winter

Abalone $15–$20, other meals $10 or less

"Unless it's February or August, or unless there is a problem with the boat or the diver is sick, we have abalone," Ida told us. The rarest of Pacific seafoods, abalone is invariably the most expensive item on a seafood restaurant's menu (when it is on the menu at all); and it is, almost without exception, frozen. Ida's is the exception.

Abalone's exalted reputation is based on a combination of taste and texture. (Although it lives in a shell, it is not a shellfish, but a snail.) While freezing does not compromise the taste, it does toughen the meat, generating a resilience similar to squid. Ida's abalone steak, tenderized by gentle pounding, is breaded and grilled just long enough to impart a quality of being cooked—yet briefly so the meat retains its distinctive milky succulence. Like some kind of ocean silk, abalone is a sumptuous experience for the taste buds, comparable to no other food.

An Ida's abalone dinner comes with a cocktail of fresh crabmeat or shrimp, salad or creamy clam chowder, and french fries. Dessert consists of ice cream or, sometimes, carrot cake.

There is other seafood on the menu, including local sole, fish and chips, and Mexican prawns. But if abalone is available, you'd be crazy to get anything else.

Ida's is an unprepossessing family-style restaurant—the last place in the world you would expect to find so precious a catch. But Princeton is a village from which divers regularly go out for abalone. Ida's son is one of the fishermen. (The Princeton Inn, on the main street of town, also sells fresh abalone when it can be had.) The village is a quaint place, with a large measure of local color. Ida's, at the turnoff for town on the scenic coast highway, has been here for more than twenty years.

Jerry's Farmhouse

10005 State Rte. #1, Olema, Calif.   At Point Reyes National Seashore
(415) 663-1264

Tues.–Sun. noon–9 p.m.

$10 or less

The Point Reyes National Seashore is a woodsy piece of the northern coast just south of Bodega Bay, where Alfred Hitchcock filmed *The Birds*. At the entrance is Olema; POPULATION 60, ELEVATION 55. The town has a very nice Mexican/eclectic inn (so eclectic it makes its own version of "oysters Mosca" —cheesier than its New Orleans inspiration, but not bad) and it has Jerry's Farmhouse, a barn of a restaurant that serves California fish with down-home biscuits on the side.

Oysters (from Drakes Bay, on the western edge of the Seashore), prawns, and calamari are pan-fried to a fine crisp. The calamari was for us a revelation; pan-frying lessened its toughness without diminishing the flavor. The oysters survived the heat well, too, still plump and sweet. These oysters are especially good in oyster stew, served (like all a la carte dinners) with hot French bread.

Halibut is a house specialty, grilled and drizzled with butter; or you can get a more luscious fish, true cod (as opposed to the leaner ling cod), from Bodega Bay. Shrimp, crab, or combination seafood salads are available with

San Francisco-style Louie dressing. A few steaks, spit-roasted chicken, and sandwiches round out Jerry's menu; and there is a fish fry every Friday.

Good seafood, capably prepared; but what we like most at Jerry's are the biscuits served with dinner. They are broad baking-powder biscuits, steamy white, begging for a little of the honey or made-here strawberry jam that comes alongside. They seem the most basic breadstuffs in the world, but Agnes Bunce, who makes them, told us the recipe is a close-kept one, passed down by her grandmother.

Jerry's is a fine place for a warming snack on the way to or from Point Reyes—oysters on the half shell (okay, so they're not warming; but they are fresh and beautiful), a bowl of oyster stew or clam chowder, or good home-made chili. Whatever else you order, get those biscuits on the side.

Lazio's Seafood

C St. on Humboldt Bay, Eureka, Calif.
(707) 442-2337

Daily 11 a.m.–10 p.m.   Until 11 p.m. in summer

$5–$15

The "local fresh" Dungeness crabs hawked on Fishermen's Wharf in San Francisco are almost all trucked down from Eureka, where not only crabbing but all kinds of Pacific fishing is great. In fact, the largest fishing fleet on the northern coast is berthed in Humboldt harbor, just outside of Lazio's restaurant.

Between late November and July, there is no better place to sample Dungeness crabs. They are literally fresh off the boats, simply steamed, cracked, and served with melted butter.

Another dish on the menu during crab season is cioppino, a specialty so distinctly San Franciscan that it seems sacrilegious to eat it in Eureka—but damned if Lazio's version isn't everything you want cioppino to be. (There is, in fact, no according-to-Hoyle recipe; cioppino is reinvented by everyone who cooks it.) It's a hearty stew made with chunks of fresh, tender crabmeat and shrimp, some finned fish too, all crowded into a tomato and olive-oil sauce. Lazio's version, true to cioppino's Italian-American ancestry, seethes with Mediterranean spices; and like paella or bouillabaisse, it calls for sturdy bread to sop up its juice. Lazio's bakes its own every day.

In the summer, before the crabs start coming in, Lazio's will serve you some of the freshest fish in northern California: fine-textured petrale sole, neatly fileted and grilled; tiny rex sole; ling cod (not cod at all, ling has a leanness unlike its juicier eastern namesake); and Pacific oysters, either broiled or on the half shell. Other than the good bread, side dishes are nothing much: french fries, salad, some fair chowders (both white and red). Breyer's ice cream is served for dessert.

One of the best things about Lazio's is its decor: a wall of raw fish, part of the seafood market with which the restaurant shares space.

Meyera

3009 Main St., Santa Monica, Calif.
(213) 399-1010

Fri. & Sat. only 6 p.m.–10 p.m.   Reservations necessary

$10–$20

Any book about American regional specialties ought to include a southern California vegetarian restaurant. But with the exception of the Orange Inn in Corona del Mar and Ratner's in New York, most vegetarian kitchens we know would qualify only if the title of this book were changed to *Smelly Unappetizing Food*.

Meyera is a third exception: a meatless restaurant that satisfies. The food is interesting; it tastes good; meals have the balance lacking in ordinary temples of rice-and-bean cookery. You come away full and happy, and not flatulent.

Some of what you'll get is completely original, like the "cauliflower parachute" in filo pastry (an occasional special appetizer), stuffed with sage dressing, accented with blue-cheese sauce. Other dishes are trompe l'oeil, and nearly fool your nose and tastebuds, too: bean stroganoff, for instance, in which legumes do a remarkable impression of beef; or fishless sushi— sweet-seasoned rice, wrapped in seaweed, served with the fiery white-radish paste called *wasabe*.

Of necessity, vegetarian is an inventive cuisine: terrine made from wild rice; an appetizer of fried wontons filled with ginger-shocked mushrooms; hearty soups made with surprisingly beefy all-vegetable stock.

Meyera's inventions work because, although flesh is banned from the kitchen, butter and cream are not. Butter-brushed filo pastry wraps many of Meyera's dishes; the stroganoff, on a bed of slippery egg noodles, is blanketed with sour cream and chives; vegetable casseroles come with robust cream sauces.

Dairy products impart weight, and ingenious seasoning makes the food interesting. Greek salad, for instance, is topped with salty goat cheese and cream dressing bright with mint. The spinach salad gets its accent from sesame seeds.

Dessert is one course never handicapped by meatlessness; and since

Meyera's cuisine is more *vegetarian* than it is *health food*, cakes and tortes, heavy with butter, cream, nuts, and fruit, are off the map.

A small, simple place—no ferns, just a few flowers on the tables, and plain white walls. Even hard-core carnivores will come away happy.

Musso and Frank Grill

6667 Hollywood Blvd., Hollywood, Calif.
(213) 467-7788

Mon.–Sat. 11 a.m.–11 p.m.

$2–$15, more for abalone

Long before Ma Maison served its fabled duck in two courses and Spago's cooked its first chichi pizza, even before Dave Chasen brewed his first bowl of chili, there was a Musso and Frank Grill.

Hollywood's oldest restaurant is on Hollywood Boulevard, the now freakish strip of yellow brick road where sidewalks decorated with brass stars are trod by roller-skating hookers and loitering weirdos with tans.

Once inside Musso's, you are back in touch with normality. A veteran waiter will competently guide you through a long but reassuring menu (printed daily) that lists, for instance, eleven different types of potatoes— boiled new, candied sweet, French fried, American fried, mashed, julienne, lyonnaise, hashed brown, cottage fried, baked, and au gratin. (If we ever do our dream book, *Great Potatoes of America*, we'll start here.) There are two dozen salads and no less than thirty entrees.

Michel Bourger, "our chef from Paris, France" (as opposed to Paris, Illinois?), does great things with Pacific seafare. Some days it is possible to spend $20 for pounded-tender abalone steaks, sauteed in butter judiciously enough to stay tender. Ours was still moist with the shimmering white juice that distinguishes this from all lesser gastropods.

For half the price, you can get sand dabs—tiny, fine-textured and deliciously sweet Pacific flounders, fileted and sauteed in butter.

Good fish, but what we really like about Musso's are its meatier American classics: the chicken pot pie (a Thursday special), corned beef and cabbage (Tuesday only), roast lamb, Welsh rarebit (the best we've had outside of Brooklyn's Gage and Tollner), minced chicken and baked ham. Steaks and lamb chops, turned on an open broiler at dinnertime, are flawless.

A loaf of sourdough bread accompanies the meal, a perfect anchor to the lighter, more distinctly southern Californian fare, such as Musso's legendary chiffonade seafood salad or a fresh mushroom omelette.

You couldn't possibly find a squarer dessert selection if the Osmonds opened a pie shop in Salt Lake City. There are two dozen desserts on Musso's menu, and not one mousse or soufflé among them: bread and butter pudding, chocolate cake, rice pudding, butterscotch sundae, fruit compote, sherbets and pies and ice creams, and, oh yes, for the sophisticate—"diplomat pudding," bread pudding with sweet strawberry topping.

If you want to pass for a native, come to Musso's before three in the afternoon and order flannel cakes, named for their thinness by the chef who invented them years ago. You get three plate-sized pancakes with maple or boysenberry syrup and melted butter. If we lived in Los Angeles, we would eat flannel cakes six mornings a week; they're the only way to start the day in glamour gulch.

Mustard's Grill

Rte. 128, Yountville, Calif.
(707) 944-2424

Daily 11:30 a.m.–9 p.m., Fri. & Sat. until 10 p.m.   Reservations essential

$10–$15

The parking lot is curb-to-curb BMWs. Inside, the bar is packed with customers waiting for their precious table. Grape growers, vintners, wine buyers, and oenophiles fell in love with Mustard's when it opened a few years back, and now the handsome grill is theirs.

For a taste of what has become classic wine-country cooking—food that the rest of us consider "California cuisine"—this is the place. It is hip and informal, waiters dressed in long white aprons, patrons in open shirts. Food is cooked in a wood-burning oven or on a mesquite grill. No liquor is served, but the wine list is strictly local, including boutique vineyard rarities you'll find nowhere else.

For us, Mustard's was a revelation. We had grown too accustomed to the rest of the country's imitations of its style of cooking, and were bored with it before the first course arrived. But we perked up quickly, because this is the real thing, not a watered-down version; here is justification for all the clichés about fresh ingredients, innovative combinations, and recherché cooking styles.

From the wood-burning oven come gorgeous half slabs of baby back ribs; gamy grilled duck leg, served with sausage and polenta; smoked, then pan-fried jumbo prawns; and a gloriously simple herbed chicken, slightly charred, accompanied by sweet mustard sauce.

Of course they have a mesquite grill, turning out fresh fish, chops, chicken with cilantro butter, etc.

For starters, check out warm goat cheese salad—a small round of creamy chèvre rolled in pulverized almonds, decorated with bright red strips of sun-dried, olive-oil–drenched tomato. You can get a cornmeal pancake with sour cream and caviar, or a whole head of roasted garlic (squeeze the heat-tempered buds out, one by one, on slices of toast provided). Hamburgers and onion rings are first-rate.

For dessert: homemade ice cream (we tried banana rum, which was swell); chocolate pecan cake with bittersweet chocolate sauce; and rice pudding, dolloped with bourbon cream sauce.

This is the food of the 1980s: modern and, by golly, good.

Nepenthe

Rte. 1, Big Sur, Calif.
(408) 667-2345

Daily 11:30 a.m.–9:30 p.m.

$5–$15

What a view! Nepenthe is more than thirty years old (it was once owned by Orson Welles), and predates local zoning laws prohibiting construction over the ocean. It is all native materials—adobe and redwood and glass, designed by a Frank Lloyd Wright student. Eight hundred feet below the stone dining terrace, waves crash against rocks. To the southwest, you can see the sun set every night.

Quite a burger, too, although nothing can compete with the drama of the architecture and the strong dose of nature. It's called an ambrosiaburger —a thick patty of ground steak on a French roll, in a basket, sided by a kosher pickle and a choice of salads (we like the herby garbanzo and kidney bean salad best). Mayonnaise sauce ("ambrosia sauce," what else?) comes with it.

Although the burger is the specialty of the house—and a worthy one it is—you can get good roast chicken at Nepenthe—called "Lolly's roast chicken," served with sage dressing. The vegetarian chef salad, crowned with sunflower seeds and sprouts, is monumental . . . and satisfying. There are steaks, fresh fish, soups, and a cheese-and-fruit board. Carrot cake is the choice dessert.

At Nepenthe, diners make themselves at ease sitting around the bar or lounging semi-prone on cushions, or cuddling in front of the enormous brick fireplace. Even a couple of crabby writers from Connecticut couldn't help but feel romantic.

Obrero Hotel

1208 Stockton St., San Francisco, Calif.
(415) 986-9850

Daily dinner 6:30 p.m.   Reservations advised

$10 or less

Find a seat at one of the long family-style tables in the small dining room. At six-thirty, the meal begins: a North Beach boarding-house feast, Basque-style.

The wine is poured (house wine or bring your own); baskets of hot sour-dough bread are passed, and soup is served from a deep tureen. The soup is a major undertaking, thick and heavily spiced—either split-pea or lemon-soured vegetable with grated cheddar cheese.

After the soup comes Basque stew, perhaps the cassoulet of white beans, sausage, lamb, pork, and several strong cloves of garlic (on Tuesday), or—the best deal of the week—shepherd's pie with a cloud of mashed potatoes for a crust (on Sunday). Other dishes filling this penultimate spot in the menu lineup are oxtail stew (Monday and Saturday), pasta with clam sauce (Wednesday), spare ribs (Thursday), and rex sole (Friday).

Following the stew, you are served the main course—roast beef, lamb, or chicken. It is accompanied by mashed potatoes or french fries—big potato logs with a startling and stupendously good garlic flavor. Along with the meat comes a salad of cabbage and zucchini in an oil and vinegar dressing.

The meal concludes with Monterey Jack cheese, a piece of fruit, and coffee.

The Obrero has always served traditional Basque meals to a varied clientele of city folks and shepherds. Its twelve rooms have recently been remodeled, and are available for approximately $30 per night for a double (no bath), including breakfast. That has to be the best hotel deal in the city —and you get the added bonus of living just upstairs from one of the best of San Francisco's legendary boarding-house meals.

The Orange Inn

7400 East Coast Hwy. (Rte. 101), Corona del Mar, Calif.
(714) 644-5411

Daily 9 a.m.–6 p.m.

$5 or less

The Orange Inn makes healthy food that tastes good. Twenty different kinds of milk shakes: fig, carob, guava, date, papaya, every kind of California fruit you want. Orange Inn "smoothies" are even better than shakes—blenderized meals in a cup made with freshly squeezed fruit juices, plus coconut milk, protein powder, bee pollen and similar thickeners. Heavy banana cake, apricot brownies, organic peanut butter sandwiches on whole-grain bread, sesame candy: luscious and sweet and fattening food—but eminently good for you.

The Orange Inn was around long before America's cereal manufacturers learned to tout products as "natural." A former tomato-packing house, it became a health-food store in the early 1930s, one of the first on the west coast; and miraculously, the land around it has stayed undeveloped. There are a few hundred head of Irvine Company cattle out back, horse stables across the street, and a clear blue sky overhead.

It's an orange-trimmed shack with no place to eat inside—but what kind of pasty-faced eastern mole would want to ingest a honey and banana smoothie indoors?

Our arms loaded with about a dozen pounds of health-giving shakes, cakes, and candies, we were directed to picnic benches, strategically placed under trees to provide a view of the sailboats skimming across the water. We breathed the palmy air, absorbed some solar rays, dispatched our smoothies, and soon began to feel just like The Orange Inn's regular customers—muscular, blond, smiling, bathing-suited beach people who appear to have never had a sad thought or suffered the heartbreak of bad skin or flabby bodies.

Original Joe's

301 S. 1st St., San Jose, Calif.
(408) 292-7030

Daily 10:30 a.m.–1:45 a.m.

$5–$15

The San Francisco Bay area has a surfeit of Joes: Little Joes, New Joes, Original Joes, Baby Joes, and just plain Joes, many in some ways related to the original Joe's Restaurant on Broadway, where the New Joe Special was invented.

A melting-pot dish that combines California love of burgers with northern Italian passion for spinach, the New Joe Special (also known as Joe's Special) is distinctly San Franciscan; and among the city's multitude of Italian restaurants, even many of those not called Joe serve their own version.

The New Joe's that invented it is long gone, but as near as we can tell, the Joes who run *this* Original Joe's (not Original Joe's Italian Restaurant on Taylor Street in San Francisco) are most directly related to New Joe's. Got that? Never mind. Here's the point: come to 301 South First Street in San Jose, and sample a superior version of a unique regional specialty.

Original Joe's "Joe's Special" is a hill of ground beef mixed with spinach, mushrooms, onions, and eggs. Heavy, oily, satisfying; a heartier dish you won't find. When you discover that you can't finish it, the waiter is ready with a take-home carton. *Nobody* finishes a meal at Original Joe's. Portions of everything are gigantic.

With the exception of a few excellent grilled steaks (the size of catcher's mitts, and expensive), the rest of the menu is boilerplate Italian—Italian-American, actually; pastas in various sauces, superior minestrone soup, marsalas, scallopinis, and cacciatores. Everything is served with hunks of bread; garlic bread is made with fresh garlic.

Original Joe's is flamboyant and fun. Food is cooked exhibition-style, waiters wear tuxedos, and there is usually a line of people waiting to eat.

Philippe the Original

1001 N. Alameda St., Los Angeles, Calif.
(213) 628-3781

Daily 6 a.m.–10 p.m.

$5 or less

It was a sad day, Los Angeles correspondent Paul Rayton told us, when the price of coffee went up at Philippe's. It now costs 10¢ a cup. Used to be a nickel.

Not much else ever changes at this septuagenarian landmark across from Union Station and the post office. The floors are strewn with sawdust, waitresses still wear tiny "cupcake hats" atop their sculpted hairdos, and you have to wonder if anyone, at any time in the last decade, has bought and eaten one of the hard-boiled eggs (dyed red) floating listlessly in brine at the counter.

This antique mess hall claims to have invented the French dip sandwich. In the same genre as Buffalo's "beef on weck," Chicago's "Italian beef," and Philadelphia's "cheese steak" (but without the cheese), the west coast's version is thin-sliced roast beef on a hard roll, called a "dip" because the inside of the roll is sopped with gravy before it sandwiches the meat, and "French" because either (a) the roll is French bread, or (b) Philippe was a Frenchman.

L.A. historian Bruce Henstell has another theory: it was not Philippe's, but Cole's P. E. Buffet that invented the French dip in 1908 for a toothless customer who asked the server to soften the roll so he could gum it.

Fortunately, our job does not require us to track down the details of such great moments in gastronomic history, only to guide you to an authentic regional meal; and for that, this joint is a pip.

The roll is a small torpedo—French bread, not sourdough—soft inside, yet with a brittle crust. The beef is tender, steam-table grey, and bland until you slather on Philippe's own hot mustard, a terrific brew (sold in bottles to take home). On the side, scoop up some milky slaw, made with fresh-cut cabbage.

The menu also lists French-dipped ham, pork, or lamb; stew and chili . . . and pigs knuckles ("Philippe's," boasts a small brochure, "is one of the very few restaurants which still prepares and serves close to 200 pounds of pigs feet a week"). For dessert, have a sturdy wedge of pie, or a fat baked-here apple. This is lunch-counter food, served by lightning-fast hash slingers. It is doled out cafeteria style, eaten at weathered wooden booths or communal waist-high tables in the center of the room.

The high chairs at the tables are populated all day long with dime-a-cup coffee hounds, geezers, neighborhood loafers, newspaper readers, and a cast of bit-part characters who seem to have wandered their way out of a Preston Sturges movie, circa 1940.

Picnique in the Pines

727 Main St., Cambria, Calif.
(805) 927-8727

Tues.–Sat. 9 a.m.–8 p.m., Sun. 10 a.m.–3 p.m.

$10 or less

This happy bauble south of San Simeon looks brand new. Blue papered walls, lace curtains, front cases with take-out food, a few tables, inside and on the sidewalk, where ladies come for luncheon and afternoon tea. Everything is immaculate and appetizing.

The cuisine is west coast health/gourmet. After weeks of travel through meat-and-potatoes states to the east, we wallowed in Picnique's "Ivory Coast Salad," a wedge of papaya serving as a boat for shrimps, avocados, orange, and grapefruit segments in a honey-sweetened sour cream dressing. There are spinach and Niçoise salads, Belgian waffles with Devonshire cream, croissant sandwiches, and quiche. You get the idea.

Mostly fresh-fruit concoctions for dessert, but the menu also lists chocolate pasta ("*REALLY!*" it says) and they stuff a wild cannoli with sweet cheese and chocolate chips. Good espresso, cappucino, and café au lait, too.

A real refresher on the coast highway.

Sam's Grill

374 Bush St., San Francisco, Calif.
(415) 421-0594

Mon.–Fri. 11 a.m.–8:15 p.m.   No reservations

$10–$15

To visit San Francisco and not eat at Sam's is like coming to New York and bypassing the Grand Central Oyster Bar. Except that Sam's, open since 1867, is about a half century older.

What's great about Sam's is that for all its history, it is still an unpretentious fish house. The walls are mahogany, the tables are covered with soft white linen, and the waiters wear formal garb; but all of those amenities are just that—old-fashioned amenities, so you should be comfortable.

The menu, printed daily to reflect what's fresh, is a roster of west coast seafood (plus a few broilings, pasta dishes, and omelettes). Sand dabs, tiny flatfish from nearby Pacific waters, are pan-fried in butter and fileted, six little pieces to an order: a delicate plate of fish, the flesh of the dabs pure snowy white. Rex sole is also sold pan-fried, fileted and drizzled with lemon butter. Petrale sole is broiled over charcoal, as is salmon (from Oregon).

You cannot go wrong with any of the simple fish preparations, but neither is it a bad idea to sample a more elaborate specialty. Deviled Crab a la Sam is one of the most delicious meals we have ever had on the west coast —a dish of crab baked in a highly spiced butter cream sauce. The turtle soup tastes *profound*—it is a stunning deep red, scented with clove.

Sam's hangtown fry—a northern California specialty of scrambled eggs and oysters—was peerless. We'll admit we consider it a waste to do anything with an oyster other than eat it raw, but a hangtown fry is one exception. Tiny, briny oysters are used; among the eggs, their textural queerness was a fascinating note.

With the main courses come California-fresh vegetables: artichokes, crunchy asparagus with a mustard-torqued mayonnaise sauce; also, a choice of nearly two dozen salads. Good cheesecake for dessert.

Sam's Grill began as a place for businessmen to lunch, and that is basically what it still is, and why it isn't open on weekends or late at night. Guys in suits monopolize the place at lunchtime; but at dinner or an odd hour, Sam's is a happy place, with a comfortable bar for waiting.

Sears Fine Foods

439 Powell St., San Francisco, Calif.
(415) 986-1160

Wed.–Sun. 7 a.m.–2:30 p.m.

$5 or less

We want to be in San Francisco when it's cold outside. We'll go to Sears about nine in the morning, when there's sure to be a line, and we'll see for ourselves if the owners really park two pink Cadillacs in front of this little coffee shop, with the radios and heaters on, for the comfort of their waiting customers. Hard to imagine hospitality like that, but reliable people swear that Sears's Cadillac Waiting Room is a reality.

If it isn't, we don't care. We'll happily wait in the cold for the city's, if not America's, best breakfast: sourdough French toast, dipped in cream-thickened eggs long enough to soften the chewy texture of the bread, grilled until tan, and served with Sears-made strawberry preserves. The toast is mildly yeasty, sour enough to thread an energetic piquance through the smoothness of the eggs and cream.

The only problem with eating a breakfast of sourdough French toast is that you are not eating Sears's superlative Swedish pancakes—eighteen airy miniatures to an order, like large floppy poker chips. (It is possible to buy the mix of three flours to take home.) Smoked ham and sausage are available on the side. There are waffles with chopped pecans mixed into the batter; banana nut bread; Swedish coffee cake; nice omelettes with crisp hashed-brown potatoes.

Don't miss the fruit bowl appetizer: bananas, peaches, watermelon, honeydew, papayas, strawberries, and whatever else is in season, marinated in orange juice.

Sandwiches, salads, and vegetable plates are made for lunch; also some stupendous pies: deep-dish blueberry, pecan, strawberry cream, and, occasionally, papaya cream.

Shields Date Gardens

Rte. 111 West, Indio, Calif.
(619) 347-0996

Daily 8 a.m.–6 p.m.

Under $5

Date shakes are a southern California tradition, and we know of no better place to taste one than Shields Date Gardens. It is in the Coachella Valley, where most of the dates eaten in America are grown—a cultivated desert that bears an uncanny resemblance to the Middle East, right down to its islands of outlandish wealth where pastel-clad desert rats cruise the streets in Rolls-Royces. Shields Date Gardens plays up the exotica by declaring itself "a bit of old Arabia in modern California."

You can watch your date shake being made at a soda fountain. It's two scoops of vanilla ice cream, a dash of milk, and a scoop of date crystals. The crystals are dry out of the jar, but when they hit moisture, they fatten to a pudgy datelike consistency. The shake is outrageously rich, hard to suck up a straw, creamy and granular—guaranteed to add at least an inch to most of your bodily measurements. Shields also serves black date ice cream, which reminded us of cherry vanilla with the cherries replaced by more voluptuous bits of date.

Aside from the date shakes and ice cream you can sample at the counter or in one of the six shellacked wooden booths along the wall, we like Shields for its ambience. It is chock full of kitsch ranging from hand-tinted photos of Ma and Pa Shields in pith helmets surveying dates, to a show for visitors entitled "The Romance and Sex Life of a Date."

It is also possible to get a list of Mrs. Shields's recipes, including such goodies as "Lazy Gal Recipe" (date crystals and miniature marshmallows—"minute dessert—try it!") and "Hungry Children's Sandwich," a schmear of moistened date crystals between two graham crackers.

Spenger's Fish Grotto

1919 4th St., Berkeley, Calif.
(415) 845-7771

Daily 8 a.m.–midnight   Reservations accepted for parties of six or more

$10 or less

When we heard about Spenger's—that it serves a million pounds of fish in a year, that it sells more meals than any other restaurant in America—we expected the worst: Mama Leone's West, but without the compensation of Mama's million-dollar art collection. We arrived early, to beat the crowds, at five-thirty in the afternoon. And the place was packed. After a half hour in the Diamond Room oyster bar, we got our table, ate fast, and just as quickly exited into a parking lot so large we couldn't find our car.

If Spenger's didn't serve good fish at bargain-basement prices, it would be a drag.

Sand dabs, tiny flounders unique to the west coast, are sweeter and more fragile-flavored than even rex or petrale sole. Spenger's sells them whole, patted with a bit of sweet crackermeal and pan-fried. Ask for yours boned: a heavenly dish of food. (Rex and petrale sole, also Pacific delicacies, are regulars on the menu, sauteed or deep-fried.)

Most local fish are available grilled—halibut, salmon, sea bass, and so forth; and that is without question the best way to savor their various flavors. But be aware that Spenger's deep-fry station is able, on a par with New Orlean's best. What the menu lists as "shrimp scatter" is a school of small bay shrimp in an audibly good gold crust. Oysters, from Spenger's beds, also sheathed in brittle gold, don't lose a bit of their savor.

Spenger's bouillabaisse is a stew of crabmeat, Tomales Bay oysters, prawns, whitefish, and scallops, all in a tomato sauce perking with a spray of Italian spice: cioppino, without shells; it is served with strong garlic toast.

There are probably four dozen entrees on the menu, and as many salads and sandwiches and soups. With so much in the way of fresh and (where we come from) rare fish to choose from, we wouldn't bother with salads (a tossed salad comes with entrees, topped with excellent anchovy dressing); but in this neighborhood, the crab Louie had to be sampled. It was a luxurious mound of fresh crabmeat and mayonnaise spiked with Worcestershire, Tabasco, and bits of pepper—second only to the pinnacle of Louies at Swan Oyster Depot.

Breakfast is the one meal of the day when, if you arrive early enough, there are no crowds. Spenger's makes a luxurious hangtown fry—scrambled eggs and oysters (supposedly invented during the Gold Rush for a newly rich miner who wanted a mess of the most expensive things in the kitchen). And on an even grander scale, there is a Pacifica omelette—a wide egg pancake of shrimp and crabmeat, spinach, and onion.

Despite the rush, Spenger's waiters are helpful, able and willing to tell you what's what.

So, come to Spenger's and expect to wait, then to be processed with as much personal attention as a Ford in the Rouge River plant receives; but *know* you are going to eat well for less money than you'd spend in almost any other fish house in America.

Swan Oyster Depot

1517 Polk St., San Francisco, Calif.
(415) 673-1101

Mon.–Sat. 8 a.m.–5 p.m.

$10 or less

Swan is a seventy-year-old fish market where you will find the best, and most expensive, raw seafood in San Francisco. In the middle of it all is a marble counter strewn with baskets of oyster crackers and lemon wedges. There are eighteen rickety stools at the counter, and you've got to be quick to nab one; but if you do, you are in for some stellar fish.

The menu is oyster-bar simple. The only hot dish is a creamy clam chowder which, while heavy with chopped clams, is a bore. Forget it, and zero in on freshly opened oysters—big steely bluepoints flown in from the east, tiny Olympias from Washington. Or have a salmon sandwich. The salmon is smoked, a mild piece of fish that falls into moist flakes atop rye or French bread.

All good stuff, but the pièce de résistance is one of Swan's salads; we like shrimps and prawns piled atop shredded lettuce, and dolloped with Louie dressing. Invented in San Francisco, Louie is a princely condiment for cold fresh seafood. Swan's version is cool and lemony, the mayonnaise enriched with hard-cooked eggs, dotted with relish and bits of olive.

Starting in November, Swan serves Dungeness crab (the rest of the year, when it is available only frozen, they don't bother). These are the freshest crabs in the city, drawn from the waters just outside the Golden Gate, or if the catch is slim down here, trucked in daily from up the coast. The meat for crab salads is freshly picked, and Swan's crab Louie is the definitive one.

But the purist wants the crab and nothing but the crab—the legs, claws, and that portion of the body with the meat. Swan serves it cool, the hard shell cracked (but not so much you don't have a fine time digging out the meat). Cold cracked Dungeness crab at the Swan Oyster Depot counter, with a beer or a glass of wine on the side, is one of California's and America's incomparable eating pleasures.

Tadich Grill

240 California St., San Francisco, Calif.
(415) 391-2373

Mon.–Sat. 11:30 a.m.–8:15 p.m.   No reservations

$8–$15

If we had time for only one meal in San Francisco, it would be at Tadich Grill, in a curtained walnut booth at a clean white-clothed table. We would order rex sole, broiled over charcoal, its delicacy accentuated by the faint perfume of the coals and a drizzle of butter and lemon. On the side would be a mound of boxy french fries, and just a tad of freshly mixed tartar sauce.

Since there are two of us, the one meal would also include sand dabs, pan-fried in a luscious nutty blend of oils that has been a Tadich specialty for more than a hundred years.

We would begin with clam chowder, a pale orange brew, Manhattan-style; and a fresh crabmeat salad. Of course, there'd be a round of sourdough bread, and we would finish off with a bowl of fresh berries, or Tadich's simple custard or motherly rice pudding.

But enough of this only-one-meal nonsense. One meal is hardly enough to savor all that is good among the four or five dozen entrees on Tadich's menu, which is printed every day to reflect what is fresh: salmon in the spring and summer (cooked on Tadich's great-looking antique broiler), Dungeness crabs beginning in November, eastern oysters except in the summer, even rare Olympias when they can be gotten from Puget Sound.

Although Tadich's hangtown fry is good, and the baked halibut Florentine in cheese sauce on a bed of spinach is better than good, we would put any preparation more elaborate than grilling or frying low on a list of Tadich priorities. You won't find better brook trout anywhere in the Rockies (except perhaps at a fisherman's campfire) than what is served here, perfectly crisped in the pan. Fried Olympia oysters come sheathed in a honey-tone crust that does not overwhelm their tang.

The charcoal grill is worked by a master, whisking halibut, sea bass, brook trout, sole, and snapper on and off with hypnotic dexterity.

Like the cooks, the waiters are fast, smooth with age, occasionally crabby. Decked out in white cotton jackets and long aprons, they are a déjà vu from another era. That's what Tadich Grill is—a piece of the past. Its mahogany walls and seasoned bar, plus an utter lack of pretense, make it one of the city's most pleasurable and comfortable dining places. . . .

With the exception of the crowds. Unless you come by five in the afternoon, you must expect to wait at Tadich Grill, then—unless you get one of the choice booths—to be seated too close to other noisy diners.

The lunch line begins forming at eleven.

(The long counter, by the way, is great for single dining.)

Tick Tock Restaurant

1716 N. Cahuenga Blvd., Hollywood, Calif.
(213) 463-7576

Tues.–Sun. lunch & dinner

$10 or less

We admit a soft spot for idiotic food data. Who can fail to be impressed, for instance, by the fact that Durgin-Park of Boston makes enough Indian pudding in a year to float the *Queen Mary?* And isn't it amazing to consider that, according to *The Total Banana,* a single-minded volume written by Alex Abella in 1979, "if all the bananas imported into the United States were placed end to end, the chain would make a loop twice the distance from the earth to the moon"?

Now, hold onto your hat, because here comes the flattener of food facts, uncovered by a reporter for the Los Angeles *Times:* all the turkey cooked each Thanksgiving at the Tick Tock Restaurant outweighs a Volkswagen!

How far will the turkey necks stretch if laid end to end? Is there enough gravy to fill the Caspian Sea? These are stories yet untold.

Trivia aside, let us consider the important fact: turkey dinner at Hollywood's Tick Tock has been served not only on Thanksgiving, but six days a week, all year around, since 1930. Always the star at the Tick Tock, the full-scale turkey dinner is usually one of several turkey dishes on the menu, including turkey pot pie, hot turkey sandwiches, and turkey hash. None of it is food to take your breath away. But you don't expect razzle-dazzle from turkey; it's more subtle than that. It offers enduring values—sustenance, reassurance, a pillow of mashed potatoes, and the gentle spice of bread stuffing.

There is a full menu, to be sure—square meals like pot roast and leg of lamb, accompanied by homey cinnamon rolls, and followed up by tall meringue pies; but somehow nothing seems as *right* at the Tick Tock as the turkey.

It's a family kind of place, lots of oldsters, children, good old-fashioned normal people the likes of which one seldom sees in trend-setting L.A. restaurants. These folks wait patiently for a table in the venerable Tick Tock because they value fast service, low prices, and food that revives meaning in the restaurant writer's overused adjective "decent."

Tony's Seafood

Highway 1, a mile south of Marshall, Calif.
(415) 663-1107

Fri.–Mon. noon–9 p.m.   Closed in December

$10 or less

How easily the shells pile up. You order the oysters a mere four at a time. They're giants on their gnarled half shells, barbecued a few moments, warm and tender. You cannot eat one in a gulp; it's at least four bites, the sweet meat of the oyster flavored with a hint of charred shell and the buttery red sauce that is brushed on as they cook. By the time you've gone through a dozen, maybe they'll clear the mess away to make room for more; then again, maybe they won't. That's the kind of place Tony's is.

You know the joint means business before you step in the door. Out in front, for all to see, is a godawful mess of a crab-cracking station, a wooden table where the staff works on crabs and oysters, heaving shells to the ground and sending the good stuff inside to be consumed immediately or run over the grill in the extension of the dining room.

We like the barbecued Tomales Bay oysters best (they're served Saturday and Sunday only); but the fresh rock crab is good, if a lot of work even after it's cracked. Clam chowder is thick and smoky, scented with a powerful bouquet of spices.

And Tony's cioppino is a stupendous idea. The mussels, shrimp, crab, calamari, etc., in a tangy red sauce, come to the table inside an entire scooped-out round of sourdough bread. It's gorgeous, except before too long, the bread sogs out, and you wish you had some dry hunks on the side.

Wedged between the highway and the Bay, Tony's is a comfortable spot, bright, local, and friendly. The Konatich family, who run it, have been barbecuing oysters here since 1948.

Whaling Station Inn

763 Wave St., Monterey, Calif.
(408) 373-3778

Daily dinner   Reservations advised

$10–$20

The Whaling Station Inn is one of many expensive dining establishments in this affluent area, and like the rest, it has gourmet food and plenty of atmo to match; but it is the one that takes the best advantage of the sea. A former

Chinese market one block above Cannery Row, it's a romantic spot: dark, all burnished woods, antiques, and stained glass. If you're looking to splurge, here's the place.

The menu is California coastline, with a dash of Italian seasoning. Some of the specialties are strictly local, pulled from Monterey Bay. The best of these are Monterey prawns, catchable only during calm weather, primarily in the fall and winter. They are gigantic, among the most delicious of all Pacific seafoods, laden with roe that gives them an unbelievable richness. They are sauteed in their shells in olive oil and garlic, served on a bed of linguine.

Nearby waters also yield squid, which the Whaling Station sautees with mushrooms, onions, garlic, and a few breadcrumbs. From farther north come Dungeness crabs, put to use here in a wine-rich cioppino, hinting of basil. Whaling Station bouillabaisse is served in a mighty casserole of brass.

Steaks of swordfish, salmon, and tuna (as well as aged beef) are cooked over an open hearth fueled with oak wood. We liked the smoke-perfumed swordfish, its meat sturdy enough to stand up to the flame and come away juicy. Spring, summer, and early fall are salmon season.

This is artichoke country, and the Whaling Station's steamed artichokes served with garlic mayonnaise as appetizers are just about the meatiest ones we've ever encountered. We were told they are from Castroville, about five miles up the coast. A good salad: baby spinach leaves dressed in a vinaigrette flavored with toasted sesame seeds and honey.

Along with the meals come hand-twisted lengths of French bread, the dough slightly sour, topped with sesame seeds.

There are cannolis and eclairs for dessert, and they're okay, but we felt our meal ended just about perfectly with a couple of dishes of strawberries and brown sugar.

Wool Growers Restaurant

609 H St., Los Banos, Calif.
(209) 826-4593

Daily lunch & dinner

$10 or less

The Wool Growers Restaurant is a Basque eating hall across from the train tracks, an old-fashioned kind of restaurant where people go for no other reason than to fill up. Long oilcloth-covered tables are designed to seat twenty or thirty people each, and when it's packed, the Wool Growers holds a couple hundred; even when the restaurant is sparsely populated, the din of eager trenchermen creates a festive air.

Meals are classic shepherds' feasts: soup (vegetable), salad, vigorously garlicked stew (chicken or lamb) followed by a hefty main course. Lamb chops, roast beef, pork chops anchor meals throughout the day. In the evening, customers can tear into a sirloin steak, accompanied by extra mounds of potato salad. Meals are concluded with ice cream and cake, or a hunk of dry jack cheese. Bottles of wine keep coming to the table, and there are baskets of good French bread.

There is a nice old-time bar in the restaurant, but it's the food and food service that create the Wool Growers' induplicable atmosphere.

IDAHO

Wolf Lodge Inn

Frontage Rd., eight miles east of Coeur d'Alene, Idaho
(208) 664-6665

Wed.–Sat. 5 p.m.–10 p.m.

$10–$25

When we began looking for regional food, we assumed there'd be great potatoes in Idaho. We were wrong. We once followed a tip to a place called The Spud Bowl, hoping it was named for its big bowls of wonderful Idaho spuds. But The Spud Bowl turned out to be a bowling-alley cafe, specializing in Soup for One. We concluded that the people of Idaho are no more interested in making something of their potatoes than the people of Maine (where, also, many are grown, but few good ones served).

We did however discover one unimpeachably great restaurant in the state, a restaurant that, if not purely Idaho, is most definitely the American west.

Where else in the world will you find a menu of steaks that starts with the "Li'l Dude" at sixteen ounces, and tops out at a 42-ounce porterhouse? Big steaks, and good steaks, too: choice meat, never frozen, never encased in cryovac, aged two and a half weeks, cut when ordered from the loin or butt, and grilled on an open pit over cherry wood.

The "Rancher" steak (the giant) is a bone-in slab, serious and heavy-textured. The tease of wood smoke imparts a tang to the crust of the beef; and the meat, although it doesn't ooze juice, is thick with character—a true taste of the west.

For an even truer taste, order Rocky Mountain oysters—bull's testicles. We listened with only slightly pained expressions as Pat Wickel (who with her husband Wally owns the Inn) described how the skin around each teste must be carefully removed and the "oyster" scrubbed clean, yielding what Pat called "a beautiful piece of meat." It is then sliced into half-inch-thick slabs, marinated, and deep-fried. The resulting crisp-crusted discs have a soft flavor that is both delicate and rich, like the cleanest sweetbreads. Rocky Mountain oysters can be ordered as a main course, but Pat explained that a lot of people like to get an order to split as a side dish.

The menu is a short one, with meat the star, but steaks and genitalia are supplemented by lobsters, shrimp, and cod filets.

After a fresh tossed salad, side dishes are the best kind of chuck-wagon grub: beans—Idaho reds, in fact—soaked, simmered, cooked, and seasoned for two days before they are ready to be served; also bread, called "krebel" on the menu, an old German-originated frontier recipe for braided sweet dough, skillet-fried. There are potatoes, too—yes, Idaho potatoes!—halved three times to form thick skin-on wedges that are then pressure-fried. Inside their leathery crusts, the potatoes are pure fluff.

For dessert, Wally and Pat have a local lady to bake cakes: walnut and double chocolate layer.

The setting is a countryish log place with a couple of fireplaces and some seats around the open flame where Wally cooks the steaks. The Wickels are proud of nearby Coeur d'Alene Lake, which their menu says is "reported to be one of the five most beautiful lakes in the world." They're proud of the Wolf Lodge Inn, too ("Generous portions are our trademark"). It is, in our book, the single best restaurant in Idaho—the only one we know worth a special trip.

NEBRASKA

Dreisbach's

1137 S. Locust St., Grand Island, Nebr.
(308) 382-5450

Daily 4:30 p.m.–11 p.m.   Reservations advised

$8–$15

Steak and potatoes. Sirloins, T-bones, filets mignon, and a pound-plus "New York strip". The meat is broiled, has an unobtrusive layer of char, is fork-tender. The sirloin runs rivulets of natural juice when opened up; the filet mignon is three inches tall, a luscious orb of silky beef with an understated flavor.

The mashed potatoes are potatoes that have been mashed, not reconstituted flakes. For a little extra you can get crusty hashed browns, or "sunflower potatoes"—long potato cross-sections, fried crisp.

Good biscuits and a salad (tossed or slaw) come with dinner. Parties of four or more can get family-style service. There is no dessert.

Dreisbach's is a windowless bunker marked by a sign with its heraldic crest: two cows' faces and a Germanic fleur-de-lis. It doesn't look like much, inside or out, but the Great Plains chow is flawless.

Fairview Cafe

1201 N. Chestnut, Wahoo, Nebr.
(402) 443-9941

Mon.–Thurs. 6 a.m.–9 p.m., Fri. & Sat. until midnight,
Sun. 7 a.m.–9 p.m.

$10 or less

Across from the cash register at the Fairview Cafe, next to the blackboard listing the morning's grain prices, hangs a plaque from the Wheat Division of the Nebraska Department of Agriculture, making honorable mention of the bread and rolls served here. They are something special! Bread alone inscribes the Fairview in our little black book.

Dinner rolls are soft and yeasty, pulling easily into fluffy halves. At breakfast the Fairview kitchen sends forth jumbo cinnamon rolls, their spice-freckled skin hidden beneath a caramelized glaze.

And look at those pies! Displayed in a case behind the counter, the meringues are six inches high. Magnificent.

We came for a mid-morning meal. Grizzly-chinned members of the overall set were lingering at the worn Formica counter over cups of coffee, and a few townsfolk started to drift in for lunch. We split a cinnamon roll, then moved on to taco salad, chicken and biscuits, and corned beef.

Taco salad has become a heartland cafe favorite in the last few years: ground beef, crumbled tortilla chips, iceberg lettuce, and shredded cheddar cheese in a deep-fried cup-shaped corn crisp ("Eat the bowl!" suggests the menu). On the side come salad dressing *and* taco sauce. Take your pick; or mix them up. The mustard-imprinted corned beef was fine, the powdery spuds alongside were not; an order of pickled beets had a fine sweet tang. We were rushing toward dessert.

The stunningly meringued raisin cream pie was loaded with stewed raisins in a strangely granular yellow custard: thick, sweet, and simple. Butterscotch pie, topped with cream and a dusting of graham cracker crumbs, spilled out from beneath its white cap. The butterscotch was bland, a disappointment.

A mixed meal. But we recommend the Fairview for its local color as much as the food. This is Wahoo's premier place to eat, to gather, to swap gossip among friends and with waitresses. Adjacent to the cafe is a table-clothed room for dinner, when the featured attraction is "Wahoo's biggest steak dinner." It is a two-pound sirloin, eighteen inches wide, with all the trimmings. Price: $8.50 for one, $10 for two. Can't beat those numbers!

Johnny's Cafe

4702 S. 27th St., Omaha, Nebr.
(402) 731-4774

Mon.–Sat. lunch & dinner   Reservations advised

Lunch about $5, dinner $10–$15

The door of Johnny's Cafe is encrusted with a baroque sculpture of cascading horned bulls. The pattern on the rug in the vestibule is a ten-foot-wide portrait of a cow. At the entrance to the coat room, a closed-circuit television shows the current futures list for beef. The salutation on the menu reads, "Omaha . . . the Steak House of the Nation; Johnny's . . . the Steak House of Omaha."

Strip steaks, bone in or out; filets mignon; heavily marbled double cuts of prime rib; chateaubriands; liver; ribs; short ribs; chicken-fried steaks cut off the heel of the prime rib; calf's tongue; even ox-tail in heavy gravy: if meat is your dish, Johnny's Cafe is your restaurant.

It isn't only a beef house; the menu is rounded out with shrimp and trout and catfish, and at lunch there are "light dishes" like tuna noodle casserole and fruit plates. But for sixty years, Johnny's Cafe has been the place to which cattle barons, bullshippers, and stockmen come after a day in the yards across the way. And what they come for is the meat.

It is bought from small, family-owned packing houses in Omaha. "I grew up with the feed lot and packing people," Tom Kawa, son of Frank "Johnny" Kawa, told us. "They know our standards, and they won't play games with me."

Government meat-grading standards have been lowered six times in the last thirty years, but Johnny's have not. The Kawas age and cut all their own steaks, which is why their beef—graded choice—is so good.

With all meals come baked (not steamed in foil) potatoes, freshly grated hash browns, or thin American fries. Salads are topped with house-made vinaigrette. The chateaubriand is served with a rich wine-and-onion mushroom sauce. The dinner rolls, the noodles for the casserole, and the dumplings that go with the stewed chicken are all made here, by expert cooks. Ditto the cakes and pies and custards.

"We are like a European hotel here," Tom put it. "We do everything—all the butchering, all the baking, even the salad-oil making."

Although it once was a small cafe, Johnny's is now a classic "red-black-and-dark" restaurant, well-cushioned, heavily air-conditioned, with oversized high-back chairs to make a man feel comfortable as he consumes pounds of beef. In the heart of Omaha's meatpacking center, it is the best of the few remaining stockyard steak houses in America.

M & M Bakery & Cafe

412 E. Douglas, O'Neill, Nebr.
(402) 336-2270

Mon.–Sat. 6 a.m.–8 p.m., Sun. 7 a.m.–2 p.m.

$5 or less

"Anything from a cup of coffee to a Nebraska sizzling T-bone steak," boasts the McMillan & Markey postcard, sent to us by the traveling duo Leslie Seeche and Tom Edmondson. Although not actually linen-finish, the card has an antique look, as though it was designed a half-century ago, depicting the bakery cafe in three separate views: the wooden booths; a long shot of the tin ceiling, marble-countered soda fountain, and display cases; and an exterior of the black-tile front.

We dwell on the postcard because its bygone style is exactly the feeling of the M & M Bakery and Cafe in 1986. Nothing's changed since who-knows-when, since perhaps the place went up, seventy-five years ago. Meals are still built around roast chicken, ham, and beef, accompanied by homemade rolls and potatoes or hand-rolled noodles.

There is a bakery's worth of desserts made every day: moist carrot bars, sweet rolls with different glazes and fillings, plus pies in every configuration this pie-wealthy part of the country has to offer. We especially favor the sour cream raisin or apricot pies; but there are also cherry, blueberry, apple, peach, coconut, chocolate . . . you get the idea.

Breadstuffs from the bakery make breakfast special, too; but don't forget to get some sausage on the side. The M & M Cafe doesn't like store-bought patties, so they grind their own.

An oasis on Highway 275.

Runza

1102 2nd Ave., Kearney, Nebr.
(308) 236-7878

Daily 10:30 a.m.–11 p.m.

Under $5

A runza is a small pocket of bread into which has been baked a blend of ground beef, onions, and cabbage; it's similar to an Acadian meat pie or a Michigan pasty.

The first runza we tasted was brought to us by a friend stationed in Lincoln, who told us that this meal in a loaf was an eastern Nebraska specialty. She had bought our runza at a fast-food stand that sold *only* runzas. The sample, if lumpish, was intriguing, and we set out for Lincoln hoping to find the really good, homemade runzas, the runzas prepared by western ladies in little farm house cafes.

When we arrived, we discovered that the word *runza* is the copyrighted name of a fast-food chain; and as much as we searched, we found no independent restaurants in the area that serve anything similar.

So, we would like to know, where does this odd regional anomaly come from? One runza waitress told us she thought it was originally German, or maybe Polish. Another said Czech, which makes some sense, since eastern Nebraska is dotted with Bohemian towns and small cafes featuring liver and dumpling soup and *kolaches* . . . but runzas? No, we've never seen runzas on the menu at Annie's Jidlike Cafe in Wilber, or any of the exemplary Czech restaurants on Cermak Road up in Chicago. Does it have an ancestry at all? Or is it simply an invented dish? We're stumped.

Wherever it comes from, here is the uniquely Nebraskan food called runza, plain or with cheese, a weighty, mildly spiced, self-contained meal.

The Runza restaurants serve it with good onion rings and pretty fair brownies for dessert.

There are several other Runza loations in eastern Nebraska.

NEVADA

Louis' Basque Corner

301 E. 4th St., Reno, Nev.
(702) 323-7203

Dinner daily

About $10

Thank heavens for the Basques; without them, there'd be nothing to eat in Nevada. Interstate 80 runs through sheep country, and in each significant town along the way (that's three—Elko, Winnemucca, and Reno), you can find a boarding house or hotel that caters to the sheepherders, all of whom are American Basques, famous for nonstop meals. A full Basque boardinghouse dinner, one of our country's grandest eating rituals, is *the* specialty of the mountain states—the results of applying Old World recipes to the vittles of the west.

Louis' is a commodious place with large tables crowded with local families, sheepherders come to town for the weekend, and tourists who crave something, anything, authentic in the unreal city of Reno.

There is no menu at a traditional Basque dinner. Every night Louis' serves a different kind of stew: tripe, beef tongue, oxtail, or lamb. We've had the lamb, which is creamy rich and surprisingly mild. "Surprisingly," because the luscious and gelatinous oxtail stew we sampled on an earlier visit —as well as nearly everything else served at Louis'—was strongly seasoned, heavy on the garlic. On Fridays, the customary stew is steamed clams and rice.

The stew follows first courses of thick vegetable soup and green salad, and an extraordinary casserole of pinto beans simmered with chunks of mutton. Of all the food served at Louis', it is this lamb and bean dish that most vividly suggests the ingenuity of the sheepherders' cuisine, which turned traditional western American grub into a savory, yet still rugged cuisine.

The soup, the stew, the salad, and the beans are merely the prelude to the main course, which is, true to the western spirit, meat—steak, a roast, sometimes leg of lamb. That's sided by potatoes (mashed or french fries) and French bread. A glass of California wine is included in the price of dinner.

From this groaning board, you won't walk away hungry. You will be lucky if you can toddle at all.

There are rooms at Louis'—stark, about $20 for a double.

Martin Hotel

Railroad & Melarkey Sts., Winnemucca, Nev.
(702) 623-3197

Mon.–Fri. lunch, daily dinner

Dinner $10, less for lunch

The Martin Hotel dining room has gussied up since we first stopped here about seven years ago. The worn tables have been covered with tablecloths; there is a buffet of Basque food offered on Sundays; and now it is even possible to order ordinary lunches—steaks, salads, sandwiches.

But we like the traditional Basque dinner, horsed down in the company of Nevadans who speak as much Spanish as English. Here in the dining room of the Martin Hotel you eat a meal that reflects the time when the Basques first came to the west. It was originally a prairie cuisine, modified by sheepherders from old country recipes to include the available produce and, of course, the available lamb.

When the sheepherders came to town during the off-season, they would stay in hotels and boarding houses that extrapolated a more elaborate cuisine from their outdoor meals. Today, in the few remaining Basque boarding houses and hotels of Nevada, the ritual hasn't changed much.

Tables are shared. Everything is served in large bowls or on platters, to be passed among strangers. The menu is always the same: lengths of French bread, a heavy bean or split-pea soup, an olive-oil salad of greens and onions, then a stew. Whatever else is in the stew, there is always garlic; perhaps it's tripe in garlic-tomato sauce, or *baccalà* (dried cod) or chicken giblets in green sauce.

At this point, the novice might think the meal is ready for its denouement; but no. You are about to face the main course, meat—either steak or prime rib, big heavy cuts.

Red wine is served throughout the meal and consumed in copious portions by these experienced trenchermen; after dinner, should you feel in need of a coup de grace, choose the traditional Basque aperitif, bittersweet *picon* punch. A couple of good slugs will put wool on your chest.

Single rooms, for men only, are available for $7 per night (shared bath).

OREGON

The Crab Broiler

Rtes. 101 & 26, Seaside, Oreg.
(503) 738-5313

Daily 11:30 a.m.–9 p.m.   Closed ten days in Jan.

Lunch $5–$10, dinner $5–$20

Hard to believe that the sumptuous Crab Broiler was once a small fish house; but its honest origins are evident when you see the food. Never mind the fireplaces and the outdoor pools for meditation. Contemplate instead the Petite Point oysters from Oregon's central coast—no bigger around than a quarter, but plump, their sensuous oiliness muscled by the snap of the ocean.

Dungeness crab is what paid for all the decor; we are told that the Broiler is the first restaurant on the coast to get it fresh, at the beginning of each season in the fall. It is available in casseroles and mayonnaise cocktails, fashioned into mild crab cakes, doused in zesty barbecue sauce, or just plain steamed and cracked. Although plain in-the-shell is the purist's choice, you won't be sorry if you save yourself the fuss of prying loose the meat. The kitchen has a way with crabs; in season, fresh-picked meat is used in the fancier preparations (which aren't so fancy that they diminish the natural sweetness of the beast).

Razor clams (deep-fried, about three lengths to an order) are first-rate. Given the choice between salad and slaw with your meal, go for slaw; it is finely chopped, creamy, but not too thick—just the ticket to accompany seafood—especially the clams. With dinner, you'll also get potatoes and bread. The bread is French, hot, spread with your choice of garlic butter or whipped blue cheese.

Oregon blackberry pie is a coastal specialty not to be missed. Wild blackberries are exquisite fruits, their royal hue promising—and delivering—a tart intensity that reminded us of the wild blueberries we had at the opposite end of the country, in northeastern Maine. Although frozen ones are used off-season, The Crab Broiler gets fresh berries through the fall, when they are picked from commercially grown "domesticated" wild berry bushes.

Up the road, the resort town of Seaside offers a wide variety of goods and services for tourists, including saltwater taffy, game parlors, souvenir shops, and an oceanside boardwalk made not of boards, but concrete.

Dan & Louis Oyster Bar

208 W. Ankeny St., Portland, Oreg.
(503) 227-5906

Sun.–Thurs. 11 a.m.–midnight, Fri. & Sat. until 1 a.m.

$5–$10

Of all the west coast oysters, we like Yaquina Bays the best, better even than the scarce Olympias. They are meaty but not gross, with an assertive but not metallic marine taste. They are just right on the half-shell—one perfect glistening mouthful; in a stew, they lace the cream and butter with a sophisticated zest; and when judiciously pan-fried they stay tender, as bracing as if straight from the shell, yet sensuously warmed by the heat.

A fringe benefit of Yaquina Bay oysters is that they are the specialty of Dan & Louis Oyster Bar, one of Portland's oldest fish houses—a *shellfish* house, really: with the exception of fish (cod) and chips, the oyster-shaped menu is all mollusks.

Founded in the early 1900s by Louis Wachsmuth, whose father wrecked a ship in Yaquina Bay and discovered the oysters, Dan & Louis is now run by the Oregon Oyster Company, which owns the beds in Yaquina Bay.

Louis's oyster stew, which the menu says he invented on a "cold, wintry day" is a legendary dish in the northwest. Like the fish stews of New England, it is merely seasoned milk and butter and oysters (single or double doses can be ordered). The oysters' liquor is no more than a whisper of flavor. No recipe is more prosaic; few bowls of food are as gruntly.

In the late fall and winter, you can order crab Louie (spelled "Louis" on the menu, but it's the familiar San Francisco Louie, made with mayo and Worcestershire and Tabasco and a few dots of pepper and scallions). Shrimp Louie is sold year-round. Of the fried foods, we recommend the pan-fried Yaquina Bays and, at least for novelty's sake, geoduck clams. These are not, of course, whole geoducks, which are so big it sometimes takes two people to bag one. What you get are little niblets, chopped geoduck—very clammy-tasting, still.

In addition to Yaquina Bays, Dan & Louis sells Pacific oysters—bigger and cheaper than Yaquina Bays, but no bargain. No verve; they're nothing but texture.

Dan & Louis is handsome, if overdecorated, done up like a ship and packed with nautical bibelots, collectible plates and beer steins.

Fuller's Restaurant

136 NW 9th St., Portland, Oreg.
(503) 222-5608

Mon.–Fri. 6 a.m.–6 p.m., Sat. to 2 p.m.

$5 or less

For forty years, Portlanders have thought of Fuller's as a breakfast place. White and cracked-wheat bread are baked daily for toast (and French toast, dipped in cream and eggs, dusted with powdered sugar). There are cinnamon rolls every morning, hot from the oven. Hashed browns to accompany the "famous omelette" (onions, tomatoes, ham, cheese, and mushrooms) are made from potatoes that are steamed and grated here. There is a fabulous German pancake, folded over on the plate like a large omelette.

There is a full lunch menu, too, including fresh salmon steaks, fish and chips made with locally caught halibut, and (usually) razor clams. Named for their resemblance to a straight razor, these northwestern clams are too tough to steam, but when they are fried, the heat turns them tender. Fuller's dips razors in egg batter, then in crumbs from the homemade bread. You get two six-inch-long clams per order: a still-chewy, but deliciously chewable meal. Good cole slaw with celery-seed dressing accompanies.

Fuller's is just a few stools around a horseshoe counter. Service is fast; the waiting line outside can be long.

Hebo Inn

Junction of Hwys. 101 & 22, Hebo, Oreg.
(503) 392-3445

Daily 6 a.m.–8 p.m.

$5 or less

The Hebo Inn was recommended to us by Portland native Paul Pintarich, originator of Pintarich's Principal of the Pretentious Pepper Mill, a theorem declaring that a restaurant's real worth is inversely proportional to the length of its peppermills. He said the Hebo Inn was "rustic but not phony," and it served hearty meals designed to "prevent hypothermia."

Bull's-eye. Thanks to Paul, we stopped in the large two-story building on Highway 101; it's old and comfortable, with a horseshoe counter and stools, a few wooden booths, and one large table. When we left, appetite was only a distant memory.

The food is hearty calorific stuff: huge breakfasts of hot biscuits and gravy, triple-egg omelettes, and pancakes doled out in stacks sized for lumberjacks. At a later lunch, we loved the clam fritters, thick clam-laced pancakes that go perfectly with a bowl of creamy chowder. The Hebo also makes fried chicken, char-broiled steaks, and, on occasion, Oregon's real stick-to-your-ribber, chicken and dumplings.

Mo's

622 SW Bay Blvd., Newport, Oreg.
(503) 265-2979

Daily 11 a.m.–10 p.m., 11 a.m.–8 p.m. at the annex

$10 or less

Mo's clam chowder is a west coast legend—a smoky soup with perfect poise —clams and cream and spice; a dish so successful it has spawned more than half a dozen more Mo's up and down the Oregon coast. This Mo's supplements its chowder with extraordinary fried food: shrimp and oysters, fish and chips made from the clean meat of ling cod. The chips are french fries, cut here. From the grill come halibut, sole, and salmon—the plainest preparations, plainly served. Seafood salads are the most elaborate dishes in the house, made with shrimp or crabmeat.

There's not much for dessert; on our last visit the choices included apple cobbler and peanut butter pie. Not bad.

Mo's long, unclothed tables are shared by strangers; its menu is scrawled on a blackboard. Decor is a riot: fish-house eclectic. It is noisy and crowded; service is sometimes confused. An endearing mess of a restaurant, with outstanding inexpensive food—just the way a coastal fish house ought to be.

Mo's Annex, across the street, has the same clam chowder, but instead of focusing on fried and grilled seafood, features casseroles of shrimp, oysters, or crabmeat; also barbecued oysters (Mo's has its own oyster beds); and a variety of sandwiches. The view is nicer, overlooking the bay.

All of the Mo's along the coast serve the renowned chowder, but the others are fancier, or at least try to be. These twin Mo's are the great ones, the originals, on Newport's old waterfront. (The truly *original* Mo's building, we have been told by an authority on such subjects, is preserved inside an old garage nearby.)

Tad's Chicken 'N' Dumplings

Rte. 30, Troutdale, Oreg.   A half-mile east of Troutdale Bridge
(503) 666-5337

Mon.–Sat. 5 p.m.–11 p.m., Sun. 2 p.m.–11 p.m.   No reservations,
but expect a wait, especially on Sun.

$10 or less

Oregonians love chicken and dumplings; and yet, because this is a homely
dish, it has never gained fame as a regional specialty. We admit that three-
alarm-chili or Michigan pasties have more sex appeal than a plate of warm
chicken, but no fancier of American food ought to head east out of Portland
without chowing down at a steaming tureen of Tad's finest. It's the perfect
food to brace you for the harrowing but scenic trip along winding Route 30
through the Columbia River gorge.

It comes to the table family-style, the chicken topped with wide biscuity
dumplings, porous enough to sop up the gravy. The chicken is in big chunks,
white and tender. The recipe for the dish, Tad's tells us, has been in the
family for more than thirty years. Other Oregon restaurants—especially
along the Pacific coast—have their own variations; none are as right as
Tad's. With it come bowls of vegetables, including some bacon-flavored
green beans that add a side of zest to the creamy chicken.

There is a lot else on Tad's menu, a predictable variety of steaks and
seafood—but note that the restaurant is not named Tad's Steaks 'N' Seafood.
The steak we ordered was okay, but nothing special. Tad's cheesecake makes
a good dessert; you might even call it light, compared to the chicken and
dumplings.

The rustic food is enhanced by the setting. Tad's is woodsy inside—
knotty pine paneling, red gingham curtains. From the tables in back, or the
deck where customers are sent to wait for a table and drink, you have a
lordly view of the Sandy River below.

SOUTH DAKOTA

Stockyards Cafe

808 E. Rice, Sioux Falls, S.D.
(605) 338-6391

Mon.–Fri. 5:30 a.m.–9 p.m.

About $10

You can breakfast at the Stockyards Cafe in the company of ranchers, truckers, and meat-packers from the nearby plant; you can come for lunch with cattlemen; or you can eat dinner with what our waitress referred to as "the fur coat crowd" of Sioux Falls. Any time of day, the star of the menu is beef, a fact you could easily deduce without even looking at a menu. Just glance across the street at the pens of cattle.

Yes, this is a real stockyards cafe, and although the lunch fare includes chicken and sandwiches, the good reason for coming here is the 30-ounce T-bone steak dinner. Thick, glistening, seared to a dark mahogany color, juicy red inside, this is steak, mid-American style, a weeklong supply of amino acid. It comes with perfunctory companions—soup or salad bar, a roll, a potato. And you can get a piece of apple or cherry pie or an ice cream sundae for dessert.

The kingly cut of beef is served without fanfare in a cinderblock restaurant on Formica tables, accompanied by bottled beer.

WASHINGTON

The Dee's Cafe

203 S. Montesano St., Westport, Wash.
(206) 268-9737

Summer daily 7 a.m.–11 p.m.   Winter Tues.–Sun. 8 a.m.–9 p.m.

$4–$8

The docks of Westport ("Salmon Capital of the World") are crowded with charter outfits for fishermen, and with restaurants catering to people with lots of money and apparently not much taste. A couple miles south is The Dee's, a cafe favored by locals, visiting clam diggers, and a few savvy summer tourists. There aren't more than forty seats in the house, decor is non-existent, service is fast, and local seafood is expertly prepared.

Of course salmon is a featured dish, fileted and grilled. Served only in season, between April and October, this salmon is *fresh*, with a flavor that is masked when the fish is smoked or cured, eradicated if it is frozen. It is served without fuss, the way a cafe in another part of the country might dish out a burger. But the plain circumstances do not detract from its nobility. It is heavy yet delicate; rich but not glutting.

Ling cod is a menu regular, as is sea bass. The bass, like the salmon, is fileted and grilled. It is finer-textured than the profound salmon—a spritely treat. Ling cod is a subtly flavored fish, leaner than its firmer-fleshed eastern namesake. Dee's fish and chips feature fresh-caught halibut. We are told that petrale sole, the best of all flounders, is often available in the fall, and is a house specialty.

With the fish comes a green salad with made-here dressing, and a choice of hash browns or baked potatoes. To start the meal, there is an agreeable clam chowder—creamy-textured, smoky, and mildly redolent of clam. For dessert, choose from a selection of homemade pies; walnut and peanut butter cream are the ones we recommend.

Dee's is open for breakfast, and while most of the menu is basic bacon and eggs, there is one peculiar local specialty that clam-lovers will want to try: razor clams, battered and fried, and served with a mess of eggs, hash browns, and toast. Razors are long and thin, their chewy meat tenderized by frying. Dee's sprinkles them with almonds—a savory complement to the meaty clam, and a fabulously different, utterly northwestern breakfast.

El Ranchito

First Avenue (Route 12), Zillah, Wash.
(509) 829-5880

Daily 8 a.m.–7 p.m.

$5 or less

Perhaps we are stretching the definition of a "regional specialty" to include a Mexican restaurant in eastern Washington, but if you are traveling through Zillah, you'll thank us. El Ranchito is in fact the closest thing there is in the Yakima Valley to a truly regional restaurant. This is fruit-growing country, populated by many Mexicans. El Ranchito is where the people who live here eat.

In back is a tortilla factory; up front a general store features herbs, cookware, and Spanish-language tabloids. Outside is a festive patio, where Mexicans, Indians, and gringos sit elbow to elbow enjoying top-quality American-style Mexican food.

By American-style, we mean that El Ranchito's cuisine is more Tex-Mex than it is Mex-Mex: tacos, enchiladas, tamales, etc.; food you'd not likely find south of the border. Ingredients are farmy; spices are hot; the freshly made tortillas are superb. With most plates comes a helping of delicious silky refried beans. We'd especially recommend El Ranchito's *menudo*, a velvety soup made with tripe and hominy; also the *barbacoa*, ropy barbecued beef out of which great tacos can be fashioned.

Bring your own beer; and skip the Mexican desserts in favor of fruit from any one of the apple stands along the road.

Emmett Watson's Oyster Bar

1916 Pike Pl., Seattle, Wash.
(206) 622-7721

Mon.–Sat. 11 a.m.–5 p.m.

$10 or less

Pike Place Market is the oldest farmers' and fishermen's market in America, a colorful bazaar of fruits and vegetables, ethnic groceries, a thousand kinds of fresh seafood, one-man flea markets, and a few restaurants. Unlike so many cities' attempted revivals of their dead urban emporia, Pike Place is authentic and unpredictable, humming with life.

At the north end of the market is Emmett Watson's, a pint-sized oyster bar with eleven seats and a little more standing room, and some fast shuckers behind the counter. On a nice day it is possible to sit at tables outside, and there is even table service, but what kind of way is that to eat oysters?

Quilcenes, Canterburies, and Middlebrooks were fresh on the day we bellied up. You order by the half dozen (they're not cheap), and the shucker goes to work. Ours were good-sized oysters, considerably meatier than the famous Olympias from farther south, beautiful steel gray with a likeable tang.

Those not satisfied with the raw bar can order chowder or steamer clams. There is also seviche, which they pronounced *sevichee*, made from true cod.

For drinks, choose from a selection of fifty different beers.

Jake O'Shaughnessey's

100 Mercer St., Seattle, Wash. In the Hansen Baking Co.
(206) 285-1897

Dinner daily

$10 or less

Salmon, slow-smoked over alder wood, the way the northwest Indians did it: the process is called cold smoke, meaning that the fish absorbs the sweet flavor of the wood smoke over a period of many hours, remaining firm and moist. The filet is heated up just before serving: a complex, and positively delicious piece of fish, the best meal in the house.

Jake O'Shaughnessey's also features something called saloon beef, a roast prepared in the old western manner by encasing it in a cast of roasting salt, then cooking it at a very low temperature for half a day. The salt both flavors the meat and holds in its juices. The results are broad scarlet slabs, warm and fully cooked however rare they are ordered, with the depth of flavor one always wishes prime rib had. The beef is served with white radish, freshly grated.

The menu offers a "Puget Sound sea stew," a hodgepodge of crabs, shrimps, oysters, etc., etc., but we had just come from farther south and were spoiled by cioppino. This gallimaufry was disconsonant, without personality —not nearly on the high level of the salmon and saloon beef.

For appetizers, we loved the "Murphy," a startling 1½-pound potato ("from Idaho," our waiter guaranteed) that is baked until fluffy white, and served with an assortment of meat and dairy fillers, such as corned beef, butter, onions, sour cream. It's far too much for one, or even two diners. A party of four will find it ideal.

Salads are served with a chilled fork. We especially like the oily wilted salad. The bread is sourdough, freshly baked, served warm in a basket.

Many desserts make use of the northwest's intensely flavorful blackberries. Blackberry ice cream is a contrast of sweet cream and tart fruit; there is a pastry made with fresh berries; you can even get "New York" cheesecake irreverently dolloped with berries.

Now we'll say it: Jake O'Shaughnessey's is a theme restaurant: an Irish saloon, circa 1900. Booze is big, the ceiling-high bar displaying more than a thousand different brands, including two dozen kinds of Scotch. It's a watering hole frequented by sports fans—the last place in Seattle we would expect to find such good food.

After dinner, take advantage of the theme and have some Irish coffee, or one of the bar's many cognacs.

Mary McCrank's Dinner House

2923 Jackson Hwy., Chehalis, Wash.
(206) 748-3662

Tues.–Sat. 11:30 a.m.–2:30 p.m., 5 p.m.–8:30 p.m., Sun. noon–8 p.m.

$10 or less

"I like a restaurant where you can smell the food cooking when you walk in," said Raeline Guy, who took over Mary McCrank's legendary dinner house when Mary died two years ago. Thank you, Raeline, a thousand thanks: you have preserved the charm that always made a meal at Mary McCrank's so extraordinarily reassuring, like a visit to a favorite Irish nanny's home for Sunday dinner.

Raeline worked for Mary eight years, so she knows how to make the panfried chicken and cream gravy just right, and the chicken and dumplings every Sunday, and the gooseberry and loganberry jam to go with homemade white or wholewheat bread. She knows that potato flakes are no substitute for real mashed potatoes, so she has the kitchen start with whole potatoes, peel them, cook them, mash and butter them: ahhh!

As always, meals begin with relishes: watermelon pickles, chow-chow, cucumbers, and onions. Fried chicken is our favorite entree, followed close by pork roast. Grilled oysters are a deliciously briny reminder that although inland, Mary McCrank's is not far from the Pacific coast. When fresh mountain trout are available, at least eleven inches long, they are pan fried. This restaurant doesn't own a deep-fryer.

In the summer, when blackberries ripen, Raeline makes them into pie. All year around, sour cream raisin pie is a house specialty, piled high into its flaky crust.

Mary McCrank's is something more than a taste of Washington and the Pacific Northwest. It is a reminder of how soul-satisfying honest American food can be.

Olympia Oyster House

320 W. Fourth Ave., Olympia, Wash.
(206) 943-8020

Mon.–Fri. 10:30 a.m.–11:30 p.m., Sat. noon–11:30 p.m., Sun. noon–
9 p.m.

Lunch about $5, dinner about $10, Olympia oysters' "market price" can be
about $20

The menu says that the Olympia Oyster House is "known 'World Wide' for
the famous Olympia Oyster which is now a bit extinct."

Just a bit, not entirely. The Oyster Bar, as this grand old restaurant is
known in Olympia, tries harder than anyone else to get the rare Olys—and
it often does, especially in the fall and winter. The oysters come to the restaurant already shucked; they are then breaded and fried—nicely fried, all
crisp and crunchy, but by this point the strong saltwater taste of the oyster
is . . . well, a bit extinct. However, if you want to eat Olys in Olympia, here
is the best you can do, other than begging a few in their shell from one of the
companies that still process them.

The dearth is because Olympias take a long time to mature and they are
tiny. Their remaining beds, between Shelton and Olympia in lower Puget
Sound, have been crowded out by Pacific oysters, a jumbo Japanese import
that makes more economic sense—but whose flavor is nowhere.

Pacific oysters are always available at the Olympia Oyster House—sauteed, deep-fried, in a stew, or "on horseback" (wrapped with bacon and
grilled). They are not a taste sensation; we like them best as a textural note
in other dishes, like, for instance, a hangtown fry—the savory scrambled egg
and oyster dish served here for lunch and dinner; or in the peppery pan roast
(lunch only).

The hidden side of the Oly Oyster House is non-oyster dishes—regionalia
like filet of salmon (baked or grilled), shrimp scatter (small batter-fried
shrimp), and baked halibut. Along with our oysters, we tasted a good crab
Louie salad, even a pretty fair version of that favorite western sandwich, the
French dip—roast beef on a hero roll *au jus*.

The Oyster House is a plain-looking place, on the water in what was the
culling house of the Olympia Oyster Company (one of the few outfits still
bothering with Olympia oysters). In nice weather, there is a patio for outdoor
dining.

Ray's Boathouse

6049 Seaview Ave. NW, Seattle, Wash.   In Ballard
(206) 789-3770

Mon.–Fri. 11:30 a.m.–3 p.m. & 5 p.m.–11 p.m., Sat.–Sun. 5 p.m.–
11 p.m.   Reservations required, sometimes weeks in advance for dinner

About $20

If you are planning a trip to Seattle (or if you live nearby) include Ray's in your itinerary. But don't expect to casually drop in. For a Friday dinner, three weeks is not too long in advance to make a reservation. It's that popular.

With good reason. Oddly, Seattle has few classy seafood restaurants. At Ray's you get suave service and good fish, plus a breathtaking view of the Olympic Mountains, Puget Sound, and the setting sun. All at a reasonable price. Only the impossibility of coming here on a whim smudges the picture.

Once you've got a valued seat in the ferny raw-wood dining room, the best way to start things off is with Ray's superior pork-enriched clam chowder; or steamed clams in melted butter, redolent of dill.

Much is made of salmon, and there are several varieties—king, coho, sockeye, etc.—whichever Pacific species are available fresh. To complicate matters, Ray's offers salmon as steaks and filets, poached or steamed or broiled over mesquite wood. We tasted—and loved—the plain broiled king salmon steak, the complex flavors of its deep red meat brought to blossom by a careful turn near the fire.

Black cod is not related to the kind of cod one gets in the east. A uniquely north Pacific creature (actually what fishermen know as sablefish), the black cod served at Ray's is lightly smoked to bring out a nearly overwhelming richness. Despite the name, the flesh of the fish, however oily-textured, is white. Alongside it came pretty melon slices and little mounds of toothsome wheatberries.

At a nearby table, a couple apparently allergic to the sea was being served rack of lamb—and it looked fabulous. But good rack of lamb is easy to come by elsewhere. Five kinds of Pacific salmon, black cod, fresh snapper, and sole will get our attention if we manage once again to book a table at Ray's.

Choose berries for dessert. Except in the dead of winter, Ray's always has fresh local berries—black-, blue-, raspberries. They are served plain, or topped with Cointreau or Grand Marnier or whipped cream, or some agreeable combination thereof.

Shuckers

4th & Seneca, Seattle, Wash.   In the Olympic Four Seasons Hotel
(206) 621-1700

Daily lunch & dinner

Lunch $5–$8, dinner about $15

An oyster bar, a couple dozen tables, walls of ornately carved mahogany: Shuckers is the bistro in the venerable Olympic Hotel. Originally, this space was a men's clothing store. What were once racks of dry goods are now booths.

Although the kitchen serves many kinds of Pacific fish (especially salmon: steaks and filets; broiled, baked, steamed, or poached), and shares a pastry chef with the ritzier hotel restaurant, it is oysters and clams, either raw or in their simplest preparations, that are the reason to come here. Three or four kinds of oysters are available every day, opened fresh—Quilcenes and Wescott Bays, bluepoints from the east, occasionally even the rare minuscule Olympias.

There are oysters Kilpatrick, casino, and Florentine, and a hearty oyster stew made with cream. The one dish that endeared Shuckers to us is a stew made from the local clam called a geoduck. Although occasionally you will find a restaurant that serves geoduck steaks, cut from the enormous body of the clam, it is the long siphon neck (sometimes three feet) that is used for stews and chowders. It is tough and resilient, and must be chopped fine, but like the flesh of its prettier eastern cousin, the quahog, the geoduck has flavor to spare, and doesn't poop out in a crowd of other ingredients.

And this stew has a multitude! Geoduck clams, diced cod, spicy ground sausage meat, bacon, peppers, onions, and chili sauce are all thrown in the stock pot, and the briny farrago is thickened with file powder and okra—turning this into a strange northwestern variation of gumbo: hearty soup rich with the taste of the sea. It's the house specialty at Shucker's, served with a made-here Irish soda roll.

From Fourth Street, you can see the fish of the day displayed, and the shucker deftly opening oysters for the raw bar.

Smokehouse Restaurant

Hwy. 101 north, Forks, Wash.
(206) 374-6258

Daily 11 a.m.–10 p.m.

About $10

Forks is near the northwest tip of the Olympic Peninsula, where for centuries the coast Indians have made their spring salmon catch last the year by smoking it over alderwood.

The Smokehouse sells alder-smoked salmon to go—by the whole vacuum-packed side of fish or in a can; you can order it by mail as a Christmas gift; or you can dine here. It's an informal restaurant—a small cedar-paneled cafe appointed with black Naugahyde booths, a help-yourself salad bar, and a case off to one side displaying salmon gift packs for sale. Upstairs, above the remodeled coffee shop, is a small bar for cocktails.

The menu includes char-broiled salmon and halibut steaks, fried clams and oysters, occasional smoked perch, cod, and tiny bay shrimp, as well as a selection of beef (available in "land & sea combos" with the various seafoods). Dinners come with hot bread and rice or potatoes. There is a good caramel custard dessert called "burnt cream" on the menu.

But it is the alder-smoked salmon from the adjacent Slathar's Smokehouse that makes the Smokehouse worth a visit. Served as an appetizer or main course, the fish is cooked by a process known as "cold smoke," which means that rather than getting broiled over a fire, the pink fish is hung for hours to absorb a maximum amount of flavor from the sizzling wood. It stays moist, complex, and satisfying—one of the northwest's not-to-be-missed specialties.

Three Crabs

Dungeness Spit, Dungeness, Wash.   On the water
(206) 683-4264

Mon.–Sat. noon–10 p.m., Sun. until 7 p.m.

About $10

The most famous crab in the west is the Dungeness, named for this tiny village at the top of the Olympic Peninsula. Unfortunately, those of us who travel out this way during the summer miss it. Oh, sure, restaurants (including this one) serve Dungeness crab year-round, but you can be sure that between April and October, it's frozen.

And there is no way frozen can compare to the steamed and cracked Dungeness crab dished out at Three Crabs in the fall and winter. It is a large creature, its legs and a small part of the body where meat resides chopped off and cracked for easy eating. The fingers of meat are tender the way no frozen seafood can ever be. It is chunky, and needs no condiment or seasoning at all, except perhaps a quick dip in drawn butter. Served hot or cold, it's a simple feast.

You'll find another regional treat on Three Crabs' menu: geoduck. The geoduck (say *gooey-duck*) is a local clam, one of the vilest-looking creatures in creation. The big ones weigh as much as ten or fifteen pounds, and their meat—seemingly too big for the shell—spills out in a long siphon neck. Disgusting. But chop the tough neck up and it makes great chowder meat. And slice the body of the clam into cutlets, pound them a bit to loosen things up, grill them like steak, and—*voilà!* The beast has become a tender beauty with a likeably oceanic flavor.

Broiled salmon, grilled halibut steak, red snapper, sole: Three Crabs has a large repertoire of northwest seafood. Jumbo omelettes, filled with crab-meat and/or oysters, are a specialty of the house. Dinners come with cabbage slaw, garlic bread, and a baked potato. And for dessert, there are excellent pies from local berries, blue and boysen.

After lunch, weather permitting, it is possible to go clamming on Three Crabs' beach.

Our waitress told us that the restaurant's name refers not to crustaceans, but to its three original owners, all humans.

The Windmill

1501 N. Wenatchee Ave., Wenatchee, Wash.
(509) 663-3478

Tues.–Sat. dinner

About $10

For your consideration, we offer this bit of roadside Americana: a windmill-shaped building where, fifty years ago, counterfeit money and bootleg booze were manufactured upstairs; and where, to our amazement, we were served one of the best steaks we had in all the west. The Windmill has been serving steak dinners to the people of Wenatchee for twenty-five years.

The Windmill is nothing but a counter with a half dozen stools, plus eleven wooden booths. When we passed through, it was about to expand. "The way it is," explained our waitress, "if we get a party of eight, we have to split them up!" Even in an expanded form, we doubt that the quality of food or the jollity of ambience will change.

Sirloins, tenderloins, and T-bones, cut from well-marbled beef, have just the right resistance to yield a full flavor. No tenderizers have been used; nothing more than a sprinkle of salt is needed to bring these thick, perfectly broiled steaks to the pink.

The baked potato is baked in foil. Choose the french fries instead. They're hand-cut—long droopy twigs, thin-sliced, fried in clean oil. The greens in the salad are predictable, but there are some good house-made dressings. A modest relish tray starts things off, and you will get some mild garlic toast.

For dessert, The Windmill offers a selection of freshly baked pies: hulking wedges of apple, berry, or cherry in masterful crusts; good coconut cream, too.

There is an esprit de corps among diners at The Windmill. Everyone here knows they're at the best place in town, an unlikely hole in the wall compared to the fancier motel restaurants in Wenatchee. The unlikeliness makes it all the better.

WYOMING

Hickory House

11th and Logan, Cheyenne, Wyo.
(307) 638-1445

Daily 7 a.m.–8 p.m.

About $5

Wyoming has no unique regional food, but it is cowboy country. In Cheyenne, where the annual Frontier Days Rodeo draws the country's finest horsemen to town each July, there is one surefire winner for a taste of cowboy cuisine.

Here's the northernmost outpost of good frontier brisket, heady with the flavor of hickory smoke. The beef comes sliced—tender cross-sections, so juicy they need no sauce or condiment; or chopped—shreds and crisp tips that are even more succulent than the slices. Sandwiches are served on rugged crusted rolls; platters are heaped high. Side dishes include corn muffins, creamy cole slaw, potato salad, and some superior beans, which are more like what we easterners would serve as chili—heavily cumin-spiked and ballasted with large cubes of meat.

Hickory House calls its dark red smoked sausages "Polish," but to us they were closer cousins to a traditional Texas hot link. They are richly flavored but not oily, so packed that the skin cracks loudly when bitten into.

You can also get pork ribs in a piquant vinegar and tomato sauce, exquisite ham, and, on occasion, smoked turkey.

Hickory House is a modernized drive-in, all tidy Formica with minimal decor. We were told about it by a saleslady in a town western-wear store, who said that they also smoke a variety of wild game. We asked, and the pitmaster said that he has smoked just about everything that cackles or crawls—but it's strictly custom cooking. You've got to bag it and bring it in yourself.

Sweet's

E. Flaming Gorge exit off I-80, six miles west of Rock Springs, Wyo.
(307) 362-3125

Fri. & Sat. 6 p.m.–10 p.m.

$10 or less

We have often thought of adopting Mrs. Sweet's philosophy as a personal motto: "If you ain't got no ribs, don't open your door." However much her dictum may or may not be applicable to life in general, it certainly holds true in much of the west, especially in the state of Wyoming where, gastronomically speaking, ribs is what it is.

Mrs. Sweet, a diminutive brown-skinned lady, smokes her ribs in an oil drum in back of a flat-fronted cafe on which the letters s-w-e-e-t-s are painted in faded red. She glazes the hickoried bones in an exhilarating sauce she learned how to brew from a Mississippi man over thirty years ago, when she first opened up for business. The ribs are served with her homemade biscuits, butter and honey, and perfunctory corn and beans. Mrs. Sweet also fries up catfish steaks and T-bones.

Eat inside this friendly roadhouse to the thump of a jukebox, or in your car, gazing over a western landscape of house trailers and stunning purple mountains.

Index of Restaurants

A Note on the Type

The text of this book was set in a film version of Aster, a type face designed by Francesco Simoncini (born 1912 in Bologna, Italy) for Ludwig and Mayer, the German type foundry. Starting out with the basic old-face letter forms that can be traced back to Francesco Griffo in 1495, Simoncini emphasized the diagonal stress by the simple device of extending diagonals to the full height of the letter forms and squaring off. By modifying the weights of the individual letters to combat this stress, he has produced a type of rare balance and vigor. Introduced in 1958, Aster has steadily grown in popularity.